Core Text Series

- Written with authority by leading subject experts
- Takes a focused approach, leading law students straight to the heart of the subject
- Clear, concise, straightforward analysis of the subject and its challenges

The University of **Law**

Com

Con:

Crin

Emp

Eurc
Mich

Evid

Fam

Inte

Lan

Med

The

The

For f
plea

OXFORD
UNIVERSITY PRESS

The Law of Trusts

Eleventh Edition

J E PENNER

Kwa Geok Choo Professor of Property Law, National University of Singapore,
Barrister of Lincoln's Inn

With contributions from

JEREMIAH LAU

Sheridan Fellow, National University of Singapore

OXFORD
UNIVERSITY PRESS

Great Clarendon Street, Oxford, OX2 6DP,
United Kingdom

Oxford University Press is a department of the University of Oxford.
It furthers the University's objective of excellence in research, scholarship,
and education by publishing worldwide. Oxford is a registered trade mark of
Oxford University Press in the UK and in certain other countries

Eighth edition 2012
Ninth edition 2014
Tenth edition 2016

Impression: 1

Published in the United States of America by Oxford University Press
198 Madison Avenue, New York, NY 10016, United States of America

British Library Cataloguing in Publication Data
Data available

Library of Congress Control Number: 2019934475

ISBN 978–0–19–879582–7

Printed in Great Britain by
Bell & Bain Ltd., Glasgow

Preface

Trusts is a gripping subject; unfortunately it grips most students with anxiety. There is good reason for this: it is difficult. Almost every topic in the law of trusts is complicated by demanding intellectual problems about the correct solutions to which academics and judges alike disagree. The consequence is that a 'Trusts Made Easy' book is like a 'Physical Chemistry Made Easy' book; a book for fools or the gullible. This is a 'Trusts Made Possible' book. It is a shorter text that explains from first principles what trusts are about, so that by the end of the book you should be 'up to speed' not only on the law, but also on the important academic controversies surrounding it, which will be of assistance to readers wishing to do well in a typical LLB exam on the subject. I do not presume that you are already an expert in any area of law. Thus I have tried in the introduction and elsewhere to provide the legal and conceptual building blocks of the subject, even if they are also taught (one hopes they are taught) in other subjects on the standard LLB syllabus. For that reason, if you are only interested in the law of trusts, and not reading for a law degree—say you've just been made a beneficiary under a trust, or your general reading tastes run to the peculiar—this book is also for you.

The law of trusts is judge-made (although it has, of course, been amended here and there by Parliament). That is, it was created by judges over time deciding actual cases, building up the body of rules and principles we today recognise as trusts law. For that reason, if you want to write a really good exam script in the subject, ie get a first, you will simply have to read some cases and not rely entirely on this book, or on any other book for that matter. Any textbook is just the author's interpretation of the law, whereas the law itself is found in the cases. To do well you must read them and interpret them by your own lights (taking into account, of course, the views of others mentioned in this book and elsewhere). And if you really want to plumb the depths and soar the heights of trusts law, feel it in your bones and exude it from your pores, reading the cases is a must. (I include a list of 'must-read' cases at the end of all the chapters save for the first two introductory ones.) Making sense out of the body of cases will try every brain cell at your command, so if you fancy yourself a true 'common lawyer', someone who is able to integrate the case decisions in an area of law while at the same time interpreting them to be humane and rational, then this is the subject for you.

Finally, trusts is not a subject you can swot up the evening before an exam. The old saw, 'You can't fatten a hog the night before slaughter', applies here in spades. Read and think; read and pause. Learn to recognise when your brain is full, and stop. Like a box of breakfast cereal, your brain will have room for more once the contents have settled. If you start to experience overload, stop, have a cup of tea and do something else for fifteen minutes. Then return, and before going on re-read what you were on before. This book proceeds pretty much step by step, and, at the end of the day, all should be reasonably clear. The only textbook that will ever make perfect sense on first reading is the one you write yourself (and often not even that one). Remember also that the different topics are all part of the same subject, so you will understand each of them better the more you understand all of the others. As Wittgenstein said, 'light dawns gradually over the whole'.

Once again, thanks for ever and ever to my brothers and sisters in trust, Tim Akkouh, Richard Barton, Mark Bennett, Rob Chambers, Sal Chowdhury, Chow Zhi Ying, Michael Crawford, Jonathan Garton, Jamie Glister, Matthew Harding, Lusina Ho, Rebecca Lee, Rachel Leow, Timothy Liau, Kelry Loi, Kelvin Low, Paul Matthews, John Mee, Ben McFarlane, Charles Mitchell, Richard Nobles, Richard Nolan, Sean Pettit, Nicole Roughan, Irit Samet, Alvin See, Lionel Smith, Rob Stevens, Bill Swadling, Charlie Webb, Sam Williams, Ian Williams, Wu Ying-Chieh, and Yip Man each of whom has made writing and revising this book much more stimulating than it otherwise would have been. My greatest thanks go to Jeremiah Lau, who was instrumental in revising this edition, in particular with respect to the new Chapter 12. I must also express my gratitude to Simon Blackett and the late Caroline Hardy for inspiring me in the first place, and to Isabel Isaacson, Tom Laidlaw, and Julian Roskams for all their help when this was a title with Butterworths, and to Liana Green, Marie Gill, and Hayley Buckley at OUP.

J E Penner
National University of Singapore

New to this edition

New material includes, but is not limited to, the following:

Chapters 3, 5, 11, and 13 (Chapter 12 in the last edition) have all been significantly revised to reflect recent developments in the law and the academic commentary on, respectively, beneficiaries' standing to sue and rights to information, resulting trusts, breach of trust, and the law governing fiduciaries.

Chapter 12 'Restitution, unjust enrichment, and the law of trusts' is new; it brings together material previously found in other chapters, organising it in a more coherent way for the better appreciation of the student reader, whilst also containing a wholly new discussion of the leading cases and academic commentary in this area of law.

Guide to using the book

There are a number of features throughout the textbook designed to help you in your studies.

SUMMARY

Express trusts and trusts arising by operation of law (TABO[...]
How beneficiaries receive their entitlements under a trust
Bare trusts, special trusts, and nomineeships
Beneficial, equitable, and legal interests
Trustees and fiduciaries
The features of the express trust
Claiming equitable title against third parties: following and [...]
The express trust in legal context
A note on the English trust for civil lawyers

Chapter summaries highlight what will be addressed in each chapter, so you are aware of the key learning outcomes for each topic.

FURTHER READING

Cullity (1975)

Nolan (2018)

Smith, L (2017)

Turner (2018)

Waters (1996)

Must-read cases: *Stephenson v Barclays Bank Trust Co Ltd* (1[...]
Lloyds Bank plc v Duker (1987); *Pitt v Holt* (2013); *IRC* [...]
Re Gulbenkian Settlement (1968); *McPhail v Doulton* [...]
(2003); *Lewis v Tamplin* (2018); *Vatcher v Paull* (191[...]

At the end of each chapter is a list of recommended **further reading.**

These suggestions include books and journal articles, and will help to supplement your knowledge, and develop your understanding of key topics.

SELF-TEST QUESTIONS

1. Explain the operation of s 53(1)(b) of the Law of Pro[...]
   Rochefoucauld v Boustead.

2. What do *Grey v IRC*, *Vandervell v IRC*, and *Re Vanderv*[...]

3. Trustbank plc holds 50,000 shares of Zinc Ltd as nom[...]
   150,000 shares of Gold Ltd to Trustbank stating that h [...]

   (i) Sam orally directs Trustbank to hold 50,000 shares [...]
   Albert, Jane, and Charlotte, in such shares as Trustb[...]
   appoint. Several months later, for revenue purpose[...]
   declaration that it holds the shares on trust for the [...]

Each chapter concludes with a selection of **self-test questions**. These allow you to check your understanding of the topics covered, and help you engage fully with the material in preparation for further study, writing essays, and answering exam questions.

Contents

Abbreviations

ART	automatic resulting trust
BFBDL	bad faith breaches of the duty of loyalty
CA	Court of Appeal
FDL	fiduciary duty of loyalty
FST	fully secret trust
HL	House of Lords
HST	half-secret trust
LPA	Law of Property Act 1925
PC	Privy Council
PRT	presumed resulting trust
TABOL	trust arising by operation of law
UA	unincorporated association
UKPC	Privy Council
UKSC	United Kingdom Supreme Court

Table of legislation

Paragraph references printed in **bold** type indicate where the Act is set out in part or in full.

Table of cases

1

The historical origins of the trust

SUMMARY

The Court of Chancery and the origin of equity
The relationship between equity and the common law
The Judicature Acts and the fusion of law and equity
Equity's creation of the use and the trust

The Court of Chancery and the origin of equity

1.1   The law of trusts is the offspring of a certain English legal creature known as 'equity'. The historical development of English law is marked by the existence of a series of different judicial institutions over time; most significant of these for the modern student are the Courts of Common Law and the Court of Chancery. The Courts of Common Law developed the basic rules and principles that we now recognise as the law of torts (civil wrongs), the law of contract, the law of restitution, and much of the law of property. The Court of Chancery generated its own rules and principles, which as a body of law are collectively known as 'equity'. Chancery developed the law of trusts, the law governing fiduciaries, also much of the law of property, much of company and commercial law, and, very importantly, a variety of legal remedies, such as the injunction, which the Courts of Common Law were unwilling or unable to provide.

1.2   The term 'equity' does not contrast with 'common law' when the latter is understood to distinguish judge-made law from legislation by Parliament. From that perspective, both equity and the common law are creations of 'common law', bodies of rules and principles developed over time as judges gave reasons for their decisions in actual cases.

1.3   The common law was developed and administered in the royal courts, those courts established by the King, in contrast to local manorial courts, which were the province of local nobles and which applied local customary law. It was called the 'common' law of England because in theory it applied universally. The origins of equity are much murkier. Equity arose out of the administrative power of the medieval Chancellor, who was at the time the King's most powerful minister. Since the King was regarded as the fount of justice, it was appropriate for him to hear pleas by his subjects concerning injustices and, kings being kings, they eventually delegated the task to their Chancellors. Since in the early days of the office the Chancellor was usually an ecclesiastic, early Chancellors felt able to concern themselves with men's immortal souls, and thus their consciences; thus it was on the basis of 'conscience' that the Chancellor exercised this royal power to remedy injustice, by ordering individuals to act in accordance with good conscience despite what their legal rights might be. In order to appreciate the character of this jurisdiction, and how it came to be in some sense opposed to the common law, certain considerations must be borne in mind.

1.4   The first is that equity, fairness, or justice were never absent from the common law courts. The difference was that from the mid-fourteenth century the complaints that the common law courts would hear became static (the categories of writs, or different forms of action, were closed), as did the procedures of the court as to pleading and evidence. Baker (2002, at 102–3) illustrates the sort of problem that could arise:

> [T]he growing strength of the substantive law could also work injustice, because the judges preferred to suffer hardship in individual cases than to make exceptions to clear rules. The stock example was that of the debtor who gave his creditor a sealed bond [a paper document recording the obligation to pay the debt], but did not ensure that it was cancelled when he paid up. The law regarded the bond as incontrovertible evidence of the debt, and so payment was no defence. Here the debtor would suffer an obvious hardship if he was made to pay twice; but the mischief was a result of his own foolishness, and the law did not bend to protect fools . . . Again, if someone granted land to others on trust to carry out his wishes, he would find that at law the grantees were absolute owners who could not be compelled to obey him. Now it was not that the common law held that a debt was due twice, or that a promise or trust could be broken; such propositions would have been dismissed as absurd. Yet those were the results which followed from observing strict rules of evidence, rules which might exclude the merits of the case from consideration but which could not be relaxed without destroying certainty and condoning carelessness.

1.5   These characteristics of the common law reflect, in part, the fact that the royal courts were 'courts of record', that is, courts whose decisions were recorded and were treated by lawyers and judges as statements of the law, ie of general rules applying to all. The Chancellor's decisions, by contrast, were not recorded. (However, from the early centuries of Chancery onward there are substantial records of the bills of complaint made by applicants to him; thus the task of recreating the principles applied by the early Chancellors is a matter of inference from the sort of complaints that were brought to him and the way they were framed.) His decisions were basically regarded as ad hoc exercises of his power to do justice in individual cases—he was not regarded as constructing a body of rules. In contrast to the procedures of proof available at common law, the Chancellor had the power of subpoena, ie the power to make litigants appear in person before him and to interrogate them. This was a quite different sort of proceeding from those which operated in the common law courts, and thus one element, perhaps a predominant one (see Macnair (2007)), in the notion that the court of equity was a court of 'conscience' is that the Chancellor made his rulings, not on the basis of various formal rules of evidence, but on the defendant's personal replies to the Chancellor's interrogation, replies that might well be adverse to the defendant's own interests. Not surprisingly, the Chancellor's decrees were treated not so much as legal decisions as they were orders directed to individuals to ensure that they acted according to good conscience in the particular circumstances of the case. This is one meaning of the phrase that 'equity acts *in personam*': equity did not determine rights under law, whether to land or anything else; rather, equity required particular individuals to comply with the Chancellor's decrees and indeed, this was reflected in the actual wording of the rulings: Chancery rulings were formulated explicitly as orders (eg 'this court doth order the defendant to give the claimant possession of … '), whereas common law rulings merely expressed that a certain state of affairs shall happen as in 'It is this day adjudged that the plaintiff shall recover against the defendant £100.' (See further Smith, S (forthcoming), chs 2 and 3. The form of these rulings also reflected the remedial consequences for defendants who failed to comply with the court's ruling (1.14).) In England, though not in other common law jurisdictions, the distinction has been abolished; since the Civil Procedure Act 1997 all court rulings in England now take the form of orders.

1.6 Secondly, the jurisdiction of the Chancellor, and his 'court of conscience', must be understood taking account of the nature of government at the time it developed. As Murphy (1991) has pointed out, throughout most of English legal history all forms of government were 'adjudicative' in the sense that governing bodies of all kinds, whether councils or courts or individual officials, basically rendered decisions to do justice in cases of conflict that came before them. One should also bear in mind,

> the multitude of forms of mediation and arbitration that existed in medieval society and Chancery's transcendence of them. Disputes in the community were resolved for both private satisfaction and public peace by the expedient of deference, wherein a cause was put by one party or both parties to a common superior executive, including the jurisdiction of a lord or a community in the manor, the hundred, and the county [all medieval units of jurisdiction]. Guilds also exercised mediatory functions, and at a high level the authority of a magnate might be invoked to arbitrate. [Haskett (1996)]

It was in response to perceived injustices arising from the decisions of any of the myriad adjudicators, arbitrators, or mediators in the medieval world that recourse to the Chancellor might be had, for his review of such decisions would have the force of the central department of state. Thus the conscience-based 'jurisdiction' of the Chancellor was not restricted to countering perceived injustices of the common law courts, but of all adjudicators of the medieval realm.

1.7 The Chancellor's conscience-based corrective role narrowed over the centuries. In time the Chancellor came to exercise a quasi-judicial function, in the Court of Chancery, which by and large was restricted to matters that were in some way covered by rules of the common law. Cases called 'suits', as opposed to 'actions' at common law, could be brought before him, the suitor appealing to the Chancellor on the basis that the rigid application of the common law rules caused injustice in his particular case. In response, the Chancellor could order a person not to act upon his common law rights if in good conscience he ought not to do so, in effect overturning the rules of common law. In theory, however, the common law was regarded as unchanged; the Chancellor merely decreed that the parties could not act upon it. The body of reasons and principles upon which the Chancellors made their decisions to temper the harsh or rigid application of common law rules became known as 'equity'. The term 'equity' reflected the idea of fairness implicit both in the 'conscience-based' administrative jurisdiction of the Chancellor, and in principles of 'equity' found in the Roman and ecclesiastical law in which many early Chancellors were learned. These principles ultimately derived from Aristotle's idea of 'equity', that there will be cases in which one must depart from the rules in order to avoid injustice (see Penner (2019a; 2019c)).

1.8 As might be expected, however, continual correction of decisions generated by a rule-based system will give rise to rules or principles of correction. It would not be conscionable for the Chancellor to give relief to one suitor unjustly dealt with by the common law, but deny it to the next whose suit was based on substantially the same facts. One of the most fundamental principles of justice, after all, is that like cases be decided alike. The widely perceived contrast between the rigid rules of the common law and the flexible conscience-based fairness of equity was a highly misleading caricature by the end of the eighteenth century. By then the *principles* of equity were fast becoming *rules* of equity as rigid and technical as any in the common law. Equity, which was once said to vary with the length of the Chancellor's foot to emphasise the personal character of the Chancellor's intervention, ie intervention on the basis of what he personally understood to be good conscience, had become a second body of law.

The maxims of equity

1.9   Although equity developed its own definite rules covering various matters, it also produced a series of 'maxims' or broad principles that manifested equity's general approach to the solution of legal problems. An example of such a maxim is 'Equity looks to intent, not form.' If, for example, two parties were to execute documents that characterised a land transaction as a sale of the land, although in substance the transaction amounted to a mortgage of the land, the court of equity would look beyond the form of the documents, which might be decisive at common law, and treat the transaction as a mortgage. We will encounter various of these maxims as we go along. Like any general legal principles, the maxims of equity have been encrusted with judicial interpretation over the centuries, so it would be a great mistake to treat these maxims nowadays as anything more than devices that assist the interpretation and organisation of particular equitable doctrines, and help explain their historical development.

The relationship between equity and the common law

Equity as a 'gloss' on the common law

1.10   Equity and the common law were not separate but equal systems of rules covering the same matters only differently. Equity has always relied on the existence of the common law, being essentially, in the terms of Maitland (a great equity scholar), a 'gloss' on the law (Maitland (1929), at 18–19). If you were to peel away all of the rules of equity, the common law could still stand alone as a comprehensive body of rules covering tort, contract, property, etc. If you were to peel away the common law from equity, however, you would not have anything like a comprehensive body of rules—equity, was, and remains, a kind of patchwork overlay modifying particular common law rules.

1.11   The two exceptions to this are the subjects of this book: the law of trusts and the law governing fiduciaries. Now, a legal system can do without trusts (civilian jurisdictions typically have no law of trusts or, to the extent they do, as in Scotland, they are imports from the common law) or the sort of law of fiduciaries found in English and commonwealth legal systems, and so could English law. So in that sense the law of trusts and fiduciary law are, like the other creations of equity, not strictly speaking necessary for a modern legal system. Peel them away and you could still have a working body of law. Nevertheless, as we shall see, they are now a vital part of English private law as a whole, and it would amount to a legal revolution if they were abolished.

Strife between equity and the common law

1.12 Equity largely worked through the issuance of 'common injunctions', by which a plaintiff at common law could be enjoined, ie stopped, by a decree of the Court of Chancery, from proceeding with his case, or restrained from enforcing the result. As one might imagine, from the point of view of the common law judges this was tantamount to the Chancellor's denying claimants access to justice. After several attempts by the common law judges to assert the dominance of the common law over the power of the Chancery, and some consequential political strife, it became settled by the end of the seventeenth century that the decrees of Chancery would prevail. Equity was here to stay. So, for about two centuries, England had a true dual system of courts with two different finely developed bodies of law.

The 'jurisdictions' of equity

1.13 Equity is said to have three jurisdictions, or areas of operation, each of which relates it to the common law: (1) equity's 'exclusive' or 'original' jurisdiction, where equity alone created a law in an area; (2) its 'concurrent' jurisdiction, where both it and the common law developed rules in relation to certain fact situations; and (3), its 'auxiliary' jurisdiction, in which equity would assist plaintiffs at common law in pursuing their common law rights. This division is controversial and its utility has been questioned. There is disagreement about whether certain areas of equitable doctrine fit into (2) rather than (3), and indeed about whether certain areas of doctrine originating in equity fit into any of these three categories (see Hohfeld (1913); Heydon et al (2015), [1-90]–[1-110]; Penner (2019c)). Even so, these classifications broadly illuminate the differing ways equity interacts with the common law. The law of trusts is the most obvious example of equity's exclusive jurisdiction. The law of trusts was developed entirely by the Court of Chancery. An example of equity's concurrent jurisdiction is one you may think of if you have studied the law of contract, that is, the law of mistake. Both the common law and equity developed rules providing remedies for contracting parties who entered into the contract labouring under some sort of mistake. To take an example of equity's auxiliary jurisdiction, you may know that as part of the litigation process, litigants can be required to disclose documents that bear on the facts of the claim. Historically, common law litigants were not afforded any right to disclosure under the procedures of the common law courts, but a common law litigant could get a decree from Chancery ordering the other party to disclose. Nowadays, this particular auxiliary jurisdiction of equity has been superseded by the statute-based codes of civil procedure. Another example of equity's auxiliary jurisdiction is equity's willingness to provide certain remedies not available at common law to common law litigants in order better to vindicate their common law rights. This aspect of equity, its range of remedies and its willingness to apply them, remains of great importance.

Remedies at common law and equity

1.14 Different remedies were available from the common law courts and the court of equity. A common law court could adjudge (1.5) that a losing defendant pay damages, a money sum, to the plaintiff, and in cases concerning land could adjudge that a defendant give up possession of the land to the plaintiff. If the defendant refused to pay damages, the judgment provided a ground for a sheriff or bailiff to come round, seize his possessions, and either hold them until he paid or sold them to raise the plaintiff's damages. Similarly, if a defendant refused to get off the land, the sheriff would come round and clear him out. Thus the common law courts had, essentially, only one means of enforcing their decisions: they could empower an official to separate a person from their property. Chancery had a much more sweeping power, which provided scope for a variety of equitable remedies. The Court of Chancery could throw anybody who disobeyed its orders (1.5) into gaol, for contempt of court. This was not a criminal sentence, where if you served your time you got out. If you refused to carry out an order of Chancery, you rotted in gaol until you decided to comply. (Nowadays, imprisonment for contempt of court is regulated by the Contempt of Court Act 1981, and the court also has powers to act in place of the defendant in certain instances, for example by executing documents, or by appointing others to act in his place: RSC Ord 45, r 8, incorporated into the Civil Procedure Rules 1998.) This gives another meaning to the phrase 'equity acts *in personam*': equity acts on your body. Equity has the power to make you do something, or to stop doing something, because if you refuse, you lose your liberty for as long as it takes. Thus injunctions have their origin in equity. Equity can also rescind contracts, ie tell people to act as if a contract was never formed, and can rectify documents, ie tell people to carry on as if the document had different terms. As a result, in many cases litigants whose substantive rights lay at common law would seek the remedial assistance of Chancery—so, for example, one suffering the smoke of a neighbour's brickworks and unsatisfied with money damages would apply to Chancery for an injunction to shut the brickworks down; or a contracting party would seek an order from Chancery for the specific performance of the contract in a case where money damages for breach would inadequately compensate.

The Judicature Acts and the fusion of law and equity

1.15 The administrative inconvenience of a dual system of courts that dealt in different fashions with the same factual issues is apparent, and by the Judicature Acts 1873–5 Parliament abolished the institutional division between the Courts of Common Law and the Court of Chancery. One High Court was established, the judges of which were henceforth to apply the rules of both common law and equity, where appropriate, in the cases before it; where the rules conflicted, the rules of equity were to prevail. What counts as equity today, therefore, is the body of rules and principles that derive from those applied in the Court of Chancery until 1875; judge-made law is a living thing, and so equity has developed since then, in just the same way as has the common law of contract or tort. Despite the abolition of the separate courts, there remain distinct traces of this institutional history that bear directly on the current state of English law.

The fusion of law and equity

1.16 Since 1875, judges apply both common law and equity in the same court at the same time. It remains an open question to what extent the rules and principles of the common law and of equity have been fashioned into one coherent, principled body of law; whether, that is, the common law and equity have 'fused'. The fusion question can be framed in this way: although judges and lawyers now deal with whatever rules of equity and common law apply to the case before them, in what sense should they maintain the distinct historical and intellectual origins of these rules in their heads? Maintaining such a notional distinction will have consequences in so far as the mere fact that a rule arose in the common law or in equity will have consequences for its application.

1.17 Consider the following old chestnut of the fusion debate: because equity arose in a 'court of conscience' it is said that, as a matter of unalterable principle, all equitable remedies are discretionary. For example, if a plaintiff seeking the equitable remedy of specific performance of a contract has acted unconscionably in some way himself, then equity will refuse to help him, leaving him to his remedies at common law. The maxim (1.9) framing this rule is 'He who seeks Equity must come with clean hands'. By contrast, it is said, common law remedies lie 'as of right', the court having no similar discretion. So we now pose the question: should it still matter which court originally devised a particular remedy when judges come to decide how they should apply it nowadays? Surely not. If it remains true that some remedies that arose in equity should only be granted on a discretionary basis (and there may be good grounds for this), this must be justified as a matter of principle that fits into a coherent rationale that explains the remedial rules in that particular area of law. This coherent rationale must, of course, also explain the various restrictions and limitations that exist today upon remedies originally given at common law. Even if an explanation is based upon concerns about justice that were originally given voice by Chancery, that does not entail that the rule must henceforth be identified as an equitable one, any more than we would identify a modern rule of the law of wills as ecclesiastical, because the law of wills was originally the province of the ecclesiastical courts. Nevertheless, this particular version of the 'history is destiny' fallacy lingers. It lingers in part almost certainly because of the theoretical difficulties that have arisen in incorporating the most important single development of equity, the law of trusts, into one coherent law of property. Fusion may seem somewhat straightforward when directed towards remedies, but the idea of ironing out the differences between the common law and equity in property law, is, as we shall see (2.118 et seq), a different kettle of fish. This issue also bears on whether equity's auxiliary jurisdiction still really exists. If we regard the law of remedies as being a coherent body of doctrine which includes not only remedies deriving from common law and equity, but statutory remedies as well, then it no longer makes sense to think of remedies originally devised by equity remaining 'equitable', brought in to 'assist' the vindication of common law rights.

Equity 'purism' and equity 'pragmatism'

1.18 These terms originate with Lionel Smith (Smith (2004)). Equity purists hold that equity reflects a distinct form or mode of reasoning that resists assimilation to common law legal reasoning, reflecting some different understanding of justice, based perhaps on some idea of an individual's 'conscience' being affected in a way that the common law disregards. By contrast, equity pragmatists respect the historical division of labour that arose with the development of the Court of Chancery, but disagree that the rules of both equity and the common law answer to different standards of reasoning, justice, or morality (see Penner (2019a; 2019c)). It is well beyond the scope of this book to adjudicate this dispute, but one point must be stressed; even equity pragmatists should respect the differences between distinct areas of doctrine both within equity and the common law themselves, and between them. As an example of the former point, as we have seen (1.11), equity devised both the law of trusts and the law governing fiduciaries, but that is no reason to think that they do not fulfil different functions, with their own distinct rules. As we shall see, not all trustees are fiduciaries and not all fiduciaries are trustees, and it would therefore make no sense to try to 'fuse' these areas of law just because of some similarities and overlap between them. As an example of the latter point, trenchantly made by Heydon et al ((2015), 47–66), the fusion of law and equity did not give the courts any 'abstractionist' marking orders, under which courts were to simplify the law based on some abstract principles of justice. Consider this sort of case: both the trustee's trust obligation and a contracting party's contractual obligation are kinds of voluntarily-undertaken obligations; but pointing this out does not give judges any ground for assimilating the law of trusts to the law of contract, as sub-species of a higher genus.

Equity's creation of the use and the trust

1.19   The most important developments of the preceding institutional history are the law of trusts and the law governing fiduciaries. These are the only branches of law studied by LLB students that arose purely in the Court of Chancery. The law of trusts and the law governing fiduciaries are worthwhile studying separately from the rest of equity for two reasons. First, the rest of equity is best studied in combination with the common law and statutory rules that govern the different substantive areas of law to which these other equitable rules apply. For example, equitable remedies are best examined in the context of studying the various substantive actions, such as breach of contract, where they are given; or, if remedies per se are the focus of inquiry, it is silly to restrict one's attention to equitable remedies, missing the important points of comparison with common law and statutory remedies. Land law courses necessarily include the substantive development by equity of the land law, and the substantive equitable wrong of breach of confidence happily fits within the study of torts generally or the law relating to industrial property. Secondly, matters of pedagogical convenience aside, the law of trusts is worthwhile studying in its own right because the 'trust'—equity's imposition of stringent personal obligations upon a legal owner to hold property for the benefit of another, with the result that he is no longer able to treat the property as his own—may be regarded as the paradigm case of equity's interference with common law rights in pursuit of justice. A similar claim may be made for the law governing fiduciaries: the legal conception of 'conflict of interest', upon which, as we shall see, fiduciary doctrine turns, very much reflects the 'conscience-based' origin of equity.

The use

1.20   The historical roots of the trust lie in a medieval property device: the 'use'. The history of the land law in the first centuries following the Conquest can be described as the process by which true property or ownership in land arose, as the influence of the social and political structure of feudalism waned. Under feudalism, rights in land basically amounted to rights in a complex hierarchical system of social and political authority and agricultural wealth distribution. This hierarchy was maintained through a system of 'tenures' of land, under which different 'tenants' had rights in the same land. At the top of this ladder was the King, at the bottom the person actually in possession of the land, and in between there might be any number of 'mesne (pronounced "mean") lords'. It was essentially a system of taxation. Each tenant, starting with the one in possession who, via the labours of his serfs, would produce agricultural goods, passed the wealth of the land upward by doing 'rent service' of various kinds to the lord immediately above him, and so on up to the King. Thus although a person might have an 'estate', an ownership interest, in some piece of land, this estate was as likely to be a 'seigneury', ie the right to a rent from a tenant immediately below on the feudal ladder, as it was to be an estate giving possession of the land itself. Different kinds of rights and duties defined the different kinds of tenure by which land could be held, such as 'knightservice', the obligation to provide knights or money for arms, or 'socage', the obligation to provide agricultural products. The use arose as a means of avoiding some of the more disgruntling rules of the tenurial feudal system. Land could not be left by will, but could only be inherited according to the rules of primogeniture, the general effect of which was that the entirety of a man's rights in land passed to his eldest son. This preserved large estates in land, but it meant that a man could not take advantage of his landed wealth to provide for all of his children on his death. Another problem arose if one wanted to benefit certain religious orders. For various reasons it was difficult, if not impossible, to provide for them by conveying land to them. Among nobles, there was also the problem that the English Crown was often bloodily contested over long periods of time, in particular during the War of the Roses. If a landowner were in the position of having backed the wrong claimant to the Crown, not only would he lose his life, being condemned as a traitorous felon by the victor, but all his lands would be forfeit to the Crown, ruining his family. Finally, certain legal incidents of feudal land-holding could themselves become very oppressive. In particular, if land held in knightservice passed to a minor heir, the lord immediately above on the feudal ladder acquired the 'right of wardship', the right to manage the estate and take all the profits of the land until the heir reached maturity. These elements (amongst others) of land tenure inspired medieval lawyers to avoid them. The avoidance mechanism was the use.

1.21 Although land could not be left by will, there were no similar restrictions on *inter vivos* transfers, ie transfers whilst the tenant was alive. At this time, the mode of transfer of freehold land was called a 'feoffment'; the transferor was called a 'feoffor', and the transferee, the person he 'enfeoffed', the 'feoffee'. Thus A, a feudal tenant, could convey his property to X, Y, and Z as co-owners. Of course, a straightforward conveyance like this would not do A any good to realise any plans for his land: by conveying the land in this way he would give up all rights to it; rather, the property was conveyed *on use*: the conveyance was written to X, Y, and Z to the use of some person or persons whom A wanted to benefit, called the 'cestui(s) que use'. (These are terms of old 'law French'—England was conquered by the Normans, after all. The way they are pronounced today would not meet with the approval of the Parisian on the street. 'Cestui(s) que use' is pronounced 'settee(s) key use'.) X, Y, and Z, taking the land subject to the use, were called 'feoffees to use'. In general, A could benefit whomever he wanted, in however complicated a fashion he wished: thus A could convey the property to the use of an order of Franciscan monks, or to his own use for his life and then to the use of his widow for her life, and then to the use of all of his children in equal shares. The common law completely ignored the words 'to the use of'. As far as it was concerned, X, Y, and Z were the owners by conveyance, subject to all the feudal duties of their estate, and could do whatever they liked with the land, regardless of the wishes of A, because A no longer held the legal estate to the lands: X, Y, and Z did.

1.22   The conveyance was made to X, Y, and Z as co-owners to exploit a particular technical common law rule. The form of co-ownership that was invariably employed was the joint tenancy. Joint tenancy has the significant feature of the right of survivorship (in Latin, the *jus accrescendi*), by which, upon the death of any joint tenant, his interest disappears—it does not pass to his heir—with the result that there is just one fewer co-owner. Thus if X were to die, his heir would not inherit a share of the property; his interest would just disappear: Y and Z would now together own the property as joint tenants. (The other common form of co-ownership is 'tenancy in common'. Here, in contrast, the tenant in common possesses an ownership share that passes to his heir.) As joint tenants of the legal title to the land, X, Y, and Z would be liable to comply with the feudal duties but, importantly, because of the right of survivorship, the particular worry of a minor heir inheriting the land could be completely avoided. The danger of inheritance would only arise if following a series of deaths only one of the original joint tenants remained, who would then be the sole owner. If he then died, his heir would inherit. But that could easily be avoided because, after the death of X for example, Y and Z could convey the land to themselves and V and W, on the same use as A originally did. In this way, whenever the number of joint tenants dropped to a low number, a simple reconveyance to another group of joint tenants ensured that the property was never inherited, and so a wardship would never arise.

1.23   The use, therefore, could be employed to avoid all of the rules of feudal tenure mentioned. The benefit of land could be passed to others than those who would inherit under the rules of primogeniture. It could be passed to those who were legally disentitled from holding property (eg religious orders and minors), and A could convey his lands to a neutral party so that if A went to the block for treason, he could do so with the comfort that he had not ruined his family dynasty—not being legal owner of his lands, they would not be forfeit to the Crown, and so his wife and children would not be destitute; the legal owners would continue to hold for them upon use. Finally, the use could be used to ensure a minor never inherited.

1.24   The term 'use' is somewhat misleading. It is a corruption of the Latin *ad opus*. What it means is 'on behalf of' or 'for the benefit of', so to grant land 'to the use' of someone meant that the feoffees to use were not entitled to treat the land as their own, but must hold it on behalf of or for the benefit of the cestui(s) que use. A typical example of an enfeoffment to uses will give something of the flavour of a medieval use.

1.25   Typically, a feoffor would grant land to feoffees 'to the use of my will'. 'Will' here did not mean the written instrument we think of today but rather simply the feoffor's expression of his intentions about where the property should go, often made on his deathbed (Mee (2010)). So uses were typically created without any express terms besides the term that the feoffor would give future directions. Now, of course, the feoffees to use were not entitled to use the property for themselves in the meantime, simply because they had the legal title. Indeed, in the vast majority of cases the feoffer continued to occupy the land and reap the profits just as he did before the feoffment to uses. Thus, the arrangement was basically one in which the feoffees to uses received the bare legal title, in essence just the 'paper' title, which they held without having to do anything until such time as the settlor gave them further directions. This sort of feoffment to uses was absolutely standard in the fourteenth, fifteenth, and sixteenth centuries. Indeed, so standard and common was this means of holding land that in 1500 Chief Justice Frowk declared that the greater part of land in England was held in use (cited in Swadling (1996a)).

1.26   Now, the attentive reader may have noticed one rather gaping potential flaw in these schemes employing the use. What could the cestuis que use do if X, Y, and Z refused to honour the use? As we have seen, the common law did not recognise the use: X, Y, and Z were the full legal owners, and so A's cestuis would get no relief in a court of common law. Here enters the Chancellor and his conscience-based power to remedy injustices. It would be unfair to allow X, Y, and Z to take the benefit of the land themselves, because they only got it in order to benefit the cestuis que use. The Chancellor would enforce the use at the suit of the cestuis, ensuring that X, Y, and Z held the land according to the use A dictated.

1.27   Now it is sometimes thought that this failure of the common law to recognise the use is indicative of the harshness or rigidity of the common law, a harshness and rigidity so severe that it would deprive A, his wife, and their children of their rights in land, thwarting the clear agreement between A and X, Y, and Z. But this is a profound misunderstanding. The common law's blindness to the use was essential for the benefits of the use to be achieved. It was only because the cestuis had no legal title to the land that the various schemes to avoid the incidents of feudal land-holding would work. If the common law were to recognise a new kind of seigneury or legal estate in the use, then it would not have put the cestuis' interests in the land beyond the reach of the very legal rules that the use was engineered to avoid. It was the very rigidity of the common law in refusing to recognise a legal estate in the use that made the use effective. The common law was not hostile to the use; undoubtedly a large number of common law judges and lawyers held land to uses and/or were cestuis que use themselves. The problem of enforcing uses against legal title holders was a real, but secondary, problem, which appears to have been met differently as time went on. It seems that when the use originated, it was understood by all that the legal title holders were bound in honour and conscience, not law, to give effect to the use, the very extra-legality of the obligation making the device effective. The non-legal sanctions for failing to comply with such an obligation cannot be discounted. Failure to meet one's conscientious obligations could and did result in social obloquy, or church-directed penance, or even excommunication. And it is natural that as the social bonds of feudalism declined in importance failures to perform uses would come before the Chancellor in greater numbers, so that his jurisdiction became the normal, then exclusive, means of enforcement, ultimately leading to the rules governing uses and trusts that make up such a large part of equity doctrine.

1.28   How should we characterise the use? One way is this: a use is a kind of 'structured gift'. A conveys property to X, Y, and Z to the use of someone to whom he wants to give the property but which for various reasons he cannot do under the common law rules of property; an obstacle in feudal times, as we have seen, was the rule of primogeniture. The use can also be characterised as a kind of feudal tax-avoidance mechanism. Transferring the benefit of land by way of use enabled feudal tenants to enhance the value of their land, by disengaging it in part from its feudal incidents, particularly those that operated upon inheritance.

The origin of the trust

1.29   This book is about the law of trusts, not the law of uses, so what happened? Very briefly: Henry VIII wanted money, and set about getting some by prosecuting with a vengeance his ancient feudal rights as the man at the top of the feudal pyramid. He even had a special court set up, the Court of Wards, to help him do so. Because by this time feudalism was essentially anachronistic, his efforts were branded 'fiscal feudalism'. Vexed at being deprived of the feudal revenues he would otherwise have got but for the employment of uses by his noble tenants, he managed to get Parliament to pass the Statute of Uses in 1535. This statute 'executed the uses':

a conveyance from A to X, Y, and Z to the use of B was, after the Act, treated as a conveyance from A to B directly. The title passed from A to X, Y, and Z, and then to B as the use was automatically 'executed', cutting out X, Y, and Z. Following the statute, then, the typical use (1.25) in which A conveyed land to X, Y, and Z to hold to his, ie A's, use, did nothing at all. A would remain the legal owner of the land. It was thenceforth impossible for someone holding the legal title to be bound to benefit another, since there was no longer any use by which he could be bound. How the trust arose in the next century and a half to replicate the use in all but name is an interesting bit of history, but not, alas, one to be gone into in detail here. But it is to be noted that the statute did not execute all uses—roughly, it only executed those uses in which the feoffees to use held the 'paper title' for a cestui que use who continued to possess the land as before the transfer. The statute did not execute 'active' uses, in which the feoffees to use had to carry out genuine positive duties. An example of an active use would be a use for the benefit of an order of Franciscan monks who were unable to own property. The feoffees to use did not merely hold the paper title, but actively participated in the management of the land. This provided one loophole in the statute, and others were soon found by industrious lawyers. Furthermore, in the next century or so the political climate changed; the monarch no longer relied primarily on his feudal rights for revenue, and so there was no political consequence if the Court of Chancery gave effect to uses which managed to evade the statute. Suffice it to say that, by the turn of the eighteenth century, where someone, now called the 'settlor', transferred a legal title to X to hold for the benefit of B, now rendered as 'in trust for B' rather than 'to the use of B', Chancery would require X to hold the land for the benefit of B, just as if he had formerly held it to B's use. B was consequently renamed the 'cestui que trust', and is now generally called the 'beneficiary', and X is now called the 'trustee'.

1.30 Since the incidents of feudalism are now abolished, you might ask why anyone would want to give a 'structured gift' today. Why do people set up trusts? For most private trusts, the basic reason is the same as in medieval times: to provide for loved ones in a way one cannot do, or it would be unwise to do, simply by transferring legal title. One cannot give minors land, so if one wants a minor to have Blackacre ('Blackacre' is the name common lawyers always give to a hypothetical piece of land—Whiteacre, Greenacre, and so on, are the colourful variations), it must be held on trust for him by someone else. One may be worried that one's son is a spendthrift, and so give money for his living expenses to a trustee to dispense, on condition that the benefit will pass to someone else if that son goes bankrupt. One may want someone, like your surviving spouse, to have the dividends, ie the income, from shares for the rest of their life, and someone else, say your children, to have the capital, title to the shares themselves, once your spouse has passed on. One cannot fragment the legal title to shares to accomplish that. In certain circumstances, the law of taxation also favours giving property by way of trust when one is alive over leaving property to others in one's will, so many trusts are essentially tax-avoidance devices.

1.31 Note that the structured gift and tax-avoidance functions of the use/trust work in essentially opposite ways. To the extent that the use/trust avoids feudal incidents or taxes, it frees property from restrictions that reduce its value to an owner. On the other hand, the structured gift burdens property, and the structure of benefits under a trust can be very complicated indeed. If the feudal use worked to free land from the institution of feudalism, its modern counterpart, the trust, also ties up property with bonds quite as tight to different social institutions, such as the family, or the workplace as in the case of pension fund trusts.

FURTHER READING

Baker (2002), chs 6, 12, 13, 14, and 16

Burrows (2002)

Haskett (1996)

Hohfeld (1913)

Jones (1997)

Maitland (1929), Lectures I–IV

Penner (2019a; 2019c)

Simpson (1986), chs I, VIII, and IX

SELF-TEST QUESTIONS

1. What features distinguish equity from the common law?

2. What does it mean to say that 'equity acts *in personam*'?

3. What does it mean to say that equity is a 'gloss' on the common law?

4. What are the 'jurisdictions' of equity, and how do these jurisdictions relate equity to the common law?

5. To what does 'fusion' refer?

6. What was a 'use', what purposes did it serve, how did it work, and how is it related to the trust?

2 The nature of the express trust

SUMMARY

Express trusts and trusts arising by operation of law (TABOLs)
How beneficiaries receive their entitlements under a trust
Bare trusts, special trusts, and nomineeships
Beneficial, equitable, and legal interests
Trustees and fiduciaries
The features of the express trust
Claiming equitable title against third parties: following and tracing trust property
The express trust in legal context
A note on the English trust for civil lawyers
Trusts in civil law jurisdictions: Quebec and Scotland
The nature of the beneficiary's right and the fusion of law and equity

Express trusts and trusts arising by operation of law (TABOLs)

2.1 In Chapter 1, we operated with the rather vague notion that a trustee 'holds property on trust' for the beneficiaries. It is now time to make this notion explicit and precise. This will take some doing, so this is a long chapter. In the first part we will look at the different kinds of trust, focusing on the express trust, ie a trust that is intentionally set up to provide different kinds of benefits to beneficiaries, and we will also look at how beneficiaries benefit from a trust. In the next part we will look at various 'structural' features of the express trust—the structure of rights and duties that essentially make the trust the sort of legal device that it is; in the third part, we will place the trust in the context of the wider law, comparing the trust with, and characterising it in relation to, testamentary gifts and security interests. Fourthly, we compare the common law trust with trusts in some civil law systems, that is, some trusts in legal systems without equity. Finally, we look at the nature of the beneficiary's right under the trust, and the fusion of law and equity. It is probably best not to try to assimilate everything here in one go; although the particular aspects of the trust we discuss are not individually difficult to grasp, pulling them all together in your head to get a proper grasp of the nature of the trust requires some intellectual digestion, so take time off at intervals to pause and think.

Express trusts

2.2   An express trust is one that is intentionally set up. The uses and trusts that we looked at in Chapter 1 were all express, set up by the feoffor to uses or the settlor, respectively. The term 'express' is not a particularly helpful one—it correctly reflects the fact that in order to create a trust intentionally the settlor must express his intentions, either orally or in writing, as in the case of a trust created by someone in his will (2.83). But it is not the expression per se that is the essence of the matter; it is the fact that the settlor exercised his power to set up a trust that is essential, as we shall see in a moment. In the case of trusts, there are two principal ways in which a settlor can create a trust: by 'self-declaration' or by transfer of the intended trust assets to another person to hold on trust. Imagine that you want to create a trust fund for your children, to be available to them to provide for their education. To remind you of the terminology set out in Chapter 1, you are called the 'settlor', because you 'settle' the property upon your children under the trust. (Confusingly, not all express trusts are nowadays properly called 'settlements'; settlements are trusts, usually family trusts, in which there are *successive* interests (3.32).) You can settle the property simply by declaring that you now hold the property, say 1,000 shares of XYZ Co Ltd, on trust for your children. That is a 'self-declaration of trust'. As the settlor, you make yourself the trustee for your children. Or you can transfer the shares to someone else—your sister, say—to hold on trust for them. In the former case, you, as trustee, the holder of the legal title of the shares, must deal with the property according to the terms of the trust; in the latter case, your sister must do so. In both cases, your children are the 'cestuis que trust', or 'beneficiaries'. Most express trusts are created in writing, and the document that contains the *terms* of the trust, ie the detailed provisions that structure the way the property is to be held by the trustee for the benefit of the beneficiaries, is normally called the *trust instrument*. Sometimes this document can also work to transfer the legal title of the property from the settlor to the trustee, but legal title in the property must be transferred to the trustee according to the correct transfer procedures for that kind of property, whether land or shares or whatever other kind of property is to be held on trust. Of course in the case of a self-declaration of trust, the settlor/trustee already holds title to the property, so no transfer is necessary.

2.3   Since, as we have just seen, a settlor can declare himself trustee of property for someone, the settlor and the trustee can be the same person. A settlor can also convey property to a trustee on trust for himself, so the settlor and beneficiary can be the same person. A trustee can also be one of several beneficiaries, as would result from, for example, a transfer of title to Blackacre to B on trust for B and C in equal shares. But what cannot exist is a lone trustee who is also a lone beneficiary. The law does not recognise a division of the individual self so that you would have an obligation to hold property for yourself in a defined way, an obligation that you could enforce against yourself.

Exercising powers to create an express trust

2.4   You should think of the express trust as the creation of the settlor; an express trust is created when a settlor *effectively exercises his powers of ownership* to do so. Understanding the significance of this will involve a brief digression.

Powers

2.5   A 'power' is the capacity to change or create rights, duties, and/or other powers. One has the power to enter into contracts: if you and I agree that I will pay you £5 for washing my car, then we give birth to a new legal relationship—we both have rights and duties that we did not have before. I have the right that you wash my car and the duty to pay you £5 for doing so, and you have, correspondingly, the duty to wash it and the right to be paid £5. Owners of property have, simply by virtue of their ownership, all sorts of associated powers. If I own Blackacre, I can exercise my powers over it to lease it, to give it away, to license you to come onto it to have dinner with me, and so on. One of the other things I can do if I own Blackacre is create a trust of it in your favour, either by self-declaration or by transferring Blackacre to a trustee to hold on trust. In the former case, I have imposed a duty upon myself to hold Blackacre for your benefit, and have conferred a right upon you to the benefit of Blackacre. In the latter case, the trustee will have undertaken a duty to hold Blackacre for your benefit, and you will have the corresponding right that he does so. Express trusts can be created by the settlor's exercise of his power gratuitously, or because he is obliged to do so under a contract. For example, occupational pension funds are held on trust and arise in fulfilment of the duties generated by employment contracts.

Trusts arising by operation of law (TABOLs)

2.6 New rights, duties, and powers are not only created by individuals exercising their legal powers, but may also arise 'by operation of law'. Consider the case of a tortious injury, ie an injury that occurs because someone has committed a civil wrong (a 'tort'). If I negligently run you down with my car, you now have the right to sue me for 'damages', ie money compensation. But it would be a dreadful mistake to think that because I was the one who ran you down, I thereby exercised a power of mine to confer upon you a right to sue me for damages. The law only recognises capacities to create new rights, duties, or powers where the law wishes to provide a facility to do things in particular ways: the law recognises a power to enter contracts, or declare trusts, or make a will, because the law is in favour of those things. The law is not in favour of my running people down, so I have no legal powers attached to that capacity. The right to sue someone for damages arises *by operation of law* on the occurrence of your negligently caused injury because the law regards it as just that you should be able to bring an action for compensation.

2.7 The distinction between rights, duties, or powers that an individual creates when he exercises a power, and those that arise by operation of law, is of great significance in the law of trusts: while express trusts are created by a settlor through the exercise of his powers of ownership, other trusts, generically called 'constructive trusts' (Chapter 4), are trusts arising by operation of law (TABOLs) on the basis of particular facts. Sometimes it is difficult to determine from the cases whether particular trusts have arisen because they were created by a settlor or by operation of law, but as we shall see when we discuss, for example, resulting trusts (Chapter 5), it is often very important to know which in order to make sense of the law.

How beneficiaries receive their entitlements under a trust

2.8 In the preceding paragraphs, I said that the trustee must hold for the benefit of the beneficiaries; the trustee is not entitled to 'use the trust property' for his own benefit. It is now imperative to make sense of this idea of 'holding' or 'using' the trust property for the benefit of the beneficiaries.

2.9   There are two paradigmatic instances of trusts. The first is the bare trust of land (sometimes with accompanying chattels such as the furniture, paintings, and so on in the place), as in the case of the trust of the mansion house of a dynastic family settlement, or in the case of the literally millions of trusts of land in England and Wales resulting from the peculiar requirement of English land legislation that any instance of co-ownership of land must take the form of a trust (see eg Burn and Cartwright (2011), ch 14). We will consider the idea of a 'bare' trust further (2.13), but a 'bare trust' is, roughly, a trust in which the trustee holds the property to the order of the beneficiaries. That is, the trustee holds title to the trust asset(s), but the beneficiaries are entitled to direct the trustee in his use of the powers that go with title. In the typical bare trust of land, the beneficiaries will require the trustee to license their possession of the property so they can occupy it for their own benefit. So in these trusts of land, the beneficiaries receive the benefit of the property by way of the trustee's exercising his power to license them to enter into possession, enjoying it '*in specie*' (enjoying the thing itself), as lawyers are wont to say.

2.10   The second is the modern wealth management trust. Typically, these trusts hold intangible assets such as shares, bonds, or bank balances, that is, financial assets. 'Intangible assets' are those whose value does not turn on the value of possessing any tangible thing, unlike the case of land, or chattels such as cars or clothes washers. True, an intangible asset might be evidenced by a document, such as a company share certificate, but the value of the share is in the rights it gives you against the company, to receive dividends, for example. So consider a wealth management trust—how do the beneficiaries receive the benefit of the trust? Let's consider a clear case and then a more complicated one. The clear case is the traditional income/capital trust. For simplicity, consider a trust of 1,200 shares of XYZ Ltd held on trust for Martha for life, and then for her children Tom, Dick, and Mary in equal shares. Because she has an interest for her life, Martha is sometimes said to be the 'life tenant', and the children the 'remaindermen', adopting the terminology of traditional land law, but it is probably better to use the modern terms: Martha is the 'income' beneficiary, and the children the 'capital' beneficiaries, as this is more descriptive of their interests. One of the things that students often fail to appreciate when considering the interests of beneficiaries under this sort of trust is that their beneficial interests 'under the trust' are, for the most part, essentially *future, legal* interests. Martha's right to income under the trust is an interest in receiving the legal title to the money that represents the trust income, in this case the dividends the trustee will receive from time to time because he owns the shares. The lesson is exactly the same for the capital beneficiaries. When they get their benefit under the trust, they get it *legally*, ie they are entitled to the transfer of the legal title to the trust assets upon Martha's death. Upon Martha's death the trustee will have a duty to transfer the legal title to 400 shares each to Tom, Dick, and Mary. At that point the trust comes to an end. So, in the case of a modern wealth management trust, no beneficiary lives on their 'equitable interest' as such; rather beneficiaries live on the *legal* proceeds of their equitable interests, in the form of the money or other property transferred to them under the trust terms.

2.11   The more complicated case arises because the terms of a trust can be more complicated than a simple income/capital trust. We will look at the basic 'tools' which allow settlors to create more complicated trusts in Chapter 3, but for now you should know that trustees often have a discretion under the terms of the trust, to pay more money to some of the trust beneficiaries than to others, and a discretion as to how to spend that money. Where there is a discretion, the trustee must show that he has '*applied* the trust property to the benefit of the beneficiaries'. 'Applying the property to the benefit of the beneficiaries' can be done in different ways; one way, as we have seen, is just to transfer the legal title to the trust assets to the beneficiaries, as when Martha is paid the money representing the dividends, or when the trustee transfers the legal title to the shares to her children in the right proportions. But there are other ways. Imagine that, under the terms of a trust, a trustee has a discretion to apply trust property to the benefit of one of the beneficiaries—call him Lionel. Suppose that the trustee thinks it would make sense for Lionel to have a new car. There are three ways in which this objective might be achieved. The trustee could just give Lionel money from the trust funds to buy a car. Or the trustee could use trust funds to buy the car for Lionel, that is pay the car seller on Lionel's behalf, so that Lionel acquires title to the car. Or the trustee could use trust funds to buy a car in his own name, ie taking title to the car as a trust asset, and then licensing the car to Lionel to use. This would be the safest way of dealing with those irresponsible or feckless Lionels of this world whose exist-ence or perceived existence preys upon the imaginations of fretful settlors—if Lionel had a bad gambling habit, for instance, keeping the car as trust property and just licensing him to use it would prevent Lionel from selling it and blowing the proceeds playing online poker.

2.12   So the application of trust funds can serve the beneficiary in different ways. In the case of minor children, it is obvious that it would rarely be a good idea simply to transfer money to them as a way of applying the trust assets for their benefit. Rather, the trustee would use the funds for their 'maintenance', say giving trust money to their parents to buy clothes for the children, or for their education by transferring trust funds to a school to cover the children's school fees. The courts in times past were well used to enforcing trusts to pay for the maintenance, edu-cation, and advancement of children. A trust for maintenance is one that will provide for the child's daily costs of living, a roof over his head and food, clothing, etc; a trust for education is straightforward; 'advancement' here is a technical term meaning to 'advance' a young adult in life—typical expenditures of this kind would be the purchase of a commission in the army for a young man or the provision of a dowry for a young woman. In this way, then, we see that by exercising his powers that go with the title to the trust assets, in particular by transferring trust moneys directly to the beneficiary or to others in a way that benefits the beneficiary (to the beneficiary's parent or guardian, to his school, and so on), the trustee discharges his obligation 'to use' or 'to apply' the trust property for their benefit.

Bare trusts, special trusts, and nomineeships

2.13   Express trusts can be divided into bare trusts and special trusts. Under a bare trust, a trustee holds property for a beneficiary on no specific trust terms; the trustee's only obligation is to transfer the property to the beneficiary or to a third party as the beneficiary directs. In contrast, a special trust is one created by a settlor with specific terms; the standard example is the typical family trust, in which the trustee has various duties, to invest the trust property, to pay the income to X, and so on. Bare trusts typically come about in three circumstances. The first is when all of the interests under a special trust 'fall into possession'. Consider the trust (2.10) in which the company shares are held for Martha for life and then for her children in equal shares. When Martha dies, Tom, Dick, and Mary are entitled to the trust assets. There is nothing left for the trustee to do. At this point, the trustee becomes a bare trustee; his only obligation is to transfer the title to the assets to them, or to someone else as they direct.

2.14   In the case of a bare trust of company shares, the trustee must exercise his voting rights in the shares as the bare beneficiary directs, but until given any instructions to do so by the beneficiary, the trustee must exercise his voting rights in good faith in the interests of the beneficiary as he judges them to be. (See *Kirby v Wilkins* (1929), 454; *Hotung v Ho Yuen Ki* (2002); *Fong Wai Lyn Carolyn v Kao Chai-Chau Linda* (2017).)

2.15   The second circumstance in which a bare trust arises is by operation of law, ie when a construct-ive trust arises (2.7). One example will suffice for the nonce: in certain circumstances, a legal title holder of land may be required by law to hold the land on trust for himself and, typically, his wife or partner, in equal shares because although the spouse's or partner's name was not put on the title when the property was acquired, their common understanding was that the property should be held for the benefit of them both (4.22 et seq). This holder of the legal title to this property never undertook to hold the property on trust for anyone, and is unlikely to think, much less know, that his partner is the beneficiary of a trust of the property of which he is, unwittingly, the trustee. Partly because of this, he has no particular duties whatsoever towards his spouse or part-ner, as would an express trustee to his beneficiary; rather, he is in the position of a bare trustee, who essentially holds the property to the order of the spouse or partner/beneficiary to the extent of the latter's co-ownership interest in equity. Thus, when the bare trustee of a constructive trust finds out he holds the legal title for the benefit of the constructive beneficiary, his only duty is to transfer the legal title to the equitable owner forthwith or, as in the example, if the equitable title holder's interest is an ownership share in the property, to treat that person as a co-owner.

2.16   The third case is the intentionally created, ie express, bare trust called a nomineeship. A nomi-neeship combines the bare trust with a contract. A nominee is a bare trustee who has con-tractually agreed to comply with various orders the beneficiary makes with respect to the trust property. Perhaps the most common example is the trust upon which a solicitor holds his cli-ent's purchase moneys prior to completion of the sale of land. The solicitor holds the money in his client trust account, and the solicitor can only disburse the money according to his client's instructions under their contract (often called a 'retainer') and, in the case of a sale of land, this will be the instruction to transfer the money to the vendor in return for the transfer of title to the land. This is not a special trust, as there are no trust terms (see *AIB Group v Mark Redler & Co* (2014, at [13])). But the solicitor here is more than a bare trustee: he has also undertaken by contract to deal with the property as the beneficiary directs. It is said that the nominee or bare trustee holds the trust property 'to the order' of the beneficiary and, while this is perfectly cor-rect, it is important to notice that in the case of a simple bare trust the only order the beneficiary can make is an order to the trustee to transfer the property to himself or someone else, whereas in the case of the nomineeship the trustee has contractually undertaken to carry out different sorts of orders, which can be very extensive (see further Matthews (2005)); in such cases the trustee is also an agent of the beneficiary (2.52). None of these cases should be confused with a trust under which (typically) the property is to be held for the settlor until such time as he declares new trusts of the property, for his children for example. This, as we have seen, was the typical form of the feoffment to uses (1.25). This is not a bare trust, but a special trust under the terms of which the settlor has a power (3.8 et seq) to declare new beneficial interests in favour of others. These days, trusts of family wealth are typically special trusts, in which the trustee has an active role to play in the management and distribution of the trust assets (see Lau (2011), ch 1).

Beneficial, equitable, and legal interests

2.17   As we have seen, the trustee must hold the property for the benefit of others; correlatively, the trustee is not entitled to use the property for his own benefit. What the trust does, then, is drive a wedge between the legal title that the trustee has, and the right to use it for his own benefit; in other words, where someone holds his title to property on trust for another, he does not have any *beneficial interest* in the property. Correspondingly, the beneficiaries, though not having the legal title to the property, *are* entitled to the benefit of it; together the beneficiaries do have the beneficial interest in the trust property. Compare this situation to the case where a legal owner of property owns it outright, ie owns it not subject to any trust; in this case the beneficial interest is the legal owner's. Now, here is the aspect of this terminology that sometimes causes confusion: the beneficiaries under a trust, as we have just said, have the beneficial interest in the trust property, but not because, like the outright owner, they have the legal title to it, but because *equity* will require their trustee to use the trust property, not for his own benefit, but for theirs. So *their* beneficial interest is an *equitable* beneficial interest. In the case of the outright legal owner, he has a *legal* beneficial interest. So the word 'beneficial' can describe the position both of a legal owner of property who owns it outright and of a beneficiary of a trust. The typical confusion that the terminology of 'beneficial interest' creates is when people (and this is very common; see eg 6.23) confuse 'beneficial' interest with 'equitable' interest. One mistake that arises from this confusion is to think that the outright legal owner of property holds both the legal *and* the equitable title to it, as if he held it 'on trust for himself'. But we have already seen (2.3) that a legal owner cannot hold property on trust for himself as a sole beneficiary. The impossibility of a legal owner being a trustee for himself alone shows that it is incorrect to think that the outright owner of a piece of property, that is the legal owner of property that is not subject to any trust, has both legal and equitable interests; he has the legal interest *simpliciter*, and there is no equitable interest at all (*Westdeutsche Landesbank Girozentrale v Islington London Borough Council* (1996) per Lord Browne-Wilkinson). This is not to say that equity is blind to the legal ownership of property: equity is perfectly aware that a legal owner of property subject to no trust has the benefit of the property himself, having no obligation to hold it for another. In determining the rights of individuals to property under the law of trusts, the pertinent question is always whether equity recognises a distinct beneficial interest in the property, ie an equitable interest, which displaces the legal owner's beneficial interest. The mistake is to think that because a legal owner has the beneficial interest, he has both a legal and an equitable title to the property. Indeed, if he didn't have the beneficial interest in the eyes of equity, he would have no power to *declare a trust over it* (2.39).

2.18   Of course, the ideas of beneficial interests and equitable interests are related: only in a legal system which had some sort of doctrine, like the law of trusts, which held that a legal owner's beneficial interest could be extinguished in favour of another, so that he held his legal title for the benefit of that other, would a concept like beneficial interest arise. It arises to describe the fact that there are different ways of having a beneficial interest in property—either as an outright legal owner, or as a beneficiary under a trust. But although the terms are related in this way, they do not have the same meaning. An equitable interest is one that is recognised because of equity's recognising an interest in property under a trust.

Trustees and fiduciaries

2.19   A trustee is under an obligation to hold the property for the benefit of the beneficiaries, and must not derive any benefit from the trust property himself (unless he is also a beneficiary (2.3)). One use of the word 'fiduciary' is in the context of powers given by the trust terms, and simply serves to indicate that the power in question is held, and must be exercised, for the benefit of the beneficiaries, not for the power-holder's own benefit. The contrasting term, where the power-holder holds the power for his own benefit, is 'personal'. The holder of a personal power may exercise it as he chooses for his own benefit. We will examine this use of the term in detail at 3.15 et seq.

2.20 But the term fiduciary generally refers to more than this. Consider the kind of obligations the trustee has under a typical express trust. The trustee *agrees* to undertake the trust, so his obligations are voluntarily undertaken. Secondly, his obligations are spelt out by the declaration of trust more or less explicitly, as in a contract: the trustee will be required to do various things with the trust property, such as invest it, pay over the income to X for his life, pay over the capital to Y if she attains the age of 30, and so on. Such trustee's duties are the essence of any trust. Beyond the trust instrument, the law of trusts itself (either in the case law or because of legislation) imposes certain duties upon a trustee. Typically, however, although not necessarily, equity will regard the trustee as having, further to his explicit obligations under the terms of the trust or the general trusts law, a special kind of overarching *fiduciary relationship* to the beneficiaries. As we shall see in Chapter 13, the precise nature and scope of the law governing fiduciaries is controversial; the brief outline given in the following few paragraphs is intended to provide the least contentious overview for the time being.

2.21 At the heart of the fiduciary relationship lie the ideas of *discretion* and *conflict of interest*. In certain cases where a person is empowered to make decisions on behalf of another, and to make these decisions using his own judgment or 'discretion', equity will seek to ensure that these decisions are not taken *in conflict of interest*. The decision-taker, the 'fiduciary', must act only in the interests of the person for whom he makes those decisions, who is called his 'principal', and must not allow his own interests, or the interests of third parties, to affect his judgment in any way. Fiduciary law is thus the origin in modern society of the legal notion of 'conflict of interest'. The fiduciary must not only act so as not to favour his own or others' interests over his principal's, but should also, if he is wise, avoid putting himself in positions of conflict of interest. (It must be noted, however, that in the same way as a trustee can also be a beneficiary and therefore someone whose own interests 'count' under the trust, it is clear from the cases that specific fiduciary liabilities, eg the fiduciary's liability to have his purchase of the trust property set aside (13.92 et seq), which would normally apply to a trustee, can be removed by the principal—see *Sargeant v National Westminster Bank plc* (1990) and *Hayim v Citibank NA* (1987)—with the result that the trustee can favour his own interests.)

2.22 Although the trustee–beneficiary relationship is the classic example of the fiduciary–principal relationship, it must be clearly understood that the law governing fiduciaries is conceptually distinct from the general law of trusts governing trustees. Agents and company directors are both examples of fiduciaries, and as we shall see when we examine the law governing fiduciaries in detail, most of the cases we will look at concern non-trustee fiduciaries, in particular company directors. The reason why we will look at fiduciary law in detail is that in the case of most trusts, trustees are fiduciaries to their beneficiaries.

2.23 Earlier I said that fiduciaries are persons who take decisions in the interests of their principals. Fiduciary relationships, at least in their core sense, are relationships in which the fiduciary must exercise judgment in the way he chooses to meet his obligations to take these decisions. Strictly defined, a fiduciary relationship exists when one person, the fiduciary, has agreed to undertake *legal* powers to affect the *legal* position—ie *the legal rights, duties, or powers*—of another, the fiduciary's principal, and the fiduciary must exercise judgment in the way he will exercise those legal powers (*legal* here meaning 'recognised by law', so *legal and/or equitable* powers). Although 'judgment' is the better word, it is common in the case law and the academic literature to use 'discretion', ie a fiduciary is one who must exercise a 'discretion' in exercising his legal powers for his principal. But think 'judgment', not 'discretion'. 'Discretion' suggests that the fiduciary has some sort of leeway, to choose one way over another. But this is misleading: the fiduciary doesn't really have a choice in the matter. The fiduciary must follow the course of action which, *in his judgment*, best advances his principal's interests. Different fiduciaries might in good faith judge differently—that's just an artefact of human judgment—but no individual fiduciary can choose to follow any course of action but the one which he judges to be best for the principal.

2.24   The two central cases are those of trustee and beneficiary, and agent and principal. A trustee has the legal title to the trust property, and therefore has the legal power to affect the position of the beneficiary. He buys and sells trust property in the course of making investments of the trust fund; he may have a discretion under the trust instrument to pay one beneficiary more than another; he may have the power to appoint successor trustees. In exercising those powers, he must bear only the beneficiaries' interests in mind. He must not buy company shares as an investment because he has an interest in the company and thinks it needs more capital; he must not exercise his discretion to give beneficiary X a great deal and beneficiary Y nothing because he is in love with beneficiary X; he must not appoint his brother as his successor trustee because the latter is down on his luck and could do with the trustee's fees.

2.25   Similarly, an agent is someone who is empowered to make contracts for his principal with third parties, and must similarly act only in consideration of the interests of his principal. He should not, for example, sell his principal's goods to a third party because the third party is willing to pay him a commission on the sale. Business partners are also generally fiduciaries to each other. Under a partnership, the partners work together to bear the costs of a business and share in the profits and, in consequence, third parties are allowed to sue an entire partnership, or firm, for breach of contract, etc. Obviously, then, a partner's individual use of his legal powers to contract will affect the legal position of all of the other partners, and therefore they are treated as fiduciaries one to another. Similarly, some company directors are agents of, and therefore fiduciaries to, their companies, and all directors in their non-agent role as members of the Board exercise their judgment in committing their companies to various courses of action. Their direction of the company's business clearly affects the company's legal position, so they must act only with the company's interests in mind. The crucial point in all these cases is that a fiduciary is one who voluntarily undertakes to act as a *decision-maker* for someone else: the fiduciary is empowered to make decisions (legally *binding* decisions) for his principal's benefit (decisions that, therefore, alter the principal's *legal* position).

2.26   As a point of contrast, the fiduciary relationship just described is thus very different from that of contracting parties to one another. While contracting parties must comply with their contractual obligations, of course, any leeway they have in the performance of those obligations amounts to a freedom to act in their own interests; in general, contracting parties are not required to act 'selflessly' when they decide precisely how they will comply with their contract, or to secure the best interests of their opposite number—what they owe the other party is strictly a matter of what rights that other has secured in negotiating the terms of the contract. (Possibly this picture of contractual obligations may have shifted. There is much talk about recognising a general obligation of 'good faith' in contractual performance. But certainly the traditional common law never imposed any such standard.)

The features of the express trust

The position of the settlor

2.27   A settlor creates the trust, determining its terms; the settlor, once having created the trust, is not the person who enforces it. It is the beneficiaries alone who are entitled to do that. Equity regards the creation of a trust as a 'disposition' of the trust property. The settlor disposes of his interest in the trust property, so that it is no longer his. In the case of a self-declaration of trust, though he retains the title to the trust property, he disposes of his legal beneficial interest by creating an equitable beneficial interest for the beneficiaries. In the case of a transfer of assets to someone else, the case is even clearer. The settlor not only disposes of his beneficial interest, but passes his legal title to the trustee, who himself will be bound by the beneficiaries' beneficial equitable interests. In this latter case, the settlor will drop out of the picture completely.

Revocability

2.28   A settlor may be able to revoke the trust, that is bring it to an end and get the trust property back, but it is important to understand the legal basis for revoking a trust where it is possible. Trusts are normally created by the settlor transferring property to a trustee while at the same time declaring the terms of the trust, thereby creating the equitable beneficial interest of the beneficiaries. And just like any other transfer or creation of an interest in property, once the act of transfer or creation is complete, the interest in the property belongs to the recipient, and that is the end of it as far as the transferor is concerned. Thus the settlor cannot think of the trust property as still 'really his'. He cannot get it back, because he is legally out of the picture, unless under a self-declaration he makes himself the trustee, but the lesson is the same; he has no right or power just to extinguish the trust and start using the assets again as if they were beneficially his own. In the same way that a donor of an outright gift has nothing to say about what the 'donee' (ie the recipient) does with the property once the gift is made, neither has the settlor anything to say about the trust, the way it is administered, etc, after the trust is created. The equitable interests under the trust belong to the beneficiaries, and they, and only they, may enforce the terms of the trust against the trustee. *But*, in setting out the terms of the trust, the settlor *may grant himself powers under it*. He can give himself a power to bring the trust to an end, that is to revoke it. He can also give himself lesser powers, such as the power to replace the trustees, or the power to direct the trustee in the making of investments, and so on. But the point to realise is this: *if* the settlor has a power to revoke the trust or to appoint new trustees, *that power must be an express or implied power under the terms of the trust itself*; the power derives from the trust terms, not from the settlor's position as the one who originally owned the property. Indeed, under the terms of the trust the settlor may give such powers to anyone he chooses.

2.29   It is also important to note that the settlor's power to revoke the trust is a personal, not a fiduciary power (2.19). This means that he holds the power for his own benefit, and this has the consequence that this power to regain title to the trust property is a valuable asset he holds. In *Tasarruf Mevduati Sigorta Fonu v Merrill Lynch Bank and Trust Co (Cayman) Ltd* (2011) the UKPC held that such a power was an asset of a bankrupt individual which he could be required to exercise (or be required to delegate the exercise of) so that receivers could claim, for the benefit of his creditors, the assets of the revocable trusts he had established.

2.30 Particularly for trusts that are administered in foreign, or 'offshore', jurisdictions (often places that offer tax and other advantages for holding property in trust there, such as Jersey or the Bahamas), a settlor may give a range of powers to individuals who have come to be called 'protectors'. These individuals monitor the trust, and by using these sorts of powers it is hoped that they can 'protect' the trust, ie ensure that its administration by the trustees is to the expected standard and coincides with the settlor's original purposes for setting it up (3.28).

The beneficiaries' interests under a trust are derivative, not possessory

2.31 Whilst equity regards the beneficiaries as having the beneficial interest in the trust property, the 'true owners' of it as it were, equity does not *disturb* the trustee's title to or possession of the property. Rather, equity requires the trustee to use his powers of title in the trust assets for the benefit of the beneficiaries. So the 'equitable ownership' of the trust property is a special kind of ownership: so long as the trust is in existence, the beneficiaries take the benefit of their rights not by dealing with the trust property directly, as if they were legal owners, but indirectly, by enforcing the terms of the trust obligation against the trustee. So, for example, a beneficiary entitled to the income from the trust property is not allowed to claim the dividends on company shares in the trust from the company himself. It is the trustee who alone is entitled to do that. The beneficiary may only demand that the trustee transfer to him trust moneys equivalent to the value of the dividends the trustee receives.

2.32 As Matthews (2005) puts it, the beneficiaries' 'equitable ownership' and the trustee's 'legal ownership' of the trust assets are not *competitive*, as if the system treated both as essentially the same sort of owner who are in constant conflict over which of them will prevail (although facile formulations such as 'in the eyes of the law, the trustee owns the property, although in the eyes of equity, the beneficiary does' can give that misleading impression). Rather, the beneficiary's title is *derivative*. It does not exist independently of the trustee's title; it *depends* upon it, because only through the obligation imposed upon the trustee to make use of *his* title in such and such a way do the beneficiaries acquire any interest in the property at all. So although it is perfectly fine in most contexts to say that a trustee 'holds property on trust', what that means is that the trustee holds the *legal title* he has to the trust assets on trust. To have title to property is to have the various rights and powers in respect of the property, which will vary with the kind of property it is. The title holder of land has a number of different rights and powers: the right to possess (or occupy) the land, the power to transfer it, the power to grant a neighbour a right of way (a kind of 'easement') over the land, the power to mortgage the land, and so on. The key point to note here about the beneficiary's interest under the trust is that it does not give the beneficiary a derivative right to possess the trust property if the trustee has title to assets such as land and chattels (which are also called 'tangible assets', in contrast to 'intangible assets' which cannot be possessed, such as the right to be paid a debt one is owed). Analogies are dangerous here, but consider the case of companies. Shareholders are said to own the company, which in turn owns its own property. As in the case of beneficiaries vis-à-vis the trust property, shareholders have no right to make use of the company property, to visit the company premises, lounge around on the furniture, and drink the company coffee, simply because they own shares. Their share ownership does not entitle them to so much as touch the company property. Any benefit they receive from the company property, and the profitable use made of it by the company directors and employees, comes to them via the defined rights to dividends and so on which comprise their rights as shareholders. Thus, the 'interest' the shareholders have in the company assets is *derivative of, not competitive with*, the company's ownership of its property.

2.33 So too in the case of trusts. We can see this by remembering the ways in which the beneficiaries take the benefit of the trust, either under a bare trust of land or under a modern wealth management trust (2.8 et seq). Just as with the case of company shareholders, surprising as this may sound, beneficiaries have no right to possession of tangible trust property just because they are beneficiaries, but only if the terms of the trust so specify. Of course, in the case of bare trusts of land, as in the typical case of co-ownership of land in England (2.9), the terms of the trust do specify this, but it is important to see how this result comes about. It is not the beneficiary's right, just as a beneficiary, that *ipso facto* entitles him to possession—it is the fact that the terms of the trust allow or require the trustee *to exercise his powers of title to apply the property to the beneficiaries' benefit by licensing the beneficiaries to take possession*. So in the millions of co-ownership trusts of land imposed in England by law, the trustee-beneficiaries apply the property to their own benefit by occupying it as a residence under a licence they grant to themselves. In *Shell UK v Total UK* (2010) the CA muddled this, holding that a beneficiary of a trust of land, though not entitled under the trust to possess the land, and not in actual possession of it, had a sufficient interest merely as a beneficiary to found a claim in tort to which, on orthodox principles of tort law, only those persons with an actual right to possession would have been entitled.

2.34 In the case of the modern wealth management trust, this point—ie that the beneficiary's interest is not an interest in the possession of the trust assets—is even clearer. Most of the trust assets will be intangible, for example bank balances, ie money held in a bank account. The banker–depositor relationship is that of debtor to creditor: the bank just owes the depositor a contractual debt, to pay on demand the balance in the account. Whilst this right is valuable, of course, it is not tangible. It cannot be possessed, taken hold of. Such intangible rights can, accordingly, give the trustee no rights to possession at all since they are unpossessible. And of course where because of the nature of the property, the trustee has no possessory right, then neither can the beneficiaries have any. Where the wealth for investment does consist of a tangible, for instance land, the trustee must 'invest' that land to generate income, for example by leasing it for a money rent. More generally, since trust law specifically prohibits the trustee from taking possession of the trust assets for his own benefit, even where a wealth management trust holds valuable tangible assets that are not to be 'invested', such as paintings, the trustee is not entitled to take possession of them for his own benefit, hanging a trust painting in his dining room, for example. They must be properly stored (perhaps in a bank vault) and insured, of course. In summary: the beneficiaries' interests lie in the trustee's exercising his powers of title to realise the value of the assets through sale and reinvestment, and also of course in the trustee's power to transfer the legal title to the assets so as to apply the assets to the beneficiaries' benefit.

The beneficiary's interest is itself a kind of property right

2.35 A trust beneficiary has the personal right that the trustee comply with his duties as set out under the terms of the trust to apply the trust property to the beneficiary's benefit. Obviously, the net re-sult of the trustee's compliance with his duties is that the beneficiary will receive whatever benefit the terms of the trust dictate. If he is an income beneficiary, for example, he has the right to receive payments when the trust investments generate income. He holds this right against the trustee, who has the correlative duty to pay the beneficiary that income. In this respect, the beneficiary has a right that the trustee pay him an amount of property at a particular time, and therefore he has a right that is very much like the right to be paid a debt, and he can transfer this right by assigning it to a third party.

2.36   Assignable personal rights of this kind, like debts, are a kind of property right in the law. So, for example, if Tom in our previous example (2.10) was being pressed by a creditor, he might reduce his debt by assigning his one-third share of the trust capital. The creditor, as his assignee, would be able to go to the trustee and require the trustee to pay him the one-third share of the capital on the death of Tom's mother. More interestingly, the beneficial interest being a property right under English law, which of course includes equity, the beneficiary can, as owner of his interest under the trust, declare a trust of that interest. For obvious reasons, the trust he creates will be called a 'sub-trust'. So, for example, Tom may decide that he wants his capital interest under the trust to be used for the benefit of his own children. He can, therefore, declare a trust over it. If he wants his sister Mary to be the trustee of this trust, he will execute an assignment of his capital interest to her on trust for the benefit of his children, so that on Martha's death Mary can claim the capital share from the trustee herself and then carry out whatever the terms of the trust for Tom's children require her to do.

2.37   Two things to note about equitable interests and sub-trusts. The first is that we now see that we have, up until this point, spoken of the trustee's *legal* title to the trust property, as if that were the only possibility. We now see that the trust property (also called the 'trust corpus' or 'trust fund') can contain equitable interests itself. Nowadays, by the way, this is not at all uncommon, because of the way that financial assets like shares are held. Typically, the right to a company share that any private individual or trustee owns is not the legal share itself—that is held by an *intermediary*, who takes legal title to the shares from the issuing company and then sells an equitable interest in the shares, holding its legal title on trust for the buyers. There may be, and often are, several layers of intermediaries, so the right the private individual has in the company shares may be under a sub-sub-sub-trust of the first intermediary's trust of the legal title to the shares.

2.38   The second thing to notice is that, now having the concept of a sub-trust in hand, we can further distinguish the concept of beneficial interests from equitable interests (2.17–2.18). When Tom creates a sub-trust in favour of his children, assigning his equitable interest to Mary, Mary now holds his equitable interest under the trust—but she does not have the beneficial interest in it, because she holds it on trust for Tom's children. So not every equitable interest in property is a beneficial interest. In the same way that a trustee who holds the legal title of trust property does not have the beneficial interest in it—the beneficiaries of that trust do—a trustee who holds an equitable interest on trust similarly has no beneficial interests in it—the beneficiaries of that sub-trust do.

2.39   This allows us to give something of a definition of a beneficial interest under English law (including again, of course, equity): a person has the beneficial interest in property when equity regards him as having the power to declare a trust over it. An outright owner of a legal title to property can declare a trust over it; in the eyes of equity, this is because he has the beneficial interest in the property. A trustee, on the other hand, who just as much has the legal title to property cannot declare a trust over those assets—the settlor has already done that. In the eyes of equity this is because he has no beneficial interest in it. In this case the beneficiaries have the beneficial interest in the property, so they can declare a trust over those assets by way of sub-trust.

The trustee's powers and duties and liability to account

The powers of the trustee

2.40   Since the trustee has title to the property in question, the trustee has all the rights and powers that go with having title to that kind of property. If the trust property is land, in which lots of different interests can be created, then because he has the title it is the trustee who can create them; he has the power to grant easements, to mortgage the land, to grant leases of the land, to license people to enter the land, and so on. If land held on trust is occupied by squatters, then it is the trustee who has the right to evict them. It is the trustee who has the power to buy and sell the trust property, so he is the one who makes the trust investments. The trustee must, however, act upon these rights and exercise those powers in accordance with his obligation to exercise his ownership of the property according to the trust terms, and in this way the trustee's exercise of his legal powers will be governed by the way the trust instrument imposes duties upon him to exercise his powers for the benefit of the beneficiaries. In general, then, the beneficiaries' rights in respect of the trust property vis-à-vis third parties are legally protected by the trustee's enforcement of his rights to the trust property. Third parties owe their duties in respect of tangible property—for example to keep off it—to the legal owner, the trustee, and the trustee enforces those rights in his own name to protect the beneficiaries' equitable beneficial interests. Similarly, if one of the trust assets is a mortgage loan over land, and the mortgagor falls behind in his payments, it is the trustee's duty to use his powers as the mortgagee to take possession of the mortgaged land and sell it so as to recover the outstanding mortgage debt.

2.41   The beneficiaries do not have any power to enforce any of these legal rights themselves; the trustee must do so, for the simple reason that he is the one who has those legal rights (see *MCC Proceeds Inc v Lehman Bros* (1998)). If the trustee for some reason were to refuse to do so, the beneficiaries could launch a legal action against a third party such as the mortgagor in the last example, *joining the trustee*, ie suing the trustee as well so as to make him participate and enforce his legal rights to the property for the benefit of the beneficiaries (see *Vandepitte v Preferred Accident Insurance Corporation of New York* (1933); *Parker-Tweedale v Dunbar Bank plc* (1991)).

2.42   One thing to notice here: as these examples illustrate, someone may have a power over property, to transfer it, for example, but be subject to a duty to exercise or not exercise that power in a certain way. A trustee has a duty to exercise his power to transfer the trust moneys representing the income of the trust assets to the income beneficiary, and a duty not to transfer the trust assets to a non-beneficiary. So duties can in this way 'control' a trustee's exercise of his powers; to the extent that a trustee complies with these duties, he will not have committed any breach of trust, any breach of his trustee's obligations. But just because there is a duty to do x or y does not mean that when a trustee exercises his power over the trust assets in a way that breaches his duty, this exercise of his power is *ineffective*. If, in breach of trust, the trustee transfers £1,000 of trust money as a birthday present to his nephew, who is not a beneficiary of the trust, that transfer is perfectly legally effective to give the nephew title to the money even though it is clearly in breach of trust. As we shall see in Chapter 11, there are a host of remedies that the beneficiaries can resort to when this sort of breach of trust occurs, but the point to be taken on board here is that the duties imposed on the trustee in the trust instrument do not 'disable' the trustee in the exercise of his powers, the powers that he has simply by virtue of having title to the trust property.

2.43 It is also vital to understand the basis upon which the trustee holds his powers over the trust property, and the way it is said that the terms of the trust 'grant' a trustee a power to do this or that. As I have rather laboured above, the trustee carries out the trust by exercising his powers over the trust property, and he has those powers simply by virtue of the fact that he has the title to that property. Undertaking to act as a trustee, being bound by the terms of the trust, does not *endow* him with those powers—his having title to the trust assets does that. But lawyers typically say that the trust instrument 'grants' the trustee a power to do this or do that. We can use the 'power of investment' as an example. Until the turn of the twentieth century, under the general law of trusts trustees were generally required to hold the particular assets they received at the creation of the trust as *the* trust assets; they were not entitled to exchange these assets for others, and so under the general law, they had a duty *not* to invest the trust assets, ie exchange the asset from time to time to realise income or capital value returns (see Nolan (2004)). In short, trustees had a duty not to transfer the trust assets in order to make investments.

2.44 But, of course, some settlors did want their trustees to exercise their power of title over the trust assets to invest them, and so they created trusts with terms that gave the trustee a 'power' to invest. But what such a provision does is to *remove* the general law duty on the trustee *not* to invest. In general, settlors have 'freedom of trust', that is, by the terms of the trust they can impose duties on the trustee greater to or different from those imposed on trustees by the general law, and can relieve trustees of duties imposed by the general law. (When we look at trust provisions which relieve trustees of liability for breach of trust (11.85 et seq), we will look at whether there are any 'core' trust obligations which a settlor could not conceivably relieve a trustee of without fundamentally undermining his position as a true trustee.) So a settlor can, in practical terms, 'empower' a trustee to do things by relieving him of a duty not to do such things that he would otherwise have under the general law. But the terms of the trust do not 'endow' the trustee with the powers which are or are not subject to those duties. He has those, as we have seen, just by virtue of his title to the assets. So while in most cases it is innocuous, I suppose, to talk about powers granted to the trustee in a trust instrument or by legislation (eg a power of advancement (10.41)), always be conscious of the fact that what these 'grants of powers' in fact do is to relieve a trustee of duties not to do this or that which he would otherwise have had under the general law.

2.45 It should also be noted that such provisions often appear in trust instruments even after the law has changed making them unnecessary, or much less necessary. Again the 'power to invest' is a good example. By virtue of the development of case law and legislation, trustees now have a broad 'power to invest', indeed, normally a duty to exercise their powers of title to invest the trust funds (10.2 et seq). So the general law now no longer imposes a ban on a trustee exercising his powers of title to invest the trust assets. But all professionally drawn trust instruments have a provision concerning investments, for two reasons: (1) such a provision allows the settlor to create a bespoke, or 'tailor-made', investment provision, so that he can direct the sorts of investments the trustee can make; and (2), as good lawyers know, the law can always change by case law development or legislation; in the absence of an express provision on investments, the trustee's power to invest would be subject to fluctuations in legal doctrine; since trusts can last a very long time, it is much better to have a clear, express provision, rather than making the trustee subject to the general law as it changes from time to time.

The trustee's liability to account, 'getting in' the trust assets, understanding
the trust terms, and keeping the trust property separate

2.46   The principal task of the trustee is to keep the trust property separate from his own (and from others') and dispose of it according to the terms of the trust. In carrying out this task, he must keep track of what he does with the trust property; this is called 'keeping the trust account(s)', and, as you would imagine, normally involves keeping the documents concerning transactions with the trust property in good order. When a beneficiary suspects that something has gone wrong with the administration of the trust, this is normally because he does not accept the trustee's account, ie his record of what he has done with the trust property, and the beneficiary's primary legal right is to bring the trustee to the Court of Chancery and have 'the account taken', ie reviewed. In a sense then, all the specific 'basic' duties of a trustee can be explained in terms of his liability to account to the beneficiaries, to show them what he has done with the trust assets.

2.47   On accepting a trusteeship, a trustee has a duty to 'get in' the trust assets. That is, he must make sure that title to the trust assets gets into his hands. So, for example, where Bernadette is appointed a trustee under Fred's will, and Bernadette accepts the trusteeship, then Bernadette must make sure that the assets in Fred's estate which are to form the trust assets get into her hands. Typically this will just mean that she ensures that the executor of Fred's will transfers the trust assets to her in a timely fashion. She cannot just do nothing for years; as someone entitled under Fred's will, she has the right to make sure that the executor administers Fred's estate in a timely fashion. Similarly, if Bernadette is taking over the trust from a trustee who wants to retire from the role, again, she must make sure that title to the trust assets is transferred to her in a timely fashion.

2.48   Bernadette must also familiarise herself with the trust terms and make sure she understands them. This is obvious—how could she properly discharge her obligations under the terms of the trust if she doesn't know what they require of her? The practical force of this duty is, in most cases, to seek legal advice about the terms of the trust if she thinks that something is unclear or awry. Unfortunately badly drawn trust instruments, cobbled-together efforts based upon precedent trust instruments, and which may not be well suited to the settlor's intentions for the beneficiaries, are not uncommon, so it is likewise not uncommon for incoming trustees to have to seek legal advice to ascertain what particular trust provisions require, or even whether they are legally valid.

2.49   Finally, Bernadette must keep the trust assets separate from her own. If she did not do that, mixing trust assets with her own assets, it would be difficult if not impossible for her to fulfil her duty to account to the beneficiaries—how could she explain what she did with the trust assets if she cannot figure out which assets those are? As we shall see (7.33, 7.73), some cases have started to nibble at the margins of this principle, but in the vast majority of trusts it would be a clear breach of trust if the trustee mixed the trust assets with his own, or did anything else the consequence of which would be that it would be difficult or impossible to identify the assets under the trust. Note, however, that the terms of a trust may allow the mixing of the assets of several beneficiaries, so long as their respective interests in the merged fund are clear. A good example of this is a solicitor's client account, which is a bank account that the solicitor holds on trust for those of his clients who deposit money with him, for example to complete the purchase of a house. The solicitor only has one client account with the bank, and deposits any client money he receives into it. But it is easy to keep track of the beneficial interests of his clients as money comes in and goes out of the client account, including allocating any interest the account earns in proportionate shares. It is essentially a bookkeeping exercise, so there is no difficulty for the solicitor in accounting for what he has done with the funds to his several clients/beneficiaries. Their respective beneficial interests are the proportionate beneficial equitable shares they have in the solicitor/trustee's title to the bank balance. Another example of such pooled beneficial interest occurs under collective investment schemes where the manager of the investments (or, more usually, a holding company) holds title to the investments, shares, bonds, and so on, but on trust for investors in proportion to the amounts they have invested.

Administrative and dispositive duties

2.50   The trustee's obligations under the trust are often subcategorised into duties of two kinds: 'administrative' and 'dispositive' duties. Roughly, administrative duties govern the trustee's power to make contracts and his powers of ownership to maintain the value of the trust property. Trustees have the duty to invest the trust property safely and so that it makes a reasonable return. A legal owner of property not subject to a trust has all the same powers, but not the duties. He can invest it, or not, as he chooses, and may engage in dangerously speculative investments. A trustee must invest the trust property and must not do so in a dangerously speculative way. Where appropriate, trustees must also insure the trust property, against fire, for example, if the trust property is a house.

2.51   Dispositive duties are those that require the trustee to dispose of the trust assets, ie distribute them by making transfers of them, to the beneficiaries according to the terms of the trust. These are the duties the trustee's compliance with which delivers to the beneficiaries the particular benefits the settlor intended. We have already gone over some examples (2.8 et seq). The trustee is not free to benefit whom he would like, as if he were the outright owner of his legal title. His duty to exercise his powers to apply the property only according to its terms is the essence of any trust.

The trustee acts in his own name, and is not an agent of the beneficiaries

2.52   In the same way that the trustee is the trust's 'face to the world' because of his ownership of the property, the same goes for the contractual obligations the trustee enters into in the course of carrying out the trust. When, for example, a trustee sells some company shares he holds on trust and buys others in the course of his investment of the trust fund, he makes these contracts to buy and sell in his own name. The trust itself has no legal personality like a company, on behalf of which agents of the company make contracts that bind the company itself as a legal person. Having no legal personality, one cannot sue the trust itself for breach of contract; one sues the trustee for his own breach of contract, even though the breach was of a contractual obligation he undertook in the course of carrying out the trust. In general, trustees are 'indemnified', have an 'indemnity', for any liabilities they incur in properly carrying out the terms of a trust, which means that they have a claim against the funds of the trust to meet any contractual obligations or expenses they incur in carrying out the trust according to its terms.

2.53   In the case of a typical trust where the contracts that the trustee enters into are investments of various kinds, and contracts of service with solicitors and financial advisors, this indemnity is generally a perfectly adequate mechanism for protecting the trustee. However, a group of late nineteenth-century cases reveals the obvious dangers for a trustee who carries on a business for the benefit of the beneficiaries of a trust in his own name. (On a trustee's power to carry on a business, see generally Mowbray et al (2008), 36–80 et seq). You can imagine that a trustee might run such a business so badly or unluckily that it goes bankrupt; in other words, all the funds of the trust may be lost. Because the trustee is liable for the business's debts himself, he will be personally liable to the creditors of the business and, there being no remaining trust funds, his indemnity against the trust funds will be worthless. In that case, he will have to dig into his own pocket to meet the claims of the creditors. Only a mad trustee would nowadays run a trust business in his own name—if a business were to be settled on trust, then a trustee would insist that the business be incorporated, the trust owning the shares of the business. Then, if the business were to go bankrupt, the trust might lose all its value (ie the value of the shares would drop to nothing), but the trustee would not himself be personally liable to the business's creditors.

2.54 Although the trust has no separate personality as a company does, notice the parallel 'limited liability' of shareholders and beneficiaries. If a company goes bankrupt, shareholders are not required to cough up to the company's creditors—their liability is limited to the value of their shares. If the company goes bankrupt, those shares will be worth nothing, but the shareholders will not have to reach into their pockets to cover the company's debts. (In the past, some company shareholders did have this liability, to pay 'calls' on their shares to keep a company solvent.) The position of beneficiaries is similar, in that they are not generally bound to indemnify a trustee for the debts he may incur in carrying out the trust business—the trustee has an indemnity out of the trust fund, but to the extent that is insufficient, he cannot go after the beneficiaries themselves to make up the shortfall.

2.55 Now, you may ask, if trusts can provide individuals with limited liability in this way, why are there not as many businesses organised as trusts as there are organised as companies? Why don't investors settle money as a trust fund for themselves as beneficiaries, the fund being used by the trustee to run a business, these investors/settlors/beneficiaries participating in the profits of the trust business according to the trust terms in proportion to the amounts they put in, just as a subscriber to company shares does? Briefly, the reason is that the law looked through this arrangement and regarded the investors as more than just beneficiaries: as joint venturers in a business enterprise, the law regarded the trustee as not only their trustee, but also as their agent, carrying out their business for them. Thus the trustee was their agent, and they were jointly the agent's principal. Thus they were all *personally* liable as parties to the contracts their agent, the trustee, made on their behalf, and so the trust arrangement did not provide them with limited liability. In consequence, limited liability for business enterprises did require legislation, because the common law (including equity) did not provide it, although the trust device did at first appear to offer just that promise (see Flannigan (1984, 1986); Cullity (1985, 1986); Ford and Hardingham (1987)). Owing to tax legislation, certain businesses nowadays, particularly in Australia, are conducted through trusts, and the absence both of limited liability and a proper legislative scheme of insolvency rules causes no end of headaches; for details see D'Angelo (2014).

2.56 The reader may find the discussion in the preceding paragraph all a little recherché—of, at most, historical interest. The reader would be mistaken. The main point to draw from it is that the trust relationship and the agency relationship are different relationships. A trustee is *not*, simply by virtue of his role as trustee, an agent for his beneficiaries. This is a good thing for beneficiaries. If the trustee was their agent, the beneficiaries would themselves be liable on any contract the trustee entered into, for when an agent makes a contract for his principal, the principal himself is held to be a party to that contract. Furthermore, in general if the trustee was an agent for his beneficiaries, this would upset the normal way in which trusts operate. In the vast majority of trusts, the benefit that the beneficiaries receive from the trust property is entirely determined by the terms of the trust; beneficiaries under most trusts have essentially no right to direct the trustee in his use of the powers he has by virtue of his legal title as if he were their legal agent. They get the benefit of the property as defined by the terms of the trust, such as it is. That is, of course, the main reason settlors benefit people through trusts in the first place, so that *they* can decide what the beneficiaries will get out of the property, in other words to give them a specified benefit from the property *without giving them the powers of an owner.*

Now, although the trust relationship and the agency relationship are distinct, nothing stops them from occurring together. It would be rare in a family trust, where property is held by a trustee for a settlor's spouse and children, for the trustee to be the spouse and children's agent as well. Normally, the trustee would not take any directions from the beneficiaries, such as entering into particular contracts concerning the trust property because they said so or running a business held by the trust at their direction. The trustee carries out the settlor's wishes as expressed in the trust terms, and the spouse and children take what they get. But trusts are used outside the family context, including where there is an agency relationship. For example, if you are an airline, in certain cases it may make sense for a ticket agent of yours to hold the money he receives on the sale of your airline tickets on trust for you (see eg *Royal Brunei Airlines v Tan* (1995), 11.105). But although he is, in this respect, your trustee, he is still acting as your agent, and as his principal you will still be liable for his acts as your agent, for example under any contracts selling your tickets he makes on your behalf. This sort of situation came up in the Canadian case of *Trident Holdings Ltd v Danand Investments Ltd* (1988, Ontario CA). Danand was the legal owner of land for six equitable co-owners who wished to develop it. Trident contracted with Danand, the trustee, to install electrics, but claiming a breach of contract, brought an action against Danand and the six equitable owners of the land. The six argued that, as beneficiaries of a trust of the land, they were not directly liable to Trident. The court noted, however, that the only terms of the trust concerning the land were that Danand as 'bare nominee and trustee' (2.13 et seq) had to follow the directions of the six. The court therefore quite properly found that the six directed Danand—Danand was their agent, and therefore as principals, they were each personally liable to Trident under the contract. The fact that Danand held property on trust for the six did not entail that Danand was not also their agent.

2.57   Occasionally the courts have to examine the facts closely to determine whether an agent is also a trustee. *Hinckley Singapore Trading Pte Ltd v Sogo Department Stores* (2001) is a nice example: the appellant paid for space in the respondent's department store to exhibit its goods for sale, and advise customers on their purchase. The purchases of the goods, however, took place when the customer paid for the goods at any of the department store's tills that were open. As a matter of sales law, the transaction at the till passed the title to the goods to the customer, and the title to the money (or credit card credit, or whatever) passed to the department store. The appellant claimed that the department store held the money it received from the sales of the appellant's goods on trust for it. The court relied heavily on the fact that under their agreement the department store had no obligation to keep the money it received from the sales of the appellant's goods separate from all the other customer money it received for the purchase of other goods for sale in the store, nor an obligation to deposit the money received for the sale of the appellant's goods in a separate account, and held that although the department store acted as the appellant's agent in transacting with the customers, it did not hold the proceeds from those sales on trust—it merely had a personal obligation to pay over the amount of the sales money it received, minus its commission, from time to time. It was a *debtor* of those amounts to the appellant, not a *trustee* of the money it received from the customers (see also *Ontario Hydro-electric Commission v Brown* (1960)).

2.58   In *Paragon Finance plc v Thakerar* (1999), Lord Millett considered the factors which would determine whether the relationship between an agent and his principal was, in respect of money received by the agent, one of trustee–beneficiary or one of debtor–creditor. He said (my emphasis):

> *Whether [the defendant] was in fact a trustee of the money may be open to doubt. Unless I have misunderstood the facts or they were very unusual it would appear that the defendant was entitled to pay receipts into his own account, mix them with his own money, use them for his own cash flow, deduct his own commission, and account for the balance to the plaintiff only at the end of the year.* It is fundamental to the existence of a trust that the trustee is bound to keep the trust property separate from his own and apply it exclusively for the benefit of his beneficiary. Any right on the part of the defendant to mix the money which he received with his own and use it for his own cash flow would be inconsistent with the existence of a trust. So would a liability to account annually, for a trustee is obliged to account to his beneficiary and pay over the trust property on demand *[emphasis added]. The fact that the defendant was [an agent and therefore] a fiduciary was irrelevant if he had no fiduciary or trust obligations in regard to the money. If this was the position, then the defendant was a fiduciary and subject to an equitable duty to account, but he was not a . . . trustee. His liability arose from his failure to account, not from his retention and use of the money for his own benefit, for this was something which he was entitled to do.*

The beneficiaries' interests 'run' with the trust property

2.59   As we have seen (2.35), as an assignable right, and as a right over which the beneficiary can declare a trust, the beneficiary's beneficial interest can be seen to be a kind of property. But the beneficiaries' beneficial interest can be seen to be a property right in other ways because the beneficiary's right is entwined with the trust property in other ways. The beneficiary's right is proprietary in so far as it is a right in the trust property itself, ie in so far as its fate is tied up with the fate of the trust property. One indication of its proprietary character is that it lasts only so long as the trust property does, that is it will only be effective so long as the trust property continues to exist. If the trust property is stolen or lost and cannot be recovered, or is destroyed, then the trust essentially evaporates, because there is no property to which the beneficiary's rights under a trust can attach (*Morley v Morley* (1678)). As a consequence of this theft or destruction the trustee's personal duty to dispose of the property in accordance with the terms of the trust likewise disappears, because he is no longer an owner of any trust property. Thus, if the property disappears, then so does the trust, and so does the beneficiary's right. There is a sharp difference between the right of the beneficiary in this respect and the right of the buyer under a contract of sale to be delivered the goods, or the right of a creditor. If the goods that the seller is bound to deliver are lost or stolen before title passes, then the buyer does not lose his contractual right to the seller's delivery of them; he may bring an action for damages for breach of contract for their full value. Similarly, if a debtor is robbed it is no skin off his creditor's nose—a debt does not attach to any specific property of the debtor, and thus not specifically to any property of his that is stolen, and the debtor cannot use the robbery as an excuse for not paying in full. In the case of the beneficiary, however, he is the one who loses if the trust property is lost or stolen, since equity regards his rights as being dependent upon his continuing equitable interest in the trust property, which attaches to the trust property from the outset of the trust (see *Ontario Hydro-electric*).

2.60   Note, however, that the complete loss of the trust property may not leave the beneficiaries absolutely bereft. If the trust property is lost through no fault of the trustee, then that is the end of the matter. But if the trust property was lost because of the trustee's fault, the trustee's liability for this breach of trust continues even if the breach caused the total loss of the trust property. For example, if the trustee commits a breach of trust by investing the trust fund improperly so that all the money is lost, the trustee is liable to reconstitute the trust by restoring property of the same value as what was lost. But this right against the trustee is a purely *personal* right, in essence to make him *recreate* the trust, to make the beneficiaries genuine beneficiaries once again. None of the trustee's own property is to be treated as trust property to which this obligation to reconstitute the trust somehow magically attaches to form a new trust fund. The trustee has a personal obligation to use his own resources to restore the trust fund, but it is up to him to use whichever of his resources he chooses to use to do so. If the trustee is bankrupt by this point (which is not uncommon), the beneficiaries are out of luck.

Claiming equitable title against third parties: following and tracing trust property

2.61   But the most important way in which the beneficiaries' interest under the trust counts as a beneficial interest in the trust assets themselves comes from the way in which the beneficiaries' interest 'runs' with the trust property in the sense that they can insist upon their beneficial interest in the trust assets being given effect to by third parties who, in breach of trust, receive the trust property from the trustee. The point about these recipients receiving in breach of trust is important. When a trustee transfers trust money in compliance with the terms of the trust—when, for example, he pays money representing trust income to the income beneficiary, or pays trust money to buy shares in the course of investing the trust property in compliance with the trust terms—of course the recipients of that money are not 'bound' by any continuing interest of the beneficiaries. As to the first example, paying money to the income beneficiary, the whole point of the trust after all, as we have seen, is to distribute the trust assets to the beneficiaries, so when that is done they must receive the outright legal title to the assets transferred. As to the person selling shares to the trust, of course he takes the outright, beneficial legal title to the money he receives; this transaction is in fulfilment of the trust terms, that is, the trustee is entitled under the terms to enter into this contract to transfer the title of the trust money to the seller of shares, extinguishing the trust interest in them, substituting the money as a trust asset with the title to the shares. (We shall return to this substitution of trust assets one for another later (2.75 et seq).)

2.62   Because a trust is an arrangement in which the title to the trust property, and therefore all the powers to deal with it, is held by someone who is not permitted to act as if he owns it for his own benefit, settling property on trust creates an obvious danger: if the trustee is an incompetent or a rogue, he is in the position drastically to harm the beneficiary's interest by transferring the trust property to a non-beneficiary. In such cases (subject to an exception (2.64 et seq)), the beneficiary can 'follow' the trust property into the hands of the person to whom the trustee wrongly transferred it, and demand that this new owner hold the property on trust for him—in other words, he can assert his equitable beneficial interest in the property against a subsequent holder of the title to it. (This does *not* mean that the recipient has to carry out the trust as if he were appointed as a replacement trustee for the wrongdoing trustee; rather, he would normally just be liable to transfer the trust assets he received to a new, honest trustee, who would carry out the terms of the trust from then on (11.188 et seq).) The only problem is that the beneficiary cannot claim his beneficial equitable interest against *every* subsequent holder of the legal title, and so the proprietary nature of the beneficiary's right in the trust assets is somewhat limited.

2.63   Historically, the law concerning which subsequent holders of the title to the trust property would be required by equity to hold the property subject to the beneficiary's equitable title developed piecemeal. Roughly, equity held first that a purchaser for value who had notice of the trust, ie knew he was buying property that the trustee held on trust for another, was obliged to give effect to the beneficiary's rights; then the trust obligation was imposed upon those who inherited the property from the trustee; then, to a donee (the recipient of a gift) with or without notice of the trust; then to creditors of the trustee who had seized the trust property in order to realise the debts owed them (roughly the equivalent of a trustee's trustee in bankruptcy (2.89)). So the development of the beneficiary's right to follow the property was conceived in equity as the transfer of the personal duty of the trustee to others where the circumstances were such that they ought not, in good conscience, take the legal title to the property free of the beneficiary's interest. Thus this aspect of the proprietary character of the beneficiary's right grew out of equity's willingness to impose personal trust obligations on subsequent takers of the legal title to the trust property (Maitland (1929), at 117–20; Smith (2008)). These subsequent takers of the title to the property can be collectively called 'successors in title' to the trustee, for they acquire title to the trust property from the trustee. But this imposition of the obligation to hold the property received by a successor in title for the benefit of the beneficiaries stopped at the door of the *bona fide purchaser of a legal interest in the trust property without notice, whether actual, constructive, or imputed, of the trust*, a person sometimes called 'equity's darling'.

The bona fide purchaser

2.64   If the trustee transfers the legal title to the trust property to someone who:

- has given good, ie valuable, 'consideration' for it, ie has given money or money's worth in exchange for it; and
- has no 'actual' notice, ie knowledge, of the beneficiary's rights; and
- has no 'constructive' notice of them either, ie knowledge of those interests that he would

have acquired if he had made all usual and reasonable investigations when purchasing that kind of property; and

- has no 'imputed notice' either, ie any agents working for him in making the purchase have no actual or constructive notice,

then this purchaser takes the property with good legal title free of any trust obligations, and the beneficiary loses his beneficial equitable interest in the trust property. The beneficiary's interest in the property is extinguished—he cannot assert that the bona fide purchaser's title is subject to his equitable interest.

2.65   We can then divide recipients of trust property into two classes. First, we have *volunteers*, the term given to persons who receive property but do not give valuable consideration for it—this class covers donees, those who take the trustee's property on his death or those who take on his bankruptcy. For these recipients, their knowledge of the trust is irrelevant, because they will take the property subject to the beneficiary's interest in any case. Secondly, we have those who have given consideration—these people can acquire beneficial ownership of the property free and clear of the trust, so long as they can establish they had no notice of it.

2.66   There are a few points worth noting. First, the rule applies to the bona fide purchaser of any legal *interest*, not just a *legal title* in the property that someone may acquire. An example is a mortgage. Where a person who bona fide and without notice lends money to the trustee and the trustee, in breach of trust, mortgages land held on trust to secure the repayment of the loan, the lender/mortgagee takes an interest that is not subject to the beneficiary's rights. The practical upshot in this situation would be that if the trustee were to fail to pay back the loan, then the lender/mortgagee could 'realise' his mortgage by taking possession of the trust land and selling it to pay off the debt. As a bona fide purchaser of this mortgage, he would prevail over the beneficiary's equitable interest in the property. In other words, the beneficiaries would only be entitled to any surplus money on the land's sale that was not needed to pay off the mortgage loan, which might be little or nothing.

Bona fide purchasers of equitable interests

2.67   Secondly, notice that the rule only applies to the case where the purchaser acquires a *legal* interest. If, for example, the trustee in breach of trust grants an *equitable* security interest in the trust property, that is, a security interest that equity will enforce but which is not recognised at common law, then the lender will take subject to the rights of the beneficiary even if he is a bona fide purchaser for value of this interest with no actual, constructive, or imputed notice of the beneficiary's rights. The bona fide purchase rule only applies in a contest between a legal interest holder and an equitable interest holder. In a contest between two equitable interest holders, like the beneficiary and the lender in this example, the general rule of equity is that the interest that was created first in time prevailed. Why is there this difference? It appears to have arisen as a kind of 'jurisdictional' curiosity. The beneficiary and the honest purchaser who has paid good value for his interest stand essentially on an equal footing with respect to their moral claims to the property. The rogue trustee has dealt dishonestly with both, selling the property out from under the beneficiary, and selling a flawed title (because impressed with a trust) to the purchaser. We have the classic case of a rogue and two innocents, and the court is faced with a choice as to whose claim should prevail. However, because the purchaser of an equitable interest was already within the jurisdiction of equity, ie his interest was equitable, equity had to deal with their competitive claims, and adopted the 'first in time' rule. On the other hand, equity did not weigh up the competing claims of the beneficiary and the bona fide purchaser of a *legal* interest. Only if that purchaser's conscience was affected could he be subject to the 'conscience-based' jurisdiction of equity; since it was not—he had done nothing unconscionable—equity regarded itself as having no power to intervene against him (see *Pilcher v Rawlins* (1872)), and this is the origin of the expression 'equity's darling'. Thus the bona fide purchaser of a legal interest got his legal title free and clear of the trust because of a sort of 'default' rule about the conscience-based jurisdiction of equity.

Where the trust property includes equitable interests

2.68   In much of the foregoing it was assumed for the sake of simplicity that the trustee always holds the *legal* title to the trust property but, as we have seen (2.35), a beneficiary's equitable interest is itself a valuable right that can be assigned; such a right can therefore form part of a trust corpus itself. Thus a beneficiary can declare a trust of it, a 'sub-trust'. Here the trustee of the legal property holds it on trust for the beneficiary, who in turn holds his right to it under the sub-trust for the sub-beneficiary. Furthermore, there are equitable property interests besides a traditional beneficial interest under a trust, in particular with respect to land. Equitable interests in land, such as equitable mortgages or leases, are well-known proprietary rights in land. Roughly, the main difference between legal mortgages and leases and their equitable counterparts is that the equitable versions are generally created informally, or less formally. Or to put this the other way around, legal interests in land typically require the observance of more or less strict formal requirements, such as being created by deed. Since 'Equity looks to intent, not form' (1.9), equity has typically been willing to give effect to informally created interests if this appeared to be required in good conscience. (Because equitable interests in land may now often be protected by registration on the land register, if registered they will bind everyone who takes the legal title, including a bona fide purchaser. For that reason, certain equitable interests in land are nowadays as secure as legal rights.) If equitable rights, as opposed to legal title to assets, are held on trust, then again we have a case, as in the preceding paragraph, where the bona fide purchaser rule does not operate, because a person cannot acquire a *legal* interest in an *equitable* interest in property; any interest in an equitable interest in property must itself be equitable. Just as in the case of the preceding paragraph, a first in time rule will operate.

2.69   But although the bona fide purchaser rule can be understood as having arisen because of the jurisdictional separation between law and equity, and equity's understanding of its own jurisdiction (ie as conscience-based) in the context of that division, are there good, practical reasons of *justice* for having a bona fide purchaser rule? An equivalent rule, called the 'holder in due course' rule, applies to negotiable instruments and money: a person who in good faith gives good value for money (eg sells goods taking money in return) or for negotiable paper—commercial rights 'reified' or 'materialised' in paper documents, like cheques—gets good title to them even if it turns out that, for example, the money was stolen, or a previous transfer of the negotiable instrument was achieved by fraud. The rule is justified on the basis that in the world of commerce it is better for the law to favour *security of receipt* over *security of title*. That is, in order to aid the practical workings of commerce the law holds that innocent purchasers of commercial paper, for example, should be protected even if that would mean that someone who has suffered by the acts of a thief or fraudster loses their title. Why? The concern is that if the bona fide recipient, the holder in due course, were the loser in this situation, individuals, to be sure they got a good title, would have to spend a great deal of time inquiring into the validity of the title of the seller, which in these contexts would be very difficult. In consequence, some transactions might not go ahead at all, and the others would be made more costly. So instead the law allows for ease of transactions, and throws the risk onto the title holder. Also, it might be more sensible for the risk of theft or fraud, say, to lie with the original owner. As the owner, he is in the best position to prevent the theft of his goods, not the bona fide purchaser from the thief or someone further down the line in a chain of transactions.

2.70   Of course, the law does not take this attitude with respect to all kinds of property. In the case of chattels, ie things such as chairs and chocolate bars, the law favours security of title over security of receipt. In the case of chattels, the rule *nemo dat quod non habet* applies (as the general rule; some exceptions apply; see eg Sale of Goods Act 1979, ss 21–5). Roughly translated, this means 'one cannot give what one hasn't got', and in the case of chattels, precisely what the thief has not got is good title to the goods, so he cannot pass a good title to anyone who buys them from him, no matter how innocent they are. So if you buy a 'hot' television from a friend of a friend, no matter how innocently, the true owner can bring an action against you for 'conversion', ie for converting *his* goods to *your* use, and you will pay him damages for the full value of the television.

2.71   We are thus faced with this question: on what side of this line ought the beneficiary's right in the trust property to fall? We know from above that the rule is already established—the bona fide purchaser takes free of the beneficiary's interest—but is there a sound reason for this in justice? The author shall not press his views on the bona fide reader for value, but will only say that no one is ever forced to put their property on trust, and putting one's property on trust, by the very nature of the device, puts one's property in a situation that presents it misleadingly to the world. We expect the legal owners of property to do with it what they want. We do not expect an owner to be bound to deal with this property only according to an obligation to benefit someone else. Trusts are entirely private (they are not, for example, recorded by the state in some central registry), and no one can tell just by looking at a piece of property or its owner that it is held on trust. Thus in creating a trust, one does expose it to the risk that one's trustee is an incompetent or a rogue who will deal with it in ways that to the rest of the world look perfectly legitimate, but are, in truth, not. Perhaps, since a settlor creates this risk, the results of things going wrong when the risk materialises should fall on the beneficiaries rather than on third parties who have acquired the trust property innocently *and* paid good value for it, ie bona fide purchasers.

'Notice' in different contexts

2.72   Finally, about the formulation of the rule: the rule as stated refers to the bona fide purchaser's having 'notice' of the trust. This formulation accurately describes the working of the rule in the context of its historical development, where land was transferred by deed. These transfers were carried out according to a standard conveyancing practice. For example, in the case of the sale of the fee simple of Blackacre, the buyer's solicitor would inspect the past title deeds and the property itself to discover any proprietary interests in Blackacre held by third parties. The neighbouring owner of Whiteacre might have an easement, such as a right of way, over Blackacre. If it were a *legal* interest, this easement would most probably have been created by deed and the solicitor should discover it when inspecting the deeds. Nevertheless, being a legal interest, the rule was that it would bind the purchaser of Blackacre whether his solicitor was able to discover it or not. (Of course, following the purchase, the buyer could bring an action against the seller for damages for not disclosing that Blackacre was subject to this ease-ment.) Blackacre might also be subject to some equitable proprietary interests. For example, the owner of Blackacre might have granted another of his neighbours an equitable right called a 'restrictive covenant' that imposed a duty upon him not to use Blackacre in some particular noxious way, as a knacker's yard, say. Such an *equitable* right would only bind the purchaser if his solicitor actually discovered it or ought to have discovered it by making the proper inves-tigations and, if so, then the purchaser would take Blackacre subject to this equitable right. In essence, then, 'notice' refers to the sort of knowledge one would normally acquire about the title to goods one wants to purchase based on standard procedures of investigating title. The pur-chaser's legal estate was limited by or subject to all the valid legal interests in the land and all the valid equitable interests in the land of which he had actual, constructive, or imputed notice—if he wanted to buy the land free of those interests, he had to deal with those interest holders themselves, to buy them out, as it were. On the other hand, those equitable rights not caught by actual, constructive, or imputed notice did not bind him at all. So the doctrine of notice here was not so much being caught out by unknown trusts of the property, but determining exactly how extensive or how limited was the property one was getting.

2.73 The rule's operation is quite different in the case of other property (see Bridge (2002), at 137–8). There is no standard 'conveyancing' practice for the sale of other property, such as chattels, or company shares. Individuals are not expected to investigate the title as they would do if they were buying land, for the simple reason that third parties do not generally have a variety of interests in chattels or shares. Therefore the practical effect of the rule in most circumstances is that the purchaser is only bound if he has actual, constructive, or imputed *knowledge* that he is dealing with a trustee of the property who is selling the property in *breach* of trust. For example, brokers who buy shares from pension fund trustees will know, of course, that the shares are the property of the pension fund. But that does not mean that they take these shares bound by the rights of the pension fund beneficiaries just because they know they are acquiring property from a pension fund trustee. Having actual notice of the trust in this case does not require them to hold any shares they buy from the pension fund trustees on trust for the pension fund beneficiaries. They will only take the shares bound by the equitable rights of the pension fund beneficiaries if they have notice that the trustees are selling the shares in a way inconsistent with the beneficiaries' rights, ie in breach of trust. (Prior to the legislative property law reforms of the late nineteenth century and 1925, a purchaser from the trust *would* have to inquire into the terms of the trust to make sure that there was no breach by the trustees, and to make sure the trustees applied the purchase money properly as part of the trust fund. For obvious reasons this rule, though imposed to protect beneficiaries, was not really to their advantage—it made it very difficult for trustees to invest trust property, because people would not deal with trustees because they did not want to expose themselves to this burden of investigation and the risk that the trustee was acting wrongfully, and so the rule operated to 'sterilise' trust assets, making them much less valuable than if they could be traded freely. For this reason the rule was changed, and nowadays there are no such duties: a purchaser from a trustee is entitled to assume that he is complying with the trust unless he has knowledge otherwise: see Swadling (1987); Harpum (1990).)

2.74 Thus in the case of sales of trust assets that are not land, like shares or other investments, which are the sort of assets trusts typically contain nowadays, with respect to the issue of notice you should think of the rule as follows: a bona fide purchaser for value of the legal title without actual, constructive, or imputed knowledge that the transaction is made in *breach of trust* will take free of the beneficiary's interests.

The trust is a fund

2.75 It is often said that the beneficiary's interest in the trust property is an interest in a 'fund', but it is important to note that the idea of a fund is an ambiguous one in the law, referring to two different cases, which I shall call 'pooled asset' funds and 'substitutional funds'. An example of a pooled asset fund is the collection of assets held by someone's trustee in bankruptcy (2.89 et seq). Take a simple case where B is bankrupt and owns a group of assets, his house, some shares, and some money, with the total value of £120,000, and has three creditors, X, Y, and Z, to whom he owes £75,000, £50,000, and £25,000 respectively. Having assets of £120,000, and debts of £150,000, B is clearly insolvent, ie has debts significantly exceeding his assets. B's trustee in bankruptcy, T, will use B's house, shares, and money, as a pool of assets to distribute to his creditors. X, Y, and Z do not have any individual rights to any of the specific assets; rather, T must realise the value of all of the assets (selling the house and the shares, for instance) to meet the claims of them all on a *pari passu* basis, ie they will receive a share of the total value of the £120,000 in proportion to the amount they are owed, so X will receive £60,000, Y will receive £40,000, and Z £20,000.

2.76 The substitutional fund concerns a different notion. On this notion of an interest in a fund, there is no requirement that there be more than one asset forming a pool. Rather, the idea is that the fund asset(s) may change over time as one is substituted for another. This is true of trust funds. If a trustee sells a trust asset, say a house, for cash, the cash will now be the trust asset in place of the house. The beneficiary's interest is not just an interest in the house, but in any asset which 'represents' the house (the original trust asset) for the time being (*Re Earl of Strafford* (1979)); so, if the trustee then uses the cash to buy shares, the beneficiary's interest in the trust property will now be in the shares. To distinguish the pooled asset and substitutional notions of the fund is not to say that they cannot occur at the same time. In the typical trust, there will be more than one trust asset, and the trustee has the power to change the individual items of property, typically so that the trustee can manage the trust for the benefit of the beneficiaries, by changing the trust investments from time to time. Although the particular investments that the trust holds change from time to time, the beneficiary's title to the property of the trust does not. The beneficiary does not have a particular right to any of the particular items in the trust fund. That is why, when a beneficiary assigns his interest (2.31) under a typical trust, he does not need to specify that he is assigning his interest in each and every particular item of trust property that happens to be in the trust at the time. He assigns his interest in the fund, which comprises (1) whatever happens to be in it at the time (the pool of assets), and (2) whatever happens to be in it in the future (property arising by any substitutions that take place). (See further Penner (2006a).)

2.77 This substitutional fund aspect of the trust does not depend upon the settlor's intentions or the terms of the trust instrument. As we have seen (2.43) in the past most trustees were required to hold the very assets first transferred to them on trust, and not exchange them for others, by way of making an investment, for example (Nolan (2004)). Nevertheless, if they used their powers of title to exchange trust assets for new assets, those assets would now be claimable by the beneficiaries, even if the transaction was in breach of trust. The principle that operates here is one that we have already discussed in detail: the beneficiary's beneficial interest in the trust assets is in the trustee's exercising his powers of title in those assets. Where the exercise of those powers of title results in the trustee's acquiring a new asset, most obviously where the trustee exchanges trust assets for other assets, the beneficiaries' beneficial interest automatically attaches to those assets, for those assets are the fruits of the trustee's exercise of his powers of title over the original trust assets. (As we shall see when we look at breach of trust in detail (Chapter 11), where a trustee commits a breach of trust the beneficiaries can refuse, or disclaim, the substitute assets, and instead require the trustee to dig into his own pocket to restore to the trust the money value of the trust asset wrongfully traded away.)

Tracing trust property

2.78   Although the beneficiary's proprietary right to follow (2.61) *the original trust property* is obliterated by its sale to a bona fide purchaser, all is not necessarily lost, because the beneficiary may acquire a substitute proprietary right by operation of law, the availability of which depends upon what are called 'tracing rules'. If my rogue trustee sells the trust property, say shares, to a bona fide purchaser for £1,000, my equitable title to the shares is extinguished. But since it is clear that the trustee has received the £1,000 in exchange for the shares, the law will trace the right to the shares into the £1,000. The principal is ancient (*Bale v Marchall* (1457)), and, as we have just seen, this is no more than an application of the idea that the trust is a fund. The law will keep track of the exchange of rights if it occurs again, for example if the trustee buys a car with that money, tracing through one exchange substitution after another. Tracing will only stop when either the proceeds of an exchange are lost or destroyed, or the evidence of what substitutions were made runs out, or the property is exchanged for non-property, for example where the trustee blows the trust money on a holiday. The rules of tracing will be discussed in detail in Chapter 11.

2.79   The thing to notice here is that the idea of having property in a fund (2.75), where one's property interest remains but the actual item or items of property change, goes hand in hand with tracing, in which the property interest of the beneficiary shifts automatically from one item of property to the proceeds acquired in exchange for it. (Such proceeds, called the 'traceable proceeds' of the exchange, are also sometimes called the 'exchange product'.) As we shall also see in Chapter 11, not only can the beneficiary trace into the exchange products where the trustee exchanges trust property, the beneficiary can also trace against any third party into whose hands he can follow the trust property. So, for example, if the trustee in breach of trust gives a trust painting to his nephew, the beneficiary can of course *follow* the painting into the nephew's possession and claim it back. (The nephew is obviously not a bona fide purchaser because he gave no consideration for the painting; it was a gift; he is a *volunteer*.) But if the nephew sells the painting for £5,000 cash, the beneficiary can also *trace* into the cash, and then into the motorcycle the nephew buys with that cash, and so on.

Personal remedies for breach of trust against third parties

2.80   Secondly, all may not be lost even if the beneficiary's proprietary rights run out because the original trust property can no longer be followed because acquired by a bona fide purchaser, or it can no longer be traced into substitute property. The beneficiary will still have *personal* rights against the original trustee, who is strictly liable for breach of trust, and must pay out of his own pocket the full value necessary to restore what was lost to the trust; the beneficiary may also be able to make similar personal claims against others. We shall discuss these rights in Chapter 11; in general they arise against anyone who dishonestly participates in a breach of trust, and against anyone who receives trust property transferred in breach of trust or its traceable proceeds and spends it having the knowledge that it was trust property.

A trust will not fail for want of a trustee

2.81   Even though the trustee's undertaking his trust obligation is necessary for the device to work— if the title holder to the intended trust assets never undertakes the trustee's obligation, there simply is no trust—this voluntary undertaking of an obligation is not regarded as essential for the exercise of a settlor's power to declare a trust. Rather, the settlor's exercise of the power to declare a trust is conceived of as essentially unilateral, in the same way that exercising the power to make a gift of the property is unilateral, rather than the bilateral act of making an agreement with a trustee as in a common law contract. But in the same way that someone can 'disclaim', that is, refuse a gift, the transferee of trust property *inter vivos*, or the person named to be the trustee of assets in a settlor's will, can refuse to take on the trusteeship. The existence of these rights of refusal do not turn the making of a gift or the declaration of a trust into a bilateral agreement (see Penner (1996a, 2014a)). (Of course in the former case of the *inter vivos* intended trustee who doesn't want to take on the trusteeship, he should try to avoid even receiving the trust assets in the first place, telling the settlor to look elsewhere to find someone to serve as trustee.) This orientation on the creation of a trust leads to the principle that 'a trust will not fail for want of a trustee'. Thus, for example, if a person in his will gives property to Fred to hold on trust for Anna, and Fred refuses to take the property on trust, the court will appoint someone else to be trustee (10.56). Think how strongly that contrasts with the law of contract. Imagine declaring that one will perform one's own version of 'Stairway to Heaven' on zither and cymbals for Prince Charles for £1m, and upon Prince Charles's (naturally) declining the offer, the court finding someone else to be the other party to the contract. But this willingness of equity to find a replacement trustee makes perfect sense if the settlor's creation of a trust is regarded as merely his exercising the powers of ownership to make a structured gift (1.28), because gifts are unilateral transactions.

The express trust in legal context

2.82   One of the ways in which the express trust is often characterised is in relation to legal devices, like gifts under wills or security interests. In this part then, we will be concerned with differentiating trusts from these other legal forms. But more than that, we will also explore how the conceptual underpinnings of these devices reveal the peculiar character of the trust, the beast that it is.

The law of succession and testamentary trusts

Testamentary gifts

2.83   A *testamentary* trust is one created as a gift under a will. (Trusts created by living settlors are called *inter vivos* trusts, trusts 'between persons alive'.) Many trusts are created in this way, so a passing familiarity with the rudiments of the law of wills and of intestate succession is very useful. The property of a dead person is called the 'deceased's estate', and it passes to the living in one of two ways: either according to the deceased's will or, if he has no valid will, that is if he dies 'intestate', then according to the rules of intestate succession. The rules of intestate succession are essentially 'default' rules that distribute the property in the way that most people would have distributed it had they made a will; to their spouse first, then to their children; if there is no spouse or children, then to their parents, siblings, and finally to more distant relations. The person who makes a will is a 'testator' (male) or 'testatrix' (female), and the will normally nominates one or more 'executor(s)' (male) or 'executrix(executrices)' (female) who will 'prove' the will, ie have the will declared valid by a Court of Probate. The title to the property of the deceased passes to the executors who will pay off the deceased's debts, and then distribute the deceased's estate to those to whom he has given it under his will. In the case of intestacy, there is no will to execute; the court will instead appoint one or more 'administrators' who will, like executors, receive title to the deceased's assets, clear up the deceased's affairs by paying his debts, and then distribute the estate according to the rules of intestate succession. Both executors and administrators are called the 'personal representatives' of the deceased. (Technically speaking, there is no longer any 'inheritance' of property under English law. The only things that are now inheritable are titles of nobility and, of course, the crown. To 'inherit' was to receive land as an 'heir' of the deceased, not by a will, but by the rules of descent existing prior to the property law reforms of 1925. We will return to the way genuine inheritance works later (2.88, 2.97).)

2.84   For historical reasons, different terms apply to testamentary gifts of different kinds of property. Land is 'devised' by will, and therefore the gift is called a 'devise' and the donees 'devisees'. Generally, personal property or 'personalty', ie anything other than land, is 'bequeathed', and such gifts are 'bequests', but gifts of sums of money are called 'legacies' and their recipients 'legatees'. 'Gifts' will suffice for a compendious term. The gifts under a will do not take effect from the time the will is made, but only when it comes into operation on the testator's death. Thus if one of the intended recipients dies before ('predeceases') the testator, his gift 'lapses'. With respect to that piece of property, it is as if the testator made no specific gift of it at all. Intended testamentary gifts, including intended trusts that are to take effect on the testator's death, may fail for a number of reasons. The testator may have failed sufficiently to specify either the recipient or the property to be given, for example. Because intended gifts under wills fail, a very important clause in any will is the one in which the testator gives 'the rest and residue' of his estate; this 'residuary' clause gives all the property left over after the specific gifts, of Blackacre to A, of 500 shares in X plc on trust to C for life and then to D absolutely, and so on, are distributed. The recipients under this clause, the 'residuary legatees' (so called whatever kind of property they get) will get more to the extent that any of the specific gifts fail. If there is no residuary gift or for some reason it fails, for example because the named residuary legatees have predeceased the testator, then any property not disposed of by specific gifts in the will will be distributed as if the testator made no will at all, ie under the rules of intestate succession. Thus it is apparent that there is always an incentive for a good fight over the validity of specific gifts in the will—the residuary legatees or, failing them, the intestate successors, will always look carefully at their validity, because they will take the property if a specific gift fails. This applies just as much to specific testamentary gifts that are trusts; indeed, most of the cases concerning the validity of trusts concern testamentary trusts.

2.85   The 'formal' requirements of wills, principally that a will be signed by the testator and attested by two witnesses, are prescribed to ensure that the will truly represents the testator's intentions and, in general, the law will allow no departures from this method. If an entire will is invalid for not being correctly formally made, the deceased's estate is distributed under the rules of intestate succession, no matter how obvious it might be that this was contrary to his actual intentions. Here again is an opportunity for a good fight. Those who would take as intestate successors, if not well provided for in the will, have the incentive to press every reasonable argument that the will is invalid.

2.86   While the main function of a will is to dispose of the testator's property, so that the power to make a will is essentially a legal power of ownership, a testator may (conditionally) impose obligations under a will, otherwise he could never create trusts, which require the creation of the duties of trusteeship. The reason why the testator can only *conditionally* impose trust obligations is that no one is ever required to take up the role of trustee; a trustee must undertake these obligations voluntarily. On the other hand, as we have seen, it is a principle of equity that a trust will never fail for want of a trustee, and so the court will find someone who will take on the trust (2.81, 10.56); so although the testator's imposition of trust obligations is in theory dependent upon their acceptance by someone, as a practical matter they will be accepted so he can impose as he likes. A testator may also direct his executors or trustees to enter into contractual obligations with respect to his property—for example, to sell some of it or to give an interest-free loan to his brother-in-law. What a testator cannot do by his will, of course, is to enter into a contract, ie undertake contractual obligations himself, for when the will takes effect he is, of course, dead.

2.87   The deceased's personal representatives are not trustees for the people who will take the property under the will or on intestate succession (*Stamp Duties Comr (Queensland) v Livingston* (1965); Maitland (1929), at 48–9); they are the full legal owners of the deceased's property, although they are under stringent obligations to dispose of his property properly, and for this reason, their role is very trustee-like. Furthermore, prospective beneficiaries under a will or under the rules of intestate succession, although they do not have an interest in the deceased's estate itself as does a beneficiary in the property of a trust, have a right against the personal representatives to administer the estate properly, and this right, like the beneficiary's right to his interest under a trust, can be assigned or bequeathed (*Re Leigh's Will Trusts* (1970)). Executors are often appointed to be the trustees of the testamentary trusts that a testator specifies in his will.

2.88   Whilst the role of a personal representative of the deceased is 'trustee-like', it is important to note the differences in his legal position from that of a trustee. The purpose of a personal representative is essentially to 'wind up' the deceased's economic existence. He takes over title to the deceased's assets, but also, in a sense, takes on the deceased's liabilities. Thus he discharges the deceased's outstanding debts, and only then distributes the surplus to the donees under his will or by the rules of intestate succession. He is not under further duties to manage the property over time in order to provide structured benefits to a class of beneficiaries. The role of the personal representative is in some ways like that of the principal heir under true regimes of inheritance as in civil law legal systems. An heir, in these systems, is regarded as immediately succeeding to the economic personality of the deceased, taking on both his assets and his liabilities. By accepting the inheritance, the heir is under an obligation to discharge the liabilities of the deceased. Also the heir must pay out of his inheritance any gifts the deceased made under his will. (The ability to make a will is not incompatible with a regime of inheritance—it is just that in regimes of inheritance the deceased is entitled to give only a portion of his assets by will.) Of course, unlike the personal representative, the heir is entitled to all the assets that remain after he has discharged the deceased's debts and distributed any assets given by the deceased's will.

Security interests and the context of insolvency

2.89   One of the main reasons why proprietary rights are valuable is that people and companies can become insolvent. One is insolvent if one has insufficient assets to meet one's liabilities—in other words, if one does not have enough financial resources to meet the demands of all one's creditors. In the case of individuals, the legal device of bankruptcy allows the insolvent individual to get out of this mess and start again afresh. It works roughly as follows: all of the property of the bankrupt, including any rights to be paid any debts owing to him or any interests he has under trusts, becomes the property of his 'trustee in bankruptcy', whose job it is to distribute these assets, the bankrupt's 'estate in bankruptcy', in proportionate shares to the bankrupt's creditors. Thus, if the bankrupt's estate is worth £10,000, and his total debts are £100,000, each creditor will receive 10 pence in the pound for the debt he is owed. Following this distribution, and after a period of time, such as three years, the bankrupt is 'discharged' from all his debts, and can begin economic life again, albeit without much in the way of assets. (Certain assets of the bankrupt remain his, and are not used to pay off his creditors: roughly, the property personally required by him in the pursuit of his employment or trade and such property as is required to meet his and his family's basic domestic needs.) The analogous process with respect to a company is called liquidation. In essence, the liquidator distributes all of the assets of the company to its creditors on a proportionate basis. Following this distribution the company no longer exists. There is no compendious term that covers both the trustee in bankruptcy and the liquidator of a company, so henceforth when the term 'trustee in bankruptcy' is used it will, for our purposes, comprise both.

2.90   Proprietary rights become very important in the case of insolvency. If a bankrupt owes you £100, then you are likely to see little money, because as a general creditor you will only be paid a proportionate share of the bankrupt's assets. You might be lucky to see any money at all. To the extent, however, that your rights against the bankrupt are proprietary, then you are in a much stronger position: an asset of the bankrupt that is subject to the proprietary right of someone else is, to the extent of that right, not the bankrupt's own property, and therefore not part of his estate in bankruptcy to be used for distribution to his general creditors—it belongs to the person with the proprietary right. The beneficiary's *equitable* rights to property held on trust stand on the same footing as legal title in this respect in the case of insolvency. The trustee has no beneficial interest in the property he holds on trust, and so neither can his trustee in bankruptcy who acquires title to all the trustee's legal assets should he become bankrupt—the trustee in bankruptcy takes these assets as a volunteer, so is not a bona fide purchaser of the assets from the trustee (2.64 et seq); thus trust property is not available to the trustee's trustee in bankruptcy for distribution to the trustee's own creditors. In other words, a beneficiary's equitable rights bind a trustee in bankruptcy. Obviously then, personal rights to be paid sums of money, for example a claim for money damages for breach of contract, are not as valuable in a bankruptcy as proprietary rights, because they give the right holder no special claim on any particular asset of the bankrupt. For this reason, claimants who have a claim for money against a bankrupt will often try to claim that their past dealings with him created a trust over some of the bankrupt's property, because then they can simply withdraw this property from the bankrupt's estate (see eg 7.25 et seq).

Security interests

2.91   A beneficiary's equitable title is, in some ways, functionally similar to a 'security interest' in the context of insolvency. A security interest is a right that a creditor holds in particular property of his debtor. The classic example is a mortgage over land. In return for providing money, the lender (the 'mortgagee') makes sure that the borrower (the 'mortgagor') grants him a mortgage over the borrower's land. (Contrary to common parlance, it is the lender, then, who gets a mortgage.) A mortgage is a right that the lender has in the land of the borrower, and it has the effect of securing repayment of the loan. If the borrower defaults on his contractual repayments of the loan, then (roughly) the lender has the right to take possession of the land and sell it to pay off the loan. All security interests work in essentially the same way. They entitle the creditor who has one, called a 'secured' creditor, to sell the property in question if the borrower defaults on his repayments and take as much of the proceeds of sale as is necessary to discharge the outstanding balance on the loan. Because security interests 'charge' the property with the repayment of a loan in this way, they are often just called 'charges'. The vital point about charges is that they are proprietary rights. They attach to the property itself. If the property passes out of the hands of the borrower into the hands of his trustee in bankruptcy, the lender will still be able to 'realise' his security, ie sell the property to pay off the debt, even though it is no longer held by the borrower. Any of the money proceeds of sale that are not required to pay off the outstanding debt belong, of course, to the trustee in bankruptcy—in other words, the security interest only charges the property to the extent of the sum owed. Security interests are not only created by two parties to a loan agreement. A court can make a 'charging order' against a defendant's property, which gives the claimant a charge over the property to secure a judgment debt (eg a court's award of damages).

2.92 The justice (or lack thereof) of the beneficiary's right to withdraw his property from the bankrupt's estate should be judged in view of the fact that a trust, like a contract, is a private arrangement. Whilst it is working, more or less, the beneficiary enforces his rights against the trustee, like a contracting party pressing for performance against the other contracting party. When things go badly wrong because the trust property is transferred away in breach of trust, the beneficiary takes the trust public, and tries to get the property back from third parties. You can make an analogy here with a secured loan. The loan contract is private, but when the borrower goes into bankruptcy, the lender goes public with the contract and claims possession of and sells the charged asset to satisfy its debt, thus removing that asset from the debtor's estate in bankruptcy, to the disappointment of all the other creditors. You can see why, in these circumstances, Parliament has tried to make things as fair as possible by putting in place public registration systems both for many equitable proprietary rights in land and for security interests, to protect third parties who would otherwise be hurt if caught out by the proprietary effect of these private arrangements. But there is no registration system as such for interests under trusts; they remain private. Thus in order to avoid surprising innocent third parties, the law must be judicious in accepting claims by those who would argue that their past dealings with a bankrupt gave rise to a trust over some of his property in their favour, as this will effectively give the claimant a priority over other creditors that may, in the circumstances, be quite unfair (7.46–7.47).

2.93 While interests under trusts and security interests share certain features in the context of insolvency, it is vital not to confuse trusts with security interests. A debtor subject to a security interest of his creditor, though subject to a powerful proprietary right, is not a 'trustee' of the asset subject to the charge. The asset is 'encumbered' to the extent of the value of the outstanding debt he owes, but the asset remains beneficially his. Therefore any increase in the value of the asset is something the debtor can realise. So, for example, if A grants to B a charge over shares worth £10,000 to secure A's repayment of a loan from B of £5,000, and the shares rise in value to £15,000, B is not entitled to any increase in the value of these shares. As the shares rise in value, B benefits practically in the sense that they are now better security for his loan, for if A defaults it is clear that by exercising a power to sell the shares in that circumstance B will get all his money back, but in any case he will have to remit to A the full surplus not needed to pay off B's loan to A. For this reason, A is sometimes called the 'residual claimant' of the assets he has charged. He gets the residual value of them, that is, he is entitled to realise the value of them after any charges on the assets are extinguished when he pays off the debts they secure. By contrast, by *extreme contrast*, a trustee is not the full beneficial legal owner of assets which are just 'encumbered' by the beneficiaries' equitable interests under the trust. The trustee is not beneficially entitled to the trust assets at all. He has no interest in any increase in the value of the trust fund—that all enures to the benefit of the beneficiaries. Unlike the chargor (the one who grants a charge over his assets), it is not the case that the trustee could possibly comply with his obligations to distribute the trust assets to his beneficiaries leaving a surplus that he could keep for himself, so he is not to be conceived of as any sort of residual claimant to them (Penner, 2014a). As we shall see (5.4, 5.50 et seq), if there is anyone who would count as a re-sidual claimant to the trust assets, ie a person who would claim any remainder after all the valid beneficial interests have been 'discharged', it is the settlor, not the trustee.

A note on the English trust for civil lawyers

2.94   It is commonly thought by lawyers from civilian legal jurisdictions, ie those whose legal con-cepts ultimately derive from Roman law, that the trust is incompatible with civilian ideas of property and ownership. The idea goes something like this: the civilian (Roman) concept of ownership is that of *dominium*, a very strong notion of ownership that requires that all rights (or almost all rights) in the property belong to one owner. Thus the idea of a divided ownership, in which there is an owner at law (the trustee) *and* an owner in equity, is simply impossible to square with the civilian idea. But, as Matthews (2002) points out, this is confused. In the first place, the trust has been taken on in some civil law jurisdictions like Quebec and Scotland (2.96). Secondly, however, it over-emphasises the use of labels. As we shall see (2.107 et seq), there has been, and in fact continues to be, controversy amongst common lawyers themselves about whether the best way of looking at the trust is from the 'obligation' side or the 'property' side. But even if one, on balance, treats the law of trusts as properly falling within the realm of English property law, as does the present author, this is a matter of determining, at a conceptual level, where the trust most properly *fits*. Neither side in the debate disputes what the *content* of the beneficiary's right or the trustee's obligation amounts to; that is, no one is confused about the rules that apply, say to whether the beneficiary's interest is defeated by a bona fide purchaser, although this might be explained either as limitation on the beneficiary's title to the trust fund, or as a limit on the extent to which equity will insist that a third party is subject to being bound by an obligation similar to the trustee's because of the circumstance in which he receives the property. The upshot is that it may well be that the beneficiary's interest does not count as an ownership interest according to the civilian concept of ownership, although it does according to the more pragmatic, or flexible, English concept of ownership. That does not prevent civilian systems from recognising the complex of rules that make the trust operate as a legal device. In Scotland, for example, as we shall see, the trust operates in basically the same way as in England although, for the Scots, the beneficiary has conventionally been taken to have only a personal right against the trustee, not a property right in the trust assets.

2.95   In any case, there may be a more basic misunderstanding fuelling the civilian lawyer's discomfort, which is the idea, canvassed earlier (2.31), that the beneficiary's equitable 'ownership' competes with the trustee's legal ownership, not only fracturing the concept of *dominium*, but requiring the law to give two different answers to the same question. But as we have also seen (2.31), this is a misunderstanding. The beneficiaries' interests are derivative of, not competitive with, the trustee's title to the trust assets. But, the civilian might persist, is it not the case that by saying that both the trustee and the beneficiaries have rights in the trust assets, the very same assets, in the sense that both, may, in particular cases, bring actions against third parties who acquire possession or title to the trust assets, one must also acknowledge that the trustees and the beneficiaries have competitive claims to the assets? The answer is 'no'. True it is that the trustee's title allows him to bring claims against, say, trespassers on the trust property. And true it also is that the beneficiaries' interests 'run' with the trust property (2.59), so that they too can bring claims against third parties who take title to the trust assets in breach of trust. But it is important to distinguish between these cases of bringing claims against third parties. In the case of a breach of trust, whereupon the beneficiary does enforce his interest in the trust property against third parties himself, it may at first appear that the beneficiary's interest is not derivative at all, in that the beneficiary enforces a right to the trust property directly against the third party. But on second glance, it is clear that the trustee's ownership and the beneficiary's ownership are not competitive so long as the temporal element of their respective rights is paid attention to. While the trust is up and running fine, with the trustee properly carrying out his duties, the trustee has all the rights of ownership, the beneficiaries none; all they have is the right to their defined benefits under the trust. Thus it is the trustee who is entitled to bring an action against, say, a trespasser on trust land. When, however, the trust property goes walkabout, ie leaves the ownership of the trustee because it was transferred in breach of trust, the beneficiaries take their interest public, and enforce the trust against all recipients save bona fide purchasers. But when this happens, one must notice that the trustee has lost his ownership interest in the trust property. It is no longer his, and whilst he may be personally liable to restore the trust out of his own pocket, this is a personal obligation of his, not an obligation to hold any property of his own as trust property. Rather, the beneficiary who enforces the trust against a third-party recipient claims that *this recipient is now the trustee in the sense of being bound by the beneficiary's interest*, in essence, claims the existence of a new trust situation, whereby the recipient now has the basic ownership right to which the beneficiary's interest can now be derivative. So there is never a time, even though the trustee and the beneficiary can both be said to have rights in the trust property itself, when these rights *compete* with each other.

Trusts in civil law jurisdictions: Quebec and Scotland

2.96   In order to understand trusts in Quebec and Scotland, it is essential to grasp the notion of a person's 'patrimonium'. In these civil law jurisdictions (the idea is not prominent in all of them), a person's patrimonium is essentially his *economic personality*. Some of the rights and duties a person has are 'patrimonial rights', others not. So a person's rights as a property holder and a creditor are patrimonial rights, and a person's economic duties—to fulfil his contractual obligations and pay his debts—are patrimonial duties. Other, non-economic rights and duties, such as the right to vote in public elections, or the duty to perform military service, are not patrimonial—these are sometimes referred to as 'personality' rights and duties, which inhere in the person irrespective of his economic wherewithal, to distinguish them from patrimonial rights.

2.97   We have already seen one example of how the notion of patrimonium works in the civil law, when we looked at civil law inheritance (2.88). The heir essentially takes over the patrimonium of the deceased, both his economic assets and economic liabilities, his right in or to, merging the deceased's patrimony with his own. If an heir takes his inheritance, not only do the deceased's assets become his, but also the deceased's liabilities, so an heir might want to disclaim an inheritance if the deceased had more debts than assets in his patrimonium, for taking on such an inheritance would make the heir a net loser. The concept of patrimonium is used in different ways in the Quebec trust and the Scottish trust. We can start with the civil law trust of Quebec.

The Quebec civil law trust

2.98   There is a general civil law principle that every person has a patrimonium, but only one. Both the Quebec civil law trust and the Scots civil law trust breach this principle, but in different ways. The English version of the Civil Code of Quebec, ss 1260 and 1261, provides:

> 1260
>
> *A trust results from an act whereby a person, the settlor, transfers property from his patrimony to another patrimony constituted by him which he appropriates to a particular purpose and which a trustee undertakes, by his acceptance, to hold and administer.*
>
> 1261
>
> *The trust patrimony, consisting of the property transferred in trust, constitutes a patrimony by appropriation, autonomous and distinct from that of the settlor, trustee or beneficiary and in which none of them has any real right.*

In Quebec, therefore, the principle is broken by allowing the existence of a patrimonium that does not belong to any person. To the common lawyer, two features of this conception of the trust stand out: first, the trust is conceived as a patrimony appropriated to a purpose, and secondly, the appropriated patrimony, ie the corpus of the trust assets, is one in which neither the trustee nor the beneficiary has any real right. In the first place, the appropriation of the trust assets to a purpose seems odd to the common law trusts lawyer, since, in general, at common law trusts are framed in terms of holding property to the benefit of individuals, not to carry out purposes as such, as if you could transfer property on trust to do any old thing, like use the trust assets to, say, support a political party. As we shall see (Chapter 9), trusts to carry out 'abstract purposes', unless they are charitable purposes to which specific rules apply, are generally void. Now this is not to say that a trustee cannot devote money to beneficiaries in a way which 'fulfils a purpose' in a casual sense. We have already seen that a trustee can apply trust funds to a beneficiary by paying his school fees, so that in this loose sense the trust funds can be thought to be spent to fulfil the purpose of the beneficiary's education. But the point here is that this application of the funds is understood to be for the benefit of the beneficiary himself. However, it is generally thought to be implicit in the understanding of the Quebec trust that the appropriation of funds to a trust patrimony for a particular purpose is for the purpose of benefiting the beneficiaries, so we can move on to the second feature, the idea that neither the trustee nor the beneficiary has any patrimonial interest, ie ownership interest, in the trust assets, ie any 'real right'.

2.99   As Macdonald (1993–4) puts it,

> Because the corpus of the trust, even if it is a single thing or single right, constitutes a patrimony which is 'autonomous and distinct' from those of the settlor, trustee, and beneficiary, it follows that the property of the trust is ownerless.

At common law, the idea that the trust property is 'ownerless' is problematic. The theoretical difficulty that the idea of the 'ownership' of the trust property has posed for common lawyers is whether the trustee, with title to the assets, is to be regarded as the owner subject to an obligation to the beneficiary to deal with those assets according to the terms of the trust—what might be called the 'obligational' view of the trust—or whether the beneficiary, as is commonly said, is the 'true' owner, the 'beneficial' owner of the property, in the 'eyes of equity'—a view that might be called the 'proprietary' view of the trust (see 2.108 et seq). Nevertheless there is some resonance of the Quebec civilian law 'ownerless' property view with the actual configuration of the rights to the trust property at common law, about which common lawyers themselves often betray confusion.

2.100   Let us consider the civilian conception of ownership of a real right ('real' meaning a right to tangible property) in comparison to common law property rights in tangibles, and then see how this comparison plays itself out in the context of the trust. For civilians, a right of ownership in a tangible is classically conceived of as a 'positive' right—to use, enjoy, and dispose of the tangible thing which is the object of ownership (eg Quebec Civil Code, Article 947). By contrast, at common law, the right of an owner of a tangible is normally seen as a 'negative right', in the sense that it focuses on the right that correlates with the duty we all have not to trespass on property that is not our own. So, as regards the 'tangible' contact of the owner to his property, this is not framed in terms of a right to use or enjoy, but rather in terms of a right to immediate, exclusive possession. This has important consequences for the way in which a trust is differently conceived in civilian versus common law systems, for as we have seen (2.8), when looking at the two paradigmatic types of trust, the bare trust of land and the modern wealth management trust, in neither case is the trustee's right to possession of tangible assets ever 'held on trust' for the beneficiaries: that is, beneficiaries have no interest in this possessory right which the trustee is entitled to by virtue of his legal title, because trust law specifically prohibits the trustee from taking advantage of his right to immediate, exclusive, possession. The trustee is never entitled to take possession of the trust assets so as to obtain any benefit from doing so. But moreover, unless the terms of the trust so specify, neither are the beneficiaries entitled to take possession of the trust property for their benefit. Of course, in the case of bare trusts of land, the terms of the trust do specify this, but the beneficiaries are not entitled to possession simply by virtue of being beneficiaries, but because the trust terms permit or require the trustee to exercise his powers of title to apply the property to the beneficiaries' benefit by licensing the beneficiaries to take possession. Where the trust holds intangible assets, the right to possession is not even at issue, since these assets are unpossessible.

2.101   Taking these considerations into account, the Quebec Civil Code's characterisation of the trust property as ownerless is not so bizarre as it might first appear from a common law perspective.

To the extent that the right to use and enjoy is a matter of the trustee or beneficiary taking possession of the trust assets and using them in some way, the corpus of a common law trust is equally 'ownerless'—that is, neither the trustee qua trustee nor the beneficiary qua beneficiary under the general law is entitled to use and enjoy the trust corpus. And given that the trustee under Quebec civil law is the 'titulary' of the trust assets, that is he has the powers of title which allow him to transfer, sell, license, evict trespassers, and so on (on the standard interpretation of Quebec Civil Code, Articles 912, 953, and 1278 al.1), then whilst this particular power to 'dispose' of the trust assets is abstracted from the full-blown ownership rights to use, enjoy, and dispose in so far as they are conceived to form a unitary whole, the conceptual picture is not so far from the common law trust as the 'ownerless' property label invites us to suppose. This conceptual issue is less pressing, or perhaps more difficult to discern, in the case of the common law trust, simply in virtue of the fact that, as we have seen, the trustee's right to the immediate, exclusive, possession of any tangible trusts assets does not entail that he is able personally to exercise this right by using or enjoying the trust assets himself. Just as in the Quebec civil law trust, it is his powers to dispose of the trust assets which are the essential feature that underlies the operation of the trust. (See further (Penner 2014a).)

2.102 This leads us to one further point, about the way in which trust property can be 'ownerless'. Consider the example of the trust for Martha and her children we discussed earlier (2.10). Under this trust the beneficial interests of Martha and her children are 'fixed' (3.4). Martha has the right to receive the income, and her children the right to receive the title to the trust assets in equal shares on her death. But as we shall look at in great detail in Chapter 3, trusts can be more complicated than this and, in particular, the trustee may have a discretion as to how to distribute the trust assets to beneficiaries. So, to modify the example, let us say that the trustee has to hold the assets for Martha for life, and then to her children 'in such shares as the trustee shall at his absolute discretion decide'. What this provision does is allow the trustee, on Martha's death, to distribute the assets to the children in any proportion he likes, giving some to each, or all to one, whatever. (This may seem an odd discretion for the settlor to give a trustee, but the basic rationale is to allow the trustee to apply the property in the best way given that Tom, Dick, and Mary may be in very different circumstances, economically and otherwise, when Martha dies.) In the meantime, when Martha is alive, and before the trustee decides how to exercise his discretion, neither Tom, Dick, nor Mary individually have any right to get anything—so they are not regarded as individually having any genuine beneficial interest in the trust assets during this time. So one might say that during this time the capital interest in trust assets has *no* specific beneficial owner. Thus even under the common law trust the idea that the property is beneficially ownerless (for a time) is not anathema, and so one should not, perhaps, sharply distinguish the Quebec civil law trust on this account, at least without some circumspection.

The Scots civil law trust

2.103 The Scots civil law trust also relies on the concept of 'patrimonium', but in a different way, breaching the principle that each person has a patrimonium and only one by allowing the trustee to hold the trust property in a separate patrimonium. So the trustee has two patrimoniums, one his own that he had from birth, and a second patrimonium that he holds for the beneficiaries (Gretton (2000)). In a sense, the Scots law trust is less interesting than the Quebec law trust, because the issue of non-ownership does not arise—the Scots trustee has legal title to the trust patrimony assets. The

Scots law trustee, as pointed out by Smith (2013b), is in a position very similar to a common law executor, who holds the deceased's estate as a kind of second economic personality which is not merged with his own, with its own assets and liabilities.

Civil law trusts and third parties

2.104 To a limited extent, the civil law trust replicates the way in which certain third-party recipients of the trust property do not take free of the beneficiaries' interests (2.61). Take the trustee's creditors, or the trustee's trustee in bankruptcy. In the Quebec case, the trustee's creditors cannot access the trust patrimony because the trustee has no ownership interest in it; likewise, on his insolvency, no trustee in bankruptcy would acquire those assets as they do not belong to the trustee; nor would his heir take on his death. Similarly with the Scots law trust: the creditors of the trustee, or his trustee in bankruptcy, only have claims against his personal patrimonium, not against the trust patrimonium. The only persons who would have claims against the trust patrimonium would be 'trust creditors', those persons who, for example, entered into contracts with the trustee when he was acting as a trustee and dealing with the trust patrimonium. And because those 'trust creditors' are only creditors vis-à-vis the trust patrimonium, they have no claim against the trustee's personal patrimonium. (Notice the difference between the 'separate patrimony' view of the trust and the English law trust principle that the trustee contracts 'in his own name' and is personally liable on any contract he enters into in the course of carrying out the trust (2.52).) Similarly, if the trustee dies his heirs inherit only his personal patrimonium.

Following and tracing

2.105 On the other hand, if the trustee *transfers* trust property to a third party, civil law beneficiaries are *not* able to follow that property into the third party's hands and require him to hold it for their benefit. The idea here is that the third party, when he received the property, did not already have some 'ownerless' trust patrimonium (Quebec) or 'second trust patrimonium' (Scotland) into which he received the transfer. It came to the only patrimony he had—his own—and so there is no civil law claim that the beneficiaries can make that would undermine his patrimonial, ie ownership right, in the asset he received: he will not be held to hold the received property on trust for the beneficiary. The general approach of the civil law in such a case is to allow the beneficiary, in certain circumstances, to *annul* the transfer, treating it as void, so getting the property back into the trust. Of course, where a transfer cannot be annulled, the beneficiary has a claim against the trustee for breach of trust, but this may not be worth much if, as is often the case, the trustee is insolvent by the time the claim is made.

2.106 What if the trustee, in breach of trust, uses trust money to buy himself a car? Can the beneficiary trace (2.78) his interest into the car, claiming that car as a trust asset? The law on this is very unclear in both Quebec and Scotland, but in theory this is possible using the civil law concept of 'real subrogation', under which one asset may stand as a substitute for another. The details are complex (Smith (2012–13)); the only point to take away is that the idea of substituting one asset for another (the idea of a substitutional fund (2.75)), is not unknown to the civil law, and might be applied in the trusts context.

The nature of the beneficiary's right and the fusion of law and equity

2.107   There is a long-standing historical debate about what sort of right the beneficiary has under a trust. In particular, the dispute concerned the application of Roman law categorisation of rights into rights *in rem* and rights *in personam* to the English law of property, where it is ill-fitting. Rights *in rem* are rights that 'bind all the world', that is all persons, because of the sort of right that they are. One example is the property right in a chattel, like a motorcycle. Because anyone can, in principle, interfere with your right to possession of your motorbike, everyone is under a duty not to do so. Another example is your right to bodily security. Again, in principle, anyone can interfere with your body, touching you or putting you in a cage, so everyone is under a duty not to interfere with your body. So because the motorbike and your body are things in the world subject to these sorts of depredations, your right *in rem* correlates with a duty imposed upon all others not to interfere with your motorbike or body. By contrast, a right *in personam* is a right that correlates with a duty that, typically, only one other person owes another. The classic example is the debtor–creditor relationship. The creditor has a right that the debtor pays him a sum that is owed, say £10, and the debtor has the correlative duty to pay the £10 to the creditor. The creditor has that right only against the debtor, and the debtor, correlatively, only owes the duty to the creditor.

2.108   For some commentators, the beneficiary's right was a right *in rem*, because it bound almost all the world, ie it bound all successors in title (2.63) to the trustee with the exception of the bona fide purchaser. For others, it could not be, because it did not bind mere successors *in possession* to the trustee of the trust assets. Where a thief stole a trust chattel or an adverse possessor took possession of trust land, the trustee, and only the trustee, could bring an action for conversion against the thief or seek to evict the adverse possessor. The trust beneficiary could not, although as we have also seen (2.40) he could by legal action require the trustee to enforce his legal rights to bring an action for conversion against the thief or require him to evict the adverse possessor. From this perspective then, the beneficiary had no right (or at least no direct right) vis-à-vis the trust property itself, or against those who interfered with it. So the right could not be a right *in rem*, so therefore, since the right had to be either a right *in rem* or a right *in personam*, it must be a right *in personam*; on this view, a trust is essentially 'obligational', not 'proprietary', the idea being that the beneficiary has no true interest in the trust assets themselves, but only has the right that the trustee, or third-party recipient from the trustee, perform a personal obligation owed to him. Perhaps the most famous advocate of this view was Maitland (Maitland (1929)).

2.109   Notice, however, that the *in rem/in personam* either/or is not particularly helpful here. From one perspective, the fact that the beneficiary's right binds all successors in title with the exception of a bona fide purchaser means that his right has a genuine *in rem* aspect, for anyone in principle might acquire the trustee's title by way of gift, or by way of contract, or as the trustee's trustee in bankruptcy, and so on. Because there is a *bona fide* purchaser exception to the *nemo dat* principle (2.70) in the case of money does not mean that we say that our title to the coins in our pockets is not a right *in rem* which binds the world. And the *in personam* characterisation of the beneficiary's right is, moreover, deeply misleading. It is simply not true that equity regards the obligation that the trustee undertook when he decided to accept the trusteeship as being a merely personal obligation to the beneficiary to use assets *he beneficially owns* for the beneficiary's benefit, as if the beneficiary had a contractual right against the trustee, or, from the opposite perspective, that the beneficiary merely has a right against *this particular* title holder to the trust assets. Although the imposition on various successors in title to the trustee of the obligation to hold the received assets on trust for the beneficiary developed piecemeal (2.63), the *only* thing that explains the imposition of these obligations is the thought that the property was not the trustee's beneficially to transmit to others—it was the beneficiary who was beneficially interested in the trust assets themselves. Furthermore, purely personal *obligations* are not 'transmissible' (although the correlative *right* to the *performance* of a personal obligation can be, as we have seen with the assignment of debts (2.35)). A creditor can assign his right to be paid, but a debtor cannot assign or otherwise pass on his duty to make the payment. (As we have seen (2.83, 2.89), a trustee in bankruptcy and the personal representative of the deceased fall under an obligation to pay the debts of the bankrupt or deceased respectively, but this is not to be explained on the basis that duties are generally transmissible.)

2.110   It was because equity regarded the assets as beneficially the beneficiary's that it was so obvious that a successor in title who was not a bona fide purchaser would be 'bound in conscience' to hold his newly acquired powers of title in the assets for the benefit of the beneficiary. This successor was not taking on the original trustee's obligation, but was bound because of the fact that, *by virtue of the original trustee's obligation not to hold the assets beneficially for himself*, the beneficial interest in the trust assets now belonged to the beneficiary, not to the trustee. So, in sum, the reason why successors in title (save for the bona fide purchaser) are bound by the beneficiary's interest in the trust assets is an equitable version of the *nemo dat* principle, that you cannot give what you do not have. Whilst the original trustee's legal title to the property can be transmitted to a successor in title, the fact that the beneficiary has the equitable right that the powers that go with that title are exercised for his benefit, means that no successor who acquires those powers of title can employ them for his own benefit, for that would be to strip the beneficiary of his beneficial interest in the trust asset, and would, of course, be against conscience. If the obligation to use the powers of title over the trust assets were merely personal to the trustee, to use assets he beneficially owned for the beneficiary's benefit, it would not be against conscience not to discharge the trustee's duty, on his behalf, when you came into the title of those assets. In the same way as you cannot transmit any obligation to me to pay your debts, however much I could afford to do so and however much I might sympathise with your creditor, it makes no sense to say that the trustee's '*in personam*' obligation to the beneficiary could be transmitted to third parties. To repeat: the trustee's undertaking of the trust obligation has the consequence that the trustee has no beneficial interest in the property, and that the beneficial interest lies with the beneficiary. Accordingly, successors in title to the trustee are also bound by the beneficiary's interest unless there is a good reason in conscience or legal policy why they should not be.

2.111   The upshot of the last paragraph was that it is not really very helpful to try to characterise the beneficiary's interest using the *in rem/in personam* terminology. Partly in response to the difficulties in applying this terminology, commentators have recently proposed a different way of characterising the beneficiary's right, as a 'right *in* a right' or a 'right *to* a right' or a 'right *against* a right' (Chambers (2013c), para 13.90; Smith (2008); McFarlane and Stevens (2010)). The idea is the following: as we have seen, the beneficiary's interest binds *successors in title* to the trustee, that is, persons who acquire the trustee's rights to the trust assets. But the beneficiary has no (direct) claim against mere *successors in possession* to the trustee, for example the thief who acquires possession of a trust asset by theft, or the adverse possessor who takes possession of trust land. Thus it is proposed that the best way to understand the beneficiary's right is as a right to the trustee's right to the property. So conceived, such a right obviously implicates certain third parties, those who acquire the trustee's right in the trust assets. And since thieves and adverse possessors do not acquire the trustee's right in the trust assets, the beneficiary has no direct claim against them when they interfere with the trustee's right.

2.112   In the view of your author, there is an innocuous way of reading the 'right to a right' characterisation of the beneficiary's interest under a trust, and a misleading one. (For further detail, see Penner (2014a).) Following on from what we have discussed throughout this chapter, you can think of the beneficiary's interest as being in, or to, or against the trustee's powers of title, and thus indirectly in the trust assets, because, of course, the trustee's obligation is to exercise his powers of title to dispose of the trust assets according to the terms of the trust so as to benefit the beneficiaries. So long as you appreciate that the beneficiary's interest under a trust is an interest in the rightful exercise of the powers that go with having title to the trust assets, you can see why the trust binds only successors in title to the trustee, for they acquire the powers to the title of the property which forms the trust assets. But there is a misleading way of taking the idea of a right to a right, one in which the trustee's right to the trust property is taken to be his right to possession of tangible trust property like chattels or land, rather than the powers of title which he must exercise to carry out the trust terms.

2.113   As we have seen, the way in which a beneficiary acquires the benefit of the trust assets is through the trustee's exercise of his powers of title to those assets. In the case of the bare trust of land, he exercises his power to license the beneficiary to take possession; in the case of a wealth management trust, he transfers income or capital to the beneficiary by exercising his power to transfer the trust assets. As we have also seen, the trustee is not entitled to take possession of any tangible trust property for his own benefit, and neither is a beneficiary, just because he is a beneficiary, allowed to take possession of the trust assets. So it is misconceived to think of a trust as a device by which the beneficiary acquires the benefit of the trust assets by virtue of either his or his trustee's possession of them (again, unless the terms of the trust require the trustee to exercise his legal powers to put the beneficiary in possession). Nevertheless, in speaking of property rights, there is a long tradition in the common law of regarding tangible assets, chattels and land, as the paradigm examples of property rights, and furthermore of taking the right of the owner of chattels or land to the immediate, exclusive possession of them as paradigmatic of ownership. On this view, the basic property right that the common law recognises is the owner's right to immediate, exclusive possession of a thing. And because the beneficiary of a trust does not have, just by virtue of being a beneficiary, the right to the immediate, exclusive possession of the trust assets, he does not have a property right or property interest in the trust assets.

2.114   Now the point here is not to argue about definitions of property. The English law notion of property sometimes refers to possessory interests, sometimes not—English law also recognises, for example, intangible property (the creditor's assignable right to be paid a debt, for instance) or intellectual property, such as a copyright. If the definition of property that you are working with is the possessory one, then it is clear that the beneficiary of a trust does not just in virtue of being a beneficiary have a property right in the trust assets; so be it. But emphasising this definition of property will mislead you if you then conclude that his interest is derivative (2.31) of the trustee's property right—is 'a right to the trustee's right'—and you conceive of the trustee's right as the right to the immediate, exclusive possession of the trust assets. That is the *wrong right of the trustee's* to take as the right of the trustee's in which the beneficiary has a right. The 'right to a right' that the beneficiary has is the trustee's title to the trust assets, that is, to the *powers* of title that he has in the trust assets, those powers which he has a duty to exercise in various ways in order to carry out the terms of the trust and benefit the beneficiaries.

2.115   Conceiving of the beneficiary's right to a right as a right to the trustee's powers of title also explains *why* the beneficiary has no direct right against the thief or adverse possessor. We know that the trustee is never entitled to take possession of tangible trust property for his own benefit. Except in the case of mansion houses and their contents, trusts these days do not typically hold much in the way of chattels, but in the case of furniture and paintings and so on, these are possessed either by beneficiaries for their use because under the terms of the trust the trustee licenses them to do so, or if the mansion house is let out furnished, by leaseholders. In both cases the beneficiaries' right lies in their right that the trustee exercise his powers of title appropriately, not in the trustee's own legal right to immediate, exclusive possession. True it is, of course, that certain investments, which have no possessory value per se, like gold bullion, are possessed by trustees, but, first of all, this possession is again not freely available to the trustee. These chattels are typically in the custody of others, ie in safe deposit somewhere. Where the trustee retains possession in such cases, as with the case of investment land not leased for rental income (let us say it is waste land held for development purposes), for the beneficiary the important power in which he is interested is the trustee's power to bring an action against thieves or trespassers, not any right of the trustee himself to possess. These assets are valuable trust assets because of their exchange value, not because of any possessory or use value that they typically do not even have.

2.116   So the trustee's right to bring an action to recover possession of land is valuable to the beneficiaries because it restores the trustee's effective power of sale. When I say 'effective power of sale' I mean to point out that, whilst it is true that an adverse possessor taking possession of the land does not in the least diminish the trustee's powers of title over the land—the trustee can still sell it, lease it, mortgage it, and so on because his title is not displaced in the least by the adverse possessor's possession—until a trustee gains possession of the land he will be unable to give possession to anyone: though he retains his title, it is diminished in value until he has possession so that he can effectively deal with the title. Similarly, a thief of a chattel acquires no title that displaces the trustee's, but if the trustee cannot secure possession of a chattel, no one will buy it from him, so his power to sell it is effectively neutralised. In view of this, the beneficiary simply does not have an interest in the trustee's possession of an asset, except in so far as the trustee's loss of possession inhibits the effective exercise of the trustee's powers of title over the asset, and so the beneficiary's concern here is to make sure that the trustee uses all the rights to legal action available to him to ensure that his effective power to deal with the title of the trust asset is restored. So the beneficiary has no interest in 'regaining possession' of the trust asset *himself* from the thief or adverse possessor, for that would not do anything to secure his interest in the trustee's exercising his powers of title to deliver his benefits under the terms of the trust. The action the beneficiary needs, and the one that he has, is to make sure the trustee himself regains possession of the trust assets to ensure that the trustee can effectively exercise his powers of title.

Trusts of assets in non-trust law jurisdictions

2.117   A trustee may hold assets in countries which do not recognise trusts. It is sometimes thought that this possibility shows that the trust is 'obligational', rather than 'proprietary', but it doesn't.

Take a simple example. T, an English trustee, holds French land on bare trust (2.13) for B. B asks T to transfer the title to him, and T refuses. What can B do? Well, one thing B cannot do is go to a French court and prove the trust relationship and get a French court order against B to transfer the title. (Under French law, B *may* be able to characterise and prove T's obligation to B as a kind of obligation, say a contractual obligation, which a French court might recognise; in that case, B may be able to obtain some kind of legal remedy in France.) But B can sue T in England and the English court will order T to transfer the land, doing whatever is necessary according to French law to do so (*Webb v Webb* (1994)). But there is a sense in which land in France or company shares in a non-trust jurisdiction are a kind of 'flawed' asset from B's perspective, because his ability to enforce his rights may be limited or non-existent. In *Akers v Samba Financial Group* (2017) the trustee transferred Saudi shares in breach of trust to a third party. Under Saudi law only legal beneficial title (2.17) to shares is recognised, so the beneficiary had no possible action against the recipient of the transfer, whether a bona fide purchaser or not. In this respect, then, one 'proprietary' facet of the beneficiary's rights, the ability to pursue third party recipients of property transferred in breach of trust, is diminished when assets are held in non-trust law jurisdictions. Does the fact that in these cases the beneficiary's only remedy is to enforce the trust obligation against the trustee himself show that the trust is primarily 'obligational'? It is hard to see how. In the first place, it tells us nothing about trusts law *per se*, which is the law of jurisdictions that *do* recognise the trust and all of the rights that law gives its beneficiaries. What it rather tells us is that there are certain sorts of assets which, by their very nature, do not allow beneficiaries to exercise what would otherwise be all the rights available to them. This can be true in trusts law jurisdictions themselves. A good example is registered land in England. Beneficiaries of a trust of land may lose their interest in the land, which would otherwise be protected, by application of the rules of 'over-reaching' (the details are unimportant), rules which favour the interests of good faith purchasers of land (*City of London Building Society v Flegg* (1988)).

Trusts and the fusion of law and equity

2.118   We are now in a position to see why the trust can appear to pose a problem for the fusion of law and equity (1.16). The trust appears to depend upon maintaining a clear distinction between legal and equitable interests, and so would appear to require that the rules of law and the rules of equity stay unfused. This, it is humbly submitted, is a pernicious non sequitur, because it appears to entail that the law of property depends for its intellectual cogency on a kind of blind adherence to the labels we use to refer to proprietary interests, rather than to the actual character of those interests themselves. The trust is, certainly, a very particular (perhaps peculiar) property device. It depends upon dividing *the powers of ownership* (the right to transfer the property, to possess it, and so on) that remain with the legal owner from *the rights to the benefit of the property* that, in usual circumstances, would follow naturally from the possession of those powers, that is, if one held those powers as an outright owner not subject to any trust. The rights to the benefit of the property go to the equitable interest holders, the beneficiaries, somewhat differently depending upon whether things are going as planned or whether things have gone wrong. When the trust is up and running and working fine, the beneficiaries take their benefits because the trustee is meeting his personal trust obligations to deliver the beneficiaries their rights as intended. But if things go awry, they then depend on their personal rights to sue the trustee for breach (or any third-party accessory to the breach of trust) or on their proprietary rights to the trust property itself in the sense of making those rights 'public', to chase the property into the hands of third-party recipients (so long as they are not equity's darlings) or to pursue the traceable proceeds of it. The point, however, is that characterising the nature of the trust in this way does not depend upon using the terms 'legal' and 'equitable', although of course these are convenient labels. We could just as easily refer, respectively, to legal interests and 'trust' interests, or 'title' interests and 'trust' interests, so long as it was clear how the labels applied, and so long as they accurately represented the various personal and proprietary rights, powers, and duties that constitute the trust as the legal creature it is. There is no reason on earth to think that it is impossible to do this without maintaining two divided 'systems' of property law or property rights.

2.119   Again, this is not a diatribe against the use of a term such as 'equitable interest'. Such a term is perfectly convenient, and it is valuable for a legal term to convey something of its historical origin. But it is one thing consciously to retain a particular term, and quite another to be blinded by it. The continuing reference to 'equitable' interests should not be regarded as a licence to say that English property law need forever be conceived as (read 'conceptually hampered by') separate systems of rules that cannot be made to work together as a single, coherent whole.

2.120   Moreover, it is doubtful whether we should want to retain the notion of an 'equitable' interest which requires all equitable interests of whatever kind, from the beneficiary's interest under a trust to the rights of an equitable easement holder to share certain features, any more than the common law should require, eg, all common law property interests to be either subject to a *bona fide* purchaser rule or not, which we have seen it does not (2.69–2.70). Consider the case of the easement., say A's right of way over Blackacre, which is owned by B. It is clearly the law that if a third party, X, blocks up the entrance to the right of way, A can bring an action for nuisance against X, *if A's easement is a legal easement*. There is no clear authority if A can do the same if his easement is an equitable one. If you hold a version of the right against the right view (2.111) that says equitable interest holders never have rights against third parties, the law should deny A a nuisance claim because his interest is 'only' equitable. But there seems to be no reason to deny this to A, just because (as will generally be the case) his easement was created informally (ie not by the execution of a deed), so long as A can prove his easement. (For discussion see Gardner (2013).)

2.121   There is a further reason, if that was not enough, to regard any continuing resistance to the progress of ironing out the rules of property into a coherent and justifiable system as pernicious. As was pointed out in the first chapter with respect to the application of common law and equitable remedies, it can easily underwrite the 'history is destiny' fallacy (1.17) that, because equitable interests arose in the Court of Chancery, their nature will forever be foreign to the perspective of the common law, and therefore in dealing with them, one must make reference to the peculiar conscience-based jurisdiction of equity, rather than the rights-based jurisdiction of the common law. Besides being historically dubious and something of an insult to judges and lawyers in both jurisdictions, it simply presumes (but gives no reason for doing so) that the two bodies of law are divided by irreconcilable intellectual foundations. Now, no one said fusion was going to be easy, and it is by no means complete a century and more after the Judicature Acts (1.15). Of course it requires a great deal of work over time, dealing with actual cases before the court, to reconcile the terms and perspectives of these bodies of doctrine one to the other, so that one finally achieves a perspective that draws as much as possible on the particular genius of each for achieving justice in particular cases. But it is no less possible than the equally important job of ironing out the difficulties between particular areas of doctrine *within* the common law or *within* equity.

2.122   Finally, your author must be allowed to make a plea on the behalf of trusts law examiners everywhere. Do not, explicitly relying on equity's historical origins (and implicitly relying on the current state of incomplete fusion), defend your answer in an exam by saying something fatuous such as 'Equity is a court of conscience … ' and continue by favouring one side of the argument or another because the result seems 'fair' to you. A court of conscience equity may have been, and certainly equitable doctrine reflects good conscience, but it is good conscience *according to law*, ie good conscience that has been made more or less explicit and precise in past decisions, and is now reflected in the current set of rules. In the same way one might say that the common law seeks to do justice, but again justice according to law. Just because equitable doctrine is called 'equity' does not let you off the hook of having to write an appropriate, legally framed, answer.

FURTHER READING

Brownbill (1992, Parts I–III)

Gardner (2013)

Gretton (2000)

Matthews (1996, 2005)

McFarlane and Stevens (2010)

Penner (2002, 2006b, 2010b, 2014a, 2014b)

Smith (2008, 2013b)

Swadling (1997)

SELF-TEST QUESTIONS

1.   What is an express trust? How is one created?

2.   What is the difference between the concepts of 'legal interest', 'equitable interest', and 'beneficial interest'?

3.   Distinguish between a bare trust, a special trust, and a nomineeship.

4.   What is a fiduciary?

5.   What is the significance of 'equity's darling'?

6.   What are the features of an express trust? How do these features together work to explain the beneficiary's interest under a trust?

7.   What is a security interest, and in what respects is it comparable to a trust?

8.   Explain the role of a deceased's personal representatives. In what respects are they like trustees?

9.   What is the concept of 'patrimonium', and how does it help explain how the Quebec and Scots civil law trusts work?

10.   How is the nature of the beneficiary's interest under a trust best described?

3

Express trusts: trusts and powers

SUMMARY

Fixed trusts, discretionary trusts, and powers of appointment

Duties and powers *virtute officii* (powers given to office holders), personal powers (powers *nominatum*), powers 'in the nature of a trust', fiduciary powers, bare and mere powers

Interests under fixed trusts

The principle in *Saunders v Vautier*

Trusts void on grounds of public policy and illegal trusts

The rule against perpetuities

Judicial control of discretionary trusts and powers of appointment

The validity of dispositive discretions: certainty of objects

Excessive and fraudulent exercises of powers

'Power to exclude' objects

Locus standi to enforce the trust and beneficiaries rights to information

Interests under discretionary trusts and powers of appointment

Protective trusts

3.1 Express trusts are very flexible devices for structuring the benefits that property can provide, in particular in ways that are impossible or inconvenient to do simply by making an outright gift. Essentially, three ways of doing so can be employed—fixed trusts, discretionary trusts, and powers of appointment.

Fixed trusts, discretionary trusts, and powers of appointment

Traditional and modern examples of express trusts

3.2 As you might expect, the terms of a trust over property of any value are often complicated, but the different provisions all do one of three things: (1) impose a fixed duty on the trustee, for example to pay the income from the trust property to Mary; or (2) impose a duty to do something which requires the trustee to make a choice, or exercise a discretion, for example to pay the income of the trust to Mary and Cecile in such proportions as the trustee chooses; or

(3) give the trustee a right, or a power, to do something, but which he is under no obligation to do, for example a power to use the trust funds to 'maintain', ie pay the living expenses, of Paul. Hence the terminology 'fixed trust' (duty with no discretion), 'discretionary trust' (duty with a discretion), and 'power' (right but no duty).

3.3 To get a sense of how these different 'devices' typically work together, consider the following simplified examples of trust instruments:

A traditional form of trust in four variations

Example 1

> All the rest and residue of my estate to my trustees ON TRUST for my beloved wife Mary for life, and then for my three sons, Jacob, Jasper, and Jeremy in equal shares.

Example 2

> All the rest and residue of my estate to my trustees ON TRUST for my beloved wife Mary for life, and then to my three sons, Jacob, Jasper, and Jeremy in such shares as my trustees shall in their absolute discretion think fit, with power to my trustees to appoint up to half the capital during my wife's lifetime to such of my sons and in such amounts as they shall in their absolute discretion think fit.

Example 3

> All the rest and residue of my estate to my trustees ON TRUST for my beloved wife Mary for life, and then to my three sons, Jacob, Jasper, and Jeremy in such shares as my wife shall appoint by her will, with power to my wife Mary to appoint up to half the capital during her lifetime to such of my sons and in such amounts as she shall in her absolute discretion think fit.

Example 4

> All the rest and residue of my estate to my trustees ON TRUST to pay or apply the income during the life of my beloved wife Mary for the benefit of Mary and my three sons Jacob, Jasper, and Jeremy in such shares as my trustees shall in their absolute discretion think fit, and then to my three sons, Jacob, Jasper, and Jeremy in equal shares, with power to my wife Mary to appoint up to half the capital during her lifetime to such of my wife's brothers and sisters and nieces and nephews in such amounts as she shall in her absolute discretion think fit.

A modern form of trust

Example 5

> 1. 'Beneficiaries'
>   The 'Beneficiaries' means
>   (i)   Unless removed under (iii) below the children and descendants of the settlor, and their spouses, widows, and widowers (whether or not remarried);

(ii) Any person, other than the Trustee or the settlor, nominated by the Trustee in writing.

(iii) During the Trust Period the trustees may at any time in writing remove any person who is a beneficiary under (i) or (ii) above, though any such person removed under this clause may at any later time be nominated as a beneficiary under (ii) above.

2. 'Trust Income'

Subject to the Overriding Powers below:

(i) The Trustees may accumulate the whole or the part of the income of the Trust Fund during the Accumulation Period. That income shall be added to the Trust Fund.

(ii) The trustees shall pay or apply the remainder of the income to or for the benefit of any Beneficiaries, as the Trustees think fit, during the Trust Period.

3. 'Overriding Powers'

Power of Appointment

(i) The Trustees may appoint that they shall hold the whole or any part of the Trust Fund for the benefit of any Beneficiaries on such terms as the Trustees think fit.

(ii) An appointment may create any provisions and in particular discretionary trusts and or dispositive or administrative powers exercisable by any person.

(iii) An appointment shall be made by deed and may be revocable or irrevocable.

4. Transfer of the Property to a new settlement

(i) The Trustees may declare by deed that they hold any Trust Property on trust to transfer it to trustees of a Qualifying Settlement, to hold on the terms of that Qualifying Settlement, freed and released from the terms of this Settlement.

(ii) A 'Qualifying Settlement' means any settlement, wherever established, under which every person who may benefit is (or would if living be) a Beneficiary of this Settlement.

5. Power of Advancement

(i) The Trustees may pay or apply any Trust Property for the advancement or benefit of any Beneficiary.

6. Default Clause

(i) Subject to the provisions 1 to 5 above, the Trust Fund shall be held on trust for such charitable objects and in such amounts as the Trustees shall in their absolute discretion think fit. [Clauses of this kind are found, eg, in Millar v Millar (2018), [6]; Foreman v Kingstone (2004), [87].]

Fixed trusts

3.4 The beneficial interests under a fixed trust are, as the name implies, fixed, which means that the *share* of the trust property the beneficiary will receive is defined by the terms of the trust. All the interests created in Example 1 for Mary, Jacob, Jasper, and Jeremy are fixed. Mary will receive the income of the trust for so long as she lives, and upon her death the trustees will distribute the trust assets to her sons in equal shares, at which point the trust will come to an end. 'Fixed' does not mean that the actual monetary value the beneficiary will receive can be determined from the outset. For example, company shares may be held on this trust. The trustees will pay the dividends to Mary during her life, and on her death the shares will be distributed in equal amounts to the boys. All know what their interests are, although the particular amounts of income that Mary may receive from the trust property will vary with the amounts of the dividends paid on the shares. 'Fixed' means 'not discretionary', and that is all it means.

Discretionary trusts

3.5 In contrast, the terms of a discretionary trust give the trustee, or indeed, someone else, a *dispositive* (2.50) discretion. In Example 2 the trustees have a discretion as to the particular amounts of capital that each of Jacob, Jasper, and Jeremy will receive on Mary's death. In Example 4 there is a discretionary trust of the income under which Mary and her three sons are the beneficiaries. Under the modern law, such a discretion will allow the trustees to choose any shares at all, even a 'zero' share, so that they might decide to distribute the capital to Jacob alone, giving the others nothing. The main reason for giving the trustee a discretion of this kind is that of *flexibility*: it allows the trustee to respond to changing circumstances. If Jeremy were to marry and have children of his own, whereas Jacob became a celibate priest, it might be sensible to give Jeremy a larger share of the capital on Mary's death. Or, to take the case of a discretionary trust of income in Example 4, if Jasper decided to become a 'trustafarian' or 'trust babe', ie to forego education, refuse employment, and try to live off whatever income he could prise out of the trustees, it might be sensible to cut him off for a time. In Example 3 we have the case of a discretionary trust where the discretion is not the trustees' but Mary's, and this is perfectly possible and sensible. Mary gets to choose the shares in which her sons will receive the capital on her death, and the settlor would undoubtedly have given her this discretion because he thought her the best judge of how much each of her sons should be given.

3.6 Under a discretionary trust, no individual who is in the class of possible beneficiaries, ie in whose favour the trustee may exercise his discretion, has any individual interest, any individual 'equitable title', in the trust property, until the trustee actually exercises his discretion and declares that such and such a share or amount will go to that individual. The possible beneficiaries have only a hope, or expectancy (sometimes referred to in Latin as a *spes*), of receiving the testator's bounty (Turner (2018), 247–56). However, the fact that the trustee has a discretion does not mean he can do anything he wants—he still has the obligation to carry out the terms of the trust, and therefore he *must* exercise his discretion within the trust terms and distribute the trust property. So, for example, in Example 4, when income is received, say dividends on shares, the trustees cannot just hang onto it for an indefinite time pondering how they will divide it between Mary and her sons; they must decide on shares and pay it out to them within a reasonable time after its receipt.

3.7 The result of the trustee's having a discretion to select only some of the possible beneficiaries means, of course, that some might not receive any money at all, in which case they will not really be 'beneficiaries' of the trust. For this reason, the term 'objects' is used, and the group of objects among whom the trustee may select is called the 'class of objects'. This is a compendious term that covers beneficiaries under a fixed trust, possible beneficiaries under a discretionary trust, and possible recipients under a power of appointment, to which we now turn.

Powers of appointment

3.8   A power of appointment under a trust allows the power holder to 'appoint', ie give, property to individuals, free of the trust, and there is such a power created in the last part of Examples 2, 3, and 4. In Example 2 the power is given to the trustees, in the latter two to Mary. Example 4 is the most straightforward: Mary is given a power of appointment to transfer up to half the trust property to her brothers and sisters and nieces and nephews before her death. If Mary exercises the power by directing the trustees to do so, they must take the property right out of the trust and give it to whichever of these relations of hers she chooses. Because a power of appointment is a power to give away property, it is a power of ownership, although limited by the trust terms. Because powers to appoint property are given to individuals, power holders are often called 'donees of the power', or 'donees' for short; this terminology is obviously confusing because one naturally thinks of the person *to whom* property is appointed as the donee, not the one who does the appointing. In any case, beware of this term when you read the cases.

3.9   As Examples 2 to 4 show, powers usually specify whether they allow the power holder to appoint income or capital; these were all powers to appoint capital, but the settlor might have given the trustees a power to appoint up to half the income as it arises from time to time to the three boys. Now, it is vital to notice who loses out when appointments are made. In Example 4, if Mary exercises the power, she will reduce the capital base from which income is earned, so it will cost her in income, and by appointing to such relations of hers as she chooses, she takes capital away that would otherwise go to her sons. Now consider Examples 2 and 3. In these cases, the class of objects of the power to appoint the capital is the same as the class of objects of trust over the capital. To the extent the trustees or Mary were to appoint the capital to one or more of the boys during her life, the less there will be to distribute to them on her death. You might consider this an odd provision, but it makes perfect sense. Mary might be a long-lived old thing, and she might have more than enough income from the trust; why not give her or the trustees a power to give some of the capital (up to half) to the boys during her lifetime (they might all be married with children and be able to use the money) rather than making them wait until she drops off her perch?

3.10 A bit of terminology: the people whose interests diminish when the property is appointed are called 'those who take in default of appointment', sometimes shortened to 'those who take in default'. So in Examples 2 to 4, in each the three sons are those who take in default because they are otherwise entitled to the capital under the prior trust terms; if the power is not exercised, they will get it.

3.11 Until the trustee actually exercises the power of appointment to appoint trust assets to an individual in the class of objects, the objects in the class have only a hope, or *spes*, (3.6) of receiving anything.

General, special, and hybrid/intermediate powers

3.12 Powers are generally restricted, essentially in the same ways that discretionary trusts are limited. As the examples show, the settlor can restrict the power so that the power holder can only appoint to a certain class of objects, the amounts that any object receives can be limited, and so on. A power to appoint to anyone in the world, including the power holder himself, is called a 'general' power. Such a power essentially amounts to absolute ownership, although a power to appoint to anyone that can only be exercised by will, which obviously cuts out the power holder himself, is still considered a general power. A 'special' power is a power to appoint to a restricted class of persons (eg the testator's children) even if that class includes the power holder; the powers of appointment in Examples 2 to 4 are all special powers. A 'hybrid' or 'intermediate' power is a power to appoint to anyone *except for* a restricted class, for example anyone except the settlor or his spouse or children (see eg *Re Park* (1932); *Re Beatty* (1990)); the power in 1(ii) in Example 5 is a hybrid or intermediate power, not to appoint directly, but to appoint to the class of 'Beneficiaries' who can receive appointments under clause 3(i).

3.13   We can now consider the much differently structured modern trust of Example 5. The first thing to notice about the terms of this trust is that those named as 'Beneficiaries' are *not* objects of the *trust of the capital* at all; the capital beneficiaries, those entitled to the trust property unless the powers of appointment found in clauses 3, 4, and 5 are exercised, are found in clause 6, the so-called 'Default Clause'. Clause 6 is a discretionary trust for charitable objects. As we will examine in detail in Chapter 14, besides trusts for people, the law allows trusts for charitable purposes. Under the discretionary trust in clause 6, the trustees have a discretion to devote the capital to charities of their choice. As regards being objects of a trust, the 'Beneficiaries' are objects only of the trust of income in clause 2(ii), although even here under clause 2(i) the trustees can decide not to pay them any income, but to add it instead to the capital. So if the beneficiaries are to receive any capital, they will receive it as objects of the powers of appointment given in clauses 3 to 5. On the other hand, under this form of modern trust, it is fully intended and expected that *all* the capital *will* be distributed under clauses 3 to 5; the charities are expected to get nothing. To summarise, then, under this form of trust, the main way in which property will be distributed is by way of powers of appointment, not by the trustees' distributing property under fixed or discretionary trusts. Why would a trust be structured in this way, with essentially 'dummy' capital beneficiaries (the charities which will likely receive nothing), and all capital distributions made by way of powers of appointment? While certain tax considerations have played their part, the main reason is maximum flexibility. What this form of trust does is create a class of objects, which can be expanded or contracted at will (clause 2(ii) and (iii)), and the provisions for distribution of both income and capital give the trustees an unfettered discretion to appoint as much or as little as they want to the clause 2 'Beneficiaries'. The trustees are expected to hold onto the fund of assets so long as they think it best to do so, distributing income or capital from time to time to the 'Beneficiaries', but when the time is right (eg all the infant beneficiaries have grown up and act responsibly) and definitely before the end of the 'Trust Period' (some selected period for the maximum lifetime of the trust (3.49, 3.53)) when the capital beneficiaries under the Default Clause would become entitled, they will distribute all the capital amongst the beneficiaries, bringing the trust to an end.

Fixed trusts, discretionary trusts, and powers compared

3.14   Fixed trusts and discretionary trusts are alike because, being trust obligations, the trustee is under a duty to distribute the property. This is obviously not the case with powers, although (as we shall see) there may be various duties that govern the power holder's exercise of the power. On the other hand, discretionary trusts and powers are alike, and different from fixed trusts, because the discretionary trustee and the power holder both have a discretion; in the case of the discretionary trustee, a discretion as to whom he will distribute the property, in the case of the power holder, generally that discretion as well (not always—one can have a 'fixed' power, where the power holder, if he chooses to exercise it, must appoint only to one individual or to specific individuals in defined shares) but always a discretion as to whether he appoints at all. Clearly, then, in the case of the discretionary trust and the power of appointment, there may be fiduciary duties that may apply to the persons who operate them, and this complicates things quite a bit, as we shall now consider.

Duties and powers *virtute officii* (powers given to office holders), personal powers (powers *nominatum*), powers 'in the nature of a trust', fiduciary powers, bare and mere powers

3.15   There are any number of ways in which a person can be instructed by the terms of a trust to transfer property in some way. The first point to emphasise here is that such instructions can be given not only to the trustees of a settlement, ie the title holders of the property who are in charge of seeing to the proper administration of the trust, but to others, like Mary in Examples 3 and 4 (see Nolan (2018)). Although Mary does not have title to the trust property, the trustees must comply with the terms of the trust, and so if she chooses to exercise the power and appoint property (usually by executing a deed that is delivered to the trustees), the trustees must follow her instructions and give the property away as she directs. The second point is that both of these sorts of operators of instructions under the trust may hold their power in as a fiduciary power (2.19), such that they must exercise the power only in the best interests of the power's objects. We can list the various options as follows.

Cases where there is a duty to distribute trust property

Duties *virtute officii*

3.16   These are the general run-of-the-mill duties to distribute property given to the trustees of the trust, whether fixed trusts or discretionary trusts. They are called duties '*virtute officii*' because they are held by a person by virtue of his holding an office, ie the office of trustee. They are, therefore, imposed upon whomsoever happens to be the trustee(s) of the trust for the time being. Where the trust is discretionary, the trustee will have to exercise judgment in choosing to distribute to the trust objects, and so holds the discretion in a fiduciary capacity, ie must choose only with the (competing) interests of the objects in mind. There is an important practical consequence of giving a power under a trust to 'the trustee' or 'the trustees': the power is exercisable by whomsoever are the trustees for the time being, ie not only by whatever particular individuals are the trustees at the outset but by any successor trustees appointed to replace them. Always remember that trustees may die, retire from the trust, or be removed, and then replaced by others (10.53 et seq). The same is true of a trust company's trust officer who looks after a number of particular trusts. So a settlor must beware of relying upon the special knowledge or particular moral integrity of the trustees he initially chooses, giving them extensive discretion because he trusts they will exercise it in a way of which he would approve; they might all be hit by a bus, and the successor trustees may not have these same attractions.

Powers 'in the nature of a trust'

3.17 Powers 'in the nature of a trust': These are 'powers' given to individuals by name ('*nominatum*'), rather than to trustees, but on the true construction of the terms of the trust the individual holder of the 'power' is under a duty to exercise the power. The discretion to appoint shares in capital amongst her sons in Example 3 is such a case. Mary is obliged to choose shares by her will just as much as the trustees in Example 2 must choose shares for the boys. Just like the trustees she must act, although unlike the trustee she is not the legal owner of the trust property. If she fails to act, in principle the court will act for her, in the same way as the court will enforce a trust should the trustees themselves fail to act (*Brown v Higgs* (1803); see also 7.11). And, just like a trustee, she will have a fiduciary obligation to exercise this power taking only the best interests of the objects into account. Thus an individual such as Mary is a kind of 'one-off' trustee, a trustee not of the whole settlement but only of her own particular power under the trust.

Cases where there is no duty to distribute trust property

Powers virtute officii

3.18 If a power of appointment is given to a trustee, he must use his judgment to decide whether to appoint the property at all, and then typically must decide upon what amounts to appoint in favour of which objects within the class of objects. Unless otherwise specified, and this would be rare, a trustee must make those choices with only the interest of the objects in mind, thus, as a fiduciary holder of the power. This has three important consequences. The first is that the trustee may not release the power, ie surrender it. It was given by the terms of the trust for the benefit of its objects, and releasing it would clearly be an act against their interests. Secondly, the trustee, although not being bound to exercise the power, must consider using it from time to time (7.91). Finally, in exercising the power, the trustee must consider not only the interests of the objects of the power, but also the interests of those beneficiaries of the trust who would take in default of appointment, because to appoint the property to the objects of the power is to take it away from them. It is sometimes said that the trustee is only a fiduciary towards, ie must only take into account the interests of, those who take in default of appointment, because they are beneficiaries of the trust, whereas the objects of the power are just that, objects of a power not objects of the trust (see Smith (2004)). But this seems wrong in principle, because under the terms of the trust the objects of fixed trusts, discretionary trusts, and powers of appointment are all equally contemplated as objects of the settlor's bounty and, although as we move from fixed trusts to powers of appointment their likelihood of receiving an actual benefit may diminish in theory, to the extent they are capable of benefiting under the trust, to that extent their interests should be taken into account by the trustee in any decision to appoint or not.

Personal fiduciary powers

3.19 In the same way that a named individual who is not a trustee may be given trust duties, he may be given powers of appointment *nominatum*, and in the same way that a trust obligation to distribute property may be imposed upon him (3.17), the trust instrument on its true construction may also indicate that he must exercise the power as a fiduciary, in the interests only of the objects and not with his own interests in mind. In that case he is in the same position as the trustee who has powers of appointment *virtute officii*—he cannot release the power, must consider using it, and must exercise it only with the objects and those who take in default in mind, but analogously with 3.17, he is a 'one-off' fiduciary power holder.

Pure personal powers

3.20   These are powers of appointment given *nominatum* where the power holder can exercise it as he chooses, considering only his own interests. Here the individual power holder may ignore the power or release it (ie inform the trustees in writing that he surrenders his right to exercise the power), and if the power confers a discretion upon him to appoint to only one or some of a class of objects, he may exercise the power in any way that suits him, favouring one object over another as he likes; he has no obligation to the objects to benefit, or even consider benefiting, them in any way. Consider the different powers of appointment given to Mary in Examples 3 and 4. In Example 3 the power to appoint capital to her sons is almost certainly fiduciary. The settlor presumably intended that Mary should consider exercising the power from time to time, and definitely not release it. But things seem quite different with the power to appoint capital away from her sons to her relations in Example 4. It is likely the settlor gave her this power *for her own benefit*, to help her relations out if she chooses, not because the settlor had any particular affection for these people. If she decided she no longer cared for these relations, there seems no good reason why she should not release the power.

'Limited powers'

3.21   In the case of pension fund trusts (see *Re the HHH Employee Trust* (2012)) a kind of power falling between a personal power and a fiduciary power has been recognised, an example being the power of the settlor of a company pension fund trust, ie the company, to amend the trust instrument. Whilst the power is not fiduciary, the company need not consider exercising it from time to time, and furthermore the company can take into account its own interests in exercising the power or not; if it does exercise the power it must do so in good faith. In so doing it must take into account the reasonable expectations of the beneficiaries in light of the fact that their benefits under the trust are not, as in the case of traditional family trusts, the result of a gift from the settlor, but are part of the remuneration package the employee receives; that is, the employees paid for these benefits through their services to the company.

3.22   Fiduciary powers are sometimes distinguished from personal powers by referring to the latter as 'bare' powers. Powers of appointment, where there is no duty to appoint, are sometimes distinguished from discretionary trusts (also known as 'trust powers') and 'powers in the nature of a trust', where there is such a duty, by being called 'mere' powers, 'mere' indicating the absence of any duty to distribute the trust property. Finally, note that there is nothing in principle preventing the settlor from giving a pure personal power to someone who is also a trustee, ie not *virtute officii*, but in his own name, although for obvious reasons this will have to be very clearly spelt out.

3.23   As Examples 1 to 5 illustrate, one whole 'trust' can combine the different devices of the fixed trust, the discretionary trust, and the power of appointment and given, as we have just seen, the various ways of distributing duties, fiduciary powers, and pure personal powers, the terms of a trust can be very complicated, involving many different actors. Trust instruments are therefore capable of giving rise to troublesome interpretive difficulties in determining whether what might on one reading be a discretionary trust is really just a fiduciary power of appointment, or whether a power conferred *nominatum* is accompanied with an obligation to exercise it, or only a fiduciary requirement to exercise it in good faith in the interests of the objects if exercised at all, or is a purely personal power.

Administrative duties and powers

3.24   Besides dispositive duties and powers, any number of administrative duties (2.50) and powers are necessary to keep the trust running while it is in existence. And just as is the case with dispositive duties and powers, there can be fixed and discretionary administrative duties, and fiduciary and personal administrative powers. For example, trustees have a fixed duty to keep the trust accounts, ie the records of trust dealings. They have a discretionary duty to invest the trust fund so as to earn a reasonable rate of return, where the discretion as to how they invest is, of course, fiduciary, so they must choose their investments with only the interests of the beneficiaries in mind. Trustees may have a power to delegate some of their functions, such as investment, though not an obligation to do so. They have a power to retire from the trust, and may have a power to appoint new trustees; as they receive these powers *virtute officii*, they are fiduciary powers.

3.25   But administrative powers may also be given to individuals *nominatum* and, again, they may be accompanied by duties to exercise them, or may be mere powers that might be fiduciary or might be purely personal. Although until recently rare, in many trusts, particularly in the 'offshore world', ie small jurisdictions which have important financial industries such as Jersey or the Cayman Islands, a named individual called a 'protector' (2.28, 3.28) might have a duty, ie might be under a trust obligation, to consider and either give or refuse consent to certain actions taken by a trustee under his powers under the trust (eg a power to 'export' the trust, ie change the jurisdiction in which the trust is administered). A named individual may be given the power to replace the trustees—this is a popular power for settlors to confer upon themselves in *inter vivos* trusts. This power may be fiduciary, in which case it may be exercised in the interests only of the beneficiaries, or purely personal, in which case the holder may exercise it as he likes. Now, given that administrative powers given to named individuals are *administrative*, ie they concern the proper running of the trust, there must be a strong initial presumption that they are fiduciary, because the purpose of a trust is to provide for and protect the interests of the beneficiaries, and so any power to enhance the trust's proper working would presumably be similarly oriented (see Hayton (1999)).

3.26   However, this might not always be the case. Assume an *inter vivos* trust of which the bulk of the trust fund is a majority shareholding in the settlor's private company, and assume the trust instrument confers upon the settlor a power to refuse consent to the trustees' voting him off the board of directors of the company. Such a provision may be inserted, not to protect the best interests of the beneficiaries, but to protect the settlor's own position. Whether an administrative power is fiduciary in such a case will depend upon the true construction of the terms of the trust. Settlors have what might be called a very broad 'freedom of trust', and the courts are generally assiduous in trying to read a trust instrument to give effect to their intentions. How a trust instrument is read in terms of the imposition of duties and the conferral of powers is very important of course, and in certain cases fine distinctions must be drawn.

3.27 Consider the following: a trust allows the trustees a discretion in dealing with the income of the trust as it arises as in Example 5, clause 2: they may either pay it directly to the income beneficiaries (3.32), or may 'accumulate' it (3.34), ie retain the income for later distribution. Now, at first glance, it may not appear important whether this is framed as a duty to distribute income as it arises with a power to depart from that duty and accumulate, or as a duty to accumulate with a power to depart from that duty and distribute, since the exercise of the power entails departure from the duty, and vice versa. On either reading, then, it appears the trustee has the same freedom of choice, so how can it matter how it is put? Here is how it matters: because trustees must comply with their duties, which task is framed as the duty sets the 'default' position from which we proceed if there is a problem of some kind. Roughly, powers are options whereas duties must be carried out. Thus in order to exercise a power to depart from a duty, trustees must agree unanimously to do so; in the absence of agreement there is no question but that they must comply with their duties. So, if on the true construction of the trust instrument we have a duty to distribute income and a power to accumulate, and the trustees cannot agree to exercise that power, then they must distribute the income. And conversely, they must carry out a duty to accumulate if they could not agree to exercise their power to distribute. So such fine distinctions can have significant practical consequences. Finally, in interpreting different trust instruments the different circumstances of different trusts, whether they are family trusts, pension fund trusts, or commercial trusts will obviously colour the initial presumptions one might apply to determining whether duties are imposed or powers conferred, and whether powers are fiduciary or personal.

Extensive power and duty holding by non-trustees: protectors

3.28 There is nothing in theory to prevent a settlor from giving extensive dispositive and administrative duties and powers to non-trustees (see Nolan (2018)), but for obvious reasons this is a dangerous thing to do if they are given to named individuals. Those named individuals may perish, or be otherwise uncooperative, and so a settlement that runs smoothly only if named third parties do their job is a precarious one. This, in general, is why most of the powers and duties needed to make the trust run are given to office holders, ie the trustees.

3.29 However, in the last few decades, a new animal has appeared called the 'protector' (2.30, 3.25), a non-trustee who under the trust is sometimes given extensive powers, in particular powers to give or refuse consent to the trustee's exercise of various of their powers and discretions. Protectors originally arose in the 'offshore' trust world: an English settlor, often with tax planning in mind, would create a trust in, say, the Cayman Islands; because the trustee in this case is far away, as a comfort the settlor would give to himself or to someone else he trusted (such as his solicitor or an old friend) the job of keeping an eye on the trustee (almost always a company specialising in trust business), and giving them sufficient powers to keep the trustee in check if it seemed the trustee might not act in the way a settlor intended. How, precisely should one treat the giving of such powers, and sometimes duties?

3.30 As a default, the protector should normally be regarded as a 'quasi-trustee', who is a fiduciary toward the beneficiaries (the Jersey Royal Court has affirmed this in a number of decisions: *In* re *Frieburg Trust* (2004); *Re the Representation of Centre Trustees (CI) Ltd* (2009); *In re A and B Trusts* (2012), and see Nolan (2016), 480–83), although in principle the trust instrument might specify or be construed such that the powers are merely personal, or that the protector holds them as fiduciary powers in favour of the settlor, to be exercised in the settlor's best interests (which raises the interesting question of whether this makes the settlor a beneficiary of some kind (and what kind?) under the trust). If there are provisions for a replacement protector, that strongly indicates that, like a trustee, the protector holds an office, and that the powers are held in a fiduciary capacity. Nevertheless, this will not invariably be so. In *JSC Mezhdunarodniy Promyshlenniy Bank v Pugachev* (2017) the court found that on the facts of the case, the powers given to the settlor, though in his position as a 'protector' of the trust, were not fiduciary, and he held those powers to use as selfishly as he wished in his own interests.

3.31   In some jurisdictions trust legislation contains provisions concerning protectors (eg Bahamas Trustee Act 1988, ss 2, 81–83), but where this is not the case, as in England, the effect of the grant of such powers and possibly duties must be determined by the court interpreting the terms of the trust (see further Waters (1996); Matthews (1995c)).

Interests under fixed trusts

Capital and income interests

3.32   Under a trust, the beneficial interests in the trust property can be carved up pretty much any way the settlor wishes. However, there are standard ways of doing so that we shall encounter again and again, in particular dividing the property between 'income' and 'capital' beneficiaries. In each of Examples 1 to 5 such a division is drawn. Mary is the income beneficiary, her sons the capital beneficiaries in Examples 1 to 3. In Example 4 the boys are also objects of the discretionary trust of income. In Example 5 the 'Beneficiaries' are entitled to the income under clause 2(ii), and clause 5 creates a discretionary trust of the capital for charities yet to be chosen. But what is income? In Example 1, can Mary insist that the trustees transfer as much of the property as she wants to her, so that her sons only get what she has not used up before she dies? No. Mary is entitled only to the income of the property, and that will depend upon the kind of property in the trust. Income on shares consists of the dividends that are paid, on bonds or other interest-bearing investments the interest payments, on land rent. During Mary's life Jacob, Jasper, and Jeremy will get nothing. They are the capital beneficiaries; after Mary's death they are entitled to the property itself, free of any trust, in equal shares. The value of their interest will fluctuate with the market price of the trust property.

Successive interests

3.33   Where there are income and capital beneficiaries, there are 'successive' interests. Successive interests are interests in the same property that take effect one after another, usually following the successive deaths of the beneficiaries. In Example 1 Mary will get the benefit for the time being, and only later will her sons get any benefit from the trust property. Traditionally, successive interest trusts, called 'settlements', were the province of dynastic families, and were used to define each successive generation's beneficial interest in a family's landed estates with a view to preserving them for subsequent generations. Because land was the subject matter of settlements, successive interests were framed in terms of two freehold estates in land: the 'life estate' and the 'fee simple'. A life estate, unsurprisingly, lasts for the lifetime of an individual, and a fee simple estate is unlimited in time, and therefore a gift of a fee simple amounts to absolute ownership. So a typical gift might be to Fred for life, then to Beatrix for life, then to Albert in fee simple. Fred will enjoy the benefit or income of the property for his life; when he dies Beatrix will get the income for as long as she lives, and when she expires Albert will take the absolute ownership. Due to the significance of the land settlement, the income beneficiary for life of a trust of any kind of property is often called the 'life tenant', the traditional land law term for the present holder of a life estate, and the capital beneficiary the 'remainderman', the corresponding term for one who took the fee simple following a life estate; so in Example 1 we can refer to Mary as the life tenant, and her sons as the remaindermen, though the latter usage is rare in the case of modern trusts. Successive interests are not, however, restricted to time periods equivalent to the life estate and fee simple. One might create a trust of shares for Richard until he attains the age of 21, and then to Tom for ten years, and then to Mary absolutely. In this case Richard and Tom will be successive income beneficiaries, and Mary the capital beneficiary. In keeping with the logic of dividing interests in property over time in this way, the final successive interest is always the capital interest, the unlimited 'forever after' interest in the property.

Exhaustive and non-exhaustive trusts of income

3.34   Trusts of the income of property can be cut down by giving the trustees a 'power to accumulate', as in clause 2(i) in Example 5, ie a power to save the income as it arises rather than distributing it to beneficiaries. The accumulations can be directed to go either to the capital beneficiary or to accumulation funds, which must later be paid over to the income beneficiaries. Trusts with a power to accumulate are called 'non-exhaustive', because when the power is exercised the distributions to the beneficiaries do not exhaust all of the income. Trusts of income with no power to accumulate are called 'exhaustive'.

Conditional and defeasible interests

3.35   Complicating matters somewhat, there may also be conditional and defeasible interests in property held under a trust. Conditions may be of two kinds: conditions precedent and conditions subsequent. A condition precedent is a condition that must be fulfilled for a gift to take effect, such as 'Blackacre to A in fee simple, on condition that he marries before the year 2010'. A condition subsequent is a condition of defeasance—the gift will come to an end if the condition occurs, such as 'Blackacre to A in fee simple, but if he should become a barrister, then to B in fee simple': if A becomes a barrister, then B will become entitled to Blackacre. Finally, a determinable interest is one that, while similar to a gift defeasible upon condition subsequent, is conceptually different. A gift defeasible upon condition subsequent is regarded as a full gift, of a life interest for example, which might come to an end before running its normal course, ie until the death of the life tenant. A determinable interest is regarded as being a gift of property for a lesser period than an estate like a life interest, this lesser interest being framed by the event by which the interest comes to an end; however, as things turn out its actual duration may extend to the full period of a normal estate (eg a full life interest) if the determining event does not occur. Thus a life interest determinable upon X's marriage will 'ripen' into a complete life interest if X never marries. The very subtle conceptual distinction between determinable interests and interests defeasible upon condition subsequent—so that the legal effect of a gift 'to Mathilda for life, but if she remarries, to Betty' (a life interest defeasible upon condition subsequent) differs from one 'to Mathilda during her widowhood' (a determinable life interest)—has been much criticised for being 'extremely artificial' (Pennycuick VC, *Re Sharp's Settlement Trusts* (1973)).

Vested, absolute, and contingent interests

3.36   Because interests can be defeasible or conditional, the interest can shift from one person to another. A person's interests are 'vested' if he is entitled to receive the benefits of the property as matters stand at present. In Example 1 both Mary and her sons have vested interests in the income and capital respectively. It is not to the point that her sons have only a future interest. Their capital interest is still vested, because they are in line to receive it and no one else is. In Example 1, because the gifts are not subject to any condition of defeasance or determining event, Mary's and the boys' interests are also 'absolute'. An absolute interest is one that cannot be defeated. An example of a person with a vested interest that is not absolute is the unmarried widow Mathilda in the example above (3.35)—the income interest is vested in her and she receives the income, but it is not absolute, because if she remarries she will lose it. Another example, perhaps, is the case of a person who will take property in default of appointment before any appointment is made. Consider a modification of the trust in Example 1, but where Mary's power to appoint to her relations in Example 4 is added to the trust terms. Under this trust the boys are in line to receive the property, but they are clearly not absolutely entitled in the sense that some of the property can be taken away from them in so far as they are entitled as capital beneficiaries, for that entitlement will (in part) be defeated by an appointment. The reason why one says 'perhaps' in this case is that the appointment does not *extinguish* their rights as capital beneficiaries per se, in the way that Mathilda's marriage extinguished her right to income entirely; it just diminishes the capital their interest relates to. On the other hand, if the power in Example 4 was a power to appoint up to *all* the capital, then an appointment of all the capital would extinguish their interest, for there would be no trust property left; such an appointment would also extinguish Mary's income interest for the same reason. Those who have vested, but defeasible interests, have counterparts in those persons who will get a vested interest if the former's are defeated. Thus, if a gift is 'Blackacre to Harry for life, but if he publishes the photographs he took at my 40th birthday party, then to Jane for life', then Jane has a *contingent* interest in Blackacre, which will vest if Harry publishes those photographs.

3.37   Although the trust device allows a settlor to distribute his bounty in a variety of ways over a period of time, the law does put limitations on this power. In particular, the law limits his ability to keep the property in the trust and out of the hands of the beneficiaries whom equity regards as the true owners of the property. The two principal means of doing so are the principle in *Saunders v Vautier* and the rule against perpetuities.

The principle in *Saunders v Vautier*

3.38   Although named after the case of *Saunders v Vautier* (1841), the principle is actually of much longer standing, and may be stated as follows: wherever a beneficiary with an absolute interest under a trust is *sui juris*, ie of full age and sound mind, he may call for the trust property that represents that interest, and the trustees are obliged to transfer the title of it to him; if he is a sole beneficiary, this will result in the complete collapse of the trust. For example, if a settlor creates a trust under which his son A is to receive the income of property until he is aged 30, at which time he is to receive the capital, that son can 'call for' the trust property, ie demand the trustees transfer the legal title to the trust property to him as soon as he reaches the age of 18.

3.39   This represents a significant limitation upon the settlor's 'freedom of trust', but it can be justified in two ways. First, there might be something of an 'anti-trust' justification, as follows: while it is fine to empower owners to create structured gifts of property where this is essentially the only means of giving the benefits of property, as for example when money is provided for minor children, this power should not be used to allow an owner to control his beneficiaries when they are fully competent to look after themselves. If you give property to someone, you naturally take the risk that they will use that property in ways that are foolish or which otherwise might defeat your hopes. But that is the price of treating people, including donees of property, as autonomous individuals. The law of trusts should not, therefore, allow settlors to treat sane adults as children, and so the principle of *Saunders v Vautier* reflects the law's desire that all individuals, once *sui juris*, should be treated as capable of running their own affairs, including their rights over property.

3.40   The second justification is related, and concerns the idea of equitable ownership. In the eyes of equity, the beneficiaries are the owners of the trust property, not the settlor. They have the rights against the trustee, and must enforce the trust themselves. When they reach full age, in essence the trust is in their hands. They can enforce their rights against the trustee or not, may consent to the trustees acting outside the terms of the trust, ie doing what would otherwise be a breach of trust (11.72), and may 'vary' (ie alter) the terms of the trust as they wish (10.65 et seq). The settlor has no say in any of this. Thus they are (in theory) in full control of the property via the office of the trustee. But, if that is so, why cannot they do with their property what they like, as can any other full owners and, in particular, take the property out of the trust completely if they so desire? (These justifications have not been found persuasive in the US, where the wishes of the settlor have often been regarded as paramount. Following *Claflin v Claflin* (1889), the principle will not apply so long as there remains a 'material purpose' of the settlor in the trust continuing. Some 'settlor-friendly' jurisdictions have adopted the 'material purpose' limitation on the principle by legislation: see, for example, the Bahamas Trustee Act, s 87.) It is important to note, however, that the principle allows the beneficiaries to collapse the trust, *not* to 'micro-manage' the trust by telling the trustee how to exercise his powers and discretions. For example, in *Re Brockbank* (1948), the court stated that while *sui juris* beneficiaries could collapse the trust and resettle the fund on new trustees, they were not entitled to direct the present trustee to exercise his power to appoint a replacement trustee (10.53 et seq) as they wished (see also *Lewis v Tamplin* (2018), [46]). In short, the principle in *Saunders v Vautier* does not turn all trustees into the *agents* of their beneficiaries (2.56). Although statute has recently conferred a power upon *sui juris* beneficiaries to replace their trustee (10.59), this does not alter the general principle that beneficiaries have no right to micro-manage the trust (see further Matthews (2006)).

3.41   The operation of the principle varies according to the type of trust. An interesting recent case is *Re Singapore Symphonia Co Ltd* (2013). The settlor settled $25m on trust, the income of which was to be distributed from time to time to support an orchestra company, but with the proviso that if there was any decline in the value of the capital sum, ie if its value dropped to below $25m, no further income could be paid. Following the 2008 financial crisis, the value of the fund fell below $25m, and there was no immediate prospect of the fund recovering its value, so the trust became useless as a support for the orchestra. There was no power granted to anyone to terminate the trust early. The only beneficiaries of the fund were the orchestra and the settlor (who was entitled to the capital after 21 years, when the trust was due to come to an end), and together they terminated the trust under the principle (having earlier agreed on a different way in which the settlor would support the orchestra in future). The principle has no application in the case of a nomineeship (2.13 et seq), where the nominee-trustee holds the property to the order of the beneficiary who can, therefore, call for the property at any time without any need to rely upon the principle. Under fixed trusts, *sui juris* beneficiaries such as the life tenant together with the remainderman may act together to call for the trust assets (*Brown v Pringle* (1845); *Quinton v Proctor* (1998)) or such portion of the assets as can conveniently be separately transferred (*Quinton v Proctor*), and *sui juris* beneficiaries of fixed shares of the trust assets may in principle demand that the trustee transfer the legal title to whatever share of the trust property is theirs, but this is subject to a general limitation that such a transfer must not result in the devaluation of the other beneficiaries' shares. In *Stephenson v Barclays Bank Trust Co Ltd* (1975) Walton J said:

> In general, the [individual sui juris beneficiary] is entitled to have transferred to him . . . an aliquot share of each and every asset of the trust fund which presents no difficulty so far as division is concerned. This will apply to such items as cash, money at the bank or an unsecured loan, Stock Exchange securities and the like. However, as regards land, certainly, in all cases, as regards shares in a private company in very special circumstances . . . the situation is not so simple, and even a person with a vested interest in possession in an aliquot share of the trust fund may have to wait until the land is sold, and so forth, before being able to call upon the trustees as of right to account to him for his share of the assets.

3.42   In *Lloyds Bank plc v Duker* (1987), the court refused the request of one beneficiary for the transfer of his proportionate interest in shares of a private company held on trust; the transfer would have given him a controlling bloc of shares in the company, and as a result his shares would be worth more per share on the open market than the remaining shares in the trust. The judge ordered the sale of all the trust shares on the open market, which, since it would give control of the company, would attract for the whole bloc of shares a higher price; the beneficiary could then claim his proportionate share of the proceeds of sale. It is important to note that the beneficiary acquired the large proportionate interest in the shares both because certain of the gifts in the original will that disposed of the shares lapsed (2.84) and through a subsequent bequest. Where a testator or settlor specifically gave one beneficiary a majority interest in a trust of shares, it might be inferred that he intended that beneficiary to take also the market value benefit of a controlling interest, in which case the principle of *Saunders v Vautier* should allow him to withdraw his shares.

3.43   The application of the principle in the case of discretionary trusts is stated in *Re Smith* (1928) by Romer J:

> What is to happen where the trustees have a discretion whether they will apply the whole or only a portion of the fund for the benefit of one person, but are obliged to pay the rest of the fund, so far as not applied for the benefit of the first named person, to or for the

benefit of a second named person? There, two people are the sole objects of the discretionary trust and, between them, are entitled to have the whole fund applied to them or for their benefit. It has been laid down by the Court of Appeal in In re Nelson (1918) that, in such a case as that you treat all the people put together just as though they formed one person, for whose benefit the trustees were directed to apply the whole fund.

Therefore, such beneficiaries may together call upon the trustees to transfer the trust property to them as co-owners. If the discretionary trust is one to pay the income only, they can demand the trustee pay the income, as it arises, to them directly as co-owners of it all. Where a beneficiary mistakenly calls for and receives the trust property under the principle, just as in the case of any other person receiving trust property transferred in breach of the trust terms, the beneficiaries can follow the property into his hands (2.61) and trace into any proceeds (2.78) he acquires with it (*Thorpe v Commissioners for HMRC* (2009)).

Trusts void on grounds of public policy and illegal trusts

3.44   Trusts, or the provisions of certain trusts, may be void on the grounds that they violate rules of public policy.

Trusts that infringe the rule against perpetuities

3.45   Until recently, in no common law jurisdiction could a settlor create a trust that was perpetual, that is, that could last forever (the exception is charitable trusts, see Chapter 14). Various rules have been put in place to invalidate such trusts, the most notorious of which was the 'rule against perpetuities'. This rule, as well as others regulating the duration of trusts, will be discussed at 3.49 et seq. The reason such rules are raised here is that what was often used to justify the rules is the idea that allowing a settlor to rule the disposition of his assets from his or her grave indefinitely violated a principle of public policy.

Private purpose trusts

3.46   A trust for pure purposes (eg a trust to devise a 40-letter alphabet for the English language, 14.21) is void, unless it is charitable (eg a trust for the relief of poverty). This is sometimes said to be because these 'private' (ie non-public or charitable) purpose trusts violate an internal principle of trusts law, the 'beneficiary principle' (9.2 et seq), but it can also be said that these trusts violate a rule of public policy (9.9).

Illegal trusts

3.47   Traditionally, neither the common law nor equity would allow a claimant to establish a claim on the basis of evidence that implicates him in an illegal purpose; thus, the equitable maxim,

'He who comes to Equity must come with clean hands.' The essentially identical principle at common law, framed in Latin, as '*ex turpi causa non oritur actio*', roughly translates as 'no action will be heard which arises from a morally turpid cause or basis'. So for example, a trust which is used to commit a fraud will not be enforced by a court of equity; two examples of the sort of fraud that a trust can be used to carry out will suffice. In *Tinsley v Milligan* (1994) two women, T and M, agreed to put a house they both paid for in the name of T so that M could deny having a beneficial interest in the house and misrepresent her assets to the Department of Social Security to claim benefits to which she would not be entitled if her beneficial interest in the house was declared. Relying on her sole legal title, T sought to evict M, and M resisted the action by claiming her beneficial interest under the trust. Thus the question arose whether M was caught by the clean hands maxim since her interest under the trust of the house was created in order to commit a fraud. In *Tribe v Tribe* (1996) a man, worried that his liabilities under two leases would be his financial ruin, transferred his shares in the family company to his son in order to safeguard these assets from his potential creditors. As it turned out, he sorted out his liabilities under the leases without having to resort to the fraudulent deception. He asked the court to hold that his son held the shares on trust for him when his son refused to reconvey them. Again, given that the transfer to the son was for the purpose of defrauding his creditors, the son argued that his father was caught by the clean hands maxim. What rankles some judges and commentators about such a rule is that, as often as not, the defendant to the action, who prays in aid this maxim, has hands just as filthy as the claimant, so as between the parties at least the rule can appear to have unfair consequences. In *Tinsley*, for example, both women devised the fraudulent scheme and both benefited from it. Thus Lord Mansfield said of the traditional rule as it applied to illegal contracts (in *Holman v Johnson* (1775), 343):

> *The objection, that a contract is immoral or illegal as between plaintiff and defendant, sounds at all times very ill in the mouth of the defendant. It is not for his sake, however, that the objection is ever allowed; but it is founded in general principles of policy, which the defendant has the advantage of, contrary to the real justice, as between him and the plaintiff, by accident, if I may so say. The principle of public policy is this; ex dolo malo non oritur actio. No court will lend its aid to a man who founds his cause of action upon an immoral or an illegal act. …[T]here the court says he has no right to be assisted. It is upon that ground the court goes; not for the sake of the defendant, but because they will not lend their aid to such a plaintiff. So if the plaintiff and defendant were to change sides, and the defendant was to bring his action against the plaintiff, the latter would then have the advantage of it.*

3.48 Prior to the recent UKSC decision in *Patel v Mirza* (2016), the illegality rules had special relevance to the law of resulting trusts (Chapter 5) because of a certain interpretation by the majority in *Tinsley* of the pleading rules in illegality cases, which in that case allowed M to succeed in establishing her beneficial interest in the house despite the fraudulent purpose. (See Penner (2016), 5.33–40.) This law has now been superseded by *Patel*, which holds that whether a claim founded upon an illegal transaction will succumb to the illegality defence will turn on the consideration of three factors: first, the purpose of, or the public policy, behind the law or rule that was breached by the claimant; second, whether there are any other public policies that would weigh in favour or against the application of the illegality defence; and finally, whether the application of the defence would be a disproportionate response to the illegality in question. The decision in *Patel* is controversial. (See Burrows (2017); Goudkamp (2017); Law & Ong (2017); Lim (2017); Virgo (2016a); for a common law jurisdiction refusing to follow the reasoning in

Patel, see the Singapore Court of Appeal decision *Ochroid Trading v Chua Siok Lui* (2018).) We shall have to see how it will apply to future trust cases.

The rule against perpetuities

3.49 As the name implies, the rule against perpetuities prevents settlors from creating perpetual trusts. The rule requires that the beneficiaries' interests in the trust property must vest in interest, and vest absolutely, within a certain period from the time the trust came into effect. Vesting in interest absolutely means that the various beneficiaries are all identified and their interests definitely determined to be theirs, and so they may individually or together require the trustees to transfer the trust property to them under the rule in *Saunders v Vautier*. The rule does not mean that by the end of the perpetuity period the trust must collapse, all legal title to trust property being transferred to individual beneficiaries. The trust must simply be in the position that this can happen.

3.50 The reason for the rule is straightforward: it prevents individuals from directing the use of their property from their grave long after they are dead. The rule ensures that within a certain time after the trust comes into effect, the full beneficial ownership of the property gets into the hands of living persons. Because the rule can be regarded as overly restrictive on the wishes of settlors (3.40) and gives rise to other inconveniences, the rule has been abolished entirely in a number of North American jurisdictions, which may lead to some quite startling results; see Waggoner (2014). England now has two different kinds of time period restricting perpetual trusts following the coming into force of the Perpetuities and Accumulations Act 2009. Trust instruments taking effect on or after 6 April 2010 will be subject to a perpetuity period of 125 years. Those taking effect before will be governed by either the common law rule which operates in terms of lives in being, or by the specification in the trust instrument of a fixed period up to 80 years under the Perpetuities and Accumulations Act 1964. Since those trusts will be around for a while, and also for the purpose of understanding some of the older cases, it is necessary still to understand the operation of the common law rule.

3.51 Applying the modern (ie post-seventeenth century) common law rule against perpetuities was a most difficult and complex process, both because of the way the time limit was calculated, and because of the way it took into account the possibility of events occurring that might make a gift fail. The time period of the rule was framed to allow testators to make gifts to their grandchildren that would not vest until the children reached the age of majority, which was 21 when the rule was devised. The rule was devised to make that possible, but also to make sure that this was the limit of what a testator could do to extend the time before his gifts actually vested; in consequence, the allowable time period was framed in a particular way, in reference to 'lives in being' plus a further period of 21 years. The way in which this limit worked is best explained by an example. If I leave property in my will to be divided equally between all my grandchildren who attain the age of 21, under the rule we calculate the time period within which the beneficiaries will become entitled to their shares of the property as follows: if I have any living grandchildren when I die, their shares will vest when they each turn 21, and so, being alive at my death, they must turn 21 within 21 years following my death. But I may end up having more grandchildren than them, because my living children may have more children. My own children who are alive at my death are lives in being for the purpose of the rule. (If my wife is pregnant with my child, a child *en ventre sa mère*, as the expression goes, that child counts as a child living at my death, thus a life in being for the purpose of the rule.) The rule now works as follows: obviously, any child born to my children must be conceived before my children die; therefore, the last grandchild of mine that could possibly be born will be conceived no later than the death of my last living child; therefore that last grandchild will turn 21 (ignoring periods of gestation) no later than 21 years after the death of the last life in being. Thus a gift to any or all of my grandchildren who attain their age of majority, 21, must vest, if it vests at all (all of my grandchildren may, as it turns out, die before 21—that makes the gift fail, but not for perpetuity), within the period determined by the lifetime of the last surviving life in being plus 21 years. Thus the rule can be stated as follows: a gift upon trust is valid if the interests in the trust property of those who are intended to benefit must vest, if they vest at all, within 21 years following the death of the last surviving life in being. The following examples will show why there were complexities and difficulties applying the rule.

3.52   Say that I had three daughters, all of whom are over the age of 60. Prior to recent technological developments in assisted reproduction, it was a certainty that they were not going to have any more children, so I would not get any more grandchildren. So if in my will I left a sum of money to be divided equally amongst my *great*-grandchildren who attain the age of 21, that gift would vest within a period determined by lives in being plus 21 years, the relevant lives in being here being those of my grandchildren. I would have no more, and the last great-grandchild of mine will come into existence (if only in the womb of his mother) no later than the death of my last surviving grandchild. And so none of my great-grandchildren would attain the age of 21 (again discounting periods of gestation) later than 21 years following the death of the last surviving life in being. Nevertheless, this gift is void for perpetuity. The courts reasoned that only death prevented anyone from having another child, and so, my daughters being alive, they might yet have another child after my death, although each was over 60 (this was taken to be a matter of 'logical' possibility—the seventeenth-century judiciary was not anticipating advances in reproductive technology). Such a grandchild would not be alive at my death, so would not be a life in being, and this grandchild could have a child after the death of the last surviving grandchild of mine who was alive at my death, thus after the death of the last surviving life in being. That great-grandchild's share would vest more than 21 years after the death of the last life in being. Thus, the gift fails because the rule was applied on the basis of what *could* happen, however unlikely something might be, not on the basis of what was likely to happen or actually happened over time. A famous trap is that of the 'unborn' widow. Consider this testamentary gift: 'Blackacre to my son A for life, then to A's widow for life, then to A's eldest child then living absolutely.' A is already alive, so is a life in being for the purpose of the rule. The problem is that A might marry someone who is not alive at my death, ie someone yet to be born when I die, and therefore someone who will not be a life in being at my death. After growing up and marrying A, she might outlive A (and anyone else alive at my death) by more than 21 years. So the gift to A's eldest son might vest more than 21 years after the death of the last life in being (ie my son), so the gift is void.

3.53   The Perpetuities and Accumulations Act 1964 changed the rules somewhat. In particular it introduced the notion of 'wait and see', by which a gift is valid if it turns out that it vests in the perpetuity period, even though it might not if some possible event or another actually occurs. Secondly, it created a provision by which a settlor can select any period of up to 80 years as the period for his gift, rather than relying on lives in being plus 21 years. The Perpetuities and Accumulations Act 2009 imposes a single perpetuity period of 125 years, and also has a 'wait and see' operation.

3.54   The rule applies not only to the vesting of fixed interests, but also to interests that arise under discretionary trusts and the exercise of powers of appointment. Special and hybrid powers of appointment must be exercised, if they are exercised at all, within the perpetuity period, and by parity of reasoning, distributions under discretionary trusts must occur within the perpetuity period as well. By contrast, since general powers are akin to ownership, the rule requires only that the power is acquired during the perpetuity period, since this acquisition in effect vests the interest in the property.

3.55   Finally, as the title of the Acts indicate, statutory rules had been introduced to limit the period in which a settlor could direct that the income of trust property may be accumulated (3.34), generally to no longer than 21 years. Restrictions on accumulations for trusts taking effect after 6 March 2010 have been abolished by s 13 of the 2009 Act.

Judicial control of discretionary trusts and powers of appointment

The enforcement of discretions generally

3.56   Duty holders, whether trustees or other individuals, may act wrongly either by *nonfeasance*, ie not carrying out their duty, or *misfeasance*, ie exercising their duty but doing so incorrectly. Because there is no duty to exercise mere powers, mere power holders can only be brought to court for misfeasance, using the power inappropriately, not for failing to use it at all (generally speaking—see 3.80). Of course, fixed duties, whether dispositive or administrative, pose no problem in this regard. If a trustee or other fixed duty-ower fails to carry out a fixed trust obligation, the court will either make him do it or will order whatever is to be done itself. The difficulties lie in controlling trustees and other power holders in the exercise of their discretions. It is noteworthy that originally, and for quite some time, the courts would not allow trustees to exercise discretions without the court's approval, though for the last couple of centuries the courts have held that the discretion is the trustee's alone, not the court's (see Lau (2011), at 4–5).

3.57   The court's control of trustees' discretions is a difficult and complex subject (see Cullity (1975)), but the following points outline the general position.

3.58   In determining what sort of bounds exist upon the trustee's or other power holder's discretion, the first thing to be done is to construe the terms of the trust. In the leading case of *Gisborne v Gisborne* (1877) the HL refused to intervene on behalf of a beneficiary where the trustees had exercised their 'uncontrollable authority' under the trust instrument to pay her less from the fund than they might have done.

3.59   Where the discretion is held by a trustee, or by an individual but the power is fiduciary, the discretion must be exercised in good faith in the interests only of the beneficiaries, although it is fair to point out that it is often very difficult to prove that a particular decision, within the scope of the trustee or power holder's discretion, was taken mala fide or not in consideration of the interests of the beneficiaries; different persons will appreciate the best interests of the bene-ficiaries differently. However there is an overarching principle here, enunciated by Templeman J in *Re Manisty's Settlement* (1974), where he said:

The court may also be persuaded to intervene if the trustees act 'capriciously', that is to say, act for reasons which I apprehend could be said to be irrational, perverse, or irrelevant to any sensible expectation of the settlor[.]

3.60   Thus, if the trustee of a trust like the modern trust of Example 5 used the power in clause 1(ii) to appoint to the class of 'beneficiaries' a waiter who had given him excellent service, and then appointed him a large sum from the trust under clause 3(i) as a very generous tip, this use of the trustee's powers would clearly be irrational, perverse, or irrelevant to any sensible expectation of the settlor, and the court would reverse it.

3.61   Relatedly, even where there is no fiduciary obligation attached to the exercise of a discretion, one should generally be able to determine from the trust instrument some *purpose* for which the power or discretion was conferred, so that an exercise of discretion for an ulterior purpose will be found to be wrongful. This standard by which to judge the exercise of a power or discretion underlies the doctrine of 'fraud on a power', which we will discuss later in this chapter (3.83–3.86).

3.62   Until 2013, under the so-called 'principle in *Re Hastings-Bass* (1975)' the court could treat the exercise of a power by a trustee as void or voidable, or the non-exercise of a power by a trustee could be treated by the court as having been exercised, where it could be shown that the trustee would not have acted as he did if he had either taken considerations into account which he ought to have done, or not taken considerations into account which he ought not to have done. In *Pitt v Holt* (2013), the UKSC held that *Hastings-Bass* was not authority for the court to undo what trustees had done or failed to do on this basis. In particular, where a trustee's exercise of a power merely leads to adverse tax consequences, that will not make the exercise voidable. In order for the court to set aside an exercise of a power which is within its terms, ie is something that is not prohibited by the terms of the trust, but where because the trustee has 'inadequately deliberated on its exercise' the exercise has led to a result the beneficiaries would like to undo, it must be shown that the trustee has breached a duty in respect of his deliberations, failing to seek expert tax advice, for instance, or failing properly to consider such advice. The court said the trustee must have breached a 'fiduciary' duty, but it does not appear from the context that the trustee must have acted in bad faith or in conflict of interest, so until the case is further interpreted it is probably best just to think that the trustee breached a 'trustee' duty, and this might be a duty to take care, so that even cases where the trustee was negligent in exercising the power in the way he did might be set aside.

3.63   *Pitt v Holt* raised another ground for setting aside a trustee's exercise of a power, that of mistake. The court held that where a trustee exercised a power in a mistaken belief about the consequences of the exercise (in this case a matter, again, about liability for tax), and the consequences of the mistake are so grave that it would be unconscionable for the court to refuse relief, the court will set aside the exercise of the power. The UKSC did not give any very precise guidance on how the notion of 'gravity' of the mistake was to be applied, and said that this would have to be determined on a case by case basis on a close examination of the facts.

3.64   In *Gany Holdings (PTC) SA v Khan* (2018), relying upon *Pitt*, the UKPC set aside an appointment made by a person with a power to appoint property under a trust where the directors of the corporate trustee were unaware that the trust held certain assets. The court held (at [58]) that the directors' failure to know what the assets of the trust were was a 'serious breach' of their fiduciary duties.

3.65   So far only in the context of pension funds, judges have assessed the validity of a trustee's exercise of discretion on the public/administrative law 'Wednesbury principle' (*Associated Provincial
Picture House Ltd v Wednesbury Corpn* (1948)). For example, in *Edge v Pensions Ombudsman*
(1998), Scott VC said a judge should refuse to interfere unless the trustee took into account improper, irrelevant, or irrational considerations, or otherwise the trustee's decision could be shown
to be one that no reasonable body of trustees could have made.

3.66   Besides relying upon recourse to the courts to control the trustee's exercise of his discretions, a
settlor may make the trustee's exercise of his discretions subject to the consent of a protector (3.29),
or provide the trustee with a 'letter of wishes' (7.16) indicating to the trustee the considerations the
settlor wishes to bear in mind when exercising his discretions.

The validity of dispositive discretions: certainty of objects

3.67   Up until the decision of the HL in *McPhail v Doulton* (1971) it was a fairly simple matter to
distinguish between the way in which the court would enforce the trustees' compliance with
a discretionary trust and the way in which it would oversee the exercise of powers of appointment. In the case of both any distribution in violation of the terms of the trust or power, ie any
misfeasance, would be invalid. The chief difference lay in the effects of nonfeasance. With respect to discretionary trusts, if the trustees failed to exercise their discretion and distribute the
property, the court would order a distribution. Before *Kemp v Kemp* (1795), the court would,
in rare cases, exercise the trustees' discretion itself to distribute the property unequally to the
objects, but following that decision the practice became to apply the maxim 'Equality is Equity'
and distribute the property equally amongst them. In the case of powers, by contrast, the case
of nonfeasance presented no problem. There was no duty for the court to enforce.

Certainty of objects

3.68   What changed in *McPhail* was the test of certainty that applied to the objects of discretionary
trusts. Normally much of what follows is covered in trust books in the chapter on 'Certainty'
(in this book, Chapter 7), but being a radical thinker I propose to include it here because it
concerns the enforceability of discretionary trusts and powers, and the rights of the objects
under them, more than it does certainty per se. Certainty of objects is a requirement of both
trusts and powers, and means nothing more than that the terms of the trust or power have to
indicate with sufficient precision who is in the class of objects.

The 'complete list' test and the 'is or is not' test

3.69   The historical test for certainty of objects for trusts, whether fixed or discretionary, was that, for
a trust to be valid, one had to be able to draw up a complete list of the objects. In a discretionary
trust for the settlor's children, for example, this could be easily accomplished since it was clear that
the class of objects comprised the settlor's children and no one else. Whether or not the 'complete

list' test was applicable to mere powers of appointment fell to be decided in *Re Gestetner Settlement* (1953). The power in question was a power to appoint property to a large and fluctuating group of objects including the settlor's former employees and their surviving spouses. It was held that the power was valid even though a complete list of the possible objects of the power could not be drawn up at any one time. Harman J stated:

> [T]he document on its face shows that there is no obligation on the trustees to do more than consider—from time to time, I suppose—the merits of such persons of the specified class as are known to them and, if they think fit, to give them something ... I cannot see [that] such a duty [makes] it essential for these trustees, before parting with any income or capital, to survey the whole field, and to consider whether A is more deserving of bounty than B ... there is no difficulty ... in ascertaining whether any given postulant is a member of the specified class. Of course, if that could not be ascertained the matter would be quite different, but of John Doe or Richard Roe it can be postulated easily enough whether he is or is not eligible to receive the settlor's bounty.

3.70   Thus was born the 'is or is not' test for certainty of objects: since the power holder has no duty to distribute the property, all that matters is misfeasance, ie if he appoints property at all, he must be sure to appoint only to those within the class of objects and not those outside it; all he need know with certainty is whether any particular person is within the class or not; in particular he does not need a complete list of all objects who are eligible to receive.

3.71   In *IRC v Broadway Cottages Trust* (1955), the CA had to decide whether the same test should apply to a *discretionary trust* for a similarly large and fluctuating class including the settlor's employees and their wives and widows. In summary, the arguments against the 'is or is not' test, and in favour of the 'complete list' test, were these: starting from the principle stated by Lord Eldon in *Morice v Bishop of Durham* (1805) that in order to be valid, a trust must be one that the court can control and execute, various factors made the court's control and execution of such a trust impossible.

- In the absence of a complete list only a subset of the whole class can be identified; such a subset cannot 'claim execution of the trust' or call for the trust property under the principle in *Saunders v Vautier* because the trustees have no duty to distribute to any subset of the whole class; as a result, where the whole class of objects cannot be identified the trustees' duties are 'illusory'.

- Since no complete list can be made, it is impossible to infer that the testator intended a trust for the entire class in equal shares in default of distribution, so the court is unable to deal with a failure of the trustees to distribute by ordering such a division; the court could not order a particular unequal division, because that would be exercising a dispositive discretion, and that discretion is the trustees' alone.

- The court's ability to execute a trust must be judged by reference to what might happen, not by reference to what is likely to happen. It must be assumed that the trustees might, for some reason, refuse to distribute, and the court be required to carry out the trust by order. This must be assumed also of new trustees replacing old ones who proved recalcitrant. Replacing one set of trustees after another is not execution of the trust by the court.

- The trustee must know or be able to ascertain all the objects whom he might select, otherwise he is merely selecting from *some* members of the class, in which case he is not carrying out the terms of the trust, ie to exercise his discretion to select from amongst *all* of the objects.

- Similarly, the court cannot mend the invalidity of a trust of this kind by imposing an arbitrary distribution amongst only some of the whole unascertainable class; to create a certain class to replace the uncertain one chosen by the settlor would amount to imposing a different trust.

3.72   The essence of the argument in favour of the 'is or is not' test was that no difficulty in practice in effectively controlling the execution of the trust would arise.

- Having undertaken the trust, the trustees can be assumed to be willing and able to carry it out.

- With respect to malfeasance by the trustees: the 'is or is not' test allows the trustees to ensure that only qualified beneficiaries take benefits, and so the trustees can distribute within the terms of the trust. Conversely, distribution to non-objects can be determined with certainty, and could be restrained by the court on the suit of any qualified member of the class.

- With respect to nonfeasance by the trustees: at the suit of any object, recalcitrant trustees could be replaced, and this process could be repeated. 'The possibility that not only the original trustees but every set of trustees appointed in their place would fail or refuse to do this is so remote that it can for practical purposes be disregarded.' In the unlikely event this occurred, the court could declare a trust in default of distribution for a modified class of whose members a complete list could be made.

3.73   The trust failed. Jenkins LJ had this to say:

> We confess to some sympathy for the appellants' argument, which has an attractive air of common sense, but we do not think that it can be allowed to prevail. We think the submissions . . . to the effect that the trust is not one which the court could control or execute, and that this objection cannot be met by urging the improbability of assistance by the court ever becoming necessary, are well founded. We also agree that . . . the court would not be executing the trust merely by ordering a change in trusteeship.

At this time, then, one important distinction between discretionary trusts and powers of appointment was their respective tests for certainty of objects, which directly reflected the court's consideration that discretionary trusts, being trusts, required possibilities of precise enforcement in the case of nonfeasance which did not apply to powers of appointment.

McPhail v Doulton

3.74   Thus the matter stood until *McPhail v Doulton* (1971), which concerned a discretionary trust for a large class comprising employees and ex-employees of a large company and their dependants and relations. Although about a year before the HL in *Re Gulbenkian's Settlement Trusts* (1970) had confirmed *obiter* that while the 'is or is not' test was appropriate for powers, the complete list test remained the appropriate test for discretionary trusts, a different panel of their Lordships in *McPhail v Doulton* decided 3:2 that the 'is or is not' test was appropriate for discretionary trusts as well. The majority decision, given by Lord Wilberforce, essentially recognised the 'common sense' arguments put in *Broadway Cottages Trusts*, accepting that in practice trusts for large classes of beneficiaries could be adequately enforced.

3.75 Lord Wilberforce emphasised that the difference between the practical tasks facing trustees who held a mere power of appointment and those of trustees who held property on a discretionary basis was a matter of degree:

> Any trustee [holding a mere power] would surely make it his duty to know what is the permissible area of selection and then consider responsibly, in individual cases, whether a contemplated beneficiary was within the power and whether, in relation to other possible claimants, a particular grant was appropriate. Correspondingly a trustee with a duty to distribute, particularly among a potentially very large class, would surely never require the preparation of a complete list of names, which anyhow would tell him little that he needs to know. He would examine the field, by class and category; might indeed make diligent and careful inquiries, depending on how much money he had to give away and the means at his disposal, as to the composition and needs of particular categories and of individuals within them; decide on certain priorities or proportions, and then select individuals according to their needs or qualifications. If he acts in this manner, can it really be said that he is not carrying out the trust? . . . Such distinction as there is would seem to lie in the extent of the survey which the trustee is required to carry out; if he has to distribute the whole of the trust fund's income, he must necessarily make a wider and more systematic survey than if his duty is expressed in terms of power to make grants. But just as, in the case of a power, it is possible to under-estimate the fiduciary obligation of the trustee to whom it is given, so, in the case of a trust (trust power), the danger lies in overstating what the trustee requires to know or to enquire into before he can properly execute his trust. The difference may be one of degree rather than of principle . . .

3.76 It is not, with respect, correct to assume that a trustee of a discretionary trust will have a wider survey to conduct than a trustee whose task is to consider exercising a power of appointment. The reverse is actually the case, for the interests of the objects of the power must be weighed against those who would take in default of appointment: the trustee therefore has two classes of objects to survey, not one. Of course, the width of the survey will vary on a case by case basis, depending on the size of the classes, the settlor's intentions in creating the trust and powers, and so on.

3.77 As regards the court's enforcement of the trust, Lord Wilberforce thought that no conclusions could be drawn from the fact that in large trusts of this kind, equal division was not a possible means of enforcement:

> As a matter of reason, to hold a principle of equal division applies to trusts such as the present is certainly paradoxical. Equal division is surely the last thing the settlor ever intended; equal division among all may, and probably would, produce a result beneficial to no one.

Rather, enforcement should be tailored to the particular trust or power, and the practicalities of the situation must be borne in mind:

> Assimilation of the validity test does not involve the complete assimilation of trust powers with powers. As to powers . . . although the trustees may, and normally will, be under a fiduciary duty to consider whether or in what way they should exercise the power, the court will not normally compel its exercise. It will intervene if the trustees

exceed their powers, and possibly if they are proved to have exercised it capriciously. But in the case of a trust power, if the trustees do not exercise it, the court will; . . . the court, if called on to execute the trust power, will do so in the manner best calculated to give effect to the settlor's or testator's intentions. It may do so by appointing new trustees, or by authorising or directing representative persons of the classes of beneficiaries to pre-pare a scheme of distribution, or even, should the proper basis for distribution appear, by itself directing the trustees so to distribute.

3.78   It should be borne in mind that *McPhail* does not appear to alter the traditional enforcement of discretionary trusts where the class of objects is small: if there are no clear indications as to how the trustee ought to exercise his discretion, the court will order an equal division amongst all the objects.

3.79   It is also to be noted that this line of cases is unlikely to be re-litigated. *McPhail*-like trusts were created by magnanimous industrialists to provide a kind of pension benefit to their employees, their employees' dependents, and so on, before the introduction of statutory pension schemes. Nowadays any class of objects however large could be made certain by the use of powers like 1(ii) and 1(iii) in the Example 5 modern trust (3.3).

3.80   Besides appointing outside the class of objects, a purported exercise of a power will be invalid if the power holders never truly applied their minds to what they were doing, as in *Turner v Turner* (1984), where the power holders blindly followed the directions of the settlor without appreciating they had a discretion to exercise.

3.81   In the case of nonfeasance, it is clear that the court must enforce the trust by one of the ways mentioned by Lord Wilberforce (3.77), according to the nature of the trust. An illustration is found in *Re Locker's Settlement Trusts* (1978). There, trustees of a discretionary trust applied to the court for its approval when they sought to distribute income which had arisen over a three-year period some eight years before, but which they had failed to distribute at the time as they ought to have done. It was argued that, having failed to comply with their duty at the relevant time, the trustees were disabled from distributing the income on a discretionary basis among the objects now, and that the court must give effect to the trust by ordering an equal division among all the objects. Goulding J disagreed. Although, following *McPhail*, the court had ample power to execute a discretionary trust upon the failure of the trustees to do so, trustees intent upon making good their past failure by subsequently exercising their discretion should be encouraged to do so, as this was more in keeping with the settlor's inten-tion than execution by the court, although in such circumstances the court should 'readily listen' to any misgivings about such a course where the trustees have failed to listen or act upon the beneficiaries' requests for distribution; in such a case the ample powers of the court to execute the trust might justifiably be invoked. Furthermore, a distinction may be drawn between powers of appointment and discretionary trusts in this regard. Failure to exercise a power of appointment results in the property going to those who take in default of appoint-ment, so a power holder's failure to act normally raises no issue of this kind.

3.82   Goulding J did not specifically consider the case of a failure of a trustee or other fiduciary power holder to act in a timely fashion. One presumes that the court might have to engage in some re-medial measures if it were shown that property went to someone who took in default of appoint-ment and the trustee or other fiduciary power holder did not even consider exercising his power of appointment as his duty requires. Indeed, in certain cases, the courts will control mere powers to the extent of requiring their exercise. Thus in *Klug v Klug* (1918), the court felt under a duty to direct a transfer of funds (under a power of advancement, 10.41 et seq) 'when one trustee very properly desires to exercise his discretion … and his co-trustee [who refused to do so because she disapproved of the beneficiary's marriage] will not'. And in the case of pension fund trusts, the beneficiaries who have earned their rights may have legitimate expectations that mere powers held by trustees to augment the benefits to which they are strictly entitled under the trust will be exercised in their favour (*Mettoy Pension Trustees Ltd v Evans* (1991); see also Nobles (1992b)).

Excessive and fraudulent exercises of powers

3.83 A purported exercise of a power will also be invalid if it is 'excessive' or constitutes a 'fraud' on the power. A power of appointment or advancement is 'excessively' exercised when the trustees purport to use trust funds to benefit an object of the power in a way that is not provided for by the power. Whether an exercise of a power is excessive often turns on the words with which the power is expressed. For example, in this passage from *Pilkington v IRC* (1964), Viscount Radcliffe discusses how applications of trust money by exercise of a power of advancement were regarded as restricted to certain kinds of expenditure:

> The word 'advancement' itself meant in this context the establishment in life of the beneficiary who was the object of the power or at any rate some step that would contribute to the furtherance of his establishment. Thus it was found in such phrases as 'preferment or advancement' . . ., '. . . advancement or preferment in the world', and 'placing out or advancement in life'. Typical instances of expenditure for such purposes under the social conditions of the nineteenth century were an apprenticeship or the purchase of a commission in the army or of an interest in business. In the case of a girl there could be advancement on marriage . . . Advancement had, however, to some extent a limited range of meaning, since it was thought to convey the idea of some step in life of permanent significance, and accordingly, to prevent uncertainties about the permitted range of objects for which moneys could be raised and made available, such words as 'or otherwise for his or her benefit' were often added to the word 'advancement'.

3.84 Similarly, the word 'appoint' has been construed as not allowing a trustee to appoint trust property on new discretionary trusts for objects within the power—that is an excessive exercise of the power, because a power to appoint is a power to transfer fixed interests to persons within the class, not to delegate that decision to the discretionary trustee under a new trust (*Re Hay's Settlement Trusts* (1981)).

3.85 A fraud on a power occurs when the appointment is made to a person who is properly within the class of objects, with the purpose, however, of benefiting someone who is not a proper object, where, for example, a power holder who could only appoint to members of her family appointed to her sister believing and intending that the sister would apply most of the funds for the benefit of a couple with whom she had lived (*Re Dick* (1953)). The leading case is the PC decision in *Vatcher v Paull* (1915), which outlines the basic principles: 'fraud' does not denote conscious immoral or dishonest wrongdoing, but merely that the power has been exercised with the intention to benefit someone outside the class of objects. Typically, this will be done under a bargain between the appointer and appointee, under which the latter will upon receipt of the property secure the benefit for someone not properly within the class, typically the appointer himself when he is a non-object, although a bargain of this kind is not essential for a fraud to occur. The test appears to be that the power holder has deliberately set out to benefit a non-object by making the appointment to a valid object, and it is irrelevant that the appointee might not, as it turned out, have complied with the appointer's wishes (*Re Dick*). Fraud does not occur simply because the appointer sets conditions on his exercise of the power; only conditions that if fulfilled result in securing the benefit of the appointment for a third party will be bad.

3.86   These principles were applied in the New Zealand case of *Wong v Burt* (2005). Under a testamentary trust, the testator's grandchildren would receive no income payments for their support if their mother were to predecease another beneficiary, which, in the event, she did. In order to fix this 'mistake', the trustee exercised a power of appointment which had as its object the testator's widow, providing her with $250,000 so that she could fund a trust for the grandchildren. The New Zealand CA held that the appointment was a clear fraud on the power, forming part of a 'deliberate scheme to subvert the terms of the will'. It is not the case however that a trustee will commit a fraud on a power where power is exercised for the benefit of an object of the power, even if the benefit is an indirect one. In R*e Clore ST* (1966) (**10.44**, **10.46**) the court approved of an appointment to a rich beneficiary to allow him to make a charitable donation he felt morally bound to make. By contrast, in *X v A* (2005), the court refused to sanction the appointment of the entire trust fund to an object who wished to donate it all to charity; the court did not think that such an advancement would allow the object to make a donation which she was morally obliged to make, if only because the amount exceeded anything she could have been obliged to give out of her own resources.

'Power to exclude' objects

3.87   The recent case of *Re New Huerto Trust* (2015) involved a discretionary trust set up by way of a trust deed that conferred power upon the trustees to appoint the trust property to one or more of the beneficiaries. The relevant clause read as follows:

> THE Trustees STAND POSSESSED of the Trust Fund and the income thereof UPON DIS-CRETIONARY TRUSTS for the benefit of the Beneficiaries or any one or more of them exclusive of the others in such shares and proportions and subject to such terms and limitations and with and subject to such provisions for maintenance, education or advancement or for accumulation of income during minority or for forfeiture in the event of bankruptcy or otherwise and such other conditions as the Trustees may from time to time appoint by Deed revocable or irrevocable executed before the Vesting Day.

3.88   The trustees sought a declaration that they had the power under the aforementioned clause to exclude permanently and irrevocably the settlor from any benefit under the trust.

3.89   The Eastern Carribean Supreme Court held that:

> [32] If the trustee can validly appoint property among two or more objects of the trust while excluding altogether one or more objects, then there is no reason why the trustee cannot, in advance of appointing any property to the objects of the trust, use the power of appointment to exclude one of them from benefiting under the trust.

3.90   There are two points here. The first, is that a power of appointment under a trust deed is capable of being exercised in an exclusionary manner. In that case, it was exercised to exclude
the settlor from benefitting under the trust, with the resulting increase in the trust property
available for distribution to the children and other more remote issue of the settlor, who were
the intended beneficiaries of the settlor's benefaction. The second point is that the power of appointment can be exercised in this exclusionary manner even before any property is appointed
to the objects of the trust.

3.91   In coming to this conclusion, the Eastern Carribean Supreme Court cited a decision of the
English Court of Appeal, *Blausten v IRC* (1972), discussed at 7.87. In that case, the trustees
exercised a power of appointment under a discretionary trust to exclude the settlor's widow
from the specified class of beneficiaries. The appointment was a resettlement on new trusts of
the capital of the trust fund, and the immediate effect was to exclude the settlor's wife from the
objects of the discretionary trusts of the income. Buckley LJ held that:

> In my judgment, however, what was done by the deed of appointment was something
> which was clearly within the terms of the power of appointment. It was an appoint-
> ment under which the capital was directed to be held upon trusts for the benefit of
> members of the specified class, and although the objective of the trustees in making
> the appointment may not have been the kind of objective which the settlor had in
> mind when he conferred the power of appointment upon the trustees, the appointment
> nevertheless in my judgment falls within the power.

3.92   Coming back to *Re New Huerto Trust*, the trustees saw the need to exercise the power of appointment in an exclusionary manner, even before appointing any property to the remaining
objects, because they desired to protect the trust property from adverse claims against it which
might diminish the property available for distribution.

Locus standi to enforce the trust and beneficiaries' rights to information

3.93   Prior to the rise in frequency of trusts like Example 5 (3.3), there was a conventional understanding that whilst objects of fixed interests had standing (or *locus standi* to use the Latin) to
enforce the trust obligations against the trustee, objects of mere powers of appointment did not.
The standing of objects of discretionary trusts seems to be somewhat in between, but there is
very little clear authority on the point; see Turner (2018), 247–50. The rationale for this conventional understanding is clearly stated by Smith ((2016), 22):

> Objects of powers do not have any right to any property. Perhaps less obviously,
> they do not have a right to enforce the [trustee's trust obligations]. This is just saying
> the same thing in a different way, because the [trustee's trust obligations] [are] the
> obligation[s] relating to the benefit of the trust property, and by definition, [those]
> obligation[s] [are] owed to the beneficiaries ... and not to the objects of any discretion-
> ary powers. Or in other words, since objects of powers do not have any right to any
> trust property, they cannot enforce obligations owed by the trustees in relation to the
> benefit of the trust property.

3.94   Indeed, this conventional understanding probably drove, in part, the development of trust structures like that in Example 5: settlors worried about their objects haranguing the trustees for benefits under the trust, or bringing actions against the trustees, would, on this conventional understanding, have no rights of enforcement, or relatedly, no rights to be provided information by the trustees, such as the trust accounts (2.46 et seq) or other trust documents. Whether this is a wise move is a question to which we will now turn.

Unwise trusts

3.95   Within the limits of the law, a settlor can create any trust he wishes, even if in several respects it is unwise. To take a very simple case, if a settlor creates a trust in favour of his children under which the trustee has a discretion to determine the shares that each child will take rather than leaving it to them in equal shares (eg Example 2–3.3), this may lead to family strife. Determining which child might be more 'worthy' of a larger share than another is obviously a fraught business, and one who receives less might (rightly or wrongly) feel resentful of his lesser portion. This is not to deny the advantages of flexibility that giving a trustee dispositive discretions affords, but just to point out flexibility is not an unmixed blessing.

3.96   In any case, the law does not invalidate a trust because it might be unwise in some respects. The classic example of such a trust was considered in the late 18th century case of *Thellusson v Woodford* (1799). In that case a truly vastly wealthy testator, after providing for his immediate family reasonably generously under his will, directed the trustees of his will to invest the vast bulk of his estate and accumulate the income (3.34), re-investing the income as it arose, the resulting fund to be distributed to his descendants then living at the end of the perpetuity period (3.49 et seq). Though some of the judges deciding the case made it clear that they thought the trust unwise or 'impolitic', the trust was held to be valid. The whole story ended badly, as Polden (1994), 14, relates:

> *Probably no testator has been so vilified by contemporaries and later writers, and few wills have given rise to such persistent and long lasting litigation. The grotesque outcome of his grandiose plan – a final distribution in 1860 which, thanks to the family's tenacious litigiousness, the insatiable appetite of the Court of Chancery and the incompetence and self-interest of the trustees, barely exceeded the initial investment – has made Thellusson a figure of ridicule as well as contumely.*

The case also led to the passage of what was known as the Thellusson Act (the Accumulations Act 1800), which limited accumulations of income to 21 years, a rule which stood until 2010 (3.55).

3.97   This possibility of unwisdom may be particularly relevant to trusts like those of Example 5, which Smith dubs 'massively discretionary trusts' (Smith, L. (2017)).

3.98   In *Re T R Technology Investment Trust plc* (1998), 263–64, Hoffmann J said:

> *... It was a typical offshore trust and since a number of these trusts feature in these proceedings, it may be useful to describe their general characteristics. The named settlor is usually a stranger to the transaction who has been requested to lend his name to a document which records (in many cases truthfully) that he has provided a nominal sum*

as the initial trust fund. Mr Sherman Chong was a chartered secretary graduate working for Frank R Mullens & Co whom Mr Mullens describes as 'willing to act as a Settlor in such circumstances', and the initial trust fund was $HK100. The name of the person providing the assets subsequently added to the fund, whom I may call 'the real settlor', does not appear. In this case the assets were the Firmandale shares. The trustees are given a wide discretion to pay income and capital to the beneficiaries, but the persons actually contemplated as beneficiaries are not necessarily named in the document. Instead, a local charity or some other person will be named and the trustee given a discretionary power to add to the list of beneficiaries. Francis Mullens and James Hinchcliffe, whom the company was told were the 'named beneficiaries' of the Firmandale trust, were the young sons of the partners in Frank R Mullens & Co. Sometimes the trustee will be given a 'letter of wishes' by the real settlor saying whom he wishes to benefit. Sometimes the real beneficiary, who may be the real settlor himself, will remain a matter of oral understanding between him and the trustee. These trusts therefore reveal very little and depend upon trust and confidence reposed in the trustee to give effect to expectations and understandings which may not be legally enforceable. The business of providing offshore financial services requires a reputation for probity, efficiency and discretion in executing such trusts in accordance with the confidential wishes of clients.

3.99   A similar trust was considered in the UKPC decision in *Schmidt v Rosewood Trust* (2003). Lord Walker said:

[34] ... It is appropriate to reflect that ... the forms and functions of settlements have changed to a degree which would have astonished Lord Eldon. By the 1930s high rates of personal taxation led some wealthy individuals to make settlements which enabled funds to be accumulated in the hands of overseas trustees or companies... . This practice increased enormously with the introduction of capital gains tax in 1965. But increasingly stringent anti-avoidance measures encouraged legal advisers to devise forms of settlement under which the true intended beneficiaries were not clearly identified in the settlement. Indeed their interests or expectations were often barely perceptible. Rarely did a beneficiary take an indefeasibly vested interest with an ascertainable market value. Tax avoidance is therefore one element which has strongly influenced the forms of settlements; and once the offshore tax-avoidance industry has acquired standard forms its inclination is to use them, subject perhaps to some more or less skilful adaptation, even for clients whose aim is not to avoid United Kingdom taxation.

[35] There is another element, also linked (though less directly) to taxation, which has encouraged the inclusion in settlements of very widely defined classes of beneficiaries. After the Second World War estate duty was charged in the United Kingdom at very high rates, with much less generous reliefs for agricultural and business property than those now available. A wealthy landowner or businessman might be advised that the safest way to preserve his fortune was to give most of it away, while he was still in the prime of life, to trustees of an irrevocable settlement in discretionary form under which the settlor himself was not a beneficiary. It is not surprising that a settlor in such a position should wish to cover as comprehensively as he could all possible current and future claims on his bounty, since he was being asked to make an immediate, irrevocable disposition of much of his wealth, rather than being able to review from time to time the ambulatory dispositions in his will and codicils. But his lawyers might also advise him that the most natural expressions for defining discretionary objects of his bounty (such as 'relatives', 'old

friends', 'dependants' or 'persons with moral claims') were of doubtful legal efficacy. So there was a tendency to define the class in the widest possible terms. The process can be seen in a long line of cases starting with In re Gestetner Settlement [1953] Ch 672. It led to In re Manisty's Settlement [1974] Ch 17, upholding the validity of an intermediate power comparable to that in clause 3.3 of the Everest Trust (that is, a power to add as beneficiaries anyone in the world apart from a very small class of excluded persons).

[36] The Board have to consider what rights or claims to disclosure the appellant has, either personally or as his father's personal representative, under two badly drafted settlements whose terms have been moulded by the sort of influences mentioned above. One possible reaction would be that Mr Schmidt and his colleagues have made their bed and they must lie on it; if they have deliberately entered into a web of camouflage, it is hardly for anyone claiming through them to complain that the position is not transparent. As Lord Greene MR observed, giving the judgment of the court in Lord Howard de Walden v Inland Revenue Comrs [1942] 1 KB 389, 397 if a taxpayer plays with fire it scarcely lies in his mouth to complain of burnt fingers.

3.100   We will return to the decision in *Schmidt*, but the present point, as these two quotations show, is that these sorts of trusts do not lend themselves to an easy application of the conventional rules of *locus standi*. The widespread existence of these sorts of trust forms an important part of the context in which courts must determine who has *locus standi* to enforce the trust terms against the trustee.

Beneficiaries' rights to information

3.101   The issue of standing almost always arises in an object bringing an action against the trustee to require the trustee to provide information about the trust, usually documents like the trust instrument, the trust accounts, and the letter of wishes (if any). If A has *locus standi* to enforce the trust, then obviously he would be in need of this sort of information to make that power to enforce the trust practically effective.

3.102   In *Armitage v Nurse* (1998), Millett LJ stated:

If the beneficiaries have no rights enforceable against the trustees, there are no trusts.

Remember that the settlor has no power to enforce the trust; it is the beneficiaries alone who are entitled to call the trustee to account in respect of his stewardship of the trust property. But the beneficiaries cannot enforce such a right if they have no information as to how the trustee has carried out the trust.

The right to be informed that one is a beneficiary

3.103   Beneficiaries of vested interests (certainly absolute vested interests) have a right to be informed of their interest (*Hawkesley v May* (1956)), and it is within the court's discretion in an appropriate case (namely where it is reasonable to assume that such beneficiary had a genuine likelihood or expectation that a dispositive discretion might be exercised in his favour) to require settlers to provide the names and addresses of trustees even to a discretionary beneficiary (*Re Murphy's Settlements* (1998)).

The right to see the trust accounts and other trust documents

3.104 In *Schmidt v Rosewood Trust* (2003) the UKPC reviewed the rights of objects of trusts to have access to the trust accounts and other trust documents, such as the minutes of trustees' meetings. Prior to that decision it was generally accepted that beneficiaries, whether of a fixed or discretionary interest (*Chaine-Nickson v Bank of Ireland* (1976); *Spellson v George* (1987)), perhaps even of a contingent interest (*Armitage*, per Millett LJ), ie objects of a trustee's dispositive duty to distribute the trust property, were entitled to copies (made at their own expense) of the trust accounts and all trust documents.

3.105 However, the basis for these rights was not clearly established. From one perspective, the trust documents being trust property, the beneficiaries had a proprietary right to them, as they were the ultimate owners in equity of the trust property (*O'Rourke v Darbishire* (1920); *Re Londonderry's Settlement* (1965)). This is clearly misguided, because whether trust documents form part of the trust property or not, beneficiaries have no rights of access to the trust property itself; they merely have rights to whatever benefits of the trust property the trust terms dictate. The better view is that these rights flow from the beneficiaries' right to make the trustee account for his stewardship of the trust (*Hartigan Nominees Pty Ltd v Ridge* (1992); *Re Rabaiotti's 1989 Settlement* (2000)).

3.106 In line with this reasoning, in *Re the HHH Employee Trust* (2012) the Jersey Royal Court held that where the settlor of a pension fund trust had fiduciary powers under the trust to appoint new trustees and to appoint a protector, the court's general supervisory jurisdiction over trusts would allow it to require the disclosure of documents from this power holder to the beneficiaries.

3.107 In *Erceg v Erceg* (2017), the New Zealand Court of Appeal considered whether a bankrupt appellant had standing to seek disclosure of information relating to two discretionary trusts (he was within the class of beneficiaries of each of the trusts). The beneficiary's status as a bankrupt brought into question whether the right to seek disclosure was 'property' or a 'right in relation to property', which would have been vested in the Official Assignee pursuant to s 3 of New Zealand's Insolvency Act 2006. The Court of Appeal found that it was unnecessary to consider whether the beneficiary's right to seek disclosure was 'property', because the appellant's standing to request disclosure of the documents derived from his 'status (or capacity) as a beneficiary of the Trusts'. Becoming a bankrupt did not alter or annul the appellant's status as a beneficiary, and it was that 'beneficiary status that entitles the appellant to have the trustees' duties to beneficiaries enforced, and to that end to request disclosure of trust documents by the trustees'.

3.108 *Schmidt* concerned a claim for rights to information, not from a beneficiary with a defined interest under the trust, but from an object of a mere power of appointment. The last paragraph of the quotation from Lord Walker's judgment in *Schmidt*, about being tempted to let the settlor lie on the bed he has made for himself, was followed by this:

> [36] … However, the Board consider that that inclination must be resisted. … It is fundamental to the law of trusts that the court has jurisdiction to supervise and if appropriate intervene in the administration of a trust, including a discretionary trust. As Holland J said in the Australian case of *Randall v Lubrano* (unreported) 31 October 1975, cited by Kirby P in *Hartigan Nominees Pty Ltd v Rydge* (1992) 29 NSWLR 405, 416:

'no matter how wide the trustee's discretion in the administration and application of a discretionary trust fund and even if in all or some respects the discretions are expressed in the deed as equivalent to those of an absolute owner of the trust fund, the trustee is still a trustee.'

3.109   Lord Walker, delivering the judgment of the PC, firmly adopted the view that the beneficiary's right to information flowed from the inherent jurisdiction of the court to ensure that trusts were properly supervised and enforced, and that, depending on the circumstances, in some cases an object of a power of appointment appropriately had such a right. In the exercise of its inherent jurisdiction, the court might refuse, in certain cases, a claim by an object for information:

> *[67] [T]he recent cases also confirm (as had been stated as long ago as In re Cowin 33 Ch D 179 in 1886) that no beneficiary (and least of all a discretionary object)) has any entitlement as of right to disclosure of anything which can plausibly be described as a trust document. Especially when there are issues as to personal or commercial confidentiality, the court may have to balance the competing interests of different beneficiaries, the trustees themselves, and third parties. Disclosure may have to be limited and safeguards put in place. Evaluation of the claims of a beneficiary (and especially of a discretionary object) may be an important part of the balancing exercise which the court has to perform on the materials placed before it. In many cases the court may have no difficulty in concluding that an applicant with no more than a theoretical possibility of benefit ought not to be granted relief.*

3.110   What does it mean to say that an applicant has 'no more than a theoretical possibility of benefit'? Consider yourself. As a student of this subject you will now know that, because of intermediate powers of appointment, or intermediate powers to appoint someone to a class, as in 1(ii) in trust Example 5, you are the object of a power of appointment in countless trusts. You decide, therefore, to go on a cycling tour of the Isle of Man, Guernsey, and Jersey, stopping at each trust company office you pass on the way. You knock on the door and tell the trust officer, 'Please provide full information on all the trusts you administer which contain intermediate powers of appointment'. You will, of course, be sent away with a flea in your ear. And quite right, too. Assuming that these trusts have been settled by strangers having nothing to do with you, any appointment to you would almost certainly be regarded as 'irrational, perverse, or irrelevant to any sensible expectation of the settlor' (3.59). This is the sense in which, though a member of the class of objects, you have no more than a theoretical possibility of benefit.

3.111   In the New Zealand case *Foreman v Kingstone* (2004) Potter J made the point this way:

> *[87] Of course what is a reasonable request for information is likely to be viewed differently by trustees conscious of their duties to administer the trusts for the benefit of all beneficiaries, and the particular beneficiaries seeking information. There are a number of factors which will bear on the situation. To take an example: the M P Foreman Trust by definition includes within the class of discretionary beneficiaries 'any charity within New Zealand'. It could be expected that trustees and the Court in the exercise of its supervisory jurisdiction, would view differently a request of the trustees for disclosure of trust documentation made by a random charity which had not, pursuant to the exercise by the trustees of their discretion, become an object of the trust, and a similar request from persons named or included by definition within the class of discretionary beneficiaries.*

3.112   The result in *Schmidt* can be questioned (see Pollard (2003); Smith (2003a) Smith, L. (2016); for a survey of the issues raised by *Schmidt*, see Ho (2010); it has been followed *Foreman v Kingstone* (2004)). The decision seems to create a good measure of uncertainty in this area, and it may be difficult for trustees to decide what information they ought properly to reveal to objects without applying first to the court, which will create an expense for the trust.

3.113   In the Australian case *McDonald v Ellis* (2007) Bryson JA held that in the case of a beneficiary with a vested entitlement the court should have no discretion; such a beneficiary should be entitled to all relevant trust information as of right.

3.114   *Schmidt* might also seem to accept the inevitability of, if not endorse, an unfortunate antagonistic attitude between trustee and beneficiary. On this latter point, Hayton (1999) has made a plea 'for more openness between trustees and beneficiaries. The more one tries to hide things from people the more suspicious they become: no one likes being treated like a mushroom, being kept in the dark and fed you know what.'

3.115   In *Breakspear v Ackland* (2008), a case concerning the disclosure of a letter of wishes to beneficiaries, Briggs J emphasised that such wishes are normally expressed to be confidential, with the result that, in general, trustees had no obligation to disclose such letters to beneficiaries, nor give reasons for not doing so.

3.116   In *Segelov v Ernst & Young Pty Ltd* (2014), which concerned discretionary payments under a pension trust, the court held that a wife of a partner of the firm nominated as an object of the discretionary trust was not owed a specific duty to be informed of her entitlement. The essence of her complaint was that she was not kept informed of the particular bank account, nominated by her husband and later ex-husband, into which her benefits were to be paid. Whether an object had a right to be informed of various things turned on the 'practical exigencies of the types of decision [the trustee] has to make' in discharging its duties (*Segelov*, [64]). The court held that the trustee discharged its duties by paying whatever distributions it made into the bank account nominated by the partner.

3.117   In another disclosure of information case, *Lewis v Tamplin* (2018), Matthews HHJ reviewed the authorities and had this to say:

> [30] Mr Adams ... expanded on his argument based on Rosewood v Schmidt [2003] 2 AC 709. He said that it was a matter of discretion for the trustees whether to give information to beneficiaries and not a matter of right. Accordingly the court should not interfere with the trustees' decision to refuse disclosure unless at least the court's suspicion had been excited. He compared the situation to that in which a court might order an account on the footing of wilful default. The court should not order the trustees to give wide ranging disclosure to the beneficiaries unless it was satisfied that there had been or would be a breach of trust, or at least if there were prima facie grounds for thinking that something may have gone wrong. Disclosure should not go any wider than that which would be necessary for an account. Here an account had already been given. He criticised the requests for disclosure as nothing more than a fishing expedition aimed at finding ammunition if possible for a claim of breach of trust against the trustees.
>
> ...
>
> [41] It is notable that Lord Walker, having referred to a person being entitled 'to a fixed and transmissible beneficial interest', immediately went on to add that '[t]he object of a

discretion (including a mere power) may also be entitled to protection from a court of equity' (emphasis supplied). He then considered the kinds of circumstances in which a discretionary object would, or would not, be likely to have disclosure ordered in his or her favour. The whole direction of travel is in equating the position of the discretionary object to that of the fixed interest beneficiary, and not the other way around [emphasis added]. The implication is that the beneficiary of a fixed, transmissible interest would normally obtain the assistance of the court.

[42] It is true that Lord Walker had by then pointed out that there were authorities making clear that even a fixed interest beneficiary would not always obtain disclosure, because there might be special circumstances in which that beneficiary's interests conflicted with the general interest of the trust: see at [48]. But it is clear that, in his opinion, absent such special circumstances, the beneficiary could normally expect the assistance of the court. In my judgment, that applies in the present case, where the claimants' interests are as fixed interest beneficiaries entitled in possession to a share in the capital of the trust fund…

[44] I turn now to the defendant trustees' other objections to giving beneficiary disclosure. First of all, I do not accept the argument for the trustees that the court should not order disclosure of particular categories of documents merely because in the opinion of the trustees the beneficiaries already have had sufficient information. The beneficiaries have the right to hold trustees to account for their stewardship of the trust fund and the performance of the trust obligations which they accepted. If the beneficiaries ask for information from the trustees and the trustees refuse, the beneficiaries may ask the court to order the disclosure of the information in the exercise of the court's jurisdiction to supervise the activities of trustees. The court will not be satisfied with the 'say-so' of the trustees that they have had sufficient information already, but will make its own mind up as to whether the information sought should be disclosed.…

[47] Thirdly, I reject the submission that the so-called Londonderry principle applies to the exercise of administrative powers of trustees. Mr Adams could cite no authority for this proposition, and I am not aware of any. Moreover, if it were correct, it would mean in practice that trustees were never obliged to disclose professional advice or even other information about (for example) dealings with the trust assets, because the relevant documents might well disclose reasons why the trustees had decided to sell this asset and buy that one. That cannot be right. In addition to that, I find that, in the case of Re Londonderry's Settlement [1965] Ch 918 itself, the members of the court made it clear that their decision was one in relation to dispositive powers of trustees. (See also [82]–[85])

[53] Lastly, I reject the submission on behalf of the trustees based on Rosewood v Schmidt to the effect that the court must get over a threshold before being entitled to interfere with the exercise of discretion of trustees to refuse disclosure. Once again the trustees could cite no authority to support their position. … [T]he supervisory jurisdiction of the court rests on a different footing, and that in the exercise of that jurisdiction the court is entitled to interfere with a disclosure decision whenever it thinks proper to do so in order that the beneficiaries may be able to hold the trustees to account.

3.118 Matthews HHJ then went on to discuss disclosure of various documents sought by the beneficiaries. Importantly, he had this to say about documents which the trustees said were privileged
by the lawyer-client relationship of confidentiality:

> [59] [T]he claimants are not entitled to production to them of any documents protected
> by legal professional privilege of the trustees in any capacity other than as trustees of
> the Tamplin Trust. Originally, the trustees sought to claim legal professional privilege
> for all the communications with their lawyers… This untenable position has wisely
> been abandoned. There is a clear distinction to make. In general, where trustees seek
> legal advice for the benefit of themselves personally, eg in relation to possible breach of
> trust liability, or of another trust of which they are trustees, and pay for it themselves, or
> out of the funds of that other trust, without recourse to the funds of the Tamplin Trust,
> that advice may well be privileged in favour of those trustees as against these benefi-
> ciaries. But, where the advice is sought for the benefit of the Tamplin Trust as a whole,
> and the trustees pay for that advice out of Tamplin Trust funds, then such advice, even
> though it may be privileged as against third parties, is not privileged as against the
> beneficiaries, and is liable to be ordered to be produced.

3.119 Based on the case *Re Londonderry's Settlement* (1965), trustees are not required to disclose
documents which reveal their reasons for exercising their dispositive discretions, eg giving
more money to object X rather than to object Y. Danckwerts LJ provided the rationale for the
rule as follows (at 935–36):

> It seems to me that where trustees are given discretionary trusts which involve a decision
> upon matters between beneficiaries, viewing the merits and other rights to benefit under
> such a trust, the trustees are given a confidential role and they cannot properly exercise
> that confidential role if at any moment there is likely to be an investigation for the pur-
> pose of seeing whether they have exercised their discretion in the best possible manner.

Salmon LJ added (at 937):

> Another ground for this rule is that it would not be for the good of the beneficiaries as a
> whole, and yet another that it might make the lives of trustees intolerable should such
> an obligation rest upon them…

3.120 But a new wrinkle has recently arisen. In *Dawson-Damer v Taylor-Wessing LLP* (2017) the CA
held that a beneficiary can apply for the information held by trustees under the Data Protection
Act 1998, and that the rights under the Act are not limited by trust law rules such as the rule in
Re Londonderry.

Interests under discretionary trusts and powers of appointment

3.121 As we have seen (3.42), the principle in *Saunders v Vautier* applies to discretionary trusts, but
this does not mean that the beneficiaries, if all *sui juris*, are treated as having a vested interest,
either individually or together; only if they exercise their *Saunders v Vautier* rights and demand

the income or trust property from the trustees do they acquire indefeasible interests (*Vestey v IRC* (1979)). Indeed, rather than 'co-owners' or 'group-owners', until such time as each object has his own individual right to retain whatever income is appointed to him, their individual interests are essentially in competition with each other (Lord Reid, *Gartside v IRC* (1968)). It is worthwhile noticing that one party in many of these cases is the IRC, the Inland Revenue Commissioners. Whether or not an object has a vested interest has been important for purposes of taxation law (see eg *Pearson v IRC* (1981); *Re Trafford's Settlement* (1985)).

3.122   Post-*Schmidt*, in the case of general or hybrid powers, merely 'theoretical' objects have no rights of enforcement whatsoever. Those entitled in default of appointment will have the only rights to ensure that the power is not improperly exercised. In the case of both powers and discretionary trusts, the distribution of property must be within the terms of the power or trust. It would appear (for discussion see Turner (2018), 247–560) that 'not merely theoretical' objects of the power and objects of discretionary trusts may enforce the trust terms where the trustee has distributed trust assets to non-members of the class of objects. So also may those who take in default of appointment: any property distributed outside the proper bounds is property not available for distribution to them too.

3.123   Objects of special powers are in a similar position to objects of a discretionary trust individually, but not collectively. Individually, they may of course retain what is appointed to them, and they can enforce the power by ensuring no invalid appointments are made, and where the power is a fiduciary power (3.15 et seq), can insist upon the power holder properly considering its exercise, although they cannot, of course, insist upon any appointments (*Re Gulbenkian's Settlement Trusts* (1968)). Their interests are in competition not only with each other, but primarily with those entitled in default of appointment, who were traditionally regarded not only as the primary objects of the settlor's bounty (*Vatcher v Paull* (1915)), but also as the persons in whom the property is vested, subject, of course, to defeat by the exercise of the power of appointment (*Re Brooks' Settlement Trusts* (1939)). This traditional view seems not to apply to the case of trusts like that of Example 5, at least in respect of the capital interest. The trust for charity here is a 'long-stop' provision which is likely only to be given effect to if all the objects named in clause 1 were to all die for some reason and there is no on suitable to be added to the class by the exercise of the power in 1(ii). It is clearly expected that the capital will be distributed to objects of the powers of appointment in clauses 3, 4, and 5.

3.124   In the case of *McPhail* trusts (how many of such trusts continue to this day is unclear) some practical difficulties arise. In a *McPhail*-type trust the beneficiaries appear to be little more than postulants, seeking the trustees' largesse but having perhaps little incentive as individuals to pursue the remedies that the HL made available to have the court replace the trustees or help devise a scheme of distribution. As regard the provision of information to beneficiaries, should the law create an exception in these cases and require trustees of a *McPhail*-type trust to publicise its existence, in order to increase the chances of enforcement (though who, prior to the publication, would be in a position to enforce an obligation to publicise)?

3.125   Besides enforcement, there is also the issue of *Saunders v Vautier* rights and equitable ownership. Whatever such rights discretionary objects have under a *McPhail*-type trust in theory, they are clearly impossible to exercise if the class of beneficiaries cannot combine together because it is unascertainable on the complete list test. The objects do not have together, nor individually, any right in the property whatsoever, but merely have a right to the enforcement of the trust. Nevertheless, given the nature of the beneficiary's interest under the trust (2.107 et seq), this does not appear to require us to say that discretionary trusts of the *McPhail* kind are radically different from other trusts. The interest that an object has is *in the powers* of title held by the trustee, not in any possessory interest in the trust assets themselves, and this realisation clarifies the case of discretionary objects of *McPhail* trusts. Because the objects of a trust never have any possessory interests in the trust assets just in virtue of being objects, it is not essential to a trust, or to the conception of a beneficial interest under a trust, that any object has any immediate, vested interests in the trust assets. All beneficial interests under trusts (excepting, again, the case where the terms of the trust require the objects to be put in possession of tangible trust assets), are essentially future interests in the sense of being able to require the trustee to exercise his power of transfer to transfer the legal title to trust assets to the objects. There is no conceptual problem of finding a 'beneficial interest' here that correlates with the trustee's absence of a beneficial interest, so long as it is understood that the interests of the objects *exhaust* the beneficial interest in the trust assets, though such interests are future or contingent interests. The essential point to notice here is that the trustee can hold trust assets not to his own benefit yet at the same time so that the benefit will enure only to the benefit of others on a future, contingent basis. Those future and contingent interests absorb all the benefit the assets have. Thus the *McPhail* trust is perfectly compatible with the idea that the trustee has no beneficial interest in the trust assets, whilst only the objects do.

3.126   One final point, which returns us to the principle in *Saunders v Vautier*. It is generally accepted that objects of non-intermediate powers of appointment, such as Mary's relations in Example 4, have interests under the trust in the sense that they must agree to any collapse of the trust under the principle (or to a variation of the terms of the trust (10.65 et seq)), although there is little clear authority here (see Smith, (2016), 41–42). Some illumination, however can be provided by Matthews HHJ's decision in *Millar v Millar* (2018). The trust instrument in question contained two blatantly contradictory provisions, and the claimants sought a favourable construction of the instrument, or its rectification. However, the instrument contained a provision as follows (at [6]):

> [6] In the event of the failure or determination of the above trusts, the capital and income of the Trust Fund shall be held upon trust for such charity or charities as the Trustees shall in their absolute discretion appoint.

3.127   Matthews HHJ emphasised that his decision could only bind those beneficiaries or possible objects that were represented in the hearing.

> [8] As I have already said, the parties to this claim are the two settlors (and trustees) as claimants, the present husband and children of the first claimant as defendants, and the Attorney-General, as representing charity under the ultimate default trust in clause 6, as fifth defendant. As a general proposition, in the absence of contrary statutory provision, it is for the claimants to decide who they wish to sue: *Dollfus Mieg v Bank of England* [1951] Ch 33. The corollary is that, again subject to contrary statutory rule (eg CPR r 19.8A), only the persons joined are bound by the order made.

> [9] However, there are two important points to bear in mind about the terms of the settlement in the present case. First, it makes a contingent gift to any spouse of either of the settlors. The spouse concerned can only be identified as at the time that the interest falls into possession and income falls to be paid to such spouse. In the case of the first claimant, who is already married, this is likely to be the first defendant. But

it may not be. In the case of the second claimant, who is not married, it may be that this gift never takes effect. But on the other hand it may. These possibilities are not in-finitesimal or illusory, but real, even if at present unlikely. Accordingly, on the face of it possible future spouses of both claimants need to be represented in these proceedings. Otherwise such possible future spouses will not be bound by any order made. However, I understand that the claimants have decided not to make application for a suitable representation order (no doubt because it is so unlikely that there would be any pos-sible future spouses), and so the order I make will not bind any that there may be.

[10] The second point is that the settlement by clause 5, coupled with the definition in clause 1.3 (c), makes both the spouses and the children of the settlors objects of a power of appointment. So far as this relates to possible spouses other than the first defendant (who is of course already a party), the same point arises as in relation to the gifts of life interests already referred to. So far as this relates to existing children of the first claimant, they also are already parties to this claim. But so far as it relates to future children of both claimants, there is a question as to whether their interests need to be represented. ...

[13] In Re Westminster Bank Ltd's Declaration of Trusts [1963] 1 WLR 820, it was held by Wilberforce J that, taking into account the applicant's age, matrimonial history, the birthdate of her children, the evidence of any possibility of the birth of further children and the medical evidence, the trustees of the trust would be authorised to deal with the trust funds on the basis that the applicant was past the age of childbearing. However, this order was made without prejudice to, and would not extinguish, any right at any future child might have. If in that case it was right for the court to give leave to trustees to ad-minister the trust fund on the footing that there would be no further children born, then in a similar case with appropriate evidence it must be possible for the court to deal with the question of construction or rectification on the footing that there will be no further children born. In accordance with principle, it must follow from what Wilberforce J said that any order made by me will not bind future children, but, as I understand the matter, given what the claimants have said in evidence about their intentions, they are not con-cerned about that, and have not asked for a suitable representation order to be made.

3.128   It seems clear that on Matthew HHJ's reasoning those with contingent interests, whether in existence (or 'ascertainable') or not, and however unlikely they are to appear or have trust assets distributed to them, have a sufficient interest under the trust to be entitled to be represented, and that this would apply just as much with respect to a claim under the principle in *Saunders v Vautier*. As we shall see, the interests of unascertainable objects are specifically provided for in the Variation of Trusts Act 1958 (10.69).

Protective trusts

3.129   A beneficiary under a fixed trust, such as a life tenant, has a vested interest in the trust property, which can be assigned, or given as security on a loan and, most significantly, will go into the ben-eficiary's estate in bankruptcy if he becomes insolvent. A settlor may be happy to give a beneficiary an interest under a trust, but may like to avoid that entitlement going to pay his creditors if he becomes bankrupt. A protective trust is a device that combines a determinable life interest with a discretionary trust to protect trust assets from just this occurrence.

A determinable life interest followed by a discretionary trust

3.130 The protective trust works as follows. There are two trusts: first, there is a gift of a determinable life interest in favour of the person the settlor wishes primarily to benefit, for example his son, who is known as the 'principal beneficiary'; on the occurrence of a determining event the trust property is then to be held on a second trust, which is a discretionary trust in favour of a class of objects, which may include the principal beneficiary himself. The determining events always include the situation in which the principal beneficiary's right to income is assigned to anyone else or goes to his trustee in bankruptcy, but typically also includes any case where the beneficiary's interest becomes charged or, more vaguely, 'payable' to anyone else. On the determining event, the secondary, discretionary, trust kicks in by operation of law, for the determinable interest automatically terminates when a defeating event occurs—no exercise of any power of revocation is necessary. The situation will now be that the income is distributable at the trustees' discretion to the objects of the secondary trust, 'the secondary objects'. Since an individual object of a discretionary trust has no vested interest in the trust property (3.121) neither can his creditors nor trustee in bankruptcy, and thus the trust property is kept out of their hands so long as the trustee chooses not to give the bankrupt object any, which, obviously, he will not, though he may apply property to this object's benefit (3.142).

3.131 It is absolutely essential that the first gift is a determinable life interest and not a life interest defeasible upon a condition subsequent, for any one of three reasons, otherwise the protective trust will not work. The chief reason is that as a matter of historical concepts of property, conditions that prevent the alienation of property, ie the assignment, charging, or transfer by operation of the law of property, are absolutely void, whereas determinable interests that determine upon an alienation are not (Burn and Cartwright (2011), at 345). Secondly, and less crucially, a condition subsequent is strictly construed and, if uncertain (eg too vague), the condition is struck down but the gift remains; thus if the condition were struck down in this way, the principal beneficiary would take an absolute life interest, which would not be protected. Finally, and least importantly, gifts defeasible upon condition subsequent do not end automatically when the condition arises; rather, the happening of the condition gives the secondary donee a right to bring the principal gift to an end; therefore the secondary donee must act. For example, in the case of land, the secondary donee acquires a right to re-enter the land if the defeating condition occurred, but the primary donee's rightful possession of the land lasts until the secondary donee actually re-enters. With respect to the protected life interest in income, that would mean that at least one of the secondary objects would be required to demand that the trustees henceforth apply the property under the secondary trust. Presumably, this would be no more than an inconvenience in most cases; nevertheless, if protective trusts could be framed in terms of conditions subsequent the primary beneficiary's life interest would remain following a forfeiting event, and the trustee would be required to apply the benefits to, for example, a trustee in bankruptcy, until a secondary object acted.

No protective trust for oneself

3.132 Although technically the protective trust works just as well for a settlor who wishes to transfer his own property on protective trusts to avoid the consequences of his own bankruptcy, this is not allowed (*Re Brewer's Settlement* (1896)). The justification is roughly as follows: A may give B a gift structured or limited in whatever ways he wishes, so if he wants B to have an interest, but not B's trustee in bankruptcy should B become insolvent, that's OK. As a donee from A, B cannot expect any particular gift, or any gift at all, and neither can his creditors; if the latter are therefore deprived of A's bounty, they have no just cause to complain. On the other hand, A may not escape his liability to his own creditors by purporting to 'give' his property to himself in the same way. His own property is absolutely his, and must retain the normal 'incident', ie conceptual attribute, of property, of being available to pay his debts. (In other jurisdictions, which offer 'asset protection trusts', such creditor avoidance may be possible: see eg Matthews (2006).)

3.133   On the other hand, a person may put his property on trust for himself, determinable on the event that he assigns or charges or otherwise alienates it—the policy is only against defeating one's creditors. If a settlor includes as one of the events his becoming bankrupt anyway, that provision will be ineffective against his trustee in bankruptcy in accordance with the general policy, but does not make the other events ineffective. So, in *Re Detmold* (1889), the occurrence of one of the other operating events terminated the trust, and therefore the settlor no longer had an interest that could pass into his estate in bankruptcy when he later became bankrupt. What happens, however, if the settlor becomes bankrupt, so that the life interest passes as one of his assets into the hands of his trustee in bankruptcy, and then another defeating condition occurs? Is the life estate subsequently defeated by the later terminating event? The secondary objects will obviously argue 'yes', since they will claim that their rights against the primary beneficiary must remain against his 'successor in title', ie anyone who takes the life estate from him. The answer, however, is 'no'. Peterson J nicely reasons it out in *Re Burroughs-Fowler* (1916):

> It is said that the result may be that the trustee in bankruptcy will be in a position to dispose of more than was vested in the bankrupt himself. That would be so in any case, because, so far as the trustee is concerned, the provisions for terminating the protected life interest upon bankruptcy are void. It seems to me that the true view is that, so far as the trustee in bankruptcy is concerned, the provisions as to bankruptcy and insolvency must be excluded from the settlement, and the trustee is therefore in a position to deal with the interest of the [bankrupt] . . . as if those provisions were excluded. So far, however, as the [secondary object] is concerned the forfeiture by reason of the bankruptcy has already taken place, and, therefore, it is no longer possible for the [bankrupt] hereafter to do or suffer something which would determine his interest. The result is that the trustee in bankruptcy is in possession of the life interest of the bankrupt, which is now incapable of being effected by any subsequent forfeiture.

The s 33 protective trust

3.134   Protective trusts can be expressly stated in a trust instrument, but may also be created by directing the trustees to hold property for X 'on protective trusts', which automatically invokes the particular protective trust formulated in s 33(1) of the Trustee Act 1925:

> 33.   *Protective trusts*
>
>   (1)   *Where any income, including an annuity or other periodical income payment, is directed to be held on protective trusts for the benefit of any person (in this section called 'the principal beneficiary') for the period of his life or for any*

*less period, then, during that period (in this section called the 'trust period')
the said income shall, without prejudice to any prior interest, be held upon the
following trusts, namely:—*

(i)   Upon trust for the principal beneficiary during the trust period or until he,
***whether before or after the termination of any prior interest, does or at-
tempts to do or suffers any act or thing, or until any event happens, other
than an advance under any statutory or express power, whereby, if the said
income were payable during the trust period to the principal beneficiary
absolutely during that period, he would be deprived of the right to receive
the same or any part thereof,*** *in any of which cases, as well as on the termination of the trust period, whichever happens first, this trust of the said income
shall fail or determine;*

*(ii)   If the trust aforesaid fails or determines during the subsistence of the trust
period, then, during the residue of that period, the said income shall be held
upon trust for the application thereof for the maintenance and support, or
otherwise for the benefit, of all or any one or more exclusively of the other or
others of the following persons (that is to say)—*

*(a)   the principal beneficiary and his wife or husband, if any, and his or her
children or more remote issue, if any; or*

*(b)   if there is no wife or husband or issue of the principal beneficiary in ex-
istence, the principal beneficiary and the persons who would, if he were
actually dead, be entitled to the trust property or the income thereof or
the annuity fund, if any, or arrears of the annuity, as the case may be;*

*as the trustees in their absolute discretion, without being liable to account for the
exercise of such discretion, think fit.*

3.135   As the s 33 formulation of the events giving rise to forfeiture (in **bold** above) shows, forfeiture
clauses are generally very widely framed so as to apply to any circumstance that might defeat the
principal beneficiaries' receipt of the benefit of the trust. Notice the initial phrase in bold, 'whether
before or after the termination of any prior interest', which indicates that if the trust initially takes
effect in circumstances where a determining event has taken place (eg any income the primary
beneficiary received would be payable to a third party), then there will be a forfeiture at the outset.
This occurred in *Re Walker* (1939): the person who would become a principal beneficiary under a
testamentary protective trust was a bankrupt who had applied for his discharge from bankruptcy.
The court granted the discharge, but suspended it for one month, and in this period the testator
died. Bad timing. Because he was still a bankrupt when the trust came into effect on the testator's
death, the interest was forfeit.

3.136   If there is a doubt as to the interpretation of a forfeiture clause, whether the s 33 formulation or an
express clause, it is resolved in favour of the principal beneficiary, not primarily because he is the first
object of the settlor's bounty—the settlor obviously considered the secondary objects to be worthy
of a benefit as well (*Re Sartoris' Estate* (1892))—but for the mundane reason that those who wish to
assert their rights based upon a forfeiture have the burden of showing that a forfeiture has occurred
(*Re Baring's Settlement Trusts* (1940)).

3.137   The actual words of the clause are all-important, as shown by the pair of cases, *Re Gourju's Will Trusts* (1943) and *Re Hall* (1944). In both cases the principal beneficiaries' income became payable to the Custodian of Enemy Property under the Trading with the Enemy Act 1939 by virtue of their residence in France during the Second World War. In effect, if there was no forfeiture, the Custodian would hold the income on behalf of the principal beneficiary until the war was over or they could return to England to claim it, so it was to the beneficiary's advantage if there were no forfeiture. In *Gourju* the will creating the trust incorporated the statutory provision, by which the life interest can terminate upon the happening of any event; Simonds J concluded that the happening of the events made the income payable to the Custodian, so the forfeiture occurred:

> It was urged upon me by council for Madame Gourju that the result of such a decision is a forfeiture by reason of an event which can never have been contemplated by the testator, an event, moreover, of a wholly different character from any event fairly within his contemplation. With that I cannot but agree, but the words of the clause are too strong for me, and I can only express the earnest hope that in the welter of legislation that peace will bring, the hard case will not be forgotten of a beneficiary who, like Madame Gourju, suffers an undeserved forfeiture of her income.

3.138   By contrast, in *Hall*, the forfeiture clause was an express provision that did not refer to the happening of events, although it did comprise the principal beneficiary's 'suffer[ing] any act or thing' whereby the property would become payable to someone else. Uthwatt J construed it this way:

> Reading the clause as a whole, it seems to me that it is directed to the forfeiture of the annuity in the event of the annuitant personally doing certain classes of things, such as alienating or charging it, or permitting an act to be done whereby she is deprived of her annuity. It appears not to be directed to a case where the annuity is subject to an alienation which is not the result of the countess's own act . . . She was in France, the normal place for a French national, when her property became subject to the provisions of the Act, and I fail to see how the fact that she was there and remained there can be said to amount to the doing of an act of the kind which is contemplated by the clause. The question whether she has 'suffered' anything is, perhaps, more open. The word 'suffer' is capable of more meanings than one. I have come to the conclusion that it is proper to attribute to the word in this clause the meaning 'permit'. It is clear that the annuitant has not permitted anything to be done.

3.139   Section 33 of the Act expressly exempts the exercise of a power of advancement from being a cause of forfeiture, and this applies to any trust that incorporates the statutory provision. A power of advancement allows the trustee to advance, or pay, capital to the income beneficiary (10.41); the obvious effect of doing so is to reduce his right to income, since as a result there is less capital upon which income can arise, and so, but for the exemption, the advancement could be seen to work a forfeiture. The exemption appears to apply to express protective trusts as well (*Re Rees* (1954)), and may simply be a matter of common sense not requiring any statutory exemption (*Re Hodgson* (1913); *Re Shaw's Settlement* (1951))—advancements simply secure the benefit of the trust property to the beneficiary by another means, not deprive him of his entitlement to it. Whether the exercise of any other power that affects the principal beneficiary's right to income, such as a power to appoint capital to a third party, causes a forfeiture, is a matter of interpretation of the instrument.

3.140   Under the Trustee Act 1925, s 57, the court may by order 'vary', ie modify, the terms of a trust (10.67), and such orders, though they may affect the life tenant's right to income, do not effect a forfeiture:

> If and when the Court sanctions an arrangement or transaction under s 57, it must be taken to have done it as though the power which is brought into operation has been inserted in the trust instrument as an overriding power. [Farwell J, Re Mair (1935)]

Orders affecting a life tenant's right to income made under the court's divorce jurisdiction to distribute property likewise do not effect a forfeiture (*General Accident Fire and Life Assurance Corpn Ltd v IRC* (1963), CA), and where the court order extinguishes one spouse's protected life interest entirely, this extinguishes the secondary discretionary trust as well—it does not arise as if the extinction of the primary trust counted as a forfeiture (*Re Allsopp's Marriage Settlement Trusts* (1959)). *Re Richardson's Will Trusts* (1958) is an anomalous exception. The case concerned a protective trust that was to operate until the principal beneficiary attained the age of 35, at which time his interest became absolute. On 3 June 1955 the court ordered that a payment of £50 per annum to his ex-wife be charged on his life interest; on 24 October 1955 he turned 35, and on 27 August 1956 he was declared bankrupt. Danckwerts J held that the court order effected a forfeiture. It is difficult not to believe that the result was motivated by the fact that, without the forfeiture, the trustee in bankruptcy would have acquired the interest in the income subject to the wife's charge, leaving the principal beneficiary nothing. Instead, under the discretionary trust upon forfeiture, the former principal beneficiary was entitled to discretionary payments, which it appears had in fact been made before his bankruptcy.

3.141   It is clear that a forfeiture should occur whenever the principal beneficiary's right to receive the income is transferred or charged either by the beneficiary himself or by operation of law or by another's exercise of his rights, as in *Re Balfour's Settlement* (1938), where by reason of the beneficiary's instigation of a breach of trust the trustees were entitled to impound the income (11.74). More difficult is the case of forfeiture upon the condition that the income becomes 'payable to' someone other than the principal beneficiary. In *Re Baring's Settlement Trusts* (1940) it was held that 'payable to' covers a broader range of cases than those where the principal beneficiary's property interest vests in a third party by reason of an assignment or charge. But a forfeiture cannot arise simply because the principal beneficiary has debts of sufficient size that he must devote some of his trust income to paying them off. The income remains payable to him, and he only has the personal duty to pay these debts out of all of his property. In order for a forfeiture to arise under the 'payable to' provision, some third party must be able to demand that the trustee must pay the trust income to him directly, and such circumstances should generally involve the state, as in the cases earlier concerning the Custodian of Enemy Property and court orders upon divorce. In *Re Baring's Settlement Trusts* an order of sequestration, which allowed third parties to demand payment of the principal beneficiary's income to enforce another order of the court, was held to forfeit the life interest. However, the cases also appear to indicate that 'payable to' will be construed narrowly, ie to the case where the third party may demand payment of the income as it arises, ie as the trustee receives it or can claim it, for example when dividends are paid on shares or rent on land falls due; a third party's right to demand income that has *already accrued* under the trust, ie funds that were already in the trustee's hands, does not effect a forfeiture (*Re Greenwood* (1901)). Furthermore, a forfeiture does not occur where a third party did acquire the right to demand payment of the income as it arose, but that right ended before any income actually accrued, on the basis that until any income arose none was actually 'payable' (*Re Longman* (1955); see also *Re Salting* (1932)). A trustee's right to require payment from the income for his charges and expenses as attorney to the principal beneficiary causes no forfeiture; it is akin to the appointment of an agent to collect one's rents who has the right to deduct his commission before paying the remainder to the beneficiary (*Re Tancred's Settlement* (1903)). In *Re Westby's Settlement* (1950) Lord Evershed MR held that even if such a right to be paid expenses was effective to create a charge over the income, the interest would not be forfeited; a forfeiture clause is directed to protect the beneficiary's net income from the trust after any proper expenses are incurred.

3.142 Following a principal beneficiary's bankruptcy and consequent forfeiture, he may be an object under the secondary discretionary trust, and will be if the s 33 provision is invoked. Following his discharge in bankruptcy, he may be paid income at the trustees' discretion. While still a bankrupt, the trustees may apply income for his benefit (2.11), by, for example, providing him with consumables such as meals or services such as accommodation, but only to the extent that this is for his 'mere support' (*Re Ashby* (1892)). Any money that is paid directly to him may be claimed by his trustee in bankruptcy, but to the extent that he receives no property in his own right, as when the trustee, at his discretion, pays third parties for services, the trustee in bankruptcy has no claim, for the bankrupt receives no property (*Re Coleman* (1888); *Re Smith* (1928)). Unless the trustee has the power to accumulate income, however, he may not retain accrued income in order to pay it to the former principal beneficiary upon his discharge from bankruptcy; the trustee must distribute the income within a reasonable time following its accrual (*Re Gourju's Will Trusts* (1943)).

FURTHER READING

Cullity (1975)

Nolan (2018)

Smith, L (2017)

Turner (2018)

Waters (1996)

Must-read cases: *Stephenson v Barclays Bank Trust Co Ltd* (1974); *Re Trafford's Settlement* (1984); *Lloyds Bank plc v Duker* (1987); *Pitt v Holt* (2013); *IRC v Broadway Cottages Trust* (1955); *Re Gulbenkian Settlement* (1968); *McPhail v Doulton* (1970); *Schmidt v Rosewood Trust* (2003); *Lewis v Tamplin* (2018); *Vatcher v Paull* (1915); *Wong v Burt* (2005); *Re Locker's Settlement* (1977); *Re Baring's Settlement Trusts* (1940); *Re Coleman* (1888); *Re Gourju's Will Trusts* (1942); *Re Westby's Settlement* (1950)

SELF-TEST QUESTIONS

1. What is a 'nomineeship' (review 2.16), a 'fixed trust', a 'discretionary trust', and a 'power of appointment', and how do the interests of the objects of each differ?

2. As regards the modern form of trust in Example 5 is it correct to say that 'The limitations [ie the gifts] in default of appointment may be looked upon as embodying the primary intention of the donor of the power' (*Vatcher v Paull* (1915))?

3. Acting as the settlor, write several provisions in a trust instrument giving dispositive and administrative discretions to trustees, to individuals *nominatum*, and to an individual *nominatum* who is also described as the 'protector of the settlement'. Then elaborate

how you think the court would determine whether these discretions must be exercised, whether they were 'mere' powers but fiduciary powers, or whether they were pure personal powers.

4. What are 'income interests', 'capital interests', 'successive interests', 'defeasible interests', 'absolute interests', 'vested interests', and 'contingent interests'? Give examples of each, and apply these terms to the various interests in Examples 1 to 5 at 3.3.

5. Following *McPhail v Doulton* (1970), the distinction between discretionary trusts and powers of appointment held by trustees is only one of degree. Discuss.

6. What is an 'excessive delegation' of a power? What is a 'fraud' on a power? Give an example of each.

7. What rights do objects of a trust have to enforce the trust, and receive information about the administration of the trust from the trustees?

8. How does a protective trust achieve its purpose?

9. Eric transfers a block of flats to trustees to hold for him on trust for life or until he 'does or attempts to do or suffers any act or thing, or until any event happens whereby Eric would be deprived of the right to receive the rental income or any part thereof', upon the happening of which they were to hold it on trust for his wife. The rent from the apartment house is collected by agents who deduct a commission. Eric is declared bankrupt, and the next day he assigns his interest under the trust to his brother Philip. Advise Eric's trustee in bankruptcy.

Constructive trusts

SUMMARY

Effectively declared trusts and trusts that arise by operation of law (TABOLs)
Varieties of constructive trust
'Anticipatory' constructive trusts
Third-party recipients of property transferred in breach of trust
Trusts of the family home
Fraud and theft
The nature of the constructive trust: 'institutional' and 'remedial' constructive trusts

Effectively declared trusts and trusts that arise by operation of law (TABOLs)

4.1 In Chapter 3 we considered express trusts, and there I advised that the way to understand express trusts is to think of them as trusts made by the settlor himself when he *effectively exercises his powers of ownership to create a trust*. In contrast to these trusts there are also trusts that arise by operation of law (TABOLs) (2.6). The law itself imposes trusts in certain circumstances, which is to say that on certain events occurring the law itself recognises that an equitable title in the property of someone arises for the benefit of someone else. The former sort of trusts might be called 'intentional trusts', because the settlor by effectively exercising his powers to create a trust has produced what he intended, but this usage can be dangerous: as we shall see in this chapter, a person's intentions are often relevant to whether a TABOL arises, and so it is probably clearer to call trusts that are effectively created by an owner's exercising his power to do so 'declared' or 'effectively declared' trusts, since the general term for the expression that counts as exercising one's power to create a trust is a 'declaration of trust'.

4.2 As we will also see in this chapter, there is controversy in some cases as to whether the trust in a particular case is a declared trust or a TABOL, and it is important to see that this sort of uncertainty has a historical aspect to it. Recall the way that uses first arose (1.20 et seq). In its origins, the obligation to hold property on use was not a legal obligation, but an obligation in honour, binding the feoffee to use morally, but not legally. The Chancellor, however, as we have seen, began to enforce uses against feoffees. At this stage in the development of the use it was clear that it was not the case that legal owners of land had a *power* (2.5) to impose an enforceable obligation upon the feoffee to use. Rather, where the feoffee to use acted unconscionably by failing to give effect to the use the Chancellor would require him to do so. It was not the case that the Chancellor regarded his intervention in these cases as the recognition of a new 'equitable power' by which legal owners were entitled to impose uses over their land. But, of course, once the Chancellor came to enforce uses on a regular basis, legal owners came to understand that they could rely upon this systematic enforcement so that by transferring their land on use, they could, in essence, *create* uses at will that the Chancellor would enforce. The transition from the Chancellor's sporadic, individualised, conscience-based intervention in particular cases, to a state of affairs whereby a legal owner came to treat the use as a particular sort of property device he could employ at will was, of course, gradual. By the time of the Statute of Uses, and the recognition of the trust (1.29) there was no doubt that the transition was complete. But one of the recurring questions concerning constructive trusts is whether what originated in the case law as the court finding that, in the circumstances, one party was bound to hold property on trust whether the parties intended that result or not now provides, in essence, a means for individual parties to arrange their affairs in order to take advantage of that case law so as to give rise to a trust intentionally (see also Gardner (2010)).

Varieties of constructive trust

4.3   Constructive trusts arise by operation of law, ie are TABOLs. Indeed, to say that a trust is constructive is, in fact, to say that it arises by 'construction of law', ie by operation of law, so 'constructive trust' and 'TABOL' are, strictly speaking, synonyms. Beyond, however, the fact that they are all TABOLs, there is little that binds the various examples of constructive trust together as a category. This chapter will very much serve as an introduction to constructive trusts, not a thorough examination, for reasons that will become apparent as we proceed.

4.4   For our purposes, we can identify three broad categories of constructive trust: (1) those in which the law anticipates the result of legal title passing at law, with the result that the legal owner is regarded as holding his title on trust for the transferee until the transfer of the legal title is effective; (2) the 'trust' under which a non-bona fide third-party recipient of property transferred in breach of trust (2.61) holds the title to the property he receives; and (3) those in which individuals acquire for the first time an interest in another's property because of their past dealings or relationship with the legal owner.

'Anticipatory' constructive trusts

4.5   As to (1), there are two different cases. The first concerns those trusts that arise on what has become known as the 'principle' in *Re Rose* (1952), at which we will look in greater detail in Chapter 8 (8.11 et seq). According to this 'principle', once a legal owner of property has done everything that he is required to do to transfer the property, say fill out the forms to transfer shares in a company and send them off to the company secretary for registration, from that moment on he will hold the property on trust for the transferee until the legal title actually passes, in this case when the transferee is registered on the books of the company as a new owner.

4.6   The second case turns on an application of the maxim (1.9) 'Equity looks upon that as done which ought to be done', and reflects the approach of equity when it deals with certain property transactions that typically have two stages. When one buys land, normally one first enters into a binding contract of sale, which is then some time later followed by the execution of the documents that transfer title (in those jurisdictions where title passes by deed) or by execution of documents which then need to be registered at a state registry for title to pass (as in England, Canada, Australia, and elsewhere); this second step is commonly known as 'completion', ie completion of the transaction of the sale of land, so the two steps are together called 'contract and completion'. Whenever the property being sold is unique in the eyes of equity, unique in the sense that a purchaser would be unable to use his money damages to go out into the market and buy the equivalent from another vendor, equity will allow the buyer specifically to enforce the contractual obligation to transfer title to property in question: if the vendor refuses to comply with his contractual obligation and transfer the title, equity will order the vendor to do so. This is the general position with contracts for the sale of land, because, in the eyes of equity, all land is unique. (Think of the estate agent's slogan, 'Location, location, location!') But moreover, because 'Equity looks upon that as done which ought to be done', equity will treat the vendor *as having transferred* the title to the land to the buyer the moment the time for completion under the contract arrives, so long as the purchaser has paid the purchase price or is ready, willing, and able to do so. From that moment on, the vendor will hold the land on a constructive trust for the buyer until he actually transfers the legal title.

4.7   It is important to notice that until the date of completion arrives, when the transfer of legal title is to take place, it is not the case that the vendor holds the legal title on trust for the purchaser, full stop. In *Jerome v Kelly (Inspector of Taxes)* (2004) Lord Walker said:

> It would ... be wrong to treat an uncompleted contract for the sale of land as equivalent to an immediate, irrevocable declaration of trust (or assignment of beneficial interest) in the land. Neither the seller nor the buyer has unqualified beneficial ownership. Beneficial ownership of the land is in a sense split between the seller and buyer on the provisional assumptions that specific performance is available and that the contract will in due course be completed, if necessary by the court ordering specific performance. In the meantime, the seller is entitled to enjoyment of the land or its rental income. The provisional assumptions may be falsified by events, such as rescission of the contract (either under a contractual term or on breach). If the contract proceeds to completion the equitable interest can be viewed as passing to the buyer in stages, as title is made and accepted and as the purchase price is paid in full.

In *Kern Corpn Pty Ltd v Walter Reid Trading Pty Ltd* (1987) Deane J of the High Court of Australia described the relationship between the vendor and the purchaser in this way:

> It is wrong to characterise the position of such a vendor as that of a trustee. True it is that, pending payment of the purchase price, the purchaser has an equitable interest in the land which reflects the extent to which equitable remedies are available to protect his contractual rights and the vendor is under obligations in equity which attach to the land. None the less, the vendor himself maintains a continuing beneficial interest in the land ... Pending completion, he is beneficially entitled to possession and use. Pending completion, he is beneficially entitled to the rents and profits. If the purchaser enters upon the land without the vendor's permission and without authority under the

> contract, the vendor can maintain, for his own benefit, an action for trespass against the purchaser.

In *Tanwar Enterprises Pty Ltd v Cauchi* (2003) the unconventional nature of the vendor–purchaser constructive trust appears to have led the High Court of Australia to go even further than Deane J, to doubt whether there was any significant equitable interest of the purchaser in the land at all, but this seems to be an overreaction to the situation's particular features, and well out of line with the authorities. As I shall suggest, one way of trying to sort this out is by determining when the vendor–purchaser constructive trust actually arises.

4.8   The pressing problem raised by the vendor–purchaser constructive trust, and for the *Re Rose* constructive trust, is why on earth do they arise when they are said to? What purpose is served by equity's anticipating the eventual transfer of legal title, by saying in the first case that the vendor holds the property on trust as soon as the time for the completion of the contract of sale arrives, or in the second case that the transferor of shares holds the property on trust for the transferee in the interval between the completion of the share transfer form and the date the share transfer is registered with the company? For his part, Swadling (2005b) does a good job of showing that the rationales or explanations for the vendor–purchaser constructive trust that have historically been given are tenuous at best. As far as I know, only Chambers (2005a) has attempted to provide a true theory of the vendor–purchaser constructive trust and *Re Rose* trust, as follows:

> The fundamental idea is that a claim to a specific asset, which prevails over the rights of the other party to the transaction [prevails, eg in the case of a sale of land, because the purchaser can get specific performance, ie ensure that he gets the land itself whatever the vendor wants], should also be enforced generally against others, so long as it does not prejudice the rights of third persons acquired for value in good faith. The basic principle is not limited to specifically enforceable contracts, but applies whenever someone has the power to obtain title to a specific asset. Generally speaking, the power to obtain title to an asset is a property right to that asset, regardless of the source of that power.

4.9   Whilst I think Chambers' explanation is on the right lines, in my view it needs modification. The authorities in this neck of the woods do not speak with one voice, to put it mildly, so what I am about to suggest cannot count as orthodoxy. But the suggestion is in line enough with the authorities to deserve consideration. (We will consider Chambers' view and mine again when we look at the case law following *Re Rose* in detail in Chapter 8 (8.14).) Let's begin with two points of law upon which everyone agrees: (1) As soon as the contract of sale is entered into the purchaser acquires a power to obtain title from the date of completion, and this power will bind third parties; if, before the date of completion, the vendor transfers the title to the land to a non-bona fide purchaser or to a donee, the purchaser will still be able to get a decree from the date of completion ordering that third party to transfer the title to him. (2) Prior to the date of completion, the vendor retains the entire beneficial interest in the land, as pointed out by Deane J above. To put this another way, the vendor is not liable, as a trustee of the land would be, to account for any of the benefit of the land to the purchaser during this time as if the purchaser was his beneficiary. Prior to the date of completion, then, the sort of right the purchaser has, capable of binding third parties in respect of a particular asset but not a 'property interest' under a trust, is close if not identical to an equitable right known as a 'mere equity' (Hayton, Matthews, and Mitchell (2006), para 2.7).

4.10   Whilst the holder of a mere equity has a power to get the asset some time in the future, it does not mean that he has the beneficial interest in the asset before that time. On this suggestion then, Deane J's formulation of the situation is preferable to Lord Walker's; once the contract has formed, the purchaser has a mere equity, to seek a decree of specific performance once the date of completion has passed.

4.11   This analysis seems to coincide with what Matthews HHJ said in *Taylor v Taylor* (2017):

> *[46] To the extent that it is properly to be regarded as a trust at all, the constructive trust arising on a contract to purchase land is simply a form of equitable protection for the purchaser. It depends on the availability of specific performance of the contract. Essentially it is a product of the contract. It anticipates the position on completion, on the footing that the purchaser is ready and willing to complete. ... The vendor's residual rights (which are in fact substantial) are together referred to as his 'lien'. But this an inapt term, because it is not really a security interest. If the purchaser does not pay the price the vendor may sell elsewhere, free from any claim by the purchaser, and is not liable to account to the purchaser if he sells for more than the purchaser contracted to pay (see Ex p Hunter (1801) 6 Ves Jr 94, 97).*

4.12   Once the date of completion has passed, the vendor is a true, bare (2.13) trustee of the land, for from that moment on the vendor is not merely subject to the power of the purchaser to get the land some time in the future, but now has a duty immediately to transfer the land; the relationship has moved from one in which the purchaser has a power and the vendor a corresponding liability to one in which the vendor has an immediate duty to the purchaser in respect of the land, a duty to hold the land for the benefit of the purchaser and account to him for any benefits he acquires in respect of it, which duties equity will specifically enforce; that, in other words, is a trust.

4.13   While typically the maxim 'equity looks upon that as done ... ' is applied to contractual obligations, it is apparently not restricted to them. In *Mountney v Treharne* (2002) the CA held that a court order imposing an obligation on a husband to transfer title to the matrimonial home to his wife gave rise to a constructive trust, so that the beneficial interest in the property passed to the wife as soon as the order was made. Laws LJ, while accepting that the result was right as a matter of authority which bound him, was unhappy with the result: while equitable maxims ought to apply so as to modify what would otherwise be the position at *common law*, as with vendors and purchasers of land, equitable maxims should not, he reasoned, similarly apply to affect court orders made under *statutory* powers.

Third-party recipients of property transferred in breach of trust

4.14   If a trustee should transfer legal title to property in breach of trust to a third-party recipient who is not a bona fide purchaser, then recipient's legal title will be bound by the beneficiary's interest (2.61). How should this recipient be described? Is he a trustee, and if so, what kind of 'trustee' is he? He was never intended to hold the property—he holds it because of a breach of trust, after all—and so he cannot be an express trustee; not being an express trustee, he is generally called a 'constructive trustee'. However, it is best to describe him more fully, if you are going to describe him as a trustee at all, as a 'constructive trustee of an express trust interest': that is, the equitable interest in the property remains throughout, and so retains its characteristic as one created by an express trust, but the trustee is not appointed a trustee of the express trust; rather his 'trusteeship' is constructive, imposed by law, so that the beneficiary can claim his equitable interest against him.

4.15   It is also worthwhile remarking that referring to this use of 'constructive trust' may be misleading on the view of the matter expressed by Lord Browne-Wilkinson in *Westdeutsche Landesbank* (1996), that no true trust arises until the recipient title holder of property subject to an equitable beneficial interest is aware of, and thus his conscience is affected by, it. While one must not push this thought too far, it does helpfully point out that in these cases the beneficiary's fundamental right is essentially a proprietary ownership interest, albeit an equitable one, in some specific property. This proprietary interest continues so long as the rules of title that govern it (ie govern how title to it can be transferred, lost, and so on) indicate that the beneficiary retains the equitable title. And if and when the recipient's conscience is affected by his knowledge of the trust, he is not in any way expected to *carry out* the original express trust as an express trustee must; rather, when he is informed of the trust he is merely required to hold the trust property to the order of the beneficiaries, ie to give it back to them or to a trustee willing to carry out the original express trust for their benefit. (We will discuss this in detail in Chapter 11, 11.188 et seq.) Consider a parallel case: a non-bona fide purchaser of land bound by an equitable mortgage is liable to the mortgagee in the sense that the mortgagee can enforce the mortgage against this third-party recipient of the land (2.95); but no one would call the third-party recipient a 'constructive mortgagor'. Therefore it may be wiser to refer to the recipient of property subject to a trust merely as a legal title holder subject to an equitable ownership interest; that may well be preferable to calling him a 'constructive trustee'.

Personal liability as 'constructive trusteeship'

4.16   Where a breach of trust occurs, the trustee is personally liable to the beneficiary to make up the loss; that is the beneficiary has a personal money claim against the trustee for whatever losses were caused by the breach. This remedy is particularly important where the trust property was transferred away in breach of trust and it can neither be followed (2.61) nor traced (2.78). Others besides the trustee, however, may be personally liable in cases of breach of trust. First, where a person dishonestly assists in a breach of trust the beneficiary will have a personal claim against such a person to make good the loss caused by the breach. Secondly, where a person receives or deals with trust property as his own knowing it was transferred to him in breach of trust, and thus that the beneficial interest in it is still the beneficiary's, the beneficiary will have a personal claim against him to the extent that he deals with the property and causes the beneficiary loss (11.188 et seq). The traditional terminology for describing the personal liability of both the dishonest assistant and the recipient who knowingly deals with the trust property causing a loss is that they become 'liable to account (2.46) as a *constructive* trustee', because they acquire the same personal liability as the trustee for equivalent breaches of trust. But, as Lord Millett argues:

> [The so-called 'constructive trustee'] is not in fact a trustee at all, even though he may
> be liable to account as if he were. He never claims to assume the position of trustee
> on behalf of others, and he may be liable without ever receiving or handling the trust

property. If he receives the trust property at all he receives it adversely to the claimant. He is not a fiduciary or subject to fiduciary obligations . . . I think we should now discard the words 'accountable as a constructive trustee' in this context and substitute the words 'accountable in equity'. [Dubai Aluminium Co Ltd v Salaam (2003)]

4.17   Our third category, those constructive trusts in which individuals acquire for the first time an interest in another's property because of their past dealings or relationship with the legal owner, is a problematic category, because the power of equity to create property rights, ie equitable title, for one individual in the property of another, in order to do justice because of his past dealings or relationship with the legal owner, has not been informed by entirely coherent principles. As an introduction, a few examples will suffice. Those familiar with land law will be aware of what are called 'constructive trusts of the family home'. If P and Q, who is usually P's spouse, come to an informal agreement or arrangement that Q is to share in the ownership of the property in which they live, the legal title to which is in P's name alone, and Q then relies on the arrangement to his detriment, Q will acquire an equitable share in the property under a constructive trust.

4.18   The second example arises in a completely different context: it has been held that an employee standing in a fiduciary relationship to his employer who accepts a bribe to breach his fiduciary duties will hold the bribe money on constructive trust for his employer. Although they do not have any informal agreement to this effect as in the case of P and Q and the family home, the fiduciary relationship, it has been argued, is sufficient to give the employer an equitable title in his employee's ill-gotten gains. This case will be examined in detail in Chapter 13.

4.19   A third example is the '*Pallant v Morgan* (1953) equity': roughly, where A and B have an arrangement or understanding (not necessarily contractually binding) that A will act to acquire property for them jointly, but A then acquires the property for himself, A will be held to hold the property on constructive trust for both of them (see *Banner Homes Group plc v Luff Developments Ltd* (2000)).

4.20   A fourth example is provided by the case of 'mutual wills': roughly, where two people make wills on the understanding that the survivor will not alter his will (eg assume a husband and wife who both leave all their property to each other first and then all their property to their children), in order to prevent any 'fraud' that might arise if the survivor were to alter his or her will (eg say the husband survived, taking all of his wife's property under her will, but then decided to alter his will to give half the property to charity rather than all to their children), the survivor will be regarded as holding his property on constructive trust to give effect to the terms of the mutual will (*Dufours v Pereira* (1769)).

4.21   A final example is the case where a person acquires property by fraud or by theft. We shall only examine in any detail the constructive trust of the family home, but we will also look at the principles which might underlie the imposition of trusts in fraud and theft cases.

Trusts of the family home

4.22   Broadly speaking, what concerns us here are the circumstances under which it is just for the law to vary the property rights between individuals in what is usually the most significant asset either one of them owns (or both of them co-own), because of their relationship to and past dealings with each other. Whilst traditionally the typical relationship was that between husband and wife where the husband was the sole legal owner of the matrimonial home, in principle and practice the relationship or dealings can be between any two or more individuals: between unmarried cohabitees, whether straight or gay, parents and (adult) children, or any others (*Cooke v Head* (1972)). Indeed, the significance of this law is now much less for married couples and civil partners than for others, because disputes over beneficial ownership typically arise on the breakdown of a relationship and the courts are empowered to vary the property rights of spouses and civil partners upon divorce (Matrimonial Causes Act 1973, s 24; Matrimonial Property and Proceedings Act 1970, s 37; Civil Partnerships Act, 2004, s 65). The court has no similar jurisdiction to vary the property rights of other cohabitees. Nevertheless, determining the beneficial interests in the family home under these rules remains important even for married couples in cases where third parties are involved. For example, if one of the couple becomes bankrupt, only that person's share will be available to his trustee in bankruptcy for distribution to creditors; therefore, regardless of the situation between the cohabitees themselves, if an informal arrangement gives rise to ownership shares not easily detected by third parties dealing with one or both cohabitees, this can have important effects on those third parties' rights.

4.23 Different common law jurisdictions have taken different theoretical approaches to the basis upon which equitable property rights arise in these circumstances. For example, in New Zealand, the courts have emphasised the reasonable expectations of the party claiming an equitable share in the property; thus a wife who in all the circumstances can reasonably claim to have expected a share in the family home given the parties' conduct, and who has relied upon those expectations, will be successful (*Gillies v Keogh* (1989)). In Canada the courts have emphasised the unjust enrichment that the defendant would obtain if the claimant were to receive no share in the property; thus, for example, a husband who has benefited throughout the marriage by his wife's raising their children and domestic work will hold the legal title upon constructive trust for himself and his wife in appropriate shares (*Pettkus v Becker* (1980); *Sorochan v Sorochan* (1986); *Peter v Beblow* (1993)). In England the foundational HL decisions in *Pettitt v Pettitt* (1970) and *Gissing v Gissing* (1971) laid down the 'common intention' approach.

4.24 *Pettitt* can in one sense be regarded as the negative side of the coin, and *Gissing* the positive. In *Pettitt* their Lordships were unanimously concerned to refute the proposition that the courts had a general jurisdiction to rearrange the property rights of cohabitees on the breakdown of their relationship in whatever way seemed 'fair and just in all the circumstances'. They revealed, however, a variety of opinions as to the circumstances in which the court could find that one party had acquired a beneficial equitable interest in the property of another. *Gissing*, in particular the speech by Lord Diplock, provided that basis: where the parties had a common intention that the beneficial interest in the property was to be shared, the best evidence of which being an actual agreement, and that common intention was acted upon by the claimant to his detriment, then the defendant would hold the property on constructive trust for them both in the intended shares.

The requirement that the claimant act to his detriment

4.25 The first question we must ask is why, if a common intention to share the property is proved or inferred from all the evidence, does this not operate as an effective *declaration of trust*, albeit an informal one? After all, as we shall see (7.4), a declaration of trust can be informal, using any words sufficient to convey the idea that the beneficial interest in the property is to be this or that. So normally mere informality is not a problem. The problem that arises for informal declarations of interests in land like the family home is a statutory provision, s 53(1)(b) of the Law of Property Act 1925, which provides that a declaration of trust of land cannot be proved in court unless the declaration is written and signed by the one declaring it. (Formality requirements will be discussed in detail in Chapter 6.) However, a person relying upon the section must plead it (6.6), and it may be the case that the reason the section has not been given more prominence in the cases is simply that it was not pleaded.

4.26   But the oral, informal, expression of intention can be a relevant fact in another way: if, in addition to showing a common intention or understanding of the parties that the claimant is to have or acquire a beneficial interest in the family home, the claimant is also able to show that he acted to his detriment in reliance on the intention or understanding, then a constructive trust in his favour will arise by operation of law (*Midland Bank plc v Dobson* (1986)). The extent and quality of reliance should match what was expected under the parties' common understanding, but in many cases this is unclear. In *Grant v Edwards* (1986) Browne-Wilkinson VC said:

> In many cases of the present sort, it is impossible to say whether or not the claimant would have done the acts relied on as a detriment even if she thought she had no interest in the house. Setting up a house together, having a baby, making payments to general housekeeping expenses . . . may all be referable to the mutual love and affection of the parties and not specifically referable to the claimant's belief that she has an interest in the house. As at present advised, once it has been shown that there was a common intention that the claimant should have an interest in the house, any act done by her to her detriment relating to the joint lives of the parties is, in my judgment, sufficient detriment to qualify . . . Accordingly, in the absence of evidence to the contrary, the right inference is that the claimant acted in reliance [on the common intention] and the burden lies on the legal owner to show that she did not do so.

4.27   Evidence of a common intention is to be read objectively, as a reasonable person would do, from the statements or conduct of the parties. In particular, a dishonest actual intention of the legal owner will not defeat an agreement or understanding objectively viewed, as, for instance, where the legal owner makes an excuse for putting the title in his name alone, as in *Eves v Eves* (1975), where the excuse was that the female partner was too young to own property, or in *Grant v Edwards* (1986), where the legal owner said placing the female partner's name on the title would prejudice her in her divorce proceedings.

4.28   The HL canvassed the issues again, in *Stack v Dowden* (2007). Writing the majority opinion, Baroness Hale held that the starting point of any inquiry was the legal title to the property. If, for example, the property had been conveyed into joint names, prima facie the beneficial title was a joint tenancy as well. The party claiming otherwise had to lead evidence that the beneficial interest was intended to be different from the legal title, and that he had relied on this intention to his detriment. Quite surprisingly, and with nothing like a thorough discussion, Baroness Hale essentially abolished the operation of resulting trusts in this area; as we shall see in Chapter 5, where someone contributes to the purchase price of an asset, they are typically entitled to a share in the asset proportionate to their contribution, in the absence of proof that they did not intend to take such a share. Many claimants of interests in family homes in the past had established such interests even though they were not on the title because they proved they had contributed to the cost of its acquisition. But Baroness Hale dismissed the application of resulting trust principles, saying that:

> the law has indeed moved on in response to changing social and economic conditions. The search is to ascertain the parties' shared intentions, actual, inferred, or imputed, with respect to the property in light of their whole course of conduct in relation to it.

4.29 Apparently, the only relevance now of contributions to the purchase price of a house is that they may indicate that the parties intended different beneficial shares than those otherwise indicated by the legal title. 'How the purchase was financed' now falls within a litany of factors that may indicate the parties' intentions. To quote again from Baroness Hale's judgment:

> In law, 'context is everything' and the domestic context is very different from the commercial world. Each case will turn on its own facts. Many more factors than financial contributions may be relevant to divining the parties' true intentions. These include: any advice or discussions at the time of the transfer which cast light upon their intentions then; the reasons why the home was acquired in their joint names; the reasons why (if it be the case) the survivor was authorised to give a receipt for the capital moneys; the purpose for which the home was acquired; the nature of the parties' relationship; whether they had children for whom they both had responsibility to provide a home; how the purchase was financed, both initially and subsequently; how the parties arranged their finances, whether separately or together or a bit of both; how they discharged the outgoings on the property and their other household expenses. When a couple are joint owners of the home and jointly liable for the mortgage, the inferences to be drawn from who pays for what may be very different from the inferences to be drawn when only one is owner of the home. The arithmetical calculation of how much was paid by each is also likely to be less important. It will be easier to draw the inference that they intended that each should contribute as much to the household as they reasonably could and that they would share the eventual benefit or burden equally. The parties' individual characters and personalities may also be a factor in deciding where their true intentions lay. In the cohabitation context, mercenary considerations may be more to the fore than they would be in marriage, but it should not be assumed that they always take pride of place over natural love and affection. At the end of the day, having taken all this into account, cases in which the joint legal owners are to be taken to have intended that their beneficial interests should be different from their legal interests will be very unusual.

> This is not, of course, an exhaustive list. There may also be reason to conclude that, whatever the parties' intentions at the outset, these have now changed. An example might be where one party has financed (or constructed himself) an extension or substantial improvement to the property, so that what they have now is significantly different from what they had then.

4.30 As will be noted from the first quotation from Baroness Hale's judgment, above, she uses the word 'impute' as well as 'infer' in respect of the court's reckoning of the parties' intentions. These are not the same thing: to infer is to deduce or determine from evidence, whereas to impute is to ascribe or attribute. In this context, to impute an intention is not to discern what the parties actually intended, but to attribute an intention, based on the court's views about what is fair or on something else, an intention that the parties themselves never had. The most one can say about Baroness Hale's decision is that it is not very clear whether she thinks the court may impute intentions or not (see further Swadling (2007)).

4.31   Although not dissenting in the result, in his separate opinion Lord Neuberger would not have abolished the operation of resulting trusts in the way the majority did. In the later CA decision in *Laskar v Laskar* (2008) resulting trust principles were applied in a case where residential property was purchased by a mother and daughter not as a home for themselves, but as an investment. Lord Neuberger would also not have accepted that intentions could be 'imputed' to the parties. Any intentions needed to be the actual intentions of the parties; otherwise the court could simply impose whatever division of the interests in the house that it felt was fair. Two decisions of the CA (*James v Thomas* (2007); *Morris v Morris* (2008)) likewise highlight the passage in Baroness Hale's speech emphasised above, affirming the view that the court is not free to impose its own view of what would be fair, but must try to discern the parties' actual intentions. These decisions also express the view that where the defendant already owned land before entering into the relationship with the claimant, 'in the absence of an express post-acquisition agreement, a court will be slow to infer from conduct alone that parties intended to vary existing beneficial interests established at the time of acquisition' (*James v Thomas per* Sir John Chadwick).

4.32   The UKSC revisited the issues again in *Jones v Kernott* (2011). Lord Walker and Baroness Hale both reaffirmed their view that the presumption of resulting trust should not apply in family homes cases, but the other three judges on the panel chose not to speak on this issue. All of the judges, however, accepted that where there was evidence of a common intention that both parties would have an interest in the family home, but there was insufficient evidence as to the shares in which the property was intended to be held, the court could not throw up its hands and do nothing. Lord Walker, Baroness Hale, and Lord Collins found that the distinction between inferring and imputing an intention to the parties was, in practice, more theoretical than real. As Lord Collins put it:

> what is one person's inference will be another person's imputation.

4.33   Lord Kerr and Lord Wilson insisted that there was a distinction between inferring an intention and imputing one which would matter in practice: to determine what was a fair share of the beneficial interest in all the circumstances would not be to infer, but to impute an intention to the parties. Lord Wilson also stated that the facts of *Jones* did not require the court to determine whether a court could impute an intention not only as to the shares of the beneficial interest in the family home, but in respect of the 'first question', ie whether there was an intention in the first place that the parties' beneficial interest in the family home would be different from that under the legal title. That question was a matter for future cases, and would 'merit careful thought'. In *O'Kelly v Davies* (2014) the CA affirmed the decision of a trial judge who held that, though there was no evidence of an express or implied agreement, he was able to find a common intention to share the beneficial interest in a residential property equally in view of the course of dealing between the parties. The following factors were taken into account by the judge:

> I find that . . . the claimant lived at number 42 when not working away from home; that a relationship continued between the parties; that by 1996 they had a child together; that the claimant worked consistently and that the defendant did not work; that the claimant provided the family income other than the benefits which were being obtained fraudulently, and that the claimant's income paid the mortgage payments. This continued for 15 years. Although the defendant disputes much of this, I note that it was conceded on her behalf that when she cashed in the endowment policy to which I have referred and paid the money in reduction of the mortgage, that must have involved a direct contribution to the mortgage by the claimant and the defendant equally.

The benefits fraud mentioned by the judge in this passage gave rise to the issue of illegality, which we have already discussed (3.47 et seq).

4.34   As a last point, it is worth noticing that detrimental reliance was not discussed in terms either in *Stack* or in *Jones*; the courts seem to be willing to give effect to the parties' common intention, whether inferred or imputed, without an explicit finding that the claimant relied to his detriment on the basis of that common intention. This is a departure from what was, prior to *Stack*, considered orthodoxy. The reason for the requirement is rather obvious—subject to the pleading point raised above (4.25) it is difficult to see why the court should allow the proof of the trust in the face of Law of Property Act 1925, s 53(1)(b) (4.25), for the defendant would not be acting unconscionably if he merely failed to give effect to a trust upon which the claimant had not relied. Even so, the courts' failure to discuss a requirement to prove detrimental reliance may be explained on the basis that in the circumstances there would be little point in doing so; it is difficult to conceive of cohabiting couples not changing their position in all sorts of ways (arranging their finances, contributing to mortgage payments and household expenses, and so on) if they shared an intention to co-own the beneficial interest in the only significant asset to which either or both of them had legal title. (Cf the quotation from Lord Browne-Wilkinson's judgment in *Grant* (4.26).) In *Curran v Collins* (2015, [78]–[79]) Lewison LJ stated that the requirement of establishing detrimental reliance had not been abolished by *Stack* and *Jones*.

The constructive trustee is a bare trustee

4.35   The legal owner holding the family home under a constructive trust is just a bare trustee vis-à-vis a partner having an equitable ownership share of the property, as are joint tenants of the legal title vis-à-vis themselves as owners of shares as tenants in common in equity (Penner (2014d)). There are no other 'terms' of the trust with which he or they have any obligation to comply. The claimant and defendant are merely co-owners in equity to the extent of their respective shares, and co-owners do not have trustee or fiduciary duties one to another.

Proprietary estoppel

4.36   While proprietary estoppel in its various forms is a much older doctrine than the common intention constructive trust, they are similar. Where a defendant represents by his words or conduct that the claimant will acquire some entitlement to his land, and the claimant acts to his detriment in reliance upon the representation, the defendant may be 'estopped', ie stopped, from standing on his strict legal rights to the land in order to withdraw the entitlement. (For a statement of the principle see the UKHL's decision in *Thorner v Major* (2009).) The two main differences between the common intention constructive trust and proprietary estoppel are, first, that the former relies upon some common understanding or agreement, while the latter is based upon the defendant's representations and, secondly, that the claim based upon a common intention detrimentally relied upon, if successful, always results in an ownership interest in equity, simply because the claimant's acquiring beneficial interest is what the common intention purports to establish, whereas in the case of a proprietary estoppel the claimant will acquire the 'minimum equity to do justice' (*Crabb v Arun District Council* (1976); *Pascoe v Turner* (1979)): the court may award not only an equitable interest in the property, but more appropriate lesser interests, such as a licence to occupy or a charge on the property for money expended. In this respect, proprietary estoppel is a more flexible doctrine. A full examination of proprietary estoppel and a comparison with the constructive trust is beyond our purposes, but even the brief comparison above is suggestive—how different in most cases will an informal 'common' understanding be from an informal representation by the defendant legal owner that is reasonably acted upon by the claimant? In *Yaxley v Gotts* (2000), the CA held that a builder who converted the defendant's house into flats on the assurance that in return he would acquire the ground-floor flat was entitled to a 99-year lease of the ground floor rent-free equally under a common intention constructive trust and by way of proprietary estoppel (see also *Banner Homes Group plc v Luff Developments Ltd* (2000)). In *Stack v Dowden* (2007), Lord Walker stated that he was:

> now rather less enthusiastic about the notion proprietary estoppel and 'common intention' constructive trusts can or should be completely assimilated. Proprietary estoppel typically consists of asserting an equitable claim against the conscience of the 'true' owner. . . . It is to be satisfied by the minimum award necessary to do justice . . . which may sometimes lead to no more than a monetary award. A 'common intention' constructive trust, by contrast, is identifying the true beneficial owner or owners, and the size of their beneficial interests.

Equitable accounting

4.37   What happens where two parties buy a house together, usually with the aid of a mortgage, and the relationship subsequently breaks down? Based on what you have read above, you already have the tools to analyse the main issue, that is, what the respective ownership shares of the parties will be. However, there are usually two other issues that crop up. The first is whether there ought to be a court-ordered sale of the property, and if so, when this sale is to occur. The second issue is whether what is called 'equitable accounting' ought to take place between the co-owners.

4.38   The starting point is to understand that co-owners of land, as between themselves, are all entitled to possession of the whole. Therefore, there generally is no action in trepass against another co-owner. However, co-owners can, through their actions, become liable to one another. This is known as the taking of accounts between co-owners, or equitable accounting.

4.39   Equitable accounting has been described as the process by which the financial burdens and benefits of land shared by co-owners are adjusted between them (*Su Emmanuel v Emmanuel Priya Ethel Anne* (2016)). Historically, it finds its origins in the Partition Acts of 1868 and 1876. These statutes empowered the English courts to order a sale in lieu of partition. In these partition actions, it was the practice of the Court of Chancery to direct an inquiry into the financial position as between co-owners at the time of sale, and make appropriate adjustments to the proceeds each party would receive upon sale.

4.40   A classic statement of this principle can be traced back to *Leigh v Dickeson* (1884), where Cotton LJ said:

> ... [I]n a suit for a partition it is usual to have an inquiry as to those expenses of which nothing could be recovered so long as the parties enjoyed their property in common; when it is desired to put an end to that state of things, it is then necessary to consider what has been expended in improvements or repairs: the property held in common has been increased in value by the improvements and repairs; and whether the property is divided or sold by

the decree of the Court, one party cannot take the increase in value, without making an allowance for what has been expended in order to obtain that increased value; in fact, the execution of the repairs and improvements is adopted and sanctioned by accepting the increased value. There is, therefore, a mode by which money expended by one tenant in common for repairs can be recovered, but the procedure is confined to suits for partition.

4.41   Equitable accounting has been applied in various contexts. These include mortgage repayments, improvements and repairs to the property, as well as rents and profits derived (*Su Emmanuel* (2016)). Specifically, in England, the concept of equitable accounting has been applied to mortgage payments in cases involving a property dispute after a breakdown of a relationship (*Bernard v Josephs* (1982); *In re Pavlou (a Bankrupt)* (1993); *Cowcher v Cowcher* (1972)).

4.42   Take the following hypothetical provided by Bagnall J in *Cowcher v Cowcher* (1972):

Suppose land be conveyed to A for £24,000 B providing in cash £8,000 and A raising on mortgage of the property the remaining £16,000; suppose A has paid off £5,000 of the mortgage and B (though under no obligation) has paid off a further £2,000 leaving £9,000 outstanding: finally, suppose the property to be sold for £60,000. The shares under the resulting trust are one-third to B and two-thirds to A; but A must account for the outstanding mortgage of £9,000 and B is entitled to be reimbursed the £2,000 paid by him in part discharge of the mortgage. Thus out of £60,000 realised £9,000 goes to the mortgagee, B takes £22,000, his one-third share of £20,000 together with £2,000 paid off the mortgage, and A takes £29,000, that is his two-thirds share of £40,000 less £9,000 outstanding on the mortgage and £2,000 repayable to B.

4.43   Commenting on the theoretical basis of equitable accounting, Bagnall J noted that he who discharges another's secured obligation is entitled to be repaid out of the security the amount paid by him. This is not the only basis for equitable accounting that has been articulated in the cases—Millett J in *In re Pavlou* preferred to see it as resting on the basis that 'neither party could take the benefit of an increase in the value of the property without making an allowance for what had been expended by the other in order to obtain it'. For Millett J, things like mortgage payments increase the value of the equity of redemption, which inures to the benefit of both co-owners. This debate over the theoretical basis of equitable accounting does have some practical significance—the court in *Su Emmanuel* noted that if Millett J is right, then the interest element of mortgage repayments may not be accounted for, as they do not directly enhance the equity of redemption. However, if Bagnall J is right, and equitable accounting is justified on the right of contribution, then the interest element may be properly taken account of.

4.44   In *Su Emmanuel*, the Singapore Court of Appeal held that 'no distinction should be drawn between payments of capital and of interest because both these payments ultimately preserve or enhance the equity of redemption and accordingly there will generally be a right of contribution as between co-owners.' This can be read as a preference of Bagnall J's explanation, or perhaps more accurately, a rejection of the idea that only capital payments increase the value of the equity of redemption. Commenting on the general principles applicable to mortgage repayments in the context of equitable accounting, the Court held:

[105] In our judgment, the extent to which each party is expected to contribute to mortgage repayments will largely depend on the common understanding or agreement between the parties at the time the mortgage is taken out. As we have noted above,

*this will usually affect the beneficial interests of the parties. If there is a material de-
parture from that common understanding, and one party repays more of the mortgage
than was initially envisaged, then equitable accounting may be brought into play, unless it is shown that at the time the mortgage repayments were made, the payor had
the intention to benefit the other co-owners. This follows from the fact that the basis
underlying the remedy of equitable accounting is a notional request to contribute so as
to restore the parties to what had been their common understanding at the time the
mortgage was taken out; but if the evidence is that the payor intended to benefit the
other co-owners, there would be no room for any such notional request for contribution
to be inferred. In these circumstances, equity will not require a co-owner to contribute.*

4.45   Ultimately, the respondent in *Su Emmanuel* was entitled to call in aid the doctrine of equitable
accounting, to take account of the mortgage repayments she had made that constituted a material departure from the common understanding at the time the loan was obtained. The remedy of equitable accounting was especially important here, as the respondent could not point
to an agreement at the time of the loan that would have enabled her to classify the repayments
as a 'direct contribution' to the purchase price, and thus claim a resulting trust interest in the
property, and neither was she successful in showing a common intention constructive trust.

4.46   It is worth noting that in England, *Stack v Dowden* (2008) has made it clear that the common
law principles applicable to one party seeking an occupation rent from another have been super-
ceded by statute (the Trusts of Land and Appointment of Trustees Act 1996).

Third parties and insolvency

4.47   The claimant's equitable proprietary interest under the constructive trust will be capable of binding third parties who deal with the legal title-holding defendant (eg *Williams & Glyn's Bank Ltd
v Boland* (1981) HL; *Kingsnorth Trust Ltd v Tizard* (1986)), although it will not do so in all cases
(eg *City of London Building Society v Flegg* (1988)); the details will not be considered here. The
standard practice of purchasers or mortgagees of land is to make such inquiries as to avoid being
caught out by the claimant's informal interest. Of greater concern, perhaps, is the position of third
parties where the legal title holder, usually the husband, goes bankrupt. For example, a wife who
acquires an equitable share of the property under a constructive trust will take the value of that
share free of the claims of her husband's creditors. Given how common it is these days for title
to the family home to be shared, it is perhaps somewhat precious to manifest much concern for
the unsecured creditors in these circumstances, since it is not very plausible that *they*, as opposed
perhaps to a mortgagee, advanced money to the husband relying on a belief that he owned the
whole of, rather than co-owned, his family home. The sale of the property now 'co-owned' by the
husband's trustee in bankruptcy, who wants to realise the husband's share in money, and the wife,
who generally wishes to remain in occupation, will not be postponed for more than a year in most
circumstances (*Re Citro* (1991)), so the trustee can get the money out of the house quite smartly.

Are common intention trusts of the family home really intentional trusts rather than TABOLs?

4.48   Are common intention trusts of the family home really informal express trusts, which are enforced in order to do justice (or at least prevent injustice) despite the fact that such trusts are

prima facie unenforceable because they are not provable by virtue of s 53(1)(b) of the Law of Property Act 1925, or are they rather trusts which arise by operation of law (TABOLs) that reflect, but do not depend upon or exactly match, the intentions of the parties? On the first view, the trust the court enforces is precisely the trust the parties informally agreed upon or understood, taking the view that a statutory provision cannot be allowed to let the legal title holder 'commit a fraud' by denying the equitable beneficial interest of his cohabitee that was the subject of their common intention (6.12 et seq). If this is correct, then the common intention trust of the family home is not, as it has so far been labelled, a constructive trust at all, because such a trust is not a TABOL, and constructive trusts are TABOLs.

4.49 The contrary view is that these are TABOLs, and the constructive trust that arises reflects the intentions of the parties, but is not, as it were, created by the parties expressing those intentions: their expressions do not amount to effective declarations of trust. Notice, this latter point of view has nothing to do with the s 53(1)(b) requirement; that section concerns proof of a declaration of trust in court, not whether an expression actually amounted to a declaration of trust. The practical consequence of the distinction is obviously that if common intention trusts of the home are informal express trusts, then the courts cannot depart from the parties' intentions in their declaration of what rights each of them have, for the declaration itself establishes those rights. Whereas on the latter view, the parties' intentions are one, but only one, factor to be taken in determining the character of the trust, in particular the size of the claiming party's beneficial share of the ownership. As we have seen, the HL decision in *Stack v Dowden* does not give anything like definitive guidance on this issue. To the extent the common intention trust is aligned with or assimilated to the doctrine of proprietary estoppel, the more it appears to be constructive, because it seems clear that the law's (or the court's) giving an interest to provide 'minimum equity' to satisfy the claimant's legitimate expectation of an interest in the property need not coincide with whatever interest the claimant expected, nor whatever interest the defendant felt he was denying by standing on his strict legal rights. The prevailing view is that the common intention trust is a constructive trust, a TABOL, which is why it is discussed in this chapter of the book. But it is worthwhile keeping the alternative interpretation in mind. It may be that in some cases, the very trust informally agreed upon by the parties is the one enforced, reflecting the former view, whereas in other cases such intentions only form one part of the picture, so that only the constructive trust perspective is explanatory.

Fraud and theft

4.50 In exercise of its concurrent jurisdiction (1.13) over frauds, equity will in some cases impose a constructive trust over the proceeds of a fraud. Frauds typically involve the abuse of contracts. I defraud you of your money if I sell you a car to which I know I have no good title, because, for example, I stole it. I use, and abuse, the legal relationship of contract in order to defraud you of your money. In certain cases equity will provide a remedy to the defrauded party (eg *Collings v Lee* (2001); *Agip (Africa) Ltd v Jackson* (1990); *Dubai Aluminium v Salaam* (2003); *Papamichael v NatWest Bank* (2003); *Westdeutsche Landesbank v Islington London Borough Council* (1996) *per* Lord Browne-Wilkinson; but see *Shalson v Russo* (2003)). In particular it may allow the wronged party to trace (2.78) into the proceeds the fraudster acquires with the property of which he defrauded the rightful owner. The basis for this right to trace appears to turn upon the right of the defrauded party to rescind the contract by which he was defrauded (*El Ajou v*

Dollar Land Holdings plc (1993); *Shalson v Russo* (2003)). It seems that the fraudster does not hold what he receives under the fraudulent contract immediately on constructive trust when he receives it, but upon rescission, at which point the voidable fraudulent contract is regarded as no longer having any validity, the fraudster will hold on constructive trust any traceable proceeds of the money he was paid by the defrauded party that can be identified in his assets. This seems to be clear where the contract can be rescinded for fraud, but it seems that equity will not impose such a constructive trust in any other case where a contract is rescinded, that is, where the right to rescission does not arise because of a fraud (see *Re Goldcorp Exchange* (1995); *Shalson v Russo* (2003)).

4.51   As to cases of theft, in *Westdeutsche Landesbank* (1996) Lord Browne-Wilkinson said:

> I agree that . . . stolen moneys are traceable in equity. But the proprietary interest which equity is enforcing in such circumstances arises under a constructive, not a resulting, trust. Although it is difficult to find clear authority for the proposition, when property is obtained by fraud equity imposes a constructive trust on the fraudulent recipient: the property is recoverable and traceable in equity.

4.52   This reasoning was criticised by Rimer J in *Shalson v Russo* (2003) (see also Matthews (1995b)), but, with respect, Rimer J did so in part on the basis of the proposition that a thief acquires no title to the stolen asset; but this is clearly wrong (*Costello v Derbyshire Constabulary* (2001)). Just like an adverse possessor of land, a thief acquires a possessor's title to the property he steals—such a title allows the thief to bring an action against anyone who wrongfully interferes with his possession of the stolen goods, in the same way that an adverse possessor can bring an action against someone who trespasses on the land he adversely possesses. Moreover, again just like the adverse possessor of land, the thief can sell the stolen property to a third party. Of course, the titles of adverse possessors and thieves are 'frail', because the 'true owner', ie the victim of the theft or the owner of the land that is adversely possessed, has a superior title which he can assert against the thief or the adverse possessor or against anyone else taking possession of the property until the true owner's title is extinguished by operation of some rule of law. For example, when a thief passes title to stolen money 'in currency', ie to pay for goods under a contract of sale, the seller, as bona fide purchaser of the money, gets good title to the money and the title of the victim of the theft is extinguished (2.69). Or, for example, by operation of a statutory limitation period (Limitation Act 1980, s 15; Land Registration Act 2002, Sch 6), the adverse possessor of land can acquire the best title to the land, and the true owner's title will thereby be extinguished. So a thief does have *a* title to the goods or money he steals. Could, therefore, such a thief hold his own thief's title on trust for the victim of the theft? There has never been such a holding, and as Crawford (2014) points out, to do so would make no sense. True it is that the thief acquires a 'thief's title', but this title is good against all *but the true owner*. If the thief held his thief's title on trust for the true owner, the true owner could call for its transfer under the principle in *Saunders v Vautier* (3.38 et seq); but this doesn't work here. This is not an asset that could be called for by the true owner, for vis-à-vis the true owner it is a nullity; it is not a right at all. So this is one 'asset', it appears, which could not be held upon trust for the true owner.

4.53   The cases concern the question whether the 'traceable proceeds' of the theft are held on trust for the thief's victim. So let us say the thief steals £10,000 in cash from his victim, and uses the cash to buy an expensive wristwatch from a bona fide watch seller. The seller, as we have just seen, will get good title to the cash, so the victim's title to the cash is extinguished. Will equity impose a constructive trust on the thief's title to the watch so that he holds it on trust for the victim of the theft?

4.54 No case in England has decided so, but this is the position in Australia (*Black v S Freedman & Co* (1910); *Helou v Nguyen* (2014)). Why this trust arises, however, is in dispute (Tarrant (2009); Chambers (2013a); Crawford (2014)). Chambers argues that there is no need to impose a constructive trust on the thief's title to the stolen property, since the victim has a superior title to the property anyway. Only a trust of the proceeds is necessary, and Chambers justifies the imposition of this trust on resulting trust principles (4.28 and, in more detail, 5.8 et seq), ie that by purchasing property with the victim's asset, the victim is entitled to claim that the title to the property the thief acquires in exchange is held on trust for the victim. Whilst ingenious, this analysis can be doubted.

4.55 In the first place, it seems to mischaracterise the actual transaction. In the typical case of a resulting trust, A pays money to B to transfer title to some asset to C; because A contributes the purchase price, C is required to hold the asset for A, for it was A's title which was used to pay for the asset. But when a thief transfers title to B in exchange for an asset, it is not the victim's superior title which is used to pay for the asset, but the thief's own 'thief's title'. We know this because if the thief steals a necklace and sells it to B for £100, B acquires the thief's title, and the victim, who retains his superior title, can sue B for conversion (2.70). B gave the £100 in exchange for the thief's title, not for the victim's title, so the proceeds, the £100, were not acquired in exchange for anything of the victim's. Despite what may appear to be the case at first glance, the same is true when the thief exchanges stolen cash with B, the bona fide seller of a wristwatch, with the result that B gets good title to the cash and the victim's title is extinguished. B gets the thief's title to the cash, which is the only title the thief has to give, and by operation of the rule that when money passes in currency to someone bona fide who gives good value for it, the victim's superior title is extinguished and B's title, despite its having come from the thief, becomes the best title. Again, nothing of the victim's went to B in exchange for the wristwatch. So Chambers' analysis does not seem to work on resulting trust principles, since their operation turns on the beneficiary of the trust property in question having contributed to its purchase price, but the victim's title to the property never in fact does contribute to the purchase price, since that is not what the third party accepts in exchange for the proceeds he provides to the thief. So it would appear that a *constructive* trust is imposed *de novo* on the traceable proceeds of the exchange of the stolen property.

4.56 There is another reason to doubt Chambers' analysis. The resulting trusts principle he cites is not normally understood to be concerned to address wrongdoing. Indeed he argues that the trust is not imposed in response to the thief's wrong, but just flows from the 'follow the money' application of the principles. If this is right then many more people than thieves will be caught by his analysis, and be required to hold proceeds on trust for 'victims', including people we might think of as innocent even though they are clearly wrongdoers in law. Many adverse possessors do not act dishonestly when they fix up and occupy vacant, derelict properties. Nevertheless it appears on Chambers' analysis that an adverse possessor who sells his title to a third party would be required to hold the purchase money on trust for the true owner. So far as I know no such claim has ever been entertained by the courts. Similarly, if I innocently buy a stolen car from a fraudulent dealer, and then sell it later, I would hold the money I receive as the seller on trust for the original owner of the car. Let's say I then use the money as a down payment to buy a flat. The true owner would then, on standard tracing principles, be a co-owner in equity of my flat. Again, I have never heard of any theft victim making such a claim against an innocent converter, and it is not clear why equity should assist one in doing so. Genuine theft seems to be a different case, because, like fraud, of the actual dishonesty involved, and if we want to confine the imposition of a trust on the thief so that any proceeds of this theft are held on trust for his victim, a specifically targeted constructive trust of the traceable proceeds would appear the only way of doing so.

The nature of the constructive trust: 'institutional' and 'remedial' constructive trusts

4.57 A 'remedial constructive trust' as opposed to an 'institutional' one, is one that is *awarded by a court* following the trial of a legal action; such a trust does not pre-exist the court award (although parties may anticipate what a court will award and act accordingly, as when a negligent driver (or more likely, his insurance company) settles the claim for damages with the person he injured so avoiding an expensive legal action). Are there remedial constructive trusts of this kind?

4.58 The term 'institutional' is unhelpful. All it means is that the trust in question arose on certain facts, and is not dependent upon a court order. The clearest example is the case of the non-bona fide recipient of trust property transferred in breach of trust (4.14), for the beneficiary's trust interest that binds the recipient arose from an express trust that pre-dated the receipt. The same is true, in principle, of common intention constructive trusts of the family home. Once it happens that the claimant detrimentally relied on the common intention, the trust is regarded as existing as from that point in time however imprecise the actual terms of the trust are. From this perspective, the vendor-purchaser constructive trust is not a trust at all, or if it is, it can only be remedial, for the 'trust' only arises as a liability to convey the property on the condition that the date of completion has passed and the purchaser is willing and able to pay—in other words, it simply amounts to a different way of saying that the vendor is liable to the remedy of specific enforcement of the contract. The only real trust that arises in such a case is a trust over any moneys the vendor receives by way of rent and profits from the land between the date of completion and his conveyance to the purchaser. The third party effects do not turn on any 'trust' reasoning. A non-bona fide purchaser third party to whom the vendor transfers the title in breach of trust will simply be liable to the same order to transfer the property to the purchaser—he is no more a trustee than the vendor himself.

4.59 Swadling (2011) has recently argued that the remedial/institutional question is conceptually confused; according to him, there are no genuine constructive trusts; what are mistakenly called 'institutional' constructive trusts are really informal but express trusts which the courts have mistakenly labelled 'constructive', and the other examples of 'constructive trusts' are merely cases where the defendant is liable to an order by a court of equity to transfer title to the claimant. The paper makes a wealth of arguments that cannot be explored here, but for 'fans' of constructive trusts, the paper is a fascinating challenge to orthodoxy. (See also Swadling (2016).)

4.60 The power of the courts to declare a trust over a defendant's assets as a form of remedial relief appears to be accepted at least theoretically in other jurisdictions (USA (American Law

Institute (1937), para 60); Canada (*Rawluk v Rawluk* (1990) and see Chambers (2001–2)); Singapore (*Wee Chiaw Sek Anna v Ng Li-Ann Genevieve* (2013)); Australia (*Muschinski v Dodds* (1985))).

4.61 As for England, although the possibility has been considered *obiter* in England (*per* Lord Browne-Wilkinson in *Westdeutsche Landesbank Girozentrale v Islington London Borough Council* (1996)), as a matter of authority, in *Polly Peck International plc (No 2)* (1998), the CA put paid to the remedial constructive trust in England following a thorough review of the cases and the academic literature. As Nourse LJ put it: 'It is not that you need an Act of Parliament to prohibit a variation of proprietary rights. You need one to permit it: see the Variation of Trusts Act 1958 [10.69] and the Matrimonial Causes Act 1973 [4.22].' So unless the UKSC decides to reverse the CA on this, it would appear that the remedial constructive trust is a dead letter in England.

4.62 On reading the cases, you might think that in reality the law of trusts gives judges such discretion that their 'finding' a constructive trust on the facts virtually amounts to 'awarding' the claimant a retrospectively effective equitable interest. Nevertheless the HL in *Pettitt* and more recently in *Stack v Dowden* certainly denied that the courts should have such a discretion.

FURTHER READING

Birks (ed) (1994b, Vol II, Part IV)

Birks (2000b)

Chambers (2001–2, 2005a, 2013a)

Piska (2008)

Rickett (1999)

Swadling (2005b, 2007, 2011)

Turner (2012)

Must-read cases: *Pettitt v Pettitt* (1969); *Gissing v Gissing* (1970); *Stack v Dowden* (2007); *Jones v Kernott* (2011)

SELF-TEST QUESTIONS

1. What are some examples of constructive trusts? Do they have any common features?

2. Phillippa and Paul, a young unmarried couple with two small children, purchased Whiteacre together for £150,000 in 1999. Phillippa contributed £10,000, Paul £5,000, to the purchase price, and the remainder was raised by way of a mortgage loan. In 2001 Paul lost his job and since that time Phillippa has paid all the mortgage instalments. From 2002 Paul stayed at home and was the primary carer of their children, and also made several DIY improvements to the property. In 2005 he started a small gardening business which he ran from Whiteacre. In the summer of 2010 the business was failing and now Paul has been declared bankrupt. The house is now worth £350,000. Discuss.

3. On your reading of the cases, does the 'intentional trust enforced despite s 53(1)(b)' interpretation or the 'constructive trust' interpretation better account for the court's recognition of the common intention trust of the family home?

4. In what circumstances does equity impose a constructive trust applying the maxim 'equity looks upon that as done which ought to be done', and why?

5. On what basis, if any, should a trust arise on the proceeds of fraud or theft?

6. What is the difference between 'remedial' and 'institutional' constructive trusts?

5

Resulting trusts

SUMMARY

Resulting uses
Automatic resulting trusts and presumed resulting trusts
Presumed resulting trusts (PRTs)
The presumption of resulting trust
The presumption of advancement
Automatic resulting trusts (ARTs)
Resulting trusteeship

Resulting uses

5.1 Resulting trusts are something of an oddity, which cannot be understood without returning to the history of the law of trusts, in particular the way that uses (1.19 et seq) were originally employed. Recall (1.25) the typical use of land, to grant land to feoffees 'to the use of my will', which were typically created without any express terms besides the term that the settlor would give future directions, and where the settlor continued to occupy the land. Thus the feoffees to use received the bare legal title, in essence just the 'paper' title, which they held without having to do anything until such time as the settlor gave them further directions. Now, of course, nothing prevents the modern day settlor from creating a trust in which the trustee holds the property for the settlor for the time being, and at some time later on trust for others when the settlor so directs (2.13; *Grey v IRC* (1960); 6.29) but this is not typical today (for various, including tax, reasons). Yet it was absolutely standard in the fourteenth, fifteenth, and sixteenth centuries.

5.2 So standard and common was this means of holding land that it led to a particular development in the law which has, somewhat surprisingly, survived to the present day. Because feoffments to use were so common, equity began to assume that this was the normal basis upon which land was conveyed. Therefore, in circumstances where the evidence was insufficient to determine the circumstances of a transfer of land from A to B, equity would hold that B held the land to A's use. This use was called a 'presumed resulting use'. Where evidence was insufficient to determine the real terms of the transaction, B would be *presumed* by equity to hold to the use of A. 'Resulting' in this context means 'jumping back' or 'rebounding'; the benefit of the property would 'jump back' to A. As we shall see (5.66–5.69), the colourful language of 'jumping back' probably misconceives what the judges understood to be going on, but the name has stuck:

these days, rather than presumed resulting uses we have presumed resulting trusts, which do the same thing. Apart from certain exceptions, where A transfers property to B and there is insufficient evidence to determine what the actual circumstances of the transaction were, equity will require B to hold the property on trust for A.

5.3   Indeed, as you can imagine, these days the most common reason why there is such a lack of evidence is that A or B are both dead, so the dispute often involves A's or B's personal representatives (2.83). A good example is *Mehta Estate v Mehta Estate* (1993) where the court had to discern the truth of the circumstances of various investment transactions involving a husband and wife where both had died in a plane crash. Now you would be right to find it surprising that even today this presumption is still applied. It has been a long time since all land, much less all property (the presumption has come to apply to property of all kinds), was held in trust. Many people think the presumption is simply anachronistic and should be abolished. The probable reason why it has not is that, in special contexts apart, it does not generally affect the result in a dispute, since in most cases there is sufficient evidence for the court to find on the balance of probabilities what the actual intentions of the parties were.

Automatic resulting trusts and presumed resulting trusts

5.4   So far I have only described presumed resulting trusts (PRTs). But resulting trusts are generally considered to be of two basic kinds, presumed resulting trusts and 'automatic' resulting trusts (ARTs). An ART will arise where the dispositive provisions in an express trust fail, or fail in part, for some reason. For example, a settlor may transfer Blackacre to trustees on trust for Barbara for life and then for her children in equal shares. As it turns out, Barbara dies without children. In consequence, the beneficial remainder interest 'results', or springs back, to the settlor, and the trustees will hold Blackacre on bare trust for the settlor (or his successors if he has died in the meantime). These trusts are said to arise 'automatically' upon the failure of the intended disposition, hence their name.

5.5   ARTs are just as ancient as PRTs. That is, just as much as presumed resulting uses there were 'automatic' resulting uses, though the use of the word 'automatic' is obviously modern (5.7). But given the history of uses, they make obvious sense. Since the standard way of disposing of property in favour of others was first to transfer the property to the feoffee to use, and only later for the settlor to express intentions about who should have it after the settlor, it is obvious that the 'use' or 'benefit' would be regarded as remaining with the settlor until he had effectively directed it elsewhere (Mee (2010, 2014, 2017)). The modern ART just does the same thing with the modern trust where the dispositions are intended to take effect from the outset. Thus in the example just given, the settlor retains the remainder interest in Blackacre (which will fall into possession when Barbara dies) under an ART since the intended gift to her children cannot operate. Well-drawn trust instruments usually provide for the possibility of failures of this kind, so ARTs should, in principle, rarely arise where a trust is created with the benefit of legal advice.

5.6   PRTs fall into two categories: voluntary transfer PRTs and purchase contribution PRTs. The first we have already encountered. If A simply transfers property he owns to B, then that will raise the presumption that B holds the property on resulting trust for A. Purchase contribution resulting trusts involve at least three parties, not just two. If A pays C to transfer property to B, ie buys property to be put in B's name, then there will be a presumption that B holds the property on resulting trust for A. This again makes perfect sense given the history. Since at the time the presumptions were developed, a person would naturally want to have all his lands held by feoffees to his use, it is entirely understandable, if he were to acquire new lands, that rather than buying the lands in his own name, and then later having to transfer the title to them to feoffees to use, he would just buy them in the names of his feoffees to begin with. It thus made just as much sense to apply the presumption in such a case as it did with the voluntary transfer case. The rule also takes into account multiple parties contributing to the purchase of an asset. Thus, if two or more persons put their money together to buy property, equity will normally hold that they share the equitable title to the property in proportion to the amount of money each contributed regardless of the way the title is held, whether in both of their names, in one of their names, or in the name of a third party. Whoever the title holders are, they will hold the property on resulting trust for the contributors in proportion to their contributions. Thus if A contributes 30 per cent and B 70 per cent of the purchase price of Blackacre, and C is registered as the owner, C will hold Blackacre on resulting trust for A and B as equitable tenants in common, A having a 30 per cent interest, B a 70 per cent interest.

5.7   The explicit terminological distinction between 'automatic' and 'presumed' resulting trusts was originally drawn by Megarry J in *Re Vandervell (No 2)* (1974) (although it was clearly foreshadowed by Lord Upjohn in *Vandervell v IRC* (1967)). According to Megarry J, the distinction turns on one essential difference between the two cases. In the presumed resulting trusts cases both the existence of the trust and the content of the trust need to be established:

> The presumption thus establishes both that B is to take on trust and also what that trust is.

In the automatic resulting trust case by contrast:

> The resulting trust here does not depend on any intentions or presumptions, but is the automatic consequence of A's failure to dispose of what is vested in him. Since ex hypothesi the transfer is on trust, the resulting trust does not establish the trust but merely carries back to A the beneficial interest that has not been disposed of.

What fundamentally distinguishes the cases is the difference in what needs to be proved. In the case of the PRT, unless rebutted the presumption establishes that the recipient, B, holds as a trustee for the transferor or contributor, and in the case of a purchase contribution PRT, the extent of A's interest (eg a 30 per cent interest if he paid 30 per cent of the purchase price). In the case of the ART B is already known to be a trustee—the only question is for whom he holds the property on trust, and what needs to be shown is that what was thought to be an effective disposition by the settlor fails. (Of course if, on a true construction of the settlor's intentions, the trustee was intended also to be a beneficiary of the trust, ie intended to take the benefit of the property not disposed of to other beneficiaries, then there is no failure by the settlor to dispose of the entire interest in the property, and no ART: see *Cook v Hutchinson* (1836); *Re Foord* (1922) for examples.)

Presumed resulting trusts (PRTs)

Law of Property Act 1925, s 60(3)

5.8   The presumption underlying voluntary transfer PRTs applied equally to transfers of land and personal property ('personalty') like chattels or company shares before 1926. Before 1926, if a gift of land was intended, it was necessary to state expressly in the deed of conveyance that the land was conveyed to the use and benefit of the donee in order to displace the presumption. Section 60(3) of the Law of Property Act 1925 provides, however, that a resulting trust is not to be implied merely because there is no express statement of this kind. Does this section effectively abolish voluntary conveyance PRTs of land? In *Lohia v Lohia* (2000) Nicholas Strauss QC decided that the section did abolish voluntary conveyance PRTs of land, but the CA (2001) refused to endorse that view on appeal, disposing of the case on other grounds. In *Ali v Khan* (2002) Morritt VC, giving the judgment of the CA, said that *Lohia* established that s 60(3) did abolish the presumption. Though the decisions can be criticised (see also Chambers (1997), at 16–19; Chambers (2001)) they probably represent the law, at least to the CA level. NB: The section has no relevance to, and so does not abolish, the presumption in *purchase contribution* PRT cases. There it remains.

5.9   Regarding personalty, the presumption still technically applies. Since, however, most gratuitous transfers are intended to be gifts, the presumption should give way to the slightest contrary evidence, including evidence of the surrounding circumstances and common-sense inferences to be drawn therefrom—the presumption fully applies when it is my round and I buy you a pint, but no judge in his right mind would say that you hold that pint on trust for me. Nevertheless, *Fowkes v Pascoe* (1875) and *Re Vinogradoff* (1935) nicely contrast the wildly varying effects that can result when different judges apply the presumption. In *Fowkes* a woman of substantial means purchased stock in the name of a son of her former daughter-in-law; the only evidence of the woman's intentions were the surrounding circumstances; since there was no conceivable reason for her transferring the stock to him to hold as her nominee, she must have intended to give it to him; thus the presumption of resulting trust was rebutted. It is important to note that this particular transaction was held to have a trust element (Mee 2014), based upon the 'universally' understood 'intent and meaning' of transactions of this kind (*per* James LJ in *Fowkes*; see also *Standing v Bowring* (1885)). The transfer by A of property into the joint names of A and B, or the purchase of property by A in the names of A and B, was not to result in A and B simply becoming joint co-owners. Rather, A was entitled to the whole benefit of the property during her lifetime; she alone would be entitled to dividends on shares for example (in *Fowkes* the son of the woman's daughter in law had to account for a dividend due in her lifetime but received after her death). On A's death, B as survivor would take the title to the property outright. Even so, where such a transaction was entered into the presumption of resulting trust would apply, and if not rebutted B would hold his interest entirely for A, so that A would not only have the whole benefit of the property during her life, but B would hold his sole title as survivor after A's death on trust for A's estate, and this latter result was what was argued for unsuccessfully in *Fowkes*.

5.10   In contrast to *Fowkes*, *Re Vinogradoff* is an atrocity of a decision. There a woman had transferred £800 of War Loan stock into the joint names of herself and her 4-year-old granddaughter. Following her death, it was successfully claimed that the child held the stock on resulting trust, there being no evidence to establish an intention to make a gift. As Mee (2014) points out, although on the 'universally' accepted construal of such a transaction the child, as we have seen, would have been a trustee of her share of the dividends for her grandmother during her life, this would not have caused any difficulty because the child would just be a passive nominee. But in the result—the finding of a resulting trust—this would not be so; on her grandmother's death she would have to account for the shares to her grandmother's personal representatives. Given that her granddaughter was aged four, the probability that the donor intended to make her a gift, not make her trustee in this way, is about as close to one as probabilities get in this life. Furthermore, any express attempt to have made her a trustee (as opposed to a passive nominee under the normal understanding of the transaction) would have been ineffective, since under the Law of Property Act 1925 an infant (ie a person under the age of majority) cannot be a trustee. Undaunted, Farwell J held that the granddaughter held the stock on resulting trust, so the executors of the grandmother's estate were entitled to it.

5.11 The idea that sensible inferences may be drawn from all the circumstances is the approach taken nowadays:

> In reality the so-called presumption of a resulting trust is no more than a long stop to pro-
> vide the answer when the relevant facts and circumstances fail to yield a solution. [Vander-
> vell v IRC (1967) per Lord Upjohn; see also Pettitt v Pettitt (1970); McGrath v Wallis (1995)]

As Raynor QC J said, 'Of course in this case I have heard the sworn evidence of both parties and I do not need to decide the case on the basis of presumptions. I decide it on the basis of my findings of fact' (*Karsten v Markham* (2009)).

5.12 The presumption has, until recently, been applied much more regularly in the case of purchase contribution PRTs, and is of particular importance where the property in question is land. Why? As we saw in the last chapter discussing the constructive trust of the family home (4.22 et seq), it is difficult to establish informally expressed trusts of land, because s 53(1)(b) of the Law of Property Act 1925 requires written proof of such trusts. And in many cases of informal under-standings as to the beneficial entitlement to a family home, both members of a couple will have contributed in some way to its purchase price. Where this has occurred, the PRT allows one to make a more straightforward claim than if one were trying to establish a common intention constructive trust; while the latter requires proof of some understanding between the parties and proof of some detrimental reliance, in the case of the PRT the only evidence one needs to provide is evidence that one contributed to the purchase price of property; that immediately puts the onus on the other party to provide evidence that no beneficial interest in the property was in-tended. Following *Stack v Dowden* (2007), however, it seems that the purchase contribution PRT no longer operates in the family home context (4.28). That is, by establishing, say, a 20 per cent contribution to the purchase price one is *not* thereby any longer entitled to a 20 per cent interest in the absence of proof to the contrary; rather, that contribution will be treated as one of perhaps many factors that together determine the beneficial interests of the parties.

5.13 The 'contribution' in purchase contribution PRTs should be read as 'purchase contribution in money or money's worth'. In *Springette v Defoe* (1992) the sitting tenant of a house was entitled to a discount from the market price; when she purchased the property with her cohabitee, the value of the discount was treated as a contribution she made to the purchase price in determining her equitable share. (This case was followed in the CA decision in *Laskar v Laskar* (2008).) In Singapore, where it is very common to buy a property and refurbish it before moving in, it has been held (*Tan Chui Lian v Neo Liew Eng* (2007)) that contributions to the 'total cost' of buying a property, both purchase money and renovation money, should be treated equally in determining the shares of the co-owners on a proportional contribution basis. This make perfect sense, for when a couple buy a residential property it hardly makes sense for them to trouble about who is paying for the property and who is paying the build-ers—both should equally be treated as contributions to the property they acquire. In the case of land purchased with the aid of a mortgage the person(s) raising money on a mortgage, and therefore liable to repay the loan, will be credited with a corresponding contribution. For example, assume A and B purchase a house in their joint names for £50,000, A contributing

£10,000 in cash, the remaining £40,000 coming from a mortgage loan under which both A and B are liable. A will therefore have an equitable share of (10 + 20 (half the loan))/50 = 60 per cent, and B a 20/50 = 40 per cent share. Note that one's equitable share is determined by the share of one's *liability to repay the loan*, not by *the value of the money one actually repays* (*Cowcher v Cowcher* (1972); *Re Gorman* (1990)). The result of this is that if the house A and B bought doubles in value in a year to £100,000, and they sell, B will acquire a much better return on the money he has actually paid than A (but note, this 'leveraging' or 'gearing up' effect is the general (and usually intended) effect of borrowing to purchase a successful investment). Assume that following the sale and the repayment of the outstanding mortgage, the profit comes to £40,000: A will receive a 60 per cent share, £24,000, in return for a £10,000 deposit and paying half the mortgage premiums for a year, while B will receive a 40 per cent share, £16,000, for having only paid half the premiums. It may not even be the case that A and B have split the premium payments in half; even if A were to have paid all the premiums, B would acquire the same £16,000 share, since it is his joint mortgage liability that determines his contribution under the PRT (see further Matthews (1994)).

5.14   Since this may appear to lead to an unjust result, the courts have on occasion varied the parties' shares via a constructive trust (see eg *Midland Bank plc v Cooke* (1995)), but it is important to keep these two kinds of trust separate. To determine the shares acquired under a purchase contribution PRT, one must precisely follow the movement of a person's beneficial ownership of money or right to value (eg a sitting tenant's discount, or the right under a mortgage agreement to have money applied to a purchase of a property in one's name) into the purchase price paid for the acquisition of the resulting trustee's title to the property. In *Goodman v Carlton* (2002) the CA denied a resulting trust share arising from the defendant's joint liability under a mortgage loan providing most of the purchase money for a house on the basis that there was never any intention on the part of either her or the other borrower under the mortgage loan that she would ever repay any part of the loan; proof of that joint intention either rebutted the resulting trust in her favour, or the parties' common intention served as a basis for reducing her share to zero. Equitable accounting (4.37) may also be invoked in such a case.

5.15   Occasionally the presumption is used as a bogus problem solver where it has no application. This happened in *Abrahams v Abraham's Trustee in Bankruptcy* (1999). A couple were each members of a syndicate, each paying a pound a week to buy lottery tickets and share the winnings. Following their break-up, the wife continued to contribute two pounds a week, initially out of habit to cover the membership shares of both her and her husband, but later with no such intention. When the syndicate had a big win, the wife took a double share of the winnings in proportion to her contributions, and the husband's trustee in bankruptcy claimed one of the shares. The court decided that since the wife contributed the money, she held the right to the husband's share on resulting trust for herself, he being unable to prove that the wife had intended to pay one of the weekly one-pound contributions for his benefit. But the presumption of resulting trust was simply not relevant here. The question simply could not turn on whether she held her second share *against him* under a purchase contribution PRT, because the money came from her, not him; he contributed nothing to the purchase price of the tickets. The only proper way to have framed the question was: given that the wife was entitled to two shares in the syndicate's winnings, could the husband establish that the wife had gratuitously made contributions for the second share on his behalf? And it was clear that by the time of the win, she had no such intention. The husband, in other words, simply failed to establish an intentional trust on his behalf. Resulting trusts do not come into it. Perhaps the court confused itself because the wife's right to the proceeds was itself equitable (a right to her share of the winnings, legal title to which was held by the 'treasurer' for the syndicate), and so, once ensconced in the consideration of equitable rights, it hastily reached for the presumption. But the husband's claim would have been the same if the wife and husband had regularly purchased second-hand books for their joint collection and, following their break-up, the wife had bought some more, one of which turned out to be a rare first edition worth £500,000. She would not defend her legal ownership of that book by claiming she held it for herself in equity under a purchase contribution PRT. She would just say she bought it for herself, and would put her husband to the strict proof of any supposed trust of the book under which he had an interest.

5.16 Is there a limit to what kind of personalty the purchase contribution or voluntary transfer PRT can apply to? It depends on the broader theory of the resulting trust that one subscribes to. If one accepts that the PRT gives effect to social conventions, then it is not immediately obvious that the PRT should be applicable to any kind of personalty.

5.17 Joint bank accounts are a troubled example of how the PRT has been applied to personalty. Across the Commonwealth, cases have arisen in which the court has to determine entitlement to funds in a joint bank account, where the depositor of the funds dies before the other joint account holder, who is a volunteer (that is, contributes no funds to the account). The contest in these cases is usually between the volunteer on the one hand, who will claim that the deceased depositor intended for him to have the balance of the funds, and personal representatives of the estate of the deceased depositor on the other hand, who will argue that a resulting trust arises. The personal representatives need to argue on the basis of the resulting trust analysis because the volunteer (who survives the depositor) will, on the depositor's death, take *legal* title to the funds by right of survivorship. Therefore, the claim of the estate of the depositor will be that the volunteer, who has legal title to the funds, is not beneficially entitled to them, and holds them on resulting trust.

5.18 When the question is whether the surviving volunteer holds the funds on resulting trust, the way this has been decided is to ascertain the intention of the depositor. The presumptions of resulting trust and advancement may come into play depending on the fact pattern, but these cases are usually decided by making a factual finding of the actual intention of the depositor. In *Pecore v Pecore* (2007), the Canadian Supreme Court found that although the lower court had wrongly applied the presumption of advancement, the depositor had the actual intention to gift away the right of survivorship when the joint account was opened. In *Lim Chen Yeow Kelvin v Goh Chin Peng* (2008), a decision of the Singapore High Court, the evidence was sufficient for the judge to make a factual finding on a balance of probability that the depositor had intended to give the moneys in the joint account to the volunteer. In this instance, the case was decided without the aid of the presumption of resulting trust.

5.19 What role does the bank documentation play in this process? In *Pecore*, it was acknowledged that previous Canadian cases characterised bank documents setting up a joint account as agreements between the account holders and the bank about legal title, not evidence of an agreement between the account holders as to beneficial title. However, *Pecore* took the step of observing that while bank documents 'do not necessarily set out equitable interests in joint accounts, banking documents in modern times may be detailed enough that they provide strong evidence of the intentions of the transferor regarding how the balance in the account should be treated on his or her death'. Similarly, in *Lim Chen Yeow*, it was held that 'bank documents including the survivorship clause governing in part the operation of the joint bank account should simply be regarded as one aspect of the overall evidence in the court's determination of the likely intention of the deceased with respect to the beneficial interest in the moneys that the deceased had contributed to the joint account in his lifetime.'

5.20   This orthodoxy has been disrupted in the recent UKPC decision of *Whitlock v Moree (Bahamas)* (2017). In that case, a majority comprising Lord Briggs, Lady Hale, and Lord Sumption held that there was a clause in the account opening agreement that dealt with the beneficial ownership of the joint account, and that this was determinative of the beneficial ownership of the account. Rejecting the view that account opening agreements only relate to legal title to the funds, they said:

> *[42] ... In the Board's view, there can be no general rule that account agreements are only about legal title, or only about the relationship between the account holders and the bank, rather than their relationship as beneficial owners inter se. In each case it will depend upon the true construction of the relevant agreement.*

5.21   In other words, the Board found that there was no need to investigate the subjective intention of the depositor in a resulting trust analysis, something the Board considered to be part of the 'ordinary equitable toolbox', but not needed in this case:

> *[50] This is, therefore, a case in which the two holders of a joint account have, by an agreement with the bank to which they were both parties, expressly set out above their signature a declaration as to the beneficial interests in that joint account which, on its true construction, provides for any balance on the account to be the beneficial property of the survivor, upon the death of the other account holder, regardless who contributed the money to the credit of the account before that date. It is, in the Board's view, a case in which there was no need to conduct an open-ended factual analysis as to the subjective intention of Mr Lennard, since the account opening forms signed by him and Mr Moree were, by themselves, dispositive of the beneficial interest in that account, subject to any contrary agreement or later variation, and there was none.*

5.22   The majority's view can be read as an avoidance of the vagaries associated with looking for the subjective intention of the depositor, who is often deceased in these cases. The obvious objection, however, to finding that the parties have by agreement expressly set out a declaration as to the beneficial interests, is that many people do not read the agreements they sign, and as a result, have no idea what they are signing. Lord Carnwath (with whom Lord Wilson agreed), had the following to say in dissent:

> *[88] the clause was part of a standard form prepared by the bank, with no input from the customers. The natural assumption is that it was designed to deal with matters in which the bank was concerned, that is in legal not beneficial interests. As Rand J observed in Niles v Lake, it is difficult to see any reason for the bank to use its standard terms to dictate to its customers how to dispose of the beneficial interests in funds held in its accounts. From the customers' point of view the primary purpose of a bank account is as a mechanism to hold and handle money. As I have said, it is not the sort of instrument one would expect to be used to make a very generous gift (in this case a half share in a fund of some $190,000) to a personal friend.*

5.23   A slightly more complicated case arises when the depositor intends that the volunteer should not have the right to withdraw funds for his own use whilst alive, but should take whatever remains in the account if he should survive the depositor. The personal representatives of the deceased are likely to argue that this amounts to a testamentary disposition, wherein the volunteer takes a beneficial interest in the joint account *for the first time* upon the death of the depositor. Being a testamentary disposition, it must be made by will, and since it has not been made by will, it is of no effect. Such a case arose in *Young v Sealey* (1949). Romer J declined to follow a line of authority that would have rendered the depositor's gift to the volunteer a testamentary disposition made otherwise than by will. However, he also found that it was hard to construe the arrangement as an immediate gift of a beneficial interest, seeing as the volunteer had no rights of withdrawal whilst the depositor was still alive, saying that the depositor 'retained the entire beneficial title to the funds' during her life. Ultimately, Romer J did not explain the basis on which he found that the volunteer could take beneficially upon the death of the depositor, other than saying that the point raised has not been conclusively dealt with by any reported English authority, and had been raised but rejected by an appellate Canadian court. A decision of Singapore's Court of Appeal (*Lau Siew Kim v Yeo Guan Chye Terence* (2008)) has construed *Young v Sealey* as a case where:

> [105] ... the intention may be that the contributing party should receive the income from the purchased property during his life – to this extent the resulting trust prevails, but the property should belong to the benefiting party after his death, ie, the resulting trust is rebutted as to the remainder.

5.24 The judge in *Lau Siew Kim* made those observations as part of a larger point about the presumption of resulting trust and the resulting trust itself—that they need not relate to the entire interest in the property. An alternative explanation of *Young v Sealey*'s result is that it has nothing to do with the presumption of resulting trust—what happens here is that the court finds an implied trust of the income for the depositor during his life, but so as to allow the principle of survivorship to operate on his death. Of course, as alluded to in the quotation from *Lau Siew Kim* above, the 'income' of a joint bank account is the right to draw upon and use the funds, which is a slightly different idea from the 'income' of say, real property or shares.

5.25 All of this talk about resulting trusts and joint bank accounts assumes that the doctrine is even conceptually applicable to joint bank accounts. Lau (2018) has argued that it is not—there is no transfer of property to which the presumption of resulting trust can apply. When you open a joint bank account, a chose in action is contractually created. The contract doesn't exist prior to its creation, and so the joint bank account is not something that the depositor can 'take' in the joint names of the parties. Therefore, accounts of how the volunteer receives his legal title to the account that depend on the idea of gift are flawed. Furthermore, one cannot 'give' another the right to enforce a contract short of an assignment. Theories of assignment (see further Lau (2018)) have also been founded to be unconvincing and contrived. The most likely explanation for how volunteers receive their legal title to the joint bank account is that they are contracting parties, pure and simple. If issue is taken with the fact that they have provided no consideration, then the answer is that they have (via their liability under overdraft liabilities) or that no consideration need move from them as it has already moved on their behalf from the depositor (the 'joint promisee' rule). Seen this way, depositors do not 'give' volunteers a legal title to the joint bank account, and one is left to wonder how the resulting trust is to apply at all. However, the courts have not addressed these conceptual problems yet, and we await the day they do with anticipation.

The presumption of resulting trust

5.26   The discerning reader will have noticed that so far I have carefully spoken of a *presumption* of resulting trust, which will determine the result of a dispute between A or B (or their personal representatives) in the *absence of sufficient evidence of the circumstances* of the transfer, or of the contribution to the purchase price of property in the name of another. Take the simple case of A transferring his Rembrandt to B. The way the presumption applies is as follows. In order to get the benefit of the presumption, all A has to do is provide evidence of the transfer itself. If B leads no evidence, then the presumption will determine the case, and the court will hold that B holds the property on bare trust (2.13 et seq) for A. B, of course, will lead contrary evidence if he can. The most obvious way of countering the presumption is if B can show that he *paid* for the Rembrandt, that is bought it from A. If B can show that, say by showing a written contract of sale, then there would be no reason to find that B held the painting on trust for A. Rather, it would establish that A just sold it to B. By leading this evidence, then, B can effectively 'rebut' the presumption of resulting trust. Now you can see why the presumption, though it exists, is in fact rarely determinative of any dispute as to who is entitled to property. In the case of property transactions there is normally sufficient evidence so that the presumption is displaced and no reliance on the presumption is needed. In the example just mentioned, assuming A and B are alive they will give evidence, produce documents and so on, and this evidence will be the basis upon which the court will determine what the nature of the transaction actually is, whether a sale, a transfer on trust, a pawn by A of his Rembrandt to secure the repayment of money he owes B, whatever.

5.27   As we have seen, all A needs to do to establish the presumption is provide evidence of a transfer or of a contribution to the purchase price of property in the name of another. Though it is often put this way, A does not have to show it was a 'gratuitous' transfer or 'gratuitous' contribution. That is, A does not have to prove that B provided no consideration for the transfer or contribution. As Sir Francis Bacon put it, 'the Chancellor thought it more convenient to put the purchaser to prove his consideration, than the feoffor and his heirs to prove the trust; and so made the intendment towards the use, and put the proof upon the purchaser'. The modern cases show the same (see *The Venture* (1908); *Mehta Estate v Mehta Estate* (1993); *Tinsley v Milligan* (1994); see also Penner (2010a)). Of course, judges do refer to the presumption arising in the case of a gratuitous transfer or a transfer without consideration (eg *Re Vandervell (No 2)* (1974) *per* Megarry J), but this is understandable; only an ill-advised claimant would advance the resulting trust argument where the transfer or contribution was obviously to fulfil a contractual obligation, since there the presumption would be trivially easy to rebut; in any case where reliance on the presumption is reasonable the absence of consideration will typically be obvious from the surrounding factual circumstances.

5.28   We must now address a thorny issue which has created a great deal of controversy (Swadling (2008); Chambers (1997, 2006, 2010a); Mee (2010, 2014); Penner (2010a)): what is the 'content' of the presumption of resulting trust, and what evidence is therefore sufficient to 'rebut' it? There are essentially three alternatives: that when the presumption applies, the law presumes (1) that the transferor/contributor A *declared an express trust* over the property now in B's hands (the view defended by Swadling); (2) that A 'had no intention' to benefit the transferee or the recipient of property purchased where A contributed to the purchase price; (the view defended in Chambers (1997, 2006)); and (3) that A intended that B should not take the property for his own benefit/

should hold it for the benefit of A, the view of Mee and your author (of Mee and me, if you like). Chambers (2010a) now endorses a different view, which does not turn on any presumption as to the intention in respect of a trust. We shall discuss this latter view in Chapter 12, because this view presents a rather revolutionary view that resulting trusts are an unrecognised species of 'unjust enrichment' trusts.

5.29   The problem with (1) is that there are too many cases which are inexplicable if this is the presumption. (We shall deal with the modern cases here; for a historical survey, see Mee (2014).)

5.30   Consider *Re Vinogradoff* (1935). Here a resulting trust arose even though an effective declaration of trust was clearly impossible on the facts, since the resulting trustee was four years old, and any express declaration that the property was transferred to her to hold on trust would have been ineffective by virtue of s 20 of the Law of Property Act 1925. Farwell J specifically held that the section 'did not operate to make any difference to the presumption'. While it is easy to criticise the case for relying upon the presumption rather than finding it was rebutted on any realistic appraisal of the facts, if the presumption is what Swadling says it is then the case simply could not have been decided as it was. But what causes the most problems for the first alternative is the court's understanding of the way the presumed resulting trust operated in the run-of-the-mill 'family home' case where a resulting trust arises on the basis of a contribution to the purchase price made by one or both cohabitees. In a number of decisions the CA considered the relevance of the intentions of a contributor to the purchase price of a shared home and in none can it realistically be argued that the presumption which gives rise to a resulting trust was that the contributor made an effective declaration of trust, much less a provable and thus enforceable declaration of trust, ie one in writing so as to comply with s 53(1)(b) of the Law of Property Act 1925.

5.31   In *Springette v Defoe* the CA held that there was no discussion between the parties of any kind, thus no declaration of trust by the contributor. Nevertheless, this did not rebut the presumption of resulting trust, which it would have done if the presumption was that an actual trust was declared. Dillon LJ put the point this way:

> [I]n the absence of an express declaration of the beneficial interests, the court will hold that the joint purchasers hold the property on a resulting trust for themselves in the proportions in which they contributed directly or indirectly to the purchase price.

Nevertheless, Dillon LJ concluded, in terms, that the presumption of resulting trust was not displaced, and therefore the presumption cannot be one of effective declaration of trust, for if that were the presumption, it would clearly have been rebutted on the facts. In *Midland Bank plc v Cooke* the CA similarly held that a wife took a proportionate beneficial interest in the house by way of purchase-contribution resulting trust even though it was accepted both by the trial judge and the CA that there was no expression by the parties to each other in respect of their beneficial interests in the house whatsoever. Both of these cases were considered by the CA in detail and approved in *Oxley v Hiscock* (2004) and the CA's reasoning in *Oxley* was approved in its essentials by the HL in *Stack v Dowden* (2007) (see also *McGrath v Wallis* (1995); *Lavelle v Lavelle* (2004)). It is, of course, open to Swadling to argue that in these cases the court was not really applying the presumption of resulting trust, but rather finding a constructive trust along the lines explained by Baroness Hale in *Stack* (4.28 et seq), where a contribution to the purchase price is regarded simply as a factor in finding a constructive trust. But given that these cases seem to suggest that simply showing that A did not effectively declare a trust does not rebut the presumption strongly suggests that this cannot be the content of the presumption.

5.32   Swadling may have a riposte (set out in personal conversation with the author). Both (1) and (3) accept that the presumption refers to the transferor or contributor's *intentions*. So (1) and (3) both accept that PRT's are intentional trusts in that sense. Given that, one might argue that in the recent cases, and the historical cases, A 'expressed' his intentions, ie declared his intentions, *by his conduct* given the background circumstances, common understandings, and context. If this is correct, there would be no real difference between alternatives (1) and (3).

5.33   (3) says that the presumption is that A had a positive intention that B should not treat the property received (or the entirety of it if A contributed part of the purchase price) as beneficially his own. This is essentially an intention that B should hold the property on trust for A. (A does not have to know what a trust is in legal terms to have this intention (7.4)—he just has to intend that B does not take the property free to deal with it as his own.) (2) takes a 'negative' formulation of this sort of intention: it says the presumption is that A had no intention to benefit B. The question posed by these different formulations is whether they are really any different in substance. What, in practical terms, is the difference between the statement 'Frank did not intend Margo to have the benefit of the property he transferred to her' and 'Frank intended to retain the benefit of the property he transferred to Margo, ie Frank transferred it to Margo intending that she would hold it for him'. If a person transfers property he must necessarily have intentions as to who is to benefit from the property transferred. And, if he has those intentions, why on earth should the court, in the absence of evidence, act on a presumption as to what was absent from his mind ('no intention to benefit Margo'), rather than what was positively there (Frank's intention to benefit himself)? This sort of consideration favours the positive intention formulation in (3). The reason why one might prefer (2), nevertheless, is that it understands the presumption to apply in a fraction of cases, such as where the transferor/contributor enters the transaction without actually settling their own intentions, as in *Dullow v Dullow* (1985) where the PRT plaintiff was basically confused about what she thought her property transaction amounted to. Our concern in such a case is with what A failed to do, or at least failed to do in the sense that there is insufficient evidence of what he did for a court to give effect to his positive intentions. The idea is that upon proof of the transfer or contribution B is presumed not to take beneficially, and in keeping with the idea underlying the ART, in such a case A, having failed effectively to dispose of the beneficial interest under this trust, B must hold the property for his benefit.

5.34   If (2) is the correct formulation, it will, of course, encompass all those cases covered by (3). But as Mee (2014) shows in detail, the courts regularly employ variants of both (2) and (3) without seeing any difference between them. The basic judicial thought seems to work like this (see also 5.69 with respect to this kind of thinking in respect of ARTs): here is a transaction by A in which B receives title to property from A, or purchased by A. The presumption is that A intended to keep or retain the beneficial interest (recall the basic feoffment to uses (5.1), that is, that B was to receive just the 'paper' title). This brings (2) and (3) together in the sense that intending to keep the beneficial interest by conferring a mere paper title is the same thing as not intending a gift/intending a trust. Mee (2014, 102–3) puts the point this way:

> [I]t is misconceived to regard the statements in the case law as reflecting two competing paradigms as to the fact being presumed. Because the courts are making a choice between the two categories of 'gift' and 'trust', a conclusion that the transferor did not intend a gift (or, to use the language of retention, did not intend to pass the beneficial interest to the transferee) is equivalent to a conclusion that the transferor did intend to create a trust . . . [T]he equivalence of the positive and negative formulations explains why the courts appear to vacillate between them.

5.35 Where the presumption is not rebutted, equity regards the beneficial interest as not having moved from A to B. As we have seen, it is a mistake to confuse the idea of a beneficial interest with an equitable interest. (2.17 – 2.18 , 2.39 , 5.3). A retains the same benefit as before, though now it is just secured via his equitable title, rather than through his prior outright legal title. A beneficial interest is not the same as a legal or equitable interest, and so the retention idea— did A intend to keep the beneficial interest or give it to B—is a perfectly sensible way of framing the presumption, the presumption of resulting trust on this formulation being that A intended to retain or keep the beneficial interest.

5.36 The 'retention' model of presumed resulting trusts has been criticised. Chambers (1997), Swadling (2008), and Mee (2017) all reject it. Mee (2017), 6–7, shows that, historically, the word 'use' had two meanings, one of which was equivalent to the notion of beneficial—not equitable—interest. This 'use' was retained by A when she transferred his property to B on bare trust, which is what a presumed resulting trust is. But Mee (2017), 9, finds this idea doctrinally unsatisfying:

> [T]he interest which the claimant holds under a resulting trust is not, strictly speaking, something that he or she previously held. Before the creation of the resulting trust, he or she held the legal title to the property, giving him or her inter alia the right to sue any-one who interferes with the property and to transfer the property to whomever he or she chooses. After the creation of the resulting trust, he or she lost these rights but gained instead inter alia the right to insist that the trustee should sue anyone who interferes with the property and to compel the trustee to transfer the property to whomever the claimant chooses.[my emphasis] Notwithstanding the rhetoric of retention, the rights that the claimant holds under the resulting trust are of a different nature to, and not 'part of', the legal title that he or she held before.

5.37 The bold portions of this passage are relevantly false. As we have seen with the historic situation of the presumed resulting trust, A never gives up possession of the property to B, giving B only a paper title. In such a case A retains the right to sue trespassers simply in virtue of her con-tinuing possession. As regards the power to transfer title, B must exercise this only in the way A directs. Although operating through B in this way may be inconvenient, on what basis can it be said that A has lost the power to transfer the title? What has A lost, and to whom has it gone? It certainly has not gone to B, who has no right to exercise the powers of title for his own benefit.

5.38 For another example, consider the case of a resulting trust of company shares that A trans-ferred to B. True, A does not directly receive any dividends from the company, nor is she allowed to vote the shares in a general meeting of shareholders. But B is obliged to transfer the dividends to A and vote the shares as A directs. Though A's *means* to get the benefit of the shares, now via a trust, are different than her means before the transfer, how has the transfer diminished her entitlement to get all the benefit of the shares that there is?

5.39 Mee is, however, on much firmer ground when we consider the purchase contribution resulting trust, for in these cases it is clear that A does not retain the interest she had before. When A contributes 50 per cent of the purchase price of land, title to which is put in B's name, A does not 'retain' the same beneficial interest she had before. Prior to the transaction, A had a right to her money, afterwards, to a equitable half-share in the title to a house. At this point, the 'reten-tion' idea must be extended, but the question is whether it is extended in a bad way. As we have seen (2.75 et seq), the law of tracing works on the basis that A's rights to one title, say to cash, can be realised by exchanging it for something else, say a car. The car is the 'exchange product' of the cash, and it belongs to A because it was A's title to the cash that was used to buy the car. Thus, A's beneficial interest in the cash, her title to the cash, is now, via the exchange, her beneficial interest in, her title to, the car. The beneficial interest in these several rights never leaves A. They never become an interest of B's. So even in the case of the purchase contribution resulting trust, the retention model holds good in the sense that the entire benefit of the transaction as regards A's actual contribution, whether 100 per cent, 50 per cent, whatever, is retained by her, even though the beneficial interest is not the beneficial interest with which A began.

5.40   Lord Millett has accepted the alternative (2) 'no intention to benefit' formulation both in his extrajudicial writing (Millett (1998a, 2000, 2005)) and in *Air Jamaica v Charlton* (1999) and *Twinsectra v Yardley* (2002).

5.41   Under the present law, the presumption will be rebutted by actual evidence of any intention which is inconsistent with the presumption, for example, that A paid the money to B to discharge a contractual obligation (*Westdeutsche Landesbank* (1996)) even if, as a matter of fact, he had no contractual obligation to discharge; that A made an express declaration of trust which determines the beneficial interests (*Pettitt v Pettitt* (1970) *per* Lord Upjohn; *Goodman v Gallant* (1986)); or, in the case of purchase money contribution, that A loaned the money to B (*Re Sharpe* (1980); *Levi v Levi* (2008)).

The presumption of advancement

5.42   The presumption does not operate in all cases of transfers or contributions to purchases in another's name. As Freud might have said, sometimes a gift is just a gift. In these circumstances, it is said that a 'presumption of advancement' or a presumption of gift operates. Under current English law (but see 5.48), the circumstances are where A gratuitously transfers property to, or contributes money to property put in the name of, his wife or fiancée (*Moate v Moate* (1948)) or his child or to someone to whom he stands *in loco parentis*, ie someone for whom he feels an obligation to provide as would a parent (*Re Paradise Motor Co Ltd* (1968)). There is no presumption of advancement in the case of a gift from mother to child (*Sekhon v Alissa* (1989)) unless the mother (eg as a widow) stands *in loco parentis* to the child (*Crown Prosecution Service v Malik* (2003)). However, the terminology 'presumption' of advancement may be misleading:

> Though normally referred to as a presumption of advancement it is no more than a circumstance of evidence which may rebut the presumption of resulting trust. [Pettitt (1970) per Lord Upjohn]

5.43   In other words, if the recipient is a man's wife or child, this fact counts as evidence that may be, and normally is, sufficient evidence to meet the evidentiary hurdle posed by the presumption of resulting trust. In view of that, in these cases if the father wishes to show that the property was not a gift but was intended to be held on trust, then it will be necessary for him to lead evidence that establishes this trust. According to this view, then, the presumption of advancement works on the basis of a standard inference from the facts where it applies; the courts, without any more evidence before them, will infer that the man is making a gift. Seen in this way, the presumption of advancement is as much an evidentiary presumption as is the presumption of resulting trust.

5.44　However, there are two ways of understanding the relationship between the presumptions. On the first, the presumption of advancement is both historically and conceptually dependent upon the existence of the presumption of resulting trust; it serves as a 'second-step' exception to the general presumption of resulting trust which *first* applies to *any* case where contributions are made to a purchase in the name of another. The importance of conceiving the relationship between the presumptions in this way is as follows. Recall again the formalities issue (5.12). Normally, trusts of land must be evidenced in writing to be enforceable, but there is a statutory exception for resulting (and constructive) trusts. Therefore, by tagging the presumption of advancement on to the presumption of resulting trust as a second-order presumption, the reasoning can proceed in this fashion: where the father leads evidence to overcome the presumption of advancement, the presumption of resulting trust, which applied but whose operation was suspended while the presumption of advancement operated, now falls back into place. He may then simply rely upon the fact that he contributed to the purchase price to establish his beneficial ownership share under a *resulting* trust, and therefore avoid the disabling effect of the formality statute.

5.45　The other way of regarding the presumption of advancement is this: all the 'presumption of advancement' means is that there is no presumption of resulting trust in cases where it applies. On this view, there are certain cases where contribution to the purchase in the name of another attracts the presumption of resulting trust, and others where it does not. On this understanding, where a father leads evidence to 'rebut' the presumption of advancement, he has more difficulty avoiding the effect of the formality statute. Because no presumptions operate at all, what the father does when he leads evidence of the trust is to try to establish an *express*, albeit informal, trust. And the statutory formality requirements would prevent his establishing his interest under such a trust, or at least that would be the starting point (5.12, 6.6 et seq). However, the father is not sunk yet; although he cannot establish this informal trust, he may be able to succeed by establishing that his share is validly held under a *constructive* trust. To establish a constructive trust further facts must be proven; roughly, that the father relied to his detriment on the trust and so therefore it would be fraudulent or unconscionable for the legal title holder to refuse to honour the trust (4.22 et seq).

5.46　Which of these views is right is actually rather difficult to determine, because having paid over his contribution to the purchase price on the understanding that he would acquire an ownership share in it is probably the best sort of evidence that one relied to one's detriment on the understanding (one paid over real money—is there any more obvious detriment than that?). In other words, given the sort of facts these cases involve, the result from applying the constructive trust analysis would almost always mimic the result of applying the resulting trust analysis. This might explain, in part, the occasional statements by judges that it is unnecessary to distinguish between resulting and constructive trusts in deciding certain cases of this kind (eg Lord Diplock in *Gissing v Gissing* (1971)). On the other hand, we can be certain that a court is applying a constructive trust analysis wherever the ownership shares the court declares are *not* in proportion to the contributions to the purchase price, or the court considers whether proportionate shares actually reflect the intentions of the parties; in those cases the court must be assuming that, or considering whether, the parties did not intend a proportionate shares trust, and a resulting trust can only be a proportionate shares trust. Once it has moved beyond the straightforward assignment of interests in proportionate shares, the court is in the world of constructive trusts, giving effect to the actual, *informal* expressions of the parties' intentions.

5.47 Founding an evidentiary inference on the theory that, in general, a husband intends to make gifts to his wife but not vice versa, and that, in general, fathers, but not mothers, intend gifts to their children, today seems exorbitantly sexist (although the courts in *Bennet v Bennet* (1879) and *Crown Prosecution Service v Malik* (2003) did hold it was easier to prove that a mother intended a gift than that a stranger did, ie that the presumption of resulting trust imposed an even weaker evidential burden in her case), but this all depends on what the rationale for the presumption is meant to be. In a thorough review of the history of the presumption, Glister (2010a) shows that there have been a number of different reasons given for it, and these would lead to applying the presumption differently. For example, if the presumption reflects a moral or legal duty to provide for a child or a spouse, historically this would make sense of the fact that fathers and husbands but not mothers and wives fall within the presumption of advancement, given the historical distribution of assets within the family. On the other hand, if the presumption is supposed to reflect family affection of one member for another, then clearly wives and mothers love their husbands and children and would make gifts to them just as much as fathers do and would as regards their wives and children. In *Pettitt* a majority of their Lordships clearly felt the presumption of advancement was a creature of the nineteenth century that was largely out of date. (A similar opinion was recently voiced by Lord Walker and Baroness Hale in *Jones v Kernott* (2011).) Lord Upjohn, while willing to apply the presumption, said:

> These presumptions or circumstances of evidence are readily rebutted by comparatively slight evidence.

While the opinions in *Pettitt* might have suggested the judicial reform or even abolition of the presumptions of advancement, it has not happened (in England) yet, though Lord Neuberger in *Laskar v Laskar* (2008) suggested that the presumption might apply between a mother and daughter, and in the PC decision in *Antoni v Antoni* (2007) Lord Scott said that the presumption applies between 'parent' and child. In Australia the presumption now applies equally to gifts from mother to child (*Nelson v Nelson* (1995)), but has not been extended to *de facto* relationships (*Ryan v Ryan* (2012)). The Supreme Court of Canada decided in *Pecore v Pecore* (2007) that the presumption of advancement would apply only between a parent (of either sex) and a *minor* child or children.

5.48 Section 199(1) of the Equality Act 2010 provides:

> 199 *Abolition of presumption of advancement*
>
> (1) The presumption of advancement (by which, for example, a husband is presumed to be making a gift to his wife if he transfers property to her, or purchases property in her name) is abolished.

It is not clear whether the parenthetical examples are intended to restrict the abolition to the presumption as it applies between wives and husbands only, or whether the presumption is abolished in all other cases (eg of a transfer from father to child). Section 199(2)(a) provides that the presumption will remain in cases involving things done before the commencement of the section, which will mean that the preceding law will be relevant for many years after the coming into force of the section. (Glister (2010b) is a scathing analysis of the legislative reasoning lying behind the provision and its problematic aspects, and repays reading in full.) One obvious criticism is simply that by abolishing the presumption of advancement, the presumption of resulting trust will now operate in these cases. The law will thus be taking a step backward into unreality: is it really to be presumed nowadays, where the evidence is unsatisfactory, that interfamilial transfers are transfers *on trust*? This is the sort of oddball thinking that would prefer the result in *Re Vinogradoff* to that in *Fowkes v Pascoe* (5.9, 5.10). At the time of writing the provision has not been brought into force.

5.49   In *McGrath v Wallis* (1995), the weak presumption of advancement of a share in a family house between father and son who both contributed to the purchase price of a house in the son's name was rebutted and a trust in favour of a father was established, on the basis, first, that putting the house in the son's name alone could be explained because it allowed the purchase to be assisted with a mortgage; secondly, that at one stage a declaration of trust formally expressing the father's and son's ownership shares in proportion to their contributions was drawn up by the father's solicitors, and although it was never executed there was no evidence that he had later given his solicitors contrary instructions; and, finally, as the father was only 63 years old and in good health, there was no obvious reason to make a gift to his son of an 80 per cent share in the house where he would himself live. However, once the court determined that the father had not intended a gift, it did not declare that the property was held on trust by the son for himself and his father in shares proportionate to their contribution to the purchase price; it did not, in other words, declare a purchase contribution PRT. Rather, the court looked at the overall intentions of the parties as to what their respective shares should be, and declared a trust in those proportions (as it happened, these intentions did coincide with the shares they would have received under a straight purchase contribution PRT, but that is not the point). What this shows is that, in cases of PRTs, the evidence led may not only confirm or upset the presumptions of resulting trust or advancement, but may be sufficient for the court to look more closely at the parties' actual intentions and find their respective interests to be determined by a constructive trust.

Automatic resulting trusts (ARTs)

The relevance of intentions to ARTs

5.50   In *Re Vandervell (No 2)* (1974) Megarry J stated that ARTs arose by operation of law independently of the settlor's intention. Lord Browne-Wilkinson doubted this in *Westdeutsche Landesbank Girozentrale v Islington London Borough Council* (1996):

> *Megarry J . . . suggests that [such a trust] does not depend on intention but operates automatically. I am not convinced this is right. If the settlor has expressly, or by necessary implication, abandoned any beneficial interest in the trust property, there is in my view no resulting trust; the undisposed-of equitable interest vests in the Crown as bona vacantia [ie goods without an owner] . . .*

5.51   There are two ways of understanding this. The first is that, despite appearances, in the vast majority of cases where resulting trusts arise on the failure of an express trust to dispose in whole or in part of the beneficial interest in the trust property, the court really does inquire into and assess whether the settlor intended a resulting trust to arise, and finds that he did. This seems fanciful, since courts appear not to make any such inquiry and it seems unlikely that settlors have any actual intentions in this regard at all. If they did, one presumes that they would express them. On the other hand, Lord Browne-Wilkinson may only be saying that despite the normal, 'intention-independent', operation of the resulting trust in these circumstances, there are cases where (1) the facts show that the settlor did actually intend to abandon any interest in the trust property if the trust failed, and (2) he did not *express* this intention *as a term* of the trust he created, ie he did not declare as he did the other terms of the trust that if the trust failed in whole or in part that he abandoned his interest, but (3), nevertheless, because of these 'collateral' intentions to abandon, the court treats the undisposed of trust property as *bona vacantia*. This does not upset Megarry J's characterisation, but only modifies it in a very minor way as follows: the ART is not wholly 'intention-independent' in that it may be *displaced* by a settlor's actual intentions to abandon to the Crown all interest in the trust property that might otherwise result to him. This surely occurs in a vanishingly small fraction of trusts, and it is not clear that there have ever been any cases of this kind (9.82–9.95).

5.52   The complicated way in which an ART can arise is shown by the attempt of a rich industrialist, one Guy Anthony Vandervell, to endow a chair of pharmacology in the Royal College of Surgeons. The facts of the case are somewhat convoluted, but the essential points are clear enough. There were three players: Vandervell himself, who controlled and owned most of the shares of a private engineering company he had founded; the Royal College of Surgeons (RCS); and Vandervell Trustees Ltd (the trust company), a company that administered two separate trusts, one for Vandervell's children, and one a retirement, profit-sharing, and savings fund trust for Vandervell's employees. The plan to endow the chair in the RCS (as devised by Vandervell's accountant to avoid tax) was to get shares of Vandervell's company into the hands of the RCS, and then Vandervell, using his control over his company, would have the company declare dividends on the shares sufficient to fund the chair; as part of the scheme, the RCS would grant an option to the trust company to purchase the shares, so that once the dividends were paid the shares could be retrieved from the RCS.

5.53   Vandervell duly instructed a bank that held some of the company shares on bare trust for him to transfer the shares to the RCS, and RCS in turn granted an option to purchase the shares for £5,000 to the trust company. The evidence was fragmentary, but at a minimum it was clear that the option was not to be granted to Vandervell himself because he did not want the beneficial ownership of the shares, which would increase his tax liability. Dividends sufficient to fund the chair were declared. In *Vandervell v IRC* (1967) a majority in the HL decided that because the option was essentially an interest in the shares that Vandervell had himself created by the arrangement, he had a beneficial interest in it; therefore, although the option was granted to the trust company, it held the option on resulting trust for Vandervell. Since he held the beneficial interest in the option under a resulting trust, he had retained a beneficial interest in the shares, because by exercising the option he could regain ownership of them. So although the RCS clearly had a beneficial interest in the shares, so did Vandervell under the option. Under the rules of taxation prevailing at the time, this beneficial interest in the shares entitled the Inland Revenue to charge Vandervell large amounts of surtax on the dividends; so, as it turned out, the grant of the option proved hugely costly to him.

5.54   Given the relative simplicity of the facts, it is startling how difficult the different judges in the CA and the HL found it to characterise adequately the transaction in which the RCS received the shares and granted the option to the trust company in a way that explains their finding a resulting trust to Vandervell. In *Re Vandervell (No 2)* (1974), where he closely analysed *Vandervell v IRC*, Megarry J gives the gist of what the judges appeared to think:

> [Quite] apart from mechanism or motive, there is the fact, of paramount importance
> in relation to any concept of resulting or implied trust, that it was Mr. Vandervell alone

who was providing the property in question. The option was an option over shares of which Mr. Vandervell was the sole beneficial owner. If Mr. Vandervell disposed of those shares in such a way that he brought about the vesting of a major benefit in the college and a minor benefit in the defendant company, then it seems to me that Mr. Vandervell was providing both those benefits, even if his provision of the minor benefit was indirect and not made under compulsion.

5.55   Now, when a judge in a trust case says things like 'Quite apart from mechanism or motive', start to worry, because if the law of trusts is about anything, it is about mechanism and motive—in other words, it concerns whether or not individuals have effectively exercised various powers of ownership, and the consequences of having done so or having failed to do so. That is what this case concerned, and so mechanism and motive are all-important. And, perhaps surprisingly, (at least) five legal mechanisms might account for the transaction in *Vandervell*:

(1) There were two entirely separate gratuitous transactions—Vandervell gave the RCS some shares, and RCS gratuitously granted the trust company an option.

(2) Vandervell made a binding contract with the RCS.

(3) Vandervell made a gift of the shares with a 'legal condition'.

(4) Vandervell made a gift of the shares upon an equitable condition.

(5) Vandervell transferred the shares to the RCS on trust to (a) set up a chair in pharmacology and (b) grant an option to the trust company.

5.56   We can dismiss (1) from the outset. While Vandervell certainly had an independent reason to grant the RCS the shares—it was how he intended to endow the chair—the RCS had no independent reason to give the trust company anything; furthermore as a charity, the RCS could not just give rights to its property away; thus (1) is simply implausible on the facts. Option (2) is more likely: the contract would be one whereby, in return for instructing his bank to transfer the legal title to the shares it held on bare trust for him to the RCS and subsequently declaring dividends upon them, the RCS would use the dividends to found a chair of pharmacology in Vandervell's name, and grant the option to the trust company. Options (3) and (4) are also possible: Vandervell made a gift of the shares (again by instructing his bank to transfer the legal title of the shares to the RCS) on condition the option was granted to the trust company. This condition would more likely be regarded as equitable (4) than legal (3). While conditional gifts of land were both perfectly valid at law and common prior to 1926, no similar facility for conditional legal gifts of personalty was ever developed (see Bell (1989), at 225–26). To the extent that a gift could be made 'conditional' at law, the 'condition' did not attach to the *property*, but was treated as a conditional *obligation* on the donee. Thus a gift of personalty upon a condition that failed neither revived the donor's title in the property nor gave him any other proprietary right in it (eg a right to repossess akin to a 'right to re-enter' land). Rather, upon failure of the condition the donee would have a personal restitutionary obligation to repay the value of the gift, so that he would not be unjustly enriched (*Re Garnett* (1905)). However, conditional gifts of any kind of property are perfectly valid in equity (3.35). Finally, (5) is also possible. Vandervell instructed the bank to transfer the shares to the RCS, the RCS agreeing to hold them on a trust that had two main terms: to found a chair in pharmacology with any dividends received and to grant an option to the trust company.

5.57   Interpreting the transaction as (3) is probably unsustainable. If the RCS were to have breached the condition to grant the option, they would have been liable only to repay the value of the shares to Vandervell because, as just mentioned, the restitutionary obligation to repay the value would be personal, and would not require the return of the shares. Since it was clear that Vandervell wanted to have the shares themselves in the hands of the trustee company (in order to facilitate a possible public flotation of the company), it seems implausible that he would have entered into a transaction where if things were to go wrong he would have no right to the return of the shares, but only a money payment for a remedy.

5.58   Options (2), (4), and (5) are all plausible, because if the RCS failed to grant the option in each of these cases, Vandervell could enforce their obligation and get the shares into the hands of the trust company. On (2), Vandervell would sue for breach of contract. Now, as stated, the grant was to be to the trust company, not Vandervell himself, and Vandervell sought no benefit from the shares. The general rule of the law of contract is that a person is only allowed damages to compensate him for his own loss, not for the losses suffered by any third party (here, the trust company to whom the option was to be granted), and so Vandervell would himself have suffered no loss under the contract, and so he would only be awarded nominal damages in an action brought against the RCS. However, because the contract involved unique property, private company shares, the court would award specific performance (4.6), and Vandervell could get specific performance so that the RCS would have to grant the option to the trust company, even though the grant was not to Vandervell's personal benefit (*Beswick v Beswick* (1968); 4.6 et seq). The problem with (2) is simply that the transaction does not look particularly like a contract. The 'consideration' that the RCS would provide would be the funding of the chair in Vandervell's name, but that seems a rather strained interpretation. The RCS clearly wanted the chair as much as Vandervell, and so the whole thing looks much more like a gift than an enforceable contract.

5.59   There is a difficulty interpreting the transaction as (4) as well. While under (4), the RCS's failure to meet the condition by granting the option would result in the retrieval of the shares, the problem is that on the failure of the condition the shares would revert in equity to the transferor, ie to the bank to hold once again on bare trust for Vandervell; again, since Vandervell intended to get the shares into the hands of the trust company, this seems an inappropriate mechanism in the circumstances. (The condition *could* have been framed such that, on failure of the RCS to grant the option, it would then hold the shares on trust for the trust company, ie so the shares would not revert to the transferor, but that seems overly convoluted, and essentially equivalent to (5).)

5.60   Option (5) probably best captures the transaction, ie that Vandervell had the legal title of the shares transferred to the RCS on trust (a) to hold any dividends on trust to found the chair, and (b) to grant an option to the trust company to purchase them. Upon granting the option, the RCS then held the shares either absolutely (subject of course to the option), or on charitable trust to further fund the chair should the option not be exercised.

5.61   This examination of the possible mechanisms for the transaction is not intended to be a mere exercise (or pointless romp) in legal technicalities. It may not be easy to adequately crystallise Vandervell's motives and acts into a workable legal transaction, but it is necessary to do so, because his motives and acts *did have legal consequences*, so *some* legal mechanism achieving those consequences must be discerned, or the case is simply unexplained.

5.62   Now, here's the crucial point that arises from this examination. On either (2) or (4) or (5), using strict 'follow the money' PRT principles, Vandervell gave value to the RCS to endow the trust company with a valuable right, the option—he either purchased it for the trust company under the contract (2), or made it an equitable condition in its favour under the grant (4), or gave it to the trust company under a trust (5)—and in the absence of any evidence of Vandervell's actual intentions the trust company would hold that option on a purchase contribution PRT for him. In other words, Vandervell provided value in the form of shares to the RCS and 'purchased', either by way of contract, equitable condition, or trust, the grant of the option to the trust company.

5.63   There was, however, evidence of Vandervell's intentions to displace the PRT. Apparently, the main rationale for requiring the RCS to grant the option was simply to ensure that the shares could be retrieved from the RCS to forestall problems in pursuing a public flotation of Vandervell's company. It was not clear that Vandervell entertained any specific intentions as to who should have the beneficial interest in the option the trustee company was to acquire, except that he did not want to retain or reacquire any interest for himself in the shares. Save for Lords Reid and Donovan, all the judges found it inconceivable that Vandervell intended the trust company to take the option beneficially (and quite right too: unless specified as a beneficiary, a person taking property as a trustee is never beneficially entitled to it (2.8 et seq))—in other words, he must have intended that the trust company was to hold the option on trust for somebody. But what trust? The majority found that the intended trust was simply too vague and undefined to be valid. Now, the court might appear a wee bit mean in its unwillingness to draw inferences from the surrounding circumstances. Both the CA and Lords Upjohn and Donovan considered the possibility that the option was transferred upon trust for the children's or employees' trust in such proportions as the settlor or the trustee company might declare, in other words a discretionary trust.

5.64   The result, then, was an ART. Vandervell had an intention to create a trust for someone else, specifically *not himself* as provider of the value, but it was an imprecise trust on the court's view—to hold the property for, well, someone, but at any rate not for himself. This express trust failed, since the objects (3.7) were not sufficiently 'certain', ie specified (7.2, 7.49 et seq), and therefore the beneficial interest resulted to Vandervell under an ART. Most ARTs arise when the settlor transfers property directly to the trustee on trusts that fail to dispose of the beneficial interest, not in the rather complicated way in which Vandervell provided the option for the trust company. Because of that, the judgments in the HL can be confusing, and Megarry J's review of them in his judgment in *Re Vandervell (No 2)*, while somewhat tedious, is preferable.

5.65   One rule of law that comes out clearly in *Vandervell v IRC* is that simply having a positive intention not to retain any beneficial ownership in property transferred to another, as Vandervell had, will not prevent the transferor from ending up with the beneficial title under an ART, since if the transferor not only has that intention but has also the intention that the transferee is to hold on trust, and the trust fails, then the only possible result is an undefined express trust, which leads to an ART (see also *Re Flower's Settlement Trusts* (1957)). As Plowman J said in *Vandervell* at first instance:

> As I see it, a man does not cease to own property simply by saying 'I don't want it'. If he tries to give it away the question must always be, has he succeeded in doing so or not?

This was cited with approval by Lord Upjohn in the HL's decision and by Lord Millett giving the advice of the PC in *Air Jamaica Ltd v Charlton* (1999).

Why do ARTs arise?

5.66   Before pursuing this question, it should be pointed out that we could abolish PRTs tomorrow, in essence leaving any person who transferred property to another or purchased property in the name of another to prove on the evidence any trust he intended to create, without the benefit of any presumption. That might be a good or bad move, but it would be perfectly feasible in law as the new rule. But the situation cannot be the same with ARTs. The law must give some answer to the case where A transfers property to B on express trust and the trusts declared fail to exhaust the benefit of the property transferred. Perhaps we could stick with the present position, where the undisposed of property results to A; alternatively, we could choose that the property goes to the crown as bona vacantia (goods without an owner); or we could say the trustee can keep it. But we cannot just leave the beneficial interest in the property 'up in the air'.

5.67 As we have just seen (5.65), the traditional reason why the ART is seen to arise is that 'what the settlor fails to give away, he keeps', and seems best to be explained as the obvious 'implied rule' which deals with cases where a settlor fails to dispose of the entire beneficial interest in property he transfers on trust (Millett (2005); Mee (2010)).

5.68 This rationale for the ART is found throughout its history. Mee (2010) shows that this understanding of the matter was crucial for the application of certain laws of succession at the time, and so as a matter of history the 'retention' model of the ART best captures the centuries-long understanding of the judges which, as we have seen, continues to this day.

5.69 Yet, as we have also already discussed, the 'retention' model of the resulting trust in the case of PRTs has been doubted (5.36). Whatever force the criticism has in the case of PRTs, it seems especially misplaced in the case of ARTs. As we have seen (5.5), originally the most common way of disposing of assets via the use was first to transfer the title to the property to the feoffee to use, and only then declare intentions as to the beneficial interests in the property. Thus, at the outset, when an intending settlor's disposition failed, it really did just fail, leaving him exactly as he was before. The equitable interests he did not dispose of, he just retained. The modern rule concerning dispositions that fail at the outset—where A transfers property to B on trust for C where the trust for C fails because, for instance, C, unbeknownst to A, has died, B will hold the property on ART for A—just seems like a sensible extension of the rule, which now forms one of the 'implied terms' which go with transferring property on trust, ie that any beneficial interest in the property one fails to dispose of is held on trust for one (see Mee (2017), 33–35). Consider this: to undertake a trust obligation is not: 'I undertake to hold these assets just in so far as you have effectively disposed of the entire interest in them, and anything not so disposed of belongs to me.' Any trustee who spelled this out as his 'trustee undertaking' to a would-be settlor (think in particular of professional trust companies) would never be accepted as a trustee, and so it would be fanciful to build a theory of ARTs on such a misunderstanding. Another way of putting the same point is that on the equitable understanding of what it means to undertake to receive property on trust, the trustee is not a 'residual claimant' (2.93). Unless expressly made a beneficiary, a trustee is not entitled to any benefit of the trust assets. On this view, the only possible residual claimant, as when a gift on trust fails, is the settlor.

Resulting trusteeship

5.70 Both the PRT and the ART are bare trusts, so the legal title holder has essentially only one duty: to hold the property for the resulting beneficiary (or his successors). This is obvious in the case of the ART. In the case of the PRT this is so because the presumption only goes so far as to presume the location of the beneficial interest—no further trust terms are presumed. Any further terms of an intentional trust must be proved without the benefit of the presumption. If they are, the trust will not properly be called a PRT, because the proof of that more complex trust will amount to the proof of an express trust.

FURTHER READING

Birks (1996b)

Chambers (1997, especially ch 1, and 2006, 2009, 2010a)

Glister (2010a, 2010b)

Matthews (1994)

Mee (2010, 2014, 2017)

Millett (1998b, 2005)

Penner (2009b, 2010a)

Swadling (1996a, 2008)

Must-read cases: *Vandervell v IRC* (1966); *Re Vandervell (No 2)* (1974); *Pettitt v Pettitt* (1971); *Cowcher v Cowcher* (1971); *Westdeutsche Landesbank v Islington London Borough Council* (1996); *Air Jamaica v Charlton* (1999)

SELF-TEST QUESTIONS

1. What are 'presumed resulting trusts' (PRTs) and 'automatic resulting trusts' (ARTs), and what distinguishes them?

2. 'The automatic resulting trust is a necessary feature of any legal system that recognises transfers of property on trust, but the recognition of presumed intention resulting trusts is inessential, and in the case of English law the presumed intention resulting trust has outlived any possible usefulness it might once have had and should be abolished.' Discuss.

3. What distinguishes 'voluntary transfer' and 'purchase contribution' PRTs?

4. What intention(s) of the voluntary transferor or contributor must be proved for a PRT to arise? How do these intentions relate to the case where the presumption of advancement applies?

5. On what basis to ARTs arise, and of what relevance is the settlor's intention?

Formalities and secret trusts

SUMMARY

The character and purpose of formalities
Declarations of trusts in land: Law of Property Act 1925, s 53(1)(b)
The doctrine of *Rochefoucauld v Boustead*
Disposition of subsisting equitable interests: Law of Property Act 1925, s 53(1)(c)
Testamentary trusts: Wills Act 1837, s 9
Informal testamentary trusts: secret and half-secret trusts

The character and purpose of formalities

6.1 The law sometimes imposes a requirement on the *form* of legal transactions before it will regard those transactions as valid, or provable, or enforceable in court, typically a requirement that the transaction be made or recorded in writing. Now consider the phrase 'valid, provable, or enforceable in court': it is important to see that different formalities provisions can have very different effects. As we shall see, s 53(1)(c) of the Law of Property Act 1925 provides that if an assignment of an equitable interest is not *made* in writing, it is void. This is the most stringent form of writing requirement; if the transaction is not made in writing, in the eyes of the law it did not occur at all. The next most stringent provision prevents the proof of a transaction unless there is written evidence of it. Section 53(1)(b) is a provision of this kind; it provides that a declaration of trust of land cannot be proved without written evidence. An oral declaration of a trust of land is not invalid, but merely cannot be proved in court. As we will see, this sort of provision gives rise to certain logical difficulties (6.10). Finally, the least stringent sort of provision merely provides that an obligation created by a transaction cannot be enforced in a court of law unless there is written evidence. This was the way the old formality requirement under s 40(1) of the Law of Property Act 1925 worked: the obligations under a contract for the sale of land could not be *enforced* unless there was a written note or memorandum of the contract signed by the party against whom the contract was being enforced. But an oral contract could still be proved in court so long as it was not being proved in order to enforce the obligations under it. So, for example, a person could prove a completed oral contract of sale of land in order to show that he was a bona fide purchaser of it (2.61 et seq). Section 40 has now been replaced by s 2 of the Law of Property (Miscellaneous Provisions) Act 1989, which imposes a 'validity' formality on contracts for the sale of land; now, a contract for the sale of land must be *made* in writing, otherwise it is void. The law may impose formalities for different purposes, but three are of particular relevance to transactions that create or transfer equitable interests in property.

As a cautionary measure

6.2 Property rights, including equitable interests under a trust, are very valuable rights. They should not be effectively dealt with in a casual or informal way, just in case the transferor did not seriously consider the consequences of his act. The formality of writing, in particular the requirement that the transferor signs his name, is suited to this purpose, because these days even the most benighted rube understands that when he signs his name to a document that is not a personal letter he is generally doing something of legal consequence.

For evidential purposes I

6.3 Writing requirements provide documentary evidence that makes frauds more difficult on the presumption that it is easier to get away with lying to the court about what someone said than it is successfully to forge documents and lie to the court about their origin.

For evidential purposes II

6.4 Documentary evidence also prevents the administrative problems that might arise when the memory of oral transactions has faded. Also, when transactions are complicated, the writing down helps the parties to be clear about what they intend. Finally, in the case of trusts, the writings are useful simply as a paper record for the trustee, which ensures that he does not commit an inadvertent breach of trust by, say, paying income to a former beneficiary who has since assigned his equitable right to the income to someone else.

6.5 It is a maxim of equity that 'Equity looks to intent not form'; equity has never itself insisted on formal requirements for any transaction (which undoubtedly once had something to do with the fact that the Chancellor could subpoena parties and interrogate them in person (1.5)). Parliament, however, has by statute imposed formalities on the creation and transfer of equitable interests, and any court must take due regard of them. Here we will be concerned, first, with the formality that applies when creating a trust—that is, bringing into existence equitable rights—and then the formality for the transfer, or assignment, or disposition of already existing equitable interests—that is, the existing rights of beneficiaries under a trust.

Declarations of trusts in land: Law of Property Act 1925, s 53(1)(b)

6.6 Section 53(1)(b) of the Law of Property Act 1925 provides:

> *A declaration of trust respecting any land or any interest therein must be manifested and proved by some writing signed by some person who is able to declare such trust or by his will.*

Section 53(1)(b) applies only to land. There is no similar provision with respect to personalty: therefore an oral declaration of a trust of personalty can be proven on the facts in a court without further ado. Thus you can orally declare that you hold your copy of this book on trust for your mother, and if you mean it, then you do, and this oral declaration, if proven, allows your mother to enforce this trust against you.

6.7 Importantly, the section must be pleaded by the party wishing to rely upon it (*James v Smith* (1891), 389). An oral declaration of trust can be proved on all admissible evidence if it is not. In particular, the court is not entitled to invoke the section of its own motion if neither side chooses to plead it.

6.8 Section 53(2) of the Act provides:

> This section does not affect the creation or operation of resulting, implied or constructive trusts.

To the extent that resulting, implied, and constructive trusts arise by operation of law, this provision is strictly speaking unnecessary, or inserted *ex abundanti cautela* (out of an abundance of caution), because there can be no formality requirements for trusts that arise by operation of law. The clause does save PRTs, however, if Swadling is right that they are express trusts, not TABOLs (5.29 et seq).

6.9 The person 'able to declare such trust' under s 53(1)(b) will be the settlor, of course. A problem arises however if A transfers land to B on an oral trust for C. Is there any writing which can be provided after the fact which satisfies s 53(1)(b)? Youdan (1984) argues that B, the legal owner, may sign the writing as the one who would be beneficial owner if there were no trust. In *Gardner v Rowe* (1828), an oral express trust was enforced against the trustee (so as to avoid claims by his creditors in bankruptcy); although the trust was evidenced by a post-transfer writing by the trustee, the case turned on the doctrine enunciated in *Rochefoucauld v Boustead* (6.12), not on the writing point, so it does not decide the issue.

6.10 But in any case, the words of s 53(1)(b) itself make it difficult to find that *any* post-oral declaration signed by anyone would be an effective writing. The point is a simple, logical one. The writing, according to the subsection, must be 'signed by some *person able to declare such trust*'; but once the trust is orally declared, it is a perfectly valid trust; s 53(1)(b) is a 'proof', not a 'validity', formality (6.1). And so once the trust has already been declared, then there just is no 'person able to declare *such* trust', for the trust already exists. A is not any such person; as the settlor, he is out of the picture; the property is no longer beneficially his. B, the trustee, has no power to declare any trust over property he already holds on trust (2.39), and C, the beneficiary, has a power to declare a sub-trust over his equitable title, but no power to declare the very trust under which he is already a beneficiary; if the subsection is ever reformulated in a review of statutory formalities, attention should be paid to this point. Even so, it is submitted that, however logical this all is, and it is perfectly logical, as a second best, the court should entertain a post-declaration writing by B in order to allow proof of the trust in at least some cases, by analogy with the writing requirement in the now-repealed s 40(1); under that section the writing had to be by the person against whom the contractual obligation was sought to be enforced; by parity of reasoning, it is the trustee's trust obligation that is sought to be enforced, so it is his writing which should be required.

6.11 Two cases, however, have not followed this approach, both giving effect to post-declaration writings of the settlor. The Singaporean case *Lai Min Tet v Lai Min Kin* (2004) concerned land which a father purchased and had placed in the names of two of his sons. Subsequent to the purchase the father on numerous occasions in personal letters stated that the land was to be held on trust for all of his four sons in equal shares, and these letters were held to satisfy the Singaporean equivalent of the section. In *Ong Jane Rebecca v Ong Siauw Ping* (2017) the UKCA held that a letter written by the settlor, two and half years after a trust of a house was supposedly declared (on very unsatisfactory evidence), a letter in which the settlor purported to 'cancel' the trust, was sufficient to satisfy the section.

The doctrine of *Rochefoucauld v Boustead*

6.12 As we have seen, s 53(1)(b)'s use of the words 'manifested and proved by some writing', indicates *not* that a purported declaration of trust is void without such a writing, but that it is *not provable* in a court of law, with the result that an oral trust of land cannot be enforced against the trustee; the express trust exists and binds the parties, but the beneficiary cannot invoke the assistance of the court to make the trustee carry it out since he cannot prove that it exists. In *Rochefoucauld v Boustead* (1897), however, the CA did enforce the oral express trust. The plaintiff, the Comtesse de la Rochefoucauld, had mortgaged her estates in Ceylon, and the mortgagee demanded payment of the mortgage debt. She had insufficient funds following her divorce, and her friend Boustead orally agreed to buy the estates from the mortgagee at a price sufficient to cover the mortgage debt and expenses, and hold the estates on trust for her, subject to her paying off the purchase price and further expenses. Since Boustead purchased the beneficial title from the mortgagee, which he impressed with the trust in the plaintiff's favour, so he should have signed the necessary writing. The rationale for the CA's enforcement of the trust is what we now call the 'doctrine of *Rochefoucauld v Boustead*': 'Equity will not allow a statute enacted to prevent fraud to be used as an instrument of fraud', and so the court will allow parol (ie oral) evidence to prove the express trust, despite s 53(1)(b) (or, in the case of *Rochefoucauld*, s 7 of the Statute of Frauds 1677, the forerunner of s 53(1)(b)).

6.13 Although there is no doubt that the CA in *Rochefoucauld* enforced the oral express trust despite the statutory formality provision (Swadling (2010)), in recent years the principle has been obscured. In *Bannister v Bannister* (1948), an elderly woman conveyed two cottages to her brother-in-law at a below market price on the understanding that she should be able to live rent-free in one of them for the rest of her days. When he tried to evict her, the CA declared that he held one of the cottages on trust to give effect to the agreement. It did not matter that the brother-in-law had no fraudulent intent when the property was transferred; the fraud consisted of relying upon the absence of writing when the sister-in-law tried to enforce her beneficial interest. So far, so much in keeping with *Rochefoucauld*. Yet Scott LJ described the trust as a constructive trust rather than the oral express trust which he was clearly enforcing despite s 53(1)(b), without, however, giving any reasons for this classification. Some commentators appear to favour the constructive trust classification because it gives an identical result without appearing to disregard the statute, since constructive trusts are specifically exempted from formality requirements by s 53(2); in this way, then, the court appears not to be disapplying the statute. But the reasoning is fallacious. One cannot both give effect to an express declaration of trust in its very terms for the very reason that not to do so would give rise to a fraud, and then say the trust is constructive, arising by operation of law.

6.14   *Rochefoucauld* and *Bannister* were both two-party cases. How should the doctrine apply in the three-party case, ie where A transfers land to B upon trust for C? If one adopts the constructive trust approach, the law may impose the result most justified in the circumstances—in some cases the constructive trust should be a bare trust for A, which merely prevents B's fraud; in others it should reflect the terms of the unenforceable express trust, so carrying out A's intention. In general, in the three-party case a bare trust in favour of A is preferable because it gives due weight to the statute, because the express trust is not enforced, yet at the same time B's fraud is prevented. Moreover, the cautionary purpose is served: if A still wishes to carry out his intentions, he can declare the trust again, providing written evidence this time; if he does not, then the statute has properly saved him from the effect of his oral declaration. Moreover, C can hardly complain that a *fraud* has been perpetrated against him simply because he has not received a gratuitous benefit from A. A constructive trust in favour of C should only be found where C relied to his detriment either because of a representation by A or because B has acted to carry out the trust, or perhaps, where A is no longer able to declare a trust in C's favour afresh, for example because he is dead, a case we shall consider when we look at secret trusts (6.51 et seq).

6.15   These considerations apply with even greater force to the case where A makes a self-declaration of trust in favour of C, because A cannot defraud himself, and appear to justify the result in *Rochefoucauld*, a self-declaration case. Boustead gratuitously promised the plaintiff to buy the estates for her benefit; thus he was the settlor of the trust, and the cautionary purpose should normally counsel the court to find no trust at all and allow him to renege, because it would be no fraud if Rochefoucauld did not receive this gratuitous benefit. The court's analysis of the facts is not well reported, but Boustead had, apparently, been giving effect to the express trust, upon which the plaintiff might have relied, and so in all the circumstances the decision was probably correct.

Disposition of subsisting equitable interests: Law of Property Act 1925, s 53(1)(c)

6.16   Section 53(1)(c) of the Law of Property Act 1925 provides:

> *A disposition of an equitable interest or trust subsisting at the time of the disposition must be in writing signed by the person disposing of the same, or by his agent thereunto lawfully authorised in writing or by his will.*

The section refers to a 'disposition' of an existing equitable interest. We shall be concerned almost entirely with what counts as a disposition for purposes of the section. 'Equitable interest or trust' refers to equitable interests in both land and personalty (*Grey v IRC* (1960)). Notice also that by this section, unlike s 53(1)(b), a disposition must *be in writing*—if not in writing it is absolutely void, not merely unprovable.

6.17   The section might be interpreted either broadly or narrowly. The predecessor section in the Statute of Frauds 1677 upon which it was based required writing for 'grants and assignments' of equitable interests; if that were taken as the intended meaning of 'disposition', then the section would have a fairly narrow compass. It would not apply to surrenders or releases of one's equitable interest, because there the beneficiary merely gives up his interest; he does not grant or assign it to another. Similarly, a beneficiary's declaration of trust over his interest in favour of someone else would not be caught, since he does not assign or grant his equitable interest but retains it in order to give effect to the sub-trust. In *Grey v IRC* (1960) the HL unanimously held that 'disposition' was to be given its natural meaning, which would appear to cover *every* transaction (not being an operation of law) by which any individual deals with his equitable interest under the trust. It has been the object of some criticism of this decision that the definition sections of the Law of Property Act 1925, which give a broad meaning to 'disposition' (s 205(1)(ii)), but which defines 'equitable interest' in terms of interests in land only (s 205(1)(x)), were neither cited to the court nor referred to in their Lordships' judgments. But as to 'disposition', the court did give a broad meaning to the section anyway, and as to the equation of equitable interest with an interest in land, the better view is that s 53(1)(c) should not be restricted to land; the section specifically mentions land in parts (a) and (b), and does not in (c), so the obvious interpretive conclusion to draw is that clause (c) is not to be confined to land. In any case, the interest in a trust is an interest in a fund (2.75), not in whatever properties constitute it. Many trusts contain both land and personalty as investments, and it would be silly to make the application of s 53(1)(c) depend upon whether, at the time any assignment is made, there happened to be some investment of the trust in land, such that an assignment would be invalid on 24 June, the day before the trustee sold an investment in land, but valid if it were made on 26 June, the day after. Beneficiaries are not expected to track the trustee's investments from day to day, after all.

6.18 How broad is broad? One could attempt to apply s 53(1)(c) not only to every act of the beneficiary by which he somehow deals with his interest, but also to the exercise by anyone of any power, such as discretion to distribute property under a discretionary trust, or the exercise of a power of appointment, which might affect the beneficiary's 'equitable interest'. So, for example, where a trustee exercised his discretion under a discretionary trust either to distribute property to Fred, or to give him nothing and all to Mabel, his sister, such an act would be a disposition of Fred's and Mabel's equitable interests, and therefore subject to s 53(1)(c). Such a wide meaning might also conceivably capture a decision of the trustee in the course of exercising his discretion to invest the trust property, because by investing in one way or another he would to some degree inevitably be enhancing the interests of the income beneficiaries over the capital beneficiaries, or vice versa (10.3).

6.19 This wider meaning of disposition is misconceived, practically and conceptually. It is misconceived as a matter of practice because it would subject to the rigours of s 53(1)(c)—remember, a transaction that does not comply with it is absolutely void—almost every exercise of any discretion by the trustee. Trustees must, of course, keep the trust accounts and therefore must record their decisions in any case, but to render void, perhaps years afterwards, perfectly sound decisions made in the course of administering the trust for failure to be put in writing at the time of the transaction, where the writing down of the particular transaction itself provides no further assistance in determining whether the trust was carried out than do the trust accounts (recording payments of money and so on) seems to be a recipe for injustice. Take another rather horrible practical example, one that clearly points to why this wide reading is bad. Consider a gift of Blackacre 'to Maria for life but if she takes up residence in the USA, then to Priscilla'. By acting to take up residence in the USA, Maria defeats her equitable interest in Blackacre, and so her act 'disposes' of her subsisting equitable interest. So in order for her disposition not to be void under s 53(1)(c), she must take up residence in the USA *in writing*. Eh? Something has gone wrong conceptually because, obviously, not every act that an individual can take under the terms of a trust that will affect the interests, ie the overall position, of the beneficiaries under the trust can even be done 'in writing'.

6.20   Consider again the section. It refers to a disposition of a *subsisting* equitable interest or trust. It must therefore refer to an existing interest under a trust. It therefore must refer to an existing interest under the specific trust under which it exists, which contours the interest in whatever ways it does. The interest, in other words, is defined by the trust, and so the interest is itself subject to whatever effects, whether positive or negative, it may be subject to under the terms of the trust. In short, the interest is whatever interest it is under the trust, warts and all. Therefore any acts by individuals rightly taken under the terms of the trust that *merely affect* a particular beneficiary's *position*, like investment decisions, or exercises by the trustee of his discretion which in various ways *give effect* to his interest, do not *dispose* of his interest. They are actions that either affect or give effect to his interest, even if they put him in a worse position, because those possible negative effects are part and parcel of the interest he has. Thus a person who takes in default of appointment who loses any chance of taking because the power is exercised has not had his interest disposed of; having a defeasible interest under the terms of the trust, the possibility was realised and it was defeated. His interest, such as it was, was *fulfilled* in one of the ways it might have been, and the fact that it's hard cheese on him that it was fulfilled to his detriment does not alter that. Similarly with a trustee's exercise of any of his discretions under the trust in ways that will affect the beneficiaries' positions. The effects of these exercises of discretion are part and parcel of having a discretionary interest. By exercising these discretions, the interest is given effect to, not disposed of. And this proper interpretation must logically extend to the possible defeat of the beneficiary's interest, either because the interest is defeasible, as with Maria's life interest in Blackacre, or because the interest is subject to a power, such as a power of appointment. Indeed, a trustee may have the power under the trust to add or delete beneficiaries *tout court* (3.3), and any beneficiaries subject to this power of deletion must likewise regard the effect of the power as part and parcel of their interest.

6.21   Thus the better interpretation of the subsection is this: A 'disposition' of an equitable interest must refer to the act of someone who is capable of disposing of the interest as it is under the terms of the trust, that is, as a property right of a particular kind. The only person who can generally do that is the owner of the property right or, as the section contemplates, his agent. Thus the subsection applies to any dealing by the beneficiary with his interest under the trust. Not only does the cautionary purpose apply in any such case, but the purpose called 'evidential II' (6.4) does also: trusts can be extremely complicated, and a paper record of various transactions concerning the equitable interests is vitally important, so important that it would be justified if the law insisted upon writing as the price of their validity (see Green (1984)). The point here is that, since the beneficiary's interest is his own, he can deal with it without any consultation or even notice to the trustee, and the trustee's being able to insist upon seeing a writing before treating a beneficiary's assignee as now entitled to the interest is a secondary valuable consequence of the subsection's application. The cases, however, do not reveal such a straightforward approach, ie applying the section to any dealing by the beneficiary with his interest. We shall consider the different possible transactions in turn.

Assignment to a third party

6.22 Assignments are clearly caught by s 53(1)(c): if A, for example, holds an equitable income interest under a trust, and wishes to assign it to X, he must do so in writing; a purported oral assignment is absolutely void.

Declaration of trust

6.23 It is generally accepted that where a beneficiary declares a trust of his equitable interest, creating a sub-trust, s 53(1)(c) does not apply. If the equitable interest is in land, any trust must be evidenced in writing by s 53(1)(b), but if the equitable interest is in personalty, such as a trust of company shares, an oral declaration of sub-trust appears to be valid. The rationale is that, whilst the declaration of the sub-trust does have the effect of extinguishing the beneficiary's *beneficial* interest in the trust, either in whole ('I declare that I hold my income interest on trust for Tim, Tom, and Tammy, in such proportions as I see fit') or in part ('I declare that I hold my income interest on trust for Trevor for life and then for myself absolutely'), and so in that sense is a disposition, it is not a disposition given that the beneficiary must *retain* his entire equitable title in order to give effect to the sub-trust. Thus, in the same way that a legal owner of property does not dispose of some 'pre-existing' equitable interest of his when declaring a trust (2.17), neither does the equitable owner dispose of any pre-existing equitable sub-trust interest when he declares a sub-trust. Thus the distinction is the difference between the *creation* of a new equitable interest over something one already has and must retain, and the *transfer* of something one has and which one thereby loses. Of course, when either a legal beneficial owner or an owner of an equitable interest declares a (sub-)trust they do shift, and thereby dispose of, their *beneficial* interest in the property concerned. But, and this cannot be repeated enough, a 'beneficial' interest is not equivalent to an 'equitable' interest (2.17), and it is to the latter that s 53(1)(c) refers. By creating the new trust interest, both the legal owner and the equitable interest owner retain their original interest—they do not dispose of it, and to repeat the point, each must retain this pre-existing interest for it is on that property right that the new trust 'bites'.

6.24 An exception to the rule that s 53(1)(c) does not apply to declarations of trust was, however, in previous years, widely accepted in the academic literature, to wit: if the beneficiary declares a *bare* sub-trust (2.13), ie 'I declare that I hold my life interest upon trust for Ted absolutely', then the declaration is void unless in writing. The idea is that the beneficiary is now a mere conduit between the trustee and the sub-beneficiary. The sub-beneficiary, it is said, should approach the trustee directly for his benefits, since it is pointless for the trustee to pay the beneficiary/sub-trustee and for him immediately to turn around and pay the sub-beneficiary. If this is right, then the declaration of a bare sub-trust amounts to an assignment of his equitable title and should count as a disposition under s 53(1)(c). Certain nineteenth-century cases (*Onslow v Wallis* (1849), *Re Lashmar* (1891), and *Grainge v Wilberforce* (1889)) seem to suggest that the beneficiary/sub-trustee drops out of the picture in this way, although whether they are actually authority for this proposition is disputed (Green (1984)). Where the trust is not a bare one, the sub-trustee will have to carry out the trust he creates, and he is said to have some 'active duties' to perform under the trust, such as the sub-trustee's discretion in the Tim, Tom, and Tammy example given earlier. Thus, not being a mere conduit, he does not drop out of the picture, and therefore the sub-trust is not in essence an assignment, and so an active duty sub-trust is valid without writing.

6.25   The bare trust/active duties distinction seems a slender reed upon which to rest a difference in the requirement of writing. The idea seems to be that, because the beneficiary drops out of the picture when he creates a bare, or no active duties, sub-trust, he has effectively assigned his interest. But even if those nineteenth-century authorities apply, it would seem that the beneficiary/sub-trustee drops out not by virtue of his own declaration of the sub-trust, but either by operation of law, which collapses the sub-trust giving the sub-beneficiary rights against the trustee automatically (the case law for which proposition, as noted above, is disputed), or because the sub-beneficiary leaps over his head to the trustee, taking his beneficial rights to the source, as it were, under the principle of *Saunders v Vautier* (3.38). But this seems wrong in principle. The beneficiary/sub-trustee could not himself insist on quitting the scene; the trustee could always choose to pay him and let him deal with his own sub-trust. After all, the trustee has no obligations under the sub-trust and so no duties to his beneficiary's sub-beneficiary. No solicitor in his right mind would advise the trustee to take over the trust of his sub-beneficiary on his own initiative: he would essentially be 'intermeddling' in a trust to which he was not appointed as a trustee, an act that would make him personally liable as a 'trustee *de son tort*' (11.103). If this is right then the beneficiary/sub-trustee does not, indeed cannot, drop out of the picture simply by declaring the sub-trust. This way of looking at the matter was accepted by the CA in *Nelson v Greening and Sykes* (2007), where Laurence Collins LJ said:

> These authorities do not bind this court to hold that as a matter of law an intermediate trustee ceases to be a trustee. I accept the submission for G&S that saying . . . that the practical effect [of declaring a sub-trust] would seem to amount to or be capable of amounting to the 'getting rid' of the trust of the equitable interest then subsisting, is not the same as saying that as a matter of law it does get rid of the intermediate trust. What he was saying was that in the case of a trust and sub-trust of personal property the trustees may decide that as a matter of practicality it is more convenient to deal directly with the beneficiary of the sub-trust.

In any case, distinguishing between these sub-trusts to alter writing requirements seems unmotivated in light of the various purposes for which formalities are imposed. Feel free, therefore, to argue that no sub-trusts should require writing, or that all should (as does Green (1984)) on the policy basis that any disposition of one's *beneficial* interest under the trust should require writing for the reasons given in 6.2–6.4. In past editions of this book I advised exam candidates to mention the bare/active sub-trust distinction in an exam answer before going on to dispute them, since the distinction would undoubtedly have attached itself limpet-like to the brain of the typical trusts law examiner; now I would advise that *Nelson* is strong authority for dismissing the distinction, disapproving as it does the 'automatic dropping out of the picture' of the sub-trustee.

Directions to the trustee to hold the equitable interest for another

6.26   If A directs his trustee to hold his equitable interest for a third party, it is generally accepted that this requires writing. This is in effect an assignment achieved, not by dealing with the third party directly, but by instructing the trustee henceforth to treat the third party as the beneficiary. *Grey v IRC* is usually cited as authority for this proposition, although as we shall see it actually concerned a different transaction. Nevertheless, the rationale for the application of s 53(1)(c) is straightforward. The beneficiary here, by his own direction, extinguishes his own equitable interest in favour of another, and so there is little to distinguish this from an assignment.

Directions to the trustee to hold the equitable interest on new trusts for another, and variations

6.27   Now we will discuss the 'big three' cases of this topic: *Grey v IRC* (1960); *Vandervell v IRC* (1967); and *Re Vandervell (No 2)* (1974). The courts made something of a hash of all of them, so it is difficult to say exactly what each decided, hence the 'and variations' above.

6.28   *Grey* involved an attempt to avoid paying *ad valorem* stamp duty on the setting up of a trust. *Ad valorem* stamp duty is a tax charged on documents that transfer the *beneficial* interest in property. For example, in England when you transfer title to a house, *ad valorem* stamp duty is payable, '*ad valorem*' indicating that the amount of the duty is a percentage of the value of the property. At the time *Grey* was decided, stamp duty was payable on the transfer of shares. So, for example, if you transferred shares to Theresa on trust for Ben, the beneficial interest passed from you to Ben, and *ad valorem* stamp duty was chargeable on the share transfer document. If by some means you could get the shares into a trust for Ben without having to use a document that transferred the beneficial title, then you could avoid paying *ad valorem* stamp duty. Furthermore, any transfer document that did not transfer a *beneficial* interest only attracted a fixed stamp duty of 50p. So a transfer of shares from one trustee to another (eg when a trustee retired), only cost 50p stamp duty, since the beneficial interest remained with the beneficiaries throughout. Say you wanted to transfer shares to Theresa on trust for Ben, but avoid *ad valorem* stamp duty. Here's how you could do it: declare that you hold the shares on trust for Ben. Shares are personalty, so you can declare such a trust orally: no document, so no stamp duty. Now retire from the trust in favour of a new trustee, Theresa, and transfer the legal title in the shares to her. The share transfer will be stampable at 50p, not *ad valorem*, because it does not transfer the beneficial interest, which already lies with Ben. (The only catch in this scheme is that if you write a document recording your declaration of trust too soon after your oral declaration, the Revenue will regard this writing as a document that transfers the beneficial interest to Ben as part of a 'composite transaction' transferring the legal title to Theresa on trust for Ben, and you will pay *ad valorem* stamp duty on it (*Cohen and Moore v IRC* (1933))). By this means, then, you could transfer the shares to Theresa on trust for Ben paying only 50p in stamp duty. The settlor in *Grey* was not so lucky.

6.29   In *Grey*, the settlor owned 18,000 company shares, which he desired to transfer in equal amounts into six trusts for his grandchildren that he had already set up. He transferred the shares to the two trustees of the grandchildren's trusts, but to hold the shares on bare trust for himself, and so, since the beneficial interest remained with him, the transfer document only attracted 50p stamp duty. He then orally directed the trustees to hold the shares in six separate and equal blocks upon the pre-existing grandchildren's trusts. Five weeks later, the trustees executed a document declaring that they held the shares on the children's trusts. The Revenue argued that this document was stampable *ad valorem* because it transferred the beneficial interest in the shares from the settlor to the grandchildren. The trustees argued that the settlor's oral direction did so, and that such a direction did not require writing under s 53(1)(c) to be valid. As we have seen (6.17), the HL read 'disposition' broadly and unanimously decided that such a direction was a disposition within s 53(1)(c) and so needed to be in writing; therefore the oral direction was void. Somewhat strangely, the later writing in which the trustees stated that they held the shares on the grandchildren's trusts was regarded as validly transferring the settlor's interest; the case therefore also appears to stand for the proposition that a later writing may retroactively validate an invalid oral disposition. Although the settlor was not expressed as a party to the deed declaring the trusts, he did sign it, and so the participation of the beneficiary is necessary for this to work.

6.30   What precisely does the case decide? The settlor's direction was clearly not a direction to the trustees to hold his equitable interest for his grandchildren in equal shares. That would simply have made them equitable co-owners of the shares under the same bare trust. Neither was it a self-declaration of trust, creating a sub-trust, in which he declared that he would henceforth hold his equitable interest in the shares on trust for the grandchildren on trusts identical to the ones he had already set up for them with the trustees. Rather, he directed his trustees in their nominee capacity to divide the shares into equal lots and thereafter hold the lots as trustees of the grandchildren's trusts, each trust to receive one lot. The important point is that the trustees were not to continue to hold the shares as nominee trustees for new beneficiaries, but to hold the shares in their quite separate capacity as trustees of the grandchildren's trusts. Because the trustees of the grandchildren's settlement were the same two persons who were the settlor's nominee trustees, the legal title did not have to be transferred, but this should not obscure the point. A trustee is a separate trustee to each of the trusts he administers, and must keep the property of the different settlements separate. For example, in this case, the trustees would be required either to divide the share certificates equally into six lots, or use the share serial numbers to allocate particular lots to each of the different grandchildren's settlements (see Green (1984)). At a minimum, therefore, the case decides that an oral direction to bare trustees to hold the trust property on different trusts that they also administer is void unless in writing, although a later writing may be effective as a 'belt and braces' device to cure a prior invalid oral direction. However, Green is clearly right to argue that the case must also be authority for the proposition that a direction to bare trustees to transfer the property to other trustees on different trusts is similarly void unless in writing, since the situations are identical except for the fact that in the former the trustees of both trusts happen to be the same persons, and this is no reason to distinguish between the two. However, in *Vandervell v IRC*, the HL unanimously decided that an oral direction to a trustee to transfer the legal title to shares to different trustees on new trusts was valid. The HL did not, apparently, realise they were deciding this, but they did.

6.31   Review the facts of *Vandervell v IRC* (5.52 et seq). The Revenue's first argument was that the first part of the transaction, the transfer of the shares held on bare trust for Vandervell by the Bank to the RCS on Vandervell's oral direction, failed because this amounted to a disposition of his equitable interest under the bare trust, and therefore it needed to be in writing under s 53(1)(c). The point their Lordships thought they were deciding was this: Is A's oral direction to his trustee to transfer the legal title to shares held on bare trust to a third party absolutely, ie so the third party acquires the beneficial legal title to them, valid, or must it be in writing under s 53(1)(c)? They all decided that s 53(1)(c) did not apply and so the oral direction was valid.

6.32   The reasoning of their various Lordships was brief and does not repay intense scrutiny (see Green (1984)). For his part, Lord Upjohn said this:

> [I]f the intention of the beneficial owner in directing the trustee to transfer the legal estate to X is that X should be the beneficial owner I can see no reason for any further document or further words in the document assigning the legal estate also expressly transferring the

beneficial interest; the greater includes the less. X may be wise to secure some evidence that the beneficial owner intended him to take the beneficial interest in case his beneficial title is challenged at a later date but it certainly cannot, in my opinion, be a statutory requirement that to effect its passing there must be writing under section 53(1)(c).

To the extent that Lord Upjohn is satisfied because the transfer of a legal title involves a document anyway, and so a 'further' document seems superfluous, he has forgotten that the rule of law he has just propounded will apply equally to chattels, which can be transferred out of the trust by delivery—the result is that a trustee may give away trust property on the basis of an oral direction with no writing whatsoever. Secondly, the point is not whether a legal transfer normally includes the beneficial interest—of course it does; the question is whether it does in this case, where the beneficiary has not expressed in writing his intention to give up the beneficial interest. Without any writing, why should we not presume that when the trustee, T, transfers the legal title to X, X takes the legal title because he has been appointed as a new trustee to replace T, in which case the beneficiary's interest would, of course, remain attached to the property? Lord Upjohn's concern that X, the recipient, might want some sort of writing is interesting, since it indicates he is somewhat aware of the kind of trouble that oral dispositions can cause, not only to the Xs of the world, but to beneficiaries, who might be defrauded on the basis of supposed oral directions, and trustees, who may later have to prove oral directions to show that their actions were not in breach of trust. (Lords Pearce and Donovan took the same line. Lord Wilberforce, in an interesting departure, decided that s 53(1)(c) did not apply on the basis of a quite different reading of the facts, roughly that the bank had effectively transferred the legal title to the shares to Vandervell before the transaction with the RCS, and so it was Vandervell himself, through the bank acting as his agent, who assigned the legal title to the RCS, not the bank acting as his trustee.)

6.33 You will recall, however, that their Lordships unanimously decided that the grant of the option from the RCS to the trust company was Vandervell's own doing, somehow part of the arrangement he set in motion, which on any plausible version of the transaction gave rise to the shares being held by the RCS on trust to grant the option to the trust company or on equitable condition to grant the option to the trust company. That was why on the failure of the express trust of the trust company's interest in the option Vandervell was found to have the beneficial interest in it under an ART (5.54 et seq). But if this is true, which it must be because that is the decision of the case, then the transfer by the bank of the shares was a transfer subject to some kind of equitable obligation or condition, that is, *subject to some trust*. In consequence, their Lordships' decision that the oral direction by Vandervell was valid is authority for the proposition that an oral direction to a trustee to transfer property held on bare trust to another person *on trust* for a third party is valid. This, of course, directly contradicts the broader basis of decision that Green (1984) argues is the right interpretation of *Grey*.

6.34 Most commentators, however, take Lord Upjohn at his word and it is textbook gospel to say that *Vandervell v IRC* decides only that an oral direction to a bare trustee to transfer the trust property to a third party absolutely for his own benefit is a valid disposition. This decision is commercially convenient, it is said, because it allows nominee trustees of shares, like brokers, to sell them on the oral directions of their beneficiaries. This justification is specious: the buying and selling of shares amounts to the trustee's exercise of his power of investment (10.2), and in general trustees never have to get the written direction of the beneficiaries to manage the trust property in this way: that is, s 53(1)(c) does not apply because these 'dispositions' of the trust property are not the disposition of anyone's equitable interest, but merely dealings with the trust corpus in which those equitable interests lie (6.20). As *Akers v Samba v Financial Group* (2017) makes clear, even a transfer of trust assets in breach of trust by the trustee does not amount to a disposition of the beneficiary's interest. *A fortiori* it cannot be the case a transfer of trust assets allowed by the terms of the trust is such a disposition. Such a transaction with the trust property is made by exercising an *administrative* power or discretion, not a *dispositive* one (2.50). The only difference the trust's being a bare trust makes is that the beneficiary has the right to tell the trustee how to exercise any of the powers he has in virtue of being the legal owner of the trust property, including the power to exchange trust property for other property. The exercise of this administrative power, then, has nothing whatever to do with the trustee's defeating or extinguishing a beneficiary's interest by *giving* the trust property away, or extinguishing part or all of the beneficiary's entitlement under the trust (whatever its specific property) on the basis of oral instructions. (For a contrary view, see Nolan (2002), who thinks oral instructions of both the administrative and dispositive kind should be treated alike in the case of a bare trust.) As with the bare sub-trust/non-bare sub-trust distinction above, feel free to make these points, but in an exam recite the accepted catechism to begin with.

6.35   The Vandervell saga continued in *Re Vandervell (No 2)*. Once the Revenue made its claim for the surtax, Vandervell and the trust company decided to exercise the option. The trustees used £5,000 from the children's trust and purchased the shares. The trustees wrote to the Revenue informing it that the shares were now held under the children's trust. As he had done for the RCS, Vandervell then exercised his control over his company and had various dividends declared on the shares over the next few years, amounting to more than a million pounds; in doing so he intended to provide for his children, and subsequently wrote a will leaving them nothing more. After his death, the executors of his will claimed that none of the preceding transactions had worked to displace Vandervell's beneficial interest in the option, nor therefore in the shares purchased through its exercise; thus the dividends declared on those shares were his property in equity as well; hence the executors claimed that the trust company held the shares on trust for Vandervell's estate.

6.36   The CA decided that a valid trust had been declared in favour of the children, and so the dividends properly belonged in the children's trust. The court gave a number of reasons, most of which are insupportable. The only plausible one, and pertinent to our discussion, is in this passage from Lord Denning MR's decision:

> A resulting trust for the settlor is born and dies without writing at all. It comes into existence whenever there is a gap in the beneficial ownership. It ceases to exist whenever that gap is filled by someone becoming beneficially entitled. As soon as the gap is filled by the creation or declaration of a valid trust, the resulting trust comes to an end. In this case, before the option was exercised, there was a gap in the beneficial ownership. So there was a resulting trust for Mr Vandervell. But, as soon as the option was exercised and the shares registered in the trustee's name, there was created a valid trust of the shares in favour of the children's settlement. Not being a trust of land, it could be created without any writing. A trust of personalty can be created without writing.

6.37   Green (1984) assumes that what makes Lord Denning's decision even possibly correct is a finding on the facts (however erroneous) that the trust company had the power to declare trusts of the option or shares purchased with it: by exercising the option and holding the shares on trust for the children the trust company declared a trust that 'filled the gap' in the beneficial interest, which declaration the court found did not attract the requirements of s 53(1)(c). On this view the case has a tiny narrow ambit, to wit: where a trustee holds property upon an almost bare trust for a settlor, but there is (oddly, it must be said) one term of the trust that gives the trustee the power to declare new trusts of the property, his exercise of that power need not be in writing.

6.38   But this interpretation cannot stand with the facts of *Vandervell v IRC*, nor with Lord Denning's own words: Vandervell held under an ART, an automatic resulting trust—a trust that simply cannot contain any special powers of this kind for the trustees or anyone else. An ART is the barest of bare trusts. So even if on the facts the express trust Vandervell had intended the trustee company to hold the option under gave the trustee company the power to declare new trusts, that trust failed for uncertainty, and nothing of it lingered in the ART that arose upon its failure. Rather, the CA decision, *per* Lord Denning MR at least, appears to be that because Vandervell was fully aware of and assented to the trustee company's exercise of the option to hold the shares on the children's trust, his assent amounted to an oral declaration of trust. So the case is authority for the proposition that where a settlor transfers personal property on trust, yet fails to make an effective oral declaration of trust, so that an ART in his favour arises, his subsequent oral declaration of trust is valid, his beneficial interest under the ART not requiring to be disposed of in writing under s 53(1)(c). This decision is not in conflict with *Grey*, since there the settlor intentionally transferred property on *express* bare trust for himself. In *Re Vandervell (No 2)*, by contrast, Vandervell had tried to do what was perfectly legitimate, ie transfer personalty to a trustee on orally declared trusts, only the oral declaration failed for uncertainty. If the settlor remedies the situation by declaring trusts that are certain, why should that declaration require writing when the first did not? This, indeed, would appear to be the one case where an exception to s 53(1)(c) is justified, since one might say that the second, valid, declaration is part and parcel of one transaction in which the holder of legal title to personal property (or the equivalent, assuming that Vandervell had the right to transfer the legal title to shares by orally directing the bare trustee bank to do so, ie that *Vandervell v IRC* is rightly decided) transfers it on trust—and that, of course, is a case of an oral declaration of trust that is provable whether there is written evidence or not, there being no equivalent to s 53(1)(b) that applies to personalty (although it should be noted that in this passage Lord Denning appears to make the common mistake of thinking section 53(1)(b) goes to *validity*, rather than *evidence*). This view is fortified by the history of the resulting trust (5.1–5.2) and the point that one receives the beneficial interest under an ART not as a beneficiary—the interest does not move forward to one as someone intended as a beneficiary—it 'remains with' or 'results to' one *as settlor*. Therefore it makes sense to think that one deals with this interest *as the settlor's*, ie declaring the trust, hopefully successfully this time, not 'disposing' of his beneficial interest as an interest properly established under a trust, in which case the formality requirements for declaring a trust of personalty should apply, ie none.

Releases, surrenders, and disclaimers

6.39   A release and a surrender are the same thing. A beneficiary surrenders his interest when he clearly indicates that he no longer wishes to benefit under the trust. If the beneficiary has a vested interest, for example a life interest in shares, what follows is an ART in favour of the settlor, if the trust is *inter vivos*, or if the trust is testamentary, to that extent the trust fails and the property falls into residue (2.84). If the beneficiary has only a contingent interest (eg he is the object of a discretionary trust or power of appointment), then his surrender just removes his name from the list of possible objects; there is no ART because he has no vested interest in any property upon which it could operate. Section 53(1)(c) should apply to surrenders or releases, since they clearly amount to the beneficiary's disposing of his entire equitable interest in favour of others, even if he does not know or care who will benefit under the trust by his surrender. There is, however, no good authority on the point, almost certainly because any careful trustee will insist that a beneficiary surrendering his interest will do so in writing. *IRC v Buchanan* (1958) is perhaps of some small assistance. There, the CA interpreted 'disposition' as used in the Finance Act 1943 to include the exercise by a beneficiary of a special power under a trust to surrender her life interest in favour of her children.

6.40   A person *disclaims* an interest under a trust when he refuses any beneficial interest from the outset. The only authority for the application of s 53(1)(c) to disclaimers is *Re Paradise Motor Co Ltd* (1968). The CA held that 'a disclaimer operates by way of avoidance, and not by way of disposition'. A person disclaiming 'avoids', that is, never obtains any equitable interest, and therefore never acquires anything to dispose of: s 53(1)(c) has no application. This characterisation of disclaimers seemed entirely ad hoc, to avoid one more complication in a case in which the beneficial ownership to shares had to be determined on vague and ill-remembered oral testimony, and the authority the court referred to (*Re Stratton's Disclaimer* (1958), CA) actually takes the *opposite* line: that a beneficiary takes the benefit of an equitable interest from the moment the gift becomes effective in his favour, and therefore his disclaimer *does* amount to a disposition extinguishing a right he presently enjoys. Little weight, then, should be given to the decision. Certainly the purposes behind the section apply just as much to disclaimers as to other dispositions, and 'disposition' under the Law of Property Act 1925, s 205(1), (2) includes a disclaimer.

Agreements to assign or vary equitable interests for consideration

6.41   As we have seen (4.6), in the case of specifically enforceable contracts for the transfer or creation of rights in property, equity will impose a vendor–purchaser constructive trust on the grantor of the interest. This doctrine operates just the same in the case of assignments of equitable interests where the interest is 'unique' in the sense that a failure to receive it under the contract cannot be adequately compensated by money damages. *Always* remember (some judges do not, eg Lord Wilberforce in *Chinn v Collins* (1981)) that this constructive trust depends on the availability of specific enforcement of the contract, and this in turn depends on whether the property is unique in this way. For example, private company shares are, since they cannot be freely purchased on the open market, but public company shares are not.

6.42   In the case of an agreement to assign equitable interests under a trust, the vendor–purchaser constructive trust that arises is a constructive sub-trust. The beneficiary holds his equitable interest on constructive sub-trust for the purchaser, subject to the right to retain the interest until the purchaser pays up; until he does, the beneficiary can refuse to assign the underlying equitable title. When the purchaser does pay up, the beneficiary holds his equitable interest on bare sub-trust for him. If it were right (which it is not) that a bare sub-trustee drops out of the picture (6.24–6.25), then this sub-trust collapses, and the equitable interest moves without any assignment by the beneficiary. The correct view is that the sub-trustee does not drop out, but the purchaser can insist upon the beneficiary assigning the equitable interest to him in writing and can get a decree of specific performance to this end.

6.43   In *Oughtred v IRC* (1960), the contractual constructive trust was employed in an attempt to avoid stamp duty. Mrs Oughtred and her son Peter both held interests in a trust of private company shares. They agreed to vary their equitable interests, as a result of which Mrs Oughtred would acquire the entire beneficial interest in the shares under a bare trust; in return she would transfer a separate block of shares to Peter. Following the agreement, Mrs Oughtred and Peter executed a deed that declared that Mrs Oughtred now had the entire beneficial interest in the shares. The trustees then formally transferred the legal title to the shares to her absolutely. The question before the court was whether the formal share transfer attracted *ad valorem* stamp duty, or only a 50p duty because by virtue of the constructive trust, she already beneficially owned the shares in equity. The HL majority held that the formal share transfer attracted *ad valorem* stamp duty, but largely on what might be called the 'principles of stamp duty law'. Lord Jenkins held that while the purchaser under a specifically enforceable agreement has a proprietary interest of some sort, that does not prevent the subsequent transfer of the property that completes the transaction from being stampable *ad valorem*. After all, *ad valorem* stamp duty was payable (and remains payable) on documents transferring title to land even though the purchaser willing and able to pay the purchase price acquires the beneficial interest in the land on the day of completion under the paradigm example of a vendor–purchaser constructive trust (4.6 et seq; see also *Taylor v Taylor* (2017), [44]–[47]). Lord Radcliffe dissented, accepting that upon the agreement being made Mrs Oughtred became the owner in equity, and so felt that the share transfer did not transfer any beneficial interest.

6.44   The view that the constructive trust arising on the specifically enforceable agreement is sufficient to create an enforceable equitable interest has been endorsed since, outside the stamp duty context (*Re Holt's Settlement* (1969); *DHN Food Distributors Ltd v Tower Hamlets London Borough Council* (1976)). In *Neville v Wilson* (1997) the CA held that the equitable interest in private company shares could pass by virtue of a contractual constructive trust arising on a specifically enforceable, although oral, agreement. In that case the equitable interest in certain shares was held by a company—the legal title in them was vested in two nominees purely for the purpose of qualifying them as directors. The company was subsequently wound up, but although the equitable interest in these shares was clearly an asset of the company it was never dealt with according to the shareholders' winding-up agreement—indeed, the nominee trustees were thereafter treated by all concerned as the beneficial owners of the shares, taking the dividends for themselves, and so on. Nevertheless, trustees they were, and so the trial judge concluded that the equitable title, as an asset of the company never transferred, remained with the company, which was, of course, now defunct having been wound up. Since by the time of trial the defunct company could not be reinstated as a legal entity, the result was that no one owned the equitable interest in the shares, and so it passed as *bona vacantia* to the Crown. On appeal it was argued that the shareholders' winding-up agreement gave rise to a constructive trust over the shares in favour of the shareholders. After reviewing the decisions in *Oughtred*, the CA agreed, reasoning that:

> So far as it is material to the present case, what subsection (2) says is that subsection (1)(c) does not affect the creation or operation of implied or constructive trusts. Just as in Oughtred v IRC the son's oral agreement created a constructive trust in favour of the mother, so here each shareholder's oral or implied agreement created an implied or constructive trust in favour of the other shareholders. Why then should subsection (2) not apply? No convincing reason was suggested in argument and none has occurred to us since. Moreover, to deny its application in this case would be to restrict the effect of general words when no restriction is called for, and to lay the ground for fine distinctions in the future. With all the respect which is due to those who have thought to the contrary, we hold that subsection (2) applies to an agreement such as we have in this case.

Reform of s 53(1)(c)

6.45   The preceding look at the cases suggests that a statutory reform making clear those dispositions to which a writing requirement should apply is a good idea. It might also be suggested that, in analogy with the Law of Property Act 1925, s 136 (the assignment of debts), for an assignment of an equitable interest to be valid, notice of the assignment must be given, in writing, to the trustee.

Testamentary trusts: Wills Act 1837, s 9

6.46   Section 9 of the Wills Act 1837 provides:

> 9.   No will shall be valid unless—
>
> (a)   it is in writing, and signed by the testator, or by some other person in his presence and by his direction; and
>
> (b)   it appears that the testator intended by his signature to give effect to the will; and
>
> (c)   the signature is made or acknowledged by the testator in the presence of two or more witnesses present at the same time; and
>
> (d)   each witness either—
>
> > (i)   attests and signs the will; or
> >
> > (ii)   acknowledges his signature,
>
> in the presence of the testator (but not necessarily in the presence of any other witness), but no form of attestation shall be necessary.

The section applies to any testamentary gift, including testamentary trusts. Unless properly signed and attested, an intended testamentary gift fails. Formalities are of obvious importance here, as a will takes effect when the testator is dead, so we will not hear any oral evidence from him as to his intentions. (It is worthwhile reviewing 2.83–2.88 at this point.)

Non-testamentary gifts giving an interest on death

6.47   Not every gift by which the donee takes an interest on the donor's death is testamentary. For example, I can declare that I hold Blackacre on trust for myself for life, and then for you. My personal representatives will hold Blackacre for you from my death. This *inter vivos* trust immediately vests in you a future interest in Blackacre. For a gift to be testamentary it must be *revocable* and *ambulatory*. A valid testamentary gift, ie one in a will, can be revoked or amended by the testator any time before his death, although he must do so in writing in compliance with s 9. A document that amends a will in part is called a 'codicil' and becomes part of the testator's whole will.

6.48   'Ambulatory' means that a will, while valid when properly made, just walks along without immediate effect, only operating when the testator dies. Thus gifts that would have been valid had they been made *inter vivos* when the testator made his will may fail at the time of his death, because in the interval things may happen to his legatees, to him, or to his property. A gift 'lapses' if the intended legatee predeceases the testator; the property goes back into the deceased's estate, and from there either to the residuary legatees or intestate successors. When a testator makes a will, he may leave specific gifts, such as his car to X or his house to Y, or pecuniary legacies, such as £10,000 to Z. The testator might be rich when he makes his will, but bankrupt when he dies. Before any property is distributed under a will, all of the testator's creditors must be paid, and some of his property might have to be sold to do this. Thus the particular items of property and the total wealth distributable under the will can never be ascertained until his estate is administered. A specific gift *adeems*, ie fails, if the testator's estate does not include the specific property; if, for example, he sells his car then any specific gift of the car in his will will fail. A gift *abates* when a legatee's gift is proportionately reduced because there is insufficient property to satisfy all the testator's gifts. Thus a pecuniary legacy may abate anywhere down to zero if the testator is not as rich at his death as he thought he would be when he made his will.

6.49   Even if the *inter vivos* trust of Blackacre (6.47) is made revocable, it is not truly ambulatory since unless and until revoked it cannot lapse by reason of your predeceasing me—if you die first, then your successors will take the fee simple in Blackacre when I die. Nor will the gift adeem or abate if it turns out that I am deeply in debt when I die—the beneficial interest in Blackacre has been disposed of *inter vivos*, and cannot form part of my estate.

6.50   Besides *inter vivos* trusts giving an interest that vests on the death of a settlor, property can 'go' to others on one's death by operation of the right of survivorship on jointly held property (1.22). Thus if I transfer Blackacre to you and me as joint owners, or set up a joint bank account in our names, and I then die before you, you become the sole owner as my joint interest just disappears on my death. I can also take out a life insurance policy naming you as the beneficiary; the policy will pay out to you on my death. In *Re Danish Bacon Co Ltd Staff Pension Fund* (1971) Megarry J held that the right of an employee to nominate someone who will receive death-in-service benefits under a pension fund was not testamentary and therefore not subject to s 9 requirements. Megarry J also held that such nominations do not require writing under s 53(1)(c), since the nominator is not disposing of any subsisting equitable interest—the benefit only arises on his death (see also *Baird v Baird* (1990)).

Informal testamentary trusts: secret and half-secret trusts

6.51   Secret and half-secret trusts are testamentary trusts that fail to comply with the Wills Act because they are not disclosed or disclosed fully in a valid will. Typically, a fully secret trust (FST) arises when T appears to take an absolute gift under A's will, but T has informally agreed with A to hold the property on trust for B. Secret trusts, however, can arise when there is no will at all: if T is A's intestate successor, he may also informally agree with A to hold the property he gets on trust for B (*Sellack v Harris* (1708)). After A's death, T, whether a legatee under A's will or A's intestate successor, is in the position to deny the informal trust and keep the property for himself fraudulently.

6.52   A half-secret trust (HST) is one in which the existence of the trust is apparent on the face of the will, but the terms of the trust are not disclosed (eg 'I leave Blackacre to X on trusts that I have communicated to him'). Unlike the fully secret trust case, X is not in the position to deny the trust, and so cannot fraudulently take the property himself, because he is clearly a trustee for someone, and of course equity will not allow him to take the property beneficially.

6.53   Why should anyone wish to make informal testamentary trusts of this kind? One possibility in the case of FSTs is simply that the legatee or intestate successor has persuaded the testator to do so, in order to perpetrate a fraud. The legatee might say: 'Don't give your property in a will—that will only lead to a great deal of squabbling in court—leave it all to me and I will do what you wish without fear of legal challenge.' Generally, however, secret trusts are intentionally created by the testator to ensure the secrecy of testamentary gifts. Since wills must be proved in a Court of Probate the contents of a will become public, and any person or member of the tabloid press can buy a copy for a trivial sum. (A brisk business was done in Princess Diana's will.) Testators wishing to provide for their secret lovers or other objects that would embarrass them or rather, harm their posthumous reputations, may instead of leaving them property by will leave property absolutely to a friend who agrees to hold the property on trust secretly for these beneficiaries. If the testator regards the obligation the legatee undertakes as only a moral obligation, and the legatee is trustworthy, then legal enforcement is not required. The imposition of such moral obligations does not interfere with the effect or policy of the Wills Act, because in law the legatee becomes the absolute owner under the will, and moral obligations to the deceased do not upset that. The question is whether and in what circumstances informal promises to a testator should be given legal effect. Should the enforcement be restricted to the case where the testator is truly a victim of an intentional fraud, or should a testator's scheme to create a secret testamentary gift, colluded in by his secret trustee, also be enforced despite the Wills Act? Originally, it appeared that equity would enforce the promise as a trust obligation over the property only in the case of actual fraud. Equity would not allow a fraudulent legatee to plead that the trust was invalid under the Act on the basis 'Equity will not allow a statute enacted to prevent fraud to be used as an instrument of fraud' (6.12). This is the 'fraud theory' of the enforcement of secret trusts, but the leading nineteenth-century HL case, *McCormick v Grogan* (1869), is ambiguous as to what counts as fraud.

6.54   In *McCormick*, the testator left all his property to his friend Grogan. On his deathbed, he told Grogan that he had left all his property to him in his will, to which Grogan replied: 'Is that right?' The testator also told him where to find the will and a letter with it. There was no further communication between the testator and Grogan. The letter to Grogan detailed a large number of gifts in pursuit of which he desired Grogan to apply the money, although he left much to Grogan's discretion. Grogan did not make all of the detailed gifts, and one non-recipient, McCormick, sought to have Grogan declared a secret trustee. The HL refused to do so, but their Lordships' conception of the fraud in response to which equity will make the legatee a trustee is ambiguous. Their reasons suggest either that the necessary fraud is (1) a fraudulent scheme on the defendant's part *to induce* the property owner either to make a will in the defendant's favour (or not revoke a will in his favour), or refrain from making a will because the defendant will take on his intestacy, in which the defendant misrepresents his true intentions, falsely promising to carry out the owner's wishes, thereby acquiring the owner's property on his death for his own benefit; or (2) merely the defendant's 'fraudulent' refusal, when he receives the property on the owner's death, to comply with an agreement with the original owner upon which the owner relied in disposing of the property as he did. (1) is obviously much narrower, and amounts to saying that a testator who attempts to make informal testamentary gifts will, by operation of the Wills Act, fail to do so unless he was fraudulently induced to avoid making a valid testamentary gift by a legatee or intestate successor who benefits from the fraud. (2) essentially allows the testator to opt out of the strictures of the Wills Act; so long as he effectively communicates his testamentary intentions to a legatee or intestate successor, who agrees to carry them out, this joint endeavour to defy the Wills Act will succeed because equity will enforce the agreement against the legatee.

6.55   Whatever the actual state of the authorities in 1869 that led to their Lordships' ambiguous characterisation, (2) is the way the law has developed. As stated by Lord Sterndale MR in *Re Gardner* (1920):

> *The obligation upon the [secret trustee] seems to me to arise from this, that he takes the property in accordance with and upon an understanding to abide by the wishes of the testatrix, and if he were to dispose of it in any other way he would be committing a breach of trust, or as it has been called in some of the cases a fraud. I do not think it matters what you call it. The breach of trust or the fraud would arise when he attempted to deal with the money contrary to the terms on which he took it.*

6.56   The more recent case of *Re Snowden* (1979) provides a good example of the current ambit of the court's willingness to enforce FSTs. There an indecisive testatrix, after making various particular gifts in her will, left the residue of her estate to her brother, he 'knowing her wishes' for the money. Her brother died six days after she did, and the question was whether on very insufficient evidence a trust of the residue was undertaken by him. Megarry VC found that the testatrix had only imposed a moral, not a legal, obligation upon her brother, so there was no secret trust. However, he pointed out that only some cases of secret trust involved the possibility of fraud, and as there was none here—the secret trustee could not personally benefit by any fraud, for he had died—the question was whether there was a secret trust that would take the property out of his estate on death. While the burden of proof that a secret trust exists lies on the person who asserts its existence, in cases where there is no fraud the normal civil standard of proof, ie what is more likely on the balance of probabilities, applies.

6.57   The state of the law now is well put by Mitchell (2010b, para 3-122):

> *Testators, today, who do not want their testamentary wishes to become public by admission to probate as part of their will can take advantage of the doctrine of secret trusts to make provision for mistresses, illegitimate children, relatives whom they do not wish to appear to be helping or organisations which they do not wish to appear to be helping. Indecisive, aged testators can also leave everything by will absolutely to their solicitors, from time to time calling upon or phoning their solicitors with their latest wishes. [On this last sentence, see further 6.80.]*

6.58   It would appear, then, that equity's enforcement of secret trusts has allowed testators to make informal, even oral, testamentary dispositions in flat defiance of the Wills Act; to opt out of it, as it were. The only 'fraud' necessary is the legatee's refusal to carry out his agreement with the testator, the agreement being to carry out an informal testamentary disposition so that the testator can bypass the provisions of the Wills Act. In its confused appreciation of fraudulent behaviour in this context equity allows a testator to make an informal will just because he uses a human instrument, ie his legatee, to do so. By reposing his informal, even oral, will in this human vessel he can succeed where another testator committing his wishes to an unattested paper cannot, because the unattested paper 'cannot commit fraud', even though the human legatee and the unattested paper are fulfilling exactly the same function. While perhaps a bit extreme, it is perhaps relevant to draw upon the law's traditional view that where property is transferred under an illegal agreement, one should allow the property interest to lie where it falls (3.47 et seq). A strict application of this principle to the 'illegality' of intentionally avoiding the Wills Act would leave the beneficial title of the property in the hands of the legatee and defeat the testator's intentions (see also Gardner (2010)). In a thought-provoking article examining the history of the Statute of Frauds 1677 and s 9 of the Wills Act, Matthews (2010) has argued that s 9 applies only to the transfer of *legal* title to the trustee; s 9 does not require testamentary trusts themselves to be in writing. Only testamentary trusts of land are required to be proved by writing under s 53(1)(b); note the last four words of the subsection: 'or by his will'. If this is right, then one needs no 'doctrine' of secret trusts at all. Any testamentary trust of personalty is valid, whether oral or not, and could be proved in court on the basis of oral evidence. While Matthews makes a persuasive case, going the other way is the fact that judges do seem to think that s 9 applies here. Otherwise, they would not have thought it necessary to create either the 'fraud' theory of the enforcement of secret trusts or, as we shall shortly see (6.61 et seq), its poor and hopeless relation, the '*dehors* the will' theory of HSTs.

Fraud and HSTs

6.59   The trustee of an HST can lie about the trust upon which he holds the property, telling the world it was for his own mistress rather than the testator's, for instance, but he cannot deny there is any trust at all and take the property for himself like the fully secret trustee can, for he is a trustee on the face of the will. As a result, because the court would only get round the Wills Act in the case of fraud, it was not settled until the 1929 HL decision in *Blackwell v Blackwell* whether HSTs should be enforced. The gift in *Blackwell* was as follows: 'I give and bequeath to my friends … the sum of twelve thousand pounds free of all duties upon trust to invest the same as they in their uncontrolled discretion shall think fit and to apply the income and interest arising therefrom yearly and every year for the purposes indicated by me to them …'. The appellants argued that where the trustee was named in the will, there could be no fraud under any version of the fraud theory in *McCormick v Grogan*; the question was merely one of for whom the trust is held: if there is no further validly expressed intention that specifies the trust terms, then the trust fails. The HL disagreed, allowing parol evidence to prove the terms of the trust. The HL removed this impediment by adopting a new variation on 'fraud'. According to Lord Buckmaster, the defendant's fraud is not falsely to induce the testator to make a gift in the defendant's favour, nor to refuse to comply with his promise to the testator, but to cheat the testator's intended donees of their intended benefits—the fraud is a fraud on the secret beneficiaries.

6.60   This reasoning is circular. As Sheridan (1951) points out, to consider the fraud as a fraud 'on the beneficiaries' begs the question. There is no fraud on an intended beneficiary if a gift intended for him 'fails' for formal invalidity, because if it is an invalid trust, he is not a beneficiary. The question is whether an HST is a valid or invalid *means* of making someone a beneficiary despite the Wills Act. If it is not, then there is no fraud. By thinking of the intended beneficiaries *as* properly entitled beneficiaries from the outset is to assume what needs to be shown, ie that failing to enforce an HST abets a fraud.

The '*dehors* the will' theory of HSTs

6.61   Viscount Sumner provided a further reason for the result, articulating what is now conventionally called the '*dehors* (ie outside) the will' theory of secret trusts:

> The limits, beyond which the rules as to unspecified trusts must not be carried, have often been discussed. A testator cannot reserve to himself a power of making future unwitnessed dispositions by merely naming a trustee and leaving the purposes of the trust to be supplied afterwards, nor can a legatee give testamentary validity to an unexecuted codicil by accepting an indefinite trust, never communicated to him in the testator's lifetime ... To hold otherwise would indeed be to 'give the go-by' to the requirement of the Wills Act, because he did not choose to comply with them. It is communication of the purpose to the legatee, coupled with the acquiescence or promise on his part, that removes the matter from the provisions of the Wills Act and brings it within the law of trusts, as applied in this instance to trustees, who happen to be legatees.

Under the '*dehors* the will' theory, secret trusts are regarded as *inter vivos* declarations of trust by the testator; the only atypical feature is that the trusts are not constituted, ie the property is not transferred into the hands of the trustee, until the testator's death, through his will. Therefore secret trusts operate outside the will, and therefore the Wills Act has no application. Do not confuse this idea with Matthews' (6.58); Matthews claims that secret trusts are outwith the province of the Wills Act because s 9 does not apply to testamentary trusts, not because secret trusts are *inter vivos*.

6.62   The *dehors* the will theory is fundamentally unsound. In the first place, the theory should be called the '*dehors* the Wills Act' theory to reflect what it means. The argument is that secret trusts are *inter vivos* trusts, therefore not testamentary, therefore not within the ambit of the Wills Act. Of course secret trusts are outside the *will*: wholly in the case of FSTs; partly in the case of HSTs. But that entails nothing whatsoever about the application of the Wills Act—every informal testamentary disposition is outside the will; if it were a formally valid testamentary disposition it would *be* a will, or part of one. So the theory depends upon establishing that secret trusts are not testamentary dispositions at all, so the formality requirements of the Wills Act simply do not apply.

6.63   But, alas, secret trusts *are* testamentary dispositions. They are perfectly revocable by the testator—he can either revoke the trust per se by communicating with his secret trustee and cancelling or modifying the arrangement, or more simply, he can execute another will deleting or modifying the gift to his legatee (or by just writing a will if the fully secret trust operates on intestacy), thus ensuring that the '*inter vivos*' trust he declared is never 'constituted' (Chapter), that is, by doing this he ensures that the specified trust property never gets into the hands of the trustee. Secondly, and more fundamentally, such a trust simply cannot be an effective *inter vivos* trust because in order to be effective the testator would be declaring a trust of 'future' property, and such a declaration is invalid, ie creates no trust. Future property just refers to property that does not exist yet. Now you might think that if I own Blackacre, and I tell you that I'm giving it to you in my will to hold on trust for Albert, then what's wrong with that? Blackacre exists, doesn't it? The point, however, is that I'm not declaring a trust over Blackacre now—I could do that, but that would *take Blackacre out of my estate on death*. But I have not done that. I am declaring a trust over property that may or may not be in my estate on death. Even if I do my utmost to ensure that Blackacre will be in my estate, it may turn out that I have to sell it before I die, or I may die in such debt that Blackacre will have to be sold by my executors. This, of course, is even more obvious in the case of a pecuniary legacy (eg a secret trust of £5,000). There is a further problem in the case of an *inter vivos* trust of a pecuniary legacy: unless you actually identify the actual money, ie the very notes and coins, the trust fails for uncertainty of subject matter. A person cannot just say, 'I now hold £5,000 on trust for you', even if he is worth millions; before the trust is valid he must segregate or otherwise identify the money that is the property of the trust (7.67 et seq). Clearly, there is no way of doing that now with money only identified some indefinite time in the future by executors following their administration of the estate. Therefore a legatee's hope of receiving any property of any kind under a will is considered by the law to be a mere hope or *spes* (3.6), which one can never count upon being fulfilled. So the fact of the matter is that secret trusts are imposed over property that will only be ascertained upon the administration of the testator's estate, and are subject to ademption and abatement like any other such gifts (for an interesting example, see *Re Maddock* (1902)). They are, therefore, ambulatory and, therefore, testamentary. Of course the Wills Act applies to them. The *'dehors* the will' theory is just an attempt to cloak the embarrassing jam equity has got itself into with its willingness to flout the Wills Act.

6.64   The theory has also proved to have confused a court in a nearby area. In *Gold v Hill* (1999) the court purported to treat the nomination of a beneficiary under a life insurance policy, the beneficiary having agreed to hold the insurance proceeds on trust for the nominator's wife and child, as a situation analogous to a secret trust. The analogy to, much less the application of, the doctrine of secret trusts is misconceived. The nomination of a beneficiary under a life insurance policy is not a testamentary gift (6.50), but akin to the assignment of a contractual right to a benefit. It is therefore not caught by the Wills Act, and any declaration of trust or undertaking of the trust by the nominee concerns the creation of a trust over a right that is personal property, so no formality requirements apply. Therefore, there is no need to import a doctrine, the purpose of which is to overcome the failure to comply with the *formality* requirements of *testamentary* gifts. The only reason one would apply the doctrine mistakenly in this way would be to assume that all informal undertakings to hold property on trust would normally fail, and so one needs some kind of '*dehors* the normal rules' equitable intervention to save the day, which is clearly false. The CA in *Kasperbaur v Griffiths* (1997) stated *obiter*, quite correctly, that the doctrine of secret trusts has no application to nominations of beneficiaries under life insurance policies.

6.65   It is submitted that the true reason for the decision in *Blackwell* has nothing really to do with the court's realising a new '*dehors*' justification for secret trusts, but is the obvious *pragmatic* reason, here stated by Viscount Sumner:

> In [both fully and half-secret trusts] the testator's wishes are incompletely expressed in his will. Why should equity, over a mere matter of words, give effect to them in one case and frustrate them in the other?

In other words, although there might be a valid *juridical* basis for enforcing FSTs but not HSTs, ie that there is no possibility of fraud in any meaningful sense in the latter, the different rules would be in *pragmatic* conflict, ie the law would look like an ass. Once equity has sold the Wills Act up the river by allowing testators to give it 'the go-by' with FSTs, it seems rather irrational to stop there and deny equity's enforcement to HSTs, and might well lead to apparent injustice, since from the testator's perspective the decision to use the words 'on trust' in his will can hardly seem to him to be of much consequence; furthermore, it would seem strange if a person who complied with the Wills Act as much as he could while keeping his gifts secret, by declaring in his will that the gift was held on trust, should be in a worse position than one who keeps everything secret. The result is, then, that both FSTs and HSTs, if properly created, are formally invalid testamentary trusts that equity will enforce.

6.66   Although the '*dehors* the will' theory is insupportable, certain decisions appear to depend upon it. In *Re Young* (1951) the testator's chauffeur was to receive a gift under an HST, but he had also attested the will; under s 15 of the Wills Act 1837, gifts to attesting witnesses and their spouses fail (attesting witnesses must be able to give unbiased evidence about the validity of the will's execution, and if a person or his spouse is to receive property under the will, that might bias him in favour of validity). Danckwerts J held that the chauffeur did not take 'under the will', so was able to receive the gift under the HST. Section 15 does not normally apply to trustees in a will because they receive no *beneficial* interest (*Cresswell v Cresswell* (1868)), but presumably, if the '*dehors* the will' theory applies, s 15 should defeat both an HST and an FST if the trustee attests the will. This may appear a bit odd in the case of the HST, for the trustee is identified as a trustee on the face of the will. But the *dehors* story says that he is not a trustee *under the will*, so s 15 should apply to him as much as to a trustee of an FST. Of course, one might argue that s 15 should not apply to any trustee, secret or not, since none takes a beneficial interest, but such a view cannot stand alongside *Re Young*, because that would be to have it both ways.

6.67   If secret trusts are *inter vivos* trusts, then s 53 should apply; in particular, s 53(1)(b) should apply to secret trusts of land. North J accepted *obiter* in *Re Baillie* (1886) that formal requirements would apply to an HST of land; an oral FST of land was found to be valid in *Ottaway v Norman* (1972), although it must be stressed that the formalities point was not raised.

6.68   An alternative version of the *dehors* theory was advanced by Romer J in *Re Gardner* (1923), which is that the secret *trustee* is the one that declares an *inter vivos* trust over the property he shall receive under the will; that, of course, is even more obviously ineffective as a declaration of trust over a mere *spes*. Such a declaration is at most a declaration of a future intention, and a mere intention will not be enforced by equity. Romer J decided that the interest that was to go to a beneficiary under a secret trust did not lapse when she predeceased the testator, because she was a beneficiary not under a testamentary trust, but under the *inter vivos* trust declared by the secret trustee. This logically follows from the finding that the legatee declares himself a secret trustee, but for the reason stated, such a trust is invalid, so the decision should not be followed.

Communication and acceptance

6.69   In order to prove an FST or an HST, the evidence must show (1) the intention of the testator to create a trust; (2) timely communication of that intention to the intended trustee; and (3) timely acceptance by the intended trustee of the trust obligation. The communication may be by the testator's agent (*Moss v Cooper* (1861)), and so long as the secret trustee *undertakes the obligation to carry out the trust*, he may 'sail under sealed orders', that is, the testator can provide him with an envelope containing the terms of the trust not to be opened until his death (*Re Keen* (1937); *Re Boyes* (1884); *McCormick*). Note the point in the italics carefully, for students regularly get this wrong in exams. Simply accepting a letter not to be opened until later which contains trust terms *does not* fulfil conditions (2) or (3); the recipient must understand that he is to hold *on trust* some property for some person(s) as specified in the letter. The testator must have decided the terms of the trust when the communication is made: 'The devisee or legatee cannot by accepting an indefinite trust enable the testator to make an unattested codicil' (*Re Boyes*). There must be an actual acceptance of or acquiescence in the trust obligation (*McCormick*); the imposition of a merely moral obligation is insufficient (*McCormick*; *Re Snowden*).

6.70   The orthodoxy governing what counts as timely communication and acceptance of the trust differs for FSTs and HSTs: an FST must be communicated to and accepted by the secret trustee before or after the execution of the will, but before the testator's death (*Moss v Cooper*); the rationale here is that because a will is revocable, he may execute his will and then communicate the trust to the intended secret trustee; if the latter refuses the trust obligation, the testator can make another will revoking the gift and leaving the property to someone else (*Re Gardner*, *per* Warrington LJ). In contrast, HSTs must be communicated before or at the same time as the making of the will.

6.71   This stricter HST rule for timely communication and acceptance arises for no good juridical reason, since the testator can still revoke the gift in the will if his intended trustee does not agree to undertake the trust just as easily as the testator of an FST can. Commentators almost universally abhor the difference in the communication rules, and, for example, in Ireland (*Re Browne* (1944)), the USA (American Law Institute (1959), para 55(c), (h)), and New South Wales (*Ledgerwood v Perpetual Trustee Co Ltd* (1997)), the rule that communication and acceptance may occur any time before the testator's death applies to HSTs as well as FSTs.

6.72   The leading case is the CA decision in *Re Keen* (1937), where £10,000 was given to two trustees:

> *to be held upon and disposed of by them among such person, persons, or charities as may be notified by me to them or either of them during my lifetime.*

The court found that before the execution of the will, one trustee was adequately notified as to the terms of the trust by being given a sealed envelope containing the name of the intended beneficiary; although told not to open it until the testator's death, he understood it to contain the terms of the trust: 'a ship which sails under sealed orders is sailing under orders though the exact terms are not ascertained by the captain till later'. The trust failed, however, for two reasons. The first, which is sometimes referred to as the 'broad' ratio, was that Lord Wright MR found that 'may' (emphasised in the quotation above) referred to future communication of the trusts, ie communication after the execution of the will. Such a clause was bad: because it contemplated future dispositions, the testator was reserving to himself the power to make future unwitnessed dispositions and so giving the 'go-by' to the Wills Act, and it therefore violated the principles laid down by Viscount Sumner in *Blackwell*. Even if the clause could be read to encompass prior communications, so long as it contemplated future ones it must be invalid.

6.73   The 'narrow' ratio was simply that the evidence of the trust, ie a trust communicated prior to the execution of the will, was inconsistent with the clause in the will as Lord Wright MR interpreted it, not necessarily defensibly, ie as encompassing only future declarations of trust. One may argue that the broad ratio was unnecessary for the decision, and therefore strictly speaking, *obiter*, so that the actual rule governing post-execution communications of HSTs remains open. Nevertheless, the rule invalidating post-execution communications is generally regarded as settled, if wrong. In *Re Bateman's Will Trusts* (1970) the rule was applied as if no doubt could be entertained about it.

6.74 The rule is typically explained as the result of a confusion of the doctrine of HSTs with the rule governing the incorporation by reference of documents into wills. Where a will refers to a document existing when the will is executed, that document becomes part of the properly attested will even though it is not itself properly attested; in other words, it is incorporated into the will. Because the existence of the half-secret *trustee* is identified in the will, the courts have confused this with a reference to a *trust declaration* that has been made when the will is executed. For this reason, the courts have seen it somehow appropriate to limit the enforcement of HSTs to those communicated and accepted prior to or contemporaneously with the will's execution. If it were not for this confusion, the argument goes, then surely the FST rule would apply, because as stated above, the FST can give the go-by to the Wills Act by allowing post-execution communications, so why not HSTs?

6.75 Perhaps, however, it is not that the judges have confused the enforcement of HSTs with the incorporation of documents, but have realised the *pragmatic* conflict that would arise between the enforcement of HSTs and the doctrine of incorporation by reference if post-execution communications were allowed. The crucial point is that both HSTs and incorporable documents are clearly referred to in the will. Whatever theory of HSTs you prefer, the proving of the HST looks like an exercise in filling in a gap in the will, much as the incorporation of an outside document does. Indeed, the practical similarities between HSTs and documents incorporated by reference are so apparent that Matthews (1979) argues that the *juridical* basis of HSTs is an expanded doctrine of incorporation by reference, ie to incorporate properly evidenced *oral* testamentary trusts. In view of this, a more expansive rule for admitting HSTs, ie allowing the proof of HSTs created after the execution of the will, would have the embarrassing consequence—embarrassing, that is, for any jurisdiction that is supposed to operate under the formalities of a Wills Act—of giving a wider ambit to unattested *oral* testamentary dispositions referred to in a will than to unattested *written* ones. As a result, the communication rules for HSTs may best be understood simply as an unprincipled but pragmatic halfway house between the doctrines of FSTs and incorporation by reference, and that it is futile to search for any more theoretically satisfying basis. The corollary is, of course, that the courts find it somewhat less embarrassing to have different communications rules for different secret trusts purely on the basis of the insertion of the words 'on trust' in the document.

Failure of a secret trust to be established

6.76 If the testator intends to create an FST, but fails to communicate it to the intended trustee so it is not accepted by him before the testator dies, then the gift under the will is not impressed with any trust, and the trustee takes absolutely (*Wallgrave v Tebbs* (1855); *Proby v Landor* (1860)). In general, if only one of two trustees is informed of and accepts the trust before the testator's death, then only he will be bound by the trust; the other receives his property absolutely, having undertaken no trust obligation. However, there appears to be a special rule for the case of trustees who receive the property as joint tenants (as opposed to as tenants in common (see 1.22)) where only one joint tenant has accepted the trust before the testator makes his will; in that case both are bound. In *Re Stead* (1900) Farwell J doubted that any good reason supported this rule, but accepted it as authoritative. Perrins (1985) argues that the uninformed legatee should only be bound by the representation of his co-legatee when that representation induced the testator either to make a gift to the two of them in his will or not to revoke a gift to the two of them in his will, on the principle that no one should profit from the fraud of another, and that nothing should turn on whether the legatees take as joint tenants or tenants in common.

6.77 If a legatee is told that he is to hold on trust, but the terms of the trust are never communicated to the trustee within the testator's lifetime, he is still a secret trustee, although the trust will obviously fail for uncertainty of objects; he will hold the property on an ART for the residuary beneficiaries or intestate successors (*Re Boyes* (1884)). The trustee will similarly hold on an ART if the trust is fully communicated, but the trust fails, like any testamentary trust might fail, for uncertainty (Chapter 7) or illegality: thus, in *Moss v Cooper*, the *residuary legatees* successfully pleaded that the legatees held the property they received on a secret trust to apply his property to charitable purposes in violation of the Mortmain and Charitable Uses Act 1736; the trust was proven, failed for illegality, and the secret trustees therefore held the property on an ART for the residuary legatees.

6.78 No cases have decided what should happen if a fully secret trustee were to renounce the gift or predecease the testator. In *Re Maddock* (1902) Cozens-Hardy LJ opined *obiter* that if the legatee renounced the gift or died during the lifetime of the testator, the secret beneficiaries would get nothing. In *Blackwell*, by contrast, Lord Buckmaster said *obiter* that he 'entertained no doubt' that if an FST were proved on the evidence, the court would not allow it to be defeated by the trustee's renunciation. He did not consider the case of a fully secret trustee who predeceased the testator. This should probably be dealt with as a problem of timing and reliance: does the testator have a realistic opportunity to alter his will? If yes, then the trust should fail if the trustee renounces, or predeceases the testator. If the testator is unable to make a new will, the trust should be proved against the secret trustee or his personal representative if dead. No such problems arise in the case of HSTs, because the court will not allow a trust to fail for want of a trustee (2.81) (assuming the terms of the trust can be proved despite the half-secret trustee's death).

6.79 In the case of HSTs, the result of any failure of the testator to specify the trusts will be that the trustee will hold the trust property for the residuary legatees, or if none, for the intestate successors. In *Re Colin Cooper* (1939) the testator made a will in which £5,000 was given to two trustees under an HST, having communicated the trust before the execution of the will. Two days before he died, he revoked the will except for the HST, but he also increased the sum to be held on the HST to £10,000; the increase was not communicated to the trustees, and the CA held (1), that the first £5,000 was to be held on the HST, because that was the extent of the subject matter communicated; the remainder went on ART into the estate, and (2) the fact that the gift of £5,000 was technically not the one in the first will, ie the will to which the communication of the trust applied, did not matter, as they were in substance the same gift. The general principle of (1), that the trust only binds to the extent communicated, applies to fully secret trusts as well. However, there the question arises, who would get the increase? One might say that, as the increase was not impressed by any communicated trust, then the trustees should take it as an absolute gift. On the other hand, by parity of reasoning with *Re Boyes*, one might argue that once obliged, even the fully secret trustee can only take *as* a trustee, so any increase that fails to get into the trust cannot go to him beneficially, but must be held on an ART.

6.80 In the case of HSTs, complications can arise between the directions given in the will and the directions communicated to the trustee—the rule is that the instructions in the will prevail in any conflict. In *Re Huxtable* (1902) £4,000 was given in the will for charitable purposes agreed by the testator and the trustee. Evidence was admissible to prove the charity was for the relief of sick and poor members of the Church of England, but not admissible to prove that only the income on £4,000 was to be spent this way, and that the trustee was to dispose of the principal as he wished on his death, because on the face of the will the whole £4,000 was given to charity, and evidence of the trustee's power to dispose of the principal would contradict the will. *Re Gardner* provides something of a contrast. The testatrix left all her property to her husband for his benefit during his life, 'knowing that he will carry out my wishes'. Thus at first glance this gift of a life estate might appear to be the subject matter of an HST (although the words do not clearly manifest an intention to create a trust: see 7.12–7.14), with an intestacy with respect to the remainder, since that was not disposed of by the will. However, in view of the evidence, the CA decided that the testatrix's intention was to give her husband the benefit of the life estate, while he held the remainder that came to him as her intestate successor under an FST to give it to certain beneficiaries under his will.

6.81   The question also arises whether evidence of the HST can show that the half-secret trustee is himself to benefit from the trust. In general a person named as a trustee may only take a beneficial interest if that is clearly indicated, and on the face of the will in an HST that is plainly not the case, so in that sense evidence proving that the trustee is to take under an HST may be regarded as contradicting the will. In *Re Rees* (1950) the testator left his entire estate to his solicitor and a friend as trustees 'they well knowing my wishes concerning the same'. The friend died shortly after the testator, and the evidence of the solicitor was that the trustees were to make certain payments and keep the surplus. The CA held that the substantial surplus went on intestacy. Lord Evershed MR said that evidence that they were to take a beneficial interest would conflict with the terms of the will, since they were named as trustees. In *Re Tyler's Fund Trusts* (1967) Pennycuick J stated *obiter* that he did not find this reasoning 'easy' and that, in principle, evidence is admissible to prove all the terms of a trust, including a trust in favour of a trustee. Evershed MR's decision undoubtedly turned in part on the consideration that:

> In the general public interest it seems to me desirable that, if a testator wishes his property to go to his solicitor and the solicitor prepares the will, that intention on the part of the testator should appear plainly in the will and should not be arrived at by the more oblique method of what is sometimes called a secret trust.

This 'public interest' issue has since been reconsidered in *Rawstron v Freud* (2014). The famous British painter Lucien Freud left a will leaving his residuary estate to two named individuals. A prior will was essentially identical except for the fact that the residue was left to the same individuals as trustees of an HST. A man claiming to be a son of Freud's argued that, on the proper interpretation of the second, operative, will, the named individuals took the residue as trustees, on an unspecified HST; his purpose in so claiming appeared to me that if he was successful on this point then he could launch another action seeking to explore whether the HST was valid (perhaps claiming it was invalid for failing to comply with the rules of timeous communication (6.70 et seq)). The court held, on interpreting the will, that the named individuals took beneficially. The issue was then raised that since one of the named individuals was Freud's solicitor, she should not take beneficially in view of the public interest considerations raised by Evershed in *Re Rees*. The court disagreed. The court argued that it was generally a good thing if a solicitor could take as an absolute legatee, for then a testator could create an FST where the trustee was a qualified professional. (Recall the quote at 6.57.) Moreover, the court admitted the solicitor's evidence that the residue was indeed to be held on an FST, and that this met any public interest concern in this case.

6.82   As is apparent from the tone of the foregoing, the present author thinks that equity should not enforce FSTs and HSTs, but should require them to fail as testamentary gifts not complying with the Wills Act, except in rare cases where a feckless testator really has been fraudulently induced to make a gift to the legatee, for example by being told that the law will not allow him to give his intended beneficiary any property under a will. No assistance should be given to any scheme by the testator to avoid the Act. *Inter vivos* trusts, joint tenancy, and insurance policies can all be used to make secret post-mortem gifts by those who cannot come clean about their preferred objects of bounty even after their death. Equity should not provide a further means that so exorbitantly flouts the policy of the Act.

FURTHER READING

Green (1984)

Hodge (1980)

Matthews (1979, 2010)

Perrins (1985)

Sheridan (1951)

Swadling (2016)

Watkin (1981)

Youdan (1984)

Must-read cases: *Rochefoucauld v Boustead* (1897); *Grey v IRC* (1959); *Vandervell v IRC* (1966); *Re Vandervell (No 2)* (1974); *McCormick v Grogan* (1869); *Blackwell v Blackwell* (1929); *Re Keen* (1936)

SELF-TEST QUESTIONS

1.   Explain the operation of s 53(1)(b) of the Law of Property Act 1925 and the doctrine of *Rochefoucauld v Boustead*.

2.   What do *Grey v IRC*, *Vandervell v IRC*, and *Re Vandervell (No 2)* decide?

3.   Trustbank plc holds 50,000 shares of Zinc Ltd as nominee trustee for Sam. Sam transfers 150,000 shares of Gold Ltd to Trustbank stating that he wishes to provide for his children.

   (i)   Sam orally directs Trustbank to hold 50,000 shares of Zinc on trust for his three children, Albert, Jane, and Charlotte, in such shares as Trustbank shall in its absolute discretion appoint. Several months later, for revenue purposes, Trustbank makes a written declaration that it holds the shares on trust for the children.

   (ii)   Sam orally directs Trustbank to transfer 50,000 Gold shares to Albert absolutely, which it does.

   (iii) Sam orally directs Trustbank to hold 50,000 of the Gold shares on trust for Jane. Sam tells Jane that he has done so, and Jane demands that Trustbank transfer the shares to her, which it does.

   (iv)   Trustbank declares that it holds the remaining 50,000 shares of Gold on trust for Charlotte.

(v)   Sam dies, leaving his entire estate to his lover, Fred. Advise Fred.

4.   In 1993, Samuel made his will, leaving £50,000 to Tina and Trish, and Blackacre to John 'on trust for such persons as I shall instruct him'. In 1994 Samuel mailed Tina a letter that enclosed a sealed envelope; the letter instructed Tina that the sealed envelope was not to be opened until after Samuel's death. Also in 1994, Samuel had lunch with John and told him that he should hold Blackacre on trust for Margaret, Samuel's mistress; John agreed to do so. Samuel died a couple of weeks ago. Tina opened the sealed envelope to discover that it states that she and Trish are to hold the £50,000 on trust for Samuel's illegitimate daughter, Francesca. Advise Margaret and Francesca.

5.   Is there a theoretical basis for secret trusts that justifies their enforcement?

7 Certainty

SUMMARY

7.1   A declaration of trust must be 'certain', which means that a settlor must declare the terms of the trust with sufficient 'certainty' or precision for the trustees to know what they must do, or the intended trust fails.

The three certainties

7.2   The traditional elements of this sufficiency of declaration are known as the 'three certainties', following *Knight v Knight* (1840): certainty of intention; certainty of subject matter; and certainty of objects. The first concerns the question whether what the putative settlor did or said amounts to a declaration of a trust over his property. The second requires that the property that is to form the trust corpus is identifiable. The third requires that the intended beneficiaries, the 'objects' of the trust, are identifiable.

7.3   One should distinguish the certainty of intention from the other two. Certainty of intention is like the 'intention to create legal relations' in contract law; it concerns the question whether the putative settlor really meant to create a trust at all. When we deal with the second and third certainties, we are past that point. We know what the person intended, whether a trust, a power of appointment, or an outright gift: these secondary certainties concern the efficacy of the settlor's expression, or the workability of his intentions—does he provide an instruction that can be carried out? Or is it too vague, or too difficult, or even impossible to implement? A severe difficulty in identifying the subject matter or objects may indicate that no trust was intended: uncertainty of subject matter (*Mussoorie Bank Ltd v Raynor* (1882)) or objects (see eg *Lambe v Eames* (1871)) has a 'reflex action' that indicates an uncertainty of intention to create a trust.

Certainty of intention: the family gift context

7.4 The maxim 'Equity looks to intent, not form' (6.5) fully applies to declarations of trust. No particular formula is necessary, not even the use of the word 'trust'. Neither is it necessary for the settlor to know that, technically, that is what he is doing. In *Paul v Constance* (1977) Mr Constance and Mrs Paul lived together as man and wife although not legally married. He opened a bank account in his own name with money received as compensation for an injury at work. Because of their dealings with the account—they both drew upon it to play bingo and deposited their winnings in it—and because on several occasions Mr Constance declared to Mrs Paul, 'the money is as much yours as mine', the court held him to have declared a trust of the property in equal shares for himself and Mrs Paul. Thus very informal declarations of trust of personalty are possible (as we have seen, there is a writing formality in the case of land (6.6)).

7.5 Many trusts are testamentary gifts, so finding a trust will often depend on construing wills to infer the testator's 'intention'. Uncertainty can arise because there are ways in which a testator may deal with his property that might superficially resemble trusts, but are not. Wills sometimes contain gifts subject to charges: for example, 'I give the leasehold interest on my factory to James, my son, absolutely, but subject to his paying £10,000 per annum to my widow, Jane.' The gift has been made subject to a charge, but James is not a trustee for his mother. Wills may also contain conditional gifts, such as 'Blackacre to James on condition he pays £10,000 per annum to my widow for life, and upon his failure to do so, to Claire for life'. If James does not comply with the condition, then the property will go to Claire. But again, James is not a trustee. In *Re Foord* (1922) the testator left shares 'absolutely' to his sister 'on trust' to pay his wife an annuity; the shares were worth considerably more than required for the annuity, and the question arose on what basis the sister held the surplus. Sargant J found the case a difficult one, but decided that the surplus was held by the sister for her own benefit, and not for the next of kin.

7.6 Occasionally it is difficult to tell whether someone intended to declare a trust or merely stated an intention to make a future gift. In *Jones v Lock* (1865) a man on return from a business trip responded to his infant child's nurse's statement that he had 'not brought baby anything' by pressing a cheque made out to him for £900 into the wee child's hand and said, 'Look you here, I give this to baby'. He later contacted his solicitor, expressing the intention to invest the £900 and more for the benefit of the child, as well as to alter his will in the child's favour. Before doing so he died. Although sympathetic, the court was unwilling to find the father's actions a declaration of trust. He intended to deal with the property in the cheque for the benefit of the son, no doubt, but not as a trustee, but as the full owner until such time as he had made his intended arrangements with his solicitor. The court regarded his 'declaration' as merely a declaration that he was now able to provide for his son and intended to do so.

Trust or power of appointment?

7.7 Trust instruments are to be interpreted or construed by applying the normal rules for the construction of documents (*Millar v Millar* (2018), [17]–[18]), although historically courts have applied some particular rules of construction with respect to trust instruments. Consider: '£100,000 to my trustees for distribution to such of my relations as my trustees shall in their absolute discretion think fit': it would seem to be unclear whether 'for distribution' means 'to be distributed', an imperative direction imposing an obligation upon them to distribute, or is rather to be interpreted as 'available for distribution', thus creating no obligation but giving the trustees a power that they may exercise if they so choose (3.8–3.10).

7.8 Several rules of construction may determine whether a trust or a power of appointment is intended:

(1) If there is an explicit 'gift over' in default of appointment, such as 'my shares in X company to my trustees, with power to appoint to my children in such portions as my trustees shall in their absolute discretion decide, *and in default of appointment to the National University of Singapore*', there is a power of appointment, because if the settlor provides for the case where the trustees do not appoint, clearly they are under no duty to do so.

(2) The second rule is a specification of the first. In order to find a power on the basis of a gift over, the gift over must specifically arise on default of appointment. For example, a residuary gift (2.84) is not a gift over for this purpose. Residuary clauses deal with failures of all kinds; nothing, therefore, can be inferred about any specific gift just because the will contains a residuary clause.

(3) Finally, if there is no gift over in default of appointment, one must determine the true intentions of the testator by construing the will or settlement as a whole. For example if the testator uses words that clearly indicate his intention to create a trust with respect to some of his gifts, but does not in the gift under consideration, the court is apt to conclude that there is no trust—the testator knew what words to use to create a trust, and in respect of this gift did not (see *Re Weekes' Settlement* (1897)). The settlor's use of the word 'power' is not determinative, but words such as 'shall' or 'to be', as in 'shall distribute' or 'to be divided amongst' seem quite clearly to be imperative, strongly indicating the imposition of a duty, and thus a trust. Finally, where a trust is intended but fails for a reason that would not invalidate a similarly framed power, the court will not save the gift by treating it as a power (*IRC v Broadway Cottages Trust* (1955); *Re Shaw* (1957)).

7.9 Settlors may create a power of appointment 'coupled' with an implied trust in default of appointment. It is perfectly possible to give someone a power to appoint certain property, in default of which appointment the property goes to the objects of the power itself, rather than to another class of objects (3.9). In cases where there is a gift over in default to the same people who are the objects of the power of appointment, then the power is, in essence, nothing more than a power to vary the shares that the objects would otherwise receive under the gift over.

7.10 In *Re Weekes' Settlement* (1897), a testatrix left property to her husband with a 'power to dispose of all such property by will amongst our children in accordance with the power granted to him as regards the other property which I have under my marriage settlements'. There was no gift over, so that did not decide the issue. The husband died intestate. The children argued that the testatrix's words indicated *a general intention* that the husband should leave the property in question to all the children in equal shares if he did not appoint particular shares to them, in other words, that he was given a power coupled with an implied trust in default of appointment. Their argument failed. The court did not find it possible to construe from the document that the property should be held on trust for all the children jointly if he did not appoint.

7.11 In *Burrough v Philcox* (1840), the pertinent instruction in the will was as follows:

> but in case my son and daughter should both of them die without leaving lawful issue, then for the said estates to be disposed of as shall be hereinafter mentioned, that is to say, the longest liver of my two children shall have the power, by a will, properly attested, in writing, to dispose of all my real and personal estates amongst my nephews and nieces or their children, either all to one of them, or to as many of them as my surviving child shall think proper.

Here the court found a general intention that the class of nieces and nephews and their children should benefit. Lord Cottenham LC said:

> [W]hen there appears a general intention in favour of a class, and a particular intention in favour of individuals of a class to be selected by another person, and the particular intention fails, from that selection not being made, the Court will carry into effect the general intention in favour of the class . . . and in such case, the Court will not permit the objects of the power to suffer by the negligence of the donee [of the power], but fastens upon the property a trust for their benefit.

Thus the property was held for the nieces and nephews and their children in equal shares.

Two problems, one old, one new: (1) precatory words and (2) 'sham' trusts and 'illusory' trusts

Precatory words

7.12 'Precatory words' are words of prayer or request in wills, for example, this testator's direction from *Mussoorie Bank Ltd v Raynor* (1882): 'I give to my dearly beloved wife . . . the whole of my property . . . feeling confident that she will act justly to our children in dividing the same when no longer required by her.' Clearly the testator had in mind that his wife would, following her use of the property, pass it on to his children, but did he intend her to hold the property on trust—for her own use for life, say, and then for their children after her death?

7.13 A run of cases leading up to the middle of the nineteenth century provided authority for a 'doctrine of precatory trusts', a rule of construction, by which such expressions were held sufficient to create trust obligations (see *Palmer v Simmonds* (1854)). In *Lambe v Eames* (1871), however, the CA refused to find that a testator's gift of his estate to his widow 'to be at her disposal in any way she may think best, for the benefit of herself and her family' was a trust. James LJ said:

> [I]n hearing case after case cited, I could not help feeling that the officious kindness of the Court of Chancery in interposing trusts where in many cases the father of the family never meant to create trusts, must have been a very cruel kindness indeed.

7.14 In *Mussoorie Bank*, the same attitude was adopted by the HL, and the 'doctrine' of precatory trusts was effectively abolished. Nevertheless in the proper context words that on their face look merely precatory may establish a trust. In *Comiskey v Bowring-Hanbury* (1905) the words 'in full confidence that . . . at her death [my wife] will devise it to such one or more of my nieces' were taken to establish a trust for the persuasive reason that immediately following this direction was a statement to the effect that in the event that the wife failed to devise the property to one or more of the nieces herself, it should be divided equally amongst them. It therefore seemed clear that the testator intended his nieces to take following her death, so the wife really held the property on trust for herself for life, and then for the nieces, with a power to vary the nieces' particular shares by her will.

Sham trusts and illusory trusts

7.15 'Sham' trusts, in the context of our interest in the certainty of intention, are equitable property transactions the written terms of which purport to divest the settlor of his interest in the trust property, but in reality do not, because he had no intention to create a trust of the kind that the written terms represent. A genuine sham involves an intent to deceive third parties, in particular, as to the extent of one's assets (see *Midland Bank v Wyatt* (1995)), and the 'sham-ming' intention may relate only to the terms of the trust, which are meant to deceive, but not to whether a trust was established at all, and a trust is not a sham just because it is created with an improper motive (*Lewis v Condon* (2013)). A second case is not really a sham, because it involves no intent to deceive; rather, it reveals that the settlor's intention does not align with the written terms of the trust. This latter situation typically arises where a rich individual is 'sold' an offshore trust as an investment vehicle offering various advantages. Recall that, in the normal case of a trust, as opposed to the case of a bare trust, the settlor cannot regard the trust property as still 'really his' (2.27). In the normal case, because the trust property is no longer beneficially the settlor's, no one having any claims against him or his estate when he dies, such as his creditors, a divorced spouse, or his heirs if the settlor comes from a jurisdiction where heirs or dependants have legal claims against his estate that cannot be defeated by his will, will be able (generally speaking) to claim any share of the property in the trust. This is regarded by some settlors as one of the *inter vivos* trust's chief advantages. But what if the 'settlor' of such a trust is told that it is equivalent to a 'living will', in which he can order the trustees to deal with the property as he orders, during his life and after his death? In that case, whatever the actual terms of the trust say, the settlor's intention was not to create a trust by which he gave up the beneficial interest in the property, but instead to create a bare trust in which he has the full control and beneficial ownership of the property (see eg the Jersey case *Rahman v Chase Bank (CI) Trust Co Ltd* (1991)). It is therefore claimable by his creditors, is treated as part of his assets on divorce, and falls into his estate at his death. Cases of this kind, then, raise the issue of certainty of intention in a different way—does the settlor intend, by entering into a transaction (whatever it may be called—remember, the particular words are not decisive (7.4)) to lose his hold over the trust assets, or does he believe, especially in consequence of the sales pitch made to him, that he will remain the beneficial owner of them? (See Willoughby (1999).)

7.16 Along similar lines is a distinction that might be drawn using the terminology of an 'illusory trust'. This is a trust in which, although appearing to be for the benefit of a class of beneficiaries, under its terms the trustee or settlor (in particular where the trustee is the settlor) has such control over the trust property in virtue of the trust provisions, he is basically able to do with the property what he likes, distributing it all to himself for instance (see eg *Clayton v Clayton* (2013) [78]–[91]) Another typical way in which 'offshore' trusts are created is by the settlor's execution of a broad discretionary trust, which gives the trustees wide dispositive powers (2.50,

3.93 et seq). However, the settlor also typically provides a 'letter of wishes' (3.66) that gives the trustee guidance on exercising his dispositive discretions, but which is not meant to be *legally binding*. But this is a matter of construction.

7.17   In *Chen v Ling* (2000) the letter of 'wishes' was in such clearly imperative terms that the court had no difficulty in finding that the settlor intended the letter to bind the trustees; hence, the real trust of the assets transferred to the trustee on trust was found to be what was said in the letter of wishes, not what the so-called 'trust document' stated. Similarly, in *Taulbut v Davey* (2018), the court held that a letter of wishes was incorporated into a testatrix's will in view of the way that the will directed her trustees to comply with the letter of wishes.

7.18   *Clayton v Clayton* (2013) went on appeal all the way up to the New Zealand Supreme Court (*Clayton v Clayton* (2016)). There, the NZSC accepted that the court can find that a deed creating a trust is a sham if the parties are shown to have intended it to be a pretence. However, the court found 'no basis to extend the sham concept to encompass a trust created under a document that was not intended to be a pretence but that the Court considers is otherwise reprehensible in some way'. Further, the court also observed that a finding that a trust deed is not a sham does not preclude a finding that the attempt to create a trust failed and that no valid trust has come into existence, in other words, that the trust is illusory. As you may have already guessed, the NZSC was ultimately of the opinion that the term 'illusory trust' used by the High Court and the Court of Appeal was unhelpful, and means nothing more than that no trust, or rather, no trust except for a bare trust in favour of the settlor was created. (See also Bennett (2017); Ho (2018).)

7.19   Most recently, in *JSC Mezhdunarodniy Promyshlenniy Bank v Pugachev* (2017), the UKHC considered the issue of illusory trusts, sham trusts, and the relation between the two. Birss J found the label 'illusory' to be unhelpful. The real question was to determine 'the true effect of the trust', ie whether the actual terms of the trust allowed the settlor to act selfishly, considering only his own interests, such that he retained effective control over the trust assets. On the facts of this case, the judge held that the settlor, in taking the role of the first protector (3.27 et seq) during his lifetime, had such extensive powers, in particular his non-fiduciary power to dismiss and replace trustees 'without cause', which gave him effective control over the assets such that he could direct how they should be used as he liked. As regards the notion of a sham, this covered the case where the actual trust document, construed according to its terms, was intended to give a false impression to third parties, false in the sense that the parties (the trustee and the settlor) never intended that the trust would be operated giving effect to those terms.

7.20   As to the relation between the two, Birss J had this to say:

> [436] Given Mr Pugachev's true intentions, the finding on the True Effect of the Trusts claim means that these trusts are not shams. They fulfil Mr Pugachev's true intention not to lose control. . . . In other words –while the trustees of these deeds are properly appointed as trustees, effective control of the actions of the trustees is held by the Protector through the Protector's powers. In this respect the Protector has ultimate control of the trusts.

> [437] However if a proper approach to the construction of these deeds was to lead to a conclusion that the Protector's relevant powers are fiduciary, as [the original trustee] now says they are, and that in turn was to lead to a conclusion that under the deeds Mr

Pugachev is not the beneficial owner, then those deeds are a sham. The settlor intended to use them to create a false impression as to his true intentions and the trustees went along with that intention recklessly.

Sham and true effect of the trusts

[438] The situation in this case reminds me of a similar phenomenon in patent law known as the Angora cat problem first identified by Professor Franzosi, an eminent academic expert in the field. It was described by Jacob LJ in the Court of Appeal in European Central Bank v Document Security Systems [2008] EWCA Civ 192 at paragraph 5. In some circumstances a patentee can argue for a narrow interpretation of a document while defending it in one context but then argue for a different wide interpretation when asserting it in another context. Jacob LJ explained that:

'Professor Mario Franzosi likens a patentee to an Angora cat. When validity is challenged, the patentee says his patent is very small: the cat with its fur smoothed down, cuddly and sleepy. But when the patentee goes on the attack, the fur bristles, the cat is twice the size with teeth bared and eyes ablaze.'

[439] This vice, that the same patent document can be presented in radically different ways in different circumstances to suit the owner's needs is not unique to patents. Both constructions may be arguable and so the canny professional who drafted the document can even salve their conscience by presenting two inconsistent but arguable interpretations on different occasions.

[440] The problem can apply to any written instrument and this case provides another example in a different context. When the validity or effect of the trust is challenged, the trustee can put forward emollient submissions about Protector's powers being confined and narrow as a result of their fiduciary nature. That has happened in these proceedings. But in other circumstances, for example when Mr Pugachev needs collateral for a bank loan, a completely different stance can be taken in relation to the very same instrument. Mr Pugachev can be presented as the owner of the trust assets.

Certainty of intention: the commercial context

7.21   There are different legal bases upon which property, in particular personalty such as goods for sale or raw materials, can be dealt with in the commercial context to serve different ends, including the trust. Which basis is used will, in general, be determined by the intentions of the parties. Here we will briefly consider bailment and agency, retentions of legal title, and equitable charges, in the case of goods and raw materials, and then consider the 'Quistclose' trust of money.

Bailment

7.22   The bailment is a common law transaction in which the owner of a chattel (bailments can only be made of chattels, never land) called the 'bailor', puts someone else into possession of his chattel, called the 'bailee' of course, with the intention that the bailee shall restore the bailor to possession at some future date. (Under the terms of the bailment or the general law, the obligation to restore the bailor to possession may be extinguished, for example in certain circumstances if the property is destroyed or stolen through no fault of the bailee, or as a term of the contract of bailment, as under a hire-purchase contract where a person buys a car on instalments; the seller (or finance company) retains title to the car until all the instalments are paid, and until they are all paid, the hirer/purchaser is merely a bailee of the car; once, however, all the instalments are paid, title to the car passes to the hirer/purchaser under the contract, and the bailment comes to an end.)

7.23   Bailments can be made for all sorts of reasons. When I lend you a book, that is a bailment. That is a bailment for the benefit of the bailee, because you want possession of the book so you can read it. But a bailment can also be for the benefit of the bailor, as when I check my coat at the theatre, or when I put a carrier in possession of my goods for shipping. Bailments can be for reward to the bailor, as when a bailee hires a car, or for reward to the bailee, as when I pay you to warehouse my goods. A bailment can be used as a form of security, as when I pledge or pawn goods. As bailor I give the bailee possession of my valuable wristwatch, and on the basis of this he agrees to lend me £100. Under the contract that attends this bailment I give the bailee, the pledgee or pawnbroker, the authority to sell my wristwatch if I do not repay the loan by the specified date.

7.24   Now what on earth has this to do with the law of trusts? Well, at a very superficial level, the bailment resembles a trust when the settlor transfers a chattel to a trustee to hold on trust for him. In the latter case, the settlor transfers legal title to the trustee, who undertakes an obligation to use his title to the chattel for the settlor's benefit. Similarly, the bailor transfers possession of the chattel to the bailee, subject to the obligation to restore possession of the chattel to him at a future date. The important thing to notice about the bailment is that though the bailee has an obligation to return the bailed chattel to the bailor, he never acquires title to the chattel from the bailor. Therefore he does not hold any title to the chattel that he must hold 'on trust' for the bailor. The bailor has the full beneficial title in the chattel, and is merely temporarily out of possession. If the bailee refuses to return the chattel at the appointed time, the bailor is entitled to bring an action against the bailee for its return, and if the bailee sells the chattel in breach of the terms of the bailment to a third party, that third party is liable for conversion (2.70). By contrast if the trustee sells the trust property to a bona fide purchaser, the beneficiary's interest is extinguished, and if the trustee transfers title to a non-bona fide purchaser, the beneficiary can enforce his equitable interest in the property against that recipient (2.64). So there is very little here either in economic reality or law that would cause most people to confuse a bailment with a trust. However, in a particular context it can be uncertain whether a transaction is a bailment or a transfer on trust for the benefit of the transferor/settlor. That context is exemplified by the sale of raw materials to a manufacturer.

Retention of legal title

7.25   A number of legal arrangements may underlie A's supplying raw materials to B, a manufacturer. A may just sell the raw materials to B, taking immediate payment, but typically, sellers do not demand payment up front for the sale of their raw materials, but allow the buyer to buy 'on credit' having to repay in, say, 90 days from receipt of the goods. Where A provides the materials to B on credit,

A may worry about B's becoming insolvent and so, in the contract of sale, A may employ what is called a reservation of title or 'Romalpa' clause (*Aluminium Industrie Vaassen BV v Romalpa Aluminium Ltd* (1976); *Clough Mill Ltd v Martin* (1984)), under which the legal title to the materials remains with A, B merely taking possession as a bailee, until (1) they lose their identity by being incorporated in B's products—if you paint a car, the paint 'accedes' to the car, so there is no longer any distinct property right in the paint; or (2) if their identity is still identifiable, they are sold by B, whereupon the title to them passes to the buyer; or (3) B has paid off all outstanding debts to A, whereupon the title passes to B himself. If B becomes insolvent, A can reclaim the materials B has on hand. There is no trust here; the legal title to the goods simply remains with A until either (1), (2), or (3) occurs.

Equitable charges

7.26   Alternatively, the legal title to the raw materials may pass to B under the contract, but A may try to establish that he has an equitable charge (2.91) on them, which will make him a secured creditor. If B is a company, however, which for obvious reasons is often the case, the equitable charge must be registered or it is void against B's general creditors or his liquidator (Companies Act 1985, s 395). Thus even if A is able to establish, through the interpretation of the contract, that he has an equitable charge over company B's property, this is unlikely to help in company B's insolvency for it is unlikely that A will have registered the charge if its creation was simply a consequence of the proper interpretation of their contract.

A trust of the materials?

7.27   A, however, may have one more string to his bow. If A can claim that he transferred the legal title to the materials to B 'on trust' for himself, so that he, A, becomes the equitable beneficial owner, then A may reclaim the property upon B's insolvency. The leading case is *Re Bond Worth Ltd* (1980). In *Re Bond Worth* the supplier purported to transfer legal title to fibre to a company for its manufacturing purposes, while retaining beneficial title for itself by requiring the manufacturing company hold the fibre it received on trust for it, as well as acquiring equitable title to the manufacturer's products incorporating the fibre and to the proceeds of sale of those products. The court held that such an arrangement effectively amounted to an equitable charge on the fibre, the products, and the proceeds. The reasoning was straightforward: it could not have been the case that, had the debtor-manufacturer paid off the amounts owing to the creditor-supplier, the latter could enforce the equitable title to the manufactured goods and proceeds of sale in any case, taking a windfall. And to the extent their value exceeded the outstanding debt owing to it, the creditor-supplier would have to account for the surplus to the debtor. Since the only commercially plausible interpretation was that the creditor-supplier was an accounting party in this way, the only plausible construction of its equitable interest in the manufactured goods and proceeds of sale was that it was a charge, not an ownership interest under a trust. It now appears to be orthodoxy that while legal retention of title clauses with respect to transferred chattels are effective, those that purport to 'retain' equitable title will be treated as charges, but the reasoning is questionable (see Worthington (1996), at 15–24). There is a sound policy reason for this position though: the registration requirement for charges against companies means these interests will be publicly ascertainable by prospective creditors.

The *Quistclose* trust of money

7.28   The position is significantly different in the case of money advanced by A to B to enable B specifically to pay off certain debts (*Barclays Bank Ltd v Quistclose Investments Ltd* (1970); *Carreras Rothmans Ltd v Freeman Mathews Treasure Ltd* (1985)); or to pursue certain projects (*Re EVTR* (1987)). Quistclose (Q) was an investment company that advanced £209,000 to Rolls Razor (RR) in order to allow the latter to pay a dividend that it had already declared. It was accepted by all concerned that if RR had used the money to pay the dividend, then RR would simply have owed Q £209,000 (plus interest); had RR paid the dividend and then gone into liquidation, Q would have been an ordinary creditor. RR was in trouble and did indeed go into liquidation, but before paying the dividend. The HL held that RR held the money on trust to pay the dividend and that, upon its failure to do so, the money was held upon trust for Q.

7.29   *Quistclose* trusts represent a departure from the 'default' position when money is lent in a commercial context. Normally if A lends money to B, the money immediately becomes B's legal property and A becomes an ordinary creditor; it does not matter that A pays the money to B under certain conditions (eg to spend it only on certain business projects). If B spends the money otherwise, he just commits a breach of contract, but not a breach of trust (the consequence of such a breach of contract may be, for example, that the loan is immediately repayable). Furthermore, it is not obvious what kind of trust this is.

7.30   We will address the nature of this trust in detail in Chapter 9 (9.47 et seq). While there remains substantial controversy, in the HL judgment of Lord Millett in *Twinsectra v Yardley* (2002) the trust was explained as a case of a loan arrangement that incorporates a 'bare trust with mandate' (9.47). The typical example is the trust under which a solicitor holds his client's funds before completing the purchase of land. If you are buying a house, the transaction normally involves two distinct steps: contract and completion. First, you and the seller will enter into a contract for the purchase. The contract will specify a date when you will hand over the money, and the seller will transfer title to the house. Both steps will normally involve the participation of your solicitor or conveyancing agent. Prior to completion, you will transfer the purchase money to your solicitor, who will hold the fund in his client account, ie a trust account. He will hold those funds on bare trust for you, *but* subject to your contractual standing order, or 'mandate', to transfer the funds to the seller on the day of completion in return for acquiring the title to the property. The contractual mandate is a term of your contract with your solicitor to carry out the purchase transaction for you.

7.31   It is important to appreciate the effect of this arrangement. Throughout the time your solicitor holds the funds in his account, he holds them on trust for you. So if your solicitor were to go bankrupt, the funds would still be yours in equity, and so could not be claimed by your solicitor's trustee in bankruptcy for distribution to his general creditors (2.89). And if your solicitor were to use the trust funds in any way inconsistent with your mandate, he would commit a breach of trust, because under a bare trust the trustee holds the funds to your order (2.13), and your mandate is your order. When your solicitor transfers the funds to the seller on completion, he carries out your order, your mandate, and thus properly disposes of the funds according to the terms of the trust, and the trust comes to an end.

7.32   In the case of a *Quistclose* trust, this arrangement is combined with a contract of loan. When the lender (L) transfers the money to the borrower (B), this transfer is on trust, a bare trust with mandate. B holds the money on trust for L until he uses the money for the purpose agreed under the loan contract. Once he does that, fulfilling the terms of the bare trust with mandate, the arrangement turns into a pure loan, with B liable to repay L the money at whatever interest rate is agreed, because there is no longer any money held on trust. But the effect of this arrangement is twofold: if B spends the money on a purpose outside the agreed loan purpose, this will be a breach of L's mandate, thus a breach of trust, and L can follow and trace this money; secondly, if B goes insolvent before spending the money according to the mandate, as happened in *Quistclose*, L retains the equitable beneficial interest in the money under the trust, and so is safe from B's insolvency.

7.33   Now to the issue of certainty of intention. The main question will be whether the parties intended the normal loan arrangement, which creates merely a debtor–creditor relationship, or a *Quistclose* trust loan. Loan contracts can, of course, stipulate a *Quistclose* trust, ie require B to hold the loan money on trust until spent properly according to purposes specified in the contract. But as we have seen, a trust can be created without the use of the word 'trust' (7.4), and the use of the word 'trust' will not create a trust if that does not represent the parties' true intentions (7.15). But every trust must comply with the necessary features of a trust, and here the most significant feature is whether or not L requires, and B understands, that B must keep the loan moneys separate from all of his other moneys. In *Quistclose* and *Carreras Rothmans*, for example, special bank accounts were set up to receive the money. Payment into B's solicitor's client account is sufficient for this purpose, because although a solicitor's client account mixes money from different clients, it is a trust account and there are specific rules by which solicitors track each client's equitable interest in the account (*Twinsectra*). If neither L nor B see anything wrong in paying the loan money into B's current account, this should give rise to a strong presumption that whatever the terms of the loan contract, including the use of the word 'trust', there was no intention to create a *Quistclose* trust. In *Cooper v PRG Powerhouse Ltd* (2008), however, Evans-Lombe J read Lord Millett in *Twinsectra* to have positively rejected the requirement that there be any intention to keep the loaned money separate and identifiable. This reasoning seems to generate a new sort of 'animal', an accounting trust or a 'tracing trust' which, with respect, does not seem to follow from Lord Millett's decision. We will look at such trusts at 7.43.

7.34   In *R v Common Professional Examination Board, ex p Mealing-McCleod* (2000) (9.54–9.56), the contract of loan between the lender and borrower included a provision in the following terms: 'You must use the cash loan for any purpose specified overleaf . . . You will hold that loan, or any part of it, on trust for us until you have used it for that purpose.' That seems straightforward enough. But one should still look at how the money was advanced. What if the bank, according to its regular practice, merely paid the loan money into its borrower/client's current account? That would strongly raise the suspicion that the contractual provision was mere boilerplate, especially if this was the bank's standard form, probably inserted on a solicitor's advice at head office to take advantage of the decision in *Quistclose*, with the local loan officer or bank manager probably having no clue as to its real significance. One can easily imagine, if the borrower/client asked what it meant, the manager's saying something like 'it means you must spend the loan money on the purpose you told us about in applying for the loan', which of course indicates no intention to create a trust as opposed to a mere contractual obligation.

7.35   *Twinsectra* itself was a very close case on the facts. Carnwath J at first instance found that the lender and the borrower never really considered a trust of the loan moneys, leaving it up to their respective solicitors; for their part, a provision that the loan money was to be used solely for the acquisition of property formed part of the loan documents; but the solicitors never discussed the provision. In this respect the case was far from the typical purchaser's instruction to a solicitor for the release of funds to acquire a specific piece of land in further-ance of a particular contract of sale. Carnwath J decided that the purpose was too vague, and did not really form part of the parties' intentions in concluding the contract. However, this decision was overturned in the CA, and the HL agreed. In both places much greater emphasis was placed on the presence of the provision in the loan documents, and it was held that 'the acquisition of property' was a trust obligation certain enough to be enforced. This is almost certainly wrong. Recall (3.68) that the test for certainty of objects is the 'is or is not' test. Applied to the case of a mandate or order, this test would require that it is certain whether *any* possible expenditure of the trust money clearly 'is or is not' with the mandate. What does 'property' mean here? Land? Business supplies? A new necklace for the borrower's wife? The CA and the HL got into a muddle over this because the original negotiations for the loan concerned the purchase of a *specific* parcel of land, which is obviously certain, and without thinking seemed to believe the certainty of that carried over to the purpose expressed in the actual loan documents.

7.36 It should be noted, as pointed out by Lord Millett in *Twinsectra*, that if the intention to create a trust is clear, then any uncertainty in the purpose or instruction would mean that B would have no right to use the money for any purpose; that is there would be no instruction on which he could act to dispose of the funds. The point about the vagueness of the purpose here is that if the intention to create a trust *as opposed to a straight loan of funds to B* is in issue, then vagueness, hence uncertainty, about the purported trust has the regular 'reflex action' (7.3) of generating a similar uncertainty as to whether a trust was genuinely intended to be part of the loan arrangement at all.

7.37 As regards the line of cases more or less directly leading to *Quistclose*, Millett (1985) gives the best explanation of when loans will be treated as giving rise to *Quistclose* trusts, ie where the in-tentions of the parties must be gathered from the circumstances as opposed to being expressed explicitly in the loan contract: if you can interpret the arrangement as one in which *B is, in essence, spending L's money to achieve a purpose that L cannot by spending his own money dir-ectly*, a *Quistclose* trust will arise. In *Quistclose* itself Q was hoping to stave off RR's bankruptcy by ensuring that RR was able to pay its declared dividend. If, however, Q had tried to do that itself, it would have revealed to the world RR's desperate circumstances. So it could only do so by putting the money in RR's hands.

7.38 While this seems a reasonable explanation of *Quistclose* and prior 'staving off bankruptcy' cases, you might well wonder whether the court should give its aid to such schemes by being astute to infer a trust where normally it would only infer a debtor–creditor relationship, a trust that by its very nature will misrepresent to the world, and in particular to prospective creditors, the true fi-nancial state of a company. It should also be noted that the prior 'staving off bankruptcy' cases were cases of trusts to pay off the troubled individual's or company's *creditors*, not to pay a *dividend to* a company's *shareholders, which, in the case of an insolvent company, would have been unlawful.* On the other hand, you may think these attempts at rescue praiseworthy, and that those who try them should not suffer unduly if they fail, as they might if rescue funds are treated like any other kind of loan. But there is a more general point here: especially in the commercial context, the law should be wary of imposing trusts willy-nilly. Where the circumstances generate uncertainty as to whether a *Quistclose* trust was intended, it makes sense to expect some reason why the parties would have thought it necessary to use this device rather than a regular loan before inferring that one was created.

'Accounting' and 'tracing' trusts

Accounting trusts

7.39   It is generally understood that, as part of the trustee's liability to account to his beneficiaries, the trustee must keep the trust property separately from his own (2.46). Nevertheless, the terms of the trust may indicate otherwise in this sense—the trust terms may provide that the trustee transform an obligation with respect to the title to the trust assets into a merely personal obligation. This was held in the UKPC case of *Space Investments Ltd v Canadian Imperial Bank of Commerce Trust Co. (Bahamas) Ltd* (1986). Under the terms of the trust, the trustee bank was entitled to transfer trust moneys to itself as a banker. The relationship of a banker to its account holder is not a trust, but creates a debtor-creditor arrangement. That means that there is no specific trust asset of the bank-trustee's assets that is trust property.

7.40   The result of this sort of arrangement is that the trustee bank is obliged to distribute any money's showing in the trust's bank account balance according to the terms of the trust, but merely had a personal obligation to do so. Take a simple example. Assume the settlor transfers $10,000 to the trustee bank on trust for A for life, and then to B on A's death. The bank trustee 'deposits' the $10,000 with itself as banker. If, after a year, the account is credited with $300 interest, then in order to discharge its trust obligation, the trustee-bank must pay that money to A. Similarly, on A's death the trustee bank can only discharge its trust obligation by paying the balance in the account to B.

7.41   The obvious risk of this sort of arrangement, a risk that materialised in *Space Investments*, is that the trustee bank might become insolvent—the trust beneficiaries merely have a personal right to be paid by the trustee bank, and so they must prove in the insolvency this 'trust debt' just like any other creditor of the bank.

7.42   We should, perhaps, not be too concerned about labels here, but there is a case for saying that this is not really a trust at all. It is merely a debt arrangement under which the proper discharge of the bank balance debt must comply with terms set out in a trust document. Here is the reason for denying that this is a true trust: under the law of banker and customer the bank cannot debit a customer's account by paying money away to a third party. In that case the bank has paid its own money in a way which doesn't discharge his debt to the customer, so if he purports to debit the customer's account on the basis of such a payment the customer can insist the debit is reversed. (Typically the third party is a fraudster who impersonates the customer—the fraud is *against the bank*, not *against the customer*.) So, unlike a regular trust—in which the trustee might wrongfully transfer trust assets to a third party, which would make him liable for breach of trust, allow the beneficiaries to follow and trace the property into the hands of third parties, and so on—it seems conceptually impossible for a true breach of trust to arise under this arrangement, because no 'trust asset' is ever transferred. A payment by a bank in this case is a payment by of the bank's own money, by definition.

'Tracing trusts'

7.43   A 'tracing trust' (see also 7.73) is one in which the 'trustee' is fully entitled to mix the trust fund with his own, but if he were to go insolvent, the 'beneficiary' can trace into expenditures from the account. In *Brothers International (Europe) (in administration) v CRC Credit Fund Ltd* (2011) the UKCA held that a company which was entitled under the applicable regulations (made under the Financial Services and Markets Act 2000) to receive money from its clients and deposit them in its current account, having the obligation only later to deposit like amounts of its own funds into a trust account for the clients, held the moneys under a trust imposed by those regulations on their proper interpretation. The court's decision did not go into the means by which the clients would establish their interests, and in what shares, of the account moneys or the traceable proceeds thereof (see also Stevens (2017)).

7.44 In contrast, in *Gabriel v Little* (2013) Gloster LJ regarded the fact that there was no requirement to segregate the funds in question as an indicator that no trust was intended by the parties, and the High Court of Australia in *Korda v Australian Executor Trustees (SA) Ltd* (2015) unanimously overturned a finding of the Victoria Court of Appeal that a commercial arrangement imposed on a company a trust of certain moneys it received in the course of the business, principally for the reason that in none of the contractual documents was there any requirement for the company to segregate those moneys and hold them as a separate fund.

7.45 In *North v Wilkinson* (2018) the UKCA found that a purported trust failed both on the ground of certainty of intention and certainty of subject matter. The intention issue was straightforward. Documents under which a businessman offered shares of his business to providers of funds clearly contemplated that they would get shares in a company incorporated to run the business, and no such company was ever formed. Quite rightly these documents could not be construed as declarations of trust. But the second issue, certainty of subject matter, was trickier. The court seemed to deny at [44] that the assets of an unincorporated business could be held on trust, but as we have seen (2.53) trusts of this kind were not uncommon in the nineteenth century. The assets of the business would be all those property rights held by the trustee which were used in the business, ie the premises, the stock in trade, the book debts, etc. If a sole trader's business assets can be determined for the purpose of tax law, there seems to be no reason why such assets cannot be made certain under the law of trusts. On the question of whether there could be a trust of the net assets, or profits of the business, David Richards LJ said ([44]), 'Net assets are an accounting entry; they are the amount of the assets less the liabilities. They cannot form the subject matter of a trust'. This is arguably sound in view of the considerations raised in (7.42), but this would not mean that there couldn't be a valid equitable obligation in respect of the profits—it is just that it would be the kind of personal 'trust' obligation found in *Space Investments*.

'Prepayment' trusts

7.46 Trusts may also protect prepayments by customers. In *Re Kayford Ltd* (1975) a mail order company unilaterally decided to place all of the money it received as prepayments for goods in a special account, only drawing upon the account when it filled an order. It was held that, upon the company's liquidation, the money in the account was held in trust for the customers even though they were unaware of the arrangement. While there is nothing particularly difficult about inferring or finding such a unilateral declaration of trust by the company, under insolvency law such a declaration appears to be an illegitimate preference of the company favouring some creditors over others. Should the court recognise a company's intentions if they have this result? (For an interesting set of facts upon which a *Re Kayford* type trust failed for uncertainty, leaving the company who tried to declare the trust with the beneficial interest in the fund so that it was available to its creditors, see *Re Challoner Club Ltd* (1997).)

7.47 A more extreme example is found in *Neste Oy v Lloyds Bank plc* (1983). An agent for ship-owners received money from them to pay various liabilities they incurred, for example to ports where their ships were berthed. The moneys were paid into the agent's general account, not held separately. One final payment by a shipowner was received by the agent after it had ceased trading. The court held that this last payment was held on *constructive* trust—in other words the court *imposed* a trust despite the actual intentions of both of the parties, on the basis that any honest recipient of the payment in these circumstances would have understood that the sum ought to be repaid immediately. It seems wrong, however, simply to find a kind of *Re Kayford* type prepayment trust rather than the ordinary debtor–creditor relationship when neither party makes the slightest gesture to declare a trust, simply because someone is unlucky given the timing of someone's insolvency. There are *always* creditors who advance that unlucky last prepayment or make that unlucky last shipment of goods on credit to a company just before it becomes insolvent. In *Japan Leasing (Europe) plc* (2000) a purchase payment was received by one co-vendor, who under the contract with the other co-vendors specifically did not hold any payments received on trust for them. At the time of the receipt of the payment, the recipient co-vendor had gone into administration and, following *Neste Oy*, the court held that the payment was held by the recipient vendor on constructive trust for all the co-vendors.

Reform

7.48 In the early 2000s the Law Commission proposed a broad reform, to create a general registration scheme for all interests that are effectively security interests (7.25 et seq) in personal property (Law Commission (2003)). If implemented then interests under retention of title clauses, charges, *Quistclose* trusts, and 'prepayment' trusts, would all need to be registered to be effective against third parties, in particular trustees in bankruptcy (see further Glister (2004a)). The proposal has gone nowhere.

Certainty of subject matter and objects: common issues

7.49 Modifying Emery's (1982) classification, we can divide up the common sources of uncertainty of subject matter and objects into three categories:

- conceptual uncertainty;
- evidential uncertainty; and
- whereabouts uncertainty.

Conceptual uncertainty concerns the problem of vagueness in the language used by the testator. For example, if a testator gives 'a lot' of his estate to 'my shorter employees' in equal shares, we appear to be faced with a problem. How much is 'a lot', and who, of all his employees, count as the 'shorter' ones?

7.50 Evidential uncertainty may arise because, while the language used to identify the property or persons is precise enough, it seems unlikely or impossible to find the evidence that will allow the trustees to carry out a settlor's, in particular a testator's, instructions. Consider 'the fishing rod that I used to catch a prize salmon on 7 September 1968, I give to the woman I had dinner with that night in celebration'. This bequest is conceptually certain both in subject matter and object—he caught the fish with only one rod, and only one woman dined with him. But determining which of the fishing rods the testator owned at his death is the prizewinning one, and who the lucky woman is, may be impossible simply because there is no reliable evidence.

7.51   Finally, the whereabouts problem; consider this bequest: 'The photograph of me with Winston Churchill I give to my nephew Paul.' On its face, there appears no problem at all. There is no conceptual or evidential uncertainty making it difficult to determine which photo is the right one and who Paul is. But what if it turns out that the testator kept the photo hidden somewhere in his 60-room mansion, Grandacre, and, secondly, that Paul emigrated somewhere (no one remembers precisely where) in 1973? It may be just impossible to locate either the photograph or Paul.

Whereabouts uncertainty

7.52   We can start with the whereabouts problem, because it is essentially no problem at all (see *Brown v Gould* (1972), *per* Megarry VC). No trust ever fails because the whereabouts of the property or the object is presently unknown. The trustees would not be required to pull down Grandacre in order to eliminate every possible hiding place for the photo. The gift is valid, and Paul may be put in possession if and when the photograph ever turns up. In a roughly similar fashion, trustees are required to hold a gift to a person whose whereabouts are presently unknown, and give it to him if and when he ever turns up. In *Re Gulbenkian* (1970) Lord Upjohn opined that, in the case of a beneficiary of a class gift whose whereabouts were uncertain, the trustees could apply to the court for a direction to pay his share into court. In short, the problem is correctly thought of as one confronting the trustees when faced with their duty to *distribute* the trust property, not as a problem concerning the very existence of the trust.

Evidential uncertainty

7.53   Evidential uncertainty of either subject matter or objects defeats an outright gift, a trust for a specified individual, or a fixed trust. The reasoning is straightforward: if the settlor expresses his gift in such a way that evidence must be adduced to identify the property or the person and that evidence is not available, then the gift or trust simply cannot be executed according to its terms. This does not mean that any requirement of evidence defeats an intended gift. There are rules that govern how evidence can be adduced to give effect to a testator's wishes expressed in his will, the general point of which is to ensure that such evidence only gives effect to the testator's declared wishes but does not serve to change or make ambiguous what the testator put in his will, and similar rules should govern the admission of evidence in the case of trusts generally. Evidential uncertainty of objects causes particular problems in the case of discretionary trusts and powers, which will be discussed at 7.77 et seq.

Conceptual uncertainty

7.54   Conceptual uncertainty arises from the settlor's use of imprecise or vague language to express his intentions. Vagueness is an ineliminable aspect of language. Vagueness can be understood as the problem of the uncertain boundaries that arise when we try to apply our words to things in the world. For example, the word 'tall' appears to have very uncertain boundaries: 'tall' is not a synonym for '5 foot 10 inches or over'; it is not that precise. People may disagree whether Jim is tall, and an individual may be in a quandary himself as to whether Jim is tall or not. Jim may be 'on the borderline' for 'tall'. Vague terms will certainly apply in some cases—Paul, who is 7 foot 8 inches, is certainly tall (heavens, he's *very* tall)—and certainly not apply in others—to Stephen who is 4 foot 10 inches—but there will be a range of cases for which the application of the term is indeterminate, or *uncertain*. We can make a rough-and-ready distinction between two kinds of vagueness. 'Degree' vagueness covers words such as 'tall': 'tall' clearly refers to a scale—height—along which we can place individuals. The second kind of vagueness is 'category' vagueness. An example is 'furniture': 'furniture' is a term that applies to certain household objects. A sofa is certainly furniture, and a dinner plate is certainly not. But what about a carpet? Or a refrigerator?

7.55   In everyday communication, vagueness is not a problem because, in context, we can draw boundaries that are sufficiently workable to understand what we are up to. When greater precision is wanted, we can stipulate a meaning for a term that provides a more precise boundary for its application. For example, we can stipulate that, for our purposes, 'tall' means '5 foot 10 inches or over', or if we run a department store, we can stipulate that furniture includes carpets if carpets are sold in the 'furniture' department. While these stipulations are arbitrary, that does not mean they are unreasonable: '5 foot 10 inches or over' is a reasonable stipulation for tall, although reasonable people might choose different measures, but '4 foot 10 inches' is not, since that boundary does not reflect anything like the normal borderline area where 'tall' is thought to be vague.

7.56   In some cases, courts are willing to determine a boundary for a vague term; in other cases, not. In *Palmer v Simmonds* (1854) the words 'the bulk of my said residuary estate' were held to indicate too uncertain a proportion of the residuary estate to establish a trust. The judge did assume that 'the bulk' meant more than half but that was still too imprecise to establish the subject matter of the trust. By contrast, in *Re Golay* (1965), the gift of a 'reasonable income', to go along with a life interest in a flat, did not fail for uncertainty. Ungoed-Thomas J said:

> The court is constantly involved in making such objective assessments of what is reasonable and it is not to be deterred from doing so because subjective influences can never be wholly excluded.

In other words, the court was willing to stipulate a meaning for 'reasonable income'. Vague words are not useless, even at the borderline. Their vagueness at the borderline just requires us to do some work, that is stipulate criteria for a term's application to give a working definition that is precise enough for the task at hand. Did the court have better reason to do this in *Re Golay* than in *Palmer*?

7.57   The same problem arises for certainty of objects. The career of the expression 'my old friends'/'my friends' is particularly interesting. Although 'my old friends' and 'my friends' were held to be conceptually certain in *Re Gibbard* (1966) and *Re Barlow's Will Trusts* (1979) respectively, in the former the court was applying a test for certainty that was later rejected by higher courts (*Re Gulbenkian* (1970)), and the latter concerned a gift subject to a condition precedent, where, apparently, a lower standard for certainty is required (7.83). In *Re Barlow's Will Trusts*, Browne-Wilkinson J denied that the meaning of 'friends' was 'too vague to be given legal effect', and he stipulated criteria for its application:

Without seeking to lay down any exhaustive definition . . . it may be helpful if I indicate certain minimum requirements: (a) the relationship must have been a long-standing one; (b) the relationship must have been a social relationship as opposed to a business or professional relationship; (c) although there may have been long periods when circumstances prevented the testatrix and the applicant from meeting, when circumstances did permit they must have met frequently.

In contrast, Lord Upjohn used 'old friend' as a paradigm example of conceptual uncertainty in *Re Gulbenkian* (1970), as did Megarry VC in *Brown v Gould* (1972):

If there is a trust for 'my old friends,' all concerned are faced with uncertainty as to the concept or idea enshrined in these words. It may not be difficult to resolve that 'old' means not 'aged' but 'of long standing'; but then there is the question how long is 'long'. Friendship, too, is a concept with almost infinite shades of meaning.

7.58   Not surprisingly, in *Re Wright's Will Trusts* (1982), CA, a trust for 'such people and institutions as [my trustees] think have helped me or my late husband' failed for uncertainty, Blackett-Ord VC at first instance observing that helping the testatrix 'could mean anything from helping the testatrix across the road to saving her from death, dishonour, or bankruptcy'.

Resolution of uncertainty by outside opinion

7.59   Should a settlor be able to express his directions as precisely as he can, but provide that if there is dispute over their meaning or application, recourse may be had to a living individual, who shall settle the matter? In *Re Coxen* (1948), the settlor made a gift of a residence to his widow, which was however to end 'if in the opinion of my trustees she shall have ceased permanently to reside therein'. Jenkins J held:

If the testator had insufficiently defined the state of affairs on which the trustees were to form their opinion, he would not I think have saved the condition from invalidity on the ground of uncertainty merely by making their opinion the criterion . . . in my view the testator by making the trustees' opinion the criterion has removed the difficulties [in deciding whether the determining event has occurred, which] may necessarily be a matter of inference involving nice questions of fact and degree.

Re Coxen thus stands for the proposition that an opinion clause cannot cure conceptual uncertainty, but may allow an individual to determine matters of fact as to whether the concept applies in any particular case. Thus Hayton (2001b, at 177) said that opinion clauses may cure evidential, but not conceptual, uncertainty.

7.60   In *Re Leek* (1969), the objects of a trust were 'such other persons as the company [acting as trustee] may consider to have a moral claim upon' the settlor. Harman LJ said:

It was argued that . . . the trust was too vague . . . If the trust were for such persons as have moral claims, I would agree with this view, but this is not the trust. The trustees are made the arbiters and the objects are such persons as they may consider to have a moral claim; and I do not see why they should not be able on this footing to make up their minds and arrive at a decision [emphasis original].

Compare this finding with that concerning persons or institutions that the trustees 'thought' had helped the testatrix in *Re Wright's Will Trusts* (1982) (7.58).

7.61   In *Re Tuck's Settlement Trusts* (1978), the CA considered a condition on the inheritance of a baronetcy, that the wife of any heir must be of 'Jewish blood' and worship 'according to the Jewish faith'; in the case of doubt the decision of the Chief Rabbi in London was to be conclusive. Lord Denning MR said:

> I see no reason why a testator or settlor should not provide that any dispute or doubt should be resolved by his executors or trustees, or even by a third person . . . if there is any conceptual uncertainty in the provision of this settlement, it is cured by the Chief Rabbi clause.

7.62   Lord Denning's view does not, however, represent the law, because although all of the judges upheld the settlement, Lord Russell and Eveleigh LJ did so on a different basis. Lord Russell did not consider the Chief Rabbi clause since he did not find the condition to be uncertain. Eveleigh LJ said that the settlor:

> is in effect saying that his definition of Jewish faith is the same as the Chief Rabbi's definition. Different people may have different views or be doubtful as to what is 'Jewish faith', but the Chief Rabbi knows and can say what meaning he attaches to the words . . . I therefore do not regard the settlor as leaving it to the Chief Rabbi to discover what the settlor meant or to provide a meaning for the expression used by the settlor when the meaning is in doubt . . . The fact is that the Chief Rabbi knows what he means by 'Jewish faith' and the testator has said that he means the same thing.

Thus in Eveleigh LJ's view the Chief Rabbi's opinion is regarded not as determining the meaning of the settlor's words by providing workable criteria for them; the Chief Rabbi's opinion is merely evidence of the settlor's opinion. In practice does this not amount to letting the Chief Rabbi determine the meaning of the settlor's words?

7.63   In *Re Tepper's Will Trusts* (1987), gifts were subject to the condition that the recipients 'shall remain within the Jewish faith and shall not marry outside the Jewish faith'. Scott J, following Eveleigh LJ, held that *Re Tuck's* established the admissibility of evidence to elucidate the meaning of terms such as 'the Jewish faith'.

7.64   In general, courts try not to invalidate trusts if a reasonable construction can be placed on the words that will make them valid (*IRC v McMullen* (1980) *per* Lord Hailsham), but individual judges vary in their willingness to find a 'benignant' construction. As a result, settlors are faced with uncertainty about the extent to which a court will allow the determination of a vague term. Examining vagueness in legal language, Endicott (1997) cites the example of the 'anti-rave' provision in the Criminal Justice and Public Order Act 1994, s 63, by which the police are empowered to shut down sound equipment at a 'gathering' where the music 'by reason of its loudness and duration and the time at which it is played, is likely to cause serious distress to the inhabitants of the locality'. To further assist the judge 'music' is defined to include 'sounds wholly or predominantly characterised by the emission of a succession of repetitive beats' (presumably to capture the essence of the music that Ecstasy-users prefer, but alas, unsuccessfully to distinguish it from the sound of a pneumatic drill). While it may be excessive to grant settlors the freedom to create legally binding obligations with the use of language as vague as that employed by Parliament, it may not be churlish to suggest that judges, given as they are to making sense of such statutory provisions, should make some reasonable effort to ensure the validity of trust provisions couched in vague language. Where an opinion clause empowers the trustees or a third party to establish criteria for applying the settlor's words, that does not mean they can choose any criteria at all. As Browne-Wilkinson J's decision in *Re Barlow's* shows (7.57), the provision of criteria, while necessarily arbitrary, can be more or less reasonable, and the courts could act if the criteria chosen were irrational or perverse; they need not, therefore, be worried that reference to opinion clauses ousts the jurisdiction of the court to determine whether a provision is conceptually certain. Of course the courts must remain the ultimate arbiters of which clauses are just so vague that any de-termination of criteria for them would, in effect, be writing the will or the settlement for the settlor. But this cannot be said of opinion clauses of the Chief Rabbi kind, which save the courts from having to determine criteria themselves for terms that should be given a deter-minate meaning, and they should welcome the help.

Certainty of subject matter: particular issues

The 'whatever is left' trust

7.65 In *Sprange v Barnard* (1789), a testatrix left £300 in securities to her husband 'for his sole use; and at his death, the remaining part of what is left, that he does not want for his own wants and use', was to be divided equally amongst three others. The court held that the husband was entitled absolutely, for a trust of what property remained after the husband's use would be impossible to be executed; similar negative attitudes to this kind of 'whatever is left' trust are found in *Lambe v Eames* (1871) and *Mussoorie Bank Ltd v Raynor* (1882).

7.66 More recently, however, in *Ottaway v Norman* (1972), the Australian (*Birmingham v Renfrew* (1936)) 'floating' or 'suspended' trust analysis was applied. The son and daughter-in-law of the deceased claimed that he had left his house, its contents, and his money to his housekeeper to her for her use so long as she lived, but on trust to leave the property to them on her death. Brightman J opined that there was a valid trust of the house and contents (the latter being subject to normal wastage and wear and tear), which he was content to assume was 'in sus-pense' during the housekeeper's lifetime, attaching to the property only upon her death. It is not clear from this 'floating trust' analysis whether the 'floating trustee' has any obligations to preserve the property during his life. May he spend as much as he wants? Could the house-keeper in *Ottaway* have sold the house and spent the proceeds living on the Costa del Sol? In *Birmingham*, the court said that gifts 'calculated to defeat' the trust could not be made, but such an obligation seems so nebulous as to be unenforceable. In *Ottaway v Norman*, the trust did not extend to the money the housekeeper received under the will. Such a trust would be 'mean-ingless and unworkable' unless the money was given with the obligation that it be kept separate from her own money, and there was none. What is most odd about trying to 'develop' a new device of the 'floating trust' is that the result can perfectly well be achieved on perfectly trad-itional trust principles. So, for example, if you want to create a floating trust in favour of Betty during her life, with whatever is left to go to Bertram, do the following: transfer the property to Betty on trust for her life, remainder to Bertram, with power to Betty to appoint capital, up to the entirety of the trust funds, to herself during her lifetime. In this way Betty can have more than a mere income interest by making use of the power, yet anything left will go to Bertram, as he has the interest in remainder. If the donee wants to ensure Bertram receives a minimum amount, he can restrict Betty's power to appoint capital accordingly.

The identification of specific property out of a larger amount

7.67 In *Boyce v Boyce* (1849), a testator left three houses to his widow, instructing her to give to his daughter Maria whichever one Maria chose and to give the other two houses to his daughter Charlotte. Maria died before choosing any house, and the court held that the gift to Charlotte failed for uncertainty, reasoning that the gift to Charlotte was of the *other* houses that remained following Maria's choice. Since she made none, the ascertainment of such *other* houses became impossible, and so the gift failed.

7.68 While *Boyce* turns on quite unusual facts, it is one instance of a more general problem that has recently arisen as an important issue in the commercial context, that of identifying which specific things, out of a larger class of things, are to be held as the subject matter of a trust. While in *Boyce* the failure turned on Maria's failure to select a property, in the commercial cases the failure generally turns on the failure of a seller of goods to choose particular goods to satisfy the buyer's contract; once identified, but only then, those goods may serve as the subject matter of a trust if one was intended by the parties. In *Re London Wine Co (Shippers) Ltd* (1986) a company that dealt in wines went into receivership. Its customers had purchased wine but left it in the company's possession for storage, and naturally assumed that they could retrieve 'their' wine and that it was not part of the insolvent company's assets. Unfortunately, the customers did not become legal owners of any wine. Although the company represented to them that it held particular cases of wine in storage for them, and even charged them storage fees, in reality the company did not allocate any particular cases of wine to any particular customers and, in general, did not ensure that it had on hand sufficient quantities to meet all the customers' purchases should they all have demanded actual delivery of their purchases all at once. Wines were only allocated to any individual customer when he actually took delivery. Under sale of goods law, legal title to goods does not pass under a contract of sale until such time as the seller actually appropriates specific property to the contract. In a thorough review of the case law, Oliver J decided that, for essentially the same reason, the company did not hold any of the wine on trust for the customers: it could not be said with any certainty which wines were the subject matter of a trust for any particular customer.

7.69 *Re London Wine* was approved by the PC in *Re Goldcorp Exchange Ltd* (1995), a case involving similar claims against a dealer in precious metals. While sympathising with the customers, Lord Mustill affirmed that a right in property, whether legal or equitable, cannot exist in the air, hovering over an undifferentiated mass of property; it can only exist in relation to property which is specifically ascertained, ie identified. For fans of fusion (1.16), the decision is also right as a matter of policy, for insisting upon one set of 'certainty of subject matter' rules that applies both to the transfer of legal title and to the creation of equitable title. If the common law and equity are ever to produce a rational law of property, they cannot diverge on matters as fundamental as this. In particular, equity should not develop its own 'flexible' notion of certainty of subject matter just in order to provide the sympathetic result in a particular case.

7.70 Unfortunately, before the decision in *Re Goldcorp* was given, the CA delivered its decision in *Hunter v Moss* (1994), which throws this area of law into some turmoil. Mr Moss was the owner of 950 shares in a private company. In order to place his finance director, Mr Hunter, on the same footing as his managing director in respect of their interests in the company, he purported to declare (as the court found) a trust of 50 of those shares. He later sold the 950 shares when the company was taken over by a larger concern, keeping all the proceeds for himself. Hunter claimed a proportionate share of the proceeds of that sale, ie the proportion that would be his in equity if the declaration of trust were valid. There was a problem, however, in that Moss had never done anything to segregate or identify any particular lot of 50 shares out of the whole 950 he was to hold on trust for Hunter. Although the case concerned 'intangible property', ie shares, not goods, there seems no good reason to distinguish the clear rule in *London Wine*, approved in *Goldcorp*, that a trust cannot exist unless and until the property to which it relates is specifically ascertained (although the CA appears to have distinguished *London Wine* on a goods/intangibles distinction without further reasoned argument). In order to have specifically ascertained the property in this case Moss would have needed either to isolate share certificates to the specified amount, or at least indicate the registration numbers of the shares to be held on trust. Nevertheless, Dillon LJ held that the trust was effectively declared. His decision was based on an analogy, to wit: since a testator may validly bequeath 50 of his 950 shares of X Ltd without previously segregating them, Mr Moss should equally be able to create an *inter vivos* trust of 50 of his 950 shares of X Ltd without previously segregating them. But under a will there is no immediate trust of any of the property for any of the intended legatees until the estate is properly dealt with by the executors, paying off the testator's debts and so on (2.88). The legatee's proprietary interest in specific items of property, whether shares or shoehorns, only arises when such property is actually identified for distribution. As Hayton (1994) points out, the *inter vivos* situation analogous to the testamentary bequest is the case where A properly transfers legal title of his 950 shares to B to hold on trust to distribute 50 of them to C, not Moss's declaration in this case.

7.71 The decision leads to obvious problems. Assume such a trust. What happens when Moss deals with the 950 shares? Say he sells 100 shares (properly transferring title) to Fred: whose shares are these? Hunter's or Moss's? If they are Hunter's, Moss has just committed a breach of trust; if they are not Hunter's, he has not. One does want to know whether a breach of trust has occurred. Martin (1997, at 96) suggested that this worry is insubstantial, since the rules of tracing (2.78, 11.123 et seq) may be notionally employed: thus, we proceed *as if* Moss did segregate 50 shares out of the 950, but then immediately mixed them again with the other 900, so we have a mixture of 950 shares, just like the case where a trustee in breach of trust mixes £50 of trust money in his bank account, raising the balance to £950. Under the rules of tracing, Hunter will be able to trace his value into particular shares in the 950, which particular shares he traces into depending upon the circumstances. But this is a strange way to deal with a certainty problem, that is by assuming that in the very act of declaring a trust a person also makes himself a trustee in breach. The better view is that Moss has not properly created a trust at all, and while he might have been contractually *obliged* to do so (under a term of Hunter's employment contract with him), it is conceptually confused to deal with his *failure to make himself* a trustee by treating him *as a trustee in breach*.

7.72 One of the strange aspects of this case was that it was argued as if Hunter was a volunteer, ie Hunter did not argue that Moss was obliged by a term of Hunter's employment contract to transfer 50 of the shares to him or hold 50 shares on trust for him. One can only speculate why: perhaps Hunter felt that he would have a difficult time proving that he had provided any new consideration for Moss's promise of the shares. But as Hayton (1994) points out, and as we shall see in Chapter 8, equity does not normally perfect imperfect transactions by creating equitable rights for people who have not paid for them. If Hunter is to be treated as a volunteer here, then he does not suffer any loss if the trust fails, and there are no obvious special factors to compel the court to bend over backwards and find an otherwise uncertain, and therefore invalid, trust valid.

7.73   The situation would be different had Hunter actually provided consideration, but the right response in that case is probably not to adopt Martin's tracing approach: Hayton suggests that the court should impose an equitable charge on Moss's shares in favour of Hunter to the value of the 50 shares. An alternative approach would be the imposition of a constructive trust on Moss over the whole 950 shares, to hold them in shares of 1/19 for Hunter and 18/19 for himself, thus creating an equitable co-ownership of the shares until such time as Moss segregated 50 for Hunter. This approach accords with the amendment to the Sale of Goods Act 1979 (Sale of Goods (Amendment) Act 1995), which holds that purchasers of unidentified goods from an identified bulk will obtain legal title to the bulk as co-owners in shares proportionate to their purchases. It seems overly fanciful to adopt a notional segregation and remixing and the immediate invocation of the rules of tracing when these other, more straightforward, techniques are available. *Hunter* was followed in *Re Harvard Securities* (1997) as representing the law in England; in *White v Shortall* (2006), Campbell J in the New South Wales Supreme Court criticised the reasoning in *Hunter* in great detail and refused to follow it; he preferred the 'proportionate shares' approach, as have the trial judge and the CA in *Re Lehman Brothers International (Europe)* (2010, 2011).

Trusts of residue

7.74   One last point on certainty of subject matter, which I stress because students regularly get this wrong in exams, is that a testamentary gift or trust of the residue under a will is NOT UNCERTAIN. In the course of executing the will, the executors will determine to the very penny the residue of the estate. 'That is certain which can readily be made certain', the saying goes, or '*id certum est quod potest reddi certum*', if you prefer Latin.

Certainty of objects: particular issues

Outright gifts, fixed trusts, and *Burrough v Philcox* trusts

7.75   In these cases, the object or each member of a class of objects must be known with certainty, or the gift or trust will fail. Thus a gift of '£1,000 to Jim' will fail if there is uncertainty as to who Jim is. The same goes for a trust of the income of 1,000 shares of ABC plc for Jim. Similarly, in the case of a gift to or fixed trust for a class, the trust fails unless the entire class can be ascertained with certainty. For example, '£100,000 on trust to pay the income to my children in equal shares' will fail unless each of the settlor's children can be ascertained. Thus the test of certainty in these cases is the 'complete list' test (recall 3.69). The same test applies to a '*Burrough v Philcox*'-type discretionary trust (7.11), because each individual in the class will take an equal share should, for some reason, the trustee fail to appoint the trust property, just as the objects of a fixed trust for a class do.

7.76   A settlor may create a trust for a class the members of which may be unborn, as in a trust for his grandchildren. Until they are born, of course, these objects are not ascertained, but that does not invalidate the trust for uncertainty of objects. These objects will be identified with certainty over the course of the trust as long as it is not perpetuitous (et seq).

Powers and *McPhail* trusts

7.77 Previously (et seq) it was discussed why the 'is or is not' test for certainty of objects was held to apply both to powers and to *McPhail*-type trusts. The *McPhail* case was remitted to the High Court for determination whether the trust was valid under the 'is or is not' test. Thence it went up to the CA as *Re Baden's Deed Trusts (No 2)* (1973). The trust was for, amongst others, employees and their 'dependants' and 'relatives'. 'Dependants' was not regarded as uncertain at all; it had been used in many other deeds and by Parliament to describe individuals financially dependent upon others for their support. 'Relatives', however, led to a difference of opinion. 'Relative' or 'relation' means a descendant from a common ancestor, and so everyone has an indefinite, although undoubtedly large, number of distant relatives about whom they have never heard; if such persons were to be included in the class, then it would be a very large class indeed, and if one thinks in grand historical terms, we may all descend from those original Australopithecines that managed to scrabble out a living in the Olduvai gorge some millions of years ago. There is nothing *conceptually* uncertain about 'descendant from a common ancestor'. The problem turns entirely on proving the connection, ie upon evidential uncertainty.

7.78 Sachs LJ made a clear distinction between conceptual and evidential certainty; the 'is or is not' test applies to the former, and 'the court is never defeated by evidential uncertainty'. It is a question of fact whether 'any individual postulant has on inquiry been proved to be within [the class]; if he is not so proved then he is not in it'. Thus it was perfectly all right that 'relative' means a descendant from a common ancestor. Someone offering sufficient proof of that 'is' within the class; someone unable to do so 'is not'. Sachs LJ did not say who has the onus of proof, although presumably if any postulant must be proved to be within it to take, then the trustees would have to be satisfied so that their decision would stand in the face of a challenge by another beneficiary. Thus, although Sachs LJ would not allow evidential uncertainty to defeat the trust, he does rely upon the existence of evidence to define the boundaries of the class.

7.79 Megaw LJ introduced a factor of substantial numbers into the 'is or is not' test: if it could be said with certainty that a substantial number of beneficiaries fell within the class, the class was certain. If this means that only those may take who are within the 'substantial numbers' within the class on the evidence available to trustees at the outset (eg a list of company employees and their spouses and children), then this appears to cut down the class contrary to the settlor's intentions and reintroduce a version of the 'complete list' test. More likely, the 'substantial numbers' merely establishes the validity of the trust. In that case, however, it gives no guidance to the trustee when considering the extent of any survey he must make of the class before distributing (   ), ie the extent of the consideration he must give to distributing to those not within the 'substantial numbers', yet who may fall within the class intended by the settlor.

7.80 Stamp LJ refused to allow evidential certainty to intrude upon or patch up the problems caused by a conceptually certain term: if 'relatives' means descendants of a common ancestor, one either glosses the word or the trust is void for uncertainty; the 'is or is not' test is a test of a class defined by the concepts the settlor used. It cannot be watered down to a test that depends upon a burden of proof, because that makes the test one of evidential certainty, not conceptual certainty, and raises the problem that only one or a few possible objects bring forward the suitable proof:

> [I]t is not enough that trustees should do nothing but distribute the fund among those objects of the trust who happen to be at hand or present themselves.

Rather, the tru\stees must survey the class of objects and so the test must indicate the scope of this duty, not merely to the validity of making a payment to a particular individual who presents himself:

> [I]t would in my judgment follow that, treating the word relatives as meaning descend-ants of a common ancestor, a trust for distribution such as is here in question would not be valid. Any 'survey of the range of the objects or possible beneficiaries' would certainly be incomplete, and I am able to discern no principle on which such a survey could be conducted or where it should start or finish.

However, Stamp LJ found authority for interpreting 'relatives' to mean next of kin, and on that basis found the trust valid.

7.81 One notes an important distinction between Stamp LJ's and Sachs LJ's opinions regarding the char-acter of the trustees' duties. Sachs LJ seems concerned only that the trustees are able, with certainty, to distribute the money only to valid recipients, and therefore he focuses the 'is or is not' test on the status of 'any given postulant'. Stamp LJ emphasises the trustees' duty to survey the class, and from this perspective he is surely right that no sensible survey could be made of the employees and all those who have descended from a common ancestor, because that would be like surveying the UK. Almost certainly the trustees will think of 'relatives', when 'surveying the field', as the employees' near relatives. This difference reflects different senses in which a large, discretionary trust is a trust. For Stamp LJ, the whole class of objects really do have the right to be considered, and therefore the trustees must have a sensible picture of them as a whole; there appears a fairly traditional right–duty relationship between the class of beneficiaries and the trustees. For Sachs LJ, the objects are much less like a class, appearing rather as applicants or postulants to a fund for which they might qualify for a distribution, and the trustees are like power holders who may benefit particular in-dividuals; their only duty is to make sure they get on with the job and distribute the funds, and so they need a solid test of whether or not any individual distribution is legitimate.

7.82 Together Sachs and Megaw LJ found that 'relative' meaning 'descendant of a common an-cestor' was not an invalidating term on the 'is or is not' test, although it remains so on the 'complete list' test. Thus a trust for one's 'relatives' in equal shares fails unless 'relatives' is read as next of kin.

Conditions precedent defining a class

7.83 One may make gifts subject to conditions precedent in equity (3.35). For example, one might give Blackacre to one's daughter conditional upon her obtaining a 2:1 degree. Notice that the condition does nothing to identify the donee. Here we are concerned with conditions precedent that do. In *Re Barlow's Will Trusts*, the testatrix directed her executor to allow any of her friends to buy paintings from her collection at below market value. Thus the condition precedent—friendship—defined *a class* of potential donees, and so the standard of certainty required here makes a useful point of comparison with that for certainty of objects of a trust. Browne-Wilkinson J held that the executor was not required to determine a class of donees defined by the term 'friends', but rather that the direction should be construed as a series of individual gifts to such persons who could satisfy the criteria for 'friendship', on which criteria he gave guidance as we have seen (7.57). As a result, the decision in *Re Barlow's Will Trusts* appears to establish that, in the case of gifts with a condition precedent that defines a class, first, an 'is or is not' rather than a 'complete list' test is appropriate and, secondly, that the court will be liberal in determining criteria for vague terms.

Administrative unworkability and capriciousness

7.84   Not knowing when to stop is a mistake anyone can make, even judges. Just before concluding his judgment in *McPhail*, Lord Wilberforce said this:

> There may be a . . . case where the meaning of the words used is clear but the defin-
> ition of beneficiaries is so hopelessly wide as not to form 'anything like a class' so that
> the trust is administratively unworkable or in Lord Eldon LC's words one that cannot be
> executed . . . I hesitate to give examples for they may prejudice future cases, but per-
> haps 'all the residents of Greater London' will serve. I do not think that a discretionary
> trust for 'relatives' even of a living person falls within this category.

Here we will try to give some kind of sensible meaning to this added condition on the validity of trusts, but it may be a hopeless enterprise.

7.85   In the first place, there is some ambiguity in respect of 'so hopelessly wide': does this refer specif-
ically to the size of the class, so that any discretionary trust for £8m or so would necessarily fail? Would that make sense given the court's willingness to validate the *McPhail* trust, where on broad reading of 'relative'—descendant of a common ancestor—the class was surely huge, certainly in the millions? Why should mere size render the trust administratively unworkable anyway? Large numbers will not entail that the trustees will be stampeded with postulants; indeed, it is more likely that the beneficiaries of a small family trust, having the incentive to harangue the trustees, give trustees more trouble than any trust of the *McPhail* kind would. If the problem is the survey the trustees must undertake, the difficulty of doing that surely has more to do with whether the class or various sub-classes within it are defined in such a way that the trustees can determine the settlor's intentions regarding how they are to distribute within it, than with absolute numbers. Or does 'hopelessly wide' refer, not to the size of the class, but to the class definition? That is what the grammar of Lord Wilberforce's statement suggests. But what is it for a definition to be 'hopelessly wide'? Hopelessly vague? 'All the residents of Greater London' is not vague at all.

7.86   The only reported case in which a trust has failed for administrative unworkability is *R v District Auditor, ex p West Yorkshire Metropolitan County Council* (1986). The council was about to be abolished, and it proposed to transfer its remaining funds, £400,000, on trust for 'any or all or some of the inhabitants of the County of West Yorkshire' in order to benefit them in various ways, which included informing all interested and influential persons of the consequences of its abolition. Lloyd LJ decided:

> A trust with as many as two and a half million potential beneficiaries is, in my judge-
> ment, quite simply unworkable. The class is far too large . . . It seems to me that the

*present trust comes within the . . . case to which Lord Wilberforce refers. I hope I am
not guilty of being prejudiced by the example which he gave. But it could hardly be
more apt, or fit the facts of the present case more precisely.*

Lloyd LJ dismissed the idea that anything but the size of the class was at work to invalidate
the power, in particular 'capriciousness', ie that the class was 'an accidental conglomeration of
persons who had no discernible link with the settlor':

*[T]hat objection could not apply here. The council had every reason for wishing to bene-
fit the inhabitants of West Yorkshire.*

Yet significantly, he stated:

What we have here, in a nutshell, is a non-charitable purpose trust.

Such trusts are normally invalid (Chapter 9), because a trust for a purpose has no beneficiaries,
and thus no one to enforce it. Therefore administrative unworkability may mean that the class
of beneficiaries is 'hopelessly wide' because the trust is not really for a class of individuals at all;
it is really a trust to carry out a purpose that is masquerading as a valid trust by the inclusion of
a bogus class of beneficiaries.

7.87   Further guidance must be gleaned from three cases dealing not with discretionary trusts, but
with 'intermediate' powers, ie powers to appoint to anyone in the world except for a specified
class: *Blausten v IRC* (1972); *Re Manisty's Settlement* (1974); and *Re Hay's Settlement Trusts*
(1981). In *Blausten* Buckley J held that such a power was only valid because under the particular provision in question any appointment by the trustees required the settlor's consent; this set
metes and bounds on the exercise of the power. Otherwise it would have been invalid.

7.88   In *Manisty*, Templeman J took quite the opposite view. As he saw it, the 'is or is not' test required
only that it could be said with certainty whether any individual was an object of the power, and
although the class of objects of an intermediate power were unlimited, there was no difficulty
determining that. This must be right: an intermediate trust passes the 'is or is not' test with flying
colours—everyone 'is' an object who is not named as one of those who cannot take, those named
individuals being the 'is nots'. On this point Buckley J in *Blausten*, like Stamp LJ in *Re Baden (No
2)*, focused on the duty to survey, while Templeman J, like Sachs LJ, emphasised the validity of any
particular appointment. On the question of whether a trustee is given any guidance in his exercise
of the power in such a case, Templeman J was not perturbed, because the expectations of the settlor
are often not difficult to discern: although 'all the beneficiaries are equal some are more equal than
others'; while the terms of the power itself may not guide the trustees, that does not mean that they
may not sensibly exercise it, which is presumably why the settlor gave them absolute discretion to
do so. And it appears that the trustees' duty to survey the entire class of objects is not onerous:

*If a settlor creates a power exercisable in favour of his issue, his relations, and the em-
ployees of his company, the trustees may in practice for many years hold regular meetings, study the terms of the power and the other provisions of the settlement, examine
the accounts and either decide not to exercise the power or to exercise it only in favour,
for example, of the children of the settlor. During that period the existence of the power
may not be disclosed to any relation or employee and the trustees may not seek or receive any information concerning the circumstances of any relation or employee. In my
judgment it cannot be said that the trustees in those circumstances have committed a*

breach of trust and that they ought to have advertised the power or looked beyond the persons who are most likely to be the objects of the bounty of the settlor.

7.89 Significantly, Templeman J directly related the concept of administrative unworkability to the idea of capriciousness by reference to Lord Wilberforce's example:

The court may also be persuaded to intervene if the trustees act 'capriciously', that is to say, act for reasons which I apprehend could be said to be irrational, perverse, or irrelevant to any sensible expectation of the settlor; for example, if they chose a beneficiary by height or complexion or by the irrelevant fact that he was a resident of Greater London . . . The objection to the capricious exercise of a power may well extend to the creation of a capricious power. A power to benefit 'residents of Greater London' is capricious because the terms of the power negative any sensible intention on the part of the settlor. If the settlor intended and expected the trustees would have regard to persons with some claim on his bounty or some interest in an institution favoured by the settlor, or if the settlor had any other sensible intention or expectation, he would not have required the trustees to consider only an accidental conglomeration of persons who have no discernible link with the settlor or any institution. A capricious power negatives a sensible consideration by the trustees of the exercise of the power.

7.90 Here we have another candidate for the meaning of administrative unworkability: the settlor's direction is so capricious that no trustee could discern a sensible way to carry it out. However, it is doubtful that there is any real standard for capriciousness that will defeat a trust. In *Bird v Luckie* (1850) Wigram VC said:

No man is bound to make a will in such a manner as to deserve approbation from the prudent, the wise, or the good. A testator is permitted to be capricious and improvident . . .

And the English case generally cited as authority for the court's power to strike down capricious directions is a purpose trust case. In *Brown v Burdett* (1882) the testator's instruction to trustees to block up the rooms of a house for 20 years was struck down.

7.91 In *Hay's*, Megarry VC opined that the width of a power per se could not invalidate it if it were given to a non-trustee. The difficulty arises when the power is given to a trustee, whose fiduciary position requires him to deal with the power responsibly. He said:

[T]he duties of a trustee which are specific to a mere power seem to be threefold. Apart from the obvious duty of obeying the trust instrument, and in particular of making no appointment that is not authorised by it, the trustee must, first, consider periodically whether or not he should exercise the power; second, consider the range of objects of the power; and third, consider the appropriateness of individual appointments.

7.92 Megarry VC specifically rejected Buckley J's view that an intermediate power (if not saved by the settlor's consent provision as in *Blausten*) would be invalid as creating a class so wide as not to form a true class:

I do not see how mere numbers can inhibit the trustees from considering whether or not to exercise the power.

He held the intermediate power valid. With regard to administrative unworkability, he simply pointed out that Lord Wilberforce's words concerning administrative unworkability were directed to discretionary trusts, not powers. With regard to capriciousness, he doubted Templeman J's analysis of a power to benefit 'residents of Greater London':

> *In saying that, I do not think the judge had in mind a case in which the settlor was, for instance, a former chairman of the Greater London Council . . .*

7.93   Unfortunately Megarry VC went on to say this:

> *Of course, if there is a real vice in a power, and there are real problems of execution or administration, the court may have to hold the power invalid.*

A *real vice in a power*? *Real problems of execution or administration*? It is hardly helpful of Megarry VC to conclude a discussion of what makes a power bad or administratively unworkable by throwing out a couple of novel criteria for invalidity, which he leaves unexplained.

7.94   Megarry VC did, however, say this regarding discretionary trusts, although the statement is clearly *obiter*:

> *I consider that the duties of trustees under a discretionary trust are more stringent than those of trustees under a power of appointment, . . . and as at present advised I think that I would, if necessary, hold that an intermediate trust [ie a trust by which the trustees could appoint to anyone save a specified class] is void as being administratively unworkable.*

But why? The mere presence of a duty to distribute neither clarifies nor muddies the trustee's task—it just means the trustee must distribute the property. If the task cannot be carried out, it would seem as impossible to carry it out for both powers and trusts, and conversely, if it can be carried out for one, it can be carried out for the other. It seems an inadequate reason to hold an 'intermediate' trust void.

7.95   McKay (1974) considers five possible interpretations of 'administrative unworkability': (1) the beneficiaries of a valid class have no common attributes; (2) the class is too large; (3) the trustees will be unable to perform their administrative duties; (4) the court will be unable to execute the settlor's directions; and (5) the trust is capricious. In view of the past cases in which trusts or powers have been held by the court to be valid, McKay argues that not only is there no discernible flaw in the trust for 'residents of Greater London' that should render it invalid, but also that:

> *None of the possible bases upon which [administrative unworkability] could or has been said to rest satisfactorily provides a substantive base for it . . . this is principally due to the disruptive influence acceptance of any of those grounds would have on both the decided cases and the presumed spirit and intention of McPhail v Doulton itself.*

7.96   Swadling (2000) suggests that the test of administrative workability requires there to be a 'core class' of objects within the larger class to which the trustees may primarily devote their survey of objects, such as the employees, not their relatives, in *McPhail*. While this is a useful suggestion, it has not been endorsed by any decision (although Templeman J's statement in *Re Manisty* that some beneficiaries are more equal than others (7.88) may lend some support), and it does not follow in any obvious way from Lord Wilberforce's actual words. To the extent, however, that the idea of core class gives a sense of what sort of appointment would be 'ir-rational, perverse, or irrelevant to any sensible expectation of the settlor', it might draw upon the same kind of reasoning employed by Templeman J in *Manisty* (7.89).

7.97   Here's a final suggestion drawn from Lord Reid's opinion in *Re Gulbenkian*, where he said:

> I could understand it being held that if the classes of potential beneficiaries were so numerous that it would cost quite disproportionate enquiries and expense to find them all and discover their needs or deserts, then the provision would fail.

Consider the following discretionary trust: '£1,000 on trust to be distributed in such amounts as my trustees shall in their absolute discretion see fit amongst those persons who have given up their seat on a bus to the settlor.' The problem here seems to be that in order to determine which persons are eligible, the trustees will have, at a minimum, to advertise, and will probably have to conduct some investigations of those coming forward to determine the validity of any payments; thus in order to carry out any survey of the objects the trustees will have to deal with evidential difficulties, and £1,000 will not be enough to enable them to do so if the recipients are going to receive any worthwhile amounts. Thus, in line with Lord Wilberforce's view that the equal division of the trust fund amongst all the beneficiaries of the *McPhail* trust would benefit no one, the costs of administering this trust would probably result in no payments being made; thus to carry out the trust would result in its defeat in practice. On that basis, one might well say that the trust is administratively unworkable. And if one does want seriously to argue that the duties of a trustee to survey the field are more onerous than those of the trustee of a mere power, we may, if we interpret administrative unworkability in this way, explain why administrative unworkability only applies to invalidate trusts and not powers: regarding this example, we might allow a power to stand, because if anyone who gave up their seat on the bus to the settlor showed up and proved that he had done so, he could be paid by the trustees. The extent of the power holder's survey would be simply to take the claims of postulants seriously, rather than to make some effort to hunt them down. Conversely, the trustee of a discretionary trust *must* carry out some sort of search simply because the trustee *must* distribute the fund and therefore *must* find someone who can be paid and, *ex hypothesi*, that search would exhaust the trust fund.

Effects of uncertainty

7.98   At the risk of stating the obvious: where property is given to a named individual, if there is un-certainty of intention in that it is uncertain as to whether a trust obligation has been imposed, then that individual takes the gift absolutely, free of any trust obligations. If property is given to a trustee *virtute officii*, ie as a trustee, it is assumed the intention was to create a trust, but if the objects or subject matter are uncertain, the trustee will hold the property on an ART (5.4 et seq) if an *inter vivos* trust or, if testamentary, the subject matter of the trust will fall into residue. If there is certainty of intention but uncertainty of subject matter, then there can be no disposition of property to found the trust, and thus the intended trust fails. If there is certainty of intention and subject matter but uncertainty of objects, ie there is no one the court is willing to hold to be beneficiaries or objects of a power, the property is held on an ART, or falls into residue if the failed trust is testamentary.

FURTHER READING

Emery (1982)

Grubb (1982)

Hayton (1994)

Hopkins (1971)

McKay (1974)

Penner (2004)

Must-read cases: *Barclays Bank v Quistclose Investments* (1970); *Twinsectra v Yardley* (2002); *IRC v Broadway Cottages Trust* (1955); *McPhail v Doulton* (1970); *Re Baden (No 2)* (1973); *Re Tuck's ST* (1978); *Re Goldcorp Exchange* (1995); *Hunter v Moss* (1994); *Re Hay's ST* (1981)

SELF-TEST QUESTIONS

1. What is 'uncertainty of intention', and how does it relate to uncertainty of subject matter or objects?

2. What is 'conceptual uncertainty' and what may be done to resolve it?

3. What, if anything, is 'administrative unworkability'?

4. Consider the validity and the effect of the following testamentary gifts.

    (A) '£100,000 to Fred for his use in his remaining days, to leave what is left to Tom by will.'

    (B) '£200,000 on trust for distribution as the trustees shall in their absolute discretion see fit, to persons or dependants of persons who have had coalminers in the family for at least three generations.'

    (C) 'One of my vintage cars to each of my old friends.'

    (D) 'The residue of my estate to my trustees for distribution to such persons and in such proportions as they in their absolute discretion see fit, save that no distribution whatsoever shall be made to my wife or children.'

5. Raymond, a builder, borrowed £20,000 from Floyd's Bank. The loan document stated 'You will hold this money on trust for us until you spend it on the Loan Purpose (see overleaf)' and under 'Loan Purpose' was written 'for business purposes'. The loan was negotiated at his local Floyd's branch and Floyd's Bank paid the money into Raymond's business account at his branch the next day (the bank's standard practice). In the next several weeks Raymond drew cheques on the account (i) to pay £3,000 in past parking fines he mostly incurred parking his van near job sites; (ii) to pay his brother £4,000 he owed him, money borrowed to buy his van; (iii) to give £1,000 to his mother as a birthday present. Discuss.

8

The constitution of trusts

SUMMARY

'Equity will not assist a volunteer'
Perfecting an imperfect gift
Covenants to settle
The enforcement of covenants to settle by equity
The enforcement of covenants to settle at common law
The trust of the benefit of a promise to settle
Fortuitous vesting of the trust property
Concluding considerations

8.1 A trust is fully set up, or constituted, only when the property is in the hands of a person who is properly bound to be a trustee. The issues that arise concerning the constitution of trusts are closely tied up with equity's general principles for dealing with gifts, and so we shall begin by considering gifts in general. A gift is any transaction that benefits an individual who has not paid, ie given any consideration, for it; such an individual is called a 'volunteer'.

8.2 In *Milroy v Lord* (1862), Turner LJ laid down three 'modes' of making a gift:

- an outright transfer of the legal title to the property (or the outright assignment of an already existing equitable interest);
- a transfer of the legal title of the property to a trustee to hold on trust;
- a self-declaration of trust.

8.3 In the case of a self-declaration, the constitution of the trust is automatic: the title to the trust property is in the hands of the trustee as soon as the declaration is made because he made the declaration. Where the settlor transfers property to B on trust for C, he must both effectively declare the trust, and effectively transfer the title to the property to B—it is this second step that constitutes the trust.

'Equity will not assist a volunteer'

8.4 The maxim 'Equity will not assist a volunteer' describes an important guiding principle of the court of equity. The principle has two main strands:

- equity will not enforce gratuitous promises; and
- equity will not perfect an imperfect gift.

Equity will not enforce gratuitous promises

8.5   If A promises B that he will give him Blackacre, or if A promises B that he will put Blackacre in trust for him, and A refuses to deliver on his promise, equity will not enforce the promise at B's request. As Hackney (1987, at 118) puts it: 'You cannot sue for presents in equity.'

Equity will not perfect an imperfect gift

8.6   In *Milroy v Lord*, a man wishing to provide for his niece gave share certificates to a Mr Lord to hold on trust for her. Now this transfer of physical possession did not pass legal title to the shares, so this act did not constitute the trust. But the uncle also gave Lord a power of attorney, which gave Lord the power to get the shares registered in his name. Unfortunately, the uncle died before Lord acted on the power of attorney to register the shares in his name, and the power of attorney was extinguished by the uncle's death, so Lord was thereafter unable to get the shares registered in his name. Thus the trust was never constituted, and the shares fell into the uncle's estate on death. Turner LJ said:

> [I]n order to render the settlement [ie the gift] binding, one or other of these modes [**8.2**] must, as I understand the law of this Court, be resorted to, for there is no equity in this Court to perfect an imperfect gift. The cases I think go further to this extent, that if the settlement is intended to be effectuated by one of the modes to which I have referred, the Court will not give effect to it by applying another of those modes. If it is intended to take effect by transfer, the Court will not hold the intended transfer to operate as a declaration of trust, for then every imperfect instrument would be made effectual by being converted into a perfect trust.

Thus the three 'modes' of conferring a benefit are three *mutually exclusive* 'modes': equity will not treat the intentions of a donor to make an outright gift, where the property for one reason or another fails to pass from the donor to the donee, as a self-declaration of trust. *Jones v Lock* (1865) and *Richards v Delbridge* (1874) are illustrative. In *Jones v Lock*, the 'cheque for baby' case (7.6), everything turned on the true intentions of the father. Although he intended to make provision for the infant in various ways, he did not intend to declare a trust of the cheque. As a result, the court found that there was no self-declaration of trust, and the court would not give aid to one claiming the benefit of an imperfect gift. Similarly, in *Richards v Delbridge*, the court would not devise a trust in order to perfect the ineffective legal assignment by Delbridge of the lease to his mill and the stock-in-trade of his business to his grandson.

8.7   Equity will also not perfect an ineffective transfer of the legal title to property to an intended trustee to constitute a trust by treating the intending settlor as having made a valid self-declaration of trust. If the property fails to get into the hands of the intended trustee, there is no trust. More recently, however, the PC in *T Choithram SA v Pagarani* (2001) generously construed the words of a rich businessman intending to transfer almost the entirety of his wealth on trust shortly before his death. Having just executed a deed of trust establishing a charitable foundation and appointing himself as one of the trustees, he orally indicated that he 'gave' all his wealth to the foundation. He never executed the necessary documents to transfer legal title in his property to the trustees. The PC held that in this context, his words of gift could be interpreted as words of declaration of trust and, being one of the trustees of the foundation, this constituted the trust, although the reasoning can be criticised (see Rickett (2001)).

8.8 But be careful to note what 'Equity will not assist a volunteer' does not mean: it does not mean that volunteers who are *already* beneficiaries under an *existing* trust have no rights in a court of equity. As beneficiaries of a constituted trust, they are fully entitled to the benefit of the trust, have equitable proprietary rights in the trust property, have the right to sue the trustees to enforce the trust, and so on. It does not matter whether they are volunteers or not at this stage. Indeed, most trusts are for volunteers, since most trusts are created by settlors to benefit family members who have certainly never paid the settlor for their benefits under the trust. Equity is not in the business of dismantling *effectively* transferred gifts, or dismantling *effectively* constituted trusts. In short, equity will not assist volunteers *to become* donees or beneficiaries under a trust, but once a person is a donee or a beneficiary, it matters not one whit whether he paid for the privilege or got it for free (*Ellison v Ellison* (1802); *Paul v Paul* (1882)).

Non-volunteers

8.9 By contrast, by *extreme contrast*, the intended non-volunteer beneficiary of a trust, ie one who has given consideration, may rely on the eager assistance of equity to constitute the trust. Obviously, an intended 'donee' who has given consideration for an 'outright gift' is in a different position as well, which is reflected in a complete change of terminology. A 'donee' who has given consideration is not a donee: he is a buyer under a contract of sale. He will therefore have common law legal rights for damages if the seller refuses to perform, and in the case of land and unique chattels, equity will not only order specific performance if the seller refuses to transfer the property, the seller will be regarded as holding the title to the property under a 'vendor–purchaser' constructive trust from the moment the date of completion of the contract arrives (4.6 et seq). In the case of a promise to create a trust for which the intended beneficiary has provided consideration, equity will again specifically enforce the promise and find a constructive trust in his favour.

Future property

8.10 Promises to transfer property on trust, or 'promises to settle', often involve 'future property', which we have already encountered (6.63); future property is property that someone *might* receive, such as a legacy under a will, or royalties from the sale of a book. It is thus no more than a *spes* (6.63) or mere 'expectancy'. The case of future property provides an example of equity's willingness to perfect an imperfect legal transaction where consideration is given. Because future property does not exist, it obviously cannot be transferred. Thus if I execute a deed whereby I purport to assign to you all the royalties from a book not yet published, that deed assigns nothing, for no royalties exist; thus at common law, an assignment of future property is totally ineffective. If the assignment is gratuitous then equity, of course, will not take any steps to make the intended assignment effective either. If, however, you give consideration for the assignment, then equity will perfect this imperfect transaction: equity will treat the assignment of future property as a contractual obligation *to* assign the future property if and when it is received (*Tailby v Official Receiver* (1888); *Re Ellenborough* (1903)). On a similar basis, in *Don King Productions Inc v Warren* (1998; aff'd CA 1999), Lightman J held that partners could hold the benefit of their individual rights under personal contracts on trust for the partnership, even though such rights could not be assigned at law. The general principle behind all of this is that equity is happy to come to the aid of someone who has given consideration for the benefit of property, but is unwilling to do so on behalf of a volunteer. Nevertheless, there are a number of exceptions to this basic rule.

Perfecting an imperfect gift

I: The *Re Rose* principle

8.11   In *Re Rose* (1952), Mr Rose properly executed a share transfer form and delivered it, with the appropriate share certificate, to his wife, who was then entitled to have the shares registered in her name. The court held that, *in equity, such a gift is valid from the time that the donor does everything he is obliged to do to transfer the shares.* This has since become known as the *Re Rose* principle. The CA distinguished *Milroy v Lord* on the basis that in that case, the uncle had not done everything in law that he was required to do to transfer his title. Under the principle, after the donor (of shares for instance) has done everything he himself is required to do to pass title, and until such time as the shares are registered in the donee's name, the donor holds the shares on trust for the donee. If a dividend were declared in the interim, the donor would accordingly hold the dividend payment upon trust for the donee as well. The case is odd, and should be read to get a sense of the judges' reasoning. At some points the judges seem to suggest that, *as between the donor and donee*, the legal title passes with the handing over of the shares and the completed transfer certificate, the company just recording the donee's legal ownership, which is just wrong in law. At other points, the judges strongly suggest that, given the form of the transfer document, Mr Rose declared an express trust of his legal title to the shares in favour of his wife until she managed to get the legal title transferred into her own name. Now, of course, a donor can perfectly well declare a trust of his legal interest in this way until legal title passes, but if this is the true reasoning in the case then there is nothing to perfect, and the 'principle' in *Re Rose* has no foundation. At other points the judges seemed to adopt a 'power analysis' (recall 4.8). That is, when Mrs Rose took possession of the transfer form and the share certificates, she was then in the position to (had, in factual terms, the 'power to') get the shares registered in her name; in equity she became the owner at that moment. Even more oddly, this was not a case where the wife needed equity to perfect this gift at all; the share transfer was duly registered in the books of the company, so the legal transfer of the title to the shares took effect in the normal way. The result of the CA's holding was that, since the beneficial interest in the shares passed at the time the donor had done everything, a tax deadline was met which would not have been met at the time the legal title passed. It is not at all clear what justifies equity anticipating the transfer of the legal title in such a case by imposing a constructive trust on the donor, the only effect of which was to allow him to escape from the application of an otherwise clear taxing statute.

8.12   *Re Fry* (1946) provides something of a contrast. In that case a donor of British company shares who was resident in America was required by law to obtain the consent of the British Treasury before he could effectively transfer his legal interest. While the donor had done everything he could, in that he had completed the transfer form in favour of his son and had submitted the necessary forms to the Treasury, he died before the Treasury had given permission for the transfer. Romer J held that the donee had obtained no interest in the shares, and applying *Milroy v Lord*, refused to treat the transaction as having passed the beneficial interest in equity. Romer J thought that it was up to the donor to obtain, not just apply for, Treasury permission, and that furthermore, since the Treasury might have sought further information before granting permission, the donor might well have had an opportunity to scuttle his own gift by failing to provide that information; therefore the donor had not done everything necessary to divest himself of his interest in the shares nor relinquished his power over them.

8.13   *Mascall v Mascall* (1984) is a case applying the *Re Rose* principle to transfers of land. There the court held that the intending donor had made a complete gift in equity to his son by executing the registered land transfer document and handing it, with the land certificate, to him. As it turned out, the father later reacquired the land certificate, thus putting him in a position not to go ahead with the gift, and indeed he did not want to having since fallen out with his son. Nevertheless, the court held that as soon as he had executed the transfer form and had given it with the land certificate the gift was complete in equity, and so he was ordered to hand over the land certificate to the son so the latter could complete the transfer of the legal title into his own name.

8.14   The ambit of the rule was expanded by the CA decision in *Pennington v Waine* (2002). There a shareholder properly completed a share transfer form in favour of her nephew, but instead of passing this to the company for registration, delivered it to one of the company's auditors; she also informed her nephew of her intention to transfer the shares. On the strength of this and a statement from the auditor, her nephew became a director of the company, a position that required a shareholding. The shareholder died before the transfer was completed. Clearly, in this case, unlike *Re Rose*, the transferor had not done 'everything in her power' to secure the share transfer. The CA held, however, that the shares were held on trust for the nephew, apparently on the basis that all that is required for the rule to operate is the execution of the transfer form with the intention that the transfer is to have immediate practical effect in circumstances where it would be 'unconscionable' for the transferor to renege on the transaction. But it is not clear how 'unconscionability' helps to explain equity's willingness to perfect imperfect gifts in these cases. There was no unconscionability whatsoever in *Re Rose* itself, although the court seemed to suggest that it would be unconscionable if Mr Rose had, for example, kept any dividends that accrued after he had executed the deed of transfer. The gift was completed, and the only effect of the rule was a tax saving. It is also not clear why it was unconscionable for the father to change his mind about making a gift of land to his son in *Mascall*. The decision makes the rule now very uncertain, and we can expect all kinds of imperfect transactions to reach the courts on the basis that it would be unconscionable if they were not perfected (see also Garton (2003)). As we have seen (4.8) Chambers (2005a) has proposed that these cases should be explained by a 'power' analysis: where the intended donee acquires the factual power to obtain the legal title— such as in *Mascall* where by acquiring the land certificate and the transfer from the son was able to have the title transferred into his own name by sending these to the Land Registry—equity will anticipate the legal transfer and require the legal title holder to hold his title on trust. As we have seen (4.8), there are reasons to question this analysis, at least in the way that Chambers puts it. In the first place, in the case where A had a power to acquire an asset from B (B being under a corresponding liability that the property will go to A), this right of A's most naturally seems to be the kind of right recognised in other areas of law as a 'mere equity'. Whilst this right is capable of binding third parties, it does not confer the beneficial ownership of the asset upon A. If this is right, then, the fact that the wife in *Re Rose* and the son in *Mascall* had the power to acquire title would not have entailed that Mr Rose or Mr Mascall senior held the shares or the land, respectively, on trust. This is not to say that this means that the cases were wrongly decided, only that the power analysis does not seem to explain them. Secondly, it is not clear that the 'power' analysis reflects the judgments in the cases. While something akin to a power analysis was adverted to in both *Mascall* and *Pennington*, the rationale of the judgments also seems to lie in 'unconscionability' of some kind (which is not to say your author approves of that rationale), and that has nothing to do with a power analysis. Furthermore, one might ask why, in *Mascall* itself, the power analysis continued to apply given that at the time of the claim, the father had recovered possession of the land certificate, so that the son no longer had the power to make the legal title his own. On a true power analysis one would expect that equity's anticipation of the result would lapse whenever the power itself lapsed, as it does in the case of the vendor–purchaser constructive trust arising on a contract for the sale of land (4.6 et seq); though the constructive trust arises as soon as the date for completion arrives, this is conditional upon the purchaser being willing and able to pay the purchase price on the appointed date; if he fails to do that, then the constructive trust evaporates because the purchaser is no longer in the position to enforce the contract and obtain title to the land. Why should the trust binding the father in *Mascall* not likewise have evaporated when he reacquired the land certificate, thereby making it impossible for the son to obtain title? Finally, we can return to *Milroy v Lord* itself. The power analysis seems to suggest that the case was wrongly decided. For Mr Lord clearly did acquire a power, his legal power of attorney from the uncle, to acquire legal title to the shares. It would seem that if the power analysis applied anywhere it was here, yet this is the reference case for the principle that equity will not perfect an imperfect gift.

II: The rule in *Strong v Bird*

8.15   At common law the appointment of a debtor to be one's executor had the effect of cancelling the executor's debts to the estate. This result was determined by the application of the following technical reasoning: the executor, on becoming the owner of the testator's property and the successor to all of the testator's rights in action, was placed in the position of having to sue himself to recover the debt; since one cannot have a right of action against oneself, the debt was effectively cancelled. Originally equity prevailed over this rule and made the executor account for the money to the deceased's estate, but in *Strong v Bird* (1874) the Court of Equity held that the common law rule should prevail, if, and only if, the testator had manifested an intention to forgive the debt in his lifetime and this intent continued up to his death. This is something like the perfecting of a gift, since the debt is regarded as discharged without a formal release of the debt being made.

8.16   The rule was extended in *Re Stewart* (1908) to apply not only to imperfectly released debts, but also to imperfect gifts, again if, and only if, the testator had manifested an intent to give the gift in his lifetime and this intent continued up to his death. Whatever the merits of this extension of the rule, it should be understood that with this extension equity is now positively assisting a volunteer. In *Strong v Bird* itself the court simply allowed the common law rule to stand in particular cases, ie where the continuing intention of the testator was to release the debt. But there has never been any common law rule whereby an ineffective attempt to make a gift during the testator's life is made effective upon the putative donee's being appointed his executor. Equity is acting off its own bat to assist a volunteer in this case.

8.17   Here are the oft-quoted words of Neville J in *Re Stewart*:

> The reasoning is first that the vesting of the property in the executor at the testator's death completes the imperfect gift made in the lifetime and secondly that the intention of the testator to give the beneficial interest to the executor is sufficient to countervail the equity of the beneficiaries under the will, the testator having vested the legal estate in the executor.

The first leg of this reasoning emphasises the 'fortuitous' vesting of the property: equity will perfect the imperfect gift just because it gets into the hands of the person it was intended for. The second leg appears to state that the rationale for perfecting the gift is that the gift was intended for the donor's executor, as if a donor's appointment of someone to be his executor has special significance in this regard. While one may presume that a testator has faith in the trustworthiness and competence of his chosen executor, it is fanciful to believe that many, or indeed any, testators pick their executors in the knowledge that in doing so they will perfect any invalid gifts or releases of personal debts made to them during their lifetime. The rule seems to work purely on the basis of the 'fortuitous' vesting of the property in the hands of the executors.

8.18   This view supports the extension of the rule in *Re James* (1935) to imperfect gifts made to someone who on the *intestacy* of the donor is appointed one of the administrators of the deceased's estate (2.83). This extension was doubted in *Re Gonin* (1979) by Walton J, who would restrict the application of the rule to executors, because they are chosen by the testator, while administrators are chosen by the court, usually from amongst a number of people who might serve. Extending the rule to administrators turned the rule into 'something in the nature of a lottery'. The rule in *Strong v Bird* itself creates an unprincipled lottery, however, because one cannot truly suppose that the appointment of a person to be one's executor indicates anything about the testator's intentions to perfect imperfect gifts—how many solicitors, do you think, advise their clients about the rule in *Strong v Bird* when instructed to draw up a will? As a rule by which imperfect gifts are perfected by fortuitous vesting, it applies just as much to the administrator as to the executor. The original reaction of equity to the common law rule regarding the release of the executor's debts is the right one: he should account to the estate for the debts he owes it. Once *Strong v Bird* overturned this sensible attitude of equity, then there could be nothing but a lottery in which some individuals will have imperfect gifts perfected, and others not, purely on the basis of who ends up, by hook or by crook, as the personal representative of the deceased. The rule has nothing to recommend it and the HL has never affirmed it; the UKSC should overrule it the first chance it gets.

8.19   Applying the rule depends upon showing that the deceased had a 'continuing intention' to release the debt or make the gift. It is important to understand what 'continuing intention' means. In *Re Pink* (1912) Kennedy LJ said:

> [A] continuing intention on the part of the testator means…a continuing intention that the gift should have been given at the time it was given.

Thus the deceased's intention must be that he had made an immediate gift that he thought was effective, and maintained that view up until his death. Thus properly understood, the deceased's intention is better framed as his *continuing belief* that he had released the debt or made an outright gift. The doctrine specifically does not cover an intention to make an *inter vivos* gift in the future, a promise to make a gift, or the intention to give the property at one's death. Hayton (2001b, at 258–59) questioned whether the restriction to failed immediate gifts is consistent, since once equity has gone so far as to assist volunteers simply because of fortuitous vesting, why should it not allow the perfection of promises or intentions to give *inter vivos* or testamentary gifts? Kodilinye (1982) points out that the present rule at least reflects the situation as the deceased understood it to be—ie his view was that he had given away the property or released the debt, while the suggested extension would enforce promises that the deceased knew full well that he had not complied with.

8.20 The rule in *Strong v Bird* requires that the property of a gift to be perfected is specific and identifiable as subject matter that might have been previously transferred in accordance with the deceased's beliefs/intentions. Thus ineffective gifts of or promises to give future property (8.10) or sums of money cannot be perfected by the rule.

8.21 Following *Re Ralli's Will Trusts* (1963), in which Buckley J made reference to the rule in *Strong v Bird* in finding that a trust was constituted when the property fortuitously came into the hands of the trustee, it appears that the rule applies to perfect not only imperfect gifts but unconstituted trusts where the deceased's personal representative is also the intended trustee. Again, the deceased must have maintained the continuing belief or 'intention' that he had constituted the trust, although in fact the transfer to the trustee was ineffective.

III: *Donationes mortis causa*

8.22 *Donationes mortis causa* (singular *donatio mortis causa*), also called 'deathbed gifts', are gifts that are made *inter vivos*, but which are conditional, only taking effect on death. If the donor revives and demands the property back, he is entitled to it. Conditional gifts of tangible personal property, like a book or a bicycle, have always been possible at common law; the gift transaction takes place in the normal way by the transfer of possession, but on condition, and on death the condition is perfected and the gift becomes absolute. The intervention of equity is necessary, however, to perfect gifts of things such as money in a bank balance or shares, which cannot simply be handed over on one's deathbed, but require more to transfer title.

8.23 *Cain v Moon* (1896) laid down the essential requirements for a valid *donatio mortis causa* (DMC):

(1) The gift must be in contemplation, although not necessarily expectation, of death. All the reported cases deal with a donor suffering from illness, but, for example, going into battle or attempting to climb the Matterhorn should do.

(2) The donee must in some respect receive the property in question before the death of the donor. What this amounts to turns on the nature of the property: for a chattel, the donee must take possession or acquire the means to do so (eg the key to a box in which it is held). Receiving some clear token of the property will suffice, as in *Woodard v Woodard* (1995), where receiving the keys to a car, although not the logbook, was sufficient. For a bank account balance,

some 'indicia of title' must be transferred, such as the deposit book; in the case of shares, the delivery of share certificates has been held to work (*Duffcy v Mollica* (1968)), and the CA recognised a DMC of land for the first time in *Sen v Headley* (1991) where the indicia of title transferred was the title deeds.

(3)   Finally, the circumstances must show that the property is to revert to the donor if it turns out that he recovers; in other words, the *gift must be made conditional on the donor's impending death*. It is a common error in exams to assume that all imperfect gifts following which the donor soon dies can be perfected as DMCs—only gifts *conditional* on the donor's death may be. A DMC was held valid where the donor died from pneumonia rather than from the incurable disease in contemplation of which the gift was made (*Wilkes v Allington* (1931)); this case is generally understood to stand for the proposition that, so long as the gift is made in contemplation of death, it does not matter whether the testator dies in the particular way he expected.

IV: Proprietary estoppel

8.24   In certain cases of proprietary estoppel (4.36) the court, to give effect to the claimant's 'minimum equity', will do what amounts to perfecting an imperfect gift. In *Pascoe v Turner* (1979) a man declared to the woman with whom he was living as her husband that the house was 'hers and everything in it'. She spent most of her savings on the house. Following their separation he tried to turn her out. The court held that the minimum equity in the case was for the man to transfer the fee simple to the woman. In both *Gillett v Holt* (2001) and *Thorner v Major* (2009) men who had worked for most of their lives on the farms of others in the expectation that they would be given the farms, or part of them, by the owner in their wills, were awarded freehold interests in the farmland on which they had laboured.

Covenants to settle

8.25   Covenants are promises formally expressed by being written in a deed. Formerly, deeds needed to be sealed, typically by a blob of wax or a red wafer affixed to the document; now (Law of Property (Miscellaneous Provisions) Act 1989, s 1), deeds must be signed and witnessed, and seals are no longer required. If the covenantor, the party who makes the promise in a deed, fails to perform what he promised, the covenantee, the party to whom the promise was made, may bring an action at common law for damages. Covenants are very much the product of formal legal thinking: the deed itself was all-important. If the seal fell off the deed, then the covenantee could not sue upon it. If after having the covenant enforced against him, the covenantor left the deed undefaced in the covenantee's possession, the covenantee could sue on it and be awarded damages again (1.4). Thus, covenants are expressions of voluntarily undertaken obligations that, because they are expressed in a particular form, can be enforced at common law.

8.26   Covenants must be distinguished from contracts. The modern law of contract developed entirely separately from the law of covenants. The modern law of contract does not require any formal expression of an agreement for it to be legally binding (except in so far as formality requirements have been imposed by statute, eg Law of Property (Miscellaneous Provisions) Act 1989, s 2 requires contracts for the sale of land to be in writing). In the course of their development of contract law, the courts developed the doctrine of consideration. Why and how it particularly arose is complicated, but in its modern formulation it essentially requires that in order for a voluntarily undertaken obligation, roughly, a 'promise', to be legally binding, the person to whom it is made, the promisee, must have given value or 'consideration' for it. The doctrine of consideration has nothing to do with the law of covenants. A covenant is a formal means by which the common law allows persons to make legally binding promises, *regardless* of consideration. In view of this, while promises under seal are sometimes called 'specialty' contracts, it is not clear that one should treat covenants as governed by the law of contract per se, rather than by their own bespoke law of covenants, which will of course in many respects be similar or identical. This is of some importance, because covenants to settle are arrangements between two parties, the covenantor/settlor and the covenantee/trustee, for the benefit of a third party, the beneficiary. If they are truly contracts, then they will be governed by the Contracts (Rights of Third Parties) Act 1999, which, basically for the first time in modern English legal history, allows third-party beneficiaries of a contract to bring an action upon it. However, if covenants are not truly contracts, then the Act will not apply. We shall see.

8.27 While equity will not assist a volunteer, equity will in many cases assist those who have given consideration by, for example, ordering the specific performance of a contract in certain circumstances. But combine the maxim 'Equity looks to intent not form' with 'Equity will not assist a volunteer' and it is clear that in equity a gratuitous promise is a gratuitous promise whether in a deed or not, and so equity will not enforce a promise just because it is in a deed even if the common law will. If I make a legally binding contract to buy your Rembrandt, I will have given good consideration, and so not only may I sue you for damages if you fail to deliver the Rembrandt, but I may also get an order for specific performance from equity (now governed by Sale of Goods Act 1979, s 52) because it is unique and money damages would be inadequate. If, however, you promise to give me the Rembrandt in a covenant, although I can still sue you at common law for money damages if you fail to deliver, I cannot get specific performance from equity, because equity will not assist a volunteer. This marked distinction looks even more odd in light of the fact that neither the common law nor equity (*Bassett v Nosworthy* (1673); *Midland Bank Trust Co Ltd v Green* (1981)) is concerned about the 'adequacy' of consideration, ie whether the amount paid for the property is substantial or trivial. Thus if I contract with you to provide you with a lease in return for your paying me a peppercorn, equity will specifically enforce that contractual obligation, indeed will treat me as having granted you the lease already (4.5 et seq), but if I make the same promise in a covenant for no consideration, it will not.

Covenants to settle and marriage settlements

8.28 A 'covenant to settle' is simply a covenant to create a trust, such as 'I, X, hereby covenant with Y that I shall transfer Blackacre to Y on trust for Z'. While X may covenant with Y to transfer property to him on trust for Z in any circumstance, covenants to settle were typical provisions in marriage settlements. A marriage settlement is a trust created by a man and a woman in contemplation of marriage. Normally the property is vested in separate trustees, but in certain cases the husband would be the trustee. Marriage settlements were popular amongst the propertied classes in the nineteenth century, and essentially allowed the wife of the marriage to have control over the property she brought into the marriage, because at common law a married woman's property became her husband's; it could thus be squandered by a wastrel husband, and if the wife were to die before her husband without 'issue', ie without having had children, the property brought into the marriage would pass to him and thence to his heirs. Thus the families of wives settled property upon them in trust, first, to allow the woman control over the property she brought into the marriage, because the settlement would give the wife certain powers over it and, secondly, the trust would direct that the property of the wife would be held on trust for her next of kin, ie her own relations, if she should die without issue.

8.29 Typically marriage settlements included covenants with the trustees of the settlement by both the husband and wife to settle 'after-acquired' property on the trusts of the settlement. 'After-acquired property' is simply property acquired after the date of the marriage, and such covenants typically restricted the obligation to property above a certain value. Coming from rich families, both the husband and wife were likely to inherit significant wealth only after the marriage began, and the inclusion of such inherited wealth in the marriage settlement would naturally be 'part of the bargain' that established their position in the dynastic line of both families. Thus both the husband and wife would make a covenant with the trustees to transfer to them, on the trusts of the marriage settlement, any property they would receive over, say, £100 in value. These covenants were not made for any consideration recognised at common law. Equity, by contrast, regarded marriage as 'the most valuable consideration imaginable' (*A-G v Jacobs-Smith* (1895)), and so, although equity would not enforce these promises to settle because they were formalised as covenants, it would enforce them because 'marriage consideration' had been provided. Furthermore, equity regarded the issue of the marriage and their issue, ie the children and grandchildren, to be within the marriage consideration, and thus able to enforce the covenants. The doctrine of marriage consideration applies *only* to marriage settlements, that is settlements made *in contemplation* of marriage. A husband and wife *who are already married* who set up a trust for themselves and their children do not create a marriage settlement, and the children are not within any marriage consideration.

The enforcement of covenants to settle by equity

Covenants in marriage settlements

8.30 Because equity recognises marriage consideration, it is willing to enforce covenants to settle in marriage settlements, that is it will order the covenantor to transfer the property to the trustees of the settlement, thus constituting the trust over the property specified in the covenant. *Pullan v Koe* (1913) is a typical case. The settlement included the usual covenant by the wife to settle after-acquired property of £100 or more. The wife received £285; she spent part of it and put the rest into bonds in her husband's name. On the husband's death, the trustees of the settlement sued his executors for the transfer of the bonds to them so they could hold them on the marriage settlement trusts. The court held that it was the duty of the trustees to enforce the covenant, and equity would order specific performance of the covenant, as there existed beneficiaries of the marriage settlement who were within the marriage consideration. The court held further that the £285 was impressed with the trust the moment the wife received it, equity looking upon that as done which ought to be done (4.6). Thus not only would equity insist on specific performance of the covenant, but that the trust was constituted by way of constructive trust the minute the covenant *could* be performed.

8.31 *Re Plumptre's Marriage Settlement* (1910) is a counterpart case: here, the next of kin, who were to take the property if there were no issue of the marriage, sued to enforce a covenant to settle after-acquired property. Their suit failed. The court would not order specific performance, as they were volunteers, not being within the marriage consideration. Eve J relied upon the unanimous CA decision in *Re D'Angibau* (1879), in which Cotton LJ emphasised the distinction between a fully constituted trust, under which volunteer beneficiaries have just as much right as beneficiaries who have given consideration, and a gratuitous promise to create a trust, which will not be enforced against the promisor at the suit of volunteers.

8.32 What happens if a wife receives after-acquired property (bound by a covenant to settle) at a time when there are children of the marriage, but she never transfers the property to the trustees, and later the children die? Can the next of kin argue that the trust was immediately constituted by way of constructive trust as in *Pullan* when the wife received the property, since at that time the covenant was specifically enforceable, there being children of the marriage within the marriage consideration? Once a trust is constituted, it is constituted for all the beneficiaries, volunteers or not (8.8); even if it is constituted as a result of a beneficiary who has given consideration suing to enforce the covenant, once the trust is constituted by the covenantor transferring the property to the trustees, it is constituted for non-volunteer and volunteer beneficiaries alike (*Davenport v Bishopp* (1843)). So if the wife had transferred the property to the trustees, the trust would have been constituted for all the beneficiaries, and if the children died the next of kin would have a perfect right to their benefits under the terms of the settlement. Therefore, does not the application of the maxim 'Equity looks upon that as done … ' to constitute the trust immediately via a constructive trust also constitute the trust for the next of kin? Alas, no. Apparently, the trust constituted by the constructive trust becomes unconstituted again, believe it or not, when those within the marriage consideration disappear, because the constructive trust evaporates. According to Eve J in *Re Plumptre's Marriage Settlement*:

> [T]he argument founded on the rule that equity looks on that as done which ought to be done is, in my opinion, met and disposed of by [the view that], this rule, although usually expressed in general terms, is by no means universally true. Where the obligation to do what ought to be done is not an absolute duty, but only an obligation arising from contract, that which ought to be done is only treated as done in favour of some person entitled to enforce the contract as against the person liable to perform it.

So volunteers such as the next of kin cannot rely upon any constructive constitution of the trust.

8.33 Although we have specifically looked at promises to settle where the consideration is marriage consideration and the promise is expressed in a covenant, the principle that equity will assist someone who has given consideration for the creation of a trust is of general application. Contracts to create trusts occur all the time in the commercial world as, for example, a contract whereby an agent is obliged to hold proceeds of sale on trust for his principal. Consideration has been given for that promise to 'settle', and equity will not hesitate to enforce it. The proceeds will be regarded as held by the agent on constructive trust when he receives them.

The enforcement of covenants to settle at common law

8.34 So far we have considered the equitable enforcement of promises to settle, and we see that where consideration has been given, equity will order the promisor to transfer property to the trustee thereby constituting the trust, and that in the meantime the promisor will hold the property in question upon constructive trust. On the other hand, where the intended benefi-ciary is a volunteer, equity will not order the constitution of the trust. This is all quite straight-forward. So far the fact that these promises to settle have been expressed in covenants has not really mattered; if these promises had been made orally, the results would have been exactly the same. Equity is not concerned with form, and its willingness to enforce promises to settle turns, as we have seen, on whether consideration (including marriage consideration) for the promise has been given, not on the form in which the promise has been expressed. Now, however, the nature of covenants does become important, because these are promises that are enforceable at common law irrespective of whether any consideration had been given.

8.35 Consider the standard covenant to settle. S, the settlor/covenantor, promises to transfer the property to T, the trustee/covenantee, on trust for B, the beneficiary, who is not himself a party to the covenant, and who is a volunteer. The question now is whether T should be able to enforce the covenant *at common law*, and what this would mean. At first glance, there appears no reason why he should not. At common law T is a covenantee, and therefore the promisee of a legally enforceable promise. Can he not therefore bring a common law action for damages for breach of covenant against the covenantor, thereby getting money to the value of the property that ought to have been transferred on trust into his hands, and thereby constitute the trust himself? The answer appears to be 'no', although the cases that establish this have been extensively criticised.

8.36 The principal case is *Re Pryce* (1917), where Eve J held that covenantees/trustees ought not to enforce a covenant to settle in favour of next of kin who were volunteer beneficiaries. Eve J reasoned as follows:

> '[V]olunteers have no right whatever to obtain specific performance of a mere covenant which has remained as a covenant and has never been performed': see per James LJ in In re D'Angibau. Nor could damages be awarded either in this Court, or, as I apprehend, at law, where, since the Judicature Acts, the same defences would be available to the defend-ant as would be raised in an action brought in this Court for specific performance or dam-ages. In these circumstances, seeing that the next of kin could neither maintain an action to enforce the covenant nor for damages for breach of it, and that the settlement is not a declaration of trust constituting the relationship of trustee and cestui que trust between the defendant and the next of kin, in which case effect could be given to the trusts even in favour of volunteers, but is a mere voluntary contract to create a trust, ought the Court now for sole benefit of these volunteers to direct the trustees to take proceedings to enforce the defendant's covenant? I think it ought not; to do so would be to give the next of kin by indirect means what they cannot obtain by any direct procedure, and would in effect be enforcing the settlement as against the defendant's legal right to [the property in question].

8.37 The statement from *Re D'Angibau* (1879) that volunteer beneficiaries may not obtain the *equitable* remedy of specific performance of a covenant, whilst true, is not obviously relevant: it does not dispose of the question whether a trustee/covenantee may sue on the covenant *at common law*. To the extent that the sentence that follows indicates that damages would not only be unavailable in equity but also at law for breach of covenant following the Judicature Acts, it is just wrong (see Elliot (1960)). If Eve J only means that the volunteer beneficiaries would be unable to get damages in equity (because volunteers) or damages at common law (because not parties to the covenant), then again, this is true, but as with the preceding statement, not obviously relevant. The real heart of the decision lies in the statement that by allowing the trustee/covenantees to sue at common law, the next of kin would achieve by indirect means what they could not achieve directly, and this would in effect allow the enforcement of the covenant to settle by volunteers, in violation of the general principle. The case is most easily criticised by pointing out that Eve J here seems to have allowed equitable principles to exceed their proper jurisdiction. The general principle, recall, is that 'Equity will not assist a volunteer', not 'Equity will stand in the way of a volunteer'. By ordering that the trustee/covenantees may not sue, Eve J appears to trench upon the trustee/covenantee's common law rights. What has equity to say about whether a covenantee at common law sues upon his covenant? The covenantee is not seeking the assistance of equity at all; he is not asking for specific performance, but for the common law remedy to which he is entitled by his common law right to enforce the covenant. From this perspective, Eve J has no jurisdiction to direct the covenantee one way or another, and so the case is wrongly decided. Two authorities that appear to go the other way, *Fletcher v Fletcher* (1844) and *Re Cavendish Browne's Settlement Trusts* (1916), will be discussed at 8.49–8.50.

8.38   It is important, however, to distinguish the question whether equity will allow a trustee to pursue his common legal rights under the covenant to constitute the trust from the case of a party to the covenant who sues, not to use the proceeds to constitute the trust, but as damages for the loss suffered when the covenant is not carried out. *Cannon v Hartley* (1949) is such a case. In *Cannon*, a man, on separating from his wife, covenanted with both his wife and daughter to settle after-acquired property upon them, but did not. The daughter, who had given no consideration but was a party to the covenant, brought an action on the covenant at common law.

8.39   Romer J awarded the daughter substantial damages for her father's failure to settle the property, stating:

> In the present case the plaintiff, although a volunteer, . . . is a direct covenantee under the very covenant upon which she is suing. She does not require the assistance of the court to enforce the covenant for she has a legal right herself to enforce it. She is not asking for equitable relief but for damages at common law for breach of covenant.

8.40   *Re Pryce* was followed in *Re Kay's Settlement* (1938) (albeit reluctantly by Simonds J), and the latter was followed in *Re Cook's Settlement Trusts* (1965), so the principle that trustee/covenantees may not sue the covenantor at common law for damages must be regarded as authoritative. Assuming, however, that these three first-instance decisions may be reconsidered in a suitable case by the higher courts, we must explore the consequences of allowing a trustee/covenantee to sue upon the covenant at common law.

8.41   If the trustee is allowed to sue upon the covenant, what remedy will he obtain? It seems quite clear that he will not be able specifically to enforce the covenant in favour of the beneficiary, that is to obtain an order that the covenantor transfer the property on trust to him, because an order of specific performance is an equitable remedy, and the trustee is a volunteer. (*Beswick v Beswick* (1968) establishes that a party to a valid contract, ie one who has given consideration, may obtain an order for specific performance that benefits a volunteer third party, but in the case we are considering both the trustee/covenantee and the beneficiary are volunteers, so this equitable remedy is unavailable.)

8.42   If the trustee/covenantee brings an action at common law for breach of covenant, he may recover on either of two bases. First, regarding the action as one particularly for breach of covenant, not breach of contract:

> for breach of a covenant to pay a certain sum, the measure of damages (if that is the appropriate expression) is the certain sum. [Elliot (1960)]

Even in contract, generally the remedy in an action for an agreed sum is the payment of that sum (see Treitel (2003), at 1013). Alternatively, according to the normal rule of common law damages for breach of contract, the damages will be measured by the covenantee's loss. Here again, the covenantee's loss is the value of the promised property. It is sometimes argued that the trustee/covenantee has suffered no real loss himself, because it is the intended beneficiary who has really suffered a loss by the covenantor's breach of covenant; therefore the covenantee's damages will be nominal (5.58) unless he can recover damages for the volunteer beneficiary as a third party, and the common law will generally not allow him to do so (*Woodar Investment Development Ltd v Wimpey Construction UK Ltd* (1980), HL). This is misconceived. Although in the deed the covenantee is to hold the property 'on trust for' the beneficiary, the common law, you will recall (1.21), has always ignored the words 'on trust for'. It is no answer to a claim in damages for breach of contract at common law that the claimant is a trustee who was contracting for others, and the same is true here.

8.43   If this is right, then the trustee/covenantee who is allowed to sue at law will recover the value of the trust property the covenantor promised to transfer. It is here where things start to fall apart, because we must now ask, does the recovery of these substantial damages constitute the trust the settlor/covenantor intended? Another way of putting this is: for whom does the trustee/covenantee hold the damages? The mere receipt of that property does not make the trustee/covenantee a trustee of it unless equity is willing to recognise the trust obligation. Or rather, the intended beneficiary will only be able to enforce a trust over that property against the trustee/covenantee if equity recognises that he holds the damages on trust for him. If this operation of securing the covenanted property is done entirely at common law, then it is still up to equity to decide whether the property is to be held on trust. In order to understand the issues at stake here, we must first make a digression.

The trust of the benefit of a promise to settle

8.44   Most commentators accept that the *Re Pryce* unenforceability problem is avoided where the covenant to settle is a special one that creates an 'immediate binding trust of the promise', perhaps like this: 'I hereby covenant to transfer £1,000 to Fred to hold on trust for Alice, and the benefit of this covenant shall forthwith be held by Fred on trust for Alice.' The idea is that in the case of the normal covenant to settle, the covenantee is not a trustee of anything until he receives the trust property, at which time the trust is constituted and he becomes a trustee. Until that time, he holds his common law rights to enforce the covenant for himself absolutely. This special kind of covenant, however, makes him a trustee at the outset, and the subject matter of the trust is his common law rights under the covenant. This might seem a strange sort of trust property, but it is not at all. The right under the covenant is a personal right, but then so is every contractual right a trustee may acquire on behalf of the trust in administering it, as, for example, the right against a bank to the balance of the trust bank account. All can serve as rights held on trust. That is not the problem with the 'trust of the benefit of the promise idea'.

8.45   The problem is that, according to this idea, in the *normal* case of a covenant to settle like those in *Re Pryce* and *Re Kay* the covenantee is *not* the trustee of his rights under the covenant for the intended beneficiary. This is entirely implausible. In the normal case, the trustee/covenantee is already a trustee of property under a settlement into which the covenanted property will go if the covenant is performed. Thus when the settlor covenants with the trustee to transfer property to him to hold on trust for the beneficiaries of the settlement, the trustee is immediately constituted trustee of the legal right to sue under the covenant. This is so simply because he undertakes in the covenant to hold the property he will receive under it *as a trustee* for the beneficiaries. As Hackney (1987, at 117) puts it:

> At no stage does the transaction operate at common law alone, giving [the covenantee] any rights under the covenant, since the covenant is made to him as a trustee, any more than would a simple transfer of property to Y on trust for Z give Y beneficial property rights at common law.

8.46   The alternative analysis, that the covenantee covenants for himself, would mean (1) that it is up to the covenantee whether or not to enforce the covenant; since he covenants for his own benefit, it is up to him whether he pursues his rights to become a trustee; and (2) that it is up to the *settlor/covenantor* to enforce the trust against the covenantee when the covenantee receives the trust property, *not* the intended beneficiary, because if, when the covenantee receives the covenanted property, he refuses to hold it on trust for the beneficiary, then he is merely acting in breach of covenant, not breach of trust, because, remember, according to this view there is no trust until the covenantee holds the property (gives effect to the intended trust terms) according to his common law obligation, ie in accord with his covenant. The intended beneficiary is not a beneficiary yet, and not being a party to the covenant himself, he has no rights to enforce it. Therefore to assume that the mere receipt of the intended trust property by the covenantee constitutes the intended trust is to confuse equitable ownership with a common law obligation.

8.47   According to this view, it would be up to the settlor (or following his death, his personal representative) to enforce the covenant and require the covenantee to hold the property on trust, and the settlor would have no obligation to the intended beneficiaries to do so. There is yet a further problem, which becomes apparent if the settlor does try to enforce the covenant. Since the intended trustee is not to hold the property for his own benefit, but as a trustee, the settlor gives him no consideration for holding the property on trust (any remuneration he might receive under the constituted trust comes from the beneficiaries, not from the settlor). Thus equity will not enforce the obligation against the trustee by an order of specific performance, requiring him to hold the property on trust. The settlor is left to his common law remedies; this will either be damages for breach of covenant, which will essentially amount to the value of the trust property, or restitution of the value of the property transferred. The upshot is that if the covenantee does not covenant as a trustee, *neither the settlor/covenantor nor the intended beneficiaries* can enforce the covenant so as *actually to constitute the trust*. These considerations strongly suggest that such covenants, in which the covenantee does not covenant as a trustee, are exceedingly rare, if not non-existent.

8.48   The courts, to their credit, have never given any explicit approval of this analysis, and certainly the decisions in *Re Pryce* and *Re Kay* do not in any way seem to depend upon it; indeed, if the judges in those cases thought that, it would be odd that they were willing to hear arguments, because the cases were applications by *trustees* seeking directions of the court as to how they should act *as trustees*. Nevertheless, it is orthodox to say that if in these cases the trustees had held the benefit of the covenant on trust from the outset, their enforcement of the covenants would have been allowed. Support for this proposition is supposedly gleaned from two cases where it is said that covenants were enforced because, exceptionally, there was an immediate binding trust of the covenant: *Davenport v Bishopp* (1843) and *Fletcher v Fletcher* (1844).

8.49   *Davenport* involved a suit by a husband against the heir of his deceased wife for the transfer of property from the heir into the husband's marriage settlement. The heir obtained the property by succession when the wife died, but it was property that the wife, when alive, was bound to transfer to the trustees of the settlement under a typical after-acquired property covenant. The husband was not a volunteer, but since there was no issue of the marriage, a relation who was a volunteer would benefit if the property was transferred into the settlement. The heir argued that while the property should go into the trust so as to give the husband his benefit, the volunteer beneficiary under the settlement should be denied any benefit from the property, having given no consideration. In other words, the heir argued that even where someone who had given consideration wished to enforce the covenant and constitute the trust, he could only constitute it for himself, as it were, not for any volunteer beneficiaries. Not surprisingly, Knight-Bruce VC found such an idea insupportable, affirming the basic principle that a trust, once constituted, is constituted for all the beneficiaries, volunteers or not. In passing, he said:

> The surviving trustee of the settlement, or his representative, may be thought to be a trustee of the covenant for the benefit both of Mr. Davenport and of the heirs of Miss Lucas [volunteers].

Put in context it is clear that Knight-Bruce VC is simply making the same point, in a different way, that the trustee, when suing on the covenant on behalf of a non-volunteer, in effect also sues for the volunteers, because by constituting the trust he does so for all the beneficiaries. It is not a statement that the trustee may sue for volunteers in special circumstances where he is a 'trustee of the covenant'. Indeed the decision turns on Knight-Bruce VC's accepting that if there was only a volunteer beneficiary, the trustee could not constitute the trust. The result, then, is that the case reiterates the *Re Pryce* line of cases—that trustees/covenantees are always trustees of the promise in a covenant, but that does not entail that equity will allow them to enforce a gratuitous covenant to settle.

8.50   In *Fletcher v Fletcher* (1844), a father had covenanted to transfer property upon trust to named persons as trustees for his sons, but did not do so. Wigram VC held that the covenant was enforceable by either the named trustees or the intended beneficiaries. The essence of his judgment on the enforceability point is in these lines:

> According to the authorities I cannot, I admit, do anything to perfect the liability of the author of the trust, if it is not already perfect. This covenant, however, is already perfect. The covenantor is liable at law, and the Court is not called upon to do any act to perfect it.

What Wigram VC has decided here is simply that a covenantee may sue a covenantor *at common law* for the trust property. In other words, the decision is simply a decision contrary to the ruling in *Re Pryce*. He only then goes on to consider an objection by counsel, that there could not be a trust of the benefit of a covenant. Wigram VC did not think 'there is any difficulty in that'. Therefore, while the case is authority, contrary to *Re Pryce*, that a trustee/covenantee may sue at common law on the covenant, it does not make the right of the trustee/covenantee to do so depend upon finding 'a trust of the benefit of the covenant' as if that were something special. *Fletcher v Fletcher* is not the only authority that contradicts *Re Pryce*. In *Re Cavendish Browne's Settlement Trusts* (1916) Younger J held that trustees were entitled to substantial damages for the breach of a covenant to settle. The case is badly reported. *Fletcher* is one of the cases listed as having been cited to the court, but there is no indication that the case turned on the particular finding of a trust of the benefit of the covenant.

8.51   In *Re Cook's Settlement Trusts* (1965), Buckley J considered an argument that the covenant created an immediate binding trust of the promise, but decided against on the ground that there cannot be a trust of a promise to transfer future property. This is simply ill founded (see eg *Lloyd's v Harper* (1880)). As a result it is difficult to know what the case stands for, but since there was no analysis of *Fletcher*, one should not draw the conclusion that the case lends weight to the thesis that *Re Pryce* prevents the enforcement of a covenant because the covenantee is not a trustee of the benefit of it.

8.52   We can now return to the question of what *Re Pryce* actually stands for, and the related question for whom the covenantee would hold the damages he was awarded if he were able, *pace Re Pryce*, to sue on the covenant at law. If the preceding consideration of the 'trust of the benefit of the covenant' idea is correct, then virtually all covenantees of covenants to settle are trustees of their rights under the covenant. If that is so, then the decision in *Re Pryce* does not mean that the court is interfering in the enforcement of a covenantee's common law right to make himself a trustee; he is a trustee already. The court is directing a trustee not to use his common law rights to 'get in', or realise a common law claim to, property, purely because the common law right is founded on a voluntary promise. By the same token, *Re Pryce* means that the court will not allow a beneficiary to enforce a common law right held by the trust, if this right is only the benefit of a voluntary promise enforceable at common law. It must be emphasised that this is a perfectly coherent position for equity to take. Equity has jurisdiction over trusts and their constitution, and if equity will not impose new equitable obligations on people who do not presently have them and do not wish to have them for the sake of those who have not paid for them, then that is fully consonant with equity's refusal to interfere against a legal owner whose conscience is not affected, and in the eyes of equity it is not unconscionable to refuse to confer a gift on someone, even if one earlier promised to do so (although this view might need to be revisited in light of *Pennington* (8.14)). In short, equity will not allow a trustee or a beneficiary to enforce a voluntary promise to bring property into the trust. It is of no moment, on this analysis, that the promise is one that the law would enforce as far as it can, ie getting property into the covenantee's hands. Equity has charge of trustees and beneficiaries, and if equity will not enforce a trust over property that results from the enforcement of a gratuitous promise, then it will insist that the trustee, who is the promisee of that promise, should not enforce it.

8.53   If this is right, it is simply not clear how equity would respond to the case of a trustee who does somehow manage to enforce his rights at common law to win substantial damages. On one hand, equity might require the trustee to hold the damages on trust for the intended beneficiary, because the covenantee is a trustee after all, and equity's refusal to assist a volunteer ought to be restricted to preventing the enforcement of a voluntary promise to settle when equity's assistance is required, or, perhaps, when its directions are sought—it may be significant that in both *Re Pryce* and *Re Kay* the trustees were seeking the advice of the court as to whether they should enforce the covenant at common law. This view might be strengthened by the attitude of the court to 'fortuitous vesting' (8.55), to which we turn shortly. If the court is willing to treat the settlor/covenantee's trust as constituted so long as the property gets into the trustee's hands, then the court may treat the trustee/covenantee's own actions that result in this as equally constituting the trust. Certainly if *Re Pryce* were overruled, and trustees were not prevented by equity from suing on covenants, the result would be that they would hold the damages on trust for the intended beneficiaries.

8.54 If, however, *Re Pryce* remains an authority, and a trustee/covenantee sues and wins damages (ie without having sought the directions of the court first as to whether he might do so), Hayton (2001b, at 253) argues that equity will step in and make the trustee/covenantee hold the damages on *resulting trust* for the settlor, ie the covenantor whom he has just successfully sued at common law. Why? Since equity will not assist a volunteer, equity will not allow the beneficiary to enforce a trust of the damages against the covenantee/trustee. This would be in line with the preceding analysis of *Re Pryce* but takes it one step further: not only will equity not enforce a constituted trust of the benefit of a promise in the volunteer's favour, but neither will it enforce a trust over the proceeds of the enforcement of that promise by a volunteer (at common law) either. But, says Hayton, neither can the trustee/covenantee keep the damages for himself, because he undertook the covenant as a trustee. Equity will therefore make him hold the damages upon resulting trust for the covenantor, putting them both back in the position they were at the beginning. This, so the argument goes, justifies *Re Pryce*. The court of equity stops the whole pointless process from the outset. Clever, don't you think?

Fortuitous vesting of the trust property

8.55 In *Re Brooks' Settlement Trusts* (1939), Lloyds Bank was trustee of a marriage settlement, under which the wife had a power of appointment. One of her sons created for himself and his wife and children a voluntary settlement, of which Lloyds Bank was also the trustee, to which settlement he assigned all his interest in any property he might receive as a result of his mother's appointing property to him from her marriage settlement. His mother did, by deed, appoint property to her son. Before this appointment, Lloyds Bank held legal title to this property as trustee for the mother; if it carried out the appointment by complying with her exercise of its power of appointment it would transfer the property to the son. But Lloyds Bank had a second role, as trustee of the son's own settlement and, according to this settlement, this self-same property was to go into it. So Lloyds Bank held the property either as trustee of the mother's settlement, under which it ought to pay the money out to the son, or it held it as trustee of the son's own settlement, as property that properly belonged in it. The question, then, was whether the son's assignment of any property he might receive by way of his mother's power of appointment, combined with the fact that the trustee had the legal title to the property, amounted to the constitution of the son's settlement. Farwell J decided it did not:

> The son had no more than a mere expectancy under the marriage settlement until the appointment was made. That being so, the son, when he assigned his interest under the [marriage] settlement to the trustees of [his own] voluntary settlement,...was assigning, or purporting to assign, something to which he might become entitled in futuro—not a contingent interest, but a mere expectancy. It is clear on the authorities that he cannot be compelled to allow the trustees to retain the appointed sum, and that he can call on the trustees to pay it over to him.

8.56 Farwell J said that in the case of an assignment for value, ie where there was consideration, the trustees could hold the property on trust, enforce the covenant as it were, on the principles of *Re Ellenborough* (8.10), ie on the basis that equity would treat the assignment of future property as a promise for consideration to assign the property if and when received. But here, as there was no consideration allowing equity to treat the invalid legal assignment of a mere expectancy as a valid promise to assign, and further that there was clearly no declaration by the son as a trustee himself, Farwell J held that the son retained beneficial ownership of the property appointed, and ordered Lloyds Bank to pay the money to him.

8.57 Farwell J viewed this result as unfortunate, and said that the law:

> *makes it impossible to enforce the [son's] voluntary settlement, even to the extent of permitting the trustees of that settlement to retain, as subject thereto, the money in their hands.*

This appears to indicate that Farwell J might have reached the opposite result had the so-called property in question not been a mere expectancy at the time of the son's assignment. In other words, had the property contemplated in the covenant not been future property, the covenant might have been held to bind the son, and the trustees could have devoted the property to the voluntary settlement. But even if that were the case, the son still would not have abided by the covenant and assigned the property into the voluntary settlement. The trustee would still have legal title only because of its multiple roles, not because the son had assigned the property, in other words merely by virtue of the fortuitous vesting of the property. But, as Hayton (2001b, at 254 et seq) argued, given the decision that Farwell J made it was not consistent of him to think there would have been a different result had the son's assignment been for existing property, because the case turns not on the law regarding the effectiveness of legal assignments, but on equity's refusal to assist a volunteer. If there had been consideration for the son's assignment, then equity would have assisted; equity would not have let the fact that this was an assignment for future property stand in its way—equity will treat an assignment of future property as an enforceable promise to assign where consideration is given (8.10). On this interpretation, then, an expansive view of the maxim 'Equity will not assist a volunteer' was taken, giving rise, according to Hayton, to the principle that 'only the settlor (or his agent) can constitute a trust'; a trust should not be regarded as constituted by mere chance, as opposed to by the settlor's own act.

8.58 The counterpart case supporting the validity of fortuitous vesting is *Re Ralli's Will Trusts* (1964). Here a wife covenanted in her marriage settlement to assign property she acquired during the course of her marriage. The after-acquired property in question was a reversionary interest under her father's will, which fell in after her mother died, but which she never assigned. She died, and as it turned out, the sole remaining trustee of the marriage settlement was also the executor of her will, so he became the legal owner of the reversion she ought to have assigned to the marriage settlement when she had first received it. Buckley J decided the case on the terms of the original marriage settlement, holding that under a clause of the settlement the wife declared that she held any existing property on trust for the marriage settlement, and further that the reversionary interest was existing property at the time of the creation of the settlement; therefore, the wife had declared herself a trustee of the reversion on the trusts of the marriage settlement from the outset; consequently her executor held the property on the same trust when he received the legal title to her estate. But Buckley J went on to state, *obiter*, that even if this were not the case, the property became subject to the settlement trusts by the fortuitous circumstance that the trustee of the settlement was the same person as the executor of the will:

> *That the [trustee] holds the fund because he was appointed trustee of the will is irrelevant. He is at law the owner of the fund and the means by which he became so have no effect on the quality of his legal ownership. The question is: for whom, if anyone, does*

he hold the fund in equity? In other words, who can successfully assert in equity against
him disentitling him to stand on his legal right?

8.59   Buckley J held that the wife, if she were alive, could not make such an assertion against the
executor/trustee (and her legatees under her will could not be in a better position) because
in order to assert her right to the fund, she would have to show that the trustee could not
conscientiously withhold it from her; but all the trustee had to do was point to the covenant
to show that in conscience he *should* withhold it from her. It was the beneficiaries under the
covenant who in equity had the superior claim upon his conscience. Buckley J accepted that the
constitution of the trust in this case would be fortuitous, and that if the executor of the wife's
will had been someone different, so would have been the result. But this naturally turned on the
fact that the operation of the maxim 'Equity will not assist a volunteer' is in a sense inherently
fortuitous, because it only goes so far as to prevent a court assisting a volunteer in transferring
property to constitute a trust; it does not compel equity to positively divest volunteers of the
benefits once their trustee obtains legal ownership. Such a view is, of course, in direct conflict
with the principle that Hayton asserts, that 'only a settlor or his authorised agent can constitute
a trust'.

8.60   There is a lurking problem in Buckley J's framing of the principle upon which fortuitous vesting
operates, which is this: he says essentially that a trustee as bare legal owner must decide who,
in equity, has the best claim upon him. Here the question was in what capacity did the trustee/
executor hold the fund: as trustee of the marriage settlement or as executor of the will? Now it
may perhaps be fair to demand that a trustee/executor in the context of a close family arrangement like this one might ask himself such a question and be bound to take cognisance of the
answer; if therefore, in this case, the trustee/executor paid out the money to the legatees under
the will he could be properly held to be in breach of trust. But is it at all sensible to make this
question-posing approach into a general principle determining whether a trustee is in breach
of trust? Take the case of Lloyds Bank in *Re Brooks' Settlement Trusts*, which is undoubtedly the
trustee for thousands of separate trusts. Qua legal owner, Lloyds Bank owns all that trust property as a single legal owner and, in Buckley J's view, Lloyds merely looks round to the various
equitable claims that can be made upon it under those thousands of trusts in order to decide
where its duty lies. But in the case of a large trustee such as a bank that is a counsel of nonsense.
Clearly it must (for accounting purposes at least) segregate the trust property it legally holds
into separate accounts relating to the different trusts it administers. Should a bank really be
in breach of trust if property is appointed under one trust, and it pays it out without knowing
that such property is also subject to a covenant in another trust, which it is administering quite
separately? Is a bank or any other professional trustee required to keep a list (if such a list could
even be kept) of actual and possible cross-references between all the trusts it administers? Can
Buckley J really be suggesting that trustees ought to be required to survey all their trusts as a
unit, treating themselves as legal owners of a big pile of property, and checking to make sure
that none of the provisions overlap?

8.61   Surely not. Trustees have the duty to treat themselves as separate trustees for separate settlements, and to keep the property in separate funds, and consequently they should not be liable
for failing to find cross-connections that give rise to fortuitous vesting, at least unless and until
a beneficiary whose equitable rights are constituted by the fortuitous vesting notifies them.
This problematic aspect of imposing an obligation to cross-check what might be very unrelated
trusts surely indicates that Buckley J's *obiter dictum*, if it is correct at all, must be restricted in its

operation to cases where the trustees are actually aware of the interlocking connection between the trusts that work to vest trust property fortuitously.

8.62   A final point: Buckley J based his decision in part on the rule in *Strong v Bird*. Even if the extension of this rule to the perfecting of trusts that the testator intended in his lifetime by the vesting of the trust property in the executor or administrator is correct, its application to the facts in *Re Ralli* is questionable. Buckley J did not refer to any evidence of a continuing intention to constitute the trust, and the requirement of continuing intention is the only thing that keeps that rule within any manageable bounds at all. The application may, perhaps, be explained, by considering the covenant itself to be evidence of a continuing intention where no other evidence is available.

Concluding considerations

8.63   The complications in this area of law arise from a failure of fusion (1.16) of equity and the common law to take place with respect to gratuitous obligations. It should not matter that the recognition of binding but gratuitous promises was first recognised by the common law. If the law (meaning the English legal system, not the common law) provides a means by which gratuitous promises can be made legally binding, then that means should be available for promises of all kinds unless good reason is given otherwise, and no reason is discernible in the cases that would rule out binding, gratuitous promises to settle. 'Equity will not assist a volunteer' is a slogan, not a reason, in this respect.

8.64   Precisely the same point applies to the availability of orders for specific performance. It should not matter that equity devised the remedy of specific performance. It should be employed by the court whenever it is just to do so, and its use or restriction should not depend upon its historical provenance, but upon principled reasons as to why its use is appropriate in one circumstance but not another. While it may well be the case that such principled reasons may be gleaned largely from past decisions of the Court of Equity, it makes no sense to say that only judges acting as equity judges have a coherent grip on the remedy and that therefore it is not a remedy of the legal system as a whole. It should be available on demand to judges to employ wherever it appears appropriate to do so. If the law treats a gratuitous promise to transfer that Rembrandt as legally binding because it is expressed in a covenant, then the enforcement of that right should turn on the same principles as apply to a right arising under a contract for consideration, unless there are good reasons why not. Specific performance is given under a contract because the Rembrandt is unique and so money damages would be an inadequate remedy. Therefore specific performance ought to be given to enforce the same obligation expressed in a covenant, although gratuitous, since money damages are just as much an inadequate remedy here and for precisely the same reason.

FURTHER READING

Chambers (2005a)

Elliot (1960)

Garton (2003)

Hackney (1987), at 110 et seq

Hornby (1962)

Kodilinye (1982)

MacNair (1988)

Rickett (2001)

Must-read cases: *Milroy v Lord* (1862); *Re Rose* (1952); *Re Stewart* (1908); *Re Pryce* (1916); *Re Kay's Settlement* (1938); *Cannon v Hartley* (1948); *Re Brooks' Settlement Trusts* (1939); *Re Ralli's Will Trusts* (1964); *Pennington v Waine* (2002)

SELF-TEST QUESTIONS

1. In 1985, Fred and Barbara created a settlement on their divorce for their then minor children, Claire and Eric. The trustee of the settlement was Tony, Barbara's brother. The settlement was originally constituted by the transfer of £100,000 to Tony, and in the trust instrument were included covenants by both Fred and Barbara to settle one half of any property either might thereafter acquire by legacy or inheritance.

    In 1987, Fred made a separate covenant with Tony to transfer one half of any royalties on his new book, to be held on the trusts of the settlement. The book earned £50,000, but Fred never transferred any money into the settlement.

    In 1988, Barbara received a legacy of £250,000 in shares of G Ltd. She has always paid the dividends to Claire, and said on numerous occasions that she intended to give the shares to Claire. On 10 July 1995, she made an appointment in early August with her solicitor for the purpose of executing the share transfer to Claire.

    On 13 July 1995, Fred and Barbara both died from food poisoning after attending Eric's university graduation. Fred left all his property to his brother Stuart, who is also the executor of his will. Barbara died intestate, and Tony and Claire have been appointed administrators of her estate.

    Advise Eric.

2. In what circumstances will equity perfect an imperfect gift? Are any reforms in the law indicated?

3. To what extent is this a correct statement of the law: 'Only a settlor can constitute a trust'?

Trusts and purposes

SUMMARY

The beneficiary principle and the invalidity of private purpose trusts
Anomalous valid purpose trusts
Powers for purposes
An enforcer principle?
Valid trusts for persons 'limited by a purpose': *Re Sanderson's Trust*
The bare trust with mandate and *Quistclose* trusts
Gifts to unincorporated associations
The dissolution of unincorporated associations
Less than unincorporated associations: the case of political parties
The rule against perpetuities

9.1 This chapter concerns how the law enables a person to devote their property to the carrying out of purposes, but restricts the ways in which that can be done. Although trusts are typically involved in legal mechanisms by which property is devoted to a purpose, this is almost always part of a mechanism that employs both the trust and a contractual obligation of some kind. In general, the law does not allow you simply to transfer property on trust to carry out a purpose, for example '£10,000 on trust to oppose UK entry into the common European currency', unless the purpose is charitable, also known as 'public'. This 'no private purpose trusts' rule is a corollary of what is known as the 'beneficiary principle'.

The beneficiary principle and the invalidity of private purpose trusts

9.2 The 'beneficiary principle' can be stated thus: for a trust to be valid, it must be for the benefit of ascertainable individuals, ie specific beneficiaries. The corollary of this rule is, roughly, that equity will not recognise a trust to carry out a purpose, since the benefits of carrying out a purpose cannot be localised to specific individuals. Hence, the principle is also framed as the 'no purpose trusts' rule.

9.3   The two most quoted statements expressing the 'no purpose trusts rule' come from the case of *Morice v Bishop of Durham* (1804, before Sir William Grant MR, 1805 on appeal to Lord Eldon LC). Both emphasise that for a trust to exist (putting charitable trusts to one side), there must be someone who will have standing to bring the trustees to court to enforce the trust obligations against the legal owner. Thus the court must find definite objects, ie beneficiaries, who can bring the trustees to court. Sir William Grant MR said:

> There can be no trust, over the exercise of which this Court will not assume a control; for an uncontrollable power of disposition would be ownership, and not trust…There must be somebody, in whose favour the court can decree performance.

Implicit in this statement is the view that only those who are intended to benefit qua beneficiaries have standing to enforce it. This rule is in essence parallel to the 'privity' rule of contract law: only those who are right holders under the trust may enforce it, not every Tom, Dick, or Mary who might like to see it carried out.

9.4   From this point of view, the beneficiary principle can be regarded as a corollary of the certainty of objects requirement: if a trust is expressed in terms of a purpose, then it will be impossible to determine any definite objects of the trust, and therefore there are no persons at whose insistence and for whose benefit the court can order the trustee to carry out the trust. Lord Eldon clearly equates the court's control over the trust with the existence of ascertainable objects and indeed, subject matter:

> As it is a maxim, that the execution of a trust must be under the control of the court, it must be of such a nature, that it can be under that control; so that the administration of it can be reviewed by the court…unless the subject and the objects can be ascertained, upon principles, familiar in other cases, it must be decided, that the court can neither reform maladministration, nor direct a due administration.

9.5   The best statement of the principle, however, is Roxburgh J's in *Re Astor's Settlement Trusts* (1952). In 1945 Viscount Astor made a settlement of most of the shares of 'The Observer Limited'. The income from the trust fund that was set up was to be applied to a number of purposes, including the maintenance of good understanding between nations, the preservation of the independence and integrity of newspapers, editors, and writers, the protection of newspapers from control by combines, and the improvement of newspapers. It was admitted that the purposes were not charitable (see Chapter 14).

9.6   Roxburgh J framed the beneficiary principle in this way:

> The typical case of a trust is one in which the legal owner of property is constrained by a court of equity so to deal with it as to give effect to the equitable right of another. These equitable rights have been hammered out in the process of litigation in which a claimant on equitable grounds has successfully asserted rights against a legal owner or other person in control of property. Prima facie, therefore, a trustee would not be expected to be subject to an equitable obligation unless there was somebody who could enforce a correlative equitable right, and the nature and extent of that obligation would be worked out in proceedings for enforcement.

9.7   According to Roxburgh J, either the legal owner of the property is under an equitable obligation or he is not. If he is, then someone else must have corresponding equitable rights against him which can be enforced. If he is not, then he can deal with the property as he wishes because he is the beneficial owner. Roxburgh J sees no ground between these two alternatives, and it is submitted that he is perfectly right not to see any. The very existence of a trust turns on there being a trust obligation to someone who, in consequence, has equitable ownership of the trust property. If we take the requirement of equitable ownership seriously, speaking about the need for someone with standing to enforce the trust is a distinctly second-order way of framing the beneficiary principle. The essence of the principle is that for a trust to exist, there must be someone other than the trustee who has the real beneficial ownership of the trust property. If there is no such person, then not only is there no person *to enforce* obligations against the trustee, but more fundamentally, there are *no trust obligations to* enforce, for the legal owner owns it for his own benefit absolutely.

9.8   Since, however, in cases of this kind the settlor has clearly intended to create a trust by transferring the property to a trustee, the trustee cannot keep the property for himself. An ART (5.4) arises, because the settlor has failed effectively to dispose of the beneficial interest in the property. In this case he fails to do so because he tries to do the impossible—create a trust without a beneficiary, which for equity is no trust at all.

9.9   There is a well-established exception to this rule in the case of trusts for charitable purposes. The duty to enforce charitable trusts fell on the King as *parens patriae*, and on to the Attorney-General as his legal representative. 'But', said Roxburgh J:

> if the purposes are not charitable, great difficulties arise both in theory and in practice. In theory, because having regard to the historical origins of equity it is difficult to visualise the growth of equitable obligations which nobody can enforce, and in practice, because it is not possible to contemplate with equanimity the creation of large funds devoted to non-charitable purposes which no court and no department of state can control . . . If the purposes are valid trusts, the settlors have retained no beneficial interest and could not initiate them. It was suggested that the trustees might proceed ex parte to enforce the trusts against themselves. I doubt that, but at any rate nobody could enforce the trusts against them.

So the trust failed.

9.10   Roxburgh J further decided that the trusts were also void for uncertainty, citing in particular the phrases 'different sections of people in any nation or community', 'constructive policies', and 'integrity of the press'.

9.11   In *Re Denley's Trust Deed* (1969) Goff J appeared to narrow the 'no purpose trusts' rule considerably, while at the same time arguing that he was not diminishing the effect of the beneficiary principle, properly understood. The case concerned an *inter vivos* trust of a piece of land:

> to be maintained and used as and for the purpose of a recreation or sports ground primarily for the benefit of the employees of the company and secondarily for the benefit of such other person or persons (if any) as the trustees may allow to use the same . . .

The gift was properly limited to a perpetuity period. Goff J held that the gift was valid:

> I think that there may be a purpose or object trust, the carrying out of which would benefit an individual or individuals, where the benefit is so indirect or intangible or

which is otherwise so framed as not to give those persons any locus standi to apply to the court to enforce the trust, in which case the beneficiary principle would, as it seems to me, apply to invalidate the trust, quite apart from any question of uncertainty or perpetuity…The present is not, in my judgment, of that character, and it will be seen that…the trust deed expressly states that, subject to any rules and regulations made by the trustees, the employees of the company shall be entitled to the use and enjoyment of the land…[I]n my judgment the beneficiary principle of Re Astor…is confined to purpose or object trusts which are abstract or impersonal. The objection is not that the trust is for a purpose or object per se, but that there is no beneficiary or cestui que trust … Where, then, the trust, though expressed as a purpose, is directly or indirectly for the benefit of an individual or individuals, it seems to me that it is in general outside the mischief of the beneficiary principle.

Goff J held that the class of 'beneficiaries' (it is not clear whether Goff J intended the word in its genuine technical sense, or meant simply people who would benefit *in fact* from the execution of the trust) was ascertainable at any given time, and thus satisfied the certainty of objects requirement on the 'complete list' test. Following *McPhail* one presumes that the class of beneficiaries need only satisfy the 'is or is not' test to be certain.

9.12   What precisely is the effect of a trust for individuals framed in terms of a purpose? While the benefited individuals have standing to enforce the trust, what does this amount to? May they enforce the trust only in order to make the trustees carry out the purpose, or may they combine to defeat the purpose under the principle in *Saunders v Vautier* (3.38), insisting that the trustee, for example, assign the lease to them so they can sublease it for profit? Have they an owner-ship interest, or just an interest in receiving whatever benefit would come to them through the serving of the purpose? Goff J does not discuss this. His only remarks concerning any disputes while the trust is up and running concern disputes between different groups of benefited indi-viduals, which give no guidance as to how a dispute between the trustees and these individuals is to be resolved, for example had the employees wanted the commercial profits of the land, not its use as a playing field.

9.13   Goff J's decision has received some *obiter* consideration. In *Re Grant's Will Trusts* (1979) Vinelott J said that the case was:

altogether outside the categories of gifts to unincorporated associations and purpose trusts. I can see no distinction in principle between a trust to permit a class defined by reference to employment to use and enjoy land in accordance with rules to be made at the discretion of trustees on the one hand, and, on the other hand, a trust to distribute income at the discretion of trustees among a class, defined by reference to, for example, relationship to the settlor. In both cases the benefit to be taken by any member of the class is at the discretion of the trustees, but any member of the class can apply to the court to compel the trustees to administer the trust in accordance with its terms.

It is not clear whether there really is 'no distinction' between the two classes of cases. In the latter case, the discretionary trust is one in which the *class* of beneficiaries is defined by the individuals' relationship to the settlor, but their *individual* shares are entirely at the trustees' discretion. In such a case the trustees' discretion is wholly dispositive, a matter of who within the class shall benefit at all, and in what amounts. By contrast, in the *Re Denley* case, the mere power of the trustees to make rules governing the enjoyment of the land does not amount to a discretion over who and in what proportion the beneficiaries may benefit from the property. This is a mere administrative discretion, to ensure that all the employees may enjoy the sports ground as much as possible; the trustees would be in breach if they framed rules governing the use of the land that intentionally excluded a particular group of employees. This view cannot stand as an interpretation of *Re Denley* that respects the actual facts and Goff J's decision. Rather, it reads down the case to the point of overturning it in substance.

9.14   *Re Denley* was also considered in *Re Lipinski's Will Trusts* (1976), which we will consider further at 9.75 et seq. Oliver J adopted the passage quoted from Goff J's decision as being 'in accord with authority and with common sense', but did not discuss precisely how *Re Denley* should be applied to the *Re Lipinski* facts, where a gift expressed to be for the purpose of constructing new buildings was given to an 'unincorporated association' (9.65 et seq), a group of individuals who together form a society, or club, bound by rules. In particular, finding the gift valid he said the following:

> [I]t seems to me that whether one treats the gift as a 'purpose' trust or as an absolute gift with a superadded direction or…as a gift where the trustees and the beneficiaries are the same persons, all roads lead to the same conclusion.

The vital point here is that on the latter two treatments of the gift, the testator's expressed purpose may be entirely ignored, either because as a 'superadded direction' it merely expresses a motive for the gift (recall 'precatory words', 7.12), or on the basis that, the trustees and the beneficiaries being the same persons, ie the members of the club, the property is absolutely owned, and thus on *Saunders v Vautier* principles the beneficiary/trustees may do with the property what they like. This seems at odds with the impression Goff J clearly gives that the trustees are to carry out the purpose.

9.15   Thus both Vinelott J's and Oliver J's interpretations appear to be killing *Re Denley* with kindness. While they are happy to agree that the *Re Denley* trust was valid, in doing so they effectively gut the decision, at least in so far as it expanded the scope of valid purpose trusts. Finally, recall *West Yorkshire Metropolitan County Council* (7.86). One of the reasons Lloyd LJ gave for finding that trust for all the residents of West Yorkshire bad was that it amounted to an invalid purpose trust, which could not be treated as a case like *Re Denley* because the class being so large, there were no ascertainable beneficiaries.

Anomalous valid purpose trusts

9.16   The most significant exception to the 'no purpose trusts' rule is charitable trusts. Charitable trusts are trusts for purposes 'beneficial to the public' as defined by the law of charities (Chapter 14). The other exceptions are all testamentary trusts. These are trusts for the maintenance of particular animals owned by the testator (a horse, *Pettingall v Pettingall* (1842); horses and hounds, *Re Dean* (1889)) and for the construction and maintenance of graves and funeral monuments (*Mussett v Bingle* (1876); *Re Hooper* (1932)).

9.17   In *Re Endacott* (1960), a testator left his entire residuary estate, which amounted to more than £20,000, 'to the North Tawton Devon Parish Council for the purpose of providing some useful memorial to myself'. The gift was not allowed as an exceptional testamentary trust to construct a monument: Lord Evershed MR said, 'It would go far beyond any fair analogy to those decisions.' There also appears to be a similarly grounded exception for the saying of private masses for the repose of the testator's relatives' souls (*Bourne v Keane* (1919); *Re Heatherington* (1990)).

9.18 These trusts are sometimes called 'trusts of imperfect obligation', because there are no beneficiaries of these trusts, and thus no obligations are owed to any persons to carry out the purpose by the legatee of the gift who, as 'trustee', is the person to carry it out. However, this does not mean that the legal holder of the money to be devoted to the purpose may spend the money as he likes. If a testamentary gift is upheld as a purpose trust of this kind, the court will make a '*Pettingall*' order (named after the order made in that case). The legatee must undertake to the court to carry out the purpose, and the 'interested' parties, ie those persons who would take if the trust were to fail and who will take any funds surplus to the requirements of carrying out the purpose, are given leave to apply to the court if the trustee applies the property outside of the intended purpose. Thus the 'enforcement' of these 'trusts' is essentially identical to the enforcement of powers of appointment.

9.19 Two final points are to be made on these exceptional trusts: one serious, one trivial. The serious point concerns a case that is regularly cited in the textbooks as a *possible* case of a valid anomalous purpose trust. In *Re Thompson* (1934) a testator left money to a friend in trust for the purpose of promoting fox-hunting. Clauson J decided that he could make a *Pettingall* order because there was a residuary legatee who as an interested party could enforce the trust by applying to the court. But on this basis any purpose trust of whatever kind could be enforced; the *Pettingall* order is devised to deal with a trust of imperfect obligation only if it is already found to fall within the class of exceptions to the general no purpose trust rule in the first place. It is getting things absolutely the wrong way round to find that a purpose trust is valid whenever one can devise a *Pettingall* order.

9.20 The trivial point is simply that leaving property for their maintenance is as much as you can do for your pets after you die. The idea that a millionaire may leave his fortune to his favourite cat is a cartoon fiction having no basis in law, in case you were wondering. Your animals are your property in law, and you cannot leave property to property. In legal terms, leaving property to your cat, Fred, is no different from leaving property to your toaster; the most you can do is leave a reasonable sum to keep Fred in the condition to which he has become accustomed.

Powers for purposes

9.21 The beneficiary principle applies to trusts, not to powers of appointment. As there is no obligation to exercise powers, there is no similar problem of finding a true beneficiary to enforce their exercise; moreover, those who take in default of appointment are the beneficial owners of the property until it is appointed away from them (3.10, 3.121), so a power for a purpose does not generate any ownerless property in equity (9.7). The courts have expressed their willingness to uphold powers to devote trust property to purposes. In *Re Douglas* (1887) the court was willing to uphold a power to appoint money to 'such charities, societies, and institutions' as the power holder should select, even if on the proper construction this allowed the appointment to non-charitable societies or institutions. Although this case concerned a power to appoint property to institutions, not to purposes per se, such institutions would themselves apply the property to particular purposes, so the case is cited as evidence of judicial willingness to uphold powers for purposes. In *Re Shaw* (1957) George Bernard Shaw had in his will devoted funds for the purpose of devising a 40-letter alphabet for the English language. Harman J accepted that a power to devote funds to the purpose would have been valid but, having decided that the provision imposed a trust to carry out the purpose, he relied on *IRC v Broadway Cottages Trust* (1955) to hold that a valid power is not to be spelled out of an invalid trust (7.8).

9.22   Those who take in default of appointment, while they can ensure that the power holder does not exercise the power improperly, cannot, however, insist that the power holder exercise the power; they would be unlikely to insist even if they could, because every such exercise will diminish the amount of property they will receive in default. Thus while a settlor can empower someone to spend the trust property on a purpose, there will be no one who is interested in ensuring that the power is exercised. Therefore a settlor creating a power cannot ensure that the trust property will be applied to the purpose he desires, although, obviously, if he gives the power to someone who is loyal to him and shares his devotion to the purpose, he may be confident that the property will be applied to it despite the absence of any legal means of enforcement.

9.23   The case of powers for purposes raises the interesting question of whether such powers can be fiduciary powers, ie whether their holders, typically the trustee of the trust, owe any fiduciary obligations in their exercise. As we have seen, fiduciary power holders owe fiduciary obligations both to those who take in default of appointment, and to the objects of the power. But here, there are no objects of the power—the power is to carry out a purpose, and a purpose cannot be owed anything. So any proposed *positive* fiduciary duty, say to consider exercising the power from time to time, which is not owed to those who take in default of appointment (their interests are best served if it is not exercised at all), has no corresponding right holder, no human object. Since there are not private duties without corresponding private rights, there cannot be any fiduciary obligations of this kind.

9.24   On the other hand, a power holder clearly has duties not to *misuse* the power, a duty that can be enforced by those who take in default of appointment. And to the extent that the fiduciary obligations binding the power holder concern wrongful acts, rather than wrongful omissions, which affect the interests of those who take in default of appointment, then such duties can be enforced. Thus, for example, if the trustee fiduciary power holder were to carry out the trust purpose, say to devise a 40-letter alphabet for English, by setting up his own company and paying the trust money to it to carry out the purpose, such an expenditure would be made in conflict of interest; those who take in default would have standing to challenge this expenditure, because to the extent that the trustee exercises the power in order to benefit himself, he exercises the power improperly, diminishing their interests under the trust, favouring his own interests over those of these beneficiaries. It would also appear that such a trustee cannot release the power; although a trustee can decide not to exercise the power at all, any purported release would be ineffective and, for example, would not bind any successor trustee. The fiduciary principle works here not because anyone has standing to enforce a fiduciary obligation not to release, but because the holder's being a fiduciary extinguishes any valid power to release. Thus it seems that there can be a fiduciary purpose power, although the fiduciary character of the power is limited.

9.25   A power to appoint property to purposes must be expressed with sufficient precision for the power holder and the court to know with certainty what will count as appointing property to the purpose, in case any person who would take in default of appointment were to challenge a particular expenditure by the power holder. As we have seen (7.35), the 'is or is not' test should apply, which is to say that any power must be expressed with a certainty sufficient to determine whether *any* proposed expenditure is within the power or not. In *Re Astor* Roxburgh J would have held the trust to fail for uncertainty if not for lack of beneficiaries. Since the capricious creation or exercise of a power may also be invalid (7.89), one presumes that a power to appoint property to purposes may founder if capricious.

An enforcer principle?

9.26   Should the law, or on an unconventional view of the case law, *does* the law, allow private purpose trusts? Hayton (2001a) argues that the cases should be read to reveal not a beneficiary principle, but rather an *enforcer* principle. An enforcer principle would allow a settlor to create a private purpose trust so long as the trust revealed a person or class of persons who could enforce the trust against the trustee, such as the employees who factually benefited from the trust in *Re Denley*, or the settlor named a particular individual as one who should have standing to enforce the trust.

9.27   While perhaps attractive in theory, there are severe difficulties with this view, in so far as it can be genuinely treated as the creation of a true private purpose trust. Remember that trusts are private, and that the only rights under the trust are those that are given to specific individuals or classes of individuals by the settlor. While the settlor can carve up the beneficial interest in the trust property in any way he likes, does he effectively create a purpose trust by giving the trustee a duty to apply the money to a purpose, and the 'enforcer' a power to enforce that duty? It is difficult to see how. Why cannot the trustee and enforcer agree to split the money between themselves? After all, no one else, no third party or the court, has any independent right to enforce any duties against the trustee (there is no equivalent of the Attorney-General who enforces charitable purpose trusts), and so no one can insist that the enforcer exercise his power to make the trustee apply the money to the purpose. The extent of the trustee's duty is the extent to which that duty will be enforced against him by the enforcer, and if the enforcer has no interest in seeing the purpose carried out, he is perfectly entitled at law to cut a deal with the trustee to split the money between themselves, in the same way that beneficiaries could consent to a distribution of trust funds that would otherwise be a breach of trust (11.72) or contracting parties can renegotiate their rights under a contract if they choose to do so, because trusts, like contracts, are purely private arrangements in which there is no public interest, and these private purpose trusts, by *definition*, generate no public interest, not being charitable.

9.28   The upshot is that while it may be perfectly sensible for the law to validate arrangements like *Re Denley* or 'purpose trusts' with named enforcers, the beneficial interest in the trust property does not 'go to the purpose'. It is distributed between the person who has the duty to spend the money on the purpose, usually, one imagines, the trustee, and any person, the 'enforcer', who has the corresponding power to enforce the duty against him. It would not help, of course, to impose a duty upon the enforcer to enforce the purpose trust against the trustee, because one would then just need a third party to enforce that duty against the enforcer, and then another to enforce his duty, ad infinitum. The result is that the 'purpose trust with enforcer' mechanism Hayton describes, while perhaps within the law, does not deliver a true purpose trust, but rather enables the settlor to give his trustee a power to apply property to purposes and a power to another to make him exercise that power.

9.29   In the preceding paragraphs, we treated the enforcer as a holder of a personal power under traditional trust rules, and concluded that he can choose to enforce the purpose or not, to release the power if he so chooses, or even to cut a deal with the trustee to divide up the trust property. According to that analysis, then, the enforcer has the right he has because he has an indirect interest in the trust property itself. But Matthews (2002) considers the nature of the enforcer's rights if we take this sort of arrangement as advertised, and we really accept that the enforcer has no interest, direct or indirect in the trust property, and has only a power to enforce the obligation the trustee undertakes to carry out the purpose. As Matthews persuasively con-tends, such a right–duty relationship between the enforcer and trustee can, on the principles of English law, be only personal between them, ie it must be seen as a contractual not a trust relationship. Why? The point is that while a settlor can, by creating a trust, give beneficial inter-ests in the property that 'run' with the trust property, and hence would bind successor trustees, or (non-bona fide purchaser) third parties who receive the property in breach of trust, a settlor has no power to bind property merely with personal rights that *do not* give an interest in the property itself. Compare the case of land. I can create an easement such as a right of way over my property, Blackacre, to you as owner of Whiteacre, and that easement will 'run' with the land, ie attach to the land. If I sell Blackacre, the new owner will be bound by the easement, and if you sell Whiteacre, its new owner will be able to use the right of way. But while I can contract with you to wash my windows each month for £50, there is no way I can make that relationship 'run' with the land so that my purchaser will be bound to pay your purchaser to wash his win-dows, because the rights under that contract do not 'run' with the land, but are merely personal between us; while 'negative' or 'restrictive' obligations or covenants (eg a covenant not to use a premises for commercial purposes) can run with the land in equity, positive obligations cannot (*Rhone v Stephens* (1994)). And Matthews says the same thing about the positive obligation of the trustee to the enforcer. While the initial trust 'agreement' between settlor, trustee, and en-forcer can create personal rights and duties as a matter of contract, because the enforcer unlike an object of a trust or power *has no interest* in the trust property, his rights do not 'run' with the trust property. So at most he could require the original trustee to carry out the purpose by bringing an action for breach of contract if he did not, but his enforcement rights could not bind successor trustees, much less third-party recipients of the trust property transferred in breach of trust. If this is right, and the logic seems impeccable, then again we find that there is no basis in English law for a true private purpose trust. It is also worth pointing out that if the enforcer mechanism *does* work as advertised so that positive obligations can be imposed upon property, then simply by using the device of the enforcer private purpose trusts can be employed to make positive obligations run with land, and centuries of case law could be over-turned in a trice. This also strongly suggests that Matthews' criticisms should be given a good deal of weight.

9.30   True private purpose trusts can only be created if the law is changed so as to give some public force to the purpose trust, so that the trust property is governed not merely by the private rights of individuals (in which case, it is no longer clear that they can be called 'private' purpose trusts). This, of course, is true of charitable purpose trusts, which are enforced by the Attorney-General. Certain 'offshore' jurisdictions, to attract trust business, have also, by legislation, cre-ated true non-charitable purpose trusts, under which the court has the power to enforce any purpose trust at the application of any interested party ((Bermuda) Trusts (Special Provisions

Act) 1989, as amended 1998), or which employ criminal sanctions to ensure that the enforcer enforces the trust ((Cayman Islands) Trust Law 2001, incorporating (Cayman Islands) Special Trusts (Alternative Regime) Law 1997).

Valid trusts for persons 'limited by a purpose': *Re Sanderson's Trust*

9.31 Certain trusts that can be thought of as 'purpose trusts' have always been allowed by equity. This is a category of trusts under which the beneficiary is only allowed to take a certain amount, which is determined by the costs of carrying out a purpose. Here's an example: '£100,000 to be paid by my trustees to my daughter Barbara in amounts equivalent to those she has expended on her education, the remaining funds to go to my son Peter.' The gift to Barbara is a gift to pay the costs of her education, and on that basis it appears that the settlor (usually, in these cases, a testator) has created a trust for the purpose of educating Barbara. Nevertheless, one should not regard this sort of gift as an anomalous valid purpose trust. Consider this gift: '£100,000 on trust to pay Julia £1,000 on each occasion that Chelsea FC wins a match during the regular football season of 2023–24, all funds remaining to be paid to Timothy.' This trust is perfectly valid, if unusual: the settlor has simply chosen an unusual way of carving up the beneficial interests between the two beneficiaries; it would be odd if such a gift were valid but a gift that limits the amount that a beneficiary receives on the basis of what it costs to educate him were not. That is why it is better to frame such a gift as a 'trust in which the subject matter is apportioned to the beneficiaries in reference to the costs of carrying out a well-defined purpose' rather than as a purpose trust. The purpose in these trusts is not to be regarded as the replacement of the human *object of the trust* with a purpose; the purpose is part of a device or formula that defines the *subject matter* of the trust for a particular object, an object, ie a beneficiary, who is fully human. True, if the beneficiary does not incur any costs of the required kind, then that beneficiary will take nothing; in that way these gifts may certainly provide an incentive for the beneficiary to achieve the purpose, although not always: consider a trust to pay the rehabilitation expenses of members of a mountaineering society who injure themselves by falling off mountains.

9.32 The leading case concerning such trusts is *Re Sanderson's Trust* (1857). Here a testator left property upon trust to 'pay and apply the whole or any part of the [income] for and towards [the] maintenance, attendance, and comfort' of his mentally disabled brother for the remainder of his life. At the death of this brother there remained unexpended income, and the question was whether those funds should be held on trust for the residuary legatees under the testator's estate, or whether the money should go into the brother's estate. In other words, the question was whether the gift was limited to such portion of the income as was required to pay for the brother's maintenance, or whether it was an absolute gift of the whole.

9.33 Page-Wood VC distinguished the two possible interpretations of testamentary gifts of this kind as follows:

> In reference to gifts of this description, there are two classes of cases between which the general distinction is sufficiently clear, although the precise line of demarcation is occasionally somewhat difficult to ascertain. If a gross sum be given, or if the whole income of the property is given, and a special purpose assigned for that gift, this Court

always regards the gift as absolute, and the purpose merely as the motive of the gift, and therefore holds that the gift takes effect as to the whole sum or the whole income, as the case may be…[If] an entire fund is given for the maintenance of children or the like, they take the whole fund absolutely, and the maintenance is treated in effect as simply the motive in making the gift; while, on the other hand, if a portion only of the fund is given for maintenance, then they are entitled to draw out so much only as may be necessary for the purpose specified.

9.34   Thus there developed a body of case law directed to determining whether the testator intended that the whole of the trust property should go to the beneficiary, the purpose of maintenance, or education, or whatever, merely indicating the motive of the gift, or whether he was creating a fund out of which money might be distributed only on the basis of meeting the costs or expenses of the purpose. In this case Page-Wood VC decided that the brother was only entitled to such part of the fund as was necessary for his maintenance, attendance, and comfort. Nevertheless, it is clear that the brother, and others who benefit under like trusts when the costs or expenses that the trusts cover are met, are just as much human beneficiaries as persons who are recipients of absolute gifts. In particular, they are not to be regarded as beneficiaries of discretionary trusts, in which the trustees, at their discretion, may or may not spend the money on the particular purpose, ie to pay the particular expenses the testator indicated. The beneficiaries are fully entitled to demand the requisite payments to meet the costs or expenses specified by the trust.

9.35   Settlors, then, may devote property to certain purposes *in the sense* that they may leave property on trust to spend any amount of the property, up to all of it, on certain well-defined expenses of named beneficiaries, and these beneficiaries can enforce these trusts, by demanding whatever amounts fall within the expenses or costs defined by the purpose from the trustees. Any property left when the purpose is accomplished will result either to the settlor or, in the case of a will, to the testator's residuary legatees, unless a specific gift over of the remainder is made.

9.36   The courts in the nineteenth century were well versed in enforcing trusts of this kind, in particular trusts to pay for the maintenance, education, and advancement of children. A trust for maintenance is one that will provide for a person's daily costs of living, a roof over his head and food, clothing, etc; a trust for education is straightforward; a trust for advancement is a trust to pay sums of money to 'advance' someone in the world, usually an infant who is approaching adulthood, by paying the costs of getting him started in his career. A typical example of a payment for advancement in the nineteenth century would be the purchase of a 'living' for a cleric, ie an appointment to an office in the Church of England, or the purchase of a commission in the army. Because the nature of these costs and expenses is so familiar it is possible, and makes sense, to treat such trusts as trusts to pay certain well-defined expenses. It is not clear that other purposes could so easily be treated in this way; indeed, it might even be regarded as a test of the validity of *Re Sanderson*-type trusts that the 'purpose' can be clearly localised to a particular beneficiary as the payment of a certain share of a fund, that share determined by well-defined expenses that he may incur—in other words, only well-defined costs or expenses will be *certain* enough, although the certainty here is the certainty of subject matter. If the 'purpose' does not provide a reasonably workable determination of the expenses, which, over the course of the trust, will define the share the beneficiary is to receive, then the testator has not defined with sufficient precision the subject matter of the trust in that beneficiary's favour. Because the subject matter is defined via the cost of carrying out a purpose, as with the certainty of other purposes, the 'is or is not' test will apply (7.35, 9.25). In *Conway v Buckingham* (1711) the life tenant was required to build a mansion house according to the testator's model; the trust was properly seen as a valid *Re Sanderson*-type trust, the effect of the testamentary instruction being to diminish the interest of the life tenant and benefit the remainderman by requiring the capitalisation of the income in a particular way. The dispute in the case between the life tenant and the remainderman was whether the amount spent by the life tenant was sufficient given the vagueness of the testator's 'design' or model, and the court held that it was.

9.37   In cases of this kind it may be difficult to determine whether a testator intended a gift of the whole fund with an attached motive or direction, or a gift of such part of the property as is required to meet the beneficiary's costs of achieving a purpose such as his education. A somewhat unusual case was *Re Skinner's Trusts* (1860). Here the Reverend Skinner left £1,000 in his will for the publication of his own work, 'intitled "An Analysis of Language, and Symbols of the Worship of the Sun" in two volumes' the profits and copyright of which were to be used to provide his grandson with funds for his education. The executors of the will set aside £1,000, and sought advice from an expert and the publisher, both of whom advised against its publication. The question was whether the grandson was entitled to the whole fund, the publication of the manuscript being only a suggested means by which he should benefit, or whether the publication of the manuscript was the essential means by which the grandson was to benefit. On the latter view, it was argued that the trust had failed because the book was unpublishable; it would be equivalent to the case where Julia in the example of 9.31 would get nothing if Chelsea FC were to go bankrupt and cease to play. Page-Wood VC, while regarding the case on the borderline, preferred the former interpretation; thus the whole amount went to the grandson.

9.38   In *Re Bowes* (1896) £5,000 was left upon trust for the purpose of planting trees on an estate. The evidence of foresters indicated that only a fraction of the land would benefit from the planting at a cost of only £800. North J decided that the paramount intention of the gift was to benefit the persons entitled to the estate, and so this intention should prevail over the specific means of planting trees where that means, if carried out, would be actually disadvantageous to the beneficiaries. Thus the owners of the estate were entitled to the £5,000 absolutely.

9.39   The problem of inferring the settlor's intention has been particularly acute in 'appeal' cases, where an appeal has been made to raise funds to provide for individuals who have suffered some misfortune. It is obviously a vexed task to determine whether an amorphous group of often anonymous contributors had one intention or the other, and perhaps these cases should be regarded as in a class of their own. In *Re Abbott Fund Trusts* (1900) one Dr Abbott of Cambridge placed money on trust for the support of his family, including two daughters who were deaf and dumb, but the trustee turned out to be a rogue and the trust money disappeared. Several persons in turn sought subscriptions on behalf of the two daughters, which were held by trustees who made quarterly payments to the two women. On the death of the survivor of the two, some £366 remained. The only evidence of the intention of the subscribers was the circular making the appeal for funds, which stated that the fund was to enable the women to reside in Cambridge and to provide for their 'very moderate wants', and, if the trustees so decided, to purchase annuities for them. Stirling J decided:

> *I cannot believe that [the fund] was ever intended to become the absolute property of the ladies so that they should be in the position to demand a transfer of it to themselves, or so that if they became bankrupt the trustee in bankruptcy should be able to claim*

> *it … I think that the trustee or trustees were intended to have a wide discretion as to whether any, and if any what, part of the fund should be applied for the benefit of the ladies and how the application should be made. That view would not deprive them of any right in the fund, because if the trustees had not done their duty—if they either failed to exercise their discretion or exercised it improperly—the ladies might successfully have applied to the Court to have the fund administered according to the terms of the circular. In the result, therefore, there must be a declaration that there is a resulting trust of the moneys remaining unapplied for the benefit of the subscribers to the Abbott fund.*

9.40   In *Re Andrew's Trust* (1905) money was raised by subscription for the children of the Bishop of Jerusalem. Again, the evidence as to the objects of the trust was slim, which was found in a letter by the now deceased canon who had initiated the appeal, who described the money as having been collected:

> *for and towards the education of Bishop Barclay's children,…[and] that it was by no means intended for the exclusive use of any one of them in particular, nor for equal division, but as deemed as necessary to defray the expenses of all, and that solely in the matter of education.*

The children's education having been provided for under their father's will, the trustees sought a declaration enabling them to distribute the fund to the children. Kekewich J decided as follows:

> *Here the only specified object was the education of the children. But I deem myself entitled to construe 'education' in the broadest possible sense, and not to consider the purpose exhausted because the children have attained such ages that education in the vulgar sense is no longer necessary. Even if it be construed in the narrower sense it is, in Wood VC's language, merely the motive of the gift, and the intention must be taken to provide for the children in the manner (they all then being infants) most useful.*

9.41   After reviewing these two decisions in *Re Osoba* (1978), Megarry VC said:

> *I think that you have to look at the persons intended to benefit, and be ready, if they still can benefit, to treat the stated method of benefit as merely indicating…the means of benefit which are to be in the forefront. In short, if a trust is constituted for the assistance of certain persons by certain stated means there is a sharp distinction between cases where the beneficiaries have died and cases where they are still living. If they are dead, the court is willing to hold that there is a resulting trust for the donors; for the major purpose of the trust, that of providing help and benefit for the beneficiaries, comes to an end when the beneficiaries are all dead and so are beyond earthly help, whether by the stated means or otherwise. But if the beneficiaries are still living, the major purpose of providing help and benefit for the beneficiaries can still be carried out even after the stated means have all been accomplished, and so the court will be ready to treat the standard means as being merely indicative and not restrictive.*

While there is obvious sense in this, Megarry VC appears to take a dangerously *ex post* view of the interpretation of testamentary gifts. Surely any interpretive strategy should be primarily devoted to figuring out the testator's intention from the outset, when the trustees who are to administer the trust receive the funds. It is then that they must be certain whether the trust is a gift of the whole with a mere motive or a *Re Sanderson* trust only of a part.

9.42 Secondly, do Megarry VC's words about the means in a gift of the whole, that they 'are intended to be in the forefront', mean that even where the gift is of the whole, the trustees *must first* apply the money according to the motive, to defray the expenses of maintenance or education or whatever, until such time as they are no longer incurred, as when the education of the beneficiary is complete? In other words, does the gift become an absolute one only upon the 'purposes' either being accomplished or no longer capable of fulfilment? (Cf *Re Bowes*.) If so, what happens if before the 'purpose' comes to an end, ie before the trustees distribute the property as an absolute gift, the beneficiaries all die? Whether the gift is a gift of the whole or only a part surely cannot simply turn on the time of the beneficiaries' deaths, because that would engender a lottery whereby the remaining surplus of a large gift for the education of Albert would go into his estate if he were to die the day after graduation (the purpose being complete, the gift of the whole would now 'take'), but would go on resulting trust if he died the day before. Megarry VC's guidance on the construction of such gifts should, then, be treated with some care.

9.43 *Re Osoba* (1978, Ch D; 1979, CA) concerned a testamentary trust of residue for the maintenance of the testator's widow and his mother, and for 'the training of my daughter Abiola up to university grade'. There was no gift over which would take effect on the completion of the purposes. The testator's mother had predeceased him, and by the time the case came before the court the testator's widow was dead, and Abiola had finished her university education; the question was whether the surplus funds were to be held on a partial intestacy, all of the trust purposes for the residue now being fulfilled. Megarry VC said he would lean toward construing a gift of residue as an absolute gift, since otherwise any surplus would go on resulting trust to those who would take on intestacy, not an intention one would normally ascribe to a testator. Megarry VC construed the instructions as to how the money should be spent as a mere indication of motive, and decided that the wife and Abiola together became entitled to the whole fund absolutely on the testator's death.

9.44 There are three reasons for having gone into these cases in some detail. The first is simply to make clear that such trusts, which are in a sense a variation on purpose trusts, exist in the law but do not violate the beneficiary principle so long as they are interpreted as 'trusts in which the subject matter is apportioned to beneficiaries in reference to the costs of carrying out a well-defined purpose'.

9.45 Secondly, however, if the subject matter of a trust can be apportioned in this way, then it is clear that well-defined purposes may be taken into account in determining how a trustee should distribute the trust property, since such purposes indicate clearly how the subject matter may be expended. Thus these trusts raise the question: even in cases where the beneficiaries' interests are not limited by the purpose, should the trustees nevertheless take the settlor's purpose into account? Should they spend the money on the stated purpose first? Should, for example, the trustees have refused to give Abiola the whole trust fund until she was either educated up to university grade, or it became clear that carrying out the purpose was impossible (ie no university would admit her)? One might suggest that the courts should at least require the trustees to comply with the settlor's directions, not so as ultimately to limit the extent of the beneficial gift, but to give effect in so far as possible to the means by which the settlor chose to give it. Thus, it might be right to say that until the beneficiaries use their *Saunders v Vautier* rights to vary or collapse the trust, individual beneficiaries should be able to insist that the trustees comply with the settlor's declared means of distribution in so far as it is certain.

9.46 This view does not detract from the beneficiary principle, because the whole gift would still be to the beneficiaries. It would only properly limit the trustee's discretion through the enforcement of the settlor's intentions by the people who are appropriately entitled to do so, ie the beneficiaries. This view might go some way to rescuing *Re Denley* from death by interpretation (9.15) for, if correct, unless and until the beneficiaries exercise their *Saunders v Vautier* rights, the trustees should apply the trust property for their benefit according to the settlor's instructions.

The bare trust with mandate and *Quistclose* trusts

9.47   The bare trust with mandate and the *Quistclose* trust have already been explained in outline (7.28–7.32), so re-read those paragraphs now. There are three issues to consider here. The first is to extend our analysis of the bare trust with mandate and look at its operation in some cases. The second is to consider alternative analyses raised by Lord Millett in *Twinsectra v Yardley* (2002). First, however, there is an initial basic question raised by Swadling (2004). The *Quistclose* arrangement seems to put the lender in the best of all possible worlds: if the borrower becomes insolvent before spending the money, the lender can rely upon the trust to retrieve the value of the loan; but if the money is lost through no fault of the borrower/trustee—say the bank where the money is held on trust fails—in which case normally the lender/beneficiary would bear the loss, here the lender can rely upon the loan element of the arrangement, and demand full repayment. It is submitted that this issue is best dealt with as a matter of construing the loan contract. Nothing in principle prevents a lender from having the best of all possible worlds in this way, because a trustee can, under the terms of the trust, be made an insurer of the trust funds, so that even if the funds are lost through no fault of his own he may be liable to restore their value. But it is submitted that the 'default' construction of the loan arrangement should be as follows: the borrower accepts the liability to pay interest on the loan money from the minute the funds are received for, whatever the delay between receiving the funds and his actual spending of them, the borrower has the use of the funds from the moment received. However, the borrower should not be liable for the innocent loss of the funds (eg through a bank failure), unless this is an explicit term of the contract. If such a thing should occur, the contract should be taken to have been frustrated, and come to an end, the lender bearing the loss of the trust funds. This would appear to be the appropriate corollary disadvantage to the lender's advantage of having the beneficial interest on the funds until expended by the borrower. Given that in most cases the lender bank will place the funds in an account the borrower has with the lender itself, this would appear to be the just result, because the loss will only arise when the lender bank itself fails; it would seem harsh if the borrower were made to repay the full amount of the loan to a lender whose own failure made the borrower's obtaining any value from the loan impossible and, as stated, any opposite conclusion should only be found where the terms of the loan arrangement explicitly provide for this.

The mandate imposes a personal obligation

9.48   The basic bare trust with mandate analysis was first explained in detail by Millett (1985). The most important feature of this analysis is that the beneficial interest in the trust property remains with the settlor, A, on bare trust, subject however to the trustee's, B's, power or duty to apply the funds according to the settlor's standing order, or mandate. There are no *trust terms* other than that B should hold the trust property to A's order. A's instructions constitute mandates that A may give, vary, and revoke from time to time—they may either impose duties on B positively to do something, or confer powers upon B to deal with the property in certain ways if he so chooses. These mandates *impose personal* obligations upon B by way of contract. If B distributes the trust property in violation of one of these mandates he certainly commits a breach of trust, but not a breach of trust because the mandate is a term of the trust; he commits a breach of the only trust term there is, the overarching duty to hold the property to A's order or mandate. By distributing the trust property in violation or outside the scope of A's orders, he fails to hold the property to A's order and thus commits a breach of trust.

9.49   In contrast, B commits no *breach of trust* if his failure to comply with a mandate is one of *nonfeasance*. In that case B still holds the property to A's order; he simply fails to carry out A's contractual mandate. For example, if I transfer £10,000 on bare trust to my broker to make investments on my behalf, and he fails to carry out my order to invest £5,000 in shares of XYZ plc, my broker will not have committed a breach of trust—he did not violate my property rights in equity—rather, he just failed to fulfil a personal contractual obligation to me, for which he will be liable for damages if I suffer a loss because of it.

9.50   Note that the bare trust with mandate does not work if one treats A's mandate as a specific term of a trust that B undertakes, imposing true trust duties, because to the extent that B is under a duty to apply the trust property in some way, to that extent is A's beneficial interest under the trust *displaced*, ie it is no longer a bare trust in A's favour. Of course, where the mandate was that B should apply the trust property to some purpose, this would be an invalid purpose trust, and so would fail (see further Penner (2004)).

The extent of the mandated purpose for the trust money

9.51   Millett (1985) pointed out that: 'The settlor's motives must not be confused with the purposes of the trust; the frustration of the former does not by itself cause the failure of the latter.' The point here is that one's ultimate goal in setting up a *Quistclose* trust may have been thwarted, but that does not mean that the trust did not operate according to its terms. In general, there is only one appropriate point at which to decide whether a trust has been properly carried out according to its terms: when the trustee applies the money by dealing with it with a third party. Thus, a trustee applies trust property according to his investment power when he makes an authorised investment, ie buys an investment such as shares from someone. A trustee correctly applies the trust property dispositively when he gives the trust property to a properly entitled beneficiary. The trust over the property, once it is transmitted correctly to the beneficiary, comes to an end, because the transfer fulfils the trust terms. Likewise, a trustee who correctly applies the trust property according to his mandate disposes of the property correctly according to the terms of the trust (to hold it to the settlor's order), and thus the trust over the property comes to an end.

9.52   Unfortunately, the confusion of ultimate goal with a proper application of the trust property according to the trust terms has dogged cases supposedly decided on *Quistclose* principles. In *Re EVTR* (1987) the appellant, who had received £250,000 following a premium bonds win, advanced £60,000 to his old employer to enable it to purchase new equipment. The employer then contracted with an equipment supplier and a leasing company, paying over the £60,000. The supplier provided temporary equipment until the new equipment could be delivered. The employer became insolvent before the new equipment arrived, and the supplier and leasing company refunded £48,000 to it. The CA held that, although the funds that had been advanced were properly paid out, the trust continued to the extent that, when the ultimate purpose failed, the refund was held for the original provider. Dillon LJ said:

> True it is that the £60,000 was paid out by the [employer] with a view to the acquisition of new equipment, but that was only at half-time, and I do not see why the final whistle should be blown at half-time.

9.53   The problem here, of course, is that the employer's payment out of the money appears to be the only appropriate point at which the trust relationship ends and its relationship with the provider of the funds becomes that of debtor and creditor. If that is not full time, what is? When the equipment has been used for a while? What if it transpires that after a year the equipment turns out not to be much use, and is sold? Are the proceeds of that sale to be held on trust for the original provider? Had the purchase gone ahead so no refund arose, the court could only have dated the transition from the trust relationship to one of debtor and creditor when the money was paid, and so should it here. It is submitted that the CA must have imposed some kind of constructive trust giving the provider an equitable title in the traceable proceeds of his loan money. There was, however, no basis in authority for such a trust, and it seems to give the provider an unjustifiable priority over the company's other creditors. Had it been found, on the true intention of the parties, that the appellant was to retain an equitable interest in the equipment and any traceable proceeds until he was paid back his loan, then the appropriate finding would have been, following *Re Bond Worth Ltd* (7.27), that he had an equitable charge, and that this was not a *Quistclose* trust at all. Such a charge would have to have been registered to be valid against the company's creditors or liquidator.

9.54   The second case, *R v Common Professional Examination Board, ex p Mealing-McCleod* (2000), decided by a panel of two in the CA, is a tissue of confusions. A law student, following several court actions against the CPE Board, was liable to it for substantial legal costs. When she pursued a further legal remedy, the Board was awarded an order for security for costs, ie the student had to pay £6,000 into court before the action would proceed. She obtained the £6,000 from her bank, with the provision in the loan agreement quoted at 7.34. The student paid the money into court, but as she was successful in her action, the money was not required to pay any costs of that action to the Board. The Board, however, claimed the money to defray the earlier costs awards against the student, which were still unpaid. Whether or not the Board's claim that money paid into court to cover the possible costs of one action should be available to pay the cost of previous ones was good in law, the basis upon which the CA refused the Board's claim was that the money was held upon a *Quistclose* trust. At trial, Hidden J got it absolutely right. He held that, while there was an express *Quistclose* trust of the money, the trust element ended when the student paid the money into court; and even if the trust endured beyond this point, the court, the recipient of the money, had no notice of it, so took free of any residual trust.

9.55   The CA, allowing the student's appeal, held that because the express agreement was that the money should only be paid as security for the student's costs in the particular action, and since the funds were not so required, the funds remained bound by the trust and could be demanded from the court by the student who would be bound in trust to return them to the bank. The trust of the money bound the court, irrespective of its notice of the trust, for the court was a volunteer, and 'effectively in the position of a stakeholder' (*per* Slade LJ). With respect, this reasoning is insupportable. It is true that a *Quistclose* trust only comes to an end when the trust money is properly applied by the trustee/lender (here the student) for the loan purpose, whereupon the trust disappears and the lender is only personally bound to repay the money. But the only 'purpose' for such a loan is to make the proper payment under the loan agreement because, once that is done, there is no longer any trust corpus upon which any trust obligation by the lender can bite. Here, that purpose was fully accomplished when the student paid the £6,000 into court to provide security for costs. Since that payment was properly made, the trust over the money came to an end. Thus the 'purpose' of the loan that defines the extent of the trust cannot be made to encompass *all the intended consequences that are expected to flow from the proper application of the loan money*. If that were the case, then the very basis of the *Quistclose* trust and the prior staving off bankruptcy cases would be rendered senseless. On the CA's broad reading of purpose in this way, the money actually paid to creditors under a staving off bankruptcy trust, or the dividend money had it been paid to the shareholders in *Quistclose* itself, would be held on trust by these payees to return to the lender if it turned out that the bankruptcy or liquidation was not averted: that was the 'purpose' of the loan broadly speaking. But if the trust attaches to that, not only is the trust an invalid purpose trust, but the whole point of the exercise would be useless, because if the creditors or shareholders were to receive their payments not as theirs beneficially, but subject to a trust that gave them no beneficial interest unless bankruptcy or receivership was averted, then these payments would not satisfy their claims against the company thus allowing it to stave off its bankruptcy or receivership, and would indeed almost certainly precipitate the bankruptcy or receivership. And this applies across the board to such trust/loans. The money is only good to the borrower if he can pay it over beneficially to third parties to accomplish the purpose of the loan. That he holds it in trust himself until he does so cannot alter his power to confer beneficial legal title on his payees if the loan is to have any value to him. Thus the terms of the trust defined by the 'purpose of the loan' must be restricted to the purpose of transferring the beneficial legal title to the money to the proper recipients as defined by the loan agreement.

9.56   Furthermore, putting these objections to one side, even if the bank were to try by its loan agreement to bind third-party recipients to hold the payments they received from the borrower on trust, it could not do that simply by making it a term of its agreement with its borrower. These third-party recipients would only hold the property on trust if they were to undertake to do so, either to the bank or to its borrower, and in none of the cases are those the facts. Accordingly, the issue of the court or any recipient being a volunteer or having notice is perfectly irrelevant, because if the borrower was entitled under the loan agreement to pay the money to the third party, then full beneficial legal title to the money was properly paid under the loan arrangement in full compliance with its trust provision. A third party could be bound only where the loan money was *improperly* paid, ie paid in breach of the trust in so far as it was specified in the loan agreement (and this happened neither in *Re EVTR* nor *R v CPE Board*), the third party being bound either as a volunteer or, having given consideration, having had notice of the breach of trust (2.64). Finally, if any more need be said, on the CA's reasoning on payment of the £6,000 into court the court would either itself have been under an obligation to keep that £6,000 separately, as trust money, or be considered a wrongdoer, since, according to the CA, the money was bound by the trust throughout. Really, however, as in *Re EVTR*, the court was merely imposing a constructive trust because it felt it was the just thing to do in all the circumstances, but with even less justification here, because at least in *Re EVTR* the holder of the property was the borrower/trustee. Here, the constructive trustee, ie the court, was a third party who was transferred the legal title to money in full compliance with the loan/trust agreement with no notice of its provisions.

9.57   It is submitted that the only conceivable way to bring the decisions in *Re EVTR* and *R v CPE Board* within workable trust law principles is to analyse them along the following lines: consider the case where the borrower transfers money from the separate bank account into which the lender pays the loan moneys to his solicitor, to hold on trust for him in the latter's client account, prior to making a purchase that will carry out the purpose of the loan. Now assume that the borrower becomes insolvent. It would seem appropriate to allow the lender to claim that the borrower's right to the money in his solicitor's client account should be held on trust for the lender, on the basis that the borrower's transfer to his solicitor was merely preparatory to his expending the money on the loan. Notice that the solicitor does not, under this analysis, hold the money on trust for the lender, as the courts in *Re EVTR* or *R v CPE Board* would have it. Rather, the borrower himself holds his right against the solicitor on bare trust for the lender, as an asset that is merely a change in form from his prior right to the money in the separate bank account. On this analysis, the rights the borrower held to the refund in *Re EVTR* and to the repayment of money deposited in court in *R v CPE Board* were held on trust for the lender. Nevertheless, this analysis still requires one to determine at which point the trust moneys are properly expended according to the trust terms, and thus it would still seem that the cases were wrongly decided, as these rights were not rights acquired merely in preparation for carrying out the trust purpose; rather, they were rights that adventitiously arose following the expenditure of the trust moneys in complete fulfilment of the trust purpose.

Alternative interpretations of the *Quistclose* trust

9.58   The judgment of Lord Wilberforce in *Quistclose* suggested that there was a primary purpose trust to pay a dividend, which purpose failed on RR's liquidation, giving rise to a resulting trust in Q's favour. There are any number of problems with this analysis (for a thorough demolition see Swadling (2004), at 9 et seq), not least of which is that, to work, non-charitable purpose trusts must be valid, and they are not. The analysis is not viable, and can be ignored. There are two other analyses of such trusts that, prior to the decision in *Twinsectra*, attracted support: Millett's (1985) analysis, the one adopted by this text above, and one by Chambers (Chambers (1997), ch 3).

9.59   Chambers' analysis, which draws support from the terms in which judges spoke in deciding these sorts of cases up to the early part of the twentieth century, in particular the use of the term 'quasi-trust', is as follows: when the lender, L, pays the loan moneys over to the borrower, B, B does not hold the money on trust for L; rather, under the loan contract that specifies the purpose(s) on which B may spend the money, L acquires an equitable right to require that B spend the money only on those purposes, a right that equity will enforce by injunction. Where it becomes impossible to carry out the purpose of the loan, a resulting trust then arises, ie at this point B holds the funds on trust for L for the first time in the course of events. This resulting trust arises because B was not intended to take the funds beneficially to use as he wishes.

9.60   The HL addressed the issue in *Twinsectra v Yardley* (2002). While the CA (1999) unanimously adopted Potter LJ's analysis, which was in most respects identical to Chambers', Lord Millett in the HL forcefully rejected this analysis and, not surprisingly, favoured his own, although it departed significantly from his 1985 analysis. Lord Millett was in a minority of one in the case, and his analysis formed part of his dissenting opinion. The leading speech was given by Lord Hutton, who agreed with both Lord Millett's and Lord Hoffmann's analysis of the *Quistclose* trust, and Lords Steyn and Slynn agreed with both Hutton and Hoffmann. So much turns on whether Lord Hoffmann's and Lord Millett's analyses were essentially the same. Unfortunately Lord Hoffmann's analysis was very brief; although it seems to be largely in keeping with Lord Millett's analysis, he nowhere adopts or refers to Lord Millett's analysis.

9.61　In *Twinsectra*, Lord Millett stated quite categorically that *Quistclose* trusts are resulting trusts that arise by operation of law. This departed in a serious way from his 1985 view that the *Quistclose* trust was an express trust, ie based on the parties' actual intentions. According to that analysis, there is no 'resulting' trust at all: A's beneficial ownership is intended from the first—he takes that interest as the intended beneficiary under the bare trust with mandate. In *Twinsectra*, however, Lord Millett said that the *Quistclose* trust is:

> an entirely orthodox example of the kind of default trust known as a resulting trust. The lender pays the money to the borrower by way of loan, but he does not part with the entire beneficial interest in the money, and in so far as he does not it is held on resulting trust for the lender from the outset.

9.62　This characterisation of the *Quistclose* trust seems to follow from Lord Millett's approval of Chambers' general theory of the resulting trust, which he endorses in *Twinsectra* as follows:

> The central thesis of Dr Chambers's book is that a resulting trust arises whenever there is a transfer of property in circumstances in which the transferor (or more accurately the person at whose expense the property was provided) did not intend to benefit the recipient. It responds to the absence of an intention on the part of the transferor to pass the entire beneficial interest, not to a positive intention to retain it. Insofar as the trans- fer does not exhaust the entire beneficial interest, the resulting trust is a default trust which fills the gap and leaves no room for any part to be in suspense. An analysis of the Quistclose trust as a resulting trust for the transferor with a mandate to the transferee to apply the money for the stated purpose sits comfortably with Dr. Chambers's thesis . . .

9.63　It is not at all clear how this analysis covers *Quistclose* trusts that are express, ie cases where the documents specifically declare that B holds the property on trust for A until properly applied for the specified purpose, because in such cases there is no question that there is merely an absence of intention on A's part that B should take the property beneficially—there is a positive intention that the property is to be held on trust for A. In *Twinsectra* Lord Millett said:

> I do not think subtle distinctions should be made between 'true' Quistclose trusts and trusts which are merely analogous to them…There is clearly a range of situations in which the parties enter into a commercial arrangement which permits one party to have a limited use of the other's money for a stated purpose, and must return it if for any reason the purpose cannot be carried out. The arrangement between the purchaser's solicitor and the purchaser's mortgagee is an example of just such an arrangement. All such arrangements should be susceptible to the same analysis.

But the arrangement between the solicitor and his purchaser's mortgagee is express, so Lord Millett's 'resulting trust arising by operation of law' simply cannot apply.

9.64 Knowing whether such trusts are express (if sometimes informal) trusts, or are rather resulting trusts arising by operation of law is a vital question, because that largely determines how
the court should properly take into account evidence of the parties' intentions in determining
whether a *Quistclose* trust has been created or has arisen. If the trust arises by operation of law
in response to the absence of intention, none of the traditional certainties for express trusts,
which might otherwise constrain a finding of trust, are relevant, because these concern the
intentional creation of trusts, not trusts arising by operation of law. There is a danger that
the resulting trust analysis will allow the court to find trusts in commercial circumstances on
flimsy evidence about what might have been *absent* to A's mind, as opposed to determining the
true intentions of the parties. It is arguable that this happened in *Twinsectra* itself (see Penner
(2004)). It is submitted that first thoughts were best thoughts, and that Lord Millett's 1985 analysis is superior to his *Twinsectra* account, which tries to bend his 1985 analysis to make it work
within Chambers' theory of resulting trusts, which he clearly admires. In *George v Webb* (2011)
following an extensive review of the case law and academic writing, Ward J took the view that
the weight of authority in Australia is that a *Quistclose* trust is an express trust.

Gifts to unincorporated associations

9.65 An 'unincorporated association' is a collective body of individuals, like a student law society,
which does not have its own legal personality as a company does, hence the name *unincorporated
association*. Unincorporated associations are of interest here because if an individual wishes to
devote his money to the carrying out of a purpose, in particular after his death, one way of
doing so is to give money to an unincorporated association the purposes of which are those
of the settlor. If the settlor wishes to promote Morris dancing with a testamentary bequest, he
might consider making a gift to a local Morris dancing association. What we will be concerned
with here is, first, the way in which these unincorporated associations hold property, given that
they have no legal personality and, secondly, whether a settlor's intention that the association
devote the gift to a specific purpose has any legal effect.

9.66 In *Conservative and Unionist Central Office v Burrell* (1982), Lawton LJ stated four criteria for
the existence of an unincorporated association. Such an association will exist where there are:

> two or more persons bound together for one or more common purposes, not being
> business purposes, [2] by mutual undertakings, each having mutual duties and
> obligations, [3] in an organisation which has rules which identify in whom control of it
> and its funds rests and on what terms and [4] which can be joined or left at will.

The existence of mutual undertakings giving rise to mutual duties and obligations is normally
read to indicate that the members are bound by a contract *inter se* (ie amongst themselves).
Each member is party to a contract that creates the legally binding rules of the association. So,
for example, the contract amongst the members of a student law society may set rules about
joining or leaving the society, about membership fees, about electing a president or treasurer,
and so on. The last requirement Lawton LJ gives, ie that the association can be joined or left
at will, is ill put. Read strictly, it must be doubted, because there may be rules limiting both
who can join the association and upon what basis, and similar rules about leaving. The idea
underlying this criterion is that any individual enters the contract *inter se* voluntarily.

9.67   The purpose trust rule applies with just the same force to gifts to unincorporated associations as it does to gifts to individuals. The problems are slightly trickier here, however, because though a settlor may give property to an unincorporated association, he may not be giving the property on trust to carry out a particular purpose he chooses or any of the general purposes of the association; rather, he may just be giving the property to the association absolutely, *in the hope* that they will spend it as he wishes. Gifts of the latter kind are perfectly valid, while those of the former are, of course, invalid, as purpose trusts.

9.68   The leading case on the application of the beneficiary principle to gifts to unincorporated associations (UAs) is the PC decision in *Leahy v A-G for New South Wales* (1959). The gift in question was of a large estate called 'Elmslea':

> upon trust for such order of nuns of the Catholic Church or the Christian Brothers as my executors and trustees shall select . . .

This wide power of selection allowed the trustees to select orders of nuns that were not charitable under the law. This trust was saved by the application of a New South Wales statute, which restricted the power of selection to charitable objects. A majority in the High Court of Australia accepted that the gift would also be valid as a gift to a UA, given to the members 'for the benefit of the community'. Viscount Simonds, giving the decision of the PC, said:

> [A]n unincorporated society…though it is not a separate entity in law, is yet for many purposes regarded as a continuing entity and, however inaccurately, as something other than an aggregate of its members. In law a gift to such a society simpliciter is nothing else than a gift to its members at the date of the gift as joint tenants or tenants in common. It is for this reason that the prudent conveyancer provides that a receipt by the treasurer or other proper officer of the recipient society for a legacy to the society shall be held a sufficient discharge to executors. If it were not so, the executors could only get a valid discharge by obtaining a receipt from every member… [But] what is meant when it is said that a gift is made to the individuals comprising the community and the words are added 'it is given to the benefit of the community?' If it is a gift to individuals, each of them is entitled to his distributive share (unless he has previously bound himself by the rules of the society that it shall be devoted to some other purpose). It is difficult to see what is added by the words 'for the benefit of the community'. If they are intended to import a trust, who are the beneficiaries? If the present members are beneficiaries, the words add nothing and are meaningless. If some other persons or purposes are intended, the conclusion cannot be avoided that the gift is void. For it is uncertain and no doubt tends to a perpetuity…it is to be noted that it is because the gift can be upheld as a gift to the individual members that it is valid, even though it is given for the general purposes of the association. If the words 'for the general purposes of the association' were held to import a trust, the question would have to be asked, what is the trust and who are the beneficiaries? A gift can be made to persons (including a corporation) but it cannot be made to a purpose or to an object…It is therefore by disregarding the words 'for the purposes of the association'…and treating the gift as an absolute gift to individuals that it can be sustained.

The testator's words could only be construed as intending a trust for the purposes of the orders that might be selected, not a gift to their individual members; so, but for the statute, the gift would have failed.

The contract-holding theory

9.69   In *Neville Estates Ltd v Madden* (1962), Cross J interpreted *Leahy* to hold that there are three possible constructions of a gift to a UA. The first is as a gift to the individual members as co-owners, whereby each may take their own share. Secondly, the gift may be to the individual members:

> but subject to their respective contractual rights and liabilities towards one another as members of the association. In such a case a member cannot sever his share. It would accrue to the other members on his death or resignation, even though such members include persons who become members after the gift took effect… Thirdly, the terms or circumstances of the gift or the rules of the association may show that the property in question is not to be at the disposal of the members for the time being, but is to be held in trust for or applied for the purposes of the association as a quasi-corporate entity. In this case the gift will fail unless the association is a charitable body.

9.70   In *Re Recher's Will Trusts* (1972), Brightman J expanded on the nature of the second kind of gift:

> In the absence of words which purport to impose a trust, the legacy is a gift to the members beneficially, not as joint tenants or as tenants in common so as to entitle each member to an immediate distributive share, but as an accretion to the funds which are the subject-matter of the contract which the members have made inter se.

A better label: the contract/trust holding theory

9.71   This analysis of the way in which unincorporated associations receive gifts and hold property is generally termed the 'contract-holding theory', although it operates through a trust of the association members' money. It is nothing other than the bare trust with mandate mechanism we have already looked at in detail. The treasurer-trustees of the association hold the association's funds on bare trust for the members of the association, to deal with the funds according to the mandates, or standing orders, which arise from time to time under rules of the association created by the contract of the members *inter se*. Such rules may allow the UA president to require the disbursement of funds for certain purposes, to require that the president and treasurer co-sign cheques for large payments, and so on. A gift that is an 'accretion to the funds' is therefore a gift to the treasurer-trustee of the UA to hold such property on the same trust as he does the other funds of the UA. Thus the given funds become subject to the bare trust with mandate that determines the way the treasurer-trustee deals with the members' funds (see *Re Ray's Will Trusts* (1936); *Abbatt v Treasury Solicitor* (1969) *per* Lord Denning; *Re Bucks Constabulary Widows' and Orphans' Fund Friendly Society (No 2)* (1979), *per* Walton J).

9.72   Certain worries have been expressed about this analysis (see eg Matthews (1995a); Gardner (1998)) but the worries may be dispelled. It is true that a person cannot give a gift *subject* to another's contract rights. I cannot by unilaterally giving £10 to you declare that you hold it under some sort of contractual obligation to someone else. But that is not what the donor does here. By making the gift to an association or its members *as* members of the association, he indicates that it is to go to the treasurer-trustee of the association to hold the property under the same trusts as he holds all the other property of the association; thus the settlor simply defines the trust he imposes by reference to a trust that exists already. That this trust is a bare trust with (contractual) mandate, and so the uses to which the property may be put may be varied by changes to the mandate, does not mean that when a settlor transfers property on this trust the terms on which he transfers the property and thus his intention to transfer the property on trust are uncertain, because the trust, being a bare trust, has perfectly certain terms, ie the treasurer is obliged to hold the funds to the order of the members, as expressed in their mandates. At all times the trust terms, which govern what the trustee is entitled to do, are certain.

9.73 Furthermore, there is no perpetuity problem with this trust any more than there is with the trust under which the trustee holds the rest of the association's property. The trust of the association's property is for the members for the time being. As members leave and join they are added to or deleted from the class of beneficiaries under an explicit or implicit power of the trustees or members to add or delete members, ie beneficiaries (6.20). Since at all times the members for the time being are fully entitled to exercise their *Saunders v Vautier* rights and collapse the trust, the trust, while it may last as long as the association does, is not perpetual, because the rights are always fully currently vested (3.49); there are no obligations to unascertained future members, because they are not beneficiaries, even contingent ones, under the trust at any time.

9.74 Finally, while it might be thought that this interpretation of the association's trust gives rise to a s 53(1)(c) problem, ie that whenever a member leaves or a new member joins all members of the old class of beneficiaries must, in writing, assign their trust interests under the trust to the new class of member/beneficiaries, this is a mistake that, as we have seen, follows from an mistakenly over-broad interpretation of s 53(1)(c) of the Law of Property Act 1925. That section does not apply to powers to add or delete beneficiaries, and every member of a UA understands that under the rules he will lose his interest in the trust property should he leave or be expelled from the association, and so this possibility is part and parcel of his interest (6.20).

9.75 The contract/trust holding theory explains how unincorporated associations may receive gifts that they can devote to their purposes, without such gifts being purpose trusts. That does not mean that a gift to an unincorporated association, properly construed, may not be on trust to carry out a purpose, and therefore invalid. *Re Lipinski's Will Trusts* (1976) concerned a gift to an unincorporated association that could well have been construed as a purpose trust. A testator left half of his residuary estate to 'the Hull Judeans (Maccabi) Association in memory of my late wife to be used solely in the work of constructing the new buildings for the Association and/or improvements to the said buildings'. Interpreting the provision, Oliver J felt that little turned on the fact that the gift was expressed as a memorial to the testator's wife—while that expressed a tribute the testator wished to pay, it did not, by itself, indicate a desire to create a perpetual endowment. Neither did the fact that money was to be available solely for construction or improvements indicate a perpetual purpose, because such money could be spent right away—'improvements' is different in this respect from 'maintenance', which may well indicate a perpetual purpose trust. Framing the legacy in terms of a sole purpose only ruled out construing the gift as one to the members absolutely in equal shares.

9.76 Oliver J considered that the members of the association for the time being were an ascertainable class of beneficiaries, and given the existence of such a class, could see no reason why the trust should fail:

> If a valid gift may be made to an unincorporated body as a simple accretion to the funds which are subject-matter of the contract which the members have made inter

se...I do not really see why such a gift, which specifies a purpose which is within the powers of the unincorporated body and of which the members of that body are the beneficiaries, should fail. Why are not the beneficiaries able to enforce the trust or, indeed, in the exercise of their contractual rights, to terminate the trust for their own benefit? Where the donee body is itself the beneficiary of the prescribed purpose, there seems to me to be the strongest argument in common sense for saying that the gift should be an absolute one within the second category, the more so where, if the purpose is carried out, the members can by appropriate action vest the resulting property in themselves, for here the trustees and the beneficiaries are the same person.

9.77   Oliver J argued that this interpretation of the law was at least consistent with *Leahy* as in that case there was no such ascertainable class. Secondly, there was authority in *Re Turkington* (1937):

> [T]here the gift was to a masonic lodge 'as a fund to build a suitable temple in Stratford'. The members of the lodge being both the trustees and the beneficiaries of the temple, Luxmoore J construed the gift as an absolute one to the members of the lodge for the time being.

9.78   Finally, Goff J's decision in *Re Denley* to uphold a purpose trust where there was such a class was, thought Oliver J, 'directly in point'. He also considered that although the gift was solely for a particular purpose, *Re Bowes*, amongst other cases, was authority for the proposition that where the entire amount of the gift was to go to the beneficiary, the purpose could be overridden as a mere motive or superadded direction. His conclusion, as we have seen (9.14), was that the gift was valid as one to the members, although expressed pretty plainly as a purpose.

Inward versus outward-looking purposes

9.79   It appears that one criterion for Oliver J's holding was that the 'donee body is itself the beneficiary of the prescribed purpose', in other words that the purpose was 'inward-looking', as a benefit to the members themselves, rather than 'outward-looking', as one that might possibly or must necessarily benefit members of the community outside the association. Such a requirement is very doubtful. On the facts of this case, the objects of the association's constitution were clearly to benefit Anglo-Jewish youth generally, so such a requirement would have made the trust fail in the present case. In *Re Bucks Constabulary Widows' and Orphans' Fund Friendly Society (No 2)* (1979) Walton J said that the analysis of the way in which a UA holds its funds is no different:

> whether the purpose for which the members of the association associate are [sic] a social club, a sporting club, to establish a widows' and orphans' fund, to obtain a separate Parliament for Cornwall, or to further the advance of alchemy. It matters not. All the assets of the association are held in trust for its members—of course subject to the contractual claims of anybody having a valid contract with the association—save and except to the extent to which valid trusts have otherwise been declared of its property.

As long as the 'purpose' framing the gift is one which the members themselves pursue by spending their own money under the rules of their association, the gift is to their 'inward-looking' benefit, and the court can construe such a gift as an accretion to the association's funds (see also *Re Recher's Will Trusts*, per Brightman J).

9.80   While requiring a gift framed as a purpose trust to be 'inward-looking' before finding it valid is, therefore, unnecessary in the case of a UA, it may well be necessary if the class of beneficiaries are not members of such an association. Recall that in *Re Denley* the purpose trust was only valid because it was considered to be directly or indirectly for the benefit of the class of ascertainable beneficiaries. If outward-looking purposes could be valid so long as the settlor named a class of beneficiaries, then *Re Astor* is essentially overthrown. For example, by naming a class of beneficiaries consisting of all the employees of national and regional newspapers in the UK, which class is ascertainable on the 'is or is not' test, Viscount Astor could have provided a class that would indirectly benefit from the outward-looking purposes he intended, members of which class would have standing to enforce it but who for all intents and purposes could never get together under the principle in *Saunders v Vautier* to vary or end the trust. Thus, it must be the case that gifts expressed as trusts for outward-looking purposes may be valid if made to unincorporated associations just for the reason that the membership, as the class of ascertainable beneficiaries is, by definition almost, capable of getting together and deciding whether to carry out the purpose or not. This prevents the possibility that a *Re Astor* abstract and impersonal trust will ever actually gain an independent life.

9.81   *Re Lipinski* raises once again the status of the settlor's purpose—as Oliver J makes quite clear, the members of the unincorporated association are free to ignore it completely if they so wish. A prospective Mr Lipinski who wishes above all to see his purpose carried out may be well advised to frame his gift as a *Re Sanderson*-type trust, such as 'to the Hull Judean (Maccabi) Association in such amounts as equal its expenditure on new buildings' with a clear gift over of any remaining funds, or as a gift on condition. A settlor should bear in mind that the certainty requirements for conditions subsequent, such as 'but if they fail to construct new buildings within five years of my death, then to the Red Cross', are strict, and if uncertain the gift will be treated as absolute (3.131); so care must be taken to frame the condition in such a way that it can clearly be applied.

The dissolution of unincorporated associations

9.82   The 'contract-holding' theory, or the 'contract/trust holding theory', which is a better label, of the way in which unincorporated associations hold their property is now generally accepted. It must, however, be distinguished from a different 'contractual' theory of UAs, which is of doubtful validity. Under this theory the property of UAs can only be explained as the holding of property on a true purpose trust, which would violate the beneficiary principle. In order to consider the merits of this theory, we must briefly return to the subject of automatic resulting trusts, or ARTs.

9.83   In *Re Gillingham Bus Disaster Fund* (1958), funds were raised on appeal to defray the cost of funerals for those who had been killed when a bus ran into a column of marching cadets, and to care for those who were disabled; any surplus funds were to be devoted to 'other worthy causes'. The gift was a *Re Sanderson*-type trust for the cadets, but the gift over 'to worthy causes' was void for being a non-charitable purpose trust (14.43). The Treasury Solicitor claimed the surplus as *bona vacantia*, ie goods without an owner. Harman J approached the question as follows:

> The general principle must be that where money is held upon trust and the trusts declared
> do not exhaust the fund it will revert to the donor or settlor under what is called a resulting

trust. The reasoning behind this is that the settlor or donor did not part with his money absolutely out and out but only sub modo to the intent that his wishes as declared by the declaration of trust should be carried into effect. When, therefore, this has been done any surplus still belongs to him. This doctrine does not, in my judgment, rest on any evidence of the state of mind of the settlor, for in the vast majority of cases no doubt he does not expect to see his money back: he has created a trust which so far as he can see will absorb the whole of it. The resulting trust arises where that expectation is for some unforeseen reason cheated of fruition, and is an inference of law based on after-knowledge of the event.

9.84 Since here the subscribers' expectations were 'cheated of fruition', an ART of the surplus arose in their favour in the proportions to which they had contributed. However, the resulting trust doctrine in appeal cases of this kind seems somewhat pointless for those who anonymously gave small amounts in collection boxes, because it means that the trustees must pay the money into court, where it will be held, essentially in perpetuity, on the off-chance that one of the anonymous subscribers of small amounts to the fund cares enough to come forward and prove that he had made a donation, hence the suggestion to treat the property as *bona vacantia*. Nevertheless, preferring to rely upon principle over matters of convenience, Harman J held firm on the resulting trust:

> *In my judgment the Crown has failed to show that this case should not follow the ordinary rule merely because there was a number of donors who, I assume, are unascertainable. I see no reason myself to suppose that the small giver who is anonymous has any wider intention than the large giver who can be named. They all give for the one object. If they can be found by inquiry the resulting trust can be executed in their favour. If they cannot I do not see how the money could then…change its destination and become bona vacantia.*

9.85 Under the contract/trust holding theory, it is clear that the members of a UA own the society's property under the terms of their association, and therefore, upon dissolution of the society, the property is clearly not *bona vacantia*, but nor is there need for any resulting trust, because the money is held under a bare trust (in their favour) with mandate. The members have owned it all along, and therefore it is theirs to be distributed amongst themselves upon dissolution. Before this theory was articulated, however, there was a line of cases in which upon the dissolution of a UA the only alternative destinations of surplus funds were thought to be an ART and *bona vacantia*. In *Re Printers and Transferrers Amalgamated Trades Protection Society* (1899) contributions from the society's members funded benefits for the contributors, in particular strike and lock-out benefits, and in *Re Hobourn Aero Components Ltd's Air Raid Distress Fund* (1946) employees contributed funds to pay benefits to members on war service or those injured in air raids. In both cases, on the dissolution of the associations the court held that there was a resulting trust of the remaining funds in favour of the members in proportion to their contributions. By contrast in *Cunnack v Edwards* (1896), where members contributed to provide widows' benefits, upon dissolution the CA reasoned that the members had received all they had contracted for, ie the relevant widows' pensions, and so the surplus was *bona vacantia*.

9.86 *Re West Sussex Constabulary's Widows, Children and Benevolent (1930) Fund Trusts* (1971) falls into this line of cases. In 1968 the West Sussex Constabulary was amalgamated with other police forces, and therefore its benevolent fund, which paid allowances to the widowed mothers, widows, and children of deceased constables who were members, was to be wound up. The forces were amalgamated from 1 January 1968, and the remaining members of the fund held a meeting in June 1968 at which it was decided that the remaining funds, some £35,000, should be used to purchase annuities for those widows, etc, who were receiving benefits, the balance to be distributed to the members.

9.87   Goff J reasoned that the amalgamation of the forces meant that there were no longer any members of the fund by June 1968, since the only persons who could be members were constables of the West Sussex constabulary, which had ceased to exist. Thus the June 1968 decision was invalid and the funds remained undisposed of. Goff J accepted that the members might have devoted the funds in this way had they met before the amalgamation, but they had simply acted too late. Now, if it were true that the contract between the members required that they be constables of the West Sussex force, then the amalgamation of the forces would have put their contract at an end. But that would only mean that the contractual rules of the association, such as a rule that by majority vote they could vary the terms upon which their property was held by the UA treasurers on trust, would no longer be operative. Any mandate to apply the property would have been extinguished, but not the bare trust of the funds. The death of this contract would do nothing to alter the *ownership rights* of the members to the fund, only their *contractual rights and duties* to deal with it in certain ways. Thus if the members were owners of the fund before 1 January 1968 (although bound by contractual mandate to deal with it under the rules), they remained owners afterward (although no longer so bound).

9.88   The former members then argued that they were the beneficial owners of the fund, as with any other UA, but Goff J rejected this argument; the fund simply did not look like a members' club, but was a pensions or dependent relatives fund; thus rather than being for the benefit of the members for the time being, only third parties could benefit.

9.89   The members then argued that there was a resulting trust in their favour. In rejecting this argument, Goff J advanced the 'contractual' basis of the decision in *Cunnack*:

> In my judgment the doctrine of resulting trust is clearly inapplicable to the contributions of [the former and surviving members]. Those persons who remained members until their deaths are in any event excluded because they have had all they contracted for, either because their widows and dependants have received or are in receipt of the prescribed funds, or because they did not have a widow or dependants…they and the surviving members alike are also in my judgment unable to claim under a resulting trust because they put up their money on a contractual basis and not one of trust . . .

The only persons who had a claim, therefore, were those surviving members who had dependants who had not received any benefits yet—they might be able to claim against the fund on the basis of total failure of consideration or frustration of the contract. This application of 'contractual' reasoning must be wrong, since it requires that the funds were held on a perpetual pure purpose trust, ie a trust to enter into contracts to provide annuities and so on for the relations of members of a constabulary—in short, a trust to carry out a (non-profit) business, the funds held not for any beneficiaries, but for the purpose of entering into and discharging contractual obligations.

9.90   In *Re Bucks Constabulary Fund*, a case with very similar facts, Walton J found himself 'wholly unable to square [Goff J's decision in *West Sussex*] with the relevant principles of law applicable', and applied the modern contract/trust holding analysis. The member/constables of the *Bucks* fund were entitled to it in equal shares on dissolution of the association. The contract/trust analysis was applied by Lewison J in *Hanchett-Stamford v AG* (2008) where a UA had dwindled to one member; Lewison J held that she was solely entitled to the association's property. Of course if the rules of a UA provide for the distribution of its assets on dissolution, these must be followed. For an example of a case where such rules were construed and applied, see *Hardy v Hoade* (2017).

9.91 There is however, a 'loose end', as Swadling (2000, at 376) puts it:

> In the case of money subscribed to a movement or campaign via its secretary, it is tolerably clear that any surplus left when the campaign is abandoned or frustrated must be returned as on a failure of consideration. This is a matter for the law of unjust enrichment. It is by no means clear that the same should not apply to property given on the basis that it be subject to the contract between the members [of a UA]. Much must depend on the precise construction of the basis on which the donations were given and, in turn, on the rules of the society. The Buckinghamshire Constabulary case certainly decides that the property in such cases belongs to the members, but it does not finally dispose of the question whether in some cases they may not come under an obligation to make restitution of its value to donors.

9.92 However, though on the modern contract/trust holding theory there should have been no 'surplus' funds to dispose of in *Re West Sussex*, Goff J's treatment of undisposed of funds is regarded as relevant if applied to cases where an ART properly arises, as in a case like *Re Gillingham Bus Disaster Fund*. The surplus is to be notionally divided in proportion to its sources, ie: (1) money raised by raffles or entertainments, whereby individuals contract with the association or trustees, the profits of which go into the fund; (2) small anonymous donations, such as those received in collecting boxes; and (3) identifiable donations, such as amounts contributed by cheque and legacies. An ART arises only for the last category. No one in the first category who contributes to the fund incidentally as a function of buying a raffle ticket or attending an entertainment has given money upon trust; he receives his full benefit from the contract. Goff J reasoned that the purchaser may or may not be interested in aiding the cause, so therefore no trust intention can be imputed to him, and secondly, his contribution is indirect, via any profit, if any, that accrues from his purchase.

9.93 This does not seem particularly justifiable. If the trustees engage in commercially viable entertainments or raffles that make profits, which they then donate to the trust, of course the purchasers are out of the picture. But if, as is common, the purchasers 'purchase' entertainment or buy raffle tickets fully realising there is a large gift element, surely the intention to be presumed of such a purchaser is that the profits certain to be made are to be applied to, and only to, the purposes of the appeal. That they doubtless do not expect any money some day to return to them on failure or completion of the purpose of the appeal would put them in the same boat as any other contributor.

9.94 Similarly, Goff J reasoned that the contributors of small anonymous donations must be assumed to have intended to part with their money absolutely in all circumstances. Again, distinguishing between large, identifiable contributors and small contributors or raffle ticket purchasers on the basis of their likely intentions is difficult to sustain. The better basis for the result is simply that the ART solution, although theoretically correct, is so patently pointless in the case of the small contributors and purchasers, none of whom will ever try to prove a valid claim to the money, that the *bona vacantia* solution is simply imposed as the most practical result in the circumstances. As Harman J points out in *Gillingham*, surely the only thing that distinguishes these classes of contributors is the possibility that they might actually be able to claim their money—there is no reason to believe that they were more or less likely to entertain any 'secondary' intentions governing the proper direction of their money if the primary trust failed. But *pace* Harman J, that fact should not prevent the *West Sussex* result, for practical reasons.

9.95   As it stands, then, neither *Gillingham Bus Disaster Fund* nor *West Sussex* disclose any factual settlor's intention that can displace the operation of an ART, and it is difficult to imagine one that realistically is likely to arise. What will displace it, apparently, is the inconvenience of the ART's effect in practice. With respect, it was, therefore, incorrect of Lord Browne-Wilkinson to have cited *West Sussex* as a case where settlors' actual intentions displaced an ART (5.50); that the ART there was supplanted by the *bona vacantia* solution is much better explained as a matter of convenience, not because the settlors' intentions so dictated.

Less than unincorporated associations: the case of political parties

9.96   In *Re Grant's Will Trusts* (1979), the testator left his entire real and personal estate to the Chertsey and Walton Constituency Labour Party. Vinelott J held that the gift was one to create a perpetual trust to further the purposes of the local Labour party, and therefore the gift failed. He held that the local Labour party was not an unincorporated association, because its rules were capable of being altered by an outside body, the national Labour Party, which could in fact direct the local party to transfer its assets to it. Furthermore, the local members could not:

> alter the rules so as to make the property bequeathed by the testator applicable for some purpose other than that provided by the rules; nor could they direct that property to be divided amongst themselves beneficially.

9.97   It is not clear whether Vinelott J's reasoning on this point is sound. While there is no other case that discusses the issue directly, Cross J in *Neville Estates* proceeded on the assumption that the Catford Synagogue was an unincorporated association although affiliated with the United Synagogue, which limited the power of the Catford members to alter their rules; moreover the United Synagogue could require the Catford Synagogue to transfer its real property to the United Synagogue.

9.98   In *Conservative and Unionist Central Office*, the CA decided that the national Conservative Party was not an unincorporated association either. The party was a historical political movement, in which the various membership constituencies, the parliamentary party, and the constituency associations had political but not contractual links. In particular, there were no rules by which the constituencies could control the leader of the party's or the central office's expenditure of the central office funds, and there was no historical point at which any contract between the members *inter se* could be said to have occurred.

9.99   If national political parties, and their local constituency parties, are not unincorporated associations, then how do they hold their property? In *Conservative and Unionist Central Office*, Brightman LJ suggested the 'mandate' theory to explain how *living* subscribers to the party donate their funds. Such funds are given upon an order from the donor, the principal, to the party treasurer, his agent; such an order is a mandate, although not a mandate over funds the treasurer takes on trust; it is a purely personal obligation to deal with property the treasurer takes as full beneficial legal owner; if the treasurer fails to apply the money as the order specifies (here for party purposes) he may be sued to so apply it, and he may be restrained from misapplying it. The mandate becomes irrevocable once the treasurer mixes it with other party funds. Brightman LJ, however, said that this analysis would not explain testamentary gifts to political parties because:

> no agency could be set up at the moment of death between a testator and his chosen agent. A discussion of this problem is outside the scope of this appeal and, although I think that the answer is not difficult to find, I do not wish to prejudge it.

But this is doubtful; true it is that a testator cannot give a mandate to someone on, much less after, his death, but there is nothing wrong with his executor doing so under an instruction given in the will--executors do carry out wishes of the testator by contracts (eg paying for the testator's funeral). However another, perhaps better, analysis may be that both *inter vivos* and testamentary gifts to political parties are conditional gifts at law or in equity (5.55), which would be subject to the unjust enrichment analysis Swadling proposes above (9.91).

The rule against perpetuities

9.100   There are two principal cases in which the rule against perpetuities (3.49 et seq) becomes relevant in the discussion of the beneficiary principle: the cases of the few, anomalous, true purpose trusts, and in the context of gifts for unincorporated associations. A true purpose trust, such as a trust for the upkeep of a grave, can last forever. Therefore, if the testator does not specifically limit his gift to a perpetuity period, the gift will be void for perpetuity. It may be the case that a testator is not entitled to choose the statutory perpetuity period of 80 years provided by the Perpetuities and Accumulations Act 1964. This turns on technical considerations regarding the interpretation of s 15(4) of the Act and the question of whether the rule against perpetuities applies in a distinct way to pure purpose trusts (see Matthews (1996)), and no case has decided the point. A testator may, however, employ a 'lives in being plus 21 years' clause to indicate a perpetuity period. For this purpose a 'royal lives' clause is appropriate, for example: '£10,000 to my trustees on trust to maintain my grave, such trust not to extend beyond the expiry of 21 years following the death of the last surviving descendant of Queen Elizabeth II alive at my death.' Since there are no lives in being that are inherently relevant to the duration of a purpose trust, the testator must choose people whose lives shall count. The purpose of picking the descendants of a king or queen is simply that, being famous, it will be easy for the trustees to determine when the last surviving life in being dies. If the testator does not use a royal lives clause, and wishes to set an exact time period, then, assuming he is not entitled to use the statutory period of 80 years or less, he may only choose a period within the definable portion of the common law rule, ie the portion not determined by the duration of any lives in being, thus periods of 21 years or less. If the testator specifies that his gift is to continue 'for as long as the law allows' or uses some similar phrase, courts have allowed the gift to last for 21 years (*Pirbright v Salwey* (1896); *Re Hooper* (1932)). Section 18 of the Perpetuities and Accumulations Act 2009 provides that the Act does not 'affect the rule of law which limits the duration of noncharitable purpose trusts', so the pre-2009 Act law will, apparently, continue to apply.

9.101   In the case of unincorporated associations, the problems are different. As we have seen, there are no valid pure purpose trusts for the purposes of an unincorporated association. For such gifts to be valid, they must be, or they must be interpreted to be, gifts to the members of the association themselves. But in some circumstances, the gift might properly be interpreted to be for the present and future members of the association, thus a gift to a class that may gain members as long as the association lasts. If the trust were not limited, the shares of any number of future individuals might vest for as long as the association lasts, hence indefinitely. Therefore, under the pre-2009 Act law, a gift in these terms must ensure that it comes to an end within a suitable perpetuity period, either a stated period of 80 years or less, or a period determined by the relevant lives in being for the gift plus 21 years (here the relevant lives in being would be the members of the association at the time the trust takes effect), or a period determined by a royal lives clause. Under the 2009 Act law, the 125 year perpetuity period will apply.

FURTHER READING

Gardner (1998)

Gravells (1977)

Green (1980)

Matthews (1995a, 2002)

McKnight (2004)

Millett (1985)

Penner (2000, 2004, 2014b)

Rickett (1980)

Smith (2004)

Swadling (2004)

Must-read cases: *Re Astor's Settlement Trusts* (1952); *Re Denley* (1968); *Re Grant's Will Trusts* (1979); *Re Lipinski's Will Trusts* (1977); *Re Sanderson's Trust* (1857); *Re Osoba* (1977); *Twinsectra v Yardley* (2002); *Leahy v A-G (NSW)* (1959); *Re Bucks Constabulary Widows' and Orphans' Fund* (1979); *Conservative and Unionist Central Office v Burrell* (1982); *Hanchett-Stamford v AG* (2008)

SELF-TEST QUESTIONS

1.   Explain the rationale of the beneficiary principle. Is this rationale less persuasive following the decisions in *Re Denley* (1969) and *McPhail v Doulton* (1970)?

2.   Should the 'beneficiary principle' be reformulated along the lines of an 'enforcer' principle?

3.   How may unincorporated associations hold property?

4.   Smith dies, leaving £100,000 to the Aylesbury Morris Dancing Society 'for the purpose of building a Morris Dancing Centre as a memorial to myself'. Shortly after Smith's death the

club decides to wind up, as most members wish to join another Morris dancing club. The treasurers report that the Society's current funds are £8,150, which amounts to a share of £163 for each of the 50 members, a figure that does not include the bequest of Smith, of which they have just been advised. Advise the treasurers.

5.   Simon is a member of his local branch of the Socialist Workers Party, and is also a member of a Marxist reading group of about 30 people who raise money to buy publications by various means and who have a treasurer who holds the group's funds in a local bank. Simon has found out that he has six months to live. On his death he wants to ensure that his considerable fortune is devoted to the furtherance of Marxist causes. Advise Simon.

6.   Brian, a collector of art, transfers £50,000 to Frances, a dealer, to 'buy antiques for me that have good investment prospects'. Brian tells Frances that she is entitled to 'take a 10 per cent commission' on any purchases she makes. Frances pays the money into her current business account, which is in overdraft, raising the balance to £40,000. She then (i) spends £30,000 on seventeenth-century furniture; (ii) draws a cheque on the account for £3,000 as her personal commission, which she pays into her personal account; (iii) uses £2,000 to pay for travel and hotel expenses to attend an antiques auction where she buys nothing; (iv) transfers £1,000 to another dealer as a deposit on a future purchase, which is not, in the end, completed. With the balance in the account at £4,000, Frances's bank fails. Advise Brian. (It would be worthwhile to review 7.33 et seq.)

10

The trust up and running

SUMMARY

The duty of investment
The Trustee Act 2000
The standard of prudence in making trust investments
'Social' or 'ethical' investing
The delegation of trustee functions
The power of maintenance
The power of advancement
Appointment, retirement, and removal of trustees
Custodian, nominee, managing, and judicial trustees
Variation of trusts

10.1 Trustees, as legal owners of the trust property, have all the rights and powers to deal with the trust property as would any other legal owner, although they must, of course, exercise these rights and powers solely in the interest of the beneficiaries. Because they are trustees, however, they have further particular powers and duties arising from their office, traditionally the most important of which are the duty of investment and the powers of maintenance and advancement.

The duty of investment

10.2 The duty of investment has two main aspects: (1) a duty to invest the trust property so as to be 'even-handed' between the different classes of beneficiary; and (2) a duty to invest so that the fund is preserved from risk yet a reasonable return on capital is made.

Even-handedness between the beneficiaries

10.3 In many trusts the benefit of the property is divided between income and capital beneficiaries (3.32). In legal terms income is whatever property actually arises as a separate payment as a result of holding the capital property. Thus on shares the dividends are the income, on land the rent is income, and so on. The income beneficiary is entitled to whatever income arises. On the other hand, if holding the property yields no new property rights, rental payments, or dividends or so forth, there is no income, even if the shares or the land double in value, making a huge economic return on the investment. Some investments produce no income, such as currency, gold, antiques. Conversely, some investments will be 'all' income, ie what are called 'wasting assets'; an example is a 20-year lease, on which the rent is income: although in economic terms it also represents the return on the initial capital investment in the lease, in legal terms the capital just slowly reduces to zero as the lease runs its course. Therefore it is obvious that the trustee may favour the income beneficiary at the expense of the capital beneficiary, or vice versa, by making particular kinds of investments. The law therefore imposes a duty of even-handedness, which requires the trustee to balance their interests fairly in making his investment decisions. (For a case where the trustees thoroughly failed to do so, see the New Zealand case of *Re Mulligan* (1998); the trustees invested so as to maximise the income of the life tenant, with the result that there was little capital left in the fund on her death.) This is a fiduciary obligation (2.19, Chapter 13), because only by being even-handed in exercising his discretion as to the trust investments does the trustee act in the best interests of all of the beneficiaries of the trust.

10.4 The two chief characteristics of any investment are risk and return, and they correlate directly. That is, the higher a risk an investment presents, the greater the percentage return on capital any investor will demand. You will (at the time of writing) win a greater sum betting on Scotland to win the next World Cup than on Brazil (alas). Historically, the law has favoured the safety, or non-riskiness, of trusts investments over high return. In particular, following the bursting of the 'South Sea Bubble' in 1720—an orgy of speculation in shares of the South Sea Company that ended, as one might expect, in tears—equity regarded investment in company shares as a risk quite beyond the pale. Therefore, until the twentieth century trustees were restricted to investment in 'consols', fixed-interest government securities.

10.5 Of course, the trust instrument itself may, and invariably does, empower the trustee to invest as the settlor allows, and in general, such investment clauses are very wide. Originally, again out of concern for the safety of the trust property, investment clauses were interpreted restrictively, but now are given their plain meaning (*Re Harari's Settlement Trusts* (1949)). If there is no express investment clause, the statutory regime provided by the Trustee Act 2000 governs the trustee's investments.

The Trustee Act 2000

10.6 Prior to 1 February 2001, the Trustee Investments Act 1961 governed the trustee's duty of investment unless the trust instrument specifically provided an investment clause. The Act was one embodiment of an approach to regulating trustee investments, which is generally called the 'legal list' approach. The legal list approach contrasts with the 'prudent investor' approach. Under the former, the state in its wisdom chooses a number of particular kinds of investment that may be made by trustees; these investments are supposed to be safe but yield a reasonable return. A trustee may not make an investment that is not on the list; if he does he will be in breach of trust. On the other hand, such a list makes things quite straightforward for trustees, especially non-professionals. So long as they choose investments from the list, they comply with their investment duties. Under the prudent investor approach, the trustees are not legally prohibited from making any particular kind of investment. They will be found in breach of trust, however, if they do not invest as a prudent investor would. The Trustee Act 2000, which now governs unless the trust instrument provides an investment clause, adopts the prudent investor approach; it thus (a) provides the trustee with a very broad power of investment, but (b) imposes a duty of care so as to ensure that the power is used prudently.

10.7   Section 3 of the Act provides a general power of investment by which:

> *a trustee may make any kind of investment that he could make if he were absolutely entitled to the assets of the trust.*

That is, he may make any investment he could make if the funds were his own. However, the various properties, securities, and so on he purchases for the trust must still count as 'investments'. What amounts to an investment is a matter of case law: it may be that certain sorts of financial products, such as derivatives or zero-dividend preference shares, although perhaps useful for managing the risk and return of trust funds (especially in light of tax considerations), may not count, for instance on the basis that they do not generate income (see Hicks (2001)). For this reason it is expected that settlors will, as was previously the norm, write trust instruments including bespoke investment clauses, rather than relying on the statutory provision. Section 8 provides the trustee with the power to acquire land, even if the land is not used to generate rental income, but is used to provide a place to live for a beneficiary or beneficiaries. This separate treatment of land is a holdover from past attitudes: in *Re Power* (1947) trustees were barred from buying a house for the beneficiaries to live in. Jenkins J said that such a purchase:

> *is not necessarily an investment, for it is a purchase for some other purpose than the receipt of income.*

10.8   Section 1 of the Act outlines a general duty of care applicable to trustees, and by Sch 1 this duty applies to the trustee when exercising any power of investment, either under the statute or conferred by the trust instrument (although the duty of care may be ousted by the trust instrument (Sch 1, s 1)). By s 1, the trustee must:

> *exercise such care and skill as is reasonable in the circumstances, having regard in particular to*
>
> (a) *any special knowledge or experience that he has or holds himself out as having, and*
>
> (b) *if he acts in the course of a business or profession, to any special knowledge or experience that it is reasonable to expect of a person acting in the course of that kind of business or profession.*

The Act does not further elaborate upon the content of this duty of care, so recourse must be had to the case law to assess how the courts will apply the duty (10.12 et seq).

10.9   Section 4 of the Act does, however, require the trustee when exercising any power of investment to have regard to 'standard investment criteria', and to review the investments from time to time with these criteria in mind. These criteria are (a) the suitability of particular kinds of investment for the trust, and (b) the need for diversification of the trust investments.

10.10   As regards diversification, investment strategy today is informed by 'modern portfolio theory', by which the risks of particular investments are balanced against the risks of others. Different investments are chosen that have offsetting risks; thus, for example, if natural gas sales rise at the expense of oil sales, investing in both offsets the risks of one against the other—if gas does well and gas shares rise, then oil shares will fall, and vice versa. Thus the overall risk of investing in both is less than the individual risk of either. The watchword, then, is 'diversification': by diversifying the investment portfolio investments that singly pose substantial risks together provide a portfolio with a much more reasonable risk. Thus the modern prudent investor is to be judged not by the individual investment vehicles he chooses but on the overall portfolio. In *Nestle v National Westminster Bank plc* (1988) Hoffmann J said:

> *Modern trustees acting within their investment powers are entitled to be judged by the standards of current portfolio theory, which emphasises the risk of the entire portfolio rather than the risk attaching to each investment taken in isolation.*

10.11   Section 5 of the Act also requires the trustee, before exercising any power of investment, to take advice from someone the trustee reasonably believes is able to provide proper advice of this kind by virtue of his ability and experience in such matters, unless it would be reasonable in the circumstances to forgo such advice. Such circumstances are not specified, but it would be reasonable not to seek advice in the case of a trust with very limited funds, such as the trust of the funds of an unincorporated association (9.65 et seq) (eg a student law society, or a trust of short duration). The only sensible option in such cases might be to place the trust funds in a bank account.

The standard of prudence in making trust investments

10.12   A standard of prudence cannot be spelled out in terms of black and white rules: like many other standards in the law, it is a standard that depends on a reasonable appreciation of the purposes the standard is to serve and the circumstances in which it applies. In the leading case of *Speight v Gaunt* (1883) the trustee paid some £15,000 to a broker on the strength of a written 'bought note', which asserted that the broker had bought securities in that amount. The broker had never purchased the securities, and his fraud was not discovered before his subsequent bankruptcy, so all the money was lost. The trustee was not liable. The payment of funds to a broker in this way was in accord with the standard business practice of purchasing securities. Jessel MR said:

> *the trustee is not bound because he is a trustee to conduct in other than the ordinary and usual way in which similar business is conducted by mankind in transactions of their own. It could never be reasonable to make a trustee adopt further and better precautions than an ordinary prudent man of business would adopt, or to conduct the business in any other way.*

The judgment was affirmed in similar terms by the HL.

10.13   In *Re Whiteley* (1886), a trustee was found liable for imprudently investing £3,000 upon a mortgage of a brickworks. The land itself was not so valuable as to provide sufficient security for the mortgage—only if the brickworks operation continued as a going concern, which, in the event it did not, was the loan likely to be repaid. In the CA Lindley LJ framed the standard thus:

> The duty of a trustee is not to take such care only as a prudent man would take if he had only himself to consider; the duty rather is to take such care as an ordinary prudent man would take if he were minded to make an investment for the benefit of other people for whom he felt morally bound to provide.

In the HL (*Learoyd v Whiteley* (1887)), Lord Watson said:

> As a general rule the law requires of a trustee no higher degree of diligence in the execution of his office than a man of ordinary prudence would exercise in the management of his own private affairs. Yet he is not allowed the same discretion in investing the moneys of the trust as if he were a person sui juris dealing with his own estate. Businessmen of ordinary prudence may, and frequently do, select investments which are more or less of a speculative character; but it is the duty of a trustee to confine himself to the class of investments which are permitted by the trust, and likewise to avoid all investments of that class which are attended with hazard.

10.14   A trustee is not required to 'beat the market' or save the trust investments from declining in value due to general economic conditions. In *Re Chapman* (1896) Lindley LJ said:

> [A] trustee is not a surety, nor is he an insurer; he is only liable for some wrong done by himself, and loss of trust money is not per se proof of such wrong…There is no rule of law which compels the court to hold that an honest trustee is liable to make good loss sustained by retaining an authorised security in a falling market, if he did so honestly and prudently, in the belief that it was the best course of action in the interest of all parties. Trustees acting honestly, with ordinary prudence or and within the limits of their trust, are not liable for mere errors of judgement.

(See also *Nestle v National Westminster Bank* (1994); 10.19 et seq.)

10.15   Special considerations apply when the trust is a controlling shareholder in a company. In *Re Lucking's Will Trusts* (1967) a majority of shares in a family business was held on trust for the family members. One trustee, one of the family members, installed his friend as manager of the company, who proved most unsuitable, drawing large amounts of the company funds for his own use. The trustee failed to detect the manager's withdrawals until it was too late to recover them, and was held liable. Cross J said:

> Now what steps, if any, does a reasonably prudent man who finds himself a majority shareholder in a private company take with regard to the management of the company's affairs? He does not, I think, content himself with such information as to the management of the company's affairs as he is entitled to as shareholder, but ensures that he is represented on the board…Alternatively, he may find someone who will act as his nominee on the board …trustees holding a controlling interest ought to ensure so far as they can that they have such information as to the progress of the company's affairs as directors would have. If they sit back and allow the company to be run by the minority shareholders and receive no more information than shareholders are entitled to, they do so at their risk if things go wrong.

10.16 In *Bartlett v Barclays Bank Trust Co Ltd* (1980), almost all the assets of the trust consisted of private shares of a company that managed real property. The company embarked on a programme of hazardous and, as it turned out, disastrous property development, of which the trust company took little notice, implicitly trusting in the 'professional calibre' of the company board. The trust company was liable for the losses. Brightman J said:

> I do not understand Cross J [in Lucking] to have been saying that in every case where trustees have a controlling interest in a company it is their duty to ensure that one of their number is a director or that they will have a nominee on the board…He was merely outlining convenient methods by which a prudent man of business (as also a trustee) with a controlling interest in a private company, can place himself in a position to make an informed decision whether any action is appropriate to be taken for the protection of the asset. Other methods may be equally satisfactory and convenient, depending on the circumstances of the individual case. Alternatives which spring to mind are the receipt of the copies of the agenda and minutes of board meetings if regularly held, the receipt of monthly management accounts in the case of a trading concern, or quarterly reports.

A higher standard for paid trustees

10.17 As we have seen, the s 1 duty of care requires a trustee who holds himself out as having special expertise, or who has such expertise by virtue of his business or profession, to be judged accordingly. Although reference to such a higher standard was made *obiter* in several decisions prior to the Act (*Bartlett v Barclays Bank Trust Co Ltd* (1980) *per* Brightman J; *Re Waterman's Will Trusts* (1952) *per* Harman J; an *obiter* statement by Romer J in *Jobson v Palmer* (1893) denied such a higher standard), it does not seem as if any higher standard for professionals was ever applied as part of the *ratio decidendi* of a case; that is a decision to hold a trustee liable or relieve him of liability has never turned on a higher standard for those with special expertise. There is, therefore, no real guidance to be gleaned from the case law as to the stringency or scope of the higher standard that is to apply to professional trustees.

10.18 It should also be borne in mind that paid trustees will invariably insist on exemption clauses before undertaking the trust (**11.85** et seq), and such clauses provide that they will be liable only for their 'wilful default', not mere negligence, so any higher standard for paid trustees will likely be of zero practical importance.

10.19 In *Nestle*, a testamentary trust was created in 1922. When the holders of the life interests had all died, in 1986, the value of the capital was some £270,000 and the plaintiff remainderman claimed that the fund would have been worth well over £1m if it had been properly invested. The trustees had failed to understand the investment clause of the trust instrument, largely because they had failed to seek legal advice as to its meaning, and in consequence they believed that their investment options were much narrower than was the case and failed to review the investments properly. Although it was clear that the real value of the fund fell dramatically, the CA was not convinced that the investment decisions the trustees actually made would have been in breach of trust even had they understood their investment powers and regularly reviewed the investments. In particular, the trustees' actions between 1922 and 1960 could not be judged by the standards of investment expertise of the post-1960 era, when modern portfolio theory favouring equity investment began to be generally applied. The CA accepted Hoffmann J's finding of fact that there was no provable loss to the fund given the advice of experts before the court on the standards of investment practice applicable over the history of the trust. It should not be assumed, however, that if a trust fund administered from the 1960s or later loses significant real value that will not indicate, at least prima facie, a failure to invest properly unless there are countervailing factors. Although that did happen to the trust in *Nestle*, there were such factors.

10.20 Roughly, from the 1960s onwards the trustee adopted a policy of investing large proportions of the funds in investments that were tax exempt for foreign residents, as both the living life tenants lived abroad. This resulted in low capital growth, but also savings in estate duty. The court did not find that the trustee breached his duty of even-handedness between the life tenants and the remainderman in adopting such a policy, because the saving in estate duty accrued to the remainderman as well. Staughton LJ said this on even-handedness generally:

> At times it will not be easy to decide what is an equitable balance. A life tenant may be anxious to receive the highest possible income, whilst the remainderman will wish the real value of the trust fund to be preserved. If the life tenant is living in penury and the remainderman already has ample wealth, common sense suggests that a trustee should be able to take that into account, not necessarily by seeking the highest possible income at the expense of capital but by inclining in that direction. However, before adopting that course a trustee should, I think, require some verification of the facts.

10.21 There are two especially significant points to be taken from *Nestle*: first, one cannot read the case without being impressed that the result very much turned on the defendant bank's winning the battle of the experts as to the investment expertise to be expected of a trustee, and this would seem to be an ineliminable element of adopting a prudent investor approach. Secondly, while the bank was clearly 'in breach' to the extent that it woefully misunderstood the scope of the investment clause, it was not 'in breach' in so far as the investment decisions that it did make were held not to cause loss, because they *could have been justified as* valid investment decisions *had they known* their actual investment powers. In *Cowan v Scargill* (1985) Megarry VC stated this general principle as follows:

> If trustees make a decision on wholly wrong grounds, and yet it subsequently appears, from matters which they did not express or refer to, that there are in fact good and sufficient reasons for supporting their decision, then I do not think that they would incur any liability for having decided the matter on erroneous grounds; for the decision itself was right.

Quaere whether, the plaintiff having proven that the trustee bank had breached its duty by failing properly to understand the investment clause, the burden of proof ought not to have shifted to the bank to show that its breach of duty caused no loss.

'Social' or 'ethical' investing

10.22 Trustees must invest in order to preserve and if possible, enhance the value of the trust property. This obligation is so strict that in *Buttle v Saunders* (1950) trustees were held to have a duty to 'gazump', that is accept a higher offer for the purchase of land they were selling even though this involved the dishonourable conduct of reneging upon their acceptance 'subject to contract' of a previous offer. Before the advent of 'social investing', the main effect of this concentration on the financial interests of the beneficiaries was simply to rule out benefits in kind as proper trust income (unless of course the trust instrument provided otherwise) (see eg *Re Power* (1947), 10.7).

10.23   *Cowan v Scargill* (1985) concerned a dispute between the trustees of the National Coal Board pension fund for miners. The trustees appointed by the National Coal Board wished to approve an investment plan that included investment in overseas securities and in the oil and gas industries. The trustees appointed by the National Union of Mineworkers (NUM) refused to consent to a plan including overseas investment and investment in industries in direct competition with the coal industry. Megarry VC held that the NUM trustees' refusal to approve the scheme would be in breach of trust:

> *When the purpose of the trust is to provide financial benefits for the beneficiaries, as is usually the case, the best interests of the beneficiaries are normally their best financial interests.*

10.24   The fact that the NUM strategy might benefit present miners by perhaps assisting the health of the coal industry, which was by no means certain, would be of no benefit at all to retired miners who depended upon the financial performance of the investment to fund their current pensions, so the NUM strategy might also be regarded as not even-handed. Megarry VC continued:

> *In considering what investments to make trustees must put to one side their own personal interests and views. Trustees may have strongly held social or political views. They may be firmly opposed to any investment in South Africa or other countries, or they may object to any form of investment in companies concerned with alcohol, tobacco, armaments or many other things. In the conduct of their own affairs, of course, they are free to abstain from making any such investments. Yet under a trust, if investments of this type would be more beneficial to the beneficiaries than other investments, the trustees must not refrain from making the investments by reasons of the views that they hold.*

10.25   However, Megarry VC also said:

> *[I]f the only actual beneficiaries or potential beneficiaries of a trust are all adults with very strict views on moral and social matters, condemning all forms of alcohol, tobacco and popular entertainment, as well as armaments, I can well understand that it might not be for the 'benefit' of such beneficiaries to know that they are obtaining rather larger financial returns under the trust by reason of investments in those activities...*

To the extent this last passage is taken to suggest that a trustee might make 'ethical' investment decisions in such circumstances, Megarry VC's words should be disregarded. If all the actual and potential beneficiaries are adults, then a trustee intending such a policy should present it to them in advance and get their consent, in which case the investment will not be in breach of trust. Otherwise it is a breach of trust, since trustees should not have the power to determine by their own lights what constitutes an 'ethical' or 'moral' benefit to their beneficiaries as a whole.

10.26   In *Evans v London Co-operative Society* (1976) trustees had regularly loaned the whole of a pension fund to the employer at below market interest rates. Although such loans were authorised by the trust instrument the trustees were liable for breach for not adequately exercising their discretion in properly negotiating an interest rate. However, Brightman J said that the trustees could:

> give the parent financial concern accommodation on preferential terms if the trustees consider that the security of the employment of their members may otherwise be imperilled.

10.27   In the Scottish case *Martin v City of Edinburgh District Council* (1989) the local authority's policy to disinvest in companies with South African interests was found to be a breach of trust, because the decision was taken without considering the best financial interests of the beneficiaries.

10.28   Charities raise particular issues. In *Harries v Church Comrs for England* (1993) the Bishop of Oxford sought a declaration that the Church Commissioners should use their assets with the objective in mind of promoting the Christian faith, and were not entitled to act in a manner inconsistent with that object; he thus proposed an active investment policy of seeking out investments to forward Christian objects. The court disagreed. As with any other trust, the normal duty of charitable trustees is to seek the maximum return while investing prudently. While the Commissioners' policy of excluding certain investments—armaments, gambling, tobacco, newspapers, and companies with interests in South Africa—was considered acceptable, a more restrictive policy of requiring them generally to invest on the basis of non-commercial considerations would create too great a risk to the trust.

10.29   It thus seems that charity trustees may rightly choose not to invest in activities that directly contradict the purposes of the trust, so a charity for cancer research may rightly not invest in the tobacco industry, because it is assumed that such restrictions will leave the charity with an adequate range of investments to diversify a portfolio. Secondly, charities may refuse to invest in otherwise sound investments if by so investing they would alienate those who give to the charity, thus reducing its overall financial position. But charities may not adopt a policy of accepting lower returns by treating their investments as a means of carrying out their charitable purpose. As Nobles (1992a) points out, however, charities generally *give* their money away in pursuit of their purposes. Why should one mode of 'giving', ie investing in activities that may earn below market returns, be disallowed, if it serves the charity's purpose? They are not, after all, trying to preserve and enhance the value of a sum of money for private beneficiaries. They should, therefore, be able to 'ethically' invest so long as the particular ethical investment furthers their *particular* charitable purpose. Note that while this licence may provide much latitude for charities such as churches, where 'Christian purposes' could be read very broadly, it would provide almost no latitude at all to, say, Dogs for the Blind.

10.30   Lord Nicholls (1995), speaking extrajudicially, has suggested that:

> The range of sound investments available to trustees is so extensive that very frequently there is scope for trustees to give effect to moral considerations…without thereby prejudicing beneficiaries' financial interests. In practice, the inclusion or exclusion of particular investments or types of investment will often be possible without incurring the risk of a lower rate of return or reducing the desirable spread of investments. When this is so, there is no reason in principle why trustees should not have regard to moral and ethical considerations, vague and uncertain though these are. The trustees would not be departing from the purpose of the trust or hindering its fulfilment.

This suggestion should be firmly resisted. In the first place, regardless of the actual financial returns to the beneficiaries, trustees should never be entitled to take into account their own moral and ethical considerations in exercising any of their trust powers. Trustees are instruments of the trust. If they were ever to act on their own views in this way, they would act in breach of their fiduciary obligation never to exercise a discretion in a way that puts themselves in conflict with the purpose of the trust; applying their ethical attitudes to investment decisions gives rise to such a conflict because the trustees' ethical views are extraneous to the consideration of serving the beneficiaries' interests. Lord Nicholls does not say that the trustees must implement the *beneficiaries'* moral or ethical views, but presumably they may act on their own. There is no warrant whatsoever to give trustees who are placed in a position of power and who are generally paid the right to engage their ethical preferences when investing so long as the beneficiaries cannot prove (see *Nestle*, 10.21) that they have caused the trust loss by doing so. Who trusts the 'ethical' perspective of a bank or trust company anyway?

10.31   Secondly, it is wrong to think that the range of investments is so great that a few ethical investment choices here and there will not affect the financial performance of the trust. As Langbein and Posner (1980) make clear, a decrease in the range of investments is not determined by the *number* of individual securities one does not invest in, but the percentage value of the investment market those securities represent:

> In 1979, Corporate Data Exchange Inc, identified ninety-nine companies that a socially responsible investor should avoid. The aggregate market value of the stocks of these companies was $342 billion. Yet the only criteria for exclusion were whether the company was predominantly non-unionised, had a poor record in occupational health and safety, failed to meet equal employment opportunity guidelines, or was a major investor or lender in South Africa. Although this is an arbitrarily limited set of criteria, it results in excluding such a large fraction (weighting numbers by market value) of listed equities as to create a degree of sampling error and sampling bias inconsistent with adequate diversification of the portfolio.

In other words 'if a trustee refuses to invest in just two things', but those two happen to be cars and alcohol, he is unlikely to adequately diversify the trust portfolio because the car and drinks industries represent such a major fraction of the overall economy. It is irrelevant that there are, in terms of numbers, thousands of other companies or securities to invest in. The resulting inadequate diversification will entail a riskier investment of the trust funds.

The delegation of trustee functions

10.32   Before 1926, unless specifically authorised by the trust instrument to do so, trustees could not delegate their administrative functions unless doing so was reasonably necessary for their administration of the trust to the standard of a prudent man of business (*Speight v Gaunt* (1883); *Learoyd v Whiteley* (1887)). Furthermore, the general rule was that trustees could not delegate any of their discretions, the idea being, first, that the settlor, by conferring discretions upon his trustees, reposed in them specifically the trust to exercise them responsibly, and, secondly, that by undertaking the trust, the trustees undertook to use their own judgment where judgment was called for, and had no right to shift the job to others. Outside specific provision in the trust instrument, a trustee's powers to delegate were governed by the Trustee Act 1925, ss 23 and 25. The Trustee Act 2000 introduced a new regime of delegation.

10.33   Under s 11(1) and (2) of the Trustee Act 2000, trustees may collectively delegate any of their functions to an agent to perform, except:

(a)   *any function relating to whether or in what way any assets of the trust should be distributed;*

(b)   *any power to decide whether any fees or other payment due to be made out of the trust funds should be made out of income or capital;*

(c)   *any power to appoint a person to be a trustee of the trust; or*

(d)   *any power conferred by any other enactment or the trust instrument that permits the trustees to delegate any of their functions or to appoint a person to act as a nominee or custodian.*

10.34   The trustees may delegate tasks to one of themselves (s 12(1)), although not to any trustee who is also a beneficiary (s 12(2)). By s 15, where the agent is to carry out any 'asset management functions' (eg investment), the trustees must first provide a written 'policy statement' to guide the agent's exercise of his powers in the best interests of the trust, so that, for example, the investments provide sufficient income to meet the level of provision the trustees intend for the income beneficiaries. By s 22, the trustees are required periodically to review any delegation arrangements, and to consider whether the 'policy statement' needs to be revised. By Sch 1, para 3, the s 1 duty of care (10.8) applies to the trustees' appointment of agents and their review of them under s 22.

10.35   By s 25 of the Trustee Act 1925 (as amended by the Trustee Delegation Act 1999, s 5) any individual trustee may, by power of attorney, delegate any or all of his duties, powers, or discretions, whether administrative or dispositive, for up to 12 months. Under s 25(4), the trustee must inform in writing any person entitled to appoint new trustees under the trust (see 10.60 et seq) and all the other trustees, which will allow them to consider whether the delegating trustee should be replaced. The trustee is liable under s 25(7) for all acts and defaults of his delegate by power of attorney as if they were his own acts or defaults.

The power of maintenance

10.36   The power of maintenance enables a trustee to spend income, but not capital, for the benefit of infant beneficiaries, ie those under 18. A settlor may specifically confer upon or deny the trustee this power, directing instead that the income should be spent on someone else or accumulated. In any other case, where property is held on trust for an infant, the Trustee Act 1925, s 31 confers on trustees a power to apply, in their sole discretion, income for the infant's maintenance. The section applies whether the infant's interest is vested (eg '10,000 shares of XYZ plc on trust for my son Benjamin absolutely'), or contingent (eg 'Blackacre to Bertram if he obtains the age of 25'). Once the beneficiary of a vested interest turns 18 then of course he is entitled to any income arising on the property, but under s 31(1)(ii) trustees must pay the income to a beneficiary even of a contingent interest upon his turning 18.

10.37   During his infancy, the trustees may pay such portions of the income for his maintenance as 'may, in all the circumstances, be reasonable', and must accumulate the rest. Unless, therefore, s 31 is excluded, even a beneficiary of an absolute interest will receive only such income as is required, in the trustees' discretion, for his maintenance. The trustees must have regard to 'the age of the infant and his requirements and generally to the circumstances of his case, and in particular to what other income, if any, is available for the same purposes' (s 31(1)). In *Wilson v Turner* (1883) the trustees paid the income to the infant beneficiary's father automatically without inquiring as to the beneficiary's actual needs, and the father's estate was required to repay the money.

10.38   Under s 31(2) income that is accumulated instead of being spent on maintenance in one year may be spent for the beneficiary's maintenance in later years. Thus income accumulated in the beneficiary's tenth and eleventh years may be spent in his seventeenth when his expenses are greater. Also under s 31(2), where a beneficiary has a vested interest or an interest that vests upon his turning 18, when he turns 18 any income that instead of being spent for his mainten-ance was accumulated will then be held on trust for him absolutely—he can demand the imme-diate payment of it. This rule does not apply, however, where the vested interest is a conditional interest in land or an interest in personalty that may in any way be defeated, such as by the exercise of a power of appointment (see *Re Sharp's Settlement Trusts* (1973)). In that case, and in any case where the beneficiary's interest in the property does not vest until later, such as where his interest is contingent upon his turning 25, these pre-age 18 accumulations are held on the same trust as is the capital. Thus they will likewise be susceptible to the same contingency as is his interest in the capital. Therefore if his interest in the capital vests only when he reaches the age of 25, then his interest in the pre-age 18 accumulations only vests when he reaches 25. In view of this, the trustees should consider making a final payment of past accumulated income shortly before the beneficiary's eighteenth birthday; after that, he will have no recourse to this money until his capital interest vests.

10.39   The income available for maintenance payments is only that income which arises on the prop-erty to which the minor beneficiary is, or will be, entitled. This is straightforward in the case of a beneficiary with a present vested interest. All of the income (ie dividends) on the shares in XYZ plc will be available to make maintenance payments to Benjamin in the earlier example (10.36). In the case of contingent or future interests, however, only income from property held on trust that 'carries the intermediate income' is available. This is best explained by example. If a testator gives Barbara a contingent pecuniary legacy, say £20,000 conditional upon her attaining the age of 25, it will be paid in due course out of the testator's residuary estate when she turns 25; Barbara will not receive any accrued income or interest since no property was set aside for her on a special account. The gift, therefore, carries no intermediate income for main-tenance payments if Barbara is a minor. The same will occur with *a future* pecuniary legacy (eg of £20,000 to Barbara on the death of her father). By contrast, in the case of any *inter vivos* trust, there is no 'residuary estate'; each gift has specific property allocated to it and therefore a contingent gift will be of specific property, and so until it vests it will carry the income that accrues on it and when the gift vests the beneficiary is entitled to that income. During the beneficiary's minority such income will therefore be available for maintenance payments. In all cases, however, any contrary indication in the terms of the trust will upset these rules, for example a direction that the income should go to a different beneficiary.

10.40   By the operation of s 175 of the Law of Property Act 1925 and a number of cases that we shall not discuss, the following rules apply to different kinds of testamentary gift to determine whether they carry the intermediate income, assuming that there is no contrary intention. A testamentary gift, whether of personalty or realty, and whether contingent or future, whether of specific property or residuary property, carries the intermediate income unless the gift is:

(1) a residuary bequest (ie a gift of residuary personalty), whether vested or contingent, which is postponed to a future date (see *Re McGeorge* (1963));

(2) a contingent or future pecuniary legacy; but such a gift *will* carry the intermediate income where:

   (i) it appears that the testator intended to maintain the beneficiary; or

   (ii) the legacy has been set aside as a separate fund from the outset; or

   (iii) the legacy is contingent upon the beneficiary's attaining the age of majority, and the testator was his parent or stood *in loco parentis* to him, and there are no other funds available for the minor's maintenance.

The power of advancement

10.41 The power of advancement is the power to expend *capital* of the trust fund to benefit a beneficiary who has only a future or contingent interest in it. Thus if Betty is entitled to the trust property for life, and Barney in remainder, Barney has a vested future interest. If he is advanced capital before Betty dies, then he receives the benefit of the capital early. If Beatrix is given trust property conditional upon her attaining the age of 30, and she is advanced property at the age of 22, not only does she receive the benefit early, but if she dies at the age of 28, she receives property she would not have received at all but for the advancement—there is no 'clawback' of advanced property if it turns out that at the end of the day the beneficiary does not meet the conditions entitling him to the contingent interest. An advancement is traditionally a significant sum intended to 'advance', or establish, a beneficiary in life (9.36), although 'benefit' is now interpreted much more broadly (10.44), and 'to advance' therefore generally simply means 'to advance' or bring forward, a beneficiary's capital interest, although this does not mean that the beneficiary will actually receive the benefit of the property sooner, since the capital may be brought forward and then resettled on trusts that actually delay the vesting of a beneficiary's interest (10.44).

10.42 A power to apply the capital of the trust to any object may be expressly given, but s 32 of the Trustee Act 1925 empowers trustees to advance capital to beneficiaries of future or contingent interests in the capital unless expressly excluded by the trust terms. Section 32 empowers trustees to advance to a beneficiary up to one half by value of the capital interest he ultimately expects, his 'presumptive share', and the value of the advancement must be taken into account when his final share is paid out. Subsequent advancements may be made over time so long as the beneficiary has not been paid out sums amounting to half of his presumptive share, but the traditional method of accounting for past money advances used in practice can be 'monstrously unjust' (Law Reform Committee (1982), paras 4.43–4.47; see Oakley (2003), at 696 for an example of the calculations). If, based on the calculation of the fund at the present time, a beneficiary is advanced an amount that, taking account of past advancements, gives him his half presumptive share in his capital interest, he may no longer be advanced any funds (*Re Abergavenny's Estate Act Trusts* (1981)), regardless of how much the value of the capital increases in future years.

10.43   In certain cases the trustees will need the prior consent of one beneficiary to advance money to another. Consider a trust of shares 'to A for life and then to B'. B has a future interest in the shares and is a candidate for advancement. But clearly, any advancement to B will reduce the capital in the trust, ie the number of shares, so A's income, which comes from the dividends on the shares, will decline. Section 32(1)(c) provides that the trustees may only make an advancement to B if A, who is said to have a 'prior' interest, is *sui juris* and consents to the advancement in writing.

10.44   What counts as 'advancement' under s 32 is very wide indeed: in *Pilkington v IRC* (1964), Viscount Radcliffe said, '[i]t means any use of the money which will improve the material situation of the beneficiary', and in that case the HL would, but for the rules against perpetuity, have approved a proposed advancement that would have resettled a 5-year-old's expected interest when she attained the age of 21 upon a new trust, which would delay the vesting of her interest in the capital until she reached the age of 30, in order to avoid the effects of death duty. In *Re Clore's Settlement Trusts* (1966) the court approved an advancement to a rich beneficiary allowing him to make a charitable donation he felt morally obliged to make; it was a material, although not decisive, consideration that by the advancement of capital the beneficiary could make the donation with much less severe tax consequences than if he did so out of his income.

10.45   Trustees have an obligation to see that the money advanced actually goes to benefit the beneficiary. In *Re Pauling's Settlement Trusts* (1964) it was held that trustees could not advance money:

> without any responsibility... even to inquire as to its application.

There, large sums were advanced that the trustees were aware were being spent by the beneficiaries' father on the family's living expenses; the advancements were therefore in breach of trust and the trustees were required to repay the money thus frittered away.

10.46   In *Pilkington*, the HL decided that an advancement on resettlement was permissible under s 32. This raises the possibility that funds advanced may be settled on discretionary trusts. A question arises as to whether an advancement under s 32 can validly be made that creates a trust under which the advanced beneficiary is, or may become (as under a protective trust), a discretionary beneficiary. The trustees under the new trust will have a discretion to benefit the beneficiary, and the general rule is that a trustee cannot delegate his discretion (10.32); by making an advancement on these terms it appears that that is just what he is doing. On the other hand, as pointed out by Oakley (2003, at 703–4), all agree that the resettlement itself might contain a power of advancement, and this confers a clear discretion on the new trustee. More to the point, however, it would seem that such a settlement should be judged by whether or not it confers a real 'benefit' on the beneficiary. Given his circumstances, it might appear that a protective trust in his favour might do that. This should be the overriding consideration, and given that the benefit in *Clore* was acceptable, it seems possible that so might being a beneficiary under a discretionary trust. The delegation point, although raised in *Pilkington*, was not considered in any detail. Any express power of advancement can, of course, be framed to permit its exercise to resettle part of the beneficiary's presumptive share on discretionary trust.

10.47   *Pilkington* also decided that, for purposes of the rule against perpetuities, a power of advancement is to be treated as a special power of appointment, and therefore an advancement on resettlement is subject to the time limitations of the original trust of the property (3.53).

Where the resettlement contains provisions void for perpetuity these will be void, of course, but the main trust for the beneficiary in whose favour the advancement is made will not fail (*Re Hastings-Bass* (1975)), unless the failure of the void provisions significantly alters the benefit the advancement was intended to achieve (*Re Abrahams' Will Trusts* (1969)).

10.48   In *Fischer v Nemeske Pty Ltd* (2016), the High Court of Australia was divided on whether a particular action by the trustee amounted to an 'advancement' under a term of the trust. A trustee purported to advance trust funds to the beneficiaries by acknowledging, in the trust accounts, a debt owed to the beneficiaries because of a loan made to the trustees. There was no evidence to suggest any such loan was ever actually made, so the case proceeded on the basis whether a trustee could simply 'create a debt' to particular beneficiaries as one way of making an advancement. The majority held that it could. In this case, the debt created reflected the entire value of certain shares (which were the principle asset of the trust) at the time the advance was made. This advance was supported by a 'Deed of Charge', subsequently executed by the trustee, which charged the shares, in favour of the beneficiaries, with the trustee's obligation to pay the debt so created.

10.49   Kiefel and Gordon JJ dissented. Kiefel J held that there was no setting aside or allocation of any property that could amount to an application of capital or income within the meaning of the trust terms, emphasising that the trust accounts confirmed this, and that:

> [88] "the importance of the accounts, not only for those having an interest in the Trust and its property, but also for third parties who may need to deal with the Trustee or rely upon Trust records, should not be lost sight of."

10.50   First, according to the minority, there was the problem of what property was the subject of the power of advancement. The only substantial assets of the trust (the shares), always remained under the ownership of the trust and were not dealt with in any way that affected the trust's title to them. In Gordon J's words, 'value' is not property held by the Trust. Therefore, an 'asset revaluation reserve', essentially a valuation of the shares at the time, was not capital or income of the Trust that could be advanced, paid, or applied.

10.51   Second, no actual trust property was advanced or applied. According to Kiefel J, property of a trust may be 'applied' under the power of advancement only in so far by allocating them in such a way that they are removed from the trust. As the assets were never set aside or allocated in any way to suggest that they were 'applied', what was done by the trustees was not an effective exercise of the power of advancement. In Gordon J's words:

> [166] whatever mechanism is adopted, the power [of advancement] operates by altering the proprietary interests in the property advanced so that the property is no longer property of the trust. It involves more than a notional 'earmarking' of property for specific beneficiaries. …
>
> [170] the power to apply was not exercised because there was no change in the beneficial ownership of any asset of the Trust

As to the deed of charge, Gordon J said at [186]:

> First, there was no effective charge as there was no debt to secure… Here, there was no debt to secure. The Deed of Charge was without legal effect.

10.52   With respect, the minority's position is preferable. Simply by earmarking in the trust accounts some amount of money to go to some beneficiary, without identifying any part of the trust assets or doing anything else to confer an actual benefit on that beneficiary, should not amount to an advancement.

Appointment, retirement, and removal of trustees

10.53   Over the course of any trust, old trustees may retire and occasionally trustees must be removed, and, in both cases, depending upon how many trustees remain, new trustees may need to be appointed. Trustees may be individual persons or companies that specialise in acting as trustees. The court of equity, in its inherent jurisdiction over trusts, has the power to remove trustees and replace them with new ones. For a recent example of a case in which the courts replaced trustees who had completely failed to appreciate their duties as trustees, and had made decisions concerning the trust property with the interests of non-beneficiaries in mind, see *Jones v Firkin-Flood* (2008).

10.54   Any number of persons may be co-trustees of a trust where the corpus is made up entirely of personalty. There are restrictions upon any trust that contains interests in land: the Trustee Act 1925, s 34 sets a maximum of four (there are exceptions for charitable and other public purpose trusts); the Act also effectively sets a minimum of two trustees. While a sole trustee, ie a lone human trustee (not a trust corporation), of land is not prohibited, s 14(2) provides that a sole trustee cannot give a valid receipt for the purchase money to a purchaser of the land, and so no purchaser will knowingly deal with a sole trustee of land.

10.55   Trustees invariably hold property as joint tenants, so if one dies the survivor(s) alone continue(s) as trustee(s) (1.22). Only if a sole trustee dies does the legal title to the trust property pass to his personal representative, who in that case becomes a trustee. In the case of a trust created by will where all the intended trustees have predeceased the testator, the testator's personal representatives will be trustees until new trustees can be appointed, who may, of course, be themselves.

10.56   A trust will not fail for want of a trustee, but neither will anyone unwilling be forced to serve as a trustee. Thus if a testator by his will transfers property to Tom on trust for Beatrix, Tom may refuse to accept the role of trustee; the court, however, will ensure that someone undertakes the trust. If there is no one else willing, as a last resort the court may appoint the Public Trustee. The office of the Public Trustee was created by the Public Trustee Act 1906, largely to ensure the administration of trusts where no other person was willing to do so. While the Public Trustee may refuse to undertake a trust, he may not do so only because of its small value (Public Trustee Act 1906, s 2(3)). The Public Trustee is entitled to charge for his administration of the trust. Alternatively, the court may appoint a trust company, authorising it to charge for its services (Trustee Act 1925, s 42).

10.57   In the first instance, trustees are appointed by the settlor when the trust is created (by the testator by his will in the case of a testamentary trust), and he can choose whomsoever he wants. Once the trust is constituted, the trust terms themselves become operative, and these may give some individual(s), typically the settlor and the trustees for the time being, the power to appoint new trustees. However, such provisions are typically supplementary to the powers to appoint provided by s 36 of the Trustee Act 1925, which are generally regarded as adequate.

10.58   The basic purpose of s 36 is to ensure that there will be someone who can appoint trustees so that a court appointment is not required. It provides that where a trustee:

- has died, which includes the case of a trustee named in a will who has predeceased the testator (s 36(8)); or
- has remained outside the UK for over a year; or
- wishes to retire from the trust; or
- refuses to act, ie disclaims the role of trustee at the outset; or
- is unfit to act (eg bankrupt); or
- is incapable of acting, ie has a personal incapacity such as mental or physical infirmity; or
- is an infant; or
- has been removed by the exercise of a power in the trust instrument (s 36(2)),

then a new appointment may be made, first, by anyone nominated to do so in the trust instrument and, failing that, by the trustees for the time being and, failing that because they have all died, by the personal representatives of the last surviving trustee. By s 36(8) refusing or retiring trustees are considered trustees for the time being so as to enable them to appoint their successors. It has been held (*Re Coates to Parsons* (1886)) that where some trustees intend to undertake the trust or continue as trustees, but some refuse or intend to retire, respectively, the appointment of new trustees by the continuing trustees without the concurrence of a refusing or retiring trustee will make the appointment invalid if it is shown that the latter was competent and willing to act. It is therefore advisable that all trustees for the time being participate in any appointment. Section 36(6) permits the appointment of additional trustees up to a maximum of four trustees in total. An appointment must be made in writing, although a last surviving trustee may not appoint a successor by will (*Re Parker* (1894)). An appointment is usually made by deed in order to vest the property in, ie transfer the legal title to, the new trustees at the same time (10.61). Nevertheless, s 36(7) provides that a new trustee becomes fully liable as a trustee as soon as he is appointed, even if the vesting of the property occurs sometime later. Even if a purported appointment is void, a new trustee who deals with the property as a trustee will be liable as one (11.103).

10.59   Section 19 of the Trusts of Land and Appointment of Trustees Act 1996 gives beneficiaries what amounts to a power to both remove and appoint trustees, although the power can be excluded by the settlor. If all are *sui juris*, the beneficiaries may unanimously direct any trustee to retire from the trust, or direct the trustees to use their power to appoint new trustees in favour of any person they choose (reversing *Re Brockbank* (3.40) on this point).

10.60   Although the court has the power to appoint trustees under its inherent jurisdiction over trusts, s 41 provides that the court may appoint trustees where it is found 'inexpedient, difficult, or impracticable to do so without the assistance of the court', and in particular to replace a trustee who is mentally incompetent, bankrupt, or where a corporate trustee is in liquidation or has been dissolved. Clearly, then, this power is regarded as a long-stop provision where no one empowered by the instrument or s 36 may practicably appoint. The court has also appointed where, for example, all the trustees nominated by will predeceased the testator (*Re Smirthwaite's Trusts* (1871)), where an elderly trustee was physically and mentally incapable of carrying on (*Re Lemann's Trusts* (1883)), and where a trustee had permanently left the UK (*Re Bignold's Settlement Trusts* (1872)). In appointing trustees the court will be guided by criteria stated by the CA in *Re Tempest* (1866): (1) the wishes of the settlor, (2) the interests of all the beneficiaries, and (3) the efficient execution of the trust. Following the enactment of s 19 of the 1996 Act, recourse to the court should be rare.

10.61   Except in the case of managing/custodian trustees (10.63), the trust property must be vested in the new body of trustees when a new trustee is appointed. Section 40 of the Trustee Act 1925 allows a deed of appointment of new trustees also to serve as a vesting instrument, which vests the legal title in the new body of trustees. In the case of registered land the Registrar must give effect to such an instrument by revising the registered title accordingly. Some property cannot be vested in this way: the most important example of this is company shares. The shares must be transferred into the names of the new trustees in the normal way so that the new trustees are registered as owners.

10.62   A person may disclaim the role of trustee from the outset, may retire from the trust, or may be removed. Although one should disclaim by deed, a disclaimer may be expressed in or implied from words or conduct. Once a person has accepted a trust, which in general is found whenever he exercises any function of a trustee in respect of the trust, he cannot disclaim—he may then only retire from the trust. Under s 36 of the Trustee Act 1925 a trustee may retire from the trust on the appointment of a replacement; under s 39, a trustee may retire by deed if there remain at least two individuals or a trust company as trustee(s), and he obtains the consent of the other trustees and anyone else entitled to appoint new trustees. The beneficiaries may now direct a trustee to retire, which is tantamount to removing him, and the court under s 41 may remove one trustee to replace him with another. The court may also remove a trustee in exercise of its inherent jurisdiction without necessarily appointing a replacement, although the grounds for doing so are not well defined. Clearly, any trustee in breach of trust or otherwise in dereliction of his fiduciary duties is a suitable candidate for removal; in *Letterstedt v Broers* (1884), the PC refused to lay down any rule governing the exercise of the power, except to say that the general interest of the beneficiaries should guide any decision.

Custodian, nominee, managing, and judicial trustees

10.63   A few particular kinds of trustee should be mentioned. 'Custodian trustees' hold the title to the trust property, but the management of the trust, ie all the trust decisions, are taken by different persons, called 'managing trustees', which the custodian trustee executes in so far as a disposition of the title to the property is required. The custodian trustee is essentially a nominee (2.13) who complies with the orders of the managing trustees. (A custodian trustee, while essentially a nominee, may differ from a nominee in some respects for particular purposes: see *IRC v Silverts Ltd* (1951).) The main advantage of a custodian trustee is that once the property is vested in him, the managing trustees may retire or be removed and new managing trustees appointed, without having to revest the property each time. A 'nominee' trustee, or just 'nominee', referred to as such in this context, is essentially identical to a custodian trustee, although 'nominee' tends to be used of trustees who hold assets of the trust for specific purposes or transactions, while 'custodian' tends to be used of a trustee intended to hold all of the assets of a trust on an ongoing basis. Under ss 16–18 of the Trustee Act 2000, trustees are empowered to appoint nominees and custodian trustees. Section 19 provides that trust corporations, corporations controlled by the trustees, or persons who carry on the business of acting as nominee or custodian, may be appointed.

10.64   A 'judicial trustee' is appointed by the court (Judicial Trustees Act 1896) in cases where some continuing court supervision is required because the administration of the trust has broken down; the court may give such directions as to the administration of the trust as it thinks fit.

Variation of trusts

10.65   In general, a settlor may set whatever terms on a trust he desires. Because trusts generally last for some years, it is not uncommon for terms that seemed reasonable at the outset to cause problems or inconvenience later, such as terms that limit the trustee's power of investment, or modes of distribution of the assets that give rise to unforeseen tax liability. Furthermore, the beneficiaries may, even from the outset, be unhappy with the distribution of their particular beneficial interests. If the beneficiaries are all ascertained and *sui juris*, they may at any time combine to exercise their *Saunders v Vautier* rights to collapse the trust or vary its terms. Where this is not the case the assistance of the court must be sought.

10.66   The court has always had an inherent jurisdiction (on the court's inherent jurisdiction generally see Nolan (2016)) to vary trusts, although the scope of this jurisdiction is limited to variations that permit the trustees greater administrative or management powers, and then only in cases of 'emergency' (*Re New* (1901)); the court will not rearrange the beneficial interests (*Chapman v Chapman* (1954)). The only true exception to this rule is that the court will empower the trustees to apply income to maintain a settlor's minor children even where he directed the income to be accumulated. A court has also always been able to sanction a 'compromise' between beneficiaries' rights where they are the subject of doubt or dispute, but this is better seen as the court's settling what the beneficial interests are, not its remoulding of the beneficial interests.

10.67   Section 57 of the Trustee Act 1925 extends the court's jurisdiction to enhance the trustee's administrative powers to cases of expediency, ie to more than emergency situations. It clearly contemplates increasing the power of trustees to deal in particular ways with the trust property, not a wholesale rewriting of the trust, nor the remoulding of the beneficial interests (*Chapman v Chapman* (1954)).

10.68   An application to extend the trustee's investment powers provides a nice example of a variation under s 57. In *Trustees of the British Museum v A-G* (1984) Megarry VC refused to follow the 1961 decision in *Re Kolb's Will Trusts*, which held that an extension of trust powers was to be approved only in special circumstances. He held that there should be a general power to widen investment powers based on a number of factors including: (1) the standing of trustees and their administrative plan for obtaining advice and controlling investments; (2) the size of the fund; and (3) the object of the fund (here capital growth was needed for the museum to be able to have an endowment for additions to the museum collection). In *Steel v Wellcome Custodian Trustees Ltd* (1988) Hoffmann J approved an extension of investment powers on similar principles.

10.69   The Variation of Trusts Act 1958 allows the variation of beneficial interests under trusts in cases where the beneficiaries are not in the position to do so by exercising their *Saunders v Vautier* rights. Essentially the Act allows the court to approve a variation on behalf of underage beneficiaries and potential beneficiaries as yet unascertained. The variation is, therefore, effected by the unanimous exercise of the beneficiaries exercising their *Saunders v Vautier* rights—those who are *sui juris* and ascertained consent for themselves, and the court consents on behalf of those who are not; the Act does not give the court a general discretionary power to vary trusts at the application of an interested party (*Re Holt's Settlement* (1969); *IRC v Holmden* (1968); *Goulding v James* (1997)). For this reason, recourse to the 1958 Act should be made only when the beneficial interests are to be varied. Variations are to be treated as 'new trusts', and the varying parties as settlors of the new trusts, such that the new trusts are subject to whatever statutory provisions apply at the time of variation (*Re Holt's Settlement*). The mere extension of trustee powers, like the power of investment, should be sought under s 57 of the 1925 Act; in such a case the trustee is the proper applicant, not the beneficiaries, and, since no need for the consent of all beneficiaries is required, the s 57 application will be less costly (*Anker-Petersen v Anker-Petersen* (1991)).

10.70   The court will not consent on behalf of beneficiaries of full age even if their interests are contingent and extremely unlikely to vest in interest, even if obtaining their consent will be very inconvenient, as in *Knocker v Youle* (1986) where there were several dozen contingent *sui juris* beneficiaries, a goodly number in Australia, who were almost certain never to take under the trust. Should Parliament amend the Act to allow the court to consent on behalf of such beneficiaries? Is a court dealing with a *McPhail*-type trust able to do this in substance already, given its power to 'implement a scheme of distribution' proposed by a representative group of beneficiaries in order to enforce such a trust (3.77)?

10.71   By s 1(1) of the Act the court may only approve an arrangement on behalf of a beneficiary if it would be to his 'benefit', unless (s 1(1)(d)) the beneficiary is an object of discretionary 'trust over' following the determination of the life interest under a protective trust (3.129) in which case no 'benefit' need be shown. 'Benefit' has been construed broadly to include not only financial but moral and social benefits (*Re Holt's Settlement*). In *Re Weston's Settlements* (1969) Lord Denning MR refused to allow the export of a trust to Jersey where the settlor and the beneficiaries had recently moved to minimise tax liability. Considering social and educational benefits he said:

> I do not believe it is for the benefit of children to be uprooted from England and transported to another country simply to avoid tax.

10.72   The court will not require an absolute certainty of benefit—where subsequent events might make the variation disadvantageous to the beneficiaries on whose behalf the court consents, the scheme will still be approved if the more likely result is an advantage to them; the court should undertake on the beneficiaries' behalf the same sort of risks that an adult would be prepared to take (*Re Cohen's Will Trusts* (1959); *Re Holt's Settlement*). However, where the effect of a variation might lead to a possible beneficiary under the old trust, even an as yet unborn individual, being excluded from the new trust entirely, the variation will not be approved because if such a person is born the variation would be wholly disadvantageous to him (*Re Cohen's Settlement Trusts* (1965)).

10.73   In *Re Steed's Will Trusts* (1960), the CA gave the testator's intentions significant weight where a life tenant under a protective trust applied for a variation to give her an absolute interest. The essence of the settlor's concern in creating the protective trust for his former housekeeper was that if absolutely entitled to the property she would be 'sponged upon by one of her brothers'. The CA refused to consent to the variation on behalf of the possible objects of the discretionary trust over, ie those who would take if the primary trust was forfeited. This decision seems quite out of line with the obvious import of the Act, which, if anything, should favour the variation of protective trusts to give the determinable life-interest holder an absolute interest: s 1 specifically provides that the court may approve a variation on behalf of the beneficiaries of the discretionary trust arising on the forfeiture of a protective trust even if the variation is of no benefit to them. In *Re Remnant's Settlement Trusts* (1970) an arrangement that overthrew the settlor's clear intentions was approved in the interest of family harmony and marital choice (a condition defeated a trust gift for objects marrying a Roman Catholic).

10.74   In *Goulding v James* (1997) the CA made clear that the settlor's intentions are only relevant in so far as they contribute to assessing whether the proposed variation is of benefit to the class on whose behalf the court consents. The *sui juris* beneficiaries, like any other beneficiaries exercising their *Saunders v Vautier* rights, may propose an arrangement that directly contradicts the settlor's wishes *for them*. Although *Re Steed* was not in terms disapproved, it was largely confined to its particular facts.

10.75   By contrast, in other jurisdictions, the *Saunders v Vautier* principle has been significantly cut down by judicial decisions and legislation, such that any proposed variation, even if consented to by all the beneficiaries, is prohibited to the extent that it would detract from a 'material purpose' of the settlor in creating the trust (see eg American Law Institute (1959), ss 337–339; Bahamas Trustee Act 1998, s 87; Matthews (2006)).

10.76   The 1958 Act empowers the court to consent to '*any* arrangement … varying or revoking *all or any* of the trusts' (my italics). Given the breadth of this language, and furthermore the courts' interpretation that variations of trusts are to be understood as the exercise of *Saunders v Vautier* rights, it would seem that the court should happily countenance the complete revocation of the old trust and resettlement of the property under a new one. Yet in *Re T's Settlement Trusts* (1964), Wilberforce J refused to approve a 'complete new resettlement' on the grounds that the Act was restricted to variations. However, in *Re Ball's Settlement* (1968), Megarry J said:

> But it does not follow that merely because an arrangement can correctly be described as effecting a revocation and resettlement, it cannot also be correctly described as effecting a variation of the trusts.

10.77   The most oft-quoted passage from the case is this, in which Megarry J quotes Martin J of the Supreme Court of Victoria in *Re Dyer* (1935):

> If an arrangement changes the whole substratum of the trust, then it may well be that it cannot be regarded merely as varying that trust. But if an arrangement, while leaving the substratum, effectuates the purpose of the original trust by other means, it may still be possible to regard that arrangement as merely varying the original trusts, even though the means employed are wholly different and even though the form is completely changed.

With respect, this is just so much verbiage. The original trust has no 'purpose' besides distributing the beneficial interests in the way it does. Any change in that changes its 'purpose', even if it does so for good reasons, such as to avoid tax. If something like the settlor's wishes is what 'purpose' means, it is clear that the statement is just wrong, since variations may freely defeat those (10.73). What *should be* quoted from Megarry J's decision is the following, which comes a couple of lines later:

> The jurisdiction of the Act is a beneficial one and, in my judgment, the court should construe it widely and not be astute to confine its beneficent operation. I must remember that in essence the court is merely contributing on behalf of infants and unborn and unascertained persons the binding assents to the arrangement which they, unlike an adult beneficiary, cannot give. So far as is proper, the power of the court to give that assent should be assimilated to the wide powers which the ascertained adults have.

Precisely.

FURTHER READING

Brownbill (1992–5)

Goodhart (1996)

Hicks (2001)

Langbein (1994)

Langbein and Posner (1980)

Law Commission (1999)

Law Reform Committee (1982)

Nicholls (1995)

Pollard (2003)

Smith (2003a)

Must-read legislation and cases: Trustee Act 2000, Pts I–IV, Sch 1; *Speight v Gaunt* (1883); *Learoyd v Whitely* (1887); *Nestle v National Westminster Bank plc* (1994); *Bartlett v Barclays Bank Trust Co Ltd* (1979); *Cowan v Scargill* (1984); *Re Holt's Settlement* (1969); *Pilkington v IRC* (1962); *Re Pauling's Settlement Trusts* (1963); *Schmidt v Rosewood Trust Ltd* (2003); *Goulding v James* (1997); *Re Ball's Settlement Trusts* (1986); *Breakspear v Ackland* (2008)

SELF-TEST QUESTIONS

1. The trustees of the substantial funds of the London Ecumenical Christian Church are given by the trust instrument a power to invest in any investments they see fit, subject only 'to their legal duty of prudent investment'. For 15 years they have left half the funds in a building society account, earning a low rate of interest. The remainder has been invested in shares of two companies. The share price of one of the companies has recently dropped by 30 per cent in line with a general collapse in the stock market. The trust has a holding of 55 per cent in the second company. The company has recently gone into receivership following the failure of a speculative venture. The trustees had not known about the venture, and generally took no interest in the company's activities.

    a.   Advise the trustees whether they have committed a breach of their duty of prudent investment.

    b.   Consider to what extent, if at all, the trustees are subject to a duty to ensure that trust funds are not invested in 'unchristian business activities'.

2.   What limitations are there on a trustee's power to delegate his functions? In what circumstances will he be liable for the defaults of his appointed agents?

3.   Bill, aged 14, and Bob, aged 23, are beneficiaries of a testamentary trust under which they are each entitled to a sum of £25,000 contingent upon their attaining the age of 25, and to a half share of a large share portfolio contingent on their attaining the age of 30. To what extent may the trustees use their statutory powers of maintenance and advancement in Bill and Bob's favour?

4.   What differences are there between the rules that govern the variation of trusts (i) to modify the administrative powers of the trustees, and (ii) to alter the beneficial interests?

5.   What powers have (i) the trustees, (ii) the beneficiaries, and (iii) the court, to appoint and remove trustees?

11
Breach of trust

SUMMARY

The array of claims that can arise when a breach of trust occurs

The difference between breach of trust and breach of fiduciary requirements

The trustee's liability to account, the performance interest in a trust, and personal claims against the trustee

Liability of trustees *inter se*

Beneficiaries' consent to a breach of trust

Trustees' relief from liability under Trustee Act 1925, s 61, trustee exemption clauses, and ouster of trustee duties

De facto trusteeship, or trusteeship *de son tort*

Liability for procuring or assisting in a breach of trust

Proprietary remedies for the misapplication of trust property

Tracing

Proprietary claims to traceable proceeds: charges and equitable ownership

Subrogation claims reliant upon tracing

Tracing at common law and the quest for a fiduciary relationship

Personal claims against recipients of trust property or its traceable proceeds: knowing receipt and knowing dealing

Limitation of actions

The array of claims that can arise when a breach of trust occurs

11.1   It is an easy thing to write a breach of trust question for an examination paper. Consider the following: Tim, the trustee of the Smith family trust, breaches the trust by giving £50,000 to Robert, his brother, telling him the money is a gift to help him with his business. Angelica, the branch manager at the bank where the trust's bank account is held, arranges for the payment from the trust account. The money is paid into Robert's business's current account, erasing his overdraft and bringing the balance to £20,000. Robert raises the balance to £25,000 by paying other funds into the account, and then he writes a cheque on the account for £30,000 to pay for new equipment.

11.2   This is clearly a case of breach of trust. The question actually tells you that Tim breached the trust. What are you supposed to say about it? Of course you would first say that Tim is liable for the breach of trust. Indeed, he is *strictly* liable, in the same way that a contracting party is strictly liable for breach of contract. In general the law does not inquire into why, or with what mental state, you breached your contract—whether you did so intentionally, or negligently, or perfectly innocently, trying your best to perform your obligation. And the same is generally true of the trustee in breach. If, for whatever reason or with whatever mental state, the trustee misapplies trust property, ie takes property from the trust and deals with it in a way that is inconsistent with the trust terms, a court of equity will require him to return it to the trust, ie hold it again as a trustee for the beneficiaries. Indeed, using a certain kind of terminology to which equity lawyers are occasionally prone (usually with poor results for the law's clarity and coherence) 'equity will not *hear* the trustee say that he misapplied trust property; it will treat him as if he never committed the misapplication, as if he held the property properly for the beneficiaries all along'. Where a trustee disposes of trust property in breach of trust so that the property is lost, or deals with the trust property in breach of trust so as to cause a loss to the trust fund, for example by making an unauthorised, losing, investment, the trustee will be strictly *personally* liable to restore the trust.

11.3   Understanding the difference between *personal* and *proprietary* liability is vital. If the trustee retains title to trust property, or acquires title to trust property (eg is paid dividends on shares), the beneficiaries are able to say that that property is theirs. Such assets do not form part of the trustee's own assets beneficially. The beneficial interest in them is the beneficiaries' equitable interest under the trust, and so their claim is essentially a 'that's ours' claim, and the court will require the trustee to hold the assets under the terms of the trust. Very much to the contrary, a personal liability does not identify any asset that the trustee has title to that belongs to the trust. In the case of an unauthorised application of the trust property, say transferring shares to his nephew in breach of trust, the trustee should first, if he can, get the very shares back from his nephew to hold them again on trust; secondly, if that is impossible (eg because his nephew has in turn sold the shares to a bona fide purchaser who will not resell them), he should, if he can, buy the same amount of those shares on the market and hold them on trust; and thirdly, if that is impossible (eg because the shares are private company shares which cannot be obtained on the open market), he must find funds from his own resources to pay into the trust the money value of the lost shares, which money he must then hold on trust (see further 11.18). Notice that there are no particular assets of the trustee that, prior to the trustee discharging this personal liability to restore the trust, are allocated to his doing so. There are no assets of the trustee, say a sum in one of his bank accounts, which the beneficiaries are entitled to make him use. Just as with the personal liability to pay a debt, the trustee may discharge the debt with any of the resources that he has, and indeed, with someone else's resources. He might get his brother to provide the required funds to reconstitute the trust, or secure a loan from a bank to do so. Because a debt or any other personal liability is not related to any particular assets of the trustee, if the trustee is insolvent by the time the breach is discovered, the claim that the beneficiaries have that the trustee restore the trust will be treated like any other debt the trustee owes—the beneficiaries will be unsecured creditors (2.89). So whatever else you can say about this fact situation, you can certainly say that Tim will be strictly liable to repay the £50,000 with interest out of his own pocket, but that this claim may be worthless because by the time the breach is discovered, Tim is insolvent.

11.4   But, alas, there is a lot more to be said. We must consider what rights the beneficiaries might have against third parties who may be somehow involved in the breach. One right they have is trivially easy to see: the beneficiaries are, after all, together the owners of the trust property in the eyes of equity, and as with all rights to property, third parties who come into possession of the trust property of others will be liable to the beneficiaries' claim, 'that's ours', and be liable to return it. This is a conceptual 'base-line' truth about equitable rights: they bind everyone except the bona fide purchaser (2.64). So if, for example, Tim had given Robert a trust painting as a birthday present, the beneficiaries could simply say to Robert, 'that's ours' and demand its return. In doing so, the beneficiaries are said to *follow* (2.61) their property into Robert's hands.

11.5 But the law allows them to do more than this: it also allows them to *trace* their equitable interest through substitutions of one kind of property right for another (2.78). The best way to think about tracing is to see how it allows the beneficiaries to continue to have property rights even when their property comes into the hands of a bona fide purchaser for value, or to put this another way, to see how tracing allows the beneficiaries to maintain a *proprietary claim* against Robert in these circumstances. Imagine Robert sells the trust painting to a dealer who gives £10,000 for the painting innocent of the fact that it came to Robert in breach of trust. As a bona fide purchaser, the dealer takes the painting free of the beneficiaries' equitable title. So the beneficiaries cannot follow their trust property, the painting, into the dealer's hands, so have no proprietary claim against him. The dealer's purchase extinguishes their equitable title to the painting. But the law allows them to trace their interest in the painting into the £10,000 that the dealer gave Robert for it—they can point to the £10,000 and say to Robert, 'that is ours'— and the law will give effect to this proprietary claim just as if the £10,000 was money that was originally in the trust. And the beneficiaries can trace from one substitution into another ad infinitum, as long as the evidence permits, or until the property is expended but not in exchange for property, such as if Robert were to spend the £10,000 on a world cruise, or, in the case of chattels (tangible things) the property traced into is destroyed (the wine is drunk, the firewood burned) or loses its identity by becoming fixed to land or to another chattel (the paint is painted onto the house or car). So the first point to take away about the relationship of following and tracing is this—one can follow trust property up to the point it is exchanged for something else with a bona fide purchaser. When you run up against the bona fide purchaser, you must 'double back', as it were, bouncing your claim from the trust property back onto the proceeds of the exchange.

11.6 It is important to realise just how valuable to beneficiaries tracing has become given the world of property in which we now live. Very few modern trusts contain large amounts of tangible property, such as land, or chattels such as paintings, or hold money *in specie*, ie in cash. What they hold are various kinds of financial instruments, such as shares and bonds and bank accounts. These days it is unlikely that beneficiaries are able to follow their property very far, if at all. If it were not for the right to trace, their property rights would be extinguished, often immediately. Consider the opening question. Angelica the bank manager arranges for the payment from the trust account to Robert's business's current account, let us assume by a BACS (Banker's Automated Credit System) transfer, which is the way most employees' money gets into their bank accounts when their employers pay them each month. In such a case, Robert never really receives any trust property at all; there is *nothing* for the beneficiaries to *follow*. What happens (the truth is slightly more complicated) is that under its banking account contract with the trust, the trust's bank agrees to pay Robert's bank £30,000 to credit Robert's account, and is entitled to reduce the trust's bank balance by the same amount; that is, the trust agrees that the trust's bank now owes the trust £30,000 less than it did before (the relationship of banker to account holder is essentially just that of debtor and creditor). In short, then, the transaction is a contractual one where the trust's right against its bank is diminished in order that the trust's bank will buy a new contractual right from Robert's bank for Robert, ie the enhanced balance in Robert's business's current account at his bank. *No title in any property of the trust passes to Robert at all.* Therefore, if there were no right to trace, the beneficiaries' equitable proprietary rights would be immediately extinguished by the very form of the breach.

11.7   The situation is not much better if Tim wrote a cheque for £30,000 on the trust account payable to Robert. The cheque is trust property, so if, before Robert deposits the cheque, the beneficiaries catch up with him, they can follow this trust property into his hands and claim back the cheque as theirs. But as soon as Robert deposits it, Robert's bank will enforce the cheque against the trust's bank, receiving money that it will immediately take as its own, and will credit Robert's account with the same amount. By crediting Robert's account, ie giving Robert a new or enhanced bank balance in his favour, Robert's bank creates a new or enhanced right for Robert—in doing so it gives good value for what it received from the trust's bank by enforcing the cheque, and so the bank is a bona fide purchaser. The beneficiaries must now trace their interest into Robert's enhanced account balance. Thus if you think about how many breaches of trust must involve transfers of money by cheque or through the banking system, you will see how important tracing is.

11.8   In the facts of the question, the trust money pulls Robert's account out of overdraft, and he then draws on the account to buy equipment, putting it into overdraft again. As we will see, tracing into and out of bank accounts raises special problems: where did the money that paid off his overdraft 'go'? As the payment and subsequent transactions with the account 'mix' Robert's money and the trust money, how do we decide which of them owns what? Whose money, or if both their moneys, in what shares, went to pay for the new equipment?

11.9   So far we have looked at Robert in terms of his proprietary liability. That is, we have looked at following and tracing to see when beneficiaries can make a 'that's ours' claim against him. But Robert may also be *personally* liable to restore the trust; that is Robert may be liable to dig into his own pocket to pay back the money value of what he received from the trust, even though he no longer has any of the trust property or its traceable proceeds—he might have blown all the trust money on a world cruise. Robert will be personally liable to dig into his pocket to replace the trust money he received if he spent the money as his own for his own purposes knowing or suspecting that the property came to him in breach of trust or, if after receiving the trust property innocently without any knowledge or suspicion, he later finds out or suspects the money is trust property and then goes ahead and spends it as if it were his own.

11.10   Now what about Angelica? As you can imagine, she is not mentioned just to add some colour to the question. Angelica carries out the transaction that breaches the trust, and in certain circumstances she may be personally liable to restore the trust on the basis that she is an accessory to the breach. Recent decisions have made it clear that accessories will only be liable for assisting a breach of trust if they do so dishonestly.

11.11   So Tom's straightforward little breach of trust, described in a few lines, has led to all of this, all of which you must deal with if you are faced with such an exam question. Before beginning to look at all of this in detail, keep a couple of points in mind. Dealing with breach of trust almost always involves working through, one by one, the array of remedies the beneficiaries may pursue. It is absolutely vital to keep these separate claims, especially proprietary and personal claims, separate.

11.12 Given that this is a large and complex area of the law of trusts, it is best to provide a bit of a roadmap for the rest of this chapter. We will first deal with the trustee's personal liability for breach of trust. A trustee can breach the trust in two basic ways. By far the most important sort of breach of trust occurs where a trustee *misapplies the trust property*. That is the trustee gives the property away to someone who is not a proper object of the trust, as in the transfer to Robert in the opening question, or enters into a contract involving the trust property that is not allowed by the trust terms, say by investing in an unauthorised investment. Secondly, there are breaches by the trustee of his duty to act with care and skill in the administration of the trust that cause the trust loss, such as the claim made in *Nestle* (10.19). Following an examination in detail of the trustee's personal liability, we will look at the various ways in which a trustee may be relieved of liability, such as by the insertion in the trust terms of an exemption clause.

11.13 We shall then consider the case where a third party dishonestly assists in the breach of trust. Such a 'stranger to the trust' (ie a third party, such as Angelica, who is neither a trustee nor a beneficiary) will be jointly and severally liable with the trustee for any loss to the trust caused by the breach. 'Joint and several' liability means that the beneficiary will be entitled to sue either the trustee or the dishonest assistant for the full amount of the loss; if he sues just one of them, that defendant must pay the full amount and is left to bring an action for 'contribution' against the other wrongdoer to recoup a money share from him. From the opening question we can see that Angelica is a candidate for this liability, although it is unclear on the facts whether she is dishonest.

11.14 This is as far as we can go in discussing the array of claims that can arise on a breach of trust without, at last, looking at tracing in detail. So that is what we shall then do. Following that, we can look at the proprietary claims that the beneficiaries can make against the trustee, and those they can make against strangers to the trust who receive trust property, like Robert, and then look at the personal liability of third parties for wrongfully disposing of trust assets they receive.

Wrongs equivalent to breaches of trust

11.15 Some of the cases that apply equity's principles for dealing with breach of trust occur in cases where there is not, strictly speaking, a breach of trust. The most common example is the case where a non-trustee fiduciary, such as an agent or company director, wrongfully exercises his powers to deal with his principal's property, say where a company director embezzles his company's funds. In this case equity will treat the company director as a trustee in breach, and give the company the same sort of remedies as it would to a wronged beneficiary (eg *John v Dodwell & Co* (1918); *Re Duckwari* (1999); *JJ Harrison (Properties) Ltd v Harrison* (2002)). On the 'beneficial interest in the trustee's exercise of his powers of title to the trust property' analysis of the beneficiary's interest under a trust (2.107), this makes perfect sense. Where a company director is empowered to transfer title to the company property this power is only to be exercised for the benefit of the company, and it is a misuse of that power over the property to misapply it, say to transfer it to himself, and equity will impose a constructive trust on him in respect to any misapplied property he receives or on anyone else who receives it, except for a bona fide purchaser. As Kay LJ put it in *Re Lands Allotment Co* (1894):

> *Now, case after case has decided that directors of trading companies are not for all purposes trustees or in the position of trustees, or quasi trustees, or to be treated as trustees in every sense; but if they deal with the funds of a company, although those funds are not absolutely vested in them, but funds which are under their control, and deal with those funds in a manner which is beyond their powers, then as to that dealing they are treated as having committed a breach of trust.*

As a consequence, we will see cases that elaborate the principles of liability for breach of trust but which do not involve trustees at all but, rather, defaulting fiduciaries.

The difference between breach of trust and breach of fiduciary requirements

11.16   If you are able to grasp this difference and bear it in mind when you consider the cases, count yourself as an intellectual of the subject, because far too often judges and commentators make a mess of it (for a number of examples see Mitchell (2013, 2014)). A trustee is strictly liable for breaches of trust, and it does not matter *why* he misapplied the trust property or neglected to invest it properly, whether because he favoured his own interests over the beneficiaries, or because of his incompetence, or for any other reason. As you will recall (2.19) and as we shall examine in detail in Chapter 13, the fiduciary relationship is a very particular and precise relationship imposed upon people who have to use their discretion in making decisions for other people, and may have other duties as well to ensure they are acting in the best interests of their principals, such as the duty to be 'even-handed' between different beneficiaries in investing the trust property (10.3). They breach the requirements of the fiduciary relationship when they fail to act entirely in the interest of their principal, in particular when they act in conflict with their own interests. The point is that if it were not for this fiduciary requirement, their actions would in many cases be perfectly correct. For example, a trustee may have the power to invest the trust property in shares. He does not breach the trust if he sells his own shares to the trust, because the trust terms allow him to invest in shares. What he breaches is the fiduciary requirement, because obviously he will be in a conflict of interest in trying to set a price for the shares—as a trustee he must try to get the shares at the lowest price possible, but as the owner of the shares himself he will try to sell them at the highest price possible. Notice, then, how the fiduciary requirement works—*it turns what would otherwise be a perfectly proper act of the trustee*, this investment in shares, *into an improper act*, because he undertakes it in conflict of interest.

11.17   There is, therefore, no point in referring to any fiduciary relationship if the act was a wrongful one in any event, as for example where the trustee in this case was not allowed to invest in shares at all. There is no *need*, and no *room*, for willy-nilly treating breaches of trust as breaches of fiduciary obligation where the breach is a breach of trust *simpliciter*. For example, if a trustee negligently invests the trust fund so that its value falls, the trustee will be liable for breach of trust, but this is not a breach of the fiduciary requirement, for negligence is not about favouring someone's interest at the expense of the beneficiaries' interests. Judges and commentators often confuse these different sorts of liabilities because, as trustees typically are fiduciaries, they tend to use the words 'trustee' and 'fiduciary' interchangeably, and then go on to call any breach of trust a breach of a fiduciary obligation. As we shall see in Chapter 13, judges such as Lord Millett have now begun to clamp down on this loose usage. NB: in 11.15 we saw that equity will treat cases where a fiduciary transfers his principal's property wrongfully as cases of breach of trust; these cases do *not* turn on breaches of any fiduciary requirement. These, just as much as other cases of breach of trust, turn on the fiduciary doing something that is wrong anyway, for example a company director embezzling his company's funds. But on the rationale canvassed in 11.15, equity will treat these wrongful exercises of the fiduciary's powers over the title to the principal's property as equivalent to breaches of trust.

The trustee's liability to account, the performance interest in a trust, and personal claims against the trustee

11.18   Traditionally, the trustee's 'liability to account' is the starting point for understanding the beneficiary's remedies for breach of trust (see Conaglen (2016); Ho (2016); Mitchell (2013, 2014); Penner (2018a)). This liability flows from the very nature of the trust relationship. The principal task of the trustee is to keep the trust property separate from his own and dispose of it according to the terms of the trust.

11.19   This reflects what might be called the beneficiary's 'performance interest' in the trust (Penner (2018a)). The essence of a trust is that the trustee perform his obligations under the terms of the trust. Trusts are settled in order for the trust obligations to be performed. This is usually the one and only reasons why trusts are created. This performance interest is protected by specific remedies, which require the trustee to do the very thing the trust terms require him to do, ie which grant the beneficiary the very performance due to him under the terms of the trust, and by 'substitutional remedies', by which the trustee is require to do something else, the next best thing, which comes closest to the intended performance.

11.20   These specific and substitutional remedies are provided under the traditional 'accounting process'. In carrying out his trust obligations, the trustee must keep track of what he does with the trust property; this is called 'keeping the trust account(s)' and, as you would imagine, normally involves keeping the documents concerning transactions with the trust property in good order. When a beneficiary suspects that something has gone wrong with the administration of the trust, this is normally because he does not accept the trustee's account, ie his record of what he has done with the trust property, and the beneficiary's primary legal right is to bring the trustee to the Court of Chancery and have 'the account taken', ie reviewed. As Lord Millett NPJ explained in *Libertarian Investments v Hall* (2012):

> 167. It is often said that the primary remedy for breach of trust or fiduciary duty is an
> order for an account, but this is an abbreviated and potentially misleading statement of
> the true position. In the first place an account is not a remedy for wrong. Trustees and
> most fiduciaries are accounting parties, and their beneficiaries or principals do not have

to prove that there has been a breach of trust or fiduciary duty in order to obtain an order for account. Once the trust or fiduciary relationship is established or conceded the beneficiary or principal is entitled to an account as of right. Although like all equitable remedies an order for an account is discretionary, in making the order the court is not granting a remedy for wrong but enforcing performance of an obligation.

168. In the second place an order for an account does not in itself provide the plaintiff with a remedy; it is merely the first step in a process which enables him to identify and quantify any deficit in the trust fund and seek the appropriate means by which it may be made good. Once the plaintiff has been provided with an account he can falsify and surcharge it. If the account discloses an unauthorised disbursement the plaintiff may falsify it, that is to say ask for the disbursement to be disallowed. This will produce a deficit which the defendant must make good, either in specie or in money. Where the defendant is ordered to make good the deficit by the payment of money, the award is sometimes described as the payment of equitable compensation; but it is not compensation for loss but restitutionary or restorative. The amount of the award is measured by the objective value of the property lost determined at the date when the account is taken and with the full benefit of hindsight.

169. But the plaintiff is not bound to ask for the disbursement to be disallowed. He is entitled to ask for an inquiry to discover what the defendant did with the trust money which he misappropriated and whether he dissipated it or invested it, and if he invested it whether he did so at a profit or a loss. If he dissipated it or invested it at a loss, the plaintiff will naturally have the disbursement disallowed and disclaim any interest in the property in which it was invested by treating it as bought with the defendant's own money. If, however, the defendant invested the money at a profit, the plaintiff is not bound to ask for the disbursement to be disallowed. He can treat it as an authorised disbursement, treat the property in which it has been invested as acquired with trust money, and follow or trace the property and demand that it or its traceable proceeds be restored to the trust in specie.

170. If on the other hand the account is shown to be defective because it does not include property which the defendant in breach of his duty failed to obtain for the benefit of the trust, the plaintiff can surcharge the account by asking for it to be taken on the basis of 'wilful default', that is to say on the basis that the property should be treated as if the defendant had performed his duty and obtained it for the benefit of the trust. Since ex hypothesi the property has not been acquired, the defendant will be ordered to make good the deficiency by the payment of money, and in this case the payment of 'equitable compensation' is akin to the payment of damages as compensation for loss.

171. In an appropriate case the defendant will be charged, not merely with the value of the property at the date when it ought to have been acquired or at the date when the account is taken, but at its highest intermediate value. This is on the footing either that the defendant was a trustee with power to sell the property or that he was a fiduciary who ought to have kept his principal informed and sought his instructions.

11.21   Before setting out how this passage shows that the process of taking the account and the making of orders in consequence thereof reflects the performance interest of the beneficiary under the trust, and the specific and substitutional remedies that protect and enforce it against the trustee, a few words must be said about a particular thing Lord Millett says. A beneficiary is entitled to an account as of right, and in pursuing the account, the beneficiary does not have to claim that the trustee has committed a breach of trust. But, obviously, if the account can be falsified or surcharged, and the court provides a remedy in consequence of that, this will be a remedy for a breach of trust, ie for a failing by the trustee to fulfil his trust obligations. Not having to plead a wrong or a breach of trust when the beneficiary initiates the accounting process does not mean that the subsequent claim, to falsify or surcharge the account, doesn't reveal or express that a wrong has taken place. In all cases where the account is falsified or surcharged, it clearly does. What the process of taking the account and the court's subsequent orders *do* is to protect and enforce the performance by the trustee of her obligations under the trust, that is, give effect to the beneficiary's interest in the performance of the trust obligations by the trustee (Mitchell (2014).

11.22   When a misapplication of trust property takes place, such as an unauthorised investment (11.2 et seq), a payment to a person who is not a proper object of the trust, or an excessive or fraudulent appointment (3.83–3.86), the account is 'falsified' and the trustee must 'restore' the trust, which will require one of two things. If possible, the trustee will be required to restore the trust '*in specie*'; that is he must return the very property misapplied, or the same kind of property, to the trust. Thus if the trustee has wrongfully transferred unique property out of the trust, such as land or a chattel such as a valuable painting, the trustee should first try to get that property back. As you can imagine, however, many breaches will involve the trustee's having wrongfully sold the trust property to a bona fide purchaser (2.64), and so it may be unlikely he can restore the trust *in specie*. In the cases of fungible property, such as shares, the trustee will most likely be unable to get back the very shares he wrongfully transferred, but he can go into the market and purchase a like number of the same shares, and if he does this he is regarded as restoring the trust *in specie*. Where the trustee cannot restore the trust *in specie*, he must restore the trust in money, obviously to the value of the misapplied trust property.

11.23   A similar order is made where the beneficiary does not ask for the disbursement to be disallowed, but adopts the trustee's application of the money and claims the proceeds thereof as trust property. The trustee will be subject to an order, a specific remedy, to thereafter hold that very property on trust and bring it into the trust account. Where the trustee cannot restore the trust *in specie*, he must restore the trust in money. An order to restore the trust by way of a money payment is a substitutional remedy.

11.24   In cases where the beneficiary surcharges the account, again, both specific performance and substitutional remedies can be awarded. Since it is sometimes not realised that a surcharging of the account can be met with an order for specific performance, we must consider the different sorts of occasion on which a claim to surcharge the account can arise.

11.25   As Lord Millett explains, a beneficiary surcharges the account when she maintains that the accounts fail to disclose trust assets which, under the terms of the trust and in fulfilment of the trustee's obligations, ought to form part of the trust fund. The right to surcharge the account can arise in a number of circumstances. First, upon taking up the office of trustee, a trustee's first obligation is to acquaint himself with the terms of the trust and 'get in' the trust property. In the case of a testamentary trust where the trustee is not also the deceased's executor, for example, the trustee must ensure that all the assets in the deceased's estate that are assets to be held on trust are transferred by the executor to him. If he fails to do so, the beneficiary can surcharge the account and the trustee will be ordered to get in those assets, by bringing an action against the executor if necessary. The same order for specific performance would be given where a successor trustee fails to get in the assets from his predecessor trustee.

11.26 Another example of this kind, probably infrequent these days, is the case of a covenant to settle after-acquired property on a marriage settlement (8.30 et seq). If the trustee of such a settlement fails to get in such property when it arises, the account can be surcharged and he will be ordered to acquire it, by action against the covenantor if necessary. These orders to get in the trust property are all specific remedies.

11.27 Even so, substitutional remedies are much more likely to arise when the account is surcharged. A few examples suffice to illustrate. In the first place, a trustee must, of course, account for all the income that is due to the trust given the trust investments. A trustee who receives funds, say dividends on trust shares, but fails to bring them into the account, or worse, fails, for example, to collect rent on trust leases, will be required to account for their money value. A trustee would normally have a duty to insure against theft or destruction of valuable chattels which form part of the trust assets. Say he fails to do so and a trust chattel, a valuable painting for instance, is destroyed by fire. Obviously, there will be no insurance payment brought into account, for there was no insurance. By way of a substitutionary remedy, the trustee will be required to pay money from his own pocket to make up for the missing insurance payment (minus the premiums that he would have paid and which would have appeared on the debit side of the account). Where a trustee has a power of investment with regard to the trust assets, he must comply with the relevant terms of the trust and invest with reasonable care (10.2). Where he fails to do so, and the trust assets suffer a fall in value as a consequence, the beneficiary can surcharge the account, and the trustee will again be subject to a subsitutionary order, to resort to his own resources to pay money into the trust fund to make up the deficiency.

11.28 There is one further feature of understanding the beneficiaries' remedy for breach of trust as invoking the trustee's liability to account: the only interest of the beneficiaries that the trustee's liability to account protects is their interest in the value of, or in the specific property in, the trust fund. It does not allow the beneficiaries any claim for *consequential loss* that they suffer which follows from the trust's being 'short of funds' owing to the breach. Take the following example: Because of the trustee's misapplication of the trust property, say making an unauthorised investment, Hazel, the income beneficiary, receives half the income in 2014 than she would have done if the authorised investment was retained. Let us also assume that Hazel can establish, on the standard 'but for' test of causation, that but for this reduction in her income she would have been able to make a profitable investment herself; instead, because of the reduced income, she could not afford it, and so can prove that the trustee's breach caused her a loss of profits. Has she any claim for this loss against the trustee? Not by way of account. By falsifying the trust account her only claim is to have the trust restored, and this will include an amount of money to ensure that she receives the missing income for 2014, plus interest. But can she 'go outside the account' and claim her consequential loss on some broader notion of the trustee's breach of trust? That would require founding a claim that would not be traditionally conceived of either as falsifying or surcharging the account, because the loss claimed is not a loss to the trust funds. No such claim has ever been argued for in any decided case (though see Glister (2014a) for a discussion about whether such a claim should be available).

11.29 At first this might seem unjust, but it is submitted that it is not. Whilst a beneficiary is entitled to ensure that she receives all the distributions from the trust fund to which she is entitled, a trust fund which has all the property in it which it should, which is what the right to falsify and surcharge the account ensures, she should not be entitled to recover any losses she suffers in her own personal affairs because she relied upon receiving such and such a distribution on a timely basis. If you have studied the law of torts, you will recognise the issue here as one about a wrongdoer's liability for consequential economic loss, or 'pure' economic loss as it is sometimes put. In general, tortfeasors are not liable to their victims for economic loss that does not directly follow from damage to the victim's person or to his tangible property. Why this is so, why a tortfeasor is not subjected to unlimited liability for all the economic losses his victim suffers that can be shown to flow from his wrong, is a controversial issue, but following Stevens (2007, chs 1–3), in the opinion of your author the most satisfactory rationale is this: the law does not protect your liberty to exploit economic opportunities for profit. It *indirectly* protects this liberty by prohibiting interferences to your person and property and, in this case, by allowing you to claim distributions under a trust to which you are entitled. But the law does not make anyone, including wrongdoers, *insurers* of your economic well-being, even if their wrongful actions alter to your detriment the economic context in which you operate. So the question in this case is whether a trustee owes his beneficiaries a duty (presumably a duty of care) to ensure that he makes distributions of the right amounts on time under the terms of the trust such that he is liable to them for any consequential losses that might eventuate if he does not (beyond any amounts of interest the beneficiaries will receive for late distributions). It is submitted that there is no good reason to impose such a duty, at least in the case of traditional trusts in which the benefits the beneficiary receives are by way of gift from the settlor; the trustee should not be liable for consequential losses you suffer because you receive the correct amount of a gift late (see Penner 2018a).

11.30   As we have seen, the beneficiary need not falsify the account if the trustee enters into *a profitable unauthorised transaction*. About this Millett (Millett 1998a) says:

> If the unauthorised investment has appreciated in value, then the beneficiary will be content with it. He is not obliged to falsify the account which the trustee renders; he can always accept it. (It goes without saying that the trustee cannot simply 'borrow' the trust money to make a profitable investment for his own account and then rely on the fact that the investment was unauthorised to avoid bringing the transaction into account.) Where the beneficiary accepts the unauthorised investment, he is often said to affirm or adopt the transaction. That is not wholly accurate. The beneficiary has a right to elect, but it is really a right to decide whether to complain or not.

11.31   The PC in *Tang Man Sit v Capacious Investments Ltd* (1996) reviewed the law governing a plaintiff's election of alternative remedies, and Lord Nicholls stated:

> The basic principle governing when a plaintiff must make his choice is simple and clear. He is required to choose when, but not before, judgment is given in his favour and the judge is asked to make orders against the defendant . . . In the ordinary course, by the time the trial is concluded the plaintiff will know which remedy is more advantageous to him . . . Occasionally, this may not be so . . . A plaintiff may not know how much money the defendant has made from the wrongful use of his property. It may be unreasonable to require the plaintiff to make his choice without further information. To meet this difficulty, the court may make discovery and other orders designed to give the plaintiff the information he needs, and which in fairness he ought to have, before deciding upon his remedy.

11.32　The requirement of election is clearly to prevent the beneficiary from having it both ways—he cannot both 'adopt' the trustee's act that turns out to be profitable, and also claim damages for a loss on the footing that he wishes to disallow the transaction. Where he elects to falsify the account, the trustee must restore the trust to the position it would have been in, but for the breach, at the time the court gives its judgment (*Re Bell's Indenture* (1980)).

11.33　Each beneficiary is entitled to elect individually whether to falsify the account or adopt the unauthorised transaction in respect of the loss or gain to his own interest under the trust. (In the case of minor beneficiaries, counsel for them or their representative in the action, called a 'guardian *ad litem*' or 'litigation friend', elects for them.) For example, where an unauthorised transaction benefits the life tenant but harms the capital beneficiary, the capital beneficiary can choose to falsify the account and make the trustee liable for the loss to the value of the capital interest (*Dimes v Scott* (1828); 11.43). However, beneficiaries have no individual right to allow the trustee to *continue* keeping the property in a state that is in breach of trust, say in investments not allowed by the trust terms. The trustee's primary duty is to carry out the terms of the trust, and so when a breach comes to light, unless the beneficiaries are all *sui juris* and consent to the unauthorised investment, the trustee must 'realise' it, ie dispose of it and apply the money to an authorised investment (*Wright v Morgan* (1926); *Re Jenkins and Randall & Co's Contract* (1903)). Otherwise, as Swinfen-Eady J pointed out in *Re Jenkins*, a trustee could never remedy a breach of trust by disposing of an unauthorised asset and replacing it with an authorised one unless he got the consent of all the beneficiaries, and he could never do that where any were minors, for minors cannot give valid consent (see also 10.65 (variation of trusts) and 11.72 (beneficiary consent in advance to a breach of trust)).

The personal liability of the trustee when the account is surcharged or falsified

11.34　As we have already seen (11.3), it is vital to distinguish between a person's personal and proprietary liability; where a trust is surcharged or falsified, the trustee's liability is *personal*. It can be nothing else where the account is surcharged, because the trustee can have no property in his hands that the beneficiaries can claim as their own if the loss does not involve a misapplication of trust property. One typically surcharges the account where the trustee *failed* to do something, such as invest the trust funds with care, or insure the trust property, and this failure causes loss. The only way the trustee can make up the loss is by digging into his own funds or, for example, borrowing some money from someone else; he thus has a purely *personal* obligation to pay. But the same kind of liability arises when the account is falsified. The particular transfer of trust property is falsified, and the trustee has either a personal obligation to pay money or by some other means to get the trust property back in order to restore the trust *in specie*, or a personal obligation to pay money out of his own pocket to restore the money value of the misapplied property. So in no case does surcharging or falsifying the account give rise to any proprietary liability against anyone. Only when the beneficiary 'adopts' the trustee's misapplication of the trust property in some form or other does any proprietary liability arise, as we shall see (11.147). Moreover, this personal liability to account must be situated in context to the other claims that might be available to a beneficiary, which we have already seen. Recall that a trustee who 'excessively' exercises a power of appointment or one who commits a fraud on a power (3.83), in fact does nothing, in the sense that the 'exercise' of the power, going beyond the scope of the power, is invalid from the outset. In such a case when, pursuant to the invalid exercise of the power, the trustee distributes property to the purported object of the power, the trustee misapplies the trust property. A distribution on the invalid exercise of power is straightforwardly an unauthorised distribution, and the beneficiary can falsify the account. But we have also seen that a distribution under a valid exercise of a power of appointment is voidable, and can be set aside by the court (3.62) if the trustee breached a duty in the exercise of a power, for example because the power was exercised on the basis of a sufficiently serious mistake as to its effect or consequence. This does not involve the falsification or the surcharging of the account. By setting aside the transaction, the trust is put into the position that it would have been in had the power not been exercised in the way that it was. This may involve a claim against third parties to recover trust property but the trustee in such a case is not liable personally to restore the trust, unless the property is irrecoverable.

'Equitable compensation' for breach of trust in contrast to equitable compensation for breach of a fiduciary duty

11.35   In certain cases, a trustee who commits a breach of trust is ordered to pay money directly to the beneficiaries because there is no point in reconstituting the trust fund itself. An example, which you will recall from 9.48, is the case of the bare trust with mandate under which a solicitor holds funds prior to the completion of a purchase of land. Imagine such a solicitor pays those funds away in breach of trust. The beneficiary, the would-be purchaser whose money has not gone to buy the land as he intended, will obviously falsify the account. The solicitor will be liable to dig into his own pocket to replace the money paid away, but there is usually no point in his paying money back into his client trust account for the beneficiary, because at this stage the land purchase transaction will probably be irredeemably compromised by the solicitor's breach, and the beneficiary would be unlikely to want this solicitor to complete the land purchase in any event. The beneficiary will simply want the money paid to him directly. A similar sort of case arises where the trustee, before misapplying the property, ought to have paid the entirety of the trust funds to the beneficiaries, if, for example, where the trust was for A for life and then to B, and A has died. The trustee would then hold the funds for B absolutely (2.13). Again, then, there is no point in the trustee's reconstituting the trust with a money payment; rather, he should pay B directly. In cases where a trustee pays his beneficiaries directly to make up for his default, he has been said to make 'equitable compensation' to the beneficiaries. The idea is that the beneficiaries are compensated directly for the loss of their interest under the trust (see also Conaglen (2016), 146–50). Similarly, in certain cases a fiduciary who has breached his fiduciary obligations will be liable directly to his principal for causing him loss (13.129–13.132), and is said to pay 'equitable compensation' for his breach of fiduciary duty. An example would be where a solicitor, in conflict of interest, advises his client to make an investment that falls in value. The solicitor will be made to compensate his client directly, and again, this is called equitable compensation. Nevertheless, it is important to understand that these cases are distinct. Though all cases where equity imposes a liability to pay an individual or individuals may be referred to as cases of 'equitable compensation', as Millett LJ does at 11.36, in the former case the trustee's liability is measured in exactly the same way as would be his liability to restore the trust under his liability to account. In the latter case, just as in the case of a tort, the fiduciary's liability is measured by the loss to the principal caused by the breach, and has nothing to do with any diminution in value of any trust fund he held for his principal. Sometimes the former version of equitable compensation is called 'substitutive' (the compensation serves as a substitute for the misapplied asset) or 'restorative'

compensation (the compensation restores the trust fund to distinguish if from the latter 'rep-
arative' compensation (the compensation repairs the loss to the beneficiary)). You, however,
should not worry overmuch about applying this terminology, so long as you understand that
the liability 'to make equitable compensation' has different grounds in the two cases, but your
author felt obliged to mention all of this so that you can make some sense of academic and
judicial writings that bandy around the term 'equitable compensation' without telling you that
it means different things in different contexts.

The measure of liability in cases where the account is surcharged

11.36   In *Bristol and West Building Society v Mothew* (1996), Millett LJ said:

> Equitable compensation for breach of the duty of skill and care resembles common
> law damages in that it is awarded by way of compensation to the plaintiff for his loss.
> There is no reason in principle why the common law rules of causation, remoteness of
> damage and measure of damages should not be applied by analogy in such a case. It
> should not be confused with equitable compensation for breach of fiduciary duty
> which may be awarded in lieu of rescission *[ie instead of a contract being set aside for
> self dealing (13.92 et seq)]* or specific restitution *[ie instead of an order to return specific
> property taken from the trust, where, for example, the property is no longer in existence].*
> *[Emphasis added.]*

Note the first two sentences of this quotation. In the case of a trustee's negligence, in principle
he should be liable for the loss due to his negligence, in exactly the same way that any person
committing the tort of negligence is liable for money 'damages' to his victim. There is no reason
why any special 'equitable' rules of causation ought to apply, because the wrong is the same as
the tort of negligence at common law. Negligence is negligence. But, as we shall see (11.37 et
seq), some very particular (and in certain cases, arguably unjust) rules of causation, ie the rules
that establish whether a particular loss should be attributed to the defendant's breach of duty,
apply when the court determines a person's liability to restore the trust in cases of falsifying the
account, and Millett LJ is rightly warning not to confuse the two situations.

11.37   Where an investment loss is caused by the trustee's negligence, the problem is to determine what
the trust property would have been worth if it had not been for his negligence. In *Nestle* (10.19),
the plaintiff beneficiary failed to prove that the trust company's negligent misunderstanding of the
trust instrument caused any loss; had she done so, however, Dillon LJ said *obiter* that the trustee
would have to pay 'fair' compensation, ie an amount sufficient to restore the trust fund to a value it
would have achieved if a proper investment policy had been followed, 'not just the minimum that
might just have got by without challenge'.

The measure of liability where the account is falsified

11.38   Where trust money is misapplied in breach of trust, in principle the calculation of loss is easy,
because the loss is simply the value of the trust property misapplied. If the trustee cannot restore
the actual trust property *in specie*, what he must pay is simply the value of that property plus
interest. The issue becomes much more complex and controversial, however, where a breach of
trust happened sometime before the beneficiaries realised a breach had occurred and took action

against the trustees. We can begin to approach this issue re-quoting the last two sentences from Lord Millett's discussion in *Libertarian Investments*, above:

> In an appropriate case the defendant will be charged, not merely with the value of the property at the date when it ought to have been acquired or at the date when the account is taken, but at its highest intermediate value. This is on the footing either that the defendant was a trustee with power to sell the property or that he was a fiduciary who ought to have kept his principal informed and sought his instructions.

Lord Millett NPJ does not cite any authority for this proposition, but authority there most assuredly is.

11.39   In such cases the rules of causation appear to make the trustee liable for all risks that attend the ownership of the property involved in the unauthorised transaction. In *Clough v Bond* (1838), Cottenham LC put it this way:

> It will be found to be the result of all the best authorities on the subject, that, although a [trustee], acting strictly within the line of his duty, and exercising reasonable care and diligence, will not be responsible for the failure or depreciation of the fund . . . yet if that line of duty not be strictly pursued, and any part of the property be invested by such [trustee] in funds or upon securities not authorised, or be put within the control of persons who ought not to be instructed with it, and loss be thereby eventually sustained, such personal representative will be liable to make it good, however unexpected the result, however little likely to arise from the course adopted, and however free such conduct may have been from any improper motive.

So, for example, if, in breach of trust, the trustee spends trust money on a painting, the beneficiaries can elect either to falsify the account or adopt the purchase of the painting. If the painting is stolen, then obviously they will falsify the account and demand that the trustee restore the money wrongfully spent on the painting. This makes perfect sense, because the trustee created the risk of the theft by purchasing a chattel that could be stolen.

11.40   But consider a case where, in breach of trust, the trustee sells one of a trust's collection of paintings and, shortly thereafter, all of the trust's paintings are stolen through no fault of the trustee's. The loss of all these paintings will be a loss to the trust, but the trustee will not be liable for the loss occurred through no fault of his. (Normally, of course, in a case like this the paintings would be insured against theft, but ignore that for the moment.) The beneficiaries now discover the breach. If the trustee has made a *good* bargain on the sale of the painting, they will of course adopt the transaction and require the trustee to hold the proceeds of the sale as trust money. But what if the trustee made a bad bargain, or the painting has risen in value, so that the present value of the painting is, say, £100,000, while the proceeds were only £50,000? The beneficiaries will falsify the account, impugning the trustee's sale of the trust painting, and demanding he restore its full value to the trust. (In 'accounting' terms, the £50,000 proceeds of sale will be treated as the trustee's own, and he will be required to pay £100,000 as the value of the painting; in practical terms, then, the trustee will have to add £50,000 in new money in addition to the £50,000 proceeds of the sale that he accounted for to the trust at the time of sale.) But notice that this falsification claim states, in theoretical or accounting terms, that the trustee never sold the painting; the beneficiaries 'falsify' the sale of the painting. So why, then, cannot the trustee, using the rules of causation that would normally apply at common law, argue that he need pay nothing in compensation, because had he continued to hold the painting on trust, it would have been stolen with all the others? In other words, if the beneficiaries choose to falsify the sale, must they then not accept all the logical consequences of that? In short, why should the trustee not argue that the trust lost nothing because of his breach; indeed the trust is £50,000 better off than it would have been, because the trust at least has the proceeds of the sale? Unfortunately, the cases do not all speak with one voice, but it is unlikely that this argument will be accepted. When the beneficiaries falsify the account, the court will regard the trustee as having the painting in his possession, which he must either restore *in specie* or pay the full value of; subsequent events such as the theft will not be taken into account to reduce his liability.

11.41 The principles under consideration here relate specifically to the risks and subsequent events concerning what happens to property and its value for the purpose of determining its 'replacement cost', ie the amount of money a trustee must pay to restore the trust when it is falsified. In other words certain questions about what happens later, or the probability of things happening later, may in certain cases, such as in a case of a continuing breach, be relevant for determining the value of a substitutional award which adequately reflects the beneficiary's performance interest in the trust.

11.42 The nineteenth-century cases waver about what ought to be done where a trustee, instead of investing the trust property as he should, wrongly transfers the property to a third party on the terms of a loan, or holds onto property instead of investing it. In *Watts v Girdlestone* (1843) the trustees lent the money to a beneficiary instead of properly investing it in real property or government stock. The court held that they were liable to restore the trust as if they had invested the property in the most favourable investment they could have made. They therefore had to pay the difference between what they received back on the loan from the beneficiary and what they would have earned investing in government stock. By contrast, in *Shepard v Mouls* (1845) the trustees wrongfully allowed one trustee to personally take the trust funds on payment of interest. Some of the beneficiaries complained, and argued, as in *Watts*, that the trustees should be charged with the difference between the interest they were paid and what they would have earned if they had made the most favourable investment they were authorised to make. Here, however, the court decided against the beneficiaries, arguing that the trustees, having a discretion in how they might invest the funds, could not be charged with the returns they would have earned on any particular investment. One can see how allowing beneficiaries to charge the trustees in this way might be unfair in certain circumstances. It would not be fair to trustees who were allowed to invest in shares, but did not, to allow the beneficiaries to say, with the full benefit of hindsight, that they should have invested in shares of some company that had done spectacularly well in the meantime. On the other hand it is a principle of the law that a wrongdoer should not benefit from uncertainties, whether of evidence or causation, ie of what might have been, which are due to his own wrongdoing (see eg *Armory v Delamirie* (1722)). Today, it is most likely that the courts would follow the approach stated by Dillon LJ in *Nestle* (11.37); the courts should try fairly to assess what the trustees might reasonably have earned by properly investing.

11.43 A different issue arose in *Dimes v Scott* (1828). The trustees, in breach of trust, held onto an unauthorised investment in an East India Company bond for ten years, which paid 10 per cent interest per annum on its face value, whereas they should have invested the money in 3 per cent Consols, government securities that paid 3 per cent interest per annum on their face value. At the end of the ten-year period the trustees did what they ought to have done in the first place, and sold the East India bond and purchased 3 per cent Consols. The trust was for a life tenant, who received the interest on the trust investments, and one remainderman, who had the interest in the capital (3.33). The remainderman falsified the account, because at first glance it seemed obvious that the life tenant had benefited from the breach at the remainderman's expense, receiving a rate of 10 per cent interest on the unauthorised investment, whereas if the trust had been properly carried out, she would have received only 3 per cent interest on the authorised investment and, normally, this would have indicated that the East India bond was a poorer capital investment. The claim against the trustees, therefore, was that they should be liable to restore what the trustees had wrongly paid out to the life tenant, ie the difference between what she was actually paid in interest on the East India bond and what she would have received from the 3 per cent Consols. However, as it turned out, when the trustees actually converted the East India bond into Consols, albeit ten years late, the price of Consols was much lower than it was ten years earlier, and so they were able to buy more Consols with the same amount of money. Thus the unauthorised investment turned out to be good for all concerned: the life tenant benefited for ten years from the higher rate of interest payments, and the remainderman ended up with more Consols as the capital of the trust than he would have done if the trustees had converted the investment at the outset. Nevertheless, when this was discovered, the remainderman maintained his claim. He argued that the trustees should still be liable for the overpayments to the life tenant (had the investment been properly converted ten years earlier the life tenant would have received about £1,000 less), and should not be able to take any credit for the 'accidental' increase in value of the capital fund owing to their mistake. The trustees argued, quite reasonably, that the remainderman could not have it both ways; he should not both 'adopt' the failure to convert in order to get the benefit of the mistake in terms of the increased capital value while at the same time falsify the account to recoup the overpayment to the life tenant. The Lord Chancellor Lord Lyndhurst decided in favour of the remainderman, and the trustees were required to pay into the trust the £1,000 the life tenant was 'overpaid'. This case is generally regarded as harsh, and points out how the equitable rules of causation for loss arguably do not properly take into account the actual facts, or indeed, the logic of the beneficiaries' electing to falsify or adopt an unauthorised transaction.

11.44 A number of other cases, besides *Watts*, support the view that a trustee may be liable for the highest interim value of the trust property between the initial breach and the time when the account is taken (*Nant-y-glo and Blaina Ironworks Co. v Grave* (1878); *McNeil v Fultz* (1906) (Supreme Court of Canada); *Re Dawson* (1966); *Guerin v The Queen* (1984) Supreme Court of Canada; see also *Michael v Hart* (1902), 488; cf *Shepard v Mouls* (1845); *Fales v Canada Permanent Trust Co.* (1977) Supreme Court of Canada). Lord Millett says this is on the 'footing' that the trustee had a power to sell the property or that he was a fiduciary who ought to have kept his principal informed and sought his instructions. It is not clear that any of the cases turned on the latter consideration, but as regards the former, that the trustee had a power to sell the property, this is normally framed somewhat differently, in terms of the trustee having the opportunity to realise the value of the unauthorised asset through the period of continuing breach.

11.45 Furthermore, it seems that the traditional view is that so long as the trustee was in such a position, he is not entitled to avoid the liability to reconstitute the trust at the highest interim value by arguing that, but for the breach, the asset would not have been realised at that value in any case. Thus, a normal principle of 'but for' causation is denied to a trustee in the case of this valuation exercise. As the point was put by Nicholas Stewart QC in *Jaffray v Marshall* (1993):

... in cases of continuing breach of trust by a failure to restore trust property, it is not necessary for the plaintiff to establish by evidence what would have happened if there had been no breach of trust. In fact they go further. It is not, apparently, open to the defendant to adduce such evidence, either ...[1290H]

The underlying point of the authorities seems to be that the breach of trust has deprived the party who ought to have had the assets throughout the relevant period of the opportunity of realising them at any point he chose. Evidence may have to be considered to see whether that opportunity was there at all; . . . But if the opportunity was there at every point during the continuing breach of trust, the defaulting party must make compensation on the footing of the lost value of the opportunity at its highest point. [1293B–C]

I do not see a distinction in principle between shares and other types of property. They are different in the sense that shares generally have no use to a trust except as a pure investment, whereas a house which provided a residence [in this case] fulfilled the basic purpose behind the trust and was in a sense only secondarily an investment. But each type of property is nevertheless a trust investment and the opportunity of selling it is normally there at any time. [1293E]

This reasoning is supported by the *Armory* 'wrongdoer principle' (11.42), and this principle was clearly applied in the Canadian Supreme Court case of *McNeil v Fultz* (1906) to require a defendant treated as a trustee of securities to pay an award calculated on the assumption that he would have sold the securities at the highest price obtainable during the period of his continuing breach.

11.46 It is fair to say that the nineteenth-century authorities do not provide a consistent guide, and may not survive the reasoning of the HL in *Target Holdings Ltd v Redferns* (1996) and the UKSC in *AIB Group v Mark Redler & Co* (2014) (11.53 et seq). In *Target*, Lord Browne-Wilkinson refused to follow *Jaffray* and the report says the case was 'over-ruled', but with respect, the judge in *Jaffray*, Nicholas Stewart QC, was unfairly characterised by Lord Browne-Wilkinson as having 'wrongly applied' 'the principles applicable in an action for an account of profits' 'to a claim for compensation for breach of trust'. He did no such thing. Lord Browne-Wilkinson also mischaracterised the claim in *Nant-y-glo* as a claim for an account of profits.

11.47 This is not to defend each of the rules set out by Nicholas Stewart QC, in particular the rule that the presumption that the investment would have been realised at its highest interim price is irrebuttable, ie that no evidence can be led by the trustee in order to rebut it. That was clearly the holding that sunk the trustee in *Jaffray*. The point is that, in the valuation exercise to determine the extent of the trustee's liability, the beneficiary has not been traditionally limited to his provable loss, nor to the trustee's provable gain, and this makes sense if the purpose of the valuation exercise is to determine the value of his performance interest under the trust. In these circumstances, it seems inevitable that in some cases some presumptions (rebuttable or not) will be necessary to ensure that a trustee restores the trust on a basis that is fair to the beneficiary.

11.48 In *Target* a solicitor of the firm Redferns acted both for Target Holdings, a mortgage lender, and Crowngate, a prospective purchaser of land (a standard bare trust with mandate (9.48)). Unbeknownst to Target, Crowngate was the final purchaser in a fraudulent land transfer scheme calculated to make the land appear much more valuable than it actually was: land purchased for £775,000 by one intermediary company was to be sold to another intermediary for £1.25m, which would then be sold to Crowngate for £2m. The solicitor was apparently fully aware of this series of transactions. Target agreed to lend Crowngate £1.5m for the final purchase in return for a mortgage over the land. Target transferred the loan money to Redferns in advance of completion on instruction to pay the money to Crowngate for the purchase in return for an execution of a charge over the land in Target's favour. In breach of this instruction, the solicitor transferred the money to the two intermediary companies in furtherance of the series of purchases. He communicated to the lender and lied, saying the transaction had been properly completed. However, the final sale to Crowngate was eventually completed and the charge in Target's favour secured. Crowngate became insolvent and, as mortgagee, Target sold the land; it fetched only £500,000. Target sued Redferns for breach of trust for paying away the loan money in breach of its instructions. In the CA Target successfully won summary judgment against Redferns for the entire £1.5m paid away less the £500,000 realised on the sale, even though, despite the breach, Target was in the same position it would have been in had the money been paid according to its instructions, since Target did receive a charge on the correct land for its loan advance of £1.5m. The reasoning advanced by the CA was that, having paid away the £1.5m in breach of trust, there was then an immediate loss to the trust of that amount, for which Redferns became immediately liable, and remained liable, to make good.

11.49   The HL reversed the decision of the CA. Lord Browne-Wilkinson, with whose opinion all their Lordships agreed, stated that both at common law and in equity the principles of compensation for loss are fundamentally the same—a plaintiff may only recover for a loss caused by a defendant's wrongful act, and the compensation is calculated to put the plaintiff in the position he would have been in but for the defendant's wrong. This principle might be called the 'compensatory principle', the principle that the plaintiff is only entitled to consequential losses caused by the breach. He further stated that the rules governing causation of loss and remoteness of damage differ between the common law claim for damages and a claim for equitable compensation:

> Even if the immediate cause of the loss is the dishonesty or failure of a third party, the trustee is liable to make good that loss to the trust estate if, but for the breach, such loss would not have occurred . . . Thus the common law rules of remoteness of damage and causation do not apply. However there does have to be some causal connection between the breach of trust and the loss to the trust estate for which compensation is recoverable, viz the fact that the loss would not have occurred but for the breach . . . Equitable compensation for breach of trust is designed to achieve exactly what the word compensation suggests: to make good a loss in fact suffered by the beneficiaries and which, using hindsight and common sense, can be seen to have been caused by the breach.

11.50   On these principles, Target obtained exactly what it would have obtained had there been no breach of trust, and so was entitled to no compensation. Target was, of course, entitled to pursue its claim that the solicitor had fraudulently procured the transaction by failing to inform Target of the deceitful series of sales; if that claim were successful Target would be able to claim the full value of the money paid away minus the money it received in the sale of the property, because, but for *that wrong*, ie the fraud, it would never have entered into the transaction at all. The HL restored the original order of the first instance judge that gave Redferns leave to defend against this claim only on the payment of £1m into court.

11.51 The decision can be criticised. The court seemed to assume that the rules for 'equitable compensation' applied in the same way to all cases of breach of trust. But as we have seen (11.36), different rules, in particular rules about causation, would appear to apply in cases where the account is surcharged, and where the account is falsified because trust property is misapplied. As Millett LJ (1998a) speaking extrajudicially points out:

> The solicitor held the plaintiff's money in trust for the plaintiff but with its authority to lay it out in exchange for an executed mortgage and the documents of title. He paid it away without obtaining these documents. This was an unauthorised application of trust money which entitled the plaintiff to falsify the account. The disbursement must be disallowed and the solicitor treated as accountable as if the money were still in his client account and available to be laid out in the manner directed. It was later so laid out. The plaintiff cannot object to the acquisition of the mortgage or the disbursement by which it was obtained; it was an authorised application of what must be treated as trust money. To put the point another way; the trustee's obligation to restore the trust property is not an obligation to restore it in the very form in which he disbursed it, but an obligation to restore it in any form authorised by the trust.

11.52 On Millett LJ's view, then, there was no loss not because the rules of causation indicated there was none, but because the misapplication was fully corrected when the trust was properly restored according to its terms. Edelman (2010), 128, has disputed Millett's reasoning, arguing that unless Target authorised or ratified the subsequent getting in of the mortgage with full knowledge of the facts, the solicitor should have remained liable. In line with Millett's criticism, Mitchell (2013, 2014) argues that in *Target* and in some following cases, the court appears to have confused the nature of the trustee's liability in cases of misapplied funds (cases of falsifying the account) with cases of surcharging, where though not misapplying trust funds, the trustee's breach of duty results in a loss to the value of the trust fund. In both cases the trustee breaches a duty, and the courts seemed to have reasoned that determining the extent of the liability should be the same in all cases of breach (see eg *Hulbert v Avens* (2003), applying the reasoning in *Target*).

11.53 The reasoning of Lord Browne-Wilkinson in *Target* was recently endorsed by the UKSC in *AIB Group v Mark Redler & Co* (2014). In 2006 the defendant solicitors were instructed by the claimant lender, AIB Group, who wished to lend £3.3m taking a first mortgage over land of the borrowers valued at £4.25m. The land was already subject to a prior mortgage from Barclays Bank of about £1.5m, which secured two different loan accounts of the borrowers, one of about £1.23m and the other of about £270,000. Prior to the date when this transaction was to take place, the solicitors erroneously overlooked the second smaller loan account, and therefore paid Barclays £1.23m. As Barclays' outstanding loan balance on the second loan account was not discharged, it did not release its security over the borrower's land, although now, of course, it only secured an indebtedness of about £270,000. The remaining funds, about £2.1m, were paid to the borrowers. For about two years, nothing much further happened, but in 2008 AIB Group negotiated with Barclays to allow it to have a second mortgage on the land to secure the loan of £3.3m to the borrower. The borrowers subsequently defaulted on its repayments, and the land was sold. The housing market had declined and the house only fetched about £1.2m, and so after paying the outstanding debt to Barclays, roughly £300,000, AIB Group recovered only £900,000.

11.54 The CA held that because of the solicitor's failure to discharge the prior mortgage, the entire outlay by the solicitors of AIB Group's £3.3m was a breach of trust, on the basis that obtaining a valid discharge of the prior mortgage (or obtaining a solicitor's undertaking from the prior mortgagee's solicitors that the mortgage would be discharged upon receipt of the payment) was a condition for paying out any funds at all. This finding was not appealed. Applying general principles of causation for loss as Lord Browne-Wilkinson did in *Target*, the UKSC held the solicitors liable only for the £300,000 the lender paid to clear Barclays' prior mortgage; even if there had been no breach and both prior mortgages had been cleared, the house would still have sold for only £1.2m because of the decline in the housing market, so AIB Group's loss owing to the breach on this 'but for' test of causation was only the £300,000-odd needed to discharge the outstanding mortgage. Whilst the result may seem, at first glance, roughly right, the reasoning of both Lords Toulson and Reed is unsatisfactory in several respects. (For an exacting analysis of the judges' reasons, see Davies (2015b) see also Conaglen (2016); Edelman (2017).) In the first place, neither clearly explained why the claimant was disentitled from falsifying the account. The court focused on determining whether *Target* was rightly decided but they did not squarely address the criticisms made of the case (11.51–11.52). Nor did they make it clear what the scope of the decision was, that is, it is not clear whether a beneficiary is now barred in all cases from falsifying the account so that the trustee's liability is to be determined on that basis, or whether only in certain cases ('commercial' cases?).

11.55 The resulting *ratio decidendi* seems to be the following: in certain circumstances, very unclearly specified (a 'commercial' context?), a beneficiary of a trust will be disentitled from falsifying the account—the unauthorised expenditure will be regarded as an expenditure of the beneficiary's funds for the beneficiary's purposes. However the trustee's breach in expending the funds on an unauthorised asset will, on the other hand, amount to a wrong sufficient to support a claim to surcharge the account, so that if the expenditure as wrongly made causally gives rise to a lower asset value than would have been obtained had the intended, authorised, asset been acquired, the trustee will be liable for the difference.

11.56 It is submitted that the better analysis of the case is this: on the disbursement of the funds, AIB Group were entitled to falsify the account because the disbursement was a misapplication of the trust money. However, it is also clear that AIB Group, when informed of the situation, proceeded to accept the disbursement, and proceeded on its own to negotiate with Barclays ultimately to acquire Barclays' consent to the second charge over the property in question to secure the full value of its loan to the borrowers. By pursuing off its own bat the second charge with Barclays, they proceeded on the basis that it was indeed their money that went to Barclays to pay off its prior mortgage, thus making it impossible for the solicitors to restore the account. In other words, at this stage they *adopted* the solicitors' expenditure of the funds as a valid expenditure of the trust moneys. At this stage they reasoned (as it turned out, wrongly), that there was sufficient value in the property to serve as security for the borrowers' entire indebtedness. On this analysis the solicitors should not have been liable at all, for the expenditure, though the breach, was effectively consented to or ratified after the fact (11.72–11.75; agency law would take the same view (Watts 2016)).

11.57 The only further question to ask is whether AIB Group could have consented to the expenditure in part, say consenting to the payment of £1.23m to Barclays, but not to the £300,000 overpayment to the borrowers. There is not much authority on the point but, as we shall see (11.73), the test is essentially one of fairness, whether it is fair given what has happened for the beneficiary to turn round and sue the trustees. It is submitted that AIB Group did not act in any way which suggested that it wanted the overpayment to the borrowers to be reversed, so they adopted the disbursement as a whole. (For a full discussion of the issue, see Penner (2017); see also Ho (2017), 171–73.)

As we shall also see (11.64), where the transactions (here the payments to Barclays and to the borrowers) form part of one composite transaction, which they surely did here, the beneficiary is not entitled to falsify one and adopt the other. Moreover, to borrow a common law analogy: whilst there is no 'duty to mitigate' one's losses, liability for damages both in contract and tort does not extend to losses which could reasonably have been avoided. AIB Group could easily have avoided the £300k loss. It had an immediate claim against the borrowers: the borrowers held the excess they received on constructive trust, and were in addition personally liable for that amount as knowing recipients (11.188 et seq); Barclays could easily have got an order against the borrowers to transfer the requisite amount to Barclays to discharge the remaining indebtedness to Barclays (at the borrowers' expense in costs) had the borrowers refused to do this themselves.

11.58 Notice also that both in *Target* and *AIB Group* the trustee was also an agent, completing the contract of sale of land on behalf of his principle. In the same way a beneficiary can adopt the breach of his trustee, a principal can 'ratify' the act of his agent who acts in breach of the instructions he has been given. On *AIB Group*, Watts (2016), 120–21, has said:

> [W]hilst the solicitors in AIB Group were initially not forthcoming about their having accidentally released the money without a first mortgage being in place, they were soon driven to reveal the facts, and indeed some negotiations then directly occurred between their client and the existing mortgagee. In those circumstances, an inference of ratification was almost irresistible.

By contrast it is not at all clear that Target adopted or ratified the breach of the solicitor. Recall that the solicitor lied to Target about what it had done, and one can only adopt or ratify in the full knowledge of the facts.

11.59 Although the ambit of *AIB Group* is not clear, it is submitted that it cannot generally be the rule that a beneficiary is no longer entitled to falsify the account and has only a remedy for consequential loss. A couple of examples show why.

11.60 The *Quistclose* trust in *Twinsectra v Yardley* (7.33–7.36, 9.47–9.64) was clearly a bare, commercial trust and yet the case proceeded on the basis that the trustee-borrower was liable for his wrongful expenditures of the trust money on falsification principles. As the borrower was insolvent by the time of the action, the lender pursued the borrower's solicitor for dishonest assistance (11.10, 11.109–11.110), claiming that the borrower's solicitor who held the loan funds in his client account should be liable for the money wrongfully paid away. There would have been no claim against either the trustee-borrower or his solicitor if the claim was limited to one for consequential loss: had the trustee-borrower disbursed all the trust money *lawfully*— ie if the money was not disbursed in breach of trust—the lender would still have recovered little or nothing, for the borrower was insolvent. It was the borrower's insolvency that caused the loss, not the misapplications of the trust property, ie not the breach of trust. Indeed, on *AIB Group* principles no *Quistclose* trustee could ever be personally liable for the misapplication of the trust money, since on pure compensation for consequential loss principles the lender would always be in the position of an unsecured creditor whether the money is spent according to the trust terms or not.

11.61 Consider another example, which draws on the logic of *Clough v Bond* (11.39–11.41): Tom the trustee, in breach of trust, removes a gemstone from the trust collection held in a secure (ha!) vault in Hatton Garden in London, and sells it for £100,000. The gems, being in what is supposed to be secure safe-keeping, are uninsured. Later that week the secure vault is burgled, and all the gems are stolen. Tom must account for the £100,000 to the trust and cannot claim that had he complied with his duty all the gems, including the one he stole, would have been lost, so again, the claim cannot be founded as one for consequential loss. If *AIB Group* is not interpreted narrowly, or found to be wrongly analysed by a future UKSC, then its scope, ie the extent to which it denies beneficiaries the power to falsify the account for misapplications of trust property, will need to be carefully examined. To the extent that *AIB Group* suggests that beneficiaries are generally denied the power to falsify the account and may only make claims on the basis of their consequential loss, it is not the law in Australia (*Youyang v Minter Ellison* (2003); *Agricultural Land Management v Jackson* (2014)) or Hong Kong (*Libertarian Investments v Hall* (2012); *Akai Holdings Ltd v Kasikornbank plc* (2011)) and your author would not recommend that judges there follow it.

11.62   One last point on the battle between applying the 'performance interest principle' and the 'compensatory principle', it may be the case that in English contract law, the latter is now becoming established as the basic remedial principal for assessing the extent of liability for breach of contract. If that is so, then the trend in *Target* and *AIB Group* might reflect a more general direction in English private law (see Penner (2018a)).

11.63   The UKCA distinguished *Target* and *AIB Group* in *Main v Giabrone* (2017). The case concerned buyers of property in Italy, and the defendant was a solicitor's firm that received the buyer's deposits under the contracts of sale. The defendant was required to transfer the funds to the Italian property developers on condition that it had received certain guarantees. It transferred the funds not having obtained them. The court said the following:

> 61. . . . In Target the solicitors were under a duty to take active steps to secure a charge over the property, before releasing the monies. In AIB the solicitors were under a duty to take active steps to secure the removal of prior charges before releasing the money.
>
> 62. In the circumstances which unfolded in the present case, I would characterise the solicitors' obligation as an obligation to act as custodians of the deposit monies indefinitely. Compliant guarantees never appeared. Therefore Giambrone should have remained as custodians of the deposit monies until the preliminary contracts were rescinded, and then paid those monies back to their clients.

This seems a rather frail basis for distinguishing the cases. Why could not the trust in both *Target* and *AIB Group* not similarly be framed in 'passive' terms, ie not to transfer the trust moneys except in so far as the solicitor's acquired the charges over the property the lenders required them to get? The essential fact in all of these cases was that the solicitors transferred funds in breach of their instructions. It does not seem helpful to introduce the terminology of active and passive failures in this context.

Setting an unauthorised gain against an unauthorised loss

11.64   What should happen where a trustee enters into two different unauthorised transactions, one of which causes a loss, but the other creates a gain for the trust? Can the beneficiary falsify only the loss-causing transaction, and adopt the successful one? In general, the answer is yes, if the transactions are distinct (*Wiles v Gresham* (1854); *Dimes v Scott* (1828)). This seems right, because the trustee should not be exonerated of particular breaches because he can say, 'overall, the trust is in good shape'. However, where the losing and gaining unauthorised transactions form part of one composite transaction, the transactions must be falsified together or not at all (*Fletcher v Green* (1864)). For example, in *Bartlett* (10.16), the court held that the disastrous investment in one property development project was part of a larger investment policy favouring land development. In taking the account, then, this decision required the beneficiary to 'falsify' both the winning and losing projects as one invalid investment, with a resulting reduction in the amount of compensation. (Note: 'falsify' here is placed in quotation marks, as *Bartlett* was not a falsification case. Recall the facts in *Bartlett*. The trustee was liable for not preventing the company in which the trust held shares from embarking on property developments. Thus the case was one of negligence, and the beneficiaries surcharged the account. But the principles of causation for loss in falsification cases were relevant because the transactions the company entered into were essentially ones that, had the company been the trustee, would have been misapplications of trust property, and so it was appropriate to think in terms of falsification when assessing the loss to the trust.)

A personal claim where the account is not falsified

11.65 Where the beneficiaries choose not to falsify the account, the trustee must, of course, treat the property he holds as a result of the unauthorised transaction as trust property, and account for it to the trust. But as Millett LJ points out (11.30), a trustee cannot 'borrow' the trust funds but treat the profits he derives from the trust money as his own. If the trustee uses trust money in his own business, it will usually, however, be impossible to trace the money into any particular property the trustee holds that the beneficiaries could adopt as trust assets. Rather, the beneficiaries will usually be in the position of having to elect whether or not to adopt the trustee's 'loan' of the trust funds to himself. If they do so, they then have a further choice: they can elect either for an accounting of the trustee's business profits, which are attributable to the use of the beneficiaries' money, or for compound interest on the 'loan' (*Docker v Soames* (1834); *Westdeutsche Landesbank Girozentrale v Islington London Borough Council* (1996)). Of course the beneficiaries will falsify the account if the authorised transaction the trustee ought to have made would have been more profitable than his business profits or compound interest.

Confusions between cases of negligence, misapplication of trust property, and breach of fiduciary obligation

11.66 When you are looking at a case where a trustee commits a wrong, you must *always* ask yourself whether the wrong is: (1) negligence or a failure to act in some way, for which a beneficiary may surcharge the account; (2) a misapplication of trust property, for which the account can be falsified; or (3) a breach of fiduciary obligation. It is a failure of analysis simply to say the trustee committed a 'breach of trust' as if this term were precise enough to explain either what went wrong or what remedy is appropriate. Two cases where a precise analysis was necessary will show the importance of this.

11.67 *Bristol and West Building Society v Mothew* (1996) concerned a claim by a building society against a solicitor who had acted both for it and the borrower, holding the funds on trust prior to completion of the purchase of land, a bare trust with mandate (9.48). The solicitor negligently failed to include facts pertinent to assessing the creditworthiness of the borrower in filling out a standard form report to the society prior to the release of the mortgage loan. Although he had been aware of the facts, he had forgotten or overlooked them when making the report. The lender claimed that the solicitor both breached the trust and breached his fiduciary obligation. Millett LJ, writing the opinion of the CA, carefully considered the nature of the solicitor's wrong, disapproving the indiscriminate use of the labels 'breach of trust' and 'breach of fiduciary obligation', in particular the latter. He held that while the solicitor's paying out the money for the purchase was certainly a payment of *trust* money (it was clearly held by him on trust), his action in paying it was not a misapplication of trust money, because the solicitor was at that time complying with his standing instructions as to how the trust money should be applied. Neither was there a breach of fiduciary duty for in paying the money away the solicitor was not acting in bad faith or in conflict of interest. Rather, the solicitor was guilty of negligence in failing to take care in the preparation of the report, which probably also constituted a breach of his contract with the lender.

11.68 The decision of the Australian High Court (the supreme appellate court in Australia) in *Alexander v Perpetual Trustees WA Ltd* (2004) shows, in contrast, a disappointing failure of analysis. In this case a solicitor acted under a bare trust with mandate (9.48) to use the beneficiary's funds to make a certain kind of investment. The solicitor-trustee paid the money to purchase the investments, but failed to acquire certain documents that provided security for the investments. At the same time, the beneficiary was also careless in failing to take notice of the fact that these security documents were never acquired, and continued to invest more sums regardless. As a result, all the money invested was lost. The main issue was whether a *beneficiary* could be partly liable for a breach of trust. (Note: the issue is not about whether a beneficiary can consent to a breach of trust (11.72); consent to an act is not the same thing as committing that act oneself.) Now, if the case is one where the trust property is misapplied, then it would seem impossible for a beneficiary to be liable, because only a trustee can commit acts, such as a transfer of the property and so on, which misapply the trust property. As we have already briefly discussed (11.10, 11.13), agents of the trustee such as his banker or his solicitor can participate in a misapplication of trust property, and if they do so dishonestly they will be liable for the loss. But a beneficiary does not usually act as an agent of the trustee, and did not in this case; it was the trustee alone who carried out all the steps in the transactions with the trust money. On the other hand, a negligent breach of trust is a very different case. Consider the case of a nomineeship (2.16). A nominee trustee essentially follows the directions of the beneficiary, and one can easily imagine a situation where both the beneficiary and the trustee carelessly contributed to a decision to make an authorised but losing investment. There would appear to be nothing in principle that would prevent the negligent trustee from claiming that the beneficiary was contributorily negligent, and should shoulder part of the loss. In *Alexander* itself, the trial judge said that if the case turned on negligence, the solicitor trustee was 60 per cent liable and the beneficiary investor, 40 per cent liable, for the resulting loss. Unfortunately, none of the judges of the High Court specified what kind of breach of trust took place, that is whether the solicitor misapplied the trust funds in purchasing the investments without obtaining the security documents, for which the account could be falsified and the solicitor made strictly liable to restore all the funds paid away, or whether the money was properly paid under the mandate for the investments, but done negligently in the sense that the documents of security were never obtained. As Millett LJ made clear in *Mothew*, this is the crucial issue, because there is all the difference in the world between a trustee who carries out the trust terms by applying the money according to his mandate, but whose negligence gives rise to loss, and one who misapplies the money in breach of his mandate. What the court failed to analyse was whether the solicitor's purchase of the investment without acquiring the security documents was a misapplication of the trust money, akin to a solicitor's paying away a mortgage lender's money on completion of a house purchase without obtaining a charge on the property (the mortgage lender's mandate is to use its money to 'buy a charge' over the property), or whether the purchase of the investments was a perfectly proper application of the money according to the mandate, the failure to get the security documents being a collateral matter owing to the solicitor's, and, as the trial judge found, the beneficiary's, negligence. Having failed to analyse the facts and explicitly render a finding on this, it is no surprise that the High Court split 3:3 (see further Penner (2005)).

Liability of trustees *inter se*

11.69 The general equitable rule is that individual trustees are only liable for their own breaches of trust, not for the breaches committed by their co-trustees. However, equity does not recognise a 'sleeping' or 'passive' trustee, ie a trustee who does not fully participate in the administration of a trust. As Cotton LJ stated in *Bahin v Hughes* (1886):

> [I]t would be laying down a wrong rule that where one trustee acts honestly, though erroneously, the other trustee is to be held entitled to an indemnity who by doing nothing neglects his duty more than the acting trustee.

On this basis a trustee would be liable for breaches of his co-trustees to the extent that he was negligent or fell below the standard of prudence in monitoring his co-trustees' behaviour.

11.70 Where two or more trustees are each liable for a breach of trust, they are jointly and severally liable (11.13). Between themselves trustees may rely upon the Civil Liability (Contribution) Act 1978, which gives the court a discretion to apportion the share of liability each defendant trustee will bear, according to their relative individual responsibilities for the loss. In certain cases a trustee, although himself liable for breach of trust, may demand that his co-trustee indemnify him for any compensation he must pay—the effect of this, where that co-trustee is solvent, is to make him alone pay for the loss. Two such circumstances were stated in *Bahin v Hughes*. The first is:

> [W]here one trustee has got the money into his own hands, and made use of it, he will be liable to his co-trustee to give him an indemnity.

Secondly, a trustee may claim an indemnity against a co-trustee who is a solicitor if, but only if, that solicitor-trustee exercised a controlling influence over the conduct of a trust (*Head v Gould* (1898)). Thirdly, where a breaching co-trustee is also a beneficiary under the trust, special considerations apply because of this dual status (11.75).

11.71 These observations should be seen against another general principle—that in the absence of an express provision in the trust instrument, beneficiaries are entitled to require that the trustees act unanimously (*Re Thompson's Settlement* (1986)). This 'unanimity principle' was reconfirmed in *Fielden v Christie-Miller* (2015), where Sir William Blackburne referred to it as 'the principle that trustees must act unanimously except and to the extent that the trust instrument makes other provision.'

Beneficiaries' consent to a breach of trust

11.72   An adult beneficiary who freely consents to, or participates in, a breach of trust, may not sue the trustee to make good any loss caused by the breach. In *Re Pauling's Settlement Trusts* (1964), the trustee of a family settlement succumbed to the pressure of the father to make 'advancements' to his children, which in reality were not advancements (10.41 et seq) at all: the money was not intended to benefit the individual children, but to defray the family's extravagant living expenses, including the cost of purchasing family homes. The children, although of full age, were not taken to have consented because, although they were aware of the true purposes of the advancements, the court held that their approval was procured by the undue influence of their father. The fact that several children received benefits to themselves from the advancements did not bar them from claiming against the trustee for breach of trust, although they did have to offset these benefits against their claim against the trustee to restore the trust fund.

11.73   To truly consent a beneficiary must be fully aware of the facts, although not necessarily of his legal rights. Wilberforce J described the court's general approach in *Re Pauling's Settlement Trusts*:

> [T]he court has to consider all the circumstances . . . with a view to seeing whether it is fair and equitable that, having given his concurrence, he should afterwards turn round and sue the trustees . . . it is not necessary that he should know that what he is concurring in is a breach of trust, provided that he fully understands what he is concurring in, and that it is not necessary that he should himself have directly benefited by the breach of trust.

These principles were adopted in *Holder v Holder* (1968). The plaintiff sued to set aside the purchase of trust property by his brother who had technically acquired the status of an executor, for breach of the 'self-dealing' rule (13.93 et seq); the plaintiff was held to have acquiesced in the sale although unaware at the time of the legal position. He had subsequently received part of the purchase price as a beneficiary under the will, and throughout had full knowledge of all the facts concerning the sale. Besides considering these facts that go to determining actual consent, in *Holder* the 'fair and equitable' requirement for allowing the beneficiary now to 'turn round and sue' was applied. Although it was clear that the plaintiff did not know his legal rights to block or set aside the sale until afterwards, the court felt that his conduct throughout, which appeared to be motivated largely by animosity towards his brother, and the fact that he failed to discover the brother's technical breach (he and his brother stood on an equal footing as both were legally advised) made it inequitable for him now to have the sale set aside.

11.74   The court has an inherent power to 'impound' the beneficial interest of a beneficiary who has requested, instigated, or consented to a breach of trust. By 'impoundment' is meant that the beneficiary's interest will be applied, to the full extent of the interest, to compensating the trust for the loss incurred by the breach. The result of this is that a beneficiary whose interest is impounded is not only prevented from suing the trustee for the breach, but is, in effect, made to indemnify the trustee for the latter's participation in it. It seems from *Chillingworth v Chambers*

(1896) that where the beneficiary merely consents to a breach initiated by the trustee, ie in circumstances where the beneficiary has not instigated or requested the breach, his interest may only be impounded if he had consented in order to benefit from the breach himself. Section 62 of the Trustee Act 1925 now supplements the inherent jurisdiction, allowing the court to impound a beneficiary's interest if he consented to a breach irrespective of any benefit to himself, so long as his consent is made in writing.

11.75   Where the beneficiary is also a trustee, two rules come into operation. Normally a trustee may claim contribution from his co-trustees for a share of the compensation to be paid (11.70). In the case of a beneficiary-trustee, the rule in *Chillingworth v Chambers* applies: where a bene-ficiary-trustee and his co-trustee are liable for a breach of trust from which the beneficiary-trustee alone has benefited, then the beneficiary-trustee's beneficial interest is impounded to its full extent, and only if his interest is insufficient to cover the loss will he be able to claim contribution from his co-trustee. Under the rule in *Re Dacre* (1916), whether his interest is impounded or not, the trustee-beneficiary is not entitled to receive any part of his beneficial interest until his breach *qua* trustee is remedied, nor, somewhat surprisingly, is any assignee of his equitable interest, even if the assignment occurred before the breach; it is thus dangerous to take an assignment from a beneficiary who is also a trustee.

Trustees' relief from liability under Trustee Act 1925, s 61, trustee exemption clauses, and ouster of trustee duties

11.76   Lord Cottenham LC once said that a person who accepted the office of trustee a second time was fit only for a lunatic asylum (Stebbings (2002), at 26). This reflected the common nine-teenth-century view that the office of trustee, which was at the time only rarely remunerated, was a burdensome and thankless task, and that the liability of trustees for breach of trust could seem very onerous, given the altruistic character of the office. It was at this time that legislative attempts were first made to empower the court to limit a trustee's liability in cases of breach. A second way to address the problem was for the settlor to include a clause in the trust instrument limiting a trustee's liability for breach of trust. Take note: these limitations on liability, whether statutory or in the trust instrument, do not authorise or validate breaches of trust—to the ex-tent that a trustee can remedy a breach, say by restoring a misapplication of trust property *in specie*, he must do so. What these limitations on liability do is remove or reduce a trustee's *per-sonal* liability to pay out of his pocket to compensate the trust for a loss. Finally, a settlor might exclude certain duties in the trust instrument that might be inclined to give rise to liability.

Trustee Act 1925, s 61

11.77   Section 61 of the Trustee Act 1925 relieves trustees of liability for breach of trust in certain circumstances. It reads:

> *If it appears to the court that a trustee, whether appointed by the court or otherwise, is or may be personally liable for any breach of trust . . . but has acted honestly and reasonably, and ought fairly to be excused for the breach of trust and for omitting to*

obtain the directions of the court in the matter in which he committed such breach, then the court may relieve him either wholly or partly from personal liability for the same.

The court's exercise of the power is not governed by hard and fast rules. In *Re Pauling's Settlement Trusts* Upjohn LJ said:

Section 61 is purely discretionary, and its application necessarily depends on the particular facts of each case.

11.78   Relief under s 61 was sought in three cases we have already considered. In *Re Pauling's Settlement Trusts* the sole trustee was a bank. Wilmer LJ opined that:

Where a banker undertakes to act as a paid trustee of a settlement created by a customer, and so deliberately places itself in a position where its duty as trustee conflicts with its interest as a banker, we think that the court should be very slow to relieve a trustee under [s 61].

Relief was refused with respect to an advancement that benefited the bank because it was used to reduce the mother's overdraft with it. This suggests that any breach carried out by a trustee acting in clear conflict of interest, although not in terms dishonest, cannot be reasonable. With respect to another transaction the court held that the bank's relying upon the consent of the children, although over 21, when clearly it was obtained by their father's undue influence, was unreasonable, and so relief under s 61 was unavailable. The court did afford the bank relief in respect of one advancement where the bank trustee's solicitors and the solicitor who separately advised the sons were largely at fault.

11.79   The trustees also sought relief under s 61 in *Bartlett* (10.16). Brightman J tersely dismissed the plea, although covering each of the three criteria of the section:

There is no doubt that the bank acted honestly. I do not think it acted reasonably. Nor do I think it would be fair to excuse the bank at the expense of the beneficiaries.

11.80   In *Re Mulligan* (1998) (10.3), a trust company and the testator's widow were trustees of a testamentary trust of which the widow was also the life tenant. They invested in fixed-interest securities, which paid a high income to the widow but resulted in severe capital depreciation. Following the death of the widow the capital beneficiaries successfully sued the trust company and the widow's estate for the decline in the capital value arising from this breach of the even-handedness rule. Applying s 73 of the New Zealand Trustee Act 1956, which is in relevant respects identical to s 61, the court held that the trust company did not act reasonably because although it realised the danger of capital depreciation, it basically accepted the widow's insistence that they invest as she desired. As regards the widow: a person of some business acumen, she could not have claimed that she did not appreciate the significance of the course of investment; furthermore, she had failed as a trustee to exercise an independent judgment, clearly favouring her own interests above those of the other beneficiaries; she therefore had not acted reasonably as a trustee, and the personal representative of her estate was denied a claim for relief under the statute.

11.81   The section was successfully pleaded in *Re Evans* (1999) by a lay administrator of her deceased father's estate, who distributed the property to herself in the reasonable belief that her brother, whom she had not heard of in years, was dead; she took out a 'missing beneficiary' insurance policy, which when her brother later turned up, only partly compensated him for what he would have received. The court excused the daughter under s 61 from having to pay over the difference. (The brother was, of course, able to claim his full share in any of their father's property that she retained, in this case the father's house.)

11.82 In *Nationwide Building Society v Davison Solicitors* (2012) Morritt C in the CA held that: 'The section only requires [the defendant] to have acted reasonably. That does not, in my view, predicate that he has necessarily complied with best practice in all respects.' *Davison* also made clear that it was only the behaviour by the trustee that was connected to his liability for the loss caused to the claimant which was to be assessed for its honesty and reasonableness. In particular, showing a trustee's unreasonable failure to take due care in matters unrelated to the loss would not be relevant to the court's application of s 61.

11.83 In *Santander UK plc v RA Legal Solicitors* (2014), the CA, unanimously reversing the decision of the trial judge, denied relief under the section. First, the court held that the burden of proof lay upon the applicant under the section, here a solicitor who had in breach of trust transferred a lender's funds to a fraudulent solicitor under a fraudulent land transaction, to establish that he had acted honestly and reasonably; it was not for the claimant to have to prove otherwise, as if he were bringing an action against the trustee for professional negligence. Secondly, the court held that although the behaviour which must be assessed for its honesty and reasonableness must be connected to the loss suffered by the beneficiary, it is up to the trustee to show that any unreasonable behaviour of his did not materially contribute to the occurrence of the beneficiary's loss or the likelihood that it would come about. In this case, the solicitor's inadequate oversight of the transaction and failure properly to apply standard conveyancing practices were held to be unreasonable, and a ground for denying relief, even though the CA accepted as a matter of probability that even if the solicitor had acted properly throughout it was likely that the fraud would still have occurred. The fact that best practice in conveyancing procedures was encouraged in part to detect such frauds, plus the fact that here the solicitor's failures basically prevented either himself or the lender from acting quickly when fraud should have been suspected, meant that in relation to the lender's loss he had acted unreasonably, and his liability would not be excused under the section.

11.84 In *P&P Property v Owen White; Dreamvar UK v Mischon de Reya (a firm)* (2018), the law on the section developed further in a new (and dangerous) direction. It was held by the UKCA that despite acting honestly and reasonably, the question whether the trustee ought reasonably to be excused turned on the issue of insurance cover. In this case the trustee, a solicitor's firm, had liability insurance, unlike the beneficiary, in this case the purchaser of land who was defrauded, who did not. The court denied relief under the section for the reason that the trustee, given his insurance cover, could better bear the loss. The reason I say this is a dangerous path to take is that finding liability, or denying relief from liability, on the basis of insurance cover, has, first, a self-defeating element to it. If the law says you are liable if you have insurance, then the thing to do to avoid liability is not to take out insurance. Secondly, there is also a strong legal-moral objection—the fact that I have had the foresight to insure myself against liability should not be a factor in determining *what* my *liability* is under the law. It is in essence no different from the idea that the extent of my liability should be determined by how much money I have. That is why having insurance is not a reason, just on its own, to make you liable for a tort. Trustees, in general, are not required to take out insurance for breach of trust but solicitors are so required, whether they are acting as trustees or not.

Trustee exemption clauses

11.85   In *Armitage v Nurse* (1998) the CA held that an exemption clause in an instrument protecting the trustees from any loss or damage 'unless such loss or damage shall be caused by his own actual fraud' was valid. The effect of this is that trustees may be relieved of liability for any loss caused by their own negligence, even gross negligence. Millett LJ pointed out that such a clause does not purport to exclude, and does not exclude, a trustee's liability as a fiduciary in certain cases. Thus it would not prevent a beneficiary setting aside a sale of trust property to a trustee (a 'self-dealing' transaction (13.93)), because that would not involve relieving a trustee for liability *for a loss*; neither, on such a view, would such a clause prevent a trustee from being stripped of an unauthorised profit. We will examine cases of this kind in Chapter 13.

11.86   Millett LJ accepted:

> that there is an irreducible core of obligations owed by the trustees to the beneficiaries and enforceable by them which is fundamental to the concept of a trust. If the beneficiaries have no rights enforceable against the trustees there are no trusts. But I do not accept the further submission that these core obligations include the duties of skill and care, prudence and diligence. The duty of trustees to perform the trusts honestly and in good faith for the benefit of the beneficiaries is the minimum necessary to give substance to the trusts, but in my opinion it is sufficient . . . [A] trustee who relied on the presence of a trustee exemption clause to justify what he proposed to do would thereby lose its protection: he would be acting recklessly in the proper sense of the term.

11.87   In his opinion, therefore, there was no basis in authority for saying that an exemption clause that relieved a trustee of liability for his gross negligence was 'repugnant', ie conceptually inconsistent with there being a trust. In his focus on good faith and honesty Millett LJ went so far as to say that an exemption clause would relieve a trustee of liability even for a deliberate breach of trust if undertaken in the honest belief that it was for the best interests of the beneficiaries. This dictum was doubted by a subsequent CA in *Walker v Stones* (2001), which held that a solicitor-trustee could not rely upon an exemption clause where his 'perception of the interests of the beneficiaries was so unreasonable that no reasonable solicitor trustee could have held such belief'. In *Bonham v Fishwick* (2008) it was held that trustees who reasonably relied upon a legal opinion could not be guilty of wilful wrongdoing, and thus were exempted from any liability by the trust's exemption clause.

11.88   Millett LJ examined the pleadings in *Armitage* and found that none clearly alleged dishonesty but, at most, negligence, and therefore the trustees were not liable. The trust arose as a variation of a previous under which both the plaintiff daughter and her mother were beneficiaries. Under the new trust, the plaintiff was the sole beneficiary. However, the trust largely consisted of a holding of farmland, and the trustees appointed a company controlled by her mother and grandmother to farm it, which also farmed the mother's own land. In essence the claim was that the trustees had managed the trust property with the interests of the family in mind, not the plaintiff, although the plaintiff was the only object of the trust. Millett LJ did not find in the pleadings sufficient particular allegations to sustain this charge, but allowed the plaintiff to re-amend her pleadings, adding:

> I express no view on whether there is material which would justify counsel in advising such a course; and I would not wish to encourage it. They will no doubt bear in mind that at the material time the trustees of the settlement consisted of one professional

man and two distant relatives; and that a charge of fraud against independent professional trustees is, in the absence of some financial or other incentive, inherently implausible.

11.89   This narrow focus on fraud, however, seems to undercut Millett LJ's previous point that such a clause would not relieve the trustee of any breach of fiduciary duty. Consider in particular the duty of even-handedness. In *Nestle* (10.19) the CA did not consider the trustee to have breached this duty by tailoring its investments to benefit the current life tenants, because the court's appreciation of the duty gave the trustee a very wide discretion, but one can imagine another court taking a somewhat narrower view. The trustee did not, apparently, give much thought to its duty of even-handedness, as the investments favouring the life tenant seemed to have been made simply in response to the hectoring of one of the life tenants. In any case, the duty of even-handedness must be regarded as one of the core trustee fiduciary obligations because only by being even-handed between the beneficiaries does a trustee meet his obligation to act in good faith and take into account the interests of *all* the beneficiaries. Indeed, the duty of even-handedness is just a specification of the duty of loyalty and good faith where there is more than one beneficiary. Therefore, an exemption clause cannot relieve a trustee from his liability to a beneficiary for failing to be even-handed towards him. If the plaintiff's claims were made out, *Armitage* is clearly *a fortiori* to *Nestle*, since the allegation was that the trustees were loyal to the interests of the plaintiff's mother, who was not a beneficiary at all.

11.90   Consider also *Re Pauling's Settlement Trusts*, where the trustee bank acted solely at the instigation of one beneficiary of the settlement, the father. It was apparently the forcefulness of his personality that largely led it to ignore the children's interests and make the advancements it did. In neither *Nestle* nor *Re Pauling's Settlement Trusts* did the professional trustees stand to gain significantly from the alleged breaches of trust; they did so in the absence of any 'financial incentive' and it is not clear what 'other incentive' they had beyond making their lives easier in the administration of the trust (see also *Wilson v Turner*, 10.37; *Re Mulligan*, 10.3, 11.80). So, although Millett J is right to suspect that any charge of actual fraud may be inherently implausible where the professional trustee gains no benefit by it, an allegation of a breach of the duty of even-handedness seems entirely plausible.

11.91   In *Armitage v Nurse*, Millett LJ suggested that statutory reform of the general law on the valid scope of exemption clauses was appropriate. The Law Commission of England and Wales (2002; see also Scottish Law Commission (2003)) took up the suggestion, producing a consultation paper on the question. (See also Matthews (1989) for the suggestion that clauses should be capable of excluding a trustee's liability for negligence, but not gross negligence; Ontario Law Reform Commission (1984), arguing against the validity of exemption clauses generally in view of the court's power to relieve trustees of liability, as under s 61.) No legislation has resulted.

11.92   We can categorise the way in which trustees may breach their duties according to different criteria:

(1) according to the way in which the breach displays the fault of the trustee, for example, whether a breach is committed intentionally, recklessly, or negligently;

(2) according to the particular sort of duty that is breached, in particular distinguishing breaches of trust duties, for example the duty to invest, the duty to keep the trust accounts, the duty to pay income as it arises in a timely fashion to the life tenant(s), etc, and breaches of fiduciary obligation (eg where a trustee invests the trust funds in a non-even-handed way).

11.93   As traditionally written, trustee exemption clauses seem clearly to relieve trustees of liability according to the fault the breach displays, that is according to the categorisation of breaches of trusts in (1). This seems to be the perspective Millett LJ takes in *Armitage*, and particularly in his characterisation of the 'irreducible core' of obligations without which a trust ceases to exist, ie an enforceable duty of good faith and honesty. If this is correct, then an exemption clause can relieve a trustee of liability for any breach of trust, from not only failing to invest the trust property properly or failing to manage the trust property well, as in *Armitage*, to paying the trust property away to wrong beneficiaries, committing frauds on powers, to failing to maintain the trust accounts or failing to keep the property separate from his own or using the trust property for his own benefit, so long as the breach is not committed dishonestly.

11.94   With respect, it would seem that this perspective, whereby the usual envisaged breach is one of failing to manage the trust property well or invest it properly, loses much of its intuitive force when other sorts of breaches are envisaged. What if one examines the effect of trustee exemption clauses according to the type of breach as in (2)? An initial distinction within this category could be between administrative and dispositive breaches. It would seem that the perspective in (1) most appropriately applies to administrative breaches, such as the breach of a duty to invest or manage the trust property, rather than to dispositive breaches, such as paying away the money to non-beneficiaries, or to committing frauds on powers. It is submitted that from this type–duty perspective, one might arrive at a different set of 'core obligations' in the absence of which a trust cannot be said truly to exist.

11.95   For example, it seems that if there is no enforceable duty to keep the trust accounts and to keep the trust property separate from the trustee's own, there cannot be a trust purely on equitable property principles, because the trust can only attach to specific property kept separate as a fund, where the various substitutions of one item of property for another from time to time in the fund are properly kept track of or accounted for (2.75). In other words, besides the core duties of good faith and honesty, there are core duties to keep the trust property separate and keep the trust accounts, which are just as much core duties in the absence of which there is simply no trust. A court might well not look favourably on an exemption clause employed to relieve trustees of liability for failure to keep the trust property separate from his own or for failure to keep the trust accounts. While at first glance it might be thought that such breaches would in every case reveal dishonesty or a lack of good faith as well, this is clearly not the case. Consider the case of a large corporate trustee the property dealings and record keeping of which fall into disarray because of negligent management (eg the failure to properly train trust officers for example). It would not seem appropriate to allow an exemption clause to relieve the trustee of personal liability for this breach, because if the trust could not be restored by a proprietary claim against the trustee because, in the event, the property was untraceable, the entire value of the trust could be lost in such a way as to benefit the trustee or its creditors. The effect of a breach in such a case is, after all, essentially a taking of the beneficiaries' property by the trustee, and can be committed negligently. It would not seem at all just for an exemption clause in whatever terms to relieve the trustee of such a liability, because in such a case the relief from liability would not only save the trustee from having to restore the trust or to compensate the beneficiaries for their loss, but because of the nature of the breach would essentially sanction the trustee's inadvertent 'theft' (see Penner (2002)).

11.96   It might be contended that the trustee in such a case might be liable under two heads: first, to restore the trust or render equitable compensation to the beneficiaries but, secondly, under the law of restitution for unjust enrichment, to repay the value of the property it acquired by its mixing of the trust property with its own so as to make it untraceable, in order to prevent its unjust enrichment at the beneficiaries' expense. If so, then whilst a trustee exemption clause could afford the trustee relief from the first liability to restore or compensate the trust, it might arguably be regarded as ineffective against the second, restitutionary, claim. However, it would be unwise to think that a court would rely upon what might appear a rather scholastic distinction in the way a case might be framed, and might rather seek to modify or embroider upon Millett's 'core obligation' thesis to find an exemption clause ineffective to discharge the trustee of such a liability, on the basis that keeping the trust accounts and the trust property separate from one's own is one of the 'core' duties of the trustee.

11.97   As to breaches of fiduciary obligations, since the breach of fiduciary obligations can be framed as a breach of one of the core obligations Millett LJ recognises, to act in good faith in the best interests of the beneficiaries, at first glance it might seem that no exemption clause can relieve a trustee of liability for breach of fiduciary obligation. The problem is simply that fiduciary breaches can be committed innocently, without negligence, and in good faith with the best interests of beneficiaries in mind. None of the defendants in *Nestle* or *Re Pauling's Settlement Trusts*, or *Re Mulligan* or *Armitage* were accused of acting in conscious bad faith (see also *Boardman v Phipps* (1967); 13.33 et seq). If the 'fault' test of (1) is applied, such non-fraudulent breaches would necessarily be relieved by any clause such as the one found in *Armitage*, and which Millett found valid. On the other hand, fiduciary obligations might well be regarded as 'core' trust obligations, and, thus once again, the decision in *Armitage* does not give certain guidance as to the effect of exemption clauses in these circumstances.

11.98   In *Barnsley v Noble* (2016), the Court of Appeal considered the proper interpretation of an exoneration clause to relieve trustees of a will trust of personal liability in respect of a breach of the fiduciary self-dealing rule. Interpreting the phrases 'wilful wrongdoing' and 'wilful fraud', the court held that 'wilful' imports a requirement of conscious wrongdoing. The court found support for this proposition in Millett LJ's exposition of what 'wilful default' meant in *Armitage*—ie that it means a 'deliberate breach of trust' and that 'nothing less than conscious and wilful misconduct is sufficient'. The terms of a trust may allow a trustee to enter into a self-dealing transaction. But where it does not, then the court rightly pointed out that the exoneration clause merely removes the trustee's personal liability for any loss suffered by a beneficiary under such a transaction; it does not remove the beneficiary's right to have that transaction 'set aside' or rescinded.

The ouster of trustee duties

11.99   A settlor may, by a provision in the trust instrument, oust, ie remove, a duty that trustees would otherwise have under the general law of trusts (*Wilkins v Hogg* (1861) (duty to see to the application of money by co-trustee); *Hayim v Citibank* (1987) (duty to deal with a specific asset, a house lived in by the settlor's siblings, as a regular trust asset prior to their death)). For example, it is nowadays common for trustees to be relieved of the duty to monitor the affairs of a company in which the trust has a substantial shareholding, avoiding the general rule described in *Bartlett* (1980) (10.16). Fiduciary obligations can also be ousted, and where a trust instrument puts someone in a situation of conflict of interest this will serve to authorise good faith exercises of discretions or powers even though taken in a situation of conflict (*Sargeant v National Westminster Bank* (1990); *Re Z Trust* (1997)).

11.100   There is a possible problem with the ouster of duties, or the use of similar 'power-extending' clauses, which permit what would otherwise be denied by a general trust duty (eg a power 'to speculate freely with the trust assets as if the assets were entirely unneeded to provide for the beneficiaries in any way whatsoever such that the entire value of the fund might be lost with no adverse consequences to the beneficiaries whatsoever'). As Millett LJ made clear in *Armitage v Nurse* (11.85) a trust requires a minimum of duties owed by the trustee to the beneficiary and enforceable by them, otherwise there is no trust. If an ouster of a duty or duties is untoward or excessive, which can only be judged in the context of the particular trust, the 'trust' may not actually be valid as a trust, leading to the rather drastic result that either the 'trustee' is regarded as the beneficial owner of the property, or that the whole trust fails, as not being an effective disposition on trust.

11.101   The Law Commission (2002) in its consultation paper on trustee exemption clauses reasoned that the ouster of a particular duty does not *pro tanto* oust a general duty to take care, nor does the extension of a power, and neither would they *pro tanto* oust the fiduciary duties of loyalty to the beneficiaries. Thus, depending very much on the nature of the particular trust, such provisions in the trust instrument may not provide the protection from a failure to fulfil the overarching duties that is normally provided by an exemption clause. The Law Commission saw no sensible way of generally limiting the ability of trustees and settlors to oust duties and extend powers; whether an ouster or extension was judged to be effective could only be determined in the context of the particular trust, and the validity of such a provision could only be assessed in light of whether the action of the trustee taking advantage of the provision was consistent with the purposes of the trust and reasonable in the circumstances. In consequence the Law Commission proposed that the court should have the power to disapply such provisions where this was not the case. It is not clear whether such a statutory power is even needed, given the general background position of equity that powers may not be exercised for purposes for which they were not conferred (3.61) and that a minimum duty to the beneficiaries is a core requirement for a valid trust. It is unlikely that a court would treat a clause ousting entirely any duty to take care in the administration of a trust as an effective provision of a valid trust.

11.102   Take note: it must always be remembered that it is one thing to relieve a trustee of liability for the breach of a trust duty, and quite another to remove a duty altogether. Whatever the trustee's liability for breach, where there is a duty a prospective or ongoing breach of it can be enjoined by a beneficiary taking the trustee to court, so that, for example, a dangerously risky investment can be prevented. Similarly, a co-trustee can make reference to such a duty in thwarting the injudicious proposals of his co-trustees. And where there is a duty, there can be an advertent or reckless breach of a duty, which an exemption clause cannot protect against. Finally, whether there is exemption clause relief or not, a breach of trust may be grounds for removal of a trustee. By contrast, where a trustee is entirely relieved of a duty, there can be no breach of it, and so no possible liability for breach. Ouster and extension clauses should be regarded as bespoke provisions providing the right latitude for action for a trustee given the general purposes and features of the particular trust. They are not equivalent, much less ideal substitutes for, valid exemption clauses.

De facto trusteeship, or trusteeship *de son tort*

11.103   Where an individual who is not a trustee 'intermeddles' with the trust affairs, although innocently, he may become liable as a trustee for any misapplication of trust property or other loss caused to the trust (*Mara v Browne* (1896)); such a person is known as a trustee *de son tort* (a trustee 'by his own wrong'), although Lord Millett (*Dubai Aluminium v Salaam* (2003)) would put it otherwise:

> *Substituting dog Latin for bastard French, we would be better to describe such persons today as de facto trustees. In their relations with the beneficiaries they are treated in every respect as if they had been duly appointed. They are true trustees and are fully subject to fiduciary obligations. Their liability is strict; it does not depend on dishonesty.*

One example of a *de facto* trustee/trustee *de son tort* is that of an agent of the trust who takes it upon himself to exercise trustee functions over the property beyond the scope of his agency. Today most cases of *de facto* trusteeship probably arise where a trustee, although not effectively appointed, believes, and therefore acts as if, he is (see eg *Re Coates to Parsons* (1886); *Jasmine Trustees Ltd v Wells & Hind* (2007); 10.58).

Liability for procuring or assisting in a breach of trust

Liability for procuring a breach of trust

11.104   In *Eaves v Hickson* (1861), the father of five children forged a marriage certificate in order to make it appear that his five children were legitimate, which he presented to the trustee of the trust, who paid each of the children the shares of the estate to which they would have been entitled had they been legitimate. Now, in a case such as this, where someone procures or induces the trustee to misapply the trust property, two principles regarding a trustee's liability come into conflict. The first is that a trustee is strictly liable for the misapplication of the trust property—the other beneficiaries should have the right to falsify the trust account and make the trustee personally liable to restore the property wrongfully paid away to these five children. The second principle, however, is that a trustee is not to be held liable for the loss or theft of the trust property through no fault of his own (*Morley v Morley* (1678)); he is not an insurer of the trust property (*Speight v Gaunt; Learoyd v Whiteley; Re Chapman* (10.12–10.14)). Here the trustee was defrauded of the trust funds through no fault of his own. Normally, of course, if the trustee is defrauded of trust funds, the second principle alone will apply, because most frauds do not involve the misapplication of trust property. Consider the case of a trustee entitled under the terms of the trust to buy works of art, and who purchases a painting from an apparently reputable dealer. If this dealer sells the trustee a stolen painting, the trust will not receive good title to the painting, and the dealer will have defrauded the trustee of the purchase money. The trustee, not being at fault, will not be personally liable for this loss, because the purchase of the painting was not a misapplication of the trust money, because the trustee was entitled to invest in art. He was defrauded in the course of *properly* applying the trust funds. But in *Eaves* the fraud induced a *misapplication* of the funds, ie a paying out to non-beneficiaries, for which the trustee would normally be strictly liable. In *Eaves* the court gave weight to both principles in the form of its order: the illegitimate children were liable to repay what they received with interest; and to the extent they could not repay the whole, then their fraudster father must pay the balance; only to the extent there was then any deficiency, would the trustee be liable.

Liability for assisting a breach of trust

11.105   The principles governing liability for assisting, or being an 'accessory' to, a breach of trust were reviewed by the PC in *Royal Brunei Airlines Sdn Bhd v Tan* (1995). Mr Tan was the principal shareholder and director of BLT, a company which was Royal Brunei Airlines' general travel agent in certain locations. Under the airline's agreement with BLT, the proceeds of ticket sales were to be held on trust for the airline. The proceeds, however, were never paid into a separate trust account, but into BLT's current account, and the money was used for BLT's general business purposes. The PC denied that an accessory could only be liable if the trustee was engaged in a dishonest or fraudulent design himself. That view derived from Lord Selborne LC's statement in *Barnes v Addy* (1874) that an accessory was not liable 'unless they assist with knowledge in a dishonest and fraudulent design on the part of the trustees'. The PC decided that the accessory's liability should turn on his own dishonest participation in the breach, whether the trustee committing the breach did so dishonestly or not.

11.106   What does 'dishonesty' mean? Lord Nicholls said that although honesty has a strong subjective element, the standard of liability was objective:

> *Honesty is not an optional scale, with higher or lower values according to the moral standards of each individual . . . Unless there is a very good and compelling reason, an honest person does not participate in a transaction if he knows it involves a misapplication of trust assets to the detriment of beneficiaries. Nor does an honest person in such a case deliberately close his eyes and ears, or deliberately not ask questions, lest he learn something he would rather not know, and then proceed regardless . . .*
>
> *Acting in reckless disregard of others' rights or possible rights can be a tell-tale sign of dishonesty. An honest person would have regard to the circumstances known to him, including the nature and importance of the proposed transaction, the nature and importance of his role, the ordinary course of business, the degree of doubt, the practicability of the trustee or the third party proceeding otherwise and the seriousness of the adverse consequences to the beneficiaries. The circumstances will dictate which one or more of the possible courses should be taken by an honest person. He might, for instance, flatly decline to become involved. He might ask further questions. He might seek advice, or insist on further advice being obtained. He might advise the trustee of the risks but then proceed with his role in the transaction. He might do many things. Ultimately, in most cases, an honest person should have little difficulty in knowing whether a proposed transaction, or his participation in it, would offend the normally accepted standards of honest conduct. Likewise, when called upon to decide whether a person was acting honestly, a court will look at all the circumstances known to the third party at the time. The court will also have regard to personal attributes of the third party such as his experience and intelligence, and the reason why he acted as he did.*

11.107   The PC found Mr Tan liable. He had assisted in the breach of trust by 'causing or permitting' BLT to undertake the transactions in breach of trust in full knowledge that the moneys were to be held on trust, and that amounted to dishonest conduct. BLT was also dishonest, since Mr Tan's state of mind as its director was to be imputed to the company.

11.108   In *Bank of Credit and Commerce International (Overseas) Ltd v Akindele* (1999; aff'd 2001, CA), the defendant, a Nigerian businessman, was found not liable for dishonest assistance for entering into a share purchase agreement with BCCI (which was part of a scheme by which directors of BCCI defrauded it) simply because the agreement was in some respects unusual or artificial and he benefited from a high rate of interest on the transaction.

11.109   After some wobbles in the case law (*Twinsectra v Yardley* (2002) (7.35, 9.60); *Barlow Clowes v Eurotrust International* (2005); *Abou-Rahmah v Abacha* (2006); *Statek Corp v Alford* (2008)), the UKHL has affirmed in *Ivey v Genting Casinos (UK) Ltd* (2017), [62], that the standard of dishonestly set out by Lord Nicholls in *Royal Brunei* is the correct standard.

11.110   Third parties or agents to the trust are not liable as accessories when they negligently, but not dishonestly, fail to discover that the transaction in which they participate is a breach of trust:

> *[B]eneficiaries cannot reasonably expect that all the world dealing with their trustees should owe them a duty to take care lest the trustees are behaving dishonestly. [Lord Nicholls, Royal Brunei]*

11.111   In *Agip (Africa) Ltd v Jackson* (1990; aff'd 1991, CA), the test of 'dishonesty' was applied to a solicitor and an agent who managed companies set up entirely for the purpose of receiving moneys obtained by fraud and then passing them on to unknown others. The only purpose of the companies was to make it difficult to detect the fraud and to follow the money that had been fraudulently obtained. With respect to finding a third party dishonest, Millett J said:

> *It is essentially a jury question. If a man does not draw the obvious inferences or make the obvious inquiries, the question is: why not? If it is because, however foolishly, he did not suspect wrongdoing or, having suspected it, had his suspicions allayed, however unreasonably, that is one thing. But if he did suspect wrongdoing yet failed to make inquiries because 'he did not want to know' . . . or because he regarded it as 'none of his business' . . . that is quite another. Such conduct is dishonest, and those who are guilty of it cannot complain if, for the purpose of civil liability, they are treated as if they had actual knowledge.*

11.112   In *Agip*, there was evidence that the defendants might have believed that they were assisting in a scheme, not to defraud a company, but to avoid the currency exchange controls of Tunisia. Millett LJ said:

> *[I]t is no answer for a man charged with having knowingly assisted in a fraudulent and dishonest scheme to say that he thought that it was 'only' a breach of exchange control or 'only' a case of tax evasion. It is not necessary that he should have been aware of the precise nature of the fraud or even the identity of its victim.*

11.113   This perspective was not adopted by Rimer J in *Brinks Ltd v Abu-Saleh* (1995). He found a woman not liable as an accessory for knowingly assisting her husband in a dishonest scheme, because she believed she was participating in a tax evasion exercise, which was false, rather than helping to transfer the proceeds of a robbery from England to the Continent, which was what was really going on. Rimer J's approach was disapproved by the PC in *Barlow Clowes*: 'Someone can know, and can certainly suspect, that he is assisting in a misappropriation of money without knowing that the money is held on trust or even what a trust means.'

11.114   In the CA decision in *Lipkin Gorman v Karpnale Ltd* (1992—the case went to the HL, but the decision on accessory liability did not form part of the appeal) a law firm sought to hold its banker liable because it allowed a partner of the firm, one Mr Cass, who was addicted to gambling, to withdraw money from the firm's client account for that purpose. The CA decided that given the contract between the banker and its client, the bank could not be liable unless it was in breach of its contract to its client to operate and monitor the account properly. In this case Cass's withdrawals were perfectly valid within the terms of the bank's contract with its customers—Cass had full authority to draw on the client account. And although the bank manager knew that Cass was a gambler, this was not a sufficient reason to suspect that he was looting the client account, and the CA held that it would impose an excessive burden on bankers to monitor all of their accounts to pick up suspicious withdrawals.

11.115   In *Finers v Miro* (1991) a firm of solicitors sought directions from the court concerning assets it held on trust for a client. The solicitors suspected that some portion of the assets represented the proceeds of a fraud the client allegedly committed by unlawfully transferring assets from a US company, now in liquidation. The CA directed the solicitors to inform the liquidator of the US company that they held assets that might be assets of the company. But for the strong suspicion of fraud, informing the liquidator would amount to a breach of their fiduciary duty of confidence to their client. The CA based its decision in part on the fact that the knowledge of the solicitors was now such that should they dispose of any of the property to the defendant they might well be liable as accessories to a breach of trust, following *Agip*. Banks are now subject to a mass of legislation that requires them to take action where they are suspicious that a customer is laundering the proceeds of crime, including rules that make it an offence to 'tip off' a customer who is or might be under investigation, and so banks must act very carefully in such circumstances (see eg *Bank of Scotland v A Ltd* (2001); for an overview, see Gleeson (1995)).

Proprietary remedies for the misapplication of trust property

11.116   Recall that in most circumstances, the trust property is a fund (2.75). It is therefore a normal part of the life of the trust that a trustee exchanges one item of trust property for another, so that the constituent properties of the trust change from time to time. The trust will also, of course, 'capture' any funds arising from its ownership of any particular trust property (eg dividends paid on shares owned by the trust). Because of this, where the beneficiaries adopt or, as Millett LJ puts it (11.30), decide not to complain about, an unauthorised transaction, the resulting property forms part of the trust fund just as would the proceeds from any authorised transaction. Therefore, where the trustee breaches the trust by making an unauthorised investment, the beneficiaries need do nothing. The trustee will hold the investment as property in the trust fund, and that is that. In one sense the beneficiaries can be said to 'trace' (2.78; 11.123 et seq) the trust funds into the unauthorised investment and claim it as their own. But this right to trace against the trustee is nothing more than the recognition that the trust is a fund, and so the proceeds of any transactions with trust funds are automatically captured by the trust unless, because of a breach, the beneficiaries exercise their right to falsify the account.

11.117   A trustee who turns out to be a rogue typically commits two different wrongs when he breaches the trust; not only does he misapply the trust property, but he treats the proceeds of that misapplication as his own, as for example when a trustee uses trust funds to buy himself a new car. He should not have used the trust funds to buy a car, and his breach is compounded by his using the car as his own, that is by failing to keep the trust property separate from his own and dealing with it properly under the trust. But these are distinct wrongs, and a trustee can commit one without committing the other. An honest trustee may misapply the trust property, as where he mistakenly makes an unauthorised investment, yet hold that investment properly as part of the trust fund. In contrast, a trustee may treat the trust property as his own without misapplying the trust property (eg where a trustee takes a trust painting to hang in his office). The painting remains an authorised trust property, but the trustee still acts in breach of trust, and should he fail to return the trust property to where it should properly be kept, the benefi-ciaries can get a court order to make him do so.

11.118 By doing so they are, in a sense, making a proprietary claim against the trustee, claiming 'that painting is ours'. But this suit does not *establish* their equitable ownership of the painting. That is taken as a given; it forms the basis of their right to make the claim they do. What they are ac-tually claiming is not equitable ownership of the painting, but *specific performance* of the trust by the trustee. They are suing to make him carry out his trust duties properly, which in this case is to treat trust property as trust property, not as his own. In this case there is no question of either falsifying the account or adopting a misapplication of trust property, for the simple reason that 'misapplication of trust property' refers not to this sort of case, but to a case where the trustee *transfers title* to the property in breach of trust (or grants to someone else a conflict-ing interest in trust property by, say, mortgaging it). Although in both cases one might frame the beneficiaries' demand as 'that property is ours!', do not be confused. Demanding that the trustee deal with the trust property properly is not the same thing as 'adopting' an unauthorised transaction, although in the typical case of a breach by a rogue trustee, beneficiaries who want to make a proprietary claim against the trustee will both 'adopt' the trustee's misapplication of the trust property so as to claim the proceeds for the trust and, of course, ask the Court of Equity to order the trustee to deal with those proceeds as trust property. In the case of a rogue trustee, this will almost always mean he will be ordered to transfer title to new trustees replacing him (recall 10.61).

11.119 The more difficult cases arise when the trustee misapplies the trust property and mixes the trust funds with his own, where for example the trustee draws cash from the trust's bank account, and then banks the cash in his own personal account. This is where the rules of 'tracing' against a trustee come into play (11.123 et seq). But wherever the tracing leads, the same basic prin-ciples apply—the beneficiaries can either adopt the transaction that produces the proceeds in one form or other, claiming the proceeds as 'theirs', or they can falsify the account so as to make the trustee personally liable to restore the trust.

Third-party recipients of trust property

11.120 Where trust property is misapplied, someone obviously receives it. The beneficiary has the right to claim the property back from a subsequent recipient, because he retains equitable title to the property unless the recipient is a bona fide purchaser for value of a legal title to the prop-erty without notice. Besides merely 'following' the trust property into the hands of third-party recipients, also known as 'strangers' to the trust, the beneficiary may trace his equitable interest in the property into the proceeds of exchanges. Finally, the beneficiary may have a *personal* claim against recipients of trust property or its traceable proceeds for its money value. We will discuss this in detail, but a few things should be said now so as to clearly distinguish the claims against third parties.

11.121   The plaintiff will be able to rely only upon a personal claim against the recipient of trust property or its proceeds (if such a claim is available, 11.188 et seq) if the recipient has destroyed or dissipated the trust property or proceeds, as no proprietary claim can be made. Obviously this personal claim will be significantly valuable only if the recipient is solvent. By contrast, a proprietary claim is most valuable in the case of the recipient's insolvency, because if the beneficiary can establish a proprietary right to property held by the recipient, that property does not form part of the recipient's estate in bankruptcy.

11.122   The preceding personal claim must be distinguished from personal liability for being an accessory to a breach of trust (11.104 et seq), although the recipient of trust property might also be an accessory. Therefore, against a stranger to the trust, the beneficiary may have three claims in respect of the misapplication of trust property. (1), a proprietary claim for the actual trust property or traceable proceeds that the stranger retains; (2), a personal claim to restore the trust, ie pay over money to the value of the trust property or traceable proceeds he received and then dissipated, ie spent as his own for his own purposes; and, (3), a personal claim for his being an accessory to the breach. Notice in particular the different basis and scope of liability between liability for 'knowing assistance' and liability for 'knowing receipt'. (For a very fine analysis of liability for knowing receipt and its difference from liability for knowing assistance see Mitchell and Watterson (2010).) The former is a kind of wrong, akin to the tort of inducing breach of contract, where the defendant is liable for participating in another's breach of duty—the assistant cannot breach the trust, only the trustee can, but he is liable for assisting the trustee in doing so. This can be a very extensive liability indeed, making the assistant liable for much more than the value of any trust property he might have received (if he received any at all), since the scheme of misapplication in which he assisted may have sent large amounts of trust property to others besides himself. The latter is not a kind of secondary liability at all; if a recipient of trust property knows that he receives it in breach of trust, or later finds this out, but uses the property for his own benefit in violation of the beneficiary's interest anyway, then he himself breaches a 'custodian' trustee relationship imposed upon him by law (11.188 et seq), and only he can breach the trust in this way, because only he has title to the trust property that he ought to hold on behalf of the beneficiaries. We now turn to consider in detail the rules of tracing. Remember throughout that tracing through different transactions may serve two purposes: (1) to allow the beneficiary to establish a *proprietary* claim to property still in the defendant's hands; and/or (2) to allow the beneficiary to say that his property was received by the defendant, in order to establish the defendant's *personal* recipient liability to restore the trust to the value of the trust property he received and then dissipated.

Tracing

11.123   It is obviously easiest to trace through direct substitutions of one item of property for another. If the trustee gives an antique chair that belongs to the trust to A who sells it for £500, then the beneficiary can claim that the £500 is the traceable proceeds of the chair. Almost all of the difficulty in tracing arises when the misapplied trust property is money, or is then traced into money, because what people tend to do with money is bank it. The reason why banking money causes problems is that bank accounts are typically *mixtures*, and tracing through mixtures raises a host of problems.

11.124 If A takes the £500 traceable proceeds and deposits them in his bank account, which has a balance of £1,000, raising the balance to £1,500, what does this new balance of £1,500 amount to in law? One view is that a bank account is a series of individual debts that add up to the current balance. Here the bank owes A at least two debts, one for £500, and as many further debts as correspond to the deposits that made up the previous balance of £1,000. The alternative view is that A and the bank agree under their contract that the bank will, in exchange for the title to the £500, replace A's right against the bank to be paid his current balance of £1,000, for a new right against the bank to be paid £1,500: in essence A exchanges the £500 plus one debt owed him by the bank for a new, more valuable debt owed him by the bank. Thus the old balance is fully replaced by a new balance, and a bank account balance at any one time is a simple whole or 'monolith', which is not made up of a series of debts. On this basis it has been contended that the bank is a bona fide purchaser of the £500 for value (Gleeson (1995) *Foskett v McKeown* (2001) per Lord Millett, 127D). The bank, either on the 'series of debts' or the 'monolithic debt' analysis, raises A's balance to £1,500, and thereby valuably enhances A's rights. Unless the bank has notice that the money is paid into the account in breach of trust, the bank is a bona fide purchaser for value of the £500 in cash, or of the rights represented in a cheque worth £500 if that is what A deposited. There is an alternative view, which is that raising the depositor's account balance is just a 'book entry', and doesn't by itself amount to giving good value *for the purposes of the* bona fide *purchaser rule*. The bank would only give good value, on this perspective, when it paid out money in accordance with the raised bank balance. The issue cannot be settled here, and we shall follow Gleeson and Lord Millett, if only because Millett took this approach in the leading tracing case. On this view, then, the beneficiary must trace the cash or cheque into the proceeds that the trustee acquires under this further exchange transaction with the bank, that is, into the new debt the bank owes him, either into the new debt of £500 on the 'series of debts' view, or into the new debt of £1,500 on the 'monolith' view. Of course a withdrawal is just the opposite of a deposit, and is just as much a purchase for value. The customer, in return for cash, or in the case of a cheque, in return for the bank's complying with his order to pay a third party, gives value since under his contract with the bank the debt the bank owes him is extinguished in whole or in part to the value of the withdrawal.

The 'first in, first out' rule

11.125 The 'series of debts' view is the common law view of bank accounts for the purposes of regulating the relations between banker and customer. When a customer withdraws money from the bank account, he extinguishes one or more of the debts the bank owes him. So for example, assume A's account has had only two transactions so far: one deposit of £1,000 and one deposit of £500. If A withdraws £400, the bank in providing him with those funds has extinguished one of these debts by that amount. Either the £1,000 debt is reduced to £600, leaving debts of £600 and £500, or the £500 debt is reduced, leaving debts of £1,000 and £100. Which debt is it? At common law *Clayton's Case* (1816) decides that in the case of current or 'running' accounts where the intentions of the parties do not determine the issue a 'first in, first out' rule applies. The first debt is paid off first, as if the debts stood in a queue waiting for extinction. So here the result of A's withdrawal is that the £1,000 debt is reduced to £600, and the £500 debt is untouched.

If A had withdrawn £1,200, that would have first fully extinguished the £1,000 debt, and then reduced the £500 debt to £300.

11.126   *Clayton's Case* establishes the rule between A and the bank as to the disposition of their serial transactions on the 'series of debts' view—should it also regulate the relations between A, if he is a trustee, and the beneficiary, for the purposes of tracing withdrawals that follow the deposit of trust money? Assume in the example above that the £1,000 deposit was A's own money, but the subsequent £500 deposit was an unauthorised deposit of trust money. If *Clayton's Case* is followed, then the £1,000 credit against the bank would be A's alone, and so the beneficiary could not trace into that; his money went into creating the £500 credit. Under the 'first in, first out' rule of *Clayton's Case*, then, A's subsequent withdrawals up to the value of £1,000 would all be withdrawals of his money only, and only withdrawals after that would represent money into which the beneficiary can trace, because only they would be substitutions for the debt in which his interest lies. Obviously, it matters what rule is adopted, because it often matters which withdrawals represent trust money and which the trustee's own. For instance, if the trustee buys a valuable painting with one withdrawal, but then withdraws all the rest of the money to spend on riotous living (giving rise to no assets one can trace into), the beneficiaries will obviously hope that the first withdrawal, to buy the painting, can be shown to have been made with their money, rather than the money that was dissipated.

11.127   The question arose in *Pennell v Deffell* (1853), and then again in *Re Hallett's Estate* (1880). Both were cases in which a trustee paid trust money into his own account. In *Pennell* the 'first in, first out' rule in *Clayton's Case* was applied by the CA in Chancery, to the detriment of the beneficiaries under the trust; *Clayton's Case* was considered to have settled what the correct approach to bank accounts was. The CA reconsidered this in *Re Hallett's*. There the trustee paid trust funds into his bank account first, and then added money of his own; he then made withdrawals of money, which he dissipated. Under the 'first in, first out' rule, the trust money went into the dissipated withdrawals. The CA decided that the 'first in, first out' rule should not be applied; rather, a presumption of honesty should be attributed to the trustee, so that he was taken to have withdrawn his own money from the account first.

11.128   Thesiger LJ dissented:

> *Equity has gone very far in aid of trust creditors when it holds that they may follow and obtain in priority to general creditors moneys paid to a banker, and, therefore, no longer existing in specie as moneys numbered and earmarked, but converted into debt, and it may be that the distinguished judges [in Pennell v Deffell] may have thought that equity had gone far enough, and that in the absence of express appropriation the general rule of appropriation of payments in and out of a bank account should apply to that debt when forming part of a larger debt made up as to the rest of moneys not trust moneys paid into the bank.*

It is always worth remembering in respect of tracing that, the more favourable the rules are to trust beneficiaries, the less favourable they are not only to the trustee, but also to his creditors.

11.129   In *Re Oatway* (1903) the trustee purchased shares with money from a bank account in which trust money and other money (treated as his own by the court) had been combined. When the shares were purchased, there was enough money in the account to buy the shares without needing any of the trust money for the purchase, so if the *Re Hallett's* presumption that the trustee spends his own money first applied the shares would be his own. The remaining funds, however, were later all withdrawn and dissipated. Joyce J refused to apply the presumption:

> [W]hen any of the money drawn out has been invested, and the investment remains in the name or under the control of the trustee, the rest of the balance having been afterwards dissipated by him, he cannot maintain that the investment which remains represents his own money alone, and that what has been spent and can no longer be traced and recovered was the money of the trust . . . the trustee must be debited with all the sums that have been withdrawn and applied to his own use so as to be no longer recoverable, and the trust money in like manner be debited with any sums taken out and duly invested in the names of the proper trustees. The order of priority in which the various withdrawals and investments have been respectively made is wholly immaterial.

11.130 The result of these decisions together is apparently to give the beneficiary the right to control the bookkeeping of the bank account to his advantage, to 'cherry-pick' the valuable expenditures, claiming his money went into any profitable investment and denying it went into any untraceable expenditure. This 'cherry-picking' result, however, is no longer justified by the interplay of the *Re Hallett* presumption and *Re Oatway* discretion not to apply it where it would disfavour the beneficiary. Rather, as put by Smith ((1997), at 158, 183 et seq), and by Lord Millett in *Foskett v McKeown* (2000) (11.156 et seq) the beneficiary may trace into such withdrawals as he pleases (within the arithmetic limits of what he and the trustee contributed) on the principle that all reasonable inferences will be made against a wrongdoer whose own act gave rise to the factual difficulty (*Armory v Delamirie* (1722)). In this case, the wrongdoing trustee created the problem by mixing the trust funds with his own, so as he 'unmixes' the funds by making various withdrawals, the beneficiary, not he, can choose which 'unmixing' withdrawals belongs to each of them.

The 'lowest intermediate balance' rule

11.131 This right to control the bookkeeping of the account extends, however, only to withdrawals. Subsequent *deposits* by the wrongdoing trustee to the bank account are not presumed to be repayments to replace any trust moneys that have been withdrawn and dissipated (*James Roscoe (Bolton) Ltd v Winder* (1915)); this makes obvious sense, because if the trustee wished to make good his breach and restore the trust, it hardly seems likely that he would do so by adding money to his own bank account. This decision leads to the 'lowest intermediate balance' rule of tracing into bank accounts. Beneficiaries cannot trace in an arithmetically impossible way. If, for example, the trustee paid £500 of trust money into his account with £500 of his own, and then £900 is withdrawn, at least £400 of trust money must have been withdrawn. A subsequent addition of the trustee's own money cannot create a new source of funds into withdrawals from which the beneficiaries can trace.

Tracing amongst innocents

11.132 Different rules apply to tracing through bank accounts when the money that the trustee mixes in one bank account comes from different trusts, or when an innocent volunteer receives trust money and adds it to his own bank account. This makes obvious sense because there are no presumptions justified by a party's wrongdoing that can lie against equally innocent parties; the rules must be neutral. Note, the wrongdoer/innocent distinction is *not* equivalent to the distinction between the trustee and third-party recipients. Of course a trustee who misapplies trust property is always treated as a wrongdoer, however 'innocent' he is; that is his state of mind is irrelevant. But the state of mind of third parties is relevant; if they have sufficient knowledge that the property they received came to them in breach of trust (a tricky question, dealt with at 11.188 et seq), then they will be treated just like a defaulting trustee, and will be subject to all the presumptions against a wrongdoer in the tracing exercise. In a case where none of a wrongdoer's money is involved, say where a trustee wrongfully mixed the funds of two trusts together, the general rule that apparently applies to tracing in and out of such a mixture is the 'first in, first out' rule of *Clayton's Case*. The application of the rule here has been criticised (see eg Smith (1997), at 193–4), and it is suggested that the innocents should be able to trace into all the withdrawals and into any money that remains in shares proportionate to the amounts that they contributed. Such a solution would be in line with the common law rule governing 'fluid' mixtures, ie mixtures of goods such as oil where the separate identity of the mixed parts cannot be ascertained—the innocent owners of the mixed goods co-own the whole in proportion to the amounts they contributed (see Birks (1992); *The Ypatianna* (1988)).

The proportionate shares solution

11.133   The applicability of the rule in *Clayton's Case* to these situations was, however, reluctantly affirmed by the CA in *Barlow Clowes International Ltd v Vaughan* (1992). The case concerned the proper means of allocating the remaining assets in a pooled investment scheme amongst the contributing investors. All three judges, however, held that the authorities indicated that the rule was not to be applied blindly in all circumstances. In this case, because the investment scheme involved the pooling of investment funds, the contributors could be presumed to intend that their interests in the fund were proportionate to their contributions, so they were entitled to be traced as co-owners into the remaining funds in proportionate shares. Leggatt LJ's dissatisfaction with the rule in *Clayton's Case* was most apparent, saying it had 'nothing to do with tracing'. In *Russell-Cooke Trust Co v Prentis* (2003) Lindsay J also refused to apply the rule in *Clayton's Case* to the remaining funds of another investment scheme where it was clear to the investors that purchased securities would not be allocated on a strict 'first come, first served' basis when their payments were received; as in *Barlow Clowes*, the 'proportionate shares' or *pari passu* solution was adopted. In *Commerzbank Aktiengesellschaft v IMB Morgan plc* (2004), Collins J refused to apply the rule where it would be impracticable and unjust to do so and, again, the proportionate shares solution was applied. In *Charity Commissioners v Framjee* (2014) Henderson J said:

> [T]he authorities establish that, although the rule in Clayton's Case is probably still the default rule in England and Wales which has to be applied in the absence of anything better, it may be displaced with relative ease in favour of a solution which produces a fairer result: see generally Barlow Clowes International Ltd (in liq) v Vaughan [1992] 4 All ER 22 and Russell-Cooke Trust Co v Prentis [2002] EWHC 2227 (Ch), [2003] 2 All ER 478. In the latter case, Lindsay J considered the possible application of Clayton's Case in relation to a shortfall in funds held in a solicitor's client account, and said at [55]:

'It is plain from all three of the judgments in the Barlow Clowes case, the third being that of Dillon LJ, that the rule can be displaced by even a slight counterweight. Indeed, in terms of its actual application between beneficiaries who have in any sense met a shared misfortune, it might be more accurate to refer to the exception that is, rather than the rule in, Clayton's Case.'

The rolling charge solution

11.134   The mode of tracing between innocents Woolf and Leggatt LJJ preferred in *Barlow Clowes* is called the 'rolling charge' or 'North American' solution (as it is applied in Canada and the USA; see eg *Re Ontario Securities Commission and Greymac Credit Corpn* (1986)). The money contributed by innocents is traced into mixtures so that they become proportionate co-owners of the whole, but the 'lowest intermediate balance' rule is properly taken account of, as is the *Foskett* presumption against the wrongdoer as between the trustee and the beneficiaries as co-owners of the trust assets. Assume a rogue trustee, T, pays into his account £500 of beneficiary A's, and then £500 of beneficiary B's, which already contains £500 of his own, raising the balance to £1,500. Now assume T withdraws £750 and dissipates the money. By *Re Hallett's*, T will be presumed to spend his own £500 first and so only £250 of the trust money. As co-owners in proportionate shares, A and B will suffer the loss equally, each now tracing into a half share of £750. Now T adds £500 from beneficiary C. Under the principle of the lowest intermediate balance, it must be the case that A and B can only trace into the £750, which is all the trust money that remains when C's money is added, not into C's contribution. From now on, however, the mixing means that C's fate is linked with A's and B's as proportionate co-owners of the entirety of their traceable money: A and B each have a $(1/2 \times £750)/£1,250 = 3/10$ share, and C has a 4/10 share of the whole of £1,250 of trust money.

11.135   Under the same scenario, the rule in *Clayton's Case* delivers the following result: the £250 trust money attributed to T's withdrawal of £750 will, under the 'first in, first out' rule of *Clayton's Case*, be £250 from A's contribution alone, so if that is the end of the story, A will receive only £250, while B will receive his full £500 back. Assume now that T adds £500 of C's, who is also an innocent. T then withdraws £500. This withdrawal will wipe out A's remaining traceable £250, will reduce by £250 B's money, and leave C's money untouched. If the money the trustee withdraws is dissipated, and the story ends there, then the timing of the deposits will mean that, although each contributed £500, A can trace into nothing, B £250 in the account, and C his full £500 in the account.

11.136   Notice that both the 'rolling charge' mode and the 'first in, first out' rule will require a careful examination of the transactions over the history of the account, which will be expensive (accountants don't work for free); expenses that will, in an insolvency, reduce the total amount of funds available for distribution. This was the case in *Barlow Clowes*, and this was the main consideration for the court's not applying the 'rolling charge' solution, despite the fact that Woolf and Leggatt thought it the most fair. Note that while the typical effect of the rule in *Clayton's Case* is to prejudice early contributors, the effect of the proportionate co-ownership solution adopted in *Barlow Clowes* prejudices late contributors. Given that we are concerned with tracing the actual contributions, the lowest intermediate balance rule ought to apply. But the proportionate shares solution ignores this rule, putting the contributor who paid in money long ago on the same footing as one who contributed last week, even though it is almost certain that, on any realistic examination of the past account withdrawals, a significant proportion of the early contributor's money was withdrawn.

11.137   In the Singapore case of *Pars Ram Brothers (Pte) Ltd v Australian & New Zealand Banking Group Ltd* (2018) the court reviewed the case law on tracing between innocents in the case of a spice company, concerning stocks of pepper and the proportions in which the receipts for the sale of these should be allocated to various claimants. There were sufficient records to give the court a choice between applying the proportionate share solution or the rolling charge solution, and the court chose the latter. The case also shows that there is a lot of money in pepper.

Tracing with respect to overdrawn accounts and backwards tracing

11.138   One 'backwards traces' when one traces into property purchased by the recipient *before* he receives the money that is traced. If a rogue trustee buys an antique table worth £3,000 *on credit*, by taking a loan from a bank, or by using his overdraft facility, or with his credit card, and then later pays off the debt incurred with trust money, logically it is clear that the antique table is the traceable proceeds of the trust money. As Smith (1997, at 146) says:

> Suppose that D buys a car from C with some money. If we were tracing the value inherent in ownership of the money, we could trace it into ownership of the car. Now change the facts slightly, so that D buys the car on credit; he takes ownership of the car, but he is C's debtor in respect of the purchase price. A day later, D pays the debt with the money being traced. Can we trace from the money into the car as before? It is difficult to see why not. There is no substantial change in the transaction; the period of credit might be reduced to a minute or a second to better make this point. If that is right, then when money is used to pay a debt, it is traceable into what was acquired for the incurring of the debt . . . . [I]nstead of tracing through substitutions in D's hands, we could trace through substitutions in C's hands. When the car is bought for cash, the car is the traceable proceeds of the money; that is the substitution in D's hands. Clearly, from the other perspective the money is the traceable proceeds of the car; that is the substitution in C's hands. It is easy to show that adding a period of credit does not change this conclusion . . . C gave up ownership of the car in exchange for a debt; that debt asset is therefore the traceable proceeds of the car. Later, the debt is paid with the money in question. This money is therefore the traceable proceeds of the debt; but since the debt was the proceeds of the car, therefore the money is the proceeds of the car, via an intermediate step.

Unfortunately, the law has not adequately recognised this logical and compelling position, in part as a result of some confusion about tracing into overdrawn bank accounts, ie about the way in which a bank receives deposits.

11.139   Normally, when money is paid into a bank account, there is no difficulty determining the substitution that has occurred. The bank takes title to the money and gives value in exchange in the form of the increased bank balance. The increased bank balance is, of course, the traceable proceeds of the payment in of the money. Where £500 is paid into an account that is £500 in overdraft, resulting in a balance of zero, what are the traceable proceeds? In exchange for the title to the money, the bank gives value in the form of the reduction of the debt it is owed by the customer to zero. No debt now exists between the bank and the customer, and therefore no rights between them that can be the traceable proceeds of the £500 payment. For this reason, it is generally but wrongly assumed that the payment of a debt is the end of the tracing exercise, since there just *are no proceeds*. While it is absolutely right to deny that anything of value *in the account* is traceable by the claimant, because there is no existing right between the bank and customer, this does not mean that the tracing exercise must end when the rights between the bank and its customer 'run out'; if you stop there you have merely given up the tracing exercise prematurely; the tracing exercise has not come to a natural conclusion by itself. The overdraft was incurred, after all, by withdrawing funds, and the payment of the overdraft is therefore traceable into those funds, and into whatever those funds were spent upon.

11.140   Of course, tracing into the proceeds of an overdraft may be evidentially difficult, and therefore may often be impossible in practice, but that is no reason to deny this form of backwards tracing in principle, especially in clear cases where it is apparent that what was purchased on credit was subsequently paid off by trust funds. Consider the case of a trustee who uses trust money to pay off his credit card bill: all the card transactions are clearly recorded in his monthly statements and receipts, and it would seem preposterous for the court to refuse to trace into the television, antique table, and suit of clothes so manifestly paid for with the beneficiary's money.

11.141   It is clear that the courts have actually backwards traced in particular cases: in *Agip* the court allowed the plaintiff to treat a payment by Lloyds Bank in London to the defendant as the transfer of his money even though the payment from the plaintiff to Lloyds' correspondent bank in New York, was made *later*. Thus Lloyds had made the payment to the defendant before, and in expectation of, receiving a corresponding amount from the plaintiff via a New York bank (see also the tracing through credit facilities in *El Ajou v Dollar Land Holdings plc* (1993)). Furthermore, backwards tracing necessarily underlies the ability of equity to trace through bank cheque clearing systems generally, since the settlement between banks is not simultaneous with the crediting and debiting of accounts. The HL conducted a backwards tracing exercise in *Foskett v McKeown* (2001) without explicitly stating as much (see 11.155–11.158) and, more recently, in *Law Society v Haider* (2003) Judge Richards QC allowed the claimant to trace from a payment discharging a mortgage into the house that was purchased with the mortgage loan, and thence into the proceeds of the sale of that house and into another house purchased with those proceeds. The decision is clearly inexplicable if not for backwards tracing. Notice that tracing into the house in such a case requires that the mortgage loan was a purchase-money mortgage, ie the mortgage loan was used to acquire the house. If a trustee had taken out a loan secured by a mortgage on a house he already owned, one would trace into whatever the trustee acquired with the loan money, not into the house in this case. The fact that the loan is secured against the trustee's house is utterly irrelevant in both cases—it is what the loan money was used to buy that is relevant.

11.142   The CA considered backwards tracing in *Bishopsgate Investment Management Ltd v Homan* (1995). At first instance Vinelott J was willing to allow backwards tracing in limited circumstances, ie:

> . . . *where an asset was acquired by [the defendant] with moneys borrowed from an overdrawn or loan account and there was an inference that when the borrowing was incurred it was the intention that it should be repaid by misappropriation of [the plaintiff's] money. Another possibility was that moneys misappropriated from [the plaintiff] were paid into an overdrawn account of [the defendant] in order to reduce the overdraft and so make finance available within the overdraft limits for [the defendant] to purchase some particular asset.*

Dillon LJ accepted this as correct, but Leggatt LJ found the contention utterly wrong on the basis that it was simply impossible for a claim to be made in respect of an asset acquired before the misappropriation took place. There is no majority decision on this point in the case, because the third judge, Henry LJ, simply agreed with both judgments. Backwards tracing was inconclusively considered again by the CA in *Foskett v McKeown* (1998) (see also *Boscawen v Bajwa* (1995) (11.165)).

11.143   As Smith (1994) points out, however, the basis for Vinelott's version of backwards tracing is deficient in any event. As to the first case he mentions, it seems to violate the general principle of tracing to require that the defendant *intends* to use the misappropriated trust property to purchase the asset. All that is generally required is that he actually acquire the asset in exchange for the plaintiff's property—his intention is entirely irrelevant. As to the second case, this is in violation of the rules of tracing, because if the payment of the overdraft is traced, it should be traced into the asset for which the debt *was incurred*, not for any new purchases enabled by the reduction of the overdraft. While those purchases might not have been possible 'but for' the payment in of the plaintiff's money, the new overdraft facility allows the defendant to use the *bank's money* to make more purchases, not the plaintiff's. The plaintiff's money can only be traced via the overdraft into what was purchased so as to give rise to the overdraft debt.

11.144   A form of backwards tracing has now been recognised, implicitly in the CA's decision in *Relfo Limited v Varsani* (2014), and explicitly in the UKPC in *Republic of Brazil v Durant* (2015). In both cases, the courts allowed the claimants to trace through a series of payments, including where the payment traced took place before the payment which was the source of the traced funds. Schematically, both cases involved payments of the following kind: A caused B to make a payment to C; A then afterward paid B with funds held on trust; in both cases, the court held that the claimant could trace the second payment to B into the first, prior payment from B to C, so that C held those funds as a recipient of trust property. Unfortunately, in neither case did the analysis make it clear whether the court was adopting the view of 'backwards tracing' endorsed *obiter* by Vinelott J which we have just seen was criticised by Smith, or whether it was pursuing principles endorsed by Smith.

11.145   Justifying the court's decision to allow backwards tracing Lord Toulson said:

> [38] The development of increasingly sophisticated and elaborate methods of money laundering, often involving a web of credits and debits between intermediaries, makes it particularly important that a court should not allow a camouflage of interconnected transactions to obscure its vision of their true overall purpose and effect. If the court is satisfied that the various steps are part of a co-ordinated scheme, it should not matter that, either as a deliberate part of the choreography or possibly because of the incidents of the banking system, a debit appears in the bank account of an intermediary before a reciprocal credit entry. The Board agrees with Sir Richard Scott V-C's observation in Foskett v McKeown [1998] Ch 265 that the availability of equitable remedies ought to depend on the substance of the transaction in question and not on the strict order in which associated events occur.
>
> ...
>
> [40] The Board therefore rejects the argument that there can never be backward tracing, or that the court can never trace the value of an asset whose proceeds are paid into an overdrawn account. But the claimant has to establish a co-ordination between the

depletion of the trust fund and the acquisition of the asset which is the subject of the tracing claim, looking at the whole transaction, such as to warrant the court attributing the value of the interest acquired to the misuse of the trust fund. This is likely to depend on inference from the proved facts, particularly since in many cases the testimony of the trustee, if available, will be of little value.

11.146 Apparently, then, the UKPC has adopted a restricted application of backwards tracing, restricted that is to cases where the debt and the payment with which it is discharged are in substance part of the same overall transaction, such that there is some sort of co-ordination between the depletion of the trust fund and the acquisition of the asset. (For discussion, see Penner (2017).)

Proprietary claims to traceable proceeds: charges and equitable ownership

11.147 Once the process or exercise of tracing succeeds in locating the beneficiary's interest, he may then make a claim in respect of that interest, whether against the trustee or a third party (see *Boscawen v Bajwa* (1995) *per* Millett LJ). Note, however, that a wrongdoing trustee may at any stage do his duty and reinstate or restore the trust. If he does so, he must do so properly. As Millett LJ points out (11.30), the trustee has no right to 'borrow' trust money for his own purposes and then just replace what he has borrowed. Thus if he used £1,000 of trust money to make an unauthorised investment in shares now worth £2,000, he will only restore the trust if he now transfers £2,000 into the trust, or if all the beneficiaries are *sui juris*, by getting them to consent to his retaining the shares (11.33). If the shares fall in value to £750, he may only restore the trust by replacing the full £1,000 plus interest. If he used £500 of trust money plus £500 of his own to buy the shares, and they rise in value to £2,000, he is similarly liable to restore the trust by a payment of £1,000 or a transfer of half of the shares into the trust if the beneficiaries are all *sui juris* and so direct. If the shares fall in value to £750, he must hold the shares as if the trust had a charge over them to secure his repayment of £500 plus interest.

11.148 This example of the trustee restoring the trust should remind you of the basic terms in which equity allows the beneficiary to deal with a misapplication of trust property against a trustee. He may either falsify the account, in which case he denies any proprietary interest in the proceeds of that transaction in the beneficiary's hands, claiming instead that the misapplication never took place and looking to the trustee personally to restore the trust *in specie* or in money, *or* he may adopt the transaction *in any form most favourable to the beneficiary* (eg as a loan at interest, *or* an investment to acquire business profits). Where the trustee misapplies the trust property so as to acquire a valuable asset, the beneficiary will adopt the transaction as an authorised purchase for the trust, ie claim that the trust owns the asset; in short he makes an equitable ownership claim.

11.149 Where, on the other hand, the asset acquired by the trustee is less valuable than the trust money misapplied to get it, there are two ways of framing the beneficiary's claim. Conventionally, it is said that the beneficiary can 'bring a personal claim against the trustee for breach of trust and enforce an equitable lien or charge on the proceeds to secure restoration of the trust fund' (*Foskett v McKeown* (2001) *per* Lord Millett). But this seems wrong in principle: by bringing the personal claim for breach of trust, the beneficiary falsifies the account, and disowns any interest in the proceeds of the falsified transaction, and thus should have no right to claim a lien over them, or any other property of the trustee for that matter. Lord Millett himself exposed the illogic here in *Foskett* itself when he criticised the CA's reasoning:

> I should now deal with the finding of all the members of the Court of Appeal that the plaintiffs were entitled to enforce a lien on the proceeds of the policy to secure repayment of the premiums paid with their money. This is inconsistent with the decision of the majority that the plaintiffs were not entitled to trace the premiums into the policy. An equitable lien is a proprietary interest by way of security. It is enforceable against the trust property and its traceable proceeds. The finding of the majority that the plaintiffs had no proprietary interest in the policy or its proceeds should have been fatal to their claim to a lien.

The better way to explain the beneficiary's right to a lien in these circumstances is as follows: a beneficiary can adopt the misapplication of trust funds in any form most valuable to him; here, he will adopt the transaction as a *secured loan to the trustee*, or as Lord Millett puts it in the quotation above, as *proprietary interest by way of security*; the beneficiary will authorise the misapplication of the trust money as a loan to the trustee, secured against the property he acquired with it. Thus the beneficiary claims an equitable lien or charge over the asset, which will in part satisfy his personal claim for repayment of the 'loan' by the trustee. To the extent the trustee fails to repay this 'loan', the beneficiary has the right, like any chargee or lien holder, to possess and sell the asset; the trustee, like any chargor or borrower giving security, is liable for the full amount of the loan, so if the sale of the asset does not generate enough money to pay back the full amount, the trustee will be personally liable to dig into his pocket to make up the shortfall.

11.150   It is sometimes suggested (eg Elliott and Mitchell (2004)) that the beneficiary may claim both the ownership of an asset and that the trustee should personally make up any shortfall if the asset's value is less than the amount that was misapplied to acquire it. This view is based on *Re Lake* (1903), but this case is in conflict with earlier authority, *Thornton v Stokill* (1855) (see also Mowbray et al (2008, at 777; Oakley (2003), at 768 fn 40), and seems wrong in principle: a beneficiary cannot logically adopt an asset as an authorised trust property and at the same time falsify the account so as to make the trustee personally liable. The beneficiary has an *election* either to adopt the transaction in any form he chooses, or falsify the account, but elect he must: he cannot have it both ways.

11.151   The same basic principles apply to the beneficiary's making a proprietary claim against a third-party recipient of trust property, except that a beneficiary is never entitled to a charge against another innocent contributor to the asset traced into. (See, however, 11.159 for the case where an innocent recipient receives property which consists of a mixture of trustee and trust money.) Where (1) an innocent third-party recipient purchases an asset with trust money and some money of his own, or (2) property is purchased by a trustee or other wrong-doer with a mixture of money from several trusts, each innocent party is entitled to a proportionate equitable co-ownership share in the proceeds. In neither case would a personal claim for the value contributed secured by a lien on the proceeds be appropriate, because this claim puts one party at an advantage as against the other party (or parties) and, as the parties are equally innocent, there is no basis for choosing between them so as to give one such an advantage.

Claiming followed property, 'clean' traceable proceeds, and 'mixed' traceable proceeds

11.152 Where there have been no substitutions of trust property requiring tracing to locate the beneficiary's interest, ie where the beneficiary is able simply to follow the trust property into the hands of the trustee (eg the case of the trustee who takes a trust painting for his office, 11.117–11.118) or a third party (not a bona fide purchaser for value), the beneficiary simply specifically enforces the trust. The trustee will be required to hold the property on trust again as he should, and the court will order any third party to deliver it up or assign the legal title back to the trustee (typically a replacement trustee). By specifically enforcing the trust, the beneficiary merely 'vindicates' his continuing equitable title in the trust property.

11.153 In the case of 'clean' substitutions, ie where the original trust property is spent to acquire traceable proceeds, but only trust property is spent—there are no mixtures of the trust value with the trustee's or a third party's—then, in the case of a trustee or a stranger who receives the trust property knowing it came to him in breach of trust, the beneficiary can adopt the misapplication either as the purchase of the proceeds for the trust, or as a secured loan of the trust funds to the wrongdoing trustee or recipient (see eg *Re Hallett's*, per Jessel MR; *Foskett v McKeown* (2000)). Where the proceeds are of equal or greater value to the property misapplied, the beneficiary will elect for the former, claiming equitable ownership of the proceeds, ie claiming that the proceeds are trust property. Where the proceeds are of lower value than the misapplied trust property, the beneficiary will make the latter claim, ie a personal claim for the return of the value of the trust property, secured with a lien on the proceeds.

11.154 In the case of an innocent third party, the beneficiary can follow any trust property or its traceable proceeds into the third party's hands; he can then specifically enforce his equitable interest in this property against this third party. Where the innocent third party then himself makes a clean substitution of the property in his hands, the beneficiary can likewise trace into this, but he can only adopt this transaction in order to make an ownership claim of the proceeds. So, for example, if a trustee writes a cheque on the trust's bank account in favour of his nephew, telling him it is a birthday present, and the nephew spends this money on a motorbike, which is now worth less than the trust money he paid for it, the beneficiary cannot adopt the nephew's purchase of the motorbike as a secured loan of the trust money, and claim a lien on the motorbike as security for the repayment by the nephew of the full amount. The beneficiary is restricted to claiming the motorbike as trust property, whatever its value. (Of course, the beneficiary will be happy with this result if the proceeds are more valuable than the trust money spent for them, but the risk of the value being lower lies with the beneficiary too.) Take note: if, *after* receiving the trust property, the innocent third party *learns* that the property came to him in breach of trust, and subsequently enters into any transaction with the trust property, he will be liable as a knowing 'dealer', that is 'spender' of the trust funds, and will be personally liable to dig into his own pocket and restore the value of the property he dissipated (11.188 et seq).

11.155 Where a trustee or a knowing recipient or dealer purchases property with a mixture of his own and trust money, the beneficiary, in accordance with the case of a clean substitution, is entitled to a lien over the proceeds, or proportionate equitable co-ownership interest in the proceeds. This was made clear by Lord Millett in *Foskett v McKeown* (2000):

> Where a trustee wrongfully uses trust money to provide part of the cost of acquiring an asset, the beneficiary is entitled at his option either to claim a proportionate share

*of the asset or to enforce a lien upon it to secure his personal claim [but see **11.149**] against the trustee for the amount of the misapplied money. It does not matter whether the trustee mixed the money with his own in a single fund before using it to acquire the asset, or made separate payments (whether simultaneously or sequentially) out of the differently owned funds to acquire a single asset.*

11.156   In *Foskett* a trustee used his own funds to purchase the first two premiums, then trust funds to pay two later premiums, on a life insurance policy in favour of his wife and children. The beneficiaries claimed that they were entitled to a share of the proceeds of the policy, which were paid when the trustee committed suicide, a share proportionate to the value of the premiums paid with trust money. The HL, by a 3:2 decision, reversing the CA (1998), agreed. In the leading judgment, Lord Millett held that the insurance company's contractual duty to pay the £1m pay-out on death was a single 'chose in action' (ie a contractual right to be paid a certain sum, which is regarded as a property right), which was acquired when the contract was formed but which was paid for in instalments. The complicating fact that obscured this analysis is that, unlike in typical purchase agreements, the number of instalment payments and thus the total price to be paid for the insurance policy cannot be known at the outset; indeed, the total purchase price is only known immediately prior to the end of the contract, ie when the insured dies and the insurer must forthwith pay the £1m (at which point the contract is at an end). Thus the beneficiaries could rightly trace from the instalment payments made with the trust moneys into the contractual right to the payoff on the assured's death, and claim a proportionate share of the proceeds.

11.157   Lords Hope and Steyn, who would have affirmed the majority decision of the CA, adopted a different analysis: the contract of insurance was to be seen as the outright purchase of a piece of property, the contractual right to the pay-off on the assured's death, with the first premium. However, that property right is subject to defeasance: the policy (the contract) and the right to be paid £1m on death (the property) will lapse if further premiums are not paid. An analogy here might be with the purchase of a long residential lease, of a flat in London, say, for £250,000, but with a requirement in the lease to pay £2,000 per annum in 'ground rent'. One is full owner of the leasehold interest with the first payment, although one might lose the lease for failure to pay the annual ground rent (assuming the failure to do so would entitle the landlord to re-enter the premises and forfeit the lease). But paying the ground rent does not constitute making a purchase payment instalment, by which one acquires a greater ownership share in the lease; it just prevents forfeiture, ie it preserves a property right, the lease, that one already fully has. Because of a wrinkle in the insurance contract, had the premiums paid with the trust money not been paid at all, the policy still would have stayed on foot. (Each premium had a savings element in it, and if a premium was missed the savings element of prior premiums was automatically employed to make up the missed premiums to keep the insurance element of the contract on foot; enough premiums had been paid before the trust money was used to cover those premiums even if they had not been made.) Therefore, the premiums paid with trust money did not save the policy from lapse, and so even had they not been made, the wife and children would have received the proceeds on death. In other words, as a matter of causation, it was not the case that *but for* the misapplication of trust money to pay the last two premiums the insurance contract would have lapsed. Lords Hope and Steyn would, therefore, have denied the beneficiaries a proportionate share.

11.158   Notice that Lord Millett's analysis depends upon the legitimacy of backwards tracing. To transfer property in return for being paid in instalments is to advance credit, and to pay for a property right in instalments is to discharge one's debt to the transferor in consideration of his transfer of the property; thus to trace the later trust money premiums into the right to the insurance pay-off is to trace backwards through the discharge of a debt into the property acquired by incurring the debt.

11.159 As in the case of a clean substitution, in the case of a mixed substitution the beneficiary's election of a co-ownership share or a charge will turn on whether the value of the proceeds has increased or declined. If £5,000 of trust money and £5,000 of the trustee's money went into the purchase of shares now worth £20,000, the beneficiary will claim a 50 per cent co-ownership of the shares. If they fall in value to £7,000, he will claim a charge over the shares, ie over *all* the shares, for the £5,000 value that went into them plus interest. Notice that in this case the lien extends to the whole of the property, not just that fraction of the property which represents the appropriate proportionate share. In essence, then, in this case the form in which the beneficiary adopts the misapplication is equivalent to the typical case of a mortgage lender; although the borrower usually puts in some money of his own, ie his 'down payment', the mortgagee's loan is secured against the whole of the property purchased with a mixture of their money. Where a third party receives an asset purchased with a mixture of the trustee's own money and trust money (as was the case in *Foskett*), the beneficiary will have the same election against the third party. In this case, unlike the case discussed in 11.151, the third party is *not a contributor* to the mixture. He is only entitled to whatever of the trustee's share of the asset is available after the beneficiary's claim is satisfied. Thus, if the beneficiary claims an ownership share because the asset has increased in value, the third party will be entitled to a share proportionate to the contribution to the mixture by the trustee. Where the beneficiary claims a lien, the third party is only entitled to whatever is left following the satisfaction of the lien. Note, however, that the third party is not personally liable to make up any shortfall if the asset does not satisfy the beneficiary's lien. Consider the following facts: in breach of trust the trustee uses £500 of his own money, £500 of trust money, to buy a painting which he gives to his nephew. The painting is now worth only £400. While the beneficiary has the right to have the painting sold to satisfy his lien over it to secure repayment of £500, the nephew is not liable for the £100 shortfall. The case is no different from one in which a person buys a house subject to a mortgage created by the vendor. The purchaser would be subject to the mortgagee's charge, so is in danger of having the house sold by the mortgagee to pay off the mortgage loan, but not being the mortgagor himself the purchaser is not personally liable under the mortgage loan to make up any shortfall if the sale price does not cover the outstanding debt.

11.160 Hayton and Mitchell ((2005), at 12–97) take the beneficiary's right to elect one step further, arguing that where the trustee buys an asset with both trust money and some of his own, but the facts indicate that *but for the use of the trust money he would not have been able to acquire the asset at all*, then if the asset rises in value the beneficiary should be able to claim ownership of the whole asset subject to a charge in favour of the trustee for the value he put in. For example, if the trustee because of his credit record is unable to borrow money to buy a house, and puts in £40,000 of trust money with £10,000 of his own to buy a house now worth £100,000, why, Hayton and Mitchell ask, should the beneficiaries be restricted to a co-ownership share of four-fifths, ie £80,000? Should they not be able to claim the whole subject to a charge in favour of the trustee for the return of his £10,000 plus interest? According to this analysis, the form in which the beneficiary adopts the misapplication of trust funds is a purchase of trust property that is assisted by a secured loan *from the trustee*. This analysis is doubtful for two reasons: one of principle, one of policy. As to the former, the analysis relies upon the correctness of a 'but for' approach to tracing (criticised at 11.143), and here, to claiming, ie on the use of a 'but for' test to determine the existence or scope of a claim, rather than upon strict transactional links in the case of tracing. The rationale of this objection is akin to that of the *James Roscoe (Bolton)* rule (11.131), which is that while the beneficiary can elect to adopt the transaction in different forms, he cannot do so in a way that presents the trustee as positively altruistic. (Why stop where Hayton and Mitchell do, treating the trustee as making a secured loan to the trust? Why not say that the trustee assisted the trust's purchase of the house by *giving* the trust £10,000 of his own?) To do that would belie the fact that the trustee was not only not altruistic in breaching the trust, but was actually taking advantage of it. As regards policy, remember also that a beneficiary most often relies upon proprietary rights against a recipient of trust property where the latter is insolvent, and so that if the ability to elect the form in which an unauthorised transaction is adopted is too generous it will be his creditors who will be harmed (11.128).

11.161   Recall (11.151) that in the case where property is the traceable proceeds of contributions made by two or more innocent parties, each party is entitled only to a co-ownership share of the proceeds in proportion to their contributions. It would be impossible to allow one an advantage over the others by giving him a lien over the whole of the proceeds to secure the repayment of his particular contribution. Hayton and Mitchell (Hayton (1990); (2001b), at 877; Hayton and Mitchell (2005)), however, argue that there might be a case of two innocents where there is a justified departure from the co-ownership share result, based on the decision in *Re Tilley's Will Trusts* (1967), in which the beneficiaries were *restricted* to a claim for a charge over assets purchased with trust money that had risen in value. The widow of a testator was trustee of his testamentary trust, and thoroughly confused the trust moneys with her own funds. She made several profitable property investments, but Ungoed-Thomas J decided that because the trustee (1) did not deliberately use the trust moneys, and (2) she had ample overdraft facilities to make the property purchase she did, and so did not, on a 'but for' basis, *rely* on any of the trust value to fund her purchases, the beneficiaries were entitled at most to a charge over the acquired property. It seems wrong in principle to allow this argument to be made by an 'innocent' *trustee*, since trustees are strictly liable for their misapplications of trust property, and should be susceptible to all the normal equitable claims regardless of their intentions or innocence. But, suggests Hayton, this decision might be justifiable in the case of an innocent volunteer recipient of trust funds who innocently mixed trust money with his own. Given his ample funds, it is not the case that 'but for' his use of trust money, he would not have made the profitable investment he made or bought the lottery ticket that won. Can he not therefore argue that the beneficiary should not benefit from his investment expertise or luck, ie that the beneficiary should be *restricted* to a personal claim for repayment of their money, secured by a lien or charge on the property?

11.162   While this argument draws upon a certain sense of fairness, it seems to prove too much. If the innocent mixer *could* have purchased the asset with all of his own funds, why should a beneficiary have any property right in the asset at all, ie even a lien, as opposed merely to a personal claim that he repays them an equivalent amount to what he received from the trust? The logic of this position seems to be that the innocent recipient was merely unjustly enriched by the receipt of the trust property, ie that following the breach he was merely more wealthy than he was before, and should return a similar amount of wealth, *not* that he was in possession of the beneficiary's property. But the logic of falsifying the account or adopting a misapplication, and of following and tracing, turns on the idea that a recipient *is* in possession of the beneficiary's property, and we can trace that property into whatever proceeds it contributes to the acquisition of. As Smith makes clear when he criticises 'but for' tracing (11.143)—and Hayton and Mitchell's position here is an example of relying upon such an approach to tracing and claiming—the intentions of the party who acquires the proceeds are irrelevant, and so should be any other facts about his general financial position.

The multiplication of claims and the 'exchange product theory' and 'power *in rem*' theories of claiming

11.163　It is perfectly possible for a beneficiary to be able to trace his equitable interest into multiplying tracks of substitutions. Consider the case where the trustee sells a trust asset, say an antique clock, to X, who is not a bona fide purchaser for value, for £2,000. The beneficiary can trace into the proceeds of that exchange, the £2,000, but at the same time can claim an ongoing equitable title in the clock. If X sells the clock to Y for £3,000, and Y is also not a bona fide purchaser, then the beneficiary's array of claims expand again, since he can trace into the £2,000, the £3,000, and still claim his equitable title in the clock. This process can go on indefinitely in principle. But, following the logic of falsifying the account or adopting the misapplying transaction at each step, the beneficiary must elect a path to one of the properties, whether he claims for an equitable charge or equitable (co-)ownership against the trustee, X, or Y. It is a difficult theoretical issue whether (1) the beneficiary has all of these property claims at once until he elects; or (2), his rights against these different defendants and their property are 'inchoate', in suspense, until he elects which party he will pursue, at which point his property right 'crystallises' as a fully fledged property right in the asset that party holds. We can refer to (1) as the 'exchange product' theory of claiming: the beneficiary is entitled to make a proprietary claim to the proceeds because the proceeds immediately become his, ie he gets an immediate equitable title to them, when they are received in exchange for the trust property; in a sense, they are automatically 'captured' by trust just like any property the trustee receives when he carries out an authorised transaction with the trust property. The election that the beneficiary is able to make against trustees and wrongdoing recipients exists because it is part and parcel of the beneficiary's equitable interest in the trust fund that he may elect to treat property acquired by a trustee or wrongdoer in breach of the trust terms either as items of the trust fund or as security for a loan to the trustee or wrongdoing recipient, ie in a form most favourable to him. We can refer to (2) as the 'power *in rem*' theory, because this theory says that the beneficiary has a power to vest himself with the equitable interest (either an ownership share or a lien) he elects, a power he exercises when he brings a claim against a recipient. The former view has been endorsed by Lord Millett in *Foskett*:

> A beneficiary of a trust is entitled to a continuing beneficial interest not merely in the trust property but in its traceable proceeds also, and his interest binds everyone who takes the property or its traceable proceeds except a bona fide purchaser for value without notice.

On this view, when a beneficiary elects to pursue one of several possible defendants, the property rights against the others are extinguished, for this amounts to his adoption of particular proceeds as *the* assets of the trust.

Subrogation claims reliant upon tracing

11.164   Subrogation is the acquisition of another person's rights against a third party upon the making of a payment: very roughly, by making a payment the plaintiff 'purchases' those rights. The classic example occurs in the insurance context—if I am insured against injuries caused by the negligence of others, my insurance company, upon paying me an insurance award compensating me for my loss, is entitled to sue the tortfeasor, ie the negligent injurer, in my name for damages. Thus acquiring my right to sue, the insurance company is said to be 'subrogated' to my claim against the tortfeasor. A different sort of subrogation is relevant here. In certain circumstances, if X pays off Y's debt to Z, X will, by operation of law, be subrogated to Z's right as a creditor. In other words, by paying off Z, X will in effect 'purchase' Z's right to the payment of the debt against Y. Notice that in the insurance example, the insurer takes over rights that the insured continues to have against his tortfeasor. The case is different where X pays off Y's debt to Z. By paying off Y's debt, X *extinguishes* the debt and thus Z's right as a creditor. The right against Y that X acquires by subrogation is a new right that arises by operation of law; in essence Y's debt is *revived* in favour of X and, in consequence, this is known as a case of 'reviving' subrogation (Mitchell (1994), at 4).

11.165   In *Boscawen v Bajwa* (1995) Bajwa intended to sell his mortgaged land for a price roughly equal to what he owed under the mortgage to the Halifax Building Society. On the sale Bajwa would be required to use the purchase money to pay off the mortgage, which would leave him with little if any proceeds for himself. The purchasers raised £140,000 on a mortgage loan from Abbey National, and the money was transferred to solicitors in advance of the completion of the sale. In breach of trust the money was advanced before completion and was applied to pay off the mortgage loan to Halifax. The sale never occurred (and the contract of sale not being in writing it was void (6.1), so there was no possibility of a decree of specific performance or a vendor–purchaser constructive trust in favour of Abbey National (4.6)) and as a result Bajwa ended up with an unmortgaged property, while Abbey National had advanced funds and received no mortgage on the property in return. The CA held that Abbey National was entitled to be subrogated to Halifax's mortgage on the land, thus entitling them to priority over a charge on the land that had been subsequently granted by the court to judgment creditors of Bajwa. The court clearly distinguished between the process of tracing, which allowed Abbey National to show that its value was received by Bajwa, and the claim to be subrogated.

11.166   Millett LJ said:

> If the plaintiff succeeds in tracing his property, whether in its original or in some changed form, into the hands of the defendant and overcomes any defences which are put forward on the defendant's behalf, he is entitled to a remedy. The remedy will be fashioned to the circumstances . . . If the plaintiff's money has been applied by the defendant, for example, not in the acquisition of a landed property but in its improvement, then the court may treat the land as charged with the payment to the plaintiff of a sum representing the amount by which the value of the defendant's land has been enhanced by the use of the plaintiff's money. And if the plaintiff's money has been used to discharge a mortgage on the defendant's land, then the court may achieve a similar result by treating the land as subject to a charge by way of subrogation in favour of the plaintiff . . . Tracing was the process by which the

Abbey National sought to establish that its money was applied in the discharge of the Halifax's charge; subrogation was the remedy which it sought in order to deprive Mr Bajwa . . . of the unjust enrichment which he would otherwise obtain at the Abbey National's expense.

11.167   The result in this case can be doubted. Note first that subrogation, while achieving a similar result in the case of a secured loan, is the opposite of backwards tracing. In backwards tracing, one traces into items purchased with the borrowed funds. In contrast, a subrogation claim allows the beneficiary claimant to stand in the shoes of the lender; in the case of an unsecured debt, for example a credit card debt that is paid off with trust money, the beneficiary will acquire by subrogation nothing more than *a personal claim* for money against the defendant, because that is all the credit card company had. In the case of a purchase-money mortgage, however, subrogation provides a result similar to backwards tracing. A backwards tracing claim would allow the beneficiary to trace his value into the property purchased with the credit given, and in the case of a mortgage of land, that will be the land itself, of course. The beneficiary might then claim a proportionate share of the value of the land or, if the recipient is a trustee or wrongdoer, elect to take a charge on it. By subrogation, the claimant will necessarily acquire a proprietary right in the land too, since the loan was a secured one, and the charge forms part of the right to which he is subrogated. But the claimant cannot acquire by subrogation an ownership or co-ownership share. So the first thing to note is that, if backwards tracing had been authoritatively recognised and applied in this case, the issue of subrogation would never have arisen, because a claim based on backwards tracing would have been superior.

11.168   There is a further 'fishy' aspect to this decision. As Millett LJ made abundantly clear in the case, the beneficiary's right to be subrogated arises by operation of law as a *restitutionary* remedy, to reverse the unjust enrichment the defendant would otherwise retain. Now, as we shall see in Chapter 12, some commentators have suggested that a stranger's proprietary and personal liability alike for receipt of trust property should be analysed as a liability arising in the law of restitution for unjust enrichment. This is in conflict with the traditional understanding of the law, which treats the beneficiary's proprietary claim against a recipient of trust property or its proceeds as a matter of his equitable title, and any personal liability of the recipient as a matter of his wrongdoing, ie as a fault-based liability. In view of this, *Boscawen* counts *either* as a revolutionary case in which the restitutionary nature of the beneficiary's claim against third-party recipients was recognised, *or* a case that mistakenly imports restitutionary principles into the property and fault-based rules governing liability for receipt of trust property. In *Primlake Ltd (in liquidation) v Matthews Associates* (2006) Lawrence Collins J held that a company was entitled to be subrogated to a mortgage loan owed by a dishonest *de facto* company director and his innocent wife following its discharge by the latter using misappropriated company funds. Backwards tracing was not considered, and *Boscawen* was not cited by the court.

11.169   You might think that this is all just a matter of theory: after all, how much difference in practice will it make whether the beneficiary (1) is entitled to be subrogated to a charge over the property, or instead (2) has the right either to elect an ownership claim or a lien following backwards tracing? Of course the latter right to elect is itself a valuable right, but since both (1) and (2) establish proprietary rights, why should we be troubled whether the rights acquired are restitutionary, or arise by electing how to deal with the asset as the proceeds of an application of trust property in the traditional way? There is a significant difference, however, when we consider the case of an innocent recipient of trust property. Why? Well, notice that the subrogation claim does not turn on the fact that the debt that was paid off with trust money was a *secured* debt. The right to be subrogated would apply to the payment of any debt the recipient makes with trust property. Of course, this right to be subrogated to the payment of an unsecured debt will only give the beneficiary a personal right against the recipient to repay the money expended on the debt, and where the recipient is a trustee this will be a pointless, additional right, because the trustee is strictly personally liable to restore the trust anyway (11.18 et seq); the same applies to the case of a third-party recipient who knows that the property in his hands is trust property; he will be strictly personally liable as well; but an innocent recipient, whilst liable to hold the trust property or traceable proceeds in his hands as trust property—ie the beneficiary can specifically enforce the trust over this property against him—is *not* personally liable to dig into his own pocket to restore the trust (11.162 et seq). But if the subrogation claim is available, then it is likely that the innocent recipient will be personally liable to restore the trust to a large extent, because if you think of the way people spend money, they almost always do so in the discharge of debts. Except for gifts and over-the-counter shop sales (see Penner (1996a)), most expenditures of money pay off contractually incurred debts of one kind or another. When you pay your restaurant bill at the end of dinner, you pay off a contractual debt incurred when you ordered the meal; when you pay for your vacation you pay off the debt incurred when you booked the holiday. Everything you ever buy on a credit card, ie on credit, creates a debt that you must ultimately discharge. Thus if a beneficiary can be subrogated to the rights of all the debtors whom a recipient pays off with trust money, and, as we have just seen, most payments a person makes discharge debts, then the beneficiary is subrogated to an array of personal claims against this innocent recipient, with the result that, contrary to what the traditional law teaches us, the innocent recipient *is* largely personally liable to restore the trust out of his own pocket.

11.170   Although those in favour of a unjust enrichment analysis of liability for receipt of trust property would be happy with, perhaps exult in, this result (see eg Hayton and Mitchell (2005), at 11–26), it cannot be the case that this general right of subrogation can stand alongside the conventional law under which an innocent recipient of trust property is *not* personally liable to restore the value of any trust property or traceable proceeds he receives. It is perhaps worth noting that Lord Millett, when giving the leading decision in *Foskett*, the most important tracing and claiming decision in a century, specifically denied that tracing had anything to do with unjust enrichment and, further, when discussing the claims available to a beneficiary when he traces his equitable interest into the hands of a recipient, did not even mention the *Boscawen* subrogation claim.

11.171   One final note about *Boscawen*: in the quoted passage Millett LJ considers that a beneficiary is entitled to a charge over land that has been improved with traceable value. In *Re Diplock* (1948) such a charge was denied beneficiaries under a will where the innocent recipient was a charity that was mistakenly paid by the executor, on the ground that a charge, being enforceable by sale, might require the charity to sell the property, and therefore the consequences of imposing a charge would do more than merely restore the plaintiff, but cause the charity a significant actual loss. The question is a difficult one because such a case is not equivalent to the usual case of an innocent recipient 'mixing' trust property or proceeds with his own; the usual case of 'mixing' is combining money in one bank account and drawing upon money from this mixed fund to buy a new asset. Spending money to make an improvement is not equivalent to 'purchasing' a share of an asset: it is paying for a service (and, usually, some materials) the performance of which does not consist in the acquisition of any new item of property, but which may, although not necessarily, raise the value of something already owned. It seems simplistic to say that a beneficiary should simply be able to trace his value into the money spent on the improvement service and materials and thence into the improved property regardless of the extent to which the property increased in value or the inconvenience to the innocent improver of charging the property. We await a rigorous examination by the courts.

11.172 In the recent case of *Bank of Cyprus UK Limited v Menelaou* (2015), the UKSC considered the law of unjust enrichment and subrogation. This case involved a claim by the Bank of Cyprus against one Melissa Menelaou. The bank had security over a first property, owned by Melissa's parents. The Menelaous wanted to buy a smaller, second property for use as the family home, and planned to purchase the property in Melissa's name. The bank released the security over the first property, and took a charge over the second property. The charge over the second property was found to be invalid, and the bank sought via these court proceedings to acquire, via subrogation, an unpaid vendor's lien on the second property.

11.173 The majority of the court held that Melissa was liable on unjust enrichment principles concerning the right to subrogation. This part of the decision has been trenchantly criticised (see Stevens (2018), 59–99; Virgo 2016b). In his own judgment, Lord Carnwarth, approving of the judgment in *Boscawen*, highlighted the importance of a 'tracing link' between the bank's money and the payment used to discharge the security (the unpaid vendor's lien). Interpreting *Boscawen* and the academic literature surrounding the area, he noted the 'close link between subrogation and the doctrine of tracing'. Therefore, Lord Carnwarth did not see that it was sufficient, as in the Court of Appeal below, to find that the bank was the source of the moneys used to purchase the second property as a matter of 'economic reality', or that there was a 'sufficiently close causal connection', by showing that 'but for' the bank's agreement to release its security over the first property, the second property would never have been purchased and the vendor of the second property would never have been paid. Only by finding a 'tracing link' between the bank and the money used to purchase the second property would the bank be able to succeed in its claim for a subrogated unpaid vendor's lien.

11.174 In Lord Carnwarth's opinion, the bank succeeded in showing that it had a 'clear and direct' interest in the purchase money, and was thus able to be subrogated to the unpaid vendor's lien. In reaching this conclusion, Lord Carnwarth seemed to have sympathy for the argument that the bank had established a *Quistclose* trust (7.28 et seq) interest in the money—the proceeds of sale of the first property were held on trust for the bank, subject to a power for the Menelaous to purchase the second property in Melissa's name, but only on condition that the outstanding debts of the Menelaous were secured by a charge over the second property (see also Stevens (2018), 599, endorsing this approach).

Tracing at common law and the quest for a fiduciary relationship

11.175 If a thief steals your watch and then sells the watch for £100, the position at common law is that the thief gets good legal title to the £100. The reason is simple. The watch buyer transferred his legal title to the £100 to the thief, intending that he should be its owner. That is how the transfer of legal title to property works. As we have seen, there may be a case for holding that the thief holds his legal title to the £100 on trust for you (4.50 et seq), but that trust depends, obviously, on the fact that the thief has good legal title to the £100, for that is the trust property he would hold for you. It has sometimes been supposed that the reason why the victim in such a case could not claim legal title to the £100 is that the common law rules of tracing were much less sophisticated than those of equity. In particular, the legal owner of property had a much harder time claiming any rights in traceable proceeds once his value had been added to a bank account, because, it was believed, the common law could not trace through mixtures of value.

11.176   The idea that the common law was mentally deficient in this respect is clearly belied by the fact that the common law developed principles to deal with the mixing of goods, as where a quantity of one individual's oil was mixed with that of another (11.132), or the rule in *Clayton's Case*, whereby a bank balance is treated as a series of individual debts. The real issue becomes clear when we pay attention to the distinction between tracing and claiming. The common law, no less than equity, was and is capable of tracing through the proceeds of exchanges; but, unlike equity, the logic of the common law resists giving the legal owner a new legal entitlement to proceeds (see Smith (1997), at 321–39). The basic logic is revealed by the thief's case. If A transfers his legal title to B, B acquires that title because that is what both A and B intended. The interests of third parties are irrelevant. Of course, the law could adopt fictions to overcome this result if it wanted to, for example imposing an agency relationship on the victim and her thief. Agency is a common law relationship under which the agent acts for his principle. If the agent enters into a contract of sale, it is the principal who becomes the party to the contract, not the agent. Here the common law could say that the thief was the victim's agent, entering into the contract of sale of the watch on her behalf. If that fiction were adopted, then the result of the transfer of £100 to the thief in exchange for the watch, the victim would acquire legal title to the £100 and the thief would simply have 'custody' of the money. But the common law does not embrace this fiction.

11.177   Recall the two different theoretical bases for the beneficiary's right to claim the proceeds of trust property following the tracing exercise (11.163), the 'exchange product' theory and the 'power *in rem*' theory. There is some very weak authority for the 'exchange product' theory in respect of legal title, ie that a legal owner may claim legal title to the proceeds acquired in exchange for his property. The foundational cases in favour of the theory are *Taylor v Plumer* (1815) and *Banque Belge pour l'Etranger v Hambrouck* (1921), but it is now generally accepted that the former case was decided on *equitable*, not common law, principles (see Smith (1995); Khurshid and Matthews (1979); Matthews (1995b)), and the latter case is unsatisfactory because two judges in the EWCA based their decision on *Taylor*.

11.178   As for the 'power *in rem*' theory, the UKHL decision in *Lipkin Gorman v Karpnale* (1991) is sometimes regarded as a case where the plaintiff was able to make a legal claim to traceable proceeds, but this reasoning has been thoroughly discredited (see Smith, (2009), 338–41; Stevens (2018), 591–92).

11.179   The last case of claiming legal title to traceable proceed we must consider is Millett LJ's decision in *FC Jones & Sons (Trustee in Bankruptcy) v Jones* (1997). Following an act of bankruptcy by a partnership, which made it unlawful for any of the partners to draw on a partnership account, one of the partners drew cheques in favour of his wife, Mrs Jones, who paid them into her account with a commodities broker, and used them to speculate on the potato futures market, making a large profit. The profits were paid into her account with the brokers, and the trustee in bankruptcy of the firm claimed them. Millett LJ held that the wife was not a trustee of the cheques or her account balance at the brokers; she did not receive the money in a fiduciary capacity. So far so good. But Millett LJ went on to say that she did not obtain *any title at all*, legal or equitable, to the cheques or the account balance at her brokers; the title remained throughout with the trustee in bankruptcy, who took over all the partnership's assets following the act of bankruptcy:

> . . . as from the date of the act of bankruptcy the money in the bankrupts' joint account . . . belonged to the trustee [in bankruptcy]. The account holders had no title to it at law or in equity. The cheques which they drew in favour of the defendant . . . were incapable of passing any legal or equitable title. They were not, however, without legal effect, for the bank honoured them. The result was to affect the identity of the debtor but not the creditor [ie the creditor, the trustee in bankruptcy, now had a claim against the brokers into the account with whom Mrs Jones banked the cheques, not the partnership's bank where the partnership's account was, and on which the cheques were drawn] and to put the defendant in possession of funds to which she had no title. A debt formally owed by [the partnership's bank] to the [partners] ultimately became a debt owed by the brokers apparently to the defendant but in reality to the trustee.

11.180 As both Birks (1997a) and Smith (1997, at 328 et seq) have pointed out, this is very difficult to reconcile with the orthodox law of property. When Millett LJ says that Mrs Jones was put 'in possession' of the funds, he seems to be making an analogy with the case of a misappropriated chattel. As we know (2.70), legal title to chattels is very robust. A thief acquires only a thief's title to what he steals from his victim, so he cannot pass the victim's superior title to a purchaser. The idea at work in this passage appears to be that Mrs Jones never acquired any title to the cheques (this is probably true, as the cheques themselves were chattels), but also acquired no title of any kind to her account balance at her brokers. But an account balance is the sort of property known as a *chose in action* or 'thing in action', a personal right to be paid a certain sum. One cannot merely 'possess' such a right without having 'title' to that right, because the right is all there is. Either Mrs Jones had a right to be paid the balance of her account at the brokers or she did not: she could not have that right but at the same time not have that right, ie have the right without having 'title' to it. In short, there is no possible conceptual distinction between 'title' and 'possession' that can make the analogy with the chattel work.

11.181 It should also be noted that if Millett's analysis is right, the position of banks and other account holders like Mrs Jones becomes impossible, because if the true title to the bank balance belongs to someone other than the person who opens the account, the bank will commit a wrong if it pays the account holder. But how is the bank to know that someone else 'really' has title to the bank balance? Thus, if Millett LJ is right, then banks are placed under an enormous risk they can do nothing to prevent every time their customers pay funds into their accounts (see further Matthews (1995b); Smith (1997), at 329–30).

11.182 Millett LJ might better have made an analogy with the legal device of the 'power of attorney', whereby one person is empowered to deal with the legal title of another person. Such an analogy does not provide a workable interpretation of Millett LJ's views as stated, however, since Millett LJ does not allow that Mrs Jones had any power of any kind over the property here. Birks (1997a) argues that nevertheless the case should be understood along the 'power *in rem*' analysis following *Lipkin Gorman*, but that would simply apply the flawed reasoning in *Lipkin Gorman* to this case as well.

11.183   On the positive side, in this case Millett LJ, emphasising the difference between tracing and claiming, argued that the tracing rules should be the same at both common law and equity:

> There is no merit in having distinct and different tracing rules at law and in equity, given that tracing is neither a right nor a remedy but merely the process by which the plaintiff establishes what has happened to his property and makes good his claim that the assets which he claims can properly be regarded as representing his property.

11.184   Because of the supposedly superior tracing process recognised in equity, and because equitable remedial rights in the form of an equitable charge or an equitable co-ownership claim are available to the plaintiff who can establish an equitable claim to traceable proceeds, the law of England has been coloured by plaintiffs arguing that the original misapplication of their property involved a breach of fiduciary duty. Like trustees, fiduciaries such as agents or company directors who misapply their principals' property are liable to account for the misapplication (11.15), and principals may trace the value of the property transferred using equitable tracing rules and avail themselves of equitable claims to the proceeds. These proprietary claims are, of course, most valuable in the case where the defendant is insolvent. The high-water mark of this development occurred in *Chase Manhattan Bank v Israel-British Bank* (1981) (12.33), in which Goulding J appeared to manufacture a fiduciary relationship out of thin air so as to allow a bank, which mistakenly paid $2m to another bank, to trace into the proceeds remaining in the recipient bank's hands.

11.185   In *Westdeutsche Landesbank Girozentrale v Islington London Borough Council* (1996) the HL held this reasoning to be wrong. However, Lord Browne-Wilkinson did state, *obiter*, that the result in *Chase Manhattan* could be justified on the basis that when the recipient bank learned of the mistaken payment, its conscience was affected, at which point equity would impose a *constructive* trust over the money received. This justification seems quite wrong, and as a mere *obiter dictum* should not be followed: the constructive trust seems to be raised on nothing more than the recipient's awareness that he owes the plaintiff a certain sum, ie that he must repay an equivalent amount to that which he received. This is just a normal everyday recognition of a legal liability to pay a debt, no different in principle from a recognition of any other kind of debt, such as a debt to pay one's credit card bill. The mere realisation that one is indebted does not turn one into a trustee, or a fiduciary, or a wrongdoer in equity, and therefore there is no basis for the imposition of a constructive trust here. The better view is simply that *Chase Manhattan* was wrongly decided (see Millett (1998a)).

Tracing from legal title to secure an equitable interest

11.186   To review where we have got to in 'tracing at common law' so far: although there seems no good reason why the rules of tracing through exchanges, whether through mixed bank accounts or not, should differ in common law from equity, there may be good reasons not to allow legal owners to acquire by operation of law legal title in the traceable proceeds that derive from exchanges with their legal title, for reasons that become apparent, as we have just seen, in the case of banks if Millett LJ's analysis in *FC Jones* is correct. As Smith (1997, at 330) argues:

> [C]ommon law rights . . . serve as a baseline. They can be transferred at will by the one who holds them. If it is necessary to change the result, one looks to equity, which can encumber legal rights in various ways . . . It is true that equitable proprietary rights

may be hidden, but for this very reason, they are fragile, always destroyed where a bona fide purchaser acquires a legal interest for value without notice of the equitable rights. [See also Matthews (1995b).]

11.187 For this sort of reason it has been suggested that a legal owner should be able to trace into the proceeds acquired in exchange for property he owned, not so as to acquire *legal* title in the proceeds, but rather an *equitable* one. As we have seen, in cases of property transferred in breach of fiduciary obligation (11.15), and in some cases of fraud (4.50), equity will allow the wronged party to trace into the proceeds acquired with the property to which he had legal title.

Personal claims against recipients of trust property or its traceable proceeds: knowing receipt and knowing dealing

11.188 A recipient of trust property transferred in breach of trust or its traceable proceeds will be personally liable to account for his handling of that property, just like the breaching trustee is, if he knowingly deals with the property as his own, ie inconsistently with the beneficiaries' equitable title to it. That is, he will be liable to dig into his own pocket and restore to the beneficiaries the money value of the property he spends as if it were his own. There are two sorts of case: the first occurs when a person receives trust property or its traceable proceeds *knowing* that it was transferred in breach of trust; clearly he should hold the property for the benefit of the beneficiaries—normally, this would involve returning the property to the trustees, unless it was clear that the trustees had fraudulently breached the trust, in which case the recipient should apply to the court for directions. If he acts properly in this way, the recipient will not be personally liable. If, however, he acts otherwise, treating the property as his own or in any other way inconsistent with the rights of the beneficiary, then he will be personally liable to restore the money value of whatever is lost. In essence, then, this *knowing* recipient will have no obligations to carry out the terms of the trust himself, but must hold the property to the order of the rightful trustees of the trust and, if he acts otherwise, will be personally liable for his breach of that trust. Mitchell and Watterson (2010) put it this way:

Liability for knowing receipt is a distinctive, primary, custodial liability, which closely resembles the liability of express trustees to account for the trust property with which they are charged.

In view of this, we can understand why the knowing recipient is traditionally called a constructive *trustee*. He is not an express trustee, of course, because he did not agree to hold the property on trust when he received it; rather, equity imposes upon him the duty of custodian trusteeship.

11.189 Swadling (2017), 322–26, disagrees with this way of putting it. He doubts, reasonably, whether the recipient really has any duties, even the duties of a 'custodian'. He suggests that, more realistically, the recipient is liable to a court order to transfer the property to a trustee who will carry out the terms of the trust, and secondarily, is liable for any wrongful dissipation of the trust property.

11.190   The second case, 'knowing dealing', is a minor variation. Where a non-bona fide purchaser receives trust property or its proceeds ignorant of the breach of trust by which it came to him, but then later learns of the breach of trust, then at that point he will be treated the same as the knowing recipient; ie as a custodian trustee. He will not be liable for any untraceable dissipations of the trust property he makes up to that point, but thereafter he is personally liable to restore the trust for any further dissipations of the trust property. Similarly, where a person receives funds perfectly properly as an agent of the trust, but then knowingly deals with the property inconsistently with the trust, he will be personally liable for any loss. A classic case is *Lee v Sankey* (1872). Solicitors received the proceeds of the sale of trust property and held it for further investment, and this was perfectly correct under the terms of the trust. However, knowing this was a breach of trust they transferred part of the funds to only one of the trustees, who dissipated the whole amount. The solicitors were personally liable for the loss. Because in these cases the constructive trusteeship arises not on the receipt of the trust property or its proceeds, but when the recipient only later learns of the trust, this liability is traditionally called liability for 'knowing dealing'.

11.191   A similar but distinct case is *Andrews v Bousfield* (1847). The case involved someone who had received a loan of the trust funds. Inconsistently with the terms of the trust, the borrower paid moneys to the trustees, which were lost. He was liable to repay the loan again, this time properly. The case is not really one of knowing dealing, because the money he paid to the trustees was not trust property. The correct way to view the case is that a debtor cannot effectively discharge his debt to the trust if he knowingly pays the trustees in circumstances where the payment would not be consistent with the trust terms. He is treated as making a payment to the trustees personally for their own benefit, not a payment to them *as trustees* that discharges his debt to the trust.

The current standard of knowledge

11.192   In preceding paragraphs we referred to *knowing* receipt and dealing. What does the recipient need to know to be fixed with the liability of a custodian trustee? The law governing the knowledge required is extraordinarily confused, largely because in a series of cases the courts did not appear to distinguish between liability for assisting a breach of trust, liability for knowing receipt or dealing, and the knowledge or notice that would prevent someone from being a bona fide purchaser of trust property, ie the knowledge which would make a purchaser for value *proprietarily* liable to the beneficiaries as a holder of trust property (see Harpum (1986)). Secondly, the issue had not reached the HL in a long time, nor has it yet been addressed by the UKSC, and there are conflicting opinions in the CA. In the case of *BCCI v Akindele* (2000) the CA tried to start afresh from first principles, but the decision is unsatisfying. First, we will undertake a brief review of the law leading up to *Akindele*.

11.193   In *Baden v Société Générale* (1992), Peter Gibson J distinguished five categories of knowledge:

> *(i) actual knowledge; (ii) wilfully shutting one's eyes to the obvious; (iii) wilfully and recklessly failing to make such inquiries as an honest and reasonable man would make; (iv) knowledge of circumstances which would indicate the facts to an honest and reasonable man; (v) knowledge of circumstances which would put an honest and reasonable man on inquiry.*

Knowledge in all of these categories is sufficient to fix the defendant with 'notice', the standard of cognisance that applies in determining whether a person has 'notice' of a breach of trust or the beneficiary's rights. Category (i), actual knowledge, is narrower than 'actual notice' (recall 2.72 et seq), but actual notice might cover categories (i), (ii), and (iv), as covering facts that would be apparent if all available information were taken into account. The 'constructive' knowledge described in (iii) and (iv) appears to be equivalent to a narrower version of constructive notice, with (iii) adding an element of dishonesty or 'want of probity', as it is sometimes put. Categories (i) to (iii) together might be regarded as 'dishonest' knowledge showing a want of probity, whereas knowledge in (iv) and (v) would not, because the defendant may fail to draw the right inferences or inquire appropriately because he was foolish or otherwise unreasonable, but not actually dishonest (see *Agip, per* Millett J, at 11.111).

11.194   The past authorities do not indicate a uniform standard of cognisance that will fix a recipient of trust property or its proceeds with the obligation to hold the property as a custodian trustee. In *Re Montagu's Settlement Trusts* (1987), Megarry VC was unwilling to fix a volunteer recipient of chattels in breach of a family trust, who later sold them, with personal liability to repay their money value. He held that even if the recipient had once known that the chattels were property of the trust, he would not be personally liable where he had honestly forgotten that they were. Megarry VC clearly distinguished between notice and knowledge; only the latter was sufficient for acquiring personal liability as a recipient, custodian trustee. Megarry clearly regarded personal liability as liability to account 'as a constructive trustee', ie on the traditional basis that the recipient himself breaches his custodian trusteeship, or to put it in an alternative way, wrongfully dissipates the trust property in his hands (11.189).

11.195   In *Agip* and *El Ajou v Dollar Land Holdings plc* (1993), Millett J appeared to hold that something less than actual knowledge is sufficient. While Millett J seemed to adopt a lower requirement for knowledge than did Megarry VC, he still applied a 'fault' standard, in that to be liable the recipient must fall below the standard of conduct of an honest and reasonable person. In *Westdeutsche Landesbank*, Lord Browne-Wilkinson specifically approved *Re Montagu's*.

11.196   The sort of inquiry such a person should undertake must be adapted to the particular circumstances of dealing; notice, as it applies to land transfers because of the standard practices of inquiry, should not apply to transactions for which there is no such practice. As Millett put the point in *Macmillan Inc v Bishopsgate Trust plc (No 3)* (1995):

> *[The plaintiff] attempted to establish constructive notice on the part of each of the defendants by a meticulous and detailed examination of every document, letter, record or minute to see whether it threw any light on the true ownership of the [relevant] shares which a careful reader—with instant recall of the whole of the contents of his files—ought to have detected. That is not the proper approach. Account officers are not detectives. Unless and until they are alerted to the possibility of wrongdoing, they proceed, and are entitled to proceed, on the assumption that they are dealing with honest men. In order to establish constructive notice it is necessary to prove that the facts known to the defendant made it imperative for him to seek an explanation, because in the absence of an explanation it was obvious that the transaction was probably improper.*

11.197   In three decisions of the CA—*Houghton v Fayers* (2000); *Bank of Credit and Commerce International v Akindele* (2000); *Brown v Bennett* (1999)—a requirement of some kind of knowledge was applied. All courts cited Hoffmann LJ's formulation in *El Ajou v Dollar Land Holdings plc* (1994):

> [T]he plaintiff must show, first, a disposal of his assets in breach of fiduciary duty; secondly, the beneficial receipt by the defendant of assets which are traceable as representing the assets of the plaintiff; and thirdly, knowledge on the part of the defendant that the assets received are traceable to a breach of fiduciary duty.

This passage would appear to indicate that the defendant must have some actual or 'naughty' knowledge of the offending transaction, but in *Houghton*, Nourse LJ, delivering the judgment of the court, went on to say (citing *Belmont Finance Corpn v Williams Furniture Ltd (No 2)* (1980)) that the defendant would be personally liable for receipt if he knew or *ought to have known* the money was paid in breach of fiduciary duty, thus adopting a standard of constructive knowledge.

11.198   We now turn to *Akindele*, which is now regarded as the leading case. The defendant, Chief Akindele, a Nigerian businessman, entered into a transaction with International Credit and Investment Company (Overseas) Limited (ICIC) (a company controlled by the BCCI group) to 'purchase' shares of BCCI Holdings for $10m, though upon the payment of the $10m the shares would continue to be held in the names of the present holders. Following a minimum period of two years, the defendant could require the 'sale' of the shares, to be arranged by ICIC, such that the defendant would receive a price equivalent to $10m plus 15 per cent per annum compounded annually. (The defendant was also entitled under the agreement to acquire any shares issued pursuant to a rights issue by BCCI holdings, which he did on one occasion, at a cost of $330,680.) Despite the framing of the transaction as the sale of BCCI Holdings shares, it was understood by all concerned that the transaction was essentially to be regarded as an investment vehicle by which the defendant could earn a high rate of interest if he left his money with ICIC for a minimum period of two years. The transaction, however, formed part of a fraudulent scheme of the claimant's employees, under which the receipt of the defendant's money, combined with the fact that he was not registered as owner of the shares during the period of the investment, meant that the employees were able falsely to represent that a dummy loan to a third party was performing normally. In due course, following the expiry of the two year period, the defendant enforced his rights under the agreement, receiving a payment of $16.679m. The plaintiffs sought to establish the defendant's personal liability as a 'knowing recipient' of money fraudulently paid in breach of fiduciary obligation. Nourse LJ, giving judgment for the CA, undertook a review of the authorities governing the requisite degree and character of knowledge necessary to fix a recipient with personal liability to restore the value of the assets received. He held that, while a defendant need not be found to have acted dishonestly in receiving the trust property, he must have known something about the breach of trust to be liable; however, he expressed 'grave doubts' about the usefulness of the *Baden* categories of knowledge in determining personal liability for receipt. He said:

> What then, in the context of knowing receipt, is the purpose to be served by a categorisation of knowledge? It can only be to enable the court to determine whether, in the words of Buckley LJ in Belmont (No 2), the recipient can 'conscientiously retain [the] funds against the company' or, in the words of Megarry VC in Re Montagu's Settlement Trusts, '[the recipient's] conscience is sufficiently affected for it to be right to bind him by the obligations of a constructive trustee'. But if that is the purpose, there is no need for categorisation. All that is necessary is that the recipient's state of

knowledge should be such as to make it unconscionable for him to retain the benefit of the receipt.

For these reasons I have come to the view that, just as there is now a single test of dishonesty for knowing assistance, so ought there to be a single test of knowledge for knowing receipt. The recipient's state of knowledge must be such as to make it unconscionable for him to retain the benefit of the receipt. A test in that form, though it cannot, any more than any other, avoid difficulties of application, ought to avoid those of definition and allocation to which the previous categorisations have led.

11.199   With respect, this is really very unsatisfactory. The term 'unconscionable', like 'unfair' or 'unjust', gives absolutely no guidance to a court trying properly to characterise the sorts of facts that must be in place for the recipient's duty of custodianship to arise. A defendant's behaviour must be unconscionable, unfair, or unjust *according to law*. The whole point of paying attention to the facts and decisions in the past cases is to acquire some understanding of what 'unconscionable' receipt or dealing amounts to. The end of the exercise cannot be the declaration of a standard—that the receipt must be 'unconscionable'—which assumes a prior grasp of the result this exercise was intended to provide; this is to beg the whole question. The *Baden* scale is not by any means perfect, but it does fulfil the useful function of pointing out some of the different ways and extents to which a defendant might have acquired knowledge of a breach of trust, and therefore requires a judge to appreciate that the question whether the defendant's awareness in the case before him is sufficient to make his treatment of the property as his own 'unconscionable' will often require a fairly subtle and nuanced appreciation of the particular facts in their surrounding context.

11.200   Nourse LJ is further mistaken to think that his declaration of a single test of knowledge for knowing receipt by reference to unconscionability is a proper parallel to Lord Nicholls' adoption of a standard of dishonesty for knowing assistance. 'Dishonest', unlike 'unconscionable', is much less a legal term of art, and it was to a common, member-of-a-jury understanding of dishonesty that Lord Nicholls appealed. Even so, as we have seen (11.106), he then went on to elaborate in some detail what should count as dishonest; Nourse LJ here undertakes no similar effort with a term that is much less likely to have any commonly well-grasped sense.

Dishonest dissipation

11.201   In summary, it is probably fair to say, subject to the issue raised at 11.202, that as things stand at the moment, a recipient who has given value for trust property will fail to be a bona fide purchaser if he has actual knowledge or some sufficiently strong suspicion of the breach of trust to 'affect his conscience'. What counts as suspicious will presumably vary according to the normal modes of carrying out the specific kind of transaction in issue, ie whether he purchases land, securities, chattels, and so on. Where he is fixed with knowledge of a breach of trust, so that even if he purchased the legal interest in the trust property for value he would not count as a bona fide purchaser, thus making him liable to the beneficiary's proprietary against the trust property, it is not clear if the recipient is thereby also immediately personally liable to account because of this knowledge, simply because the recipient might have some sort of 'constructive knowledge' of the breach of trust that does not equate to the sort of knowledge which would make it 'unconscionable' to 'retain the benefit of the receipt', in other words, to have been able to deal with the property received as his own. Despite the recent CA decision in *Akindele*, it is probably wisest to make reference to the range of views expressed by different judges that we have seen, as even if Nourse LJ's 'unconscionability' test prevails in name, much will have to be done to sort out exactly how knowledge and/or notice are relevant to its application.

11.202   In *Criterion Properties v Stratford UK Properties* (2004), the HL more or less said that *Akindele* was decided on an entirely faulty legal analysis. Lord Nicholls made the point this way:

> I respectfully consider the Court of Appeal in Akindele's case fell into error . . . If a company (A) enters into an agreement with B under which B acquires benefits from A, A's ability to recover these benefits from B depends essentially on whether the agreement is binding on A. If the directors of A were acting for an improper purpose when they entered into the agreement, A's ability to have the agreement set aside depends upon the application of familiar principles of agency and company law. If, applying these principles, the agreement is found to be valid and is therefore not set aside, questions of 'knowing receipt' by B do not arise. So far as B is concerned there can be no question of A's assets having been misapplied. B acquired the assets from A, the legal and beneficial owner of the assets, under a valid agreement made between him and A. If, however, the agreement is set aside, B will be accountable for any benefits he may have received from A under the agreement.

Thus in *Akindele* the CA failed first to determine whether BCCI was bound by the investment agreement with Akindele. Given that the CA did not set that contract aside, it appears that they understood the contract to be binding on BCCI, in which case Chief Akindele was perfectly entitled to what he received, and no issue of knowing receipt arose. This certainly weakens the authority of *Akindele*, but as stated at 11.201, we are probably stuck with its 'unconscionability test' until the UKSC visits the issue.

11.203   It is submitted, however, (see also Swadling (2017)), that the appropriate standard for knowledge here should be 'dishonesty', as set out by Lord Nicholls in *Tan*, including of course wilful blindness and reckless disregard for the beneficiaries' rights. The recipient commits a wrong by dissipating the assets, ie, treating them as if they were his own, flouting the rights of the beneficiaries of which he is aware. If this logic were adopted, we could get past the terminology of 'knowing receipt' and 'knowing dealing', and focus on the beneficiaries' true grievance, that the recipient spent the assets actually knowing they were the beneficiaries', not his own, or recklessly not caring if they were.

Limitation of actions

11.204   The Limitation Act 1980 provides:

> 21. (1) No period of limitation prescribed by this Act shall apply to an action by a beneficiary under a trust, being an action—
>
> (a)   in respect of any fraud or fraudulent breach of trust to which the trustee was a party or privy; or
>
> (b)   to recover from the trustee trust property or the proceeds of trust property in the possession of the trustee, or previously received by him and converted to his use.

11.205   The application of these subsections, which allow a defendant no statutory limitation period, was considered the UKSC in *Williams v Central Bank of Nigeria* (2014). By a majority of 4:1, the court held that s 21(1)(b) applies only to those who undertake the obligations of a trustee or a fiduciary in respect of the claimant's property, that is, only to cases where a person who has in a lawful transaction undertaken fiduciary obligations to the claimant, or can be implied to have put himself in a position where he owes such obligations, and *then* goes on to breach those obligations by wrongfully retaining his principal's property or converting his principal's property to his own use. The rationale for this absence of a limitation period is simply that the trustee or other fiduciary can never hold *adversely* to his beneficiary or principal; his title to the trust assets is always a title held on trust.

11.206   This clearly covers the case of an express trustee who misappropriates trust property, or a company director who misappropriates company property, because in both of these cases the fiduciary obligation arises independently of, and prior to, the wrong of retaining the principal's property or converting it to his use or holding it inconsistently with the beneficiary's or principal's rights. Similarly, the liability of a trustee '*de son tort*' or *de facto* trustee (11.103), will fall under this subsection, for such a person *de facto* undertakes the obligations of trusteeship.

11.207   However, the section does not apply to persons called 'constructive trustees' because held 'liable to account as a constructive trustee'. Thus, a knowing recipient (11.188) will be subject to a limitation period of six years (s 21(3)), and for others who do not receive trust property transferred in breach of trust but are otherwise subject to the remedial jurisdiction of equity as are fraudsters in some cases (4.50), equity will apply by analogy the limitation periods under the statute that applies to corresponding actions at common law (in this case six years).

11.208   By a slimmer majority of 3:2 the UKSC decided that s 21(1)(a) applies only to the same defendants who fall under s 21(1)(b), ie express trustees, fiduciaries, or *de facto* trustees. The claimant argued for a broader interpretation of the subsection, under which defendants guilty of dishonest assistance would (11.105) likewise not have the benefit of a limitation period, but this was denied.

11.209   As applied to company directors, in *First Subsea Ltd v Balltec Ltd* (2017) the CA decided that no limitation would run where a director fraudulently breached any of his fiduciary duties, in this case forming a company which then bid for contracts in competition with the company of which he was a director. A company director acting fraudulently cannot escape the effect of s 21(1)(b) by not receiving company assets himself directly, but having them transferred to a company that he owns or controls: *Burnden Holdings (UK) Ltd v Fielding* (2016).

11.210   Cases that fall under s 21(1)(a) and (b), so that no statutory limitation periods apply are, however, subject to the equitable doctrine of laches (pronounced 'lay-cheese'), or delay. A suit may not succeed in equity if by reason of the claimant's delay the defendant would be unfairly disadvantaged.

FURTHER READING

Birks and Pretto (2002)

Brownbill (1993, Pt VI)

Davies (2015b)

Elliott and Mitchell (2004)

Glister (2014a, 2014b)

Millett (1998a)

Mitchell (2013, 2014)

Mitchell and Watterson (2010)

Penner (2002, 2009b, 2010a, 2014a, 2017, 2018a)

Smith (1994, 1997, 2000, 2009)

Swadling (1994, 1996b, 1997, 1998, 2017)

Trust Law Committee (1999, 'Trustee Exemption Clauses')

Watts (2016)

Must-read cases: *Re Pauling's Settlement Trusts* (1963); *Armitage v Nurse* (1997); *Target Holdings v Redferns* (1995); *AIB Group v Redler* (2014); *Main v Giambrone* (2017); *Bristol & West Building Society v Mothew* (1996); *Royal Brunei Airlines v Tan* (1995); *Re Hallett's Estate* (1880); *Boscawen v Bajwa* (1995); *Foskett v McKeown* (2000); *Pars Ram Brothers (Pte) Ltd v Australian & New Zealand Banking Group Ltd* (2018); *Westdeutsche Landesbank v Islington London Borough Council* (1996); *Re Montagu's Settlement Trusts* (1987); *Twinsectra v Yardley* (2002); *Bank of Credit and Commerce International (Overseas) Ltd (in liquidation) v Akindele* (1999); *Republic of Brazil v Durant* (2015); *Williams v Central Bank of Nigeria* (2014)

SELF-TEST QUESTIONS

1. What does it mean for a beneficiary to (a) 'falsify the account'; and (b) 'surcharge the account'? How are these ways of dealing with breaches of trust related to the concept of 'equitable compensation'? Give examples from actual cases where these terms can be employed to explain the decisions.

2. Tom is the trustee of the Higgins family trust. He misappropriates £30,000, which he pays into his bank account raising the balance to £40,000. He makes the following payments from his account. He buys shares for £5,000, which are now worth £10,000. He uses £20,000 to pay off the mortgage on his flat. He then adds £10,000 of his own to the account, raising the balance to £25,000. He gives £10,000 to his son, Ted, who is ignorant of the source of the money. Ted uses it to buy ten cases of vintage wine; he drinks up five of the cases, and lays down the rest. Tom dissipates the remaining funds in the account.

   With the knowledge of Harry Higgins, one of the beneficiaries, Tom misappropriates another £10,000, which they together spend on a world cruise.

   Discuss the liability of Tom, Harry, and Ted.

3. In 1990, Pavlos, a solicitor, received £40,000 from Nicos on discretionary trusts for Nicos's relations. He paid the money into a separate bank account, and in each of 1990, 1991, and 1992 drew £1,000 a year from the account to pay premiums on a life insurance policy on his own life. Having fallen in love with Nicos's daughter in 1991, he exercised his discretion under the trust to make large payments to her. In 1993, he exercised a power of appointment under the trust in favour of Christos, one of the proper objects of the power, giving him £2,000 on condition that Christos and he split the money 50/50. In late 1993, Nicos realised that he did not much like his relations any more, and exercised his power under the trust to revoke the trust, telling Pavlos to hold the remaining money in the account to his order. Instead of doing that, Pavlos immediately withdrew the money

from the account and dissipated it. Early in 2000, Nicos demanded the transfer of the funds from Pavlos, who committed suicide in response. Advise Nicos.

4. In breach of trust, Max ordered his broker, Bob, to invest £50,000 of the Simpson family trust in junk bonds. Bob complied with the order although he was surprised that a trust fund would permit such a hazardous investment. The bonds were defaulted upon almost immediately, becoming worthless. Max then transferred £100,000 from the trust account into his own bank account, raising the balance to £150,000, immediately using £120,000 to buy a London flat. Six months later, he sold the flat for £180,000 and spent the entire amount at auction for a painting that has since been independently appraised to be worth only £100,000. Of the remaining £30,000 in his account, Max (a) used £10,000 to clear a gambling debt with Horatio, (b) used £10,000 to make a support payment to his ex-wife, Fran, which was in arrears, and (c) gave £10,000 to his son, Philip, who used the money to pay off his credit card bill, the charges on which he had mostly incurred in taking holidays over the past several years. Max is now bankrupt. Advise the beneficiaries.

Restitution, unjust enrichment, and the law of trusts

SUMMARY

Introduction

12.1   Chapters 1 to 11 covered the basic principles and doctrine of the law of trusts. In the next chapter we shall look at the law governing fiduciaries, for the reason that many trustees are also fiduciaries. The fiduciary relationship is not restricted to the trust–beneficiary relationship, but covers a broader set of relationships, such as that of agent and principal. The lesson is that different areas of the law overlap. This chapter concerns the possible overlap between the law of trusts and the law of restitution, or the law of 'unjust enrichment'. The notion of overlap here is somewhat ambiguous. As we shall see, some commentators would say that certain areas of traditional trust law doctrine are 'really' part of a different area of law, the law of restitution/unjust enrichment. Less ambitiously, others might say that the law of trusts is informed or shaped by restitutionary/unjust enrichment principles of analysis. The purpose of this chapter is to examine whether some traditional trust law principles and doctrines are best coherently framed within a restitutionary/unjust enrichment analysis.

12.2   So what is the law of restitution, or the law of unjust enrichment, and what is a legal analysis which draws upon these areas of legal doctrine? As you can tell from the cagey way in which we have just spoken of the law of restitution/law of unjust enrichment, it is not entirely clear what this area of law should be called. The leading English practitioner text, 'Goff & Jones', was called *The Law of Restitution* up to its 7th edition, and then changed its name to *The Law of Unjust Enrichment*. The difference is basically the difference between a *remedy*, and a *cause of action*. 'Restitution' describes a remedy: X has to give a money payment to Y, returning the same amount that Y previously transferred to X. A standard example is a payment by Y made by mistake. Y pays the gas company £50 for her August bill, forgetting that she had paid it earlier. Y now has a restitutionary remedy, for return of the money, against the gas company.

12.3   But just saying this does not explain Y's 'cause of action'. A cause of action consists of the facts that Y must prove which, under the relevant law, entitle her to a remedy against X. In this example, the explanation of the cause of action was historically obscured by the form in which the action proceeded, as a claim for 'money had and received'. That label isn't very helpful. 'Unjust enrichment' provides a way in which we can make sense of the facts Y must prove to entitle her to a remedy. She has to prove (1) the payment and (2) that it was made by mistake. Because of the mistake, the law holds that X is unjustly enriched by the payment—he shouldn't be enriched in this way, and so he has to pay Y back.

12.4   But consider a different case. X buys goods from Y on credit. X now owes Y £50 as the price of the goods. X fails to pay. Y clearly has claim against X for the price of the goods, for that contractually incurred debt. But even though one could say, morally speaking, the reason why X has to pay is that if he didn't, he would be unjustly enriched by having the goods without paying for them, Y's claim is not a claim in unjust enrichment. It is a claim under the law of contract that X do what he agreed to do, ie pay for the goods.

12.5   Now consider a trickier case, which is on the borderline. Y contracts with X, a builder, to re-model Y's kitchen. Y pays £5,000 to X up front, with a further payment of £5,000 due when the work is finished. Before starting work, X dies. This contract is frustrated, and thereby terminated, by X's death. Y has a clear claim against X's estate for the repayment of £5,000. Is Y's claim a claim under the law of contract, or under the law of unjust enrichment? In the opinion of your author, it is a claim under the law of contract. It seems obvious that an implied term of a contract of this kind is that if a contract is frustrated, any payments going from one party to the other must be reversed (cf Stevens (2018), 584-86). So this is a restitutionary claim in the remedial sense, but not an unjust enrichment claim in the 'cause of action' sense. Yet (owing largely to the fact that these claims were brought as 'money had and received' claims), most unjust enrichment scholars claim that this is an example of an unjust enrichment claim. X, or rather X's estate, would be unjustly enriched if it were able to keep the £5,000 when there is no performance of the contract by X.

12.6   This last example is pertinent to our purposes because, as we shall see, in certain areas of trusts law, unjust enrichment scholars have claimed that certain parts of trusts law doctrine, such as the doctrine of presumed resulting trusts, or the law of tracing, are only explained, or better explained, on the basis of unjust enrichment reasoning.

12.7   The fact that it has become necessary to include a chapter on unjust enrichment and restitution in a trusts text should be telling of the direction of modern developments. Graham Virgo (2018, v) describes equity as 'another country', and 'an ancient country with rich resources'. Virgo goes on to say:

> *The territory of Equity is itself under threat. Some people wish to invade it and impose their will on its running, despites its many years of peaceful, benevolent existence. One group appear to have particular designs on Equity. This is a strange evangelical sect known as the 'unjust enrichmentarians'. The members of this sect are mostly benign, but they have their own strange dialect and wish to reform what they consider to be the unsophisticated attitudes of the ancient Equity people, not realizing that the new structures they wish to impose typically replicate what Equity already has and in a much less sophisticated way.*

When you are done with this chapter you should be equipped to assess if equity truly is (or should be) losing parts of its bailiwick to unjust enrichment.

A brief history of unjust enrichment and restitution

12.8   Unjust enrichment was only recognised relatively recently as a distinct branch of law. The decision of *Lipkin Gorman v Karpnale Ltd* (1991) is seen as a moment where the subject came into
its own. In that case, Lord Templeman quoted an earlier statement of Lord Wright from *Fibrosa
v Fairbairn* (1943):

> It is clear that any civilised system of law is bound to provide remedies for cases of
> what has been called unjust enrichment or unjust benefit, that is to prevent a man
> from retaining the money of or some benefit derived from another which it is against
> conscience that he should keep.

12.9   It is not to our purposes whether *Lipkin Gorman* was adequately reasoned. It has been subjected to severe criticism (Smith, (2009), 338–41; Stevens (2018), 591–92). It does, however
stand for the proposition that there is a principle of unjust enrichment in English law which
founds a cause of action leading to a restitutionary remedy.

12.10   What facts need to be shown to make out the cause of action in unjust enrichment? Can the
phrase 'unjustly enriched at the expense of the claiment be broken down into component parts,
and articulated in the form of a test? In the literature on unjust enrichment, this is often referred to as the 'stable set of large questions'. The articulation of a stable set of large questions is
one of Peter Birks' major contributions to this area of the law. In the most recent edition of *The
Law of Restitution* (Burrows (2011), 27), these questions are expressed as follows:

(i)   *Has the defendant been benefited (ie, enriched)?*

(ii)   *Was the enrichment at the claimant's expense?*

(iii)   *Was the enrichment unjust?*

(iv)   *Are there any defences?*

If the first three questions are answered affirmatively, and the last is answered negatively, the
claimant will be entitled to restitution.

12.11   The four questions that make up the 'unjust enrichment' cause of action are simply phrased,
and this four-question test is regularly invoked by judges addressing claims purporting to be
founded on the defendant's unjust enrichment. Although questions (i), (ii), and (iv) have given
rise to many controversial issues, (iii) is obviously the heart of the matter. What makes an
enrichment unjust? Orthodox English law takes what is called an 'unjust factors' approach;
the claimant must claim and prove that his enrichment of the defendant, say by a payment of
money, was unjust because it was made by mistake, or under duress, or under undue influence.
The alternative approach is the 'absence of basis' approach, which derives from certain readings
of the law in civil law juridictions. Here the claimant need only to show that there was no legal
basis, or legal reason, for the payment of money.

12.12   Given the now prevalent use of the four-question approach, one could be forgiven for thinking
that the law of unjust enrichment has always been this way. This is not true. For a long time, the
law of unjust enrichment lurked in the shadows of other areas of private law.

12.13   Historically, restitutionary obligations were seen to arise from implied contracts. Blackstone
supported this view in his *Commentaries on the Laws of England*, saying that restitutionary

obligations in the common law depend on implied contracts, or quasi-contracts ('*quasi ex contractu*').

12.14   *Moses v Macferlan* (1760) was one such case that employed this kind of reasoning. Lord Mansfield, the judge in the case, identified several classic 'restitutionary' situations including money paid by mistake, and said that the law gives relief '*as it were upon a contract ('quasi ex contractu,' as the Roman law expresses it)'.*

12.15   It is likely that this early identification of restitution with contract was for reasons of pleading and procedure, as opposed to reasons of substance. When early restitutionary claims emerged, they were brought under the form of action known as *indebitatus assumpsit*. This form of action was for an implied promise or contract to repay money, and was pleaded, as we have seen (12.3, 12.5) under a particular 'count' within *indebitus assumpsit*, the action 'for money had and received to the plaintiff's use'. (See Smith L (2009) for a discussion of the variety of claims that could be brought under this action, including 'equitable debt' claims against a trustee who held assets on bare trust for a beneficiary.) Therefore, where a claim for money paid by mistake was brought under the *indebitatus assumpsit* action, the promise to repay was fictitious.

12.16   The quasi-contract theory and terminology persisted for most of the subject's history, culminating perhaps in the decision of the HL in *Sinclair v Brougham* (1914). The quasi-contract theory was decisively rejected in *Westdeutsche Landesbank Girozentrale v Islington LBC* (1996). It is safe to say, as the CA noted in *Cleveland Bridge UK Ltd v Multiplex Constructions (UK) Ltd* (2010), that the implied contract theory is now a 'ghost of the past'.

12.17   Therefore, in more modern times, as opposed to seeing the rules of unjust enrichment (and restitution) as part of the law of quasi-contract (whatever that really is), or as isolated bits of legal miscellany, the tendency has been to see the law of unjust enrichment as 'one of the main sources of rights and obligations in English private law' (Goff & Jones (2016), 3)

12.18   Much of the credit for the emergence of the law of unjust enrichment and restitution as an area in its own right must surely go to Robert Goff and Gareth Jones with their publication of *The Law of Restitution* (Goff & Jones (1966)) in 1966, and later on, Peter Birks's *An Introduction to the Law of Restitution* (Birks (1985)). As Lord Rodger put it, 'Goff and Jones are the Romulus and Remus of the English law of restitution … out of a few weak and scattered settlements they founded a powerful city whose hegemony now extends far and wide' (Goff & Jones (2016), vii). One speaks of the *English* law of restitution because powerful developments were occurring in the United States with the American Law Institute's publication of its *Restatement of Restitution* in 1937, predating and influencing the English revival.

12.19   However, the publication of *The Law of Restitution* in 1966 was by no means the end of the story. In fact, the four stage test we saw earlier was only endorsed conclusively by the House of Lords in *Banque Financière de la Cite v Parc (Battersea) Ltd* (1998). As late as 1977, Lord Diplock was still saying that 'no general doctrine of unjust enrichment [is] recognized in English law' (*Orakpo v Manson Investments Ltd* (1978), 104).

12.20   Recent scholarship has cast doubt on the proposition that unjust enrichment ought to be thought of as a coherent area of law at all (Watts (2016); Stevens (2018); Smith (2018). Stevens (2018) argues that unjust enrichment as a legal subject has no single reason (what he refers to as a 'consideration of justice') unifying it. Take for example contract law. According to Stevens, 'contract takes its unity from the consideration of justice that agreements, subject to various conditions, create legal rights that ought to be enforced'. If unjust enrichment were a single subject, Stevens argues, then it would have a reason of this kind unifying it. The development of the omnibus four-question test for liability assumes that the subject is unified to some extent— it assumes that the elements of the test are capable of being articulated in a way that captures all situations of liability. This would mean that what constitutes an 'enrichment', for example, would be the same in all cases. Stevens argues that this is not true (Stevens (2018), 576):

> in some cases we are reversing a performance rendered, sometimes the value of a right received, in others a right retained, in some what it would have cost to discharge an obligation, and in still others the expense compelled to incur on another's behalf. The subject lacks even the weak formal unity of being concerned with the same kinds of 'enrichment'. There is no genus to which these species belong.

12.21   To give a brief flavor of Stevens's thinking, consider an example Stevens ((2018), 579) raises:

> C and D each own one of only two examples of a rare collectible stamp worth thousands of pounds. C, by mistake, destroys his stamp, which causes D's stamp to more than double in value. D sells his stamp. C seeks restitution from D of the enrichment D has made at C's expense.

12.22   The elements of the four stage test for liability seem to be satisfied here. If the correct result is that there should be no liability, then the omnibus test has led us into error. Stevens explains that the problem is that the relevant 'enrichment' is wrongly identified. What needs to be reversed, he argues, is the *performance* from C to D, and not the consequences of the performance. To Stevens, 'a defendant who receives a performance from a claimant does so either on the basis that it is made for some justified reason, or that it is not.' If the recipient knows that there is no justifying reason for the performance, then restitution must be made. In this case, when C destroys his stamp by mistake, there has been no performance rendered by C to D at all, and therefore there is nothing to reverse.

12.23   For his part, Watts (2016) argues that the four-question test obscures the analysis of restitutionary claims, and has induced in judges a 'well-meaning sloppiness of thought' that has led to unjust claims being upheld, and just restitutionary claims to be denied. Smith (2018) similarly claims the four-question test 'overgeneralises', and argues for a 'smaller unjust enrichment' framed in terms of discrete, specific, causes of action akin to the different causes of action found in the law of torts.

12.24   It is beyond our purposes here to examine these criticisms in detail, but it should be recognised that there is no consensus about some of the very fundamental basics of the 'unjust enrichment' analysis (see also Penner (2018b)). If Stevens, Watts, and Smith right that there really are irreconcilably different justificatory reasons for restitution, then we do not have a big 'unified' law of unjust enrichment after all.

Unjust enrichment and restitution

12.25   In the introduction to this chapter, we saw that the difference between restitution and unjust enrichment is basically the difference between a remedy and a cause of action. Here we will touch on (i) whether unjust enrichment is the only cause of action that can lead to restitution, and (ii) the difference between restitution of an unjust enrichment and restitution for wrongs.

12.26   If restitution is a remedy and unjust enrichment is a cause of action, do the two match up perfectly? That is, is it only unjust enrichment that triggers restitution? At one point, it was thought that restitution and unjust enrichment were like two opposite sides of a square. In an earlier work, Birks ((1985), 17) asserted that:

> restitution and unjust enrichment identify exactly the same area of law. The one term simply quadrates with the other. That is, if one thinks of the area as a square, the name at the top is unjust enrichment, the causative event, and the name at the side is restitution, the response. There are not many areas of law in which such perfect quadration is practicable.

12.27   However, in a later work, Birks ((2005), 17 et seq) recanted his views on this issue. He recognised that it is *not only unjust enrichment that can lead to restitution*. A fancy term for this is the 'multi-causality' of restitution. The examples we have discussed thus far are examples of restitution of unjust enrichment 'by subtraction', as it is sometimes said. When Y mistakenly pays the gas company twice for her August bill, Y now has a claim for restitution because the money went *from* Y *to* the gas company; importantly, Y's claim is not founded upon any civil wrong committed by the gas company. But restitution can be triggered by civil wrongs, thus there can be restitution for wrongs. The availability of true restitutionary claims based on wrongdoing is a disputed territory in itself (for an overview, see Stevens (2007), 79–84). Sometimes, the claimant has the choice between restitution for an unjust enrichment and restitution for a wrong. Consider the following example of a breach of contract that Burrows ((2011), 10) uses to distinguish between restitution of an unjust enrichment and restitution for wrongs:

> One can illustrate the distinction between restitution of an unjust enrichment and restitution for wrongs by reference to where there has been a breach of contract. Let us assume that the innocent party has paid money to the defendant under the contract and that the defendant has also made profits from dealings with third parties as a direct result of breaking the contract. A claim for restitution of money paid under the contract has been recognized for centuries and has traditionally required that the claimant establish that the money was paid for a consideration that has totally failed. That is a claim for restitution of an unjust enrichment. In contrast, a claim to strip the profits made by the contract-breaker—which was for the first time openly accepted as a valid claim in A-G v Blake is a claim for restitution for the wrong of breach of contract. The cause of action is the breach of contract.

12.28   Now that you know the difference between 'restitution for unjust enrichment' and 'restitution for wrongs', there is a final term to understand, purely because you may encounter it when reading further about this subject. This is the 'principle of reversing unjust enrichment', which is distinct from unjust enrichment as a specific cause of action. This principle is said to underlie both 'restitution for unjust enrichment' and 'restitution for wrongs'. The law of restitution, on one view, is the law that is based on the 'principle of reversing unjust enrichment'.

Personal and proprietary restitution

12.29   Just saying that someone has a claim to restitution leaves a lot unsaid. In our mistaken payment example, if Y mistakenly pays her gas bill of £50 twice, and the gas company becomes insolvent, then it would matter very much to Y whether her claim to restitution is 'personal' or 'proprietary'. If Y only has a personal remedy, it means that the gas company simply has to pay her £50 from its funds, so Y's claim will be on the same footing with all the gas company's other unsecured creditors, and she may end up getting very little or nothing at all. If Y has a proprietary remedy, she asserts a claim over the very £50 that she paid (assuming of course, it can be followed or traceable substitutes of the money can be identified), and that £50 or its traceable proceeds will not be available to satisfy the claims of the other competing creditors. A personal restitutionary remedy is given for claims made for money had and received. Proprietary restitutionary remedies are the norm in equity. The classic example is the claim available against a non *bona fide* purchaser who receives property transferred in breach of trust. Such a person will be liable to an order to transfer the very property, or its traceable proceeds, to a trustee to hold the property on trust as before. The important thing to note here is that we are focussing only on the restitutionary remedy, not the cause of action for which it is a remedy. In the latter case, of property transferred in breach of trust, the restitutionary remedy is not traditionally regarded as responding to the recipient's unjust enrichment—it responds to the fact that the beneficiary has a continuing equitable interest in the assets transferred.

Unjust enrichment and resulting trusts

Presumed resulting trusts

12.30 Although Chambers (1997) was the originator of the 'absence of intention to benefit' reading of the presumption of resulting trust, he now (Chambers (2010a)) denies that resulting trusts respond to any presumption at all; cases where the so-called 'presumption' applies are really just cases where there is no legal reason or basis for the transfer. Chambers thus embraces the 'no legal basis' (12.11) reading of what makes a transfer unjust. B, having received the property either directly from A (as in the case of an ART or a voluntary transfer PRT) or indirectly from A (in the case of a purchase contribution PRT), would be *unjustly* enriched, because *inexplicably* enriched, at A's expense, if he were allowed to keep the property for his own benefit.

12.31 On this view, the current categories of PRTs and ARTs do not exhaust the cases in which resulting trusts (should) arise. They are just the most well-recognised historical situations in which they do. This formulation encompasses a much wider range of cases than is captured by PRTs and ARTs.

12.32 Take our familiar example: I mistakenly pay my gas bill a second time, simply forgetting that I have done so already. Assume, for simplicity, that I pay in cash. The gas company acquires legal title to the cash when I pass it to one of its employees, even though I do so under a mistake, because I voluntarily hand it over intending title to pass. At common law I am entitled to a restitutionary personal claim against the gas company for the amount I mistakenly paid. On Chambers' thesis, however, equity steps in to give me more: although I intended to pay the money to meet a contractual debt to the gas company, because I owed the company no money there was no legal basis for the transfer; therefore the gas company should hold the money it received on an 'unjust enrichment trust' for me. Obviously, I will be very happy about acquiring this equitable proprietary right if, following my mistaken payment, the gas company becomes insolvent (2.89 et seq). If this is right, many common law personal restitutionary claims may be elevated to equitable proprietary rights via this restitutionary resulting trust, because it makes any B who receives A's property when A had no valid legal obligation for transferring it, and A intended no gift, a trustee of that property.

12.33 This result occurred in *Chase Manhattan Bank v Israel-British Bank* (1981). Goulding J held that the plaintiff bank, which mistakenly paid the defendant bank $2m, not only had the normal common law restitutionary personal claim against the recipient of a mistaken payment; in addition, immediately upon receiving the money the recipient bank incurred a fiduciary obligation to return that very money; therefore the recipient bank held it on trust for the paying bank. Accordingly, the paying bank could claim any traceable proceeds acquired with the money as its in equity, thus withdrawing the proceeds from the pool of assets on the recipient's insolvency. The case is poorly reasoned, as Chambers admits (2010a), and the HL in *Westdeutsche Landesbank v Islington London Borough Council* (1996) disapproved of the reasoning.

12.34 The 'unjust enrichment trust' thesis has not been accepted by the courts. In *Westdeutsche Landesbank* the HL unanimously adopted Swadling's view that proof of any intention inconsistent with A's intention that B hold the received property on trust defeated the PRT. Since that time Lord Millett has accepted the alternative 'no intention to benefit' formulation both in his extrajudicial writing (Millett (1998a, 2000, 2005)) and in *Air Jamaica* (1999) and *Twinsectra v Yardley* (2002), but has also stated extrajudicially (Millett (1998a)) that *Chase Manhattan* was wrongly decided. His difference from Chambers lies in what it means to have 'no intention to benefit'. In the mistaken payment case, for example, there is no doubt on the facts that the payor *did* intend to confer on the recipient a beneficial interest in the property. When I pay money to you to discharge a debt, I transfer the money to you to use as your own. In other words, I intend that you should take the money beneficially, to bank in your current account, to spend it as you please—if that wasn't my intention, if I intended that the money should remain mine beneficially, then I wouldn't be discharging the debt; for me to discharge a debt I must make the money beneficially yours. In such a case then, the evidence clearly shows that the transferor (to employ a necessary but clumsy double negative) genuinely did not have 'no intention to benefit the recipient'.

12.35 As Virgo has pointed out, (Virgo (2006), 598):

> ... [I]f the absence of intention analysis [of resulting trusts] is to be recognized, it is vital to define the notion of the vitiation of the claimant's intent restrictively. ... [J]ust because the claimant's intention to benefit the defendant has been vitiated for the purposes of identifying a ground of restitution for unjust enrichment, it does not necessarily mean that the claimant's intention to benefit the defendant has been vitiated for the purposes of identifying a resulting trust. A more restrictive interpretation of when the claimant's intention will be vitiated needs to be adopted before a resulting trust can be recognized.

12.36 Therefore, just because the claimant's intention has been vitiated for one purpose (ie for identifying a ground of restitution for unjust enrichment), does not mean that the claimant's intention to benefit the defendant is vitiated for the purposes of finding a resulting trust. (For other criticisms of Chambers' thesis see Mee (2014, 2017)).

12.37 A final criticism of the unjust enrichment trust theory is that it doesn't really seem to effect restitution of the unjust enrichment. This is most clearly seen in the case of a purchase money PRT. A pays C £1m to transfer C's title in a house to B. If A has no intention to benefit B, then the transaction ought to be reversed; A's claim is that he should get an equivalent sum of money back from B. That would be true restitution, because it would put the parties in the position in which they started. If A is entitled to a trust interest in the house under the PRT, then this gives A a right which, according to the unjust enrichment thesis, *he never intended to have*, and which is a *new and different right to the one he gave up*. Whatever this is, it is not restitution in any conventional sense.

Automatic resulting trusts

12.38   We have seen (5.66 et seq) that the ART is fully explicable on trust law principles. Chambers (2009) argues for an alternative explanation: ARTs arise to reverse the unjust enrichment of B, the trustee. But according to this view, in order to reverse the unjust enrichment created by the receipt of an asset, the claimant is entitled to the very asset back from the recipient. This places the unjust enrichment view on the horns of a dilemma. If the ART gives A, the settlor, an interest which is regarded as different than the one he had before—he started with legal title, and the ART gives him an equitable interest under the ART—then the ART does not effect restitution, for A is not getting the same interest he gave up. But if the interest he acquires *is* the same interest he had at the outset—ie the beneficial interest he started with—then that is as much as to say that he *retained* the same interest he had at the outset, ie that which he did not effectively give away, he kept, which is just the traditional view.

12.39   Another way in which the alternative, unjust enrichment, analysis can be criticised is as follows: if the rules governing the creation of an express trust are that where a person receives title to property he takes a beneficial interest in that property unless and only to the extent that the transferor effectively imposes a trust obligation upon him, then under the rule he is *entitled* to whatever beneficial interest that rule gives him; what the transferor does not 'take away from him' by imposing a valid trust, he keeps. But if that is the rule, then he is not *unjustly* enriched. That is just what the rule gives him. It would seem to go without saying that this is not the way that a trustee's undertaking to hold property on trust is understood. Consider this: to undertake a trust obligation is not: 'I undertake to hold these assets just in so far as you have effectively disposed of the entire interest in them, and anything not so disposed of belongs to me' (2.93). Any trustee who spelled this out as his 'trustee undertaking' to a would-be settlor (think in particular of professional trust companies) would never be accepted as a trustee, and so it would be fanciful to build a theory of ARTs on such a misunderstanding.

12.40   What seems to make most sense of the law is to remember that equity looks to the substance of the matter, not its form. When in the early days of the use, the Chancellor began to enforce uses, it was on the basis that the feoffee to use, bound as he was by the use, had only the 'paper' title, but no right to benefit from the property; it was the settlor who *retained* that. Obviously then, if we keep our focus on the beneficial interest that the settlor had before and after the feoffment to use, nothing has changed in terms of the beneficial interest the settlor had. Mee (2010) shows that this understanding of the matter was crucial for the application of certain laws of succession at the time, and so as a matter of history the 'retention' model of the ART best captures the centuries-long understanding of the judges which, as we have seen, continues to this day.

Tracing and restitution

12.41   At first glance, there appears to be a very strong argument for saying that only by relying upon an unjust enrichment analysis can one explain the process of tracing and claiming. The unjust enrichment theorist asks, why does the property that is the proceeds of a transaction with trust property become in turn the property of the trust? In the case of the trustee, one could argue that the trustee, by undertaking the trust, agrees to hold substitute property as trust property. But this only works if the terms of the trusts allow substitutions (say the investment of the trust assets); the trustee cannot consent, at least as part of his undertaking of the trust, to hold unauthorised substitutions on trust. But the law doesn't care whether the traceable proceeds are the result of an unauthorised substitution or not. Therefore, reasons the unjust enrichment lawyer, whenever a new interest in property arises, ie the interest in the substitute asset, the law must have a reason in justice for awarding it, and the most obvious reason is that otherwise the trustee would be unjustly enriched, because he would acquire an unencumbered legal title to property purchased with trust money. So the law imposes a trust over the proceeds. The same reasoning goes *a fortiori* in the case of tracing through substitutions made by a third-party recipient of the trust funds, who never undertook to act as a trustee at all.

12.42   This characterisation of tracing was rejected by the HL in *Foskett v McKeown* (2001), most forcefully by Lord Millett who said:

> The transmission of a claimant's property rights from one asset to its traceable proceeds is part of our law of property, not of the law of unjust enrichment. There is no 'unjust factor' to justify restitution (unless 'want of title' be one, which makes the point). The claimant succeeds if at all by virtue of his own title, not to reverse unjust enrichment.

12.43   Unfortunately, Lord Millett presented the picture in his decision in *Foskett* without sufficient elaboration. In order to counter the unjust enrichment theorist's argument, and defend the view that the right to claim traceable proceeds flows from the rules of the law of property, one must focus on the nature of the beneficiary's title. As Lord Millett (2005) has since explained extra-judicially, the rules of tracing only make sense on the understanding that the beneficiary's right to claim traceable proceeds flows from the fact that the beneficiary's interest is an interest in a fund (2.75). Recent work by Smith (2009) and your humble author (Penner (2009b, 2014a)) elaborates on the reasons why equitable ownership interests are fund interests. The basic idea is that ownership not only comprises the right to use an asset, ie to realise its use-value, but also the power to exchange it for other property, to realise its exchange-value. If I own the legal title to property outright, and I decide to exchange it for other property for my own benefit, then I become the owner of the property I receive in exchange. It could hardly be otherwise given what ownership means. But now let us consider the case of property held on trust. It is axiomatic that the trustee, having legal title to the property, has the power as legal owner to exchange it for other property. But, in the eyes of equity, the beneficiary is the true beneficial owner of the property. But if this is so, and it is, then any realisation of the ownership of the property through the use of the power to exchange it must be a realisation for the benefit of the beneficiary. The trustee is not entitled to use his legal power to exchange the property otherwise than for the benefit of the beneficiary. Or rather, in any case where the trustee does use his legal power to exchange the trust property for some new asset, that asset is the proceeds of that power and thus belongs to the beneficiary. Equity's recognition of the beneficiary's right to the proceeds is ancient (*Bale v Marchall* (1457)).

12.44   Another way of putting the present point is to say that it would be inconceivable for equity to allow the trustee to defeat the beneficiary's interest by using the very powers that go with title to the trust assets to exchange those assets for others. And the situation is no different for a recipient of trust property transferred in breach of trust. The property this recipient receives is bound by the beneficiary's equitable beneficial interest unless the recipient is a bona fide purchaser. If so bound, just like the trustee the whole beneficial interest in the property is the beneficiary's. And so just as in the case of an express trustee, any use of the powers that go with his legal title to that property to exchange it for some other property, whether innocently or not, is just as much a realisation of the beneficiary's right to the exchange value of the property as is the case when the express trustee exchanges it. The upshot is that equitable ownership interests go hand in hand with understanding those interests as interests in a fund, as interests not only in the assets held in trust for the time being but in any proceeds of those assets, because of the way the trust splits the benefit of the property, which belongs to the beneficiary, from the powers over the title to that property, which are in the hands of the trustee. There is, thus, no need to invoke any unjust enrichment reasoning to explain the rules of tracing.

The restitutionary analysis of recipient liability

The impulse towards fusion

12.45   The way third-party recipients of trust property or its traceable proceeds may be liable to the beneficiaries, via proprietary liability and/or fault-based personal liability for knowing receipt, is a remedial approach unique to equity. It does not match up with the way that recipients of another's property are dealt with at common law. At common law, a person who receives the property of another in flawed circumstances will be liable either for the tort of conversion, and be required to pay compensation for loss, or will be liable to make personal restitution for unjust enrichment. For many commentators, this difference in treatment between equity and the common law suggests that like cases are not being treated alike, and thus that the current law does not provide a workable, coherent, justice—we need a good dose of 'fusion' (1.16) here. The most forceful arguments that have been made have come from restitution lawyers, who argue that liability for receipt of trust property should be analysed in harmony with common law liability for unjust enrichment. The basic question that must be asked is whether the case of receipt of trust property is really a case sufficiently like the traditional cases of restitution, such that their assimilation really makes sense in terms of coherence and justice.

The unjust enrichment analysis of recipient liability

12.46   From the unjust enrichment perspective, the recipient of trust property is liable simply because he has been *unjustly enriched*, ie is now wealthier than he should be, at the beneficiary's expense. Thus he should reverse this situation, by paying back the same amount to the beneficiary, thus restoring the *status quo ante*. This claim, then, is not for compensation for a wrong as in conversion, but restitutionary, ie the recipient must give up the gain he received. The analogy here is with common law restitutionary actions, such as the action 'for money had and received'. As with the standard of knowledge applicable to conversion, the recipient's knowledge about Y's mistake is irrelevant.

12.47   To review Y's mistaken payment of her gas bill under the four-question formula, we can see that the gas company was enriched by receiving £50, it came from Y, and the enrichment is unjust because of the 'unjust factor' of Y's paying the money by mistake. As we shall see (12.61), one of the problematic aspects of treating liability for the receipt of trust property under a restitutionary analysis is that of determining the unjust factor. Now to question (iv). The most wide-ranging defence available to a defendant otherwise liable to make restitution is the defence of 'change of position'.

The defence of change of position

12.48   This defence was firmly established as part of English law in the HL's decision in *Lipkin Gorman* (12.8). Lord Goff said:

> *Where an innocent defendant's position is so changed that he will suffer an injustice if called upon to repay or to repay in full, the injustice of requiring him so to repay outweighs the injustice of denying the plaintiff restitution. If the plaintiff pays money to the defendant under a mistake of fact, and the defendant then, acting in good faith, pays the money or part of it to charity, it is unjust to require the defendant to make restitution to the extent that he has so changed his position . . . I am most anxious that, in recognising this defence to actions of restitution, nothing should be said at this stage to inhibit the development of the defence on a case by case basis, in the usual way.*

12.49   The law has indeed since developed on a case-by-case basis, but it is beyond our purposes to examine the law in detail—you should merely be aware of it in outline. The main points to be aware of are, first, that the defence arises on the basis that the defendant has made an extraordinary expenditure on the faith of his greater wealth due to the enrichment, or has suffered an extraordinary loss because of it. Lord Goff gives the example of a person who celebrates his new-found wealth by making a gift to charity he would not otherwise have made. Other stock examples are organising a more lavish wedding for one's child, or taking a world cruise. The defence applies because the recipient can argue that had he not received the money, he would not have spent it on these things, and it would now be unjust to require the full amount back, because that would leave him in a worse position than if he had never received the money at all. The change of position defence does not arise when one merely spends in the normal way—paying one's rent is an expense one would have had to meet anyway, so there is no change of position that flows from the enrichment. Secondly, the defence is only available to innocent recipients. A person who realises that he has been unjustly enriched and will have to return his newly acquired wealth has no justification for making any extraordinary expenditures. Finally, as to the notion of extraordinary loss, consider this case: you receive a mistaken payment of cash of £1,000, and on the way to bank it you are robbed. The receipt of this much cash exposed you to an extraordinary risk of theft, and it may not be just to require you to pay it back if the risk materialises.

Judicial support for the restitutionary analysis

12.50   There have been a number of *obiter* and extrajudicial statements by judges that argue for treating liability for the receipt of trust property as liability for unjust enrichment leading to a claim for restitution. In *Royal Brunei Airlines* (1995), for instance, Lord Nicholls sharply distinguished accessory liability and recipient liability:

> *Different considerations apply to the two heads of liability. Recipient liability is restitution-based, accessory liability is not.*

In *El Ajou v Dollar Land Holdings plc* (1993) Millett J said:

> [Knowing receipt] is the counterpart in equity of the common law action for money had
> and received. Both can be classified as receipt-based restitutionary claims.

In *Lipkin Gorman* Lord Goff said the following:

> [T]he recognition of the [change of position] defence should be doubly beneficial. It will
> enable a more generous approach to be taken to the recognition of the right to resti-
> tution, in the knowledge that the defence is, in appropriate cases, available; and, while
> recognising the different functions of property at law and in equity, there may also in
> due course develop a more consistent approach to tracing claims, in which common de-
> fences are recognised as available to such claims, whether advanced at law or in equity.

12.51   In respect of the final sentiment, Millett LJ in *Boscawen*, dealing with the claims of an owner in
equity for recipient liability against a defendant into whose hands he has traced his value, made it
clear that the change of position defence should apply. Moreover, he said:

> The introduction of the defence not only provides the court with a means of doing justice in
> future, but allows a re-examination of many decisions in which the absence of the defence
> may have led judges to distort basic principles in order to avoid injustice to the defendant.

12.52   Writing extrajudicially Lord Nicholls (1998) takes *Lipkin Gorman* to be a catalyst in the development of the law, and has argued vis-à-vis recipient liability:

> In this respect equity should now follow the law. Restitutionary liability, applicable
> regardless of fault but subject to a defence of change of position, would be a better
> tailored response to the underlying mischief of misapplied property than personal
> liability which is exclusively fault-based. Personal liability would flow from having
> received the property of another, from having been unjustly enriched at the expense of
> another. It would be triggered by the mere fact of receipt, thus recognising the endurance
> of property rights. But fairness would be ensured by the need to identify a gain, and by
> making change of position available as a defence in suitable cases when, for instance,
> the recipient had changed his position in reliance on the receipt.

Moreover, in *obiter* remarks in *Criterion Properties v Stratford UK Properties* (2004) Lord
Nicholls reasserted the restitutionary analysis in cases of knowing receipt.

12.53   The move toward a restitutionary analysis has not been unanimous, of course. In *Westdeutsche
Landesbank Girozentrale v Islington London Borough Council* (1996) Lord Browne-Wilkinson
quite clearly affirmed, *obiter*, the traditional formulation:

> Even if the third party [recipient of trust property], X, is not aware that what he has
> received is trust property B [the beneficiary] is entitled to assert his title in that property.
> If X has the necessary degree of knowledge, X may himself become a constructive trustee
> for B on the basis of knowing receipt. But unless he has the requisite degree of knowledge
> he is not personally liable to account as trustee.

However, viewed in its context, the statement may be taken to be directed only to the question
whether the third-party recipient should, without knowledge, be regarded as having a trustee's

duties and liabilities such as the liability to account (the answer being 'no'), leaving entirely open whether the third-party recipient might have personal liabilities arising on a different basis, ie on the basis of his unjust enrichment or his interference with the beneficiary's proprietary rights.

12.54   Nourse LJ in *Akindele* (11.198) strongly doubted whether knowing receipt should be reframed along restitutionary lines; although in *Grupo Torras v Al Sabah* (2001) the CA appeared to leave the question more open.

12.55   Originally it was argued by unjust enrichment lawyers that liability under the 'knowing receipt' label was not truly fault-based, but was an unrealised form of liability for unjust enrichment, and this appears to have been the view of judges found in most of the preceding quotes. The currently favoured view (see eg Birks (2002)) is that there is concurrent liability, both fault-based liability for knowing receipt, and strict restitutionary liability for unjust enrichment. This is the view advanced *obiter* by Lord Millett in *Dubai Aluminium v Salaam* (2003):

> Dishonest receipt gives rise to concurrent liability, since the claim can be based on the defendant's dishonesty, treating the receipt itself as incidental, being merely the particular form taken by the defendant's participation in the breach of fiduciary duty; but it can also be based simply on the receipt, treating it as a restitutionary claim independent of any wrong doing . . .

12.56   In terms of authority, however, this more recent view seems no more plausible than the former view. As Smith (2000) puts it:

> It has been said that the claim in knowing receipt belongs to the law of unjust enrichment, and since claims in unjust enrichment do not depend on fault, therefore it cannot be right that the knowing receipt claim should depend on fault. The startling consequence is that not some but all of the cases on the subject are wrong. More recently, another line has been taken, to the effect that even if the claim in knowing receipt is based on wrongdoing rather than unjust enrichment, nonetheless there is no reason that a plaintiff cannot put to one side the claim based on wrongdoing, and sue instead in unjust enrichment. The consequences of this view are only slightly less startling: the cases may be right, but all of the lawyers and judges involved failed to notice that there was another claim available to the plaintiff, and moreover one which renders otiose any inquiry into cognition. That of course is the inquiry with which the cases are most concerned. It is important to stress that no defendant appears ever to have been made strictly liable for the receipt of trust property.

12.57   More recently, the High Court of Australia has weighed in, in *Farah Constructions Pty Ltd v Say-Dee Pty Ltd* (2007), rejecting, pretty much root and branch, the restitutionary analysis of the recipient's personal liability. In a unanimous decision of the five-judge panel, the court echoed the just-quoted views of Smith:

> [T]he restitution basis is unhistorical. There is no sign of it in clear terms in any but the most recent authorities. It is inherent in the Court of Appeal's conclusion that for many decades the courts have misunderstood the tests for satisfying [personal recipient liability]: that is improbable. It is inherent in the conclusion advocated by Say-Dee that for many decades the courts have failed to notice the existence of a form of liability co-existing with [it]: that is equally improbable.

Perhaps more importantly, the court also rejected the theoretical approach of the proponents of the restitutionary approach:

> The restitution basis reflects a mentality in which considerations of ideal taxonomy prevail over a pragmatic approach to legal development. As Gummow J said [in Roxborough v Rothmans of Pall Mall Australia Ltd (2001) at 544 [72]]:

> 'To the lawyer whose mind has been moulded by civilian influences, the theory may come first, and the source of the theory may be the writings of jurists not the decisions of judges. However, that is not the way in which a system based on case law develops; over time, general principle is derived from judicial decisions upon particular instances, not the other way around.'

> The restitution basis was imposed as a supposedly inevitable offshoot of an all-embracing theory. To do that was to bring about an abrupt and violent collision with received principles without any assigned justification.

12.58   One is unlikely to get a more brutal rejection of the theory than that. Unsurprisingly, restitutionary analysis proponents find the result deplorable (see eg Chambers (2007)).

The recipient's enrichment

12.59   As we have seen, in order for a claimant to establish the restitutionary liability of the defendant, he must first show that he has been enriched at the expense of the claimant, and then point to an unjust factor that makes the defendant's enrichment unjust. We will deal with each point in turn.

12.60   There is a long-running dispute amongst commentators on the law of restitution as to whether someone in the position of the recipient of trust funds is enriched. As we know, unless the recipient is a bona fide purchaser, the beneficiary retains his equitable interest in the property the recipient receives. In view of this it seems impossible to say that the recipient is enriched, because the beneficiary retains his beneficial, equitable, title and the recipient acquires no beneficial title at law or in equity. This contrasts sharply with the case of the typical mistaken payment. If you pay your gas bill a second time, the gas company acquires beneficial legal title to your money, since you transferred it with the intention that title should pass. The gas company is clearly enriched because it now has beneficial title to money that was once yours, and at your expense. But the very opposite is the case with the third-party recipient of trust property. Traditionally, if a third party is in possession of property that is beneficially yours, one brings a 'title' claim, not a restitutionary claim, such as a claim for damages for interference with your beneficial title if the property is a chattel, a claim to be put into possession if the property is land, or a claim to specifically enforce the trust against a recipient of trust property. From a traditional perspective, there would seem to be no room for a restitutionary claim in these circumstances, and this distinction between title claims and restitutionary claims appeared to be endorsed by Lord Millett in *Foskett v McKeown*, and was explicitly endorsed in Millett (2005). (But see Chambers (2009) for a sophisticated reappraisal of the issue.)

The unjust factor

12.61   What is the unjust factor making the receipt by the third party of trust property unjust? The problem here is that the trustee, in transferring the property in breach of trust, does not make a mistake, nor does the recipient (at least in the vast majority of cases) acquire the property by acting unconscionably or by putting the trustee under duress (and, if he did, the trustee would simply have a common law claim for restitution against the third party, which he would be bound to pursue on behalf of the trust). Birks ((1985), 140) claims that the unjust factor is 'ignorance': the beneficiary's property is transferred away from the trust and he does not even know about it. This, argues Birks, is clearly a stronger case of injustice than that of the mistaken payor who pays his gas bill twice, because here the beneficiary could do nothing to prevent the transfer; his ignorance of the transfer makes the stranger's receipt of the trust property unjust.

12.62 There is, however, a glaring problem with saying that ignorance is the unjust factor, which is simply that the beneficiary is typically ignorant of all the dispositions of the trust property the trustee makes, whether unauthorised or authorised (except, of course, payments to that beneficiary himself under the terms of the trust, and sometimes not even those). The argument therefore proves too much. If the beneficiary was entitled to reverse any disposition of the trust property of which he was ignorant, he could reverse any transaction a trustee undertook, whether it was authorised or not. The beneficiary's 'ignorance' of the trustee's dealing is simply part and parcel of the way trusts work, of the fact that it is the trustee who has all the legal powers to deal with the trust property and is expected to use them according to the terms of the trust, not according to the beneficiary's instructions (see also Swadling (1996b); Grantham and Rickett (1996); Bant (1998)). One might reply that, in the case of authorised transactions, the 'ignorance' factor is displaced by the beneficiary's implicit 'consent' to authorised transactions, ie transactions within the terms of the trust—to the extent that the beneficiary claims any benefit under the trust at all, it is only to such a benefit as is within its terms, and therefore he must consent to any transaction within the terms. But this argument revises the unjust factor to 'unauthorised or wrongful transactions of which the beneficiary is ignorant', and this does not describe the cases. A breach is a breach of trust whether the beneficiary is ignorant of or knows about it (a beneficiary's mere knowledge does not amount to consent (11.72)), so clearly the operative factor here is that the transaction is unauthorised; the beneficiary's knowledge or ignorance is irrelevant. Thus the only unjust factor that would appear to operate is the trustee's want of authority in carrying out the transaction. (For a much more thorough exploration of the problems of 'ignorance' as an unjust factor, see Chambers and Penner (2008).) But if want of authority is the 'unjust factor', then plausibly the appropriate analogy to the common law is liability for conversion, not liability for unjust enrichment, because dealing with the trust property without authority would appear to amount to committing a wrong commensurate to interfering with the beneficiary's property rights. Liability for conversion is strict, and so differs from knowing receipt, which depends upon fault. But in view of the battery of claims that a beneficiary can make in cases of breach (he always has a strict liability claim against the trustee, may have a claim for knowing assistance against a third party, etc), it may make sense that the 'conversion' claim in equity is more restrictive, fault-based rather than strict.

12.63 A similar point is put by Smith (2000):

> Writing on this subject, [Lord Nicholls (1998)] deploys the following example. A defendant innocently receives some money, trust property, as a gift from the trustee. He spends it on something which he would have bought anyway, and which leaves no traceable product. If fault is required, there is no claim; if fault is not, then there probably is, because the facts are intended to imply that the defendant cannot use the

defence of change of position. Lord Nicholls takes the view that this defendant should repay; he has been made better off out of the claimant's trust fund, and if the defendant is required to repay, he will only be back to where he started. But of course the fact that someone is only back to where he started does not justify liability. Otherwise all gifts would be recoverable, subject only to a defence of change of position. Presumably Lord Nicholls would say, this is not a gift; the plaintiff never intended the defendant to be enriched. But in another sense, it was a gift; it was a gift from the trustee. Ignoring that amounts to ignoring that there is a trust. This defendant might reasonably ask why he should be required to account in court for what he has done over the preceding several years with money that was legally his own (subject only to the [plaintiff's] undiscoverable equitable interest), failing which he will have to dig into his pocket to repay. He might ask why the plaintiff should not instead look for relief to his trustee, the one to whom the money was entrusted in the first place. But the argument for strict liability consistently ignores the essential fact that there is a trust, and seeks to treat the trust beneficiary like a legal owner.

12.64 Put another way, there are certain attendant risks with utilising the trust, and one of these risks is that the trustee is truly the legal owner of the trust property, and his actions are not without consequence.

12.65 The difficulty of identifying and defending a workable unjust factor which would underpin the restitutionary analysis is not a merely academic issue. One of the most trenchant criticisms of the High Court in *Farah v Say-Dee* of the lower court's decision was its failure to do just that—the New South Wales Court of Appeal failed to identify any unjust factor at all.

Untraceable expenditure of the trust property

12.66 The preceding considerations would seem to undercut the idea that a third-party recipient of trust property should be strictly personally liable to transfer a sum of money equivalent in value to that of the property she received on the basis that she was unjustly enriched at the beneficiary's expense. They would seem to suggest that the present law, whereby the beneficiary can enforce the trust against the recipient in respect of any trust property or traceable proceeds in his hands, is both sufficient and just. However, what if the recipient dissipates the trust property or proceeds, ie spends it on something that does not generate any traceable proceeds in exchange, say blows it all on a holiday? Cannot the restitutionary lawyer intervene at this stage? By spending the money in this way, the beneficiary's title is extinguished (the holiday agent is a bona fide purchaser) in a way that legally, not just factually, benefits the recipient, because he acquires the contractual right to the performance of the holiday agent, which he benefits from when he takes the holiday.

12.67 The problem again comes down to the unjust factor: there is no mistake, duress, unconscionability and, as we have seen, 'ignorance' does not work either. The transaction is not 'vitiated' in any way on any of these bases. What has happened here is simply that the recipient has bought his holiday with trust money—that is, he has defeated the beneficiary's equitable interest in that property. So if the recipient should be liable, he would be primarily liable for committing this wrong, not for being unjustly enriched at the beneficiary's expense. But coming to this conclusion depends upon saying that the innocent recipient of trust property does commit a wrong when he spends the trust property, ie commits a wrong in the eyes of equity. But this is precisely what the cases do not say. Smith (2000) again (see also Hayton (2007)):

> *The argument that suggests that personal claims based on receipt of trust property must line up with the strict liability in Lipkin Gorman v Karpnale seems to ignore a very basic truth: a beneficiary's interest under a trust is not legal ownership. Equitable proprietary rights are not protected in the same way as legal ones. In general, they are protected less well. They are always subject to destruction by bona fide purchase of a legal interest or overreaching, and wrongful interference with them is dependent on fault . . . The argument for strict liability would make the most sense as part of an agenda which sought the abolition of the trust, and the return to a regime in which only one person can claim to be the owner of a given asset. That would be an odd agenda to pursue, when civilian systems all over the world, aware of the flexibility which the trust device offers, are introducing it in various forms. Certainly as the law is now, the beneficiary's interest under a trust attracts different incidents from legal ownership. It is not clear that it would make sense to abolish some of the characteristics of equitable property rights while leaving others intact. If liability for receiving trust property is strict, why should equitable interests be subject to destruction by the defence of bona fide purchase of a legal interest?*

> *The trustee is (usually) the legal owner. If he makes, for example, a mistaken payment, or is defrauded . . ., he will have at his disposal all of the strict liability claims which protect his legal title and protect him from defective transfers. On the other hand, he might not have a claim; he might have given the trust money away in breach of trust. But it does not follow from this that we must give the beneficiaries the same rights that the trustee would have had, had he acted properly. It is in the nature of the trust institution that beneficiaries are vulnerable to breaches of trust, in ways which they would not be if they were the legal owners of the trust property. To complain about this is to complain about the incidents of the institution of the trust.*

12.68   The contrast with the typical two-party case of restitution at common law (eg where you pay your gas bill twice) and the situation of breach of trust can be further sharpened by pointing out that, in the case of breach of trust, the beneficiary has, besides the recipient, a defendant who is always strictly liable for the entire loss to the trust, with no change of position defence, that is, the trustee. So while the beneficiary's remedial protection can look weaker from a restitutionary point of view, this is so only if one focuses only on the third-party recipient. Recall the array of claims that can arise in a case of breach of trust (11.1 et seq).

12.69   Another point to consider is that it seems fair that beneficiaries should take the bad with the good regarding the fact that their property interest in equity is an interest in a fund. It is only because equity conceives of the beneficiary's property interest as an interest in a fund that the third-party recipient is bound by the beneficiary's interest not only in the property he receives but in anything he receives in exchange for it. This is an advantage of one's property interest being treated as an interest in the fund, not in the individual items of property in that fund. But there is a corresponding disadvantage. One cannot treat the recipient's transaction with any one of the items in the fund as the disposition of one's title in that property, as if one were the legal owner of it, equivalent to conversion.

12.70   One final consideration: to make the recipient strictly liable to pay for any loss in the value of the beneficiaries' interest when he innocently dissipates the trust assets (albeit subject to a change of position defence, which he must claim and also prove) would be to make the recipient equivalent to an insurer of the beneficiaries' interest, insuring the beneficiaries against the consequence of breaches of trust by their trustee. That cannot be right. To adapt what Lord Nicholls said in *Tan*, 387EF, when discussing imposing strict liability on someone who participates in a breach of trust:

> *The recipient's only sin is that he interfered with the due performance by the trustee of the fiduciary obligations undertaken by the trustee by innocently dissipating property transferred to him on a basis he did not know to be wrongful. Beneficiaries could not reasonably expect that third parties should deal with trustees at their peril, to the extent that they should become liable to the beneficiaries even they were unaware and had no reason to suppose that they were dealing with trust property.*

FURTHER READING

Birks (2002)

Chambers (1997, 2009, 2010a)

Chambers and Penner (2008)

Mee (2014, 2017)

Millett (1998a, 2000, 2005)

Nicholls (1998)

Penner (2009b, 2014a, 2018b)

Smith (2000, 2009, 2018)

Stevens (2018)

Swadling (1996b)

Watts (2016)

Must-read cases:

Westdeutsche Landesbank Girozentrale v Islington LBC (1996); *Chase Manhattan Bank v Israel-British Bank* (1981); *Twinsectra v Yardley* (2002); *Foskett v McKeown* (2001); *Farah Constructions Pty Ltd v Say-Dee Pty Ltd* (2007)

SELF-TEST QUESTIONS

1. Owing to a serious computer error, the London School of Econometrics mistakenly directs its bank to pay £1,500 into several hundred of its employees' bank accounts with the payment reference 'performance bonus'. Is there any basis in law for the School to claim that these employees hold these mistaken payments on trust for it?

2. What examples are there of personal restitutionary remedies and how are they different from proprietary restitutionary remedies?

3. X pays Y to convey Blackacre to Z. What kind of interest does X have now in Blackacre, and how is that interest best explained?

4. On what basis does an ART arise, and is this basis illuminated by an 'unjust enrichment trust' analysis?

5. What insights, if any, arise from the restitutionary analysis of a third party recipient of trust property or its traceable proceeds?

13

The law governing fiduciaries

SUMMARY

The 'duty of loyalty': fiduciaries, employees, and others
The 'no conflict' rule
Authorised profits
Unauthorised profits and the liability to account for them
The self-dealing and fair dealing rules
The proprietary and personal nature of the liability to account
Equitable compensation for breach of fiduciary obligation
Secondary liability for breach of fiduciary obligation

13.1 To begin with, review the descriptions of the fiduciary relationship at 2.19 and 11.16.

The 'duty of loyalty': fiduciaries, employees, and others

13.2 At its core, the fiduciary relationship is founded upon the fiduciary's voluntary undertaking to exercise powers which are conferred upon him by the principal, the exercise of which will involve his making judgments about how specifically to exercise those powers, judgments which require him to take into consideration only the principal's interests. This is sometimes called the 'discretionary' theory of the fiduciary relationship (Conaglen (2007), 39–40; Miller (2011, 2013, 2014); Penner (2014a, 2014b, 2019b); Smith, (2014a, 2014b); Smith, S (2016); Valsan (2016); Sitkoff (2014); Weinrib (1975)). It responds to the fact that the voluntary obligation (or 'contract,' loosely speaking), which underlies the relationship, is 'incomplete' in the important following sense: the actual exercises of the agent's powers to enter into contracts on her principal's behalf, or a trustee's making investment decisions regarding the trust assets, or in exercising a dispositive discretion under a trust, cannot be specified in advance under the objective legal terms of the agency or trust.

13.3 The now classic judicial formulation of this view in the US is found in Justice Breyer's judgment in the US Supreme Court decision *Varity Corp v Howe* (1996), 504; (see also *Perez v Galambos* (2009), [50]–[84], [83]–[84]; *Hospital Products Ltd v United States Surgical Corporation* (1984), 96–97 (Mason J)):

> [T]he primary function of the fiduciary duty is to constrain the exercise of discretionary powers which are controlled by no other specific duty imposed by the trust instrument or the legal regime. If fiduciary duty applied to nothing more than the activities already controlled by specific legal duties, it would serve no purpose [emphasis added].

13.4 Although 'discretion' and 'discretionary' are the standard terms used to describe the 'leeway' the fiduciary has in exercising her powers, the better word for describing this 'leeway' is 'judgment', not discretion, at least in so far as the word 'discretion' suggests that the fiduciary has any sort of personal freedom in these cases. The fiduciary is required to choose that course of action which, in her judgment, is in the best interests of her principal. Because the literature tends to use the word 'discretion' and 'discretionary' powers rather than saying 'judgment' and powers 'whose exercise requires the prior exercise of judgment in determining which, among more than one authorised exercise of the power, is to be chosen,' I shall use the 'discretion' formulation as well, though in doing so it is with the 'exercise of judgment' meaning in mind.

13.5 Sometimes the exercise of an agent's or trustee's powers can be objectively specified, and no judgment on the part of the fiduciary is necessary to determine when and how the powers ought to be exercised. An agent may be given precise instructions. A trustee may have no power to sell trust assets and invest the proceeds elsewhere. A trust may not involve any dispositive discretions. In such cases there is no need to invoke any fiduciary relationship to explain the nature of the agent's or trustee's duties and her liability for breach of those duties. In the case where the agent breaches his instruction, or the trustee breaches the trust by misapplying the trust property, there is obvious and straightforward liability in agency and trust law, based on an objective analysis of the facts in the sense that the agent's or trustee's liability in these cases is strict and his or her state of mind irrelevant (just like in a breach of contract case), and it is confusing to treat any such breach of agency or trust as a breach of any fiduciary relationship. The same can be said for a breach of a trustee's duty of care in, say, making investment decisions. The liability for careless investments is determined upon an objective basis, and the motives or state of mind of the trustee is irrelevant to her liability.

13.6 Nevertheless, courts and commentators routinely describe the duties of trustees involving no requirement of judgment as 'fiduciary duties', one supposes simply on the principle that a trustee is (typically) a fiduciary, and so why not just call all of his duties 'fiduciary duties'? This can only lead to confusion. As Millett LJ makes clear in *Bristol and West Building Society v Mothew* (1996), just because A stands as a fiduciary to B, that does not mean that every duty he owes B is a fiduciary duty:

> The expression 'fiduciary duty' is properly confined to those duties which are peculiar to fiduciaries and the breach of which attracts legal consequences differing from those consequent upon the breach of other duties. Unless the expression is so limited it is lacking in practical utility. In this sense it is obvious that not every breach of duty by a fiduciary is a breach of fiduciary duty . . . It is . . . inappropriate to apply the expression to the obligation of a trustee or other fiduciary to use proper skill and care in the discharge of his duties . . . A fiduciary is someone who has undertaken to act for or on behalf of another in a particular matter in circumstances which give rise to a relationship of trust and confidence. The distinguishing obligation of a fiduciary is the obligation of loyalty.

> The principal is entitled to the single-minded loyalty of his fiduciary. This core liability has several facets. A fiduciary must act in good faith; he must not make a profit out of

his trust; he must not place himself in a position where his duty and his interest may conflict; he may not act for his own benefit or the benefit of a third person without the informed consent of his principal . . . [Where] the fiduciary deals with his principal . . . he must prove affirmatively that the transaction is fair and that in the course of the negotiations he made full disclosure of all facts material to the transaction. Even inadvertent failure to disclose will entitle the principal to rescind the transaction . . . The nature of the obligation determines the nature of the breach. The various obligations of a fiduciary merely reflect different aspects of his core duties of loyalty and fidelity. Breach of fiduciary obligation, therefore, connotes disloyalty or infidelity. Mere incompetence is not enough. A servant who does his incompetent best for his master is not unfaithful and is not guilty of a breach of fiduciary duty.

13.7   Mitchell (2013), 311, (footnotes omitted) elaborates:

As Matthew Conaglen has written (Conaglen (2007), ch 2,) the corollary of Millett LJ's argument is that the other duties which a fiduciary can owe to his principal are not fiduciary duties, because they are not duties of loyalty. These include the duty to perform an engagement according to its terms (which includes the duty owed by a trustee to adhere to the trust terms), the duty to act for a proper purpose, the duty to take relevant matters into account and to exclude irrelevant matters from account when exercising a power, the duty of skill and care, and the duty of confidence. At one time or another, these have all been described as 'fiduciary duties', but this is to misunderstand their content. It also makes it harder to understand the content of the duty of undivided loyalty and the remedial consequences of breaching this duty. Describing different duties as though they were a single duty can lead to the false conclusion that the remedies consequent on breach of the duties are always the same.

13.8   As Millett LJ also points out, the duty of loyalty has been elaborated in the form of a number of more particular duties, concerning profits from the trust, conflicts of interest, and transactions with the principal's property. We shall examine each in turn. First however, we have to come to terms with the fact that the 'duty of loyalty' has two distinct meanings in the law, one fiduciary, and one not.

The employee's duty of loyalty and bad faith breaches of the duty of loyalty (BFBDL)

13.9   Employees owe their employers a 'duty of loyalty', though merely having this duty does not make them fiduciaries to their employers. The basis of the duty is the fact that, in relying upon or 'trusting', in a colloquial sense, or placing faith in, the employee to deal with the employer's property and carry out his employer's instructions, the employer places the employee in a position that enables the employee to take advantage of the factual circumstances. That position differentiates him from a mere stranger to the employer. So, for example, both a stranger and an employee can steal property from the employer, but in the latter's case this is also (again, colloquially, not legally) a breach of trust, or a breach of faith. In law this would amount to the employee's breach of his 'duty of loyalty'.

13.10   Here is an example which combines both the breach of an employer's right to his property and his right that the employee follows his instructions. I (the employer) hand you (my employee) a

£10 note and instruct you to buy a bottle of wine with it. In deliberate breach of my instructions, you take the money (of which you have mere custody, not any title to the note) and instead buy yourself lunch. As far as the law of property is concerned you have committed a conversion. (You will also have committed theft, but let us leave the criminal law to one side). Your liability to me will be the value of the note you have converted, £10. Your contractual liability will be much more serious. On the basis of your deliberate breach of my instructions you have breached your duty of loyalty, and I may summarily dismiss you. Moreover, it may be the case that I can refuse to pay you your wages for that day and any day that follows to which you would otherwise be entitled, a sum which is likely to be much more than the £10 I can claim for your conversion.

13.11   Although in this case you are probably also acting as my agent, as well as my employee, you are not a fiduciary. As we have seen, the fiduciary relationship involves the fiduciary having a legal or practical power in respect of the principal which requires the fiduciary to exercise judgment in relation to the principal's interests, and that is not the case here. You are simply required to follow my instructions, and establishing whether you have done that or not is entirely an objective exercise; your state of mind is irrelevant as regards that liability; your liability is strict. The way in which your mental state is relevant, your *deliberate* disregard of my instructions, is for the purpose of establishing your breach of the duty of loyalty. Though you had *no power to exercise judgment on my behalf,* you were in a position, unlike third parties, to wrong me in a particular way, by having custody of my money and spending it contrary to my instructions. Your mental state, your deliberate act contrary to my instructions, shows you breached your duty of loyalty, because you acted contrary to my instructions in bad faith, ie so as to breach the faith I placed in you. This the bad faith breach version of the duty of loyalty, or BFBDL, for short.

13.12   But the employee's duty of loyalty only extends to this sort of case, a breach of the contract of employment or a misuse of the employer's property. It is not a general duty to exercise whatever discretions she has under her contract of employment with only the interests of her employer in mind. She may exercise whatever discretions she has in her own interests, in the same way that her employer may exercise whatever discretions it has in its. For example, if an employee is entitled to four weeks' holiday under her contract, she can take all of that holiday, as and when she chooses, even if the employer is inconvenienced by her choice in one way or another. The employee is not required to think about taking her holiday at this time or that with only with her employer's best interests in mind. Similarly, an employee entitled to maternity leave need not plan her pregnancies with her employer's best interests in mind.

BFBDL also applies to fiduciaries

13.13   Fiduciaries are also under an obligation to act in good faith. Fiduciaries have legal or practical powers in respect of their principals. A fiduciary agent has discretionary powers to enter into contracts on her principal's behalf. A trustee may be a fiduciary because he has dispositive powers with respect to the trust assets. The fiduciary must exercise these powers with only the interest of the principal(s) in mind. One way of exercising these powers in a flawed fashion is to exercise them in a situation of conflict of interest, which we shall discuss presently. Bad faith raises a different issue. Having legal or practical powers over others puts one in a situation in which one may act against those persons' interests in a particular way, and the duty of good faith, or the duty not to act in bad faith, is one obvious norm ensuring that those others' interests are not negatively affected.

13.14   So, how does one act in bad faith? Like a breach of the employee's duty of loyalty, bad faith reflects the state of mind of the person exercising the power in question. It is not aptly described as an act undertaken by acting in conflict of interest, unless every thief, who clearly favours his own interests over his victim's, is regarded too as acting in conflict of interest; rather it evokes a state of mind in which the fiduciary positively and deliberately acts against the principal's interest in some way.

13.15   *Klug v Klug* (1918) provides an illustration. There, one of two trustees, the beneficiary's mother, refused to agree to an advancement to her daughter, even though it was within the terms of the trust and the other (professional) trustee thought it right to make the advancement, because the mother disapproved of her daughter's marriage. This was an irrelevant consideration in deciding whether to exercise the power. In taking it into account, it is right to say that the mother was acting in bad faith even if, all things considered, she thought deliberately refusing to exercise the power for its intended purposes was an appropriate way of teaching her daughter a lesson. In so acting, the mother was not acting in conflict of interest, but was rather intentionally not taking account of her daughter's interests for reasons that she ought to have understood to be irrelevant.

The duty to act in the principal's best interests

13.16   This duty, or at least the way it is framed, seems almost designed to generate confusion. It suggests that there is an objective standard of 'best interests' which the fiduciary must meet. It has even been suggested that it entitles a trustee to commit 'judicious' breaches of trust, so long as these breaches are undertaken in the beneficiaries' best interests (*Armitage v Nurse* (1998), 251, per Millett LJ). As pointed out by Smith (See Smith, (2014), 143–45, 148–58), this is confused. What the duty requires is that the fiduciary exercise her legal and/or practical powers with only the principal's interests in mind, and because benefitting the principal is the point of the whole exercise, the fiduciary must act in the way that, in her judgment, best serves the principal's interests given the options for action that are available to her. There is, in general, no standard of 'due diligence' that applies, except in so far as the terms of the trust, the contract, or the general law specifies a duty of care or a duty of 'best efforts'. A fiduciary must act so as to reasonably discharge such latter duties in terms of pursuing information and so on, but there is no background mandatory or default rule or standard of law imposing a 'best efforts' duty with which a fiduciary must comply. Nor is there any applicable objective standard of 'best interests' which would make a fiduciary liable if the principal were able to show that, in hindsight, the fiduciary could have entered into a better contract for the principal or made a better investment decision or, finally, a 'better' distribution of the trust assets, whatever that might mean.

The fiduciary duty of loyalty (FDL)

13.17   'Loyalty' in the sense of the *fiduciary* duty of loyalty, is distinct from the duty of loyalty owed by employees, agents, and others under BFBDL. From your present author's perspective, it would probably have been better had the term 'loyalty' never been applied in this context (Penner (2014a, 2014b); Smith, S (2016)), but the term is so regularly used to explain the nature of the fiduciary relationship that all we can do is notice what it means in this context.

13.18   The 'no-conflict rule' is the heart and soul of FDL, because it addresses a problem peculiar to fiduciaries. It addresses the case where an exercise of a power is taken in cases where the trustee's judgment is impaired. This idea of impairment follows from the recognition that, even with the best intentions in the world, where one is interested in a transaction one cannot be sure that one has made an unbiased decision; judgment in these circumstances is moreover compromised by the human propensity to rationalise a decision favouring oneself.

13.19   Here is one particular pitfall in applying our commonsense notion of loyalty to the fiduciary relationship. Under our commonsense notion, loyalty relates to a relationship in which the loyal person must emotionally identify with the object of her loyalty, friend with friend, teammate with team, citizen with country. Such relations of loyalty give rise to the possibility of 'epistemic bias'; the identification involved lends itself to forming favourable but false or at least dubious beliefs about the object of loyalty. (This may be particularly true in the case of loyalty to one's country, eg 'My country, right or wrong.') While there is a weak sense in which fiduciaries should identify with their principals, generally thinking that their role in serving their principals is worthwhile, discharging the role of fiduciary does not require any sympathy or identification of this kind. Being a fiduciary, an agent or a trustee, is just a job, after all. Once again, the case of the trustee-fiduciary makes this point particularly clearly. One of the main tasks of the trustee-fiduciary of a family wealth-management trust is to stand back and take a clear-eyed view of the beneficiaries, untainted by personal 'identification', drawing upon personal knowledge of the beneficiaries of course, but not being swayed by personal likes or dislikes. And beneficiaries, just like some of the rest of the population, can be perfectly dreadful people, with whom it would be unseemly to identify. It is not in any way part of the remit of a trustee to think of her identity as bound up with that of the beneficiaries.

13.20   As to epistemic bias, a fiduciary in law undertakes a duty to exercise various powers in the interests of her principal. This duty will not be discharged properly if, in the exercise of those powers, the fiduciary forms false beliefs, however congenial those false beliefs may be to her. Indeed, in the case of family trusts, one of the whole purposes of placing powers in the hands of impartial trustees is to provide an antidote to the false beliefs which persons close to the beneficiaries might form based on their identification with them. While it is not uncommon for one of a number of trustees in a family trust to be one of the family members, often a beneficiary, any properly advised settlor should choose a trustee (typically a trust company) that is impartial vis-a-vis the several beneficiaries; if loyalty in the commonsense notion of loyalty were genuinely prized in a fiduciary one would see the reverse—settlors would choose close family members to be the only trustees in family trusts, but this, as wise settlors recognise, is normally a very inadvisable thing to do.

The true fiduciary holds two duties of loyalty: BFBDL and FDL

13.21   In both the case of the employee and the fiduciary, the employer and the principal have reposed trust in the colloquial sense, and have thereby made themselves vulnerable in a way that mere strangers to the employee or fiduciary are not. They are both, therefore, governed by the BFBDL. To take advantage of their employer's or principal's vulnerable position as a means of harming the employer or principal is indeed morally iniquitous. The mere wrong is compounded or aggravated because of the person who did it. The overlap here is not merely theoretical. Like the employee who steals from her employer, the trustee who intentionally misappropriates trust property (besides being liable for breach of trust, of course) is liable to the equivalent of summary dismissal: the court will remove her from her position as trustee. Other breaches of trust that do not reveal bad faith do not, generally, lead to trustee removal.

The 'duty of loyalty' and family relationships

13.22   In *M (K) v M (H)* (1992) the Canadian Supreme Court held that a parent stood in a fiduciary relationship with his child. A daughter was sexually abused by her father; she brought an action against her father for damages for the tort of assault, which the trial judge dismissed on the basis that the claim was barred by the Ontario Limitations Act. On appeal to the Supreme Court of Canada, the daughter claimed that for various reasons the Limitations Act should not apply to bar her claim in tort, and her appeal on this ground succeeded. But she also claimed that her father's assault also constituted a breach of fiduciary obligation; in view of the fact that there was no statutory limitation period in respect of breach of a fiduciary obligation, if she succeeded on this ground she would have been in a much better position to avoid any bar based upon the lapse of time between the assaults and her launching her action against her father. The court accepted her argument that her father had breached a fiduciary obligation in assaulting her.

13.23   Child abuse is of course a terrible wrong, and is also a dreadful breach of loyalty and good faith when committed by a parent or guardian. It seems that the latter consideration is what drove the court to accept the abuse as a breach of fiduciary obligation. But this 'duty of loyalty', which, it is submitted, does apply to parents vis-à-vis their children (and vice versa for that matter), is nothing more or less than BFBDL. It had nothing to do with FDL. In particular, it seems positively odd if the father's wrong in this case breached a genuinely *fiduciary* relationship between him and his daughter.

13.24   In the first place, child abuse is a crime and a civil wrong. No one has a legal power or discretion to commit child abuse, a power or discretion that should be exercised only in the interests of the victim. FDL is intended to ensure that a fiduciary takes decisions that he is *legally empowered or obliged to undertake under his trust, agency, or retainer* only in ways that best serve the interests of his principal. In view of a fiduciary's position, an otherwise *legitimate* use of a *legitimate* power or discretion may be 'turned into a wrong', and set aside, because it was made when the trustee's judgment was compromised by a conflict of interest. A breach of any old obligation, whether the commission of a tort like assault or child abuse, or a breach of contract, does not become a breach of FDL because, besides being wrong in its own right, it also reveals self-interested bad faith; otherwise every thief would be branded as a fiduciary in breach. As Valsan (2016), 8, writes: 'The decision of whether to appropriate another's property or opportunities is not an exercise of discretion in any meaningful sense of the term.' Those acts are not within the range of decisions that make up the extent of the fiduciary's discretion, to which, and only to which, FDL applies. As Lord Millett has said in another context (*Dubai Aluminium v Salaam* (2002), [123]): 'Sexually assaulting a boy is not an improper mode of looking after him. It is an independent act in itself, not an improper mode of doing something else.' Similarly, as I have just discussed, where a trustee intentionally misappropriates trust property, this is a breach of loyalty equivalent to that of an employee who steals from his employer, a breach BFBDL.

13.25   To put this another way, the existence of a genuine fiduciary relationship turns something a fiduciary would otherwise be perfectly allowed to do into a wrong because it is done in conflict of interest. Things that are already straightforwardly wrongs are not within the scope of a fiduciary's action, because they are wrongs already. Just because a wrong manifests, in addition to its wrongness per se, a bad faith breach of duty does not turn it into a breach of FDL as well. Thus the parent in *M (K) v M (H)* did not commit a breach of FDL because the act of sexual assault is straightforwardly a wrong, whoever does it. It *aggravates* the wrong that it is committed by a parent, a person the child should be able to trust; it is clearly a breach of BFBDL. Indeed, from this point of view, it belittles the gravity of the wrong to say that the essence of the wrong is its being a breach of a genuine fiduciary relationship—what is wrong about sexual assault is the heinous violation of the victim's bodily integrity, whereas the essence of a breach of FDL is that the fiduciary is the *wrong party* to take a particular decision because he is conflicted. But the wrong of sexual assault is not wrong because it was the wrong person who made the decision to carry out the assault. It is a wrong because assault itself is wrong, whoever does it.

13.26   In *M (K) v M (H)*, the father's wrong was a breach of BFBDL, and only that. It is, it is submitted, identical in structure and purpose to the BFBDL version of the duty of loyalty an employee owes her employer, and a fiduciary owes her principal, and I would also say that a child caring for a parent owes that same duty to the parent. In each of these cases a breach of the bad faith breach norm should be subject to the equivalent of 'summary dismissal': in *M (K) v M (H)*, the child should be placed in care and the father's parental rights and duties terminated. The equivalent should happen to child 'carer' who abuses his parent.

Contending interests and conflicts of interests

13.27   Typically people who have to use their judgments to make decisions have to face contending interests, especially in terms of the allocation of resources. The manager of a business has to weigh the interests of its shareholders as against its employees in deciding how much employees should be paid, for the more they pay the employees the less profit for shareholders. A Dean of a law faculty has a budget and, in consultations with others, must use his judgment to allocate resources to teaching, to research, to administration, to IT improvements, to renovations of the classrooms, and so on. We can call these cases of 'contending' interests.

13.28   These are not situations of conflict of interest (see Getzler (2014), 44). A conflict arises when A must exercise his judgment to make a decision for or on behalf of B, where only B's interests may be taken into account, but A's interests are implicated in the decision.

13.29   In the rest of this chapter we shall primarily restrict our attention to FDL and the various rules which give effect to it, since this chapter concerns the law governing true fiduciaries, although consideration of BFBDL will arise in several places where the courts seemed to have failed to distinguish between the two.

The 'no conflict' rule

13.30   The 'no conflict' rule is the basic rule governing fiduciaries. (See Conaglen (2007), especially ch 3, for a robust defence of the view that the 'no conflict' is the core of the law governing fiduciaries.) The idea that the no conflict rule is a rule is significant. It is sometime said that a fiduciary must not place himself in a position where his own interests might conflict with those of his principal, so that where a trustee acts in conflict of interest he breaches his fiduciary duty to his principal. But this is almost certainly a misconception (Mitchell (2013); Smith (2014a); Penner (2014c)). The better way of understanding this is that, in equity, any transaction the fiduciary undertakes which, on examination, turns out to be taken by him in conflict of interest, is liable to be set aside. In other words, the fiduciary is liable to a rule which reverses any transaction undertaken in conflict of interest, however little he appreciated the conflict. The leading case in this respect is *Boardman v Phipps* (1967) which we shall look at in detail. Though the defendants were liable, it is difficult to claim they breached any duty they owed their principal. This is not to say that there are no genuine fiduciary duties, which a fiduciary owes his principal. A fiduciary has a duty to act in good faith, and as we have seen, it is an application of a trustee/fiduciary's relationship that he acts with an even hand vis-à-vis the different beneficiaries (10.3–10.5), for only by doing so does he properly take into account the fact that he holds his powers and discretion for all of them. Another case, which we will consider (13.129 et seq), is where the fiduciary is an advisor to his principal. In such cases, for obvious reasons, the fiduciary has an obligation to disclose any interest he has in the transaction upon which he is advising his principal, so that the principal knows that his advice may be tainted by his interest. Where he fails to disclose his interest, the fiduciary is quite rightly normally liable to compensate his principal for any loss he suffers from entering into the transaction. As we shall see, the no conflict rule underlies all the more specific rules governing fiduciaries. Under the no conflict rule, a fiduciary is liable to account for any profit he obtains in circumstances where his interests *may* conflict with his duty to his principal. The rule is exceptionally stringent, in that it is framed—'*may* conflict'—in terms of the possibility of conflict, not in terms of there being an actual conflict of interest.

13.31 Perhaps the extreme example of the no conflict rule is *Keech v Sandford* (1726). A trustee held a lease for a minor beneficiary, which he sought to renew. The lessor refused to renew the lease in favour of the minor. The trustee took the new lease for his own benefit. King LC required the trustee to hold the lease on trust for the beneficiary, even though his interest when he acquired it could not, strictly speaking, be in conflict with his duty to the beneficiary, since the lessor absolutely refused to renew to a minor. Lord King accepted that the consequence of the rule's application was that:

> the trustee is the only person of all mankind who might not have the lease; but it is very proper that the rule should be strictly pursued, and not in the least relaxed; for it is very obvious what would be the consequences of letting trustees have the lease, on refusal to renew to the cestui que trust.

13.32 In *Protheroe v Protheroe* (1968) the CA, without a review of the relevant authorities, held that the rule in *Keech* applied to a trustee's purchase of the reversion upon a lease held by the trust so that it was automatically to be held on trust for the beneficiary. While on the authorities this would be a clear extension of the rule, Hayton (1996, at 342) argues that the decision is right on a strict application of the no conflict rule, because the trustee would, as landlord, have interests in conflict with his role as fiduciary holder of the lease, or 'trustee-lessee', for the beneficiary.

13.33 The leading modern case is *Boardman v Phipps* (1967). The defendants were Boardman, the solicitor to trustees of the Phipps family trust, and Tom Phipps, one of the beneficiaries. The trust held a significant holding in a private company, which was ailing. Boardman and Phipps decided that with new and effective management the company could generate significant profits for the shareholders. With the informed consent of the two active trustees (a third trustee was the settlor's widow, who was suffering from dementia, and took no part in the administration of the trust), Boardman and Phipps, as proxy holders of the trust shares, tried to get Phipps elected to the board, and failed. They also failed to negotiate a splitting up of the business between the Phipps holding and the other major bloc of shareholders. The two active trustees made it clear that they would not buy any more shares of the company for the trust. Finally, Boardman and Phipps purchased sufficient shares with their own money to enable them, with the support of the trustees, to take control of the company. As a result, they were able to sell off certain of the company assets, paying out large dividends while at the same time maintaining a high share price. Tom's brother, John Phipps, another beneficiary under the family trust, then sued Boardman and Tom Phipps, calling upon them to account for the profits they had earned on the shares they had purchased, as profits acquired in conflict of interest with 'the trust'. The HL, by a 3:2 margin, found Boardman and Phipps liable to account for the profits they earned.

13.34   Clearly Boardman stood in a fiduciary position as solicitor to the trustees; but there is no position of 'solicitor to the trust', and it was an unfortunate aspect of the case that the court did not specify clearly how or when Boardman came under a fiduciary obligation to John Phipps, one of the beneficiaries, who brought the suit. The case was argued and decided on the basis that Tom Phipps should be treated equally with Boardman whatever the outcome, although Phipps, as a beneficiary under the trust, obviously did not stand in the same fiduciary capacity. Lord Guest's finding that Boardman was liable was straightforward:

> In the present case the knowledge and information obtained by Mr Boardman was obtained in the course of the fiduciary position in which he had placed himself. The only defence available to a person in such a fiduciary position is that he made the profits with the knowledge and assent of the trustees. It is not suggested that the trustees had such knowledge or gave such consent.

13.35   Thus, because the information was acquired in the course of his dealings with the trust, and he was a fiduciary 'to the trust', any profits made from using that information would be profits arising from his fiduciary office; unless authorised, they must be accounted for. Simple. Two points should be noted. First, this simple equation of liability with Boardman's having profited from information acquired in his conduct of the trust would not have led to the liability of Tom Phipps, because as a beneficiary under the trust he could well argue that he obtained any information in that capacity, not as a fiduciary to the trust. Secondly, Lord Guest speaks of the consent of the *trustees*. (There was no informed consent by *all* the trustees, since the third, inactive, trustee, was not informed at all.) This poses something of a puzzle. Normally, the consent of the beneficiaries is required to authorise any act that would otherwise be a breach of trust. Where a trustee employs a fiduciary agent, the agent owes his duties to the trustee, and the trustee may then authorise what would otherwise be a breach of that agent's fiduciary duty. But, if the trustee does so for insufficient reasons, then he would be liable to the beneficiaries for a breach of trust, ie for failing himself to carry out his duties properly. However, in this case Boardman was liable to the beneficiaries directly, so it can only be the case that because of his close relationship with the trustees and the beneficiaries he stood as fiduciary directly to them.

13.36   Lord Hodson took a similar line to that of Lord Guest. Pointing out that in *Keech* the beneficiary could not have acquired the disputed assets himself, it was irrelevant that the trustees had decided not to purchase further shares in the company. Any profit obtained by a fiduciary made possible by his fiduciary position was to be accounted for unless consented to, although Lord Hodson made it clear that the consent required was that of the complaining beneficiary.

13.37   Unlike Lords Guest and Hodson, Lord Cohen did not wholly rely upon the *Keech* rule, as if any use of information acquired in the course of dealing with the trust to generate a profit for the fiduciary automatically entailed that the profit was to be accounted for. He stated:

> [I]n my opinion, Mr Boardman would not have been able to give unprejudiced advice if he had been consulted by the trustees [about acquiring further shares for the trust] and was at the same time negotiating for the purchase of the shares on behalf of himself and Mr Tom Phipps. In other words, there was, in my opinion, at the crucial date ... a possibility of a conflict between his interest and his duty.

13.38   Lord Cohen's opinion thus has the virtue of specifying the precise way in which Boardman's purchase of the shares for himself can be interpreted as an act undertaken in conflict of interest, because given Boardman's personal intention to acquire the shares, counselling the trust to acquire the rest of the shares would conflict with his own interests.

13.39   Lord Upjohn dissented and said:

> The phrase 'possibly may conflict' requires consideration. In my view it means that the reasonable man looking at the relevant facts and circumstances of the particular case would think that there was a real sensible possibility of conflict; not that you could im-agine some situation arising which might, in some conceivable possibility in events not contemplated as real sensible possibilities by any reasonable person, result in a conflict ... it has been assumed that it has necessarily followed that any profit made by [a fidu-ciary] renders him accountable to the trustees. This is not so.

In Lord Upjohn's opinion the 'no conflict' rule was not to be applied automatically, because that would only lead to the harsh and inequitable consequences of the majority decision. In order for a fiduciary to be accountable, he reasoned, the fiduciary must have made a profit (1) earned within 'the scope and ambit of his duty', and (2) in circumstances where he had placed himself in a position where there was a 'real sensible possibility of conflict' between his duty and his interest.

13.40   Viscount Dilhorne also dissented. He reasoned that when the trustees firmly insisted they would purchase no further shares, the trustees no longer sought to rely upon Boardman as an advisor as to the shares' value, but rather from that time forward Boardman and Phipps and the trustees acted in a sort of joint venture to get the value out of the company. Viscount Dilhorne's reasoning is plausible on the facts, and delivers the same result Lord Upjohn preferred without watering down the 'no conflict' rule, requiring the court to engage in an inquiry as to whether a conflict arose in the eyes of a 'reasonable' person. The essence of Viscount Dilhorne's argu-ment is that a fiduciary can be released from his fiduciary role by his principal(s) (ie the acting trustees) if done in full knowledge of the circumstances, as was the case here; thenceforward the principal is no longer relying on the trustee to make his decisions for him, or rely on his advice. The former principal and fiduciary are now free to act as partners or joint venturers who, while they have fiduciary obligations as business partners to each other (2.25), do not have the fiduciary obligations of advisor to advisee. Bryan (2012) has argued that, as found at trial and not overturned, Boardman and Phipps essentially became agents *de son tort* (11.103), that is, not properly appointed but *de facto* agents of those who were interested in the Phipps shareholding in the company, including, of course, John Phipps. Whilst they provided some information to the trustees and John, they did not fully inform them of their activities, but throughout represented to the shareholders of the other holdings that they were acting not only for their own benefit, but on behalf of the Phipps shareholders. They therefore took upon themselves a fiduciary position which made them liable for any gain that they acquired in conflict of interest that was not properly authorised by their principals. Viewed from this perspective, the conflict was clear: by seeking to acquire shares in the company themselves, they were taking advantage of their position as representatives of all of the Phipps beneficiaries to acquire a gain on their own behalf. Unless this taking advantage was authorised by those others interested in the Phipps shareholding, including John, they were liable to account for their gains; the court found that they had not been so authorised, and so they were. Viscount Dilhorne's dissent shows that this application of the law to the facts was not necessarily correct, and also explains why readers of the case often have conflicting intuitions about the result. If, when the trustees firmly insisted they would purchase no further shares, Boardman and Phipps were not acting *on behalf of* the Phipps beneficiaries, but on behalf of themselves and the Phipps beneficiaries in a sort of joint venture to get the value out of the company, in which Boardman and Tom Phipps did all the work, and the trustees agreed to vote their shares along with Boardman and Phipps to get control of the company, then they ought not to have been liable.

13.41   The majority decision in *Boardman* can certainly be criticised for what appears to be an unjustifiably harsh result. Although Boardman and Tom Phipps were allowed remuneration for their efforts on a liberal scale, they were stripped of all their profits from investing their own money in an endeavour that hugely profited the trust beneficiaries.

13.42   What should a fiduciary do who finds himself in a position of conflict of interest? In *Public Trustee v Cooper* (2001), Hart J laid out three ways in which a conflict might 'in theory, successfully be managed'; Hart J speaks only of trustees, but one presumes his views apply *mutatis mutandis* to other fiduciaries:

> One is for the trustee concerned to resign. This will not always provide a practical or sensible solution. The trustee concerned may represent an important source of information or advice to his co-trustees or have a significant relationship to some or all of the beneficiaries such that his or her departure as a trustee will be potentially harmful to the interests of the trust estate or its beneficiaries.

> Secondly, the nature of the conflict may be so pervasive throughout the trustee body that they, as a body, have no alternative but to surrender their discretion to the court.

> Thirdly, the trustees may honestly and reasonably believe that, notwithstanding a conflict affecting one or more of their number, they are nevertheless able fairly and reasonably to take the decision. In this third case, it will usually be prudent, if time allows, for the trustees to allow their proposed exercise of discretion to be scrutinised in advance by the court, in proceedings in which any opposing beneficial interests are properly represented, and for them not to proceed until the court has authorised them to do so. If they do not do so, they run the risk of having to justify the exercise of their discretion in subsequent hostile litigation and then satisfy the court that their decision was not only one which any reasonable body of trustees might have taken but was also one that had not in fact been influenced by the conflict.

Hilton v Barker, Booth & Eastwood (2005) is a forceful reminder that a fiduciary who acts in conflict of interest does so at his peril. Solicitors acted for parties on both sides of a property development transaction. Solicitors under their contract of retainer owe a duty, which Lord Walker regarded 'as rooted in the fiduciary relationship between solicitor and client', to inform a client of any information relevant to any transaction on which they were giving advice. Here the solicitors failed to inform their client, Mr Hilton, a property developer, that entering into the contract with their other client posed a serious financial risk owing to the latter's past behaviour, which included an offence of fraudulent trading for which, amongst other offences, he had been imprisoned. The court found that, had they informed Mr Hilton of these facts, he would never have entered into the transaction with this other client of the firm (which, in the end, turned out to be a financial calamity). Overturning the decision of the High Court and a unanimous CA, the HL unanimously held that the fact that it would *also* have been a breach of their duty of confidentiality to their other client to impart this information provided no excuse: the solicitors had placed themselves in this position of conflict and failed to deal with it properly by refusing to act for one of the parties; they therefore put themselves in the position that they had no choice but to breach their contract of retainer to one of their clients, and were liable for any consequences of doing so. They were therefore liable to Mr Hilton for his entire loss resulting from his entering into the contract.

The 'no conflict' rule and company directors

13.43   The leading case applying the 'no conflict' rule to company directors is *Regal (Hastings) Ltd v Gulliver* (1942). The defendants were directors of a company, Regal, which owned and operated a cinema. Two other local cinemas were available for lease, and the directors decided to create a subsidiary company that would acquire leases to these cinemas, and that Regal would then sell its holding in all three cinemas as a going concern. The landlord of the two cinemas was not prepared to grant the leases to the subsidiary unless either a personal guarantee was given by the directors, or the subsidiary had paid-up capital of £5,000. The directors were reluctant to provide personal guarantees, so the second route was chosen. However, the directors decided that Regal could not put up more than £2,000 of the required £5,000. Four directors then each subscribed for shares worth £500, as did the solicitor to Regal at the request of the director; one director acquired £500 worth of shares for third parties. With £5,000 paid-up capital, the subsidiary acquired the leases. As it turned out, Regal did not sell its interest in the three-cinema business; rather, the shareholders of Regal and the subsidiary sold their shares to a purchaser. The directors who had put up part of the capital for the subsidiary company received a handsome profit for their investment. The purchaser installed a new board of directors, and Regal, now under their control, launched this action against the former directors, calling for them to account for the profits they had made on their sale of the subsidiary shares. Regal succeeded in the HL. In the lower courts the directors successfully defended the claim, by arguing that the decision they made for Regal to invest no more than £2,000 in the subsidiary was bona fide— indeed it might have been a breach of trust to have risked more of Regal's money; therefore, the directors putting up their own money *secured a benefit* for Regal *that it could not otherwise have obtained*, and so there was no basis for holding them liable to account for the profits they had personally made.

13.44   The HL unanimously rejected this interpretation of the case, applying the rule in *Keech* in its full rigour. Lord Russell said:

The rule of equity which insists on those, who by use of a fiduciary position make a profit, being liable to account for that profit, in no way depends on fraud, or absence of bona fides; or upon such questions or considerations as whether the profit would or should otherwise have gone to the plaintiff, or whether the profiteer was under a duty to obtain the source of the profit for the plaintiff, or whether he took a risk or acted as he did for the benefit of the plaintiff, or whether the plaintiff has in fact been damaged or benefited by his action. The liability arises from the mere fact of a profit having, in the stated circumstances, been made. The profiteer, however honest or well intentioned, cannot escape the risk of being called to account.

13.45 None of the non-director subscribers of shares in the subsidiary, including the solicitor, was accountable, because none was a fiduciary subject to the rule. The solicitor took up his shares at the request of the company (a request made, of course, through its directors), and Lord Russell said:

I know of no principle or authority which would justify a decision that a solicitor must account for profit resulting from a transaction which he has entered into on his own behalf, not merely with the consent, but at the request of his client.

13.46 Note that the effect of the decision was to give the new purchasers of the company and subsidiary shares a windfall, because they were, by this action by Regal, able to secure the return of part of their purchase price to Regal's coffers—had the company itself just sold the cinema business, the purchasers would not have been able to make such a claim, because the 'injured company' which suffered by the directors' breach, would not have been in their hands. Recognising this, Lord Porter said:

This, it seems, may be an unexpected windfall, but whether it be so or not, the principle that a person occupying a fiduciary relationship shall not make a profit by reason thereof is of such vital importance that the possible consequence in the present case is in fact as it is in law an immaterial consideration.

13.47 Lord Russell suggested that the directors' liability might easily have been avoided. Their decision to take up shares in the subsidiary could have been approved by the vote of a general meeting of the company, ie a general shareholders' meeting, and being in control of the company, they doubtless would have controlled the voting to ensure the result they desired. Such approval in the case of a company is equivalent to the informed consent of the beneficiaries under a trust. But as pointed out by Lowry (1997), the fact that company directors are typically able to control the voting at a general meeting makes the court's ringing endorsement of the application of the rule in *Keech* somewhat hollow, because if Lord Russell's suggestion is correct then any well-advised company directors who control by proxy a sufficient number of the company's shares may, by ensuring the approval of a general meeting, engage in profit-taking of this kind as they please. However, Lord Russell's view seems to conflict with the PC's decision in *Cook v Deeks* (1916), where such a resolution was held to be ineffective.

13.48 The *Regal Hastings* principle was applied in *Industrial Development Consultants Ltd v Cooley* (1972). Cooley was the former chief architect of the West Midlands Gas Board. He joined IDC as its managing director, principally in order to procure work in the gas industry. He was approached by representatives of the Eastern Gas Board with respect to some large contracts for work to be done in the near future. The evidence indicated that the Eastern Gas Board would not have entered into contracts with IDC, as they disagreed in principle with 'the set-up' of IDC; the Board was willing, however, to enter into contracts with Cooley personally. Cooley secured his release from his position at IDC by lying to them that he was seriously ill, and secured the lucrative contracts for himself. Roskill J found that Cooley had clearly placed himself in actual conflict with IDC; it was his fiduciary duty to inform IDC of the Eastern Gas Board's plans and not to keep secret his dealings with the Board to his own advantage; the court declared that he held the profits of the contracts on trust for IDC. Roskill J realised that his decision secured for IDC a profit that it never would have obtained if Cooley had complied with his fiduciary duty, but he accepted that:

> It is an over-riding principle of equity that a man must not be allowed to put himself in a position in which his fiduciary duty and his interests conflict.

13.49   In the middle of the last century, North American courts began to take the view that a genuinely good faith decision by a board of directors not to take up a corporate opportunity frees individual directors or other company fiduciaries to take up such opportunities themselves. For example, in *Peso Silver Mines v Cropper* (1966), the Supreme Court of Canada held that a director was not liable to his company for acquiring mining properties and profitably exploiting them when they had previously been offered to the company and the board of directors had bona fide decided not to take up the offer. It is noteworthy that in *Peso* the court clearly approved the following statement of Lord Greene, MR, from his judgment in the CA in *Regal Hastings*:

> To say that the Company was entitled to claim the benefit of those shares would involve this proposition: Where a Board of Directors considers an investment which is offered to their company and bona fide comes to the conclusion that it is not an investment which their Company ought to make, any Director, after that Resolution is come to and bona fide come to, who chooses to put up the money for that investment himself must be treated as having done it on behalf of the Company, so that the Company can claim any profit that results to him from it. That is a proposition for which no particle of authority was cited; and goes, as it seems to me, far beyond anything that has ever been suggested as to the duty of directors, agents, or persons in a position of that kind.

13.50   In *Canadian Aero Services v O'Malley* (1971), Laskin J reviewed the English, Commonwealth, and US authorities, and said:

> In holding that . . . there was a breach of fiduciary duty by [officers of a company for pursuing and capturing a contract for surveying work which their company was actively seeking to acquire itself, even though the officers had resigned their offices prior to the award of the contract] I am not to be taken as laying down any rule of liability to be read as if it were a statute. The general standards of loyalty, good faith and avoidance of a conflict of duty and self-interest to which the conduct of a director or senior officer must conform, must be tested in each case by many factors which it would be reckless to attempt to enumerate exhaustively. Among them are the factor of position or office held, the nature of the corporate opportunity, its ripeness, its specificness and the director's or managerial officer's relation to it, the amount of knowledge possessed, the circumstances in which it was obtained and whether it was special or, indeed, even private, the factor of time in the continuation of fiduciary duty where the alleged breach occurs after termination of the relationship with the company, and the circumstances

under which the relationship was terminated, that is whether by retirement or resigna-
tion or discharge.

13.51   Notice the effect of this ruling: henceforth the bright line 'prophylactic' strictness of the rule, as enunciated in *Keech*, is replaced by the very inquiry into a number of factors to determine the good faith and reasonableness of the fiduciary that a strict rule is meant to avoid. One of the main reasons for applying the rule stringently is so as not to make the rule turn on difficult inferences from facts difficult to establish, lest the fiduciary obligations of directors be weakened, in practice, as a result. (For an argument that courts should abandon the bright line rule in favour of this sort of inquiry on a case-by-case basis, because of the greater fact-finding ability of the modern court, see Langbein (2005).) One might argue that the substantial compensation that directors and senior officers of companies receive partly reflects the fact that they are denied the right to exploit corporate opportunities, even those that the company itself decides to refuse; thus they are compensated for the stringent application of the rule. By contrast, Langbein (2005) argues that the rule should be flexibly applied so as not to discourage entrepreneurial risk-taking.

13.52   In the USA, the courts have similarly developed a 'corporate opportunity doctrine', the purpose of which is to determine which opportunities for profit 'belong' to a company, from which directors may not personally profit (*Guth v Loft Inc* (1939); *Broz v Cellular Information Systems Inc* (1996)).

13.53   In something of a departure from the stringent application of the rules, the PC, in an appeal from Australia, *Queensland Mines Ltd v Hudson* (1978), decided that Hudson, a former managing director of a company who had resigned from the board to take up mining licences personally, which the company had decided, due to its financial difficulties, not to pursue itself, was not liable to account to the company for the profits he earned. The court reasoned that although the opportunity came Hudson's way in his role as a fiduciary to the company, the company board knew of his interest and had given their fully informed consent. This decision directly contradicts both *Regal Hastings* and the received wisdom generally, since it is not the directors but the shareholders in a general meeting who are capable of giving such consent. The PC also decided that the good faith rejection of the opportunity placed the opportunity 'outside' the scope of Hudson's fiduciary duty.

13.54   However, as Sullivan (1979) points out:

> *This [ground for the decision] enables the directors when exercising their managerial prerogative to reject corporate opportunities to thereby remove those opportunities from the restrictions imposed by their fiduciary duties ... The orthodoxy is that the director's legal powers of management are subject to the equitable obligations imposed by their fiduciary role; Queensland stands this on its head in allowing a managerial decision to delineate the scope of a fiduciary duty.*

This aspect of the decision is particularly significant since, if it represents the law, a board's rejection of an opportunity may now be challenged only on the basis that it was not in good faith, raising all the difficulties of proof that such a charge may entail. However, the CA's decision in *O'Donnell v Shanahan* (2009) shows a fondness for the strict application of the no conflict rule in the context of business opportunities. The court emphasised a distinction between the rule as it applies to partners (see *Aas v Benham* (1891)) and company directors: the fiduciary duties of a partner may be limited by the terms of the partnership, restricting the ambit of the business opportunities which a partner must pursue only for the partnership; a director's duties are not similarly circumscribed. The nature of a director's duty is akin to a 'general trusteeship' on behalf of the company, and so any business opportunity that comes to a director in the context of his directorship must be pursued only for the company.

13.55 As you might imagine, a trustee may not, of course, operate a business in competition with the trust (*Re Thomson* (1930)), and this applies to other fiduciaries vis-à-vis their principals as well. A recurring issue is the extent of a director's liability in the context of his departure from the board of directors. In *Island Export Finance Ltd v Umunna* (1986), Hutchison J decided that, while a director's fiduciary obligations did not cease utterly upon the termination of his post, the mere fact that he entered into competition with his former company following his departure did not make him liable, so long as he did not capture a 'maturing business opportunity' of the company. (The phrase comes from *Canadian Aero Services*.) Hutchinson J said:

> In this context counsel for the defendants rightly stresses the fundamental principles relating to contracts in restraint of trade. It would, it seems to me, be surprising to find that directors alone, because of the fiduciary nature of their relationship with the company, were restrained from exploiting after they ceased to be such any opportunity of which they had acquired knowledge while directors. Directors, no less than other employees, acquire a general fund of knowledge and expertise in the course of their work, and it is plainly in the public interest that they should be free to exploit it in a new position.

13.56 Similarly, in *Balston Ltd v Headline Filters Ltd* (1987), Falconer J stated:

> [A]n intention by a director of a company to set up business in competition with the company after his directorship has ceased is not to be regarded as a conflicting interest within the context of the principle, having regard to the rules of public policy as to restraint of trade, nor is the taking of any preliminary steps to investigate or forward that intention so long as there is no actual competitive activity, such as, for instance, competitive tendering or actual trading, while he remains a director.

13.57 In *Plus Group Ltd v Pyke* (2002), the CA took a firm line on conflicts of interest in respect of individuals who serve as a director of different companies whose businesses compete. Sedley LJ said:

> [T]he fiduciary must not only not place himself in a position (of conflict of interest); if, even accidentally, he finds himself in such a position he must regularise it [ie get the consent of his principal(s)] or abandon it . . . [It is not the case that] a director can go cheerfully to the brink so long as he does not fall over the edge. [I]f he finds himself in a position of conflict he must resolve it openly or extract himself from it.

13.58 The CA also affirmed that every decision on the principle governing conflict of interest is fact-specific. In *Plus Group*, a director was not found to have been liable for acting in conflict of interest for engaging in business with a client of the company of which he was formerly a director, where his dealings with the client began six months after he had been effectively expelled from the management of the company. The CA in *Foster Bryant Surveying Ltd v Bryant* (2007) again emphasised the fact-sensitive application of the rules, while approving as perceptive and useful the following summary of the principles of the law in this area by Livesey QC, sitting as a deputy High Court judge in *Hunter Kane Ltd v Watkins* (2003):

1. A director, while acting as such, has a fiduciary relationship with his company. That is he has an obligation to deal towards it with loyalty, good faith and avoidance of the conflict of duty and self-interest.

2. A requirement to avoid a conflict of duty and self-interest means that a director is precluded from obtaining for himself, either secretly or without the informed approval of the company, any property or business advantage either belonging to the company or for which it has been negotiating, especially where the director or officer is a participant in the negotiations.

3. A director's power to resign from office is not a fiduciary power. He is entitled to resign even if his resignation might have a disastrous effect on the business or reputation of the company.

4. A fiduciary relationship does not continue after the determination of the relationship which gives rise to it. After the relationship is determined the director is in general not under the continuing obligations which are the feature of the fiduciary relationship.

5. Acts done by the directors while the contract of employment subsists but which are preparatory to competition after it terminates are not necessarily in themselves a breach of the implied term as to loyalty and fidelity.

6. Directors, no less than employees, acquire a general fund of skill, knowledge and expertise in the course of their work, which is plainly in the public interest that they should be free to exploit it in a new position. After ceasing the relationship by resignation or otherwise a director is in general (and subject of course to any terms of the contract of employment) not prohibited from using his general fund of skill and knowledge, the 'stock in trade' of the knowledge he has acquired while a director, even including such things as business contacts and personal connections made as a result of his directorship.

7. A director is however precluded from acting in breach of the requirement at 2 above, even after his resignation where the resignation may fairly be said to have been prompted or influenced by a wish to acquire for himself any maturing business opportunities sought by the company and where it was his position with the company rather than a fresh initiative that led him to the opportunity which he later acquired.

8. In considering whether an act of a director breaches the preceding principle the factors to take into account will include the factor of position or office held, the nature of the corporate opportunity, its ripeness, its specificness and the director's relation to it, the amount of knowledge possessed, the circumstances in which it was obtained and whether it was special or indeed even private, the factor of time in the continuation of the fiduciary duty where the alleged breach occurs after termination of the relationship with the company and the circumstances under which the breach was terminated, that is whether by retirement or resignation or discharge.

9. The underlying basis of the liability of a director who exploits after his resignation a maturing business opportunity 'of the company' is that the opportunity is to be treated as if it were the property of the company in relation to which the director had fiduciary duties. By seeking to exploit the opportunity after resignation he is appropriating to himself that property. He is just as accountable as a trustee who retires without properly accounting for trust property.

10. It follows that a director will not be in breach of the principle set out as point 7 above where either the company's hope of obtaining the contract was not a 'maturing business opportunity' and it was not pursuing further business orders nor where the director's resignation was not itself prompted or influenced by a wish to acquire the business for himself.

11. As regards breach of confidence, although while the contract of employment subsists a director or other employee may not use confidential information to the detriment of his employer, after it ceases the director/employee may compete and may use know-how acquired in the course of his employment (as distinct from trade secrets—although the distinction is sometimes difficult to apply in practice).

13.59   As the US case law reveals (see in particular *Broz v Cellular Systems Inc* (1996)), and Lowry and Edmonds point out (1997; 1998), the common law rules are likely to have little influence in many cases, simply because (subject to the reservation in reference to *Cook v Deeks*, **13.47**) the directors, if agreeing that all or some or one of them may exploit a corporate opportunity, will be able to secure the ratification of their decision at a general meeting.

Authorised profits

13.60   Most trusts are today undertaken by professional trustees, so it is clear that there is no rule of equity that prevents a trustee from profiting from his position as trustee. The rule is that a trustee may not obtain any *unauthorised* profits. Most trusts contain express remuneration clauses in the trust instrument. Formerly if there was no such provision the trustee was not entitled to any remuneration whatsoever; however, under s 29 of the Trustee Act 2000, where the trust instrument is silent on this point a professional trustee or trust company, although not a lay trustee such as a family friend, is entitled to 'reasonable remuneration' for services provided. All trustees are, however, entitled to the reimbursement of their out-of-pocket expenses incurred in carrying out the trust terms, such as the costs of employing solicitors or brokers, or to pay those expenses directly from the trust funds (Trustee Act 2000, s 31).

The rule in *Cradock v Piper*

13.61   The only true exception to the rule disallowing unauthorised profits is the rule in *Cradock v Piper* (1850). Just like any other trustee, unless authorised by the trust instrument a solicitor-trustee cannot charge for any professional legal work done for the trust. Nor may he retain his own firm to do any such work, because he will indirectly benefit from the firm's revenue (*Christophers v White* (1847)), although he may employ a partner of his firm on the basis that he will receive no share of the profits (*Clack v Carlon* (1861)). Under the rule in *Cradock v Piper*, a solicitor-trustee is allowed his usual charges for litigation work done for the body of trustees, which include himself, so long as his being one of the parties has not added to the expense of the litigation. This limited exception for litigious work is illogical and has not been extended to other cases. The rule is of limited practical importance since any competent solicitor undertaking a trust will insist that the instrument contain an appropriate provision allowing him to charge for his professional services.

The inherent jurisdiction to authorise remuneration

13.62   The court has inherent jurisdiction to authorise remuneration for trustees and other fiduciaries, and to increase the remuneration beyond that provided in the trust terms. The general principles were examined in the leading case, *Re Duke of Norfolk's Settlement Trusts* (1982). In this case a trust's charging clause provided a level of payment well below the current market standard; furthermore, due to changes in the nature of the trust holdings, the work required by the trustee had increased significantly. The CA decided that the inherent jurisdiction covered not only the power to allow remuneration for past services, and to allow remuneration for future services upon the appointment of a trustee, but to increase the level of remuneration beyond that fixed in the trust instrument.

13.63   Two arguments stood in the way of the court's increasing the trustee's remuneration: first, if one regards the remuneration provision as a contract between the settlor and the trustee, then the trustee should, on contractual principles, live with the bargain he has made; secondly, it was argued that by increasing the level of remuneration the court would in effect vary the beneficial interests under the trust because less would then go to the beneficiaries, and the court had no inherent jurisdiction to vary beneficial interests (10.65 et seq). The CA rejected both arguments.

13.64   Fox LJ said this of the contractual analysis:

> It might have some appearance of reality in relation to a trustee who, at the request of the settlor, agrees to act before the settlement is executed and approves the terms of the settlement. But very frequently executors and trustees of wills know nothing of the terms of the will until the testator is dead ... It is difficult to see with whom, in such cases, the trustees are to be taken as contracting. The appointment of a trustee by the court also gives rise to problems as to the identity of the contracting party. The position, it seems to me, is this. Trust property is held by the trustee upon the trusts and subject to the powers conferred by the trust instrument and the law. One of those powers is the power given to the trustee to charge remuneration ... [I]t seems to me to be quite unreal to regard them as contractual. So far as they derive from any order of the court they simply arise from the court's jurisdiction and so far as they derive from the trust instrument itself they derive from the settlor's power to direct how his property should be dealt with.

13.65   Brightman LJ said:

> [The contractual conception] also seems to me, in the context of the present debate, to give little weight to the fact that a trustee, whether paid or unpaid, is under no obligation, contractual or otherwise, to provide future services to the trust. He can at any time express his desire to be discharged from the trust and in that case a new trustee will in due course be appointed ... The practical effect therefore of increasing the remuneration of the trustee (if the contractual conception is correct) will merely be to amend for the future, in favour of a trustee, the terms of a contract which the trustee has a unilateral right to determine.

13.66   In so far as these reasons are intended to justify the court's power to increase a trustee's remuneration, they are inadequate. Although Fox LJ emphasises that a trustee may have no say in determining the particulars of a remuneration clause, still, trust obligations are always voluntarily undertaken (no one is forced to become a trustee of any particular trust), and when a trustee does undertake a trust with an express remuneration clause, he must be assumed to accept the clause as adequate. In this respect his agreement to take on the trust is very like his agreeing to enter into a contract. The voluntariness of the trustee's undertaking is made clear by Brightman LJ's observation that a trustee has an escape route, retirement, if he later feels underpaid. Therefore the court should be slow to upset the 'bargain' represented by the remuneration clause, because, especially in the case of a professional trustee, his voluntary acceptance of the trusts is very close to contractual. The court should not exercise its inherent jurisdiction simply to allow him to escape from a bad bargain, ie an agreement to undertake a trust that later turns out not to be as profitable as expected. If he wishes to retire, so be it, and if a new trustee will only undertake the trust on better remuneration terms, it may be better to consider increasing the remuneration for him, not for the original trustee. Such an approach would prevent a trustee from being in the position, by reason of his incumbency, to hold the trust to ransom.

13.67   With regard to the second argument, the CA held, quite rightly, that in authorising a trustee's increased remuneration the court was exercising its jurisdiction to ensure the adequate administration of the trust. In doing so the court did not concern itself with the beneficial interests as such, and so cannot be regarded as varying them.

13.68   When considering increasing the remuneration of an incumbent trustee, Fox LJ said this:

> [T]he court has to balance two influences which are to some extent in conflict. The first is that the office of trustee is, as such, gratuitous; the court will accordingly be careful to protect the interests of the beneficiaries against claims by the trustees. The second is that it is of great importance to the beneficiaries that the trust should be well administered. If therefore the court concludes, having regard to the nature of the trust, the experience and skill of a particular trustee and to the amounts which he seeks to charge when compared with what other trustees might require to be paid for their services and to all the other circumstances of the case, that it would be in the interests of the beneficiaries to increase the remuneration, then the court may properly do so.

13.69   In his opinion Brightman LJ referred to the court's 'power to increase *or otherwise vary* the future remuneration of a trustee who has already accepted office' (my italics). It would be interesting to see in what circumstances the court will exercise its inherent jurisdiction to *reduce* the remuneration provided by the trust instrument, and whether a trustee opposing such an application would fare any better with the contractual argument, insisting that a bargain is a bargain.

13.70   Finally, although it has been said that the jurisdiction 'should only be exercised sparingly, and in exceptional cases' (*Re Worthington* (1954) *per* Upjohn J), Fox LJ in his reasons said that he and Brightman LJ were both of the impression that orders authorising increases in remuneration had been made in chambers since the 1950s, which might suggest that the exercise was not, in practice, all that exceptional.

13.71   These principles were applied in *Foster v Spencer* (1996) in which trustees of a cricket club were awarded remuneration for having tackled various problems 'vigorously and unremittingly' over the course of 20 years to enable the club to sell its ground. The court disagreed with the proposition that it could only allow remuneration, whether for past or future service, in order to engage or retain the services of the particular trustees for the future, ie to obtain the future services of trustees who would not act unless remunerated:

> *Where, as in this case, there were no funds out of which to pay remuneration at the time of their appointment, nor was a true appreciation of the extent of the task possible, a prospective application would be impracticable, if not impossible. The refusal of remuneration . . . would result in the beneficiaries being unjustly enriched at the expense of the trustees. The right of a trustee to remuneration for his past services cannot depend upon the circumstance that at the time he seeks it, his services are further required so that he is in a position to demand remuneration for the past as a condition of continuing in office.*

13.72 Here, one trustee was awarded a retrospective annual fee, and another a percentage of the sale price of the ground, which took into account his successful effort in obtaining planning permission for the development of the site.

13.73 Take note: a trustee seeking remuneration, or an increase in remuneration, is clearly not in a situation where his interest and duty *may* conflict; they definitely are in *actual* conflict. The court, therefore, must be astute to assess the trustee's claims that he 'requires' such and such a level of remuneration. In the case of an increase of remuneration, taking a strict *Keech* approach would mean that the only person who could not benefit from the trustee's advice to the court that the remuneration of the trust was insufficient would be that trustee himself, because of the 'very obvious consequences' that would ensue if a trustee were able to argue for an increase in remuneration, which would be to his own benefit; thus a court would only accept a trustee's argument that the proper administration of the trust required an increase on the basis that a new trustee who would take advantage of the increased remuneration would be appointed. To state this is not to argue that the court should adopt such a rule, but only to question whether the court's strict and automatic application of the 'no conflict' rule is justifiable when *Re Norfolk's Settlement Trusts* shows that the court thinks itself fit to determine an appropriate division of benefits between the beneficiary and the trustee in a clear situation of actual conflict of interest.

13.74 Finally, the court may even award unauthorised remuneration to trustees or fiduciaries who are liable to account for gains acquired in conflict of interest. We have already seen this (13.41) in *Boardman v Phipps* (1967). And in *O'sullivan v Management Agency and Music Ltd* (1985) remuneration including a profit element was allowed for management and production companies that had procured a contract from an artist through undue influence, but the efforts of which were clearly in part responsible for the artist's financial success.

13.75 In *Guinness plc v Saunders* (1990) a director who had negotiated on behalf of a company in a takeover bid sought an allowance from the court for his efforts. The HL questioned whether the court should ever authorise exceptional remuneration to a director, since the company articles specifically provided for the payment of directors—the exercise of the inherent jurisdiction:

> *may be said to involve interference by the court in the administration of a company's affairs when the company is not being wound up. [per Lord Goff]*

The court would definitely not do so in this case where the director had plainly put himself in a position of conflict of interest by agreeing to provide his negotiation services for a fee the size of which depended on the price his company would pay in the takeover.

Unauthorised profits and the liability to account for them

13.76 The rule regarding unauthorised profits is boldly framed in the oft-quoted statement of Lord Herschell in *Bray v Ford* (1896):

> It is an inflexible rule of the court of equity that a person in a fiduciary position . . . is not, unless otherwise expressly provided, entitled to make a profit; he is not allowed to put himself in a position where his interest and duty conflict. It does not appear to me that this rule is, as has been said, founded on the principles of morality. I regard it rather as based on the consideration that, human nature being what it is, there is danger, in such circumstances, of the person holding the fiduciary position being swayed by interest rather than by duty, and thus prejudicing those whom he was bound to protect.

13.77 It is clear from this statement that the prohibition on unauthorised profits arises to avoid conflicts of interest. If a trustee were entitled to profit from the trust as he saw fit, his own interests would be in conflict with his fiduciary duty to act solely in the interests of the beneficiaries. It is sometimes suggested that the 'no unauthorised profits' rule is a 'free-standing' rule, separate from the 'no conflict' rule. Smith (2013a) says:

> [The no-profit rule] is a direct implication of the fact that a fiduciary acts, within a sphere of activity, for and on behalf of the principal. The implication is that whatever may be extracted from that sphere of activity is attributed, as between the fiduciary and the beneficiary, as a matter of primary right, to the beneficiary; including that which was extracted without authority, should the beneficiary so choose.

But, with respect, this seems wrong in principle and leads to perverse results. Consider the case of a trustee of a trust which has a majority shareholding in a private company, allowing him to determine the appointment of the company directors. And assume that, taking his responsibilities seriously (10.15–10.16), he thinks it would be in the best interest of the beneficiaries if he were to appoint himself to the board. Realising that his entitlement to directors' fees would place him in conflict of interest in making this decision, he waives his directors' fees. He thus resolves the conflict of interest and his decision is now unimpeachable (a case similar to *Clack v Carlon* (1861) (13.61)). On the proposed 'attribution rule' reading of the no-profit rule, the trustee cannot resolve his conflict of interest in this way, because the opportunity to acquire the directors' fees fell within the sphere of activity in which he acts for the beneficiaries. Instead, on this reading of the rule, the trustee should act so as to ensure he takes advantage of his power to elect board members and elect himself to acquire the directors' fees just because he will have to account for them to the beneficiaries. This would have the perverse result that the trustee has a reason (a duty?) to appoint himself even if he did not think this would be in the best interest of the beneficiaries, because, for example, he felt he could monitor the company perfectly well without taking a seat on the board (10.16) and that other individuals would better serve as directors. It is submitted then, that the no-profit rule is an expression or application of the no-conflict rule, in that it makes trustees liable, as we shall see, to account for profits acquired in conflict of interest. Indeed, as we have seen (*Keech v Sanford* (1726), 13.31; *IDC v Cooley* (1972), 13.48), a fiduciary is so accountable even if there was no possibility that the profit could have been obtained with the authorisation of the principal, because it was outside the proper sphere of his activity—it cannot be within the proper sphere of a fiduciary's activity to accomplish the impossible. What makes him accountable is that the profit was received in conflict of interest, and these cases show that something that a fiduciary can only acquire for himself but not for his principal can nevertheless put him in a conflict of interest with his principal (see further Penner (2014d)). This is emphatically the case with bribes, as we shall later see in detail.

13.78   You will recall (11.18 et seq) that the primary duty of a trustee is to 'account' for his stewardship of the trust, ie reveal his dealings with the trust property and so afford a beneficiary a right to surcharge or falsify the account. Normally, it is said that a fiduciary is 'liable to account' for any unauthorised profits that he receives as a result of his fiduciary position. The difficult question that this formulation of the fiduciary's liability raises is whether the principal's right to make his fiduciary account for an unauthorised profit is personal or proprietary. Does the fiduciary merely have an obligation to pay the value of the unauthorised profit to his principal, or does the fiduciary hold the unauthorised profit on trust for the beneficiary from the moment he receives it, as in *Keech* with respect to the lease that the trustee obtained? Clearly, if the fiduciary is insolvent, only the trust will ensure that he receives the value of the property; furthermore, if the property rises in value, a right to the property itself will be superior to a merely personal claim against the fiduciary that he pay the value of the property at the time he received it. We will consider the issue in detail at 13.105 et seq.

Incidental profits

13.79   A typical example of an incidental unauthorised profit is a commission a trustee receives by directing the trust business to a particular company. In *Williams v Barton* (1927), a trustee had a contract with a brokerage firm under which he received a commission on work for clients that he had introduced to them; he was accountable to the trust for the commission he earned by directing trust business to the firm. In *Swain v Law Society* ((1981), CA; rev'd (1983), HL), a solicitor claimed that the Law Society was acting as a fiduciary vis-à-vis solicitors when it procured liability insurance for the profession, and so it held its share of a broker's commission on trust for the members of the Society. The argument succeeded in the CA, but it was decided in the HL that the Law Society was acting under a statutory duty to secure insurance cover and not as a fiduciary for the members; there was, however, no doubt that had the Society been acting as a fiduciary the commission would have been an incidental profit for which it would have been accountable to the members.

13.80   Another example is directors' fees. Trustees must safeguard the trust investments and it will be appropriate and sometimes necessary for a trustee to be appointed to the board of directors of a company in which the trust has a large shareholding (10.15–10.16). The general rule is that their directors' fees are incidental profits of their position for which they must account to the trust (*Re Macadam* (1946)), unless of course their retention of the fees is authorised. The decision in *Re Dover Coalfield Extension Ltd* (1907) is problematic. In that case, two directors of the Dover company were appointed to the board of the Kent company, in which Dover held shares. In order for the appointments to be effective, the directors were required to hold a certain minimum number of shares in Kent. Sufficient shares were transferred from Dover into their names as trustees for Dover; although the beneficial interest remained with Dover, their legal title to the shares was sufficient to qualify them as directors. The CA held that the directors were not liable to account for their directors' fees. The basis of the decision is unclear, although the judgments seem to rest on two grounds: first, since they became directors of Kent at Dover's request, this amounted to an authorisation from Dover to retain their fees; secondly, because the appointment to Kent was obtained before they acquired Dover's shares in Kent, and the fact that 'they did the work' as directors, the contract between the directors and Kent was a bona fide agreement for their services, ie so that they were not on the board simply as trustee-monitors of Dover's interests.

13.81   In *Re Gee* (1948), Harman J, after reviewing the authorities, explained the law as follows:

> [A] trustee who either uses a power vested in him as such to obtain a benefit (as in Re Macadam) or who (as in Williams v Barton) procures his co-trustees to give him, or those associated with him, remunerative employment must account for the benefit obtained. Further, it appears to me that a trustee who has the power, by the use of trust votes, to control his own appointment to a remunerative position, and refrains from using them with the result that he is elected to a position of profit, would also be accountable. On the other hand, it appears not to be the law that every man who becomes a trustee holding as such shares in a limited company is made ipso facto accountable for remuneration received from that company independently of any use by him of the trust holding, whether by voting or refraining from so doing. For instance, A who holds the majority of shares in a limited company becomes the trustee of the estate of B, a holder of a minority interest; this cannot, I think, disentitle A to use his own shares to procure his appointment as an officer of the company, nor compel him to disgorge the remuneration he so receives, for he cannot be disentitled to the use of his own voting powers, nor could the use of the trust votes in a contrary sense prevent the majority prevailing.

13.82   In *Re Gee*, the trustee-director was not liable to account for his remuneration as a director because the company resolutions to appoint and pay him were unanimously voted by the shareholders, and since there was only a minority of shares held on trust, the resolutions did not turn on the voting of the trust shares—even if the trust shares had been voted against the resolutions, that would not have changed the result.

'Secret' profits

13.83   One important subset of incidental profits is what are sometimes called 'secret' profits; while the term might be regarded simply as a synonym for unauthorised commission or profits, including, for example, the commission in *Williams v Barton*, it is useful to restrict the term to bribes and hidden commissions that the trustee knowingly obtains in breach of his fiduciary position. These latter cases are cases of the fiduciary's breach of BFBDL. As we shall see, this has often failed to have been recognised, especially in clear cut bribe cases.

13.84   It must be acknowledged, however, that the distinction may not be sharp. In *Imageview Management Ltd v Jack* (2009) an agent negotiating a contract for a football player also entered into an undisclosed contract with the football club under which it obtained a commission for getting the footballer a UK work permit. The CA held that where an agent takes a benefit in this way, there is a clear conflict of interest and, not having disclosed it, he is liable to account for it to his principal. This sort of commission was to be distinguished from a benefit honestly acquired in a collateral way (for example where an agent in selling goods for his principal receives a discount from an advertiser when advertising the goods) or a benefit from an honest breach of the contract with the principal. The agent's failure to disclose the contract to obtain the work permit in *Imageview* had the further result that he 'forfeited' the commission he was entitled to for (successfully) negotiating the footballer's contract with the club. This forfeiture arises on the principle that where the agent receives a payment from the 'other side' when he is meant to be negotiating for his principal, he is acting so adversely to his principal that he no longer is entitled to any payment from him. This result, it is submitted, can only be justified on the basis that the agent here breached the BFBDL.

13.85 In *A-G for Hong Kong v Reid* (1994), Reid, the acting Director of Public Prosecutions, accepted bribes to obstruct the prosecution of criminals. Reid was liable to account for the bribe money to the Crown. Lord Templeman said:

> *Where bribes are accepted by a trustee, servant, agent, or other fiduciary, loss and damage are caused to the beneficiaries, master, or principal whose interests have been betrayed. The amount of loss or damage resulting from the acceptance of a bribe may or may not be quantifiable. In the present case the amount of harm caused to the administration of justice in Hong Kong by Mr Reid in return for bribes cannot be quantified.*

13.86 Note that a bribee (someone bribed) is accountable for the money to his employer whether or not the employer has himself suffered loss; the effect of the rule is to strip the bribee of his profits, not compensate the employer for any loss.

13.87 In *Islamic Republic of Iran Shipping Lines v Denby* (1987), a solicitor accepted a 'commission' of $200,000 from the opposite side for securing the settlement of a legal action brought by his client. Leggatt J said, '[w]hat he received was, quite simply, a bribe', and he was liable to pay the sum to his client.

13.88 The CA muddled the liability of the fiduciary to account for secret profits with liability to make equitable compensation, ie to compensate a principal for a loss caused by a breach of fiduciary duty (13.129 et seq), in *Murad v Al-Saraj* (2005). The defendant entered into a joint venture with the claimants to purchase and run, and then eventually sell, a hotel. The venture was profitable both as a hotel business and on the final sale of the hotel. The court held that the claimants relied upon the defendant's experience and advice in the venture, and so the defendant acted in a fiduciary capacity towards the claimant, and there was no appeal as to this finding. The fiduciary knowingly breached his fiduciary obligations in two ways: first, he took a secret commission from the vendor on the sale of the hotel; secondly, he failed to disclose to the claimants that his share of the acquisition price of the hotel would not be paid in cash—rather, the vendor would simply set off debts that he owed to the defendant, including the value of the secret commission. The trial judge found as a fact that, had the claimants been informed, as they ought to have been, that the defendant intended not to put any cash into the purchase of the hotel, they would still have entered into the joint venture but would have demanded a greater share of the profits. In the CA, Arden LJ, with whom Jonathan Parker LJ agreed, held that the defendant was liable to account for all the profits he earned under the joint venture agreement. The decision appeared to turn on the view (at [49]) that it did not matter whether the case was analysed as one of a failure to disclose, or the making of a secret profit. In other words, Arden LJ failed to distinguish the two ways in which the defendant had breached his fiduciary obligation. On any view, the defendant was liable to account for the secret commission—the liability for that has nothing to do with a failure to disclose, and the defendant would have been liable for that even if he could prove that the claimants would have consented to his receiving it if he had disclosed it. That is straightforward, and is supported by a wealth of authority.

13.89   But the second breach, the failure to explain the way in which he was contributing to the purchase of the hotel, had nothing to do with any secret profits. Here the defendant had made a misrepresentation that was material to the agreement as to the terms of profit sharing. He therefore ought to have been liable for any loss this caused, which in this case was the *lower share of profits the claimants received* under the agreement, which, of course, would have equalled the higher share of the profits he received. He should have been liable to pay equitable compensation in this amount. But on no basis should the defendant have been liable to account for all of his profits he received under the contract, in particular the profits that represented the share he would have received but for the breach, because his receiving those did not flow from the breach, but from the successful joint venture that the judge found would have gone forward in any event.

13.90   Arden LJ seems to have reasoned (at [71]) that because of the non-disclosure, which bore on the profit shares under the joint venture, no profit of any kind for the defendant was thus authorised, and he should be stripped of it all, and Arden LJ seemed to welcome this result as an aspect of the policy of holding fiduciaries to a high standard of behaviour. But this is to act punitively, and the policy of stringent fiduciary standards was never intended to *punish* anyone; the strictness simply ensures that a fiduciary is stripped of any gains acquired in breach of the fiduciary relationship, not all profits he earned in the course of acting as a fiduciary so as to inflict the greatest punishment possible. If, as a trustee, I take a secret commission, I am certainly to be stripped of that gain; but I will not be stripped of all the authorised trustees fees that I have earned until then or after that. In this case, putting the matter this way, the defendant should disgorge any profits owing to his failure to disclose, which, as the trial judge found, were those greater profits he would not have acquired but for this failure. The rest of the profits owing to him under the agreement did not flow from any breach, but from the joint venture. (To take a different angle on the case, as Chambers (2005b) points out, had the claimants pursued the remedy of rescinding the contract for misrepresentation, the most they would have received would have been the money back that they put into the venture in the first place, with perhaps a share of the profits from the sale of the hotel as representing the traceable proceeds of their contribution to its purchase price; only by treating the misrepresentation as a breach of fiduciary duty can the wildly different result seem to be justified. Why should the effect of a misrepresentation material to the formation of a contract be magnified in this way simply because the defendant was a fiduciary?) Arguably, this punitive remedy could only be justified by holding that the defendant in this cased breached the BFBDL, in the same way in which the harsh remedy in *Imageview Management* might be justified (13.84).

13.91   Clarke LJ would have held that, while the claimants were entitled to an account of profits, the defendant would have been entitled to argue that, on the basis that the claimants would have agreed to his taking a profit even if he had disclosed, it would be inequitable for him to be stripped of his entire profit. As explained earlier, however, the better route to this result would have been to distinguish the two distinct breaches, and appreciate that the first, the secret commission, required the defendant to account for that receipt no questions asked, while the second, the non-disclosure, was a matter of equitable compensation requiring full attention to issues of 'but for' causation.

The self-dealing and fair dealing rules

13.92   The self-dealing rule and fair dealing rule apply to all fiduciaries, but they are most easily ex-plained in the case of the trustee–beneficiary fiduciary relationship, so we will deal with that case first, and then elaborate the rules briefly in respect of other fiduciaries.

The self-dealing rule

13.93   The self-dealing rule makes voidable any transaction in which a trustee purchases the trust property or, more unusually, sells his own property to the trust, unless the transaction is specifically authorised, and explicit authorisations are strictly construed (*Wright v Morgan* (1926)). The rationale, as explained by Lord Eldon in *Ex p Lacey* (1802) (see also *Ex p Bennet* (1805)), is that because the trustee acts both as vendor for the beneficiaries and purchaser or vice versa, he places himself in an obvious conflict of interest and it is impossible to determine whether he has served the beneficiaries' interests properly in securing the best price for them. The rationale of the self-dealing rule was confirmed in *Fenwick v Naera* (2015), where the New Zealand Supreme Court stated that 'at its most basic level, the self-dealing rule is based on the no-conflict rule: having an interest or duty on both sides of a transaction'. In consequence, if a trustee sells trust property to himself, the sale may be set aside, ie is voidable, at the insistence of any beneficiary, regardless of how fair the transaction is. The principle in all its rigour was affirmed and applied in *Re Thompson's Settlement* (1986) to a trustee-landlord's consent to the assignment of a lease; the principle essentially applies to all trust property transactions.

13.94   *Holder v Holder* (1968) is an exceptional case where the purchaser from a testator's estate, al-though not proving the will, admitted at trial that by having performed certain minor acts in the administration of the estate he had become an executor, and therefore a fiduciary. Innocent of his fiduciary status, he purchased the property at fair value at a public auction. The CA re-fused to set aside the sale, and in this respect the case appears to be an extension from previous authority where sales were not set aside where a purchaser had retired from the trust 12 years prior to the sale (*Re Boles and British Land Co's Contract* (1902)), or where a purchaser was en-titled to but did not take up the office of trustee (*Clark v Clark* (1884)). Harman LJ argued that the purpose of the rule was to prevent any sale by a person acting as both vendor and purchaser, but here the property was prepared for sale by the two proving executors of the will with no input from the purchaser:

> I feel the force of the judge's reasoning that if the [purchaser] remained an executor he is within the rule, but in a case where the reasons behind the rule do not exist I do not feel bound to apply it.

13.95   Danckwerts and Sacks LJJ both went further and questioned whether the rule should ever be applied automatically, doubting that it was beyond the court to determine whether the trustee had taken unfair advantage of his position. Vinelott J, in *Re Thompson's Settlement*, clearly pre-ferred the traditional approach. Note that the problems of determining a trustee's good faith in the face of an actual conflict are just the same here as they were in *Regal Hastings*, where the court refused to mitigate the severity of the rule on evidence that the director's decision that Regal could invest no more than £2,000 in the subsidiary was bona fide.

13.96   The self-dealing rule does not apply to a trustee's exercise of a personal right he acquired prior to appointment as a trustee. In *Newman v Clarke* (2016) a man acquired a lease, which gave him a statutory right to acquire the freehold. Subsequently the freehold reversion was purchased by the trustees of a settlement as trust property, and the man was appointed one of the trustees. The fact that he became a trustee did not bring his subsequent exercise of his right to acquire the freehold under the self-dealing rule.

The fair dealing rule

13.97   The fair dealing rule applies to purchases not of the trust property itself, but of a beneficiary's interest in the trust property. So, the rule comes into play when, for example, a capital beneficiary assigns (2.35–2.39) his capital interest under the trust to his trustee. The rule is less harsh, for the simple reason that the danger here is less: since there are two real parties to the transaction with their own interests at stake, not a trustee selling to himself, the bargain is much more likely to be a real one. Therefore if a trustee purchases the beneficial interest of a beneficiary the transaction may not be set aside automatically at the beneficiary's insistence, but only if the trustee cannot show (and the onus is on him to do so) that he has taken no advantage of his position, has fully disclosed all relevant information to the beneficiary, that the beneficiary did not rely solely on his advice, and that the price was fair. (See eg the characterisation of Megarry VC in *Tito v Waddell (No 2)* (1977), cited in *Re Thompson's Settlement* (1986); *Edwards v Meyrick* (1842).)

The application of the self-dealing and fair dealing rules to other fiduciaries

13.98   The rules apply to other fiduciaries who, like trustees, have the discretion or power to enter into property sales or other contracts on behalf of their principals. So, for example, the self-dealing rule applies to a company director who enters into a contract to buy goods for his company from another company in which he is interested (see eg *Aberdeen Railway Co v Blaikie Bros* (1854)). The rule also applies where someone close to the director, such as his spouse, has an interest in the second company. The fair dealing rule would apply where the director enters into a contract between himself and the company, so long as the company is represented by some other person or persons, such as where the director sells land he owns to a company for development by negotiating the contract with the board of directors. Because it is not uncommon for company directors to have outside interests of various kinds, company law and company articles generally provide for a director to escape liability for breach of these rules by making full disclosure of his interests under such a transaction (see Dignam and Lowry (2010), ch 14).

13.99   The self-dealing rule applies to all contracts, not just contracts for the sale of property. In *Fenwick v Naera* (2015), the New Zealand Supreme Court confirmed this principle, observing that the self-dealing rule has been applied to commercial transactions other than sales, including leases of trust property to trustees. Therefore, if your literary agent signs a book contract for you with a publisher in which he has an interest, this breaches the self-dealing rule.

13.100   The fair dealing rule typically applies only to property transactions. Thus, if your agent negotiates to buy the movie rights for the book from you, unless he can discharge the onus of showing that the deal was fair, he will breach the fair dealing rule. The reason why the fair dealing rule usually applies only to property transactions is that in other cases the principal will typically be negotiating with the fiduciary to perform a further service for the principal, and this will not usually involve a transaction involving the existing fiduciary relationship, but will be a contract establishing a new one. On the other hand, in certain circumstances one can imagine the fair dealing rule applying: where an agent's contract is renewed, for example, it is easy to conceive a court setting aside the new contract if the agent failed to disclose that he had breached the prior contract in significant ways, ways difficult for the principal to detect.

13.101   If a fiduciary attempts to circumvent the application of either the self-dealing or the fair dealing rules by collusively selling to a third party, the sale is liable to be set aside as if the fiduciary were a party himself. In *Re Postlethwaite* (1888) the court did not set aside a sale to a third party just because the trustee entertained a hope of purchasing the property himself from him. Sales to family members or spouses will be viewed suspiciously, and a trustee will not be entitled to avoid the application of the rule by retiring from the trust in order to purchase trust property (*Re Boles and British Land Co's Contract* (1902)).

13.102   Where a sale is liable to be set aside, the transaction is voidable, not void at the outset, so an innocent third-party purchaser of the property from the fiduciary before a principal acts will take a good title; in these circumstances the fiduciary will be liable to account for any profits made on the resale, or if it is shown that the resale was at an undervalue, the difference between the sale price and the true value. Where the transaction is avoided while the property is still in the hands of the fiduciary, the principal may require the return of the property in return for the purchase price received, or may require a resale of the property on the open market—if the property fetches more on the open market than the price paid by the fiduciary the difference is the principal's, of course (see *Holder v Holder* (1968); Conaglen (2003)).

13.103   Is there a 'limited beneficial interest' exception to the self-dealing rule? This was considered in *Fenwick v Naera*, but the court preferred not to rule on the issue, deciding instead that even if it does exist, Mrs Fenwick would not have had recourse to it. Glazebrook J said:

> The rationale for such a general exception, should it exist, is as such that where there is only a very small conflicting interest in the transaction, it may not have influenced it, as long as the person is not also negotiating 'on both sides of the transaction' by being a trustee or director of both contracting parties.

13.104   The court commented that the existing cases and texts do not provide strong support for the existence of this general exception. Furthermore, other recent cases (*Movitex Ltd v Bulfield* (1986)) have also doubted the existence of a general limited interest exception, preferring to explain the cases that seem to have recognised such an exception (see *Farrar v Farrars Ltd* (1888)) on other grounds.

The proprietary and personal nature of the liability to account

13.105   Where a trustee is liable to account for an unauthorised profit, one might understand this as a claim that the trustee has failed to bring trust property into the account. That is, his liability to account is simply a recognition of the fact that the property is trust property in his hands for which he has not properly accounted, ie included in the trust accounts as an addition to the trust funds, and thus the beneficiary's claim amounts to a claim to specifically enforce the trust over that property (11.118–11.119, 11.142 et seq). It would follow from this analysis that the particular profit, as trust property, is held on trust for the beneficiary from the moment the trustee receives it—as the beneficiary's interest in the trust is an interest in a fund, the interest will comprise all those items of property that from time to time are 'captured' by the trust.

13.106   It is important to realise that on this view the property should be regarded as being held under an *express* trust, the express trust under which all of the other trust property is held. Such a profit would stand on the same footing as would the proceeds of the sale of any of the trust property, or the income from trust property, which a trustee might wilfully or inadvertently have paid into his own bank account. Such property, just like capital proceeds or income, is captured by and is within the terms of the express trust. On this view, then, there is no question of the court's *imposing* a constructive trust on the particular profits or the income earned on it, and of course the profit can be traced into the proceeds of substitutions. The trustee will, of course, also be personally liable to the trust for the value of the property if it has disappeared or cannot be traced, because that will be how he will satisfy the account if he cannot do so with the actual property itself or its traceable proceeds.

13.107   But this perspective cannot apply easily to all fiduciaries, because as I have rather pounded into the reader's head, not all fiduciaries are trustees (see further Penner (2014d)). Indeed, not all fiduciaries are even accounting parties, much less trustees. An accounting party is someone who is obliged to render an account. Besides trustees, accounting parties are generally so as a matter of contract. A book publisher has to account to an author for the sales of the book, for this is the basis upon which the author receives his royalties. But the publisher is not a trustee, holding the proceeds of book sales on trust to give the author his cut. The publisher is just personally liable to 'account for', ie pay over, the right amount based on the sales figures. Neither, in this case, is the publisher a fiduciary to the author. The publisher is not acting as an agent, entering into book sales on the author's behalf. The publisher sells its own books, and the author is merely contractually entitled to be paid on the basis of the publisher's sales. So a liability to account is not purely the province of fiduciaries, nor is the liability to account necessarily proprietary. A true agent may sell his principal's property but not be obliged to hold those proceeds on trust (2.57–2.58). Now we can see that not all fiduciaries are accounting parties. A solicitor is a fiduciary to his client, but unless he is dealing with his client's property—holding in his client account for example—he is not an accounting party because his service is to provide legal advice, not to manage his client's property or sell his client's goods on his client's behalf. As we have seen, of course, in certain cases equity does tend to treat fiduciaries who are not trustees as if they were (11.15), and one might do so here, arguing that a non-trustee fiduciary who receives an unauthorised profit should hold it on trust for the principal, in this case the court imposing a constructive trust in order to provide parity of treatment with the trustee fiduciary. But this perspective, which seems to be espoused by Lord Millett (13.111), assumes the correctness of the view that the fiduciary's liability to account should be modelled on that of the express trustee, whose liability to account flows from his stewardship of the beneficiary's property. But as we also know, the essence of the fiduciary obligation does not lie in the stewardship of property—it lies in the fiduciary's discretionary powers to alter his principal's legal position. And so, in determining whether the fiduciary holds any unauthorised profit on trust, or rather is personally liable to pay over the value of such a profit, we should look to the basic rationale of the fiduciary's liability for unauthorised profits. We will return to this following a review of the way that the courts have dealt with the issue.

13.108 In *Williams v Barton* (13.79), Russell J decided that the trustee held the commission as a 'constructive trustee' and was 'liable to account' as if this meant much the same thing. In *Boardman*, when the HL affirmed the order of Wilberforce J at first instance, it affirmed that the shares were held on trust, although apart from Lord Guest all of their Lordships spoke only of the defendant's liability to account. Similarly, in *Industrial Development Consultants Ltd v Cooley*, the court declared that Cooley was a trustee of the profits he earned from his contracts, and liable to account for those profits plus interest.

13.109 It does appear that whenever judges refer to the trust over a fiduciary's profits, even in the case of an express trustee, they always speak of a *constructive* trust, but the use of 'constructive' in these circumstances may be little more than a judicial tic—it may be that the court has a tendency, when it must decide the entitlement in equity to a piece of property that the legal owner disputes belongs in equity to another, and it finds against him, to say that he holds it on 'constructive' trust. For example, if the trustee himself appropriates property that clearly belongs to the trust, any profits or income on the property are clearly trust property, ie property under the express trust because, as we have seen (11.116 et seq), if beneficiaries wish to claim property acquired in breach of trust they 'adopt' the transaction giving rise to it, thereby capturing the property as trust property. Yet, it has been said that such profits are held on 'constructive' trust (eg Martin (2001), at 624).

13.110 In *Lister & Co v Stubbs* (1890), the CA held that a non-trustee fiduciary agent's liability to account for a bribe to be personal, not proprietary. Stubbs was a purchaser for Lister & Co, who received large secret commissions from one of Lister's suppliers, Varley & Co, for ordering goods from it. Stubbs had invested part of the commission money in land, and Lister sought an interlocutory injunction restraining Stubbs from dealing with the land, arguing that the land, as an investment purchased with the commission money, belonged in equity to it. The UKCA refused. Here is the famous passage from Lindley LJ's judgment:

> Then comes the question, as between Lister & Co and Stubbs, whether Stubbs can keep the money he has received without accounting for it? Obviously not. I apprehend that he is liable to account for it the moment he gets it. It is an obligation to pay and account to Messrs. Lister & Co, with or without interest, as the case may be. I say nothing at all about that. But the relation between them is that of debtor and creditor; it is not that of trustee and cestui que trust.

13.111 In 1994, the UKPC in *A-G for Hong Kong v Reid* (1994) decided that the recipient of a bribe held it on trust for his principal. There were three bases for the decision. On one hand, Lord Templeman quoted with approval the words of Sir Peter Millett, speaking extrajudicially:

> [The fiduciary] must not place himself in a position where his interest may conflict with his duty. If he has done so, equity insists on treating him as having acted in accordance with his duty; he will not be allowed to say that he preferred his own interest to that of his principal. He must not obtain a profit for himself out of his fiduciary position. If he has done so, equity insists on treating him as having obtained it for his principal; he will not be allowed to say that he obtains it for himself. He must not accept a bribe. If he has done so, equity insists on treating it as a legitimate payment intended for the benefit of the principal; he will not be allowed to say it was a bribe.

13.112 This analysis, of course, leads to a finding that the bribe is held as trust property from the outset, under an express trust, just as much as any other trust 'income', such as the dividends on shares, would be. On this reckoning, the liability to account is a proprietary liability per se, as considered in 13.105–13.109, and *Lister* must be wrong because it is conceptually in error—there is just no such thing as a liability to account which means that the fiduciary has only a personal obligation to pay over the value of the property in question. The problem with this view is that it is fictional: as we have seen (13.107), the fiduciary's pre-existing liability to account cannot be the ground or justification for preferring proprietary over personal liability, for not all fiduciaries have a pre-existing proprietary liability to account—for some fiduciaries their liability to account is only personal—and in some cases fiduciaries are not accounting parties at all.

13.113   But Lord Templeman *also* stated that the fiduciary was subject primarily only to an equitable obligation to pay the money over to the principal, ie was a 'debtor in equity', not a trustee of the bribe money at all. But he further reasoned:

> Equity considers as done that which ought to have been done. As soon as the bribe was received, whether in cash or in kind, the false fiduciary held the bribe on constructive trust for the person injured.

13.114   The application of this maxim in these circumstances is nonsensical (see Crilley (1994)), because as Swadling (1997) points out, the maxim does not work in the case of a debt:

> [T]hat debt can be satisfied by the payment of money belonging to the fiduciary taken from any source. It is not only discharged by the handing over of the very money received. And since there is no duty to pay over the bribe in specie, the application of the maxim 'equity considers as done that which ought to have been done' cannot give rise to any proprietary rights over those moneys, for the payment over of the bribe itself is not that 'which ought to have been done'.

13.115   The judgment is certainly subject to criticism for depending upon these two apparently incompatible grounds for the decision, but Lord Templeman seems to have added a third. Recall the quotation from his judgment in 13.85. The liability to account Lord Millett describes and the 'equitable debt' subject to the 'equity looks upon that as done … ' maxim could apply only to fiduciaries. But if the reason for the decision was to ensure that bribees are stripped of their wrongful gains, then the liability to account laid down by the decision applies to anyone who takes a bribe, and *anyone*, whether a fiduciary or not, can be bribed; a security guard is not a fiduciary of any kind, but he can certainly be bribed by thieves to let them in. Bribes, then, seem clearly to be breaches of BFBDL, and have nothing in particular to do with whether a person is a fiduciary or not.

13.116   In short, the decision, if taken at face value, pretty much abolished the merely personal liability to account for an unauthorised profit—it is essentially proprietary in all cases, and this has now been confirmed in the UKSC decision in *FHR European Ventures v Cedar Capital Partners* (2014).

13.117   Between the decisions in *Reid* and *FHR* the CA refused to follow *Reid* in two cases. In *Halifax Building Society v Thomas* (1996) the CA refused to hold that the profit a fraudster had acquired as the result of purchasing land with a fraudulently acquired mortgage was held by him on constructive trust for the mortgagee, although the court accepted that he was liable to pay the value of the profit to the mortgagee. There are clear parallels between this sort of case and that of a person who profits from a bribe, and yet *Reid* was not applied. In *Sinclair Investments (UK) Ltd v Versailles Trade Finance Ltd* (2011), the CA refused to follow *Reid* and indeed cast doubt on its reasoning, Neuberger MR saying:

> [I]t seems to me that there is a real case for saying that the decision in Reid [1994] 1 AC 324 is unsound. In cases where a fiduciary takes for himself an asset which, if he chose to take, he was under a duty to take for the beneficiary, it is easy to see why the asset should be treated as the property of the beneficiary. However, a bribe paid to a fiduciary could not possibly be said to be an asset which the fiduciary was under a duty to take for the beneficiary. There can thus be said to be a fundamental distinction between (i) a fiduciary enriching himself by depriving a Claimant of an asset and (ii) a fiduciary enriching himself by doing a wrong to the Claimant.

13.118 Nevertheless in the UKSC in *FHR*, Lord Neuberger giving the unaminous judgment of the court, followed *Reid*. The defendant was an agent who organised the claimant's purchase for about €200m of a hotel in Monaco. The defendant was entitled to receive on the sale a commission of about €10m under a brokerage agreement with the hotel owner, and at trial the judge found that the defendant had not sufficiently disclosed the right to the commission to the claimant, so finding that this was an unauthorised profit for which the defendant was liable to account to the claimant, and this finding was not appealed. The UKSC held that the defendant held this commission on trust for his principal. It is important to note that, unlike *Reid*, this was not a case of a bribe, although in his judgment Lord Neuberger did not seem to distinguish between bribes and unauthorised or undisclosed commissions.

13.119 The reasoning in the decision is less than satisfactory. The court quite rightly showed that there were lines of authority going both ways, and so the court had to decide on the basis of principle and, perhaps, policy. But the discussion of principle was not thorough, and it seems the court adopted the rule that any unauthorised profit should be held on trust because of its simplicity and clarity. But it is one thing for equity to require a fiduciary to hold on trust a profit acquired by misappropriating his principal's property, or the income arising on it, and quite another thing to do the same for any property acquired in an unauthorised fashion, especially in the case of someone like Reid who was not an accounting party at all, much less a trustee; in the case of a non-accounting party like Reid, there was no prior basis in his relationship with the Attorney-General of Hong Kong that would of itself justify his having to hold anything he received and was accountable for on trust for the Attorney-General. Furthermore, if the evil in the case which needed a remedy was bribery (amongst the opening lines of Lord Templeman's judgment one finds: 'Bribery is an evil practice which threatens the foundations of any civilised society') then it is one which can be and is committed by non-fiduciaries; it is a breach of BFBDL.

13.120 Moreover, consider this sort of case: a fiduciary agent who is liable to account personally on a regular basis, say half-yearly, receives an unauthorised commission from a third party. Realising he cannot keep it for himself, he records it in his accounts and pays it over at the next accounting date. According to *FHR*, he does wrong here. Because it is unauthorised, he cannot account for it like any other gain he makes for his principal, but must treat this particular gain as special, segregating it and holding it on trust. On what principle of justice does this make sense?

13.121 What, after all, is the rationale for stripping the fiduciary of his unauthorised profit? It cannot be to *compensate* the principal for a loss, because in most cases (there are exceptions that we shall consider in a moment) the principal does not suffer any loss when his fiduciary acquires an unauthorised profit, earning a commission or directors' fees or taking a bribe: the rule applies across the board to all unauthorised profits. Rather, the rationale is to *strip* the fiduciary of any *gain* he earns *in conflict of interest*: this is typically called a 'disgorgement' remedy, and its purpose is to ensure that the fiduciary who places himself in a situation of conflict of interest cannot benefit thereby. It is a rule put in place to prevent fiduciaries from personally profiting in an unauthorised fashion, not to generate any extra resources for the principal. The goal of the rule is that fiduciaries *never* earn profits of this kind in the first place, *not* to create a new source of revenue for their principals when they do. Understanding this 'prophylactic' nature of the rule explains why it is often questioned why the principal should have the right to the profit anyway—should it not be forfeited to the state, as proceeds of a wrong? Why shouldn't the Attorney-General as representative of the Crown have the right to claim the profit? The most compelling justification for according the right to the principal is simply that, as a matter of private law rights, he is the only appropriate plaintiff, because he has been wronged by the fiduciary's act, and although the principal suffered no loss, if given the incentive of claiming the profit, he will be likely to enforce the claim and strip the fiduciary of the profit. Understood this way, the rationale for stripping the fiduciary's profit follows the maxim 'No one should profit from his own wrong', and the principal's claim is one for 'disgorgement' or 'restitution' for a profit acquired in the commission of a wrong. This topic is, therefore, typically discussed in restitution texts under the heading 'restitution for wrongs' (see eg Burrows (2011), Part 4). But if these are really restitution for wrongs cases, there is nothing special about the fiduciary relationship in such a case; and breach of a civil wrong must *prima facie* qualify. In particular in the case of bribes, only an examination of BFBDL across the range of cases where it applies, to employees, to agents, etc, would allow us to determine whether gain-stripping should be allowed in all cases of wrongs. *Prima facie*, it is attractive to say that a gain, such as a bribe, acquired in breach of BFBDL, can be stripped by the employer or principal. But again, that would tell us nothing about whether such a gain should be held on trust as soon as it is received.

13.122   It is submitted that the primary remedy against the fiduciary should be personal, not proprietary. Consider the consequences in the context of insolvency (2.89 et seq). If B has the obligation to pay A money, and B goes bankrupt, then A is an unsecured creditor; if B has breached his fiduciary obligations to A and has earned a profit from a third party in doing so, our goal should be to ensure that B does not profit from his wrong against A. In order to accomplish that there is no need for A *to acquire* a proprietary interest in those profits, for that simply allows A to gain a priority over B's other creditors when B, *ex hypothesi*, has not appropriated or interfered with A's property. Where a trust is automatically imposed on B's unauthorised profit, however innocently it was acquired, as in *Boardman*, A gains an unjustified advantage merely because the obligation that was breached was a fiduciary one; it is difficult to say that John Phipps' right to Boardman's profits is any more compelling than C's common law right to be paid by Boardman for the property C has provided him under a contract, because C has thereby increased the value of Boardman's estate, or D's common law right to be compensated for Boardman's running him down with his car, because in this case Boardman's wrong has caused D to suffer an actual (monetarily quantifiable) loss at Boardman's hands. C and D have no proprietary claim, of course. (See further Swadling (2005a).) In *Boardman*, Boardman did not appropriate any property of the beneficiaries, unless the use of the information was itself an acquisition of trust property. While Lords Hodson and Guest treated the information as trust 'property', the majority did not, and there is little to recommend that view (see Lord Upjohn's dissent on the point). In such a case it would be right to strip Boardman of his profits (assuming the case was rightly decided), but the profits should not be regarded as trust property from the outset.

13.123   Because of these considerations, restitution lawyers typically argue that, except in cases where the fiduciary's profit can be treated as in some way a misappropriation of his principal's property, the remedy should be personal, not proprietary. Is a trust over property in the breaching fiduciary's hands that is not originally property of the trust, or its traceable proceeds, or income of that property, ever justified? A trust over some unauthorised profits may be justified. If an agent acquires an unauthorised commission that was really part of the consideration in the contract between his principal and the third party, then the money, this 'rebate' on the purchase price, should have gone to the principal in the first place. On this view, the trust over the commission prevents an unjustified distinction between a case of embezzlement and fraudulent conversion: one should not allow the agent to avoid holding the property on trust from the outset simply because he embezzled it (ie prevented property that should have gone to his principal from getting there by treating it as his own) rather than fraudulently converted it (ie existing property of his principal to his own benefit); both are equally examples of theft. The argument is that this 'rebate' is akin to the income on property, like dividends on shares. The agent 'intercepts' this payment to his principal, treating it as his own (ie embezzling it) rather than paying it over to his principal. This is the rationale of making the fiduciary liable as a constructive trustee in the corporate opportunity cases, such as *IDC v Cooley*. The fiduciary in such cases appropriated or intercepted an opportunity which, if he pursued it at all, he was bound to pursue only for his principal.

13.124   In *Mahesan v Malaysia Government Officers' Co-operative Housing Society Ltd* (1979) an agent of the housing society took a one-quarter share of an overvalue of $488,000 on a price of $944,000 paid for a piece of land the agent purchased for the society from the briber. The bribe of $122,000 clearly represented the agent's 'cut' of the overvalue. The housing society sued the agent for its loss on the purchase, $443,000, which was the amount of the overvalue minus certain costs. Having elected for that remedy, the society was unable also to claim the value of the bribe, since the value of the bribe clearly formed part of the total overvalue. In other words, both the bribe and the rest of the overpayment element of the purchase price were equally treated, quite rightly, as different kinds of appropriations by the fiduciary resulting in loss to his principal.

13.125   But there are bribes and bribes. Certainly the Attorney-General for Hong Kong could hardly claim that he should have received the profits from Reid's suborning of the judicial process, ie that Reid took bribes that in justice the Attorney-General should have himself received to corrupt the criminal justice system. In that sort of case, the principal, by having a claim against the fiduciary, is really just stripping him of the profits of his wrong, not demanding property that was his from the outset, or was a payment made to him intercepted by his fiduciary. A useful thought experiment is always to ask what should happen if the 'unauthorised profit' or bribe is stolen before the principal has a chance to claim it. If the money is really trust money, then the principal's claim should lapse with the theft, because the theft was of *his* property; if you think the principal should be able to sue the false fiduciary for the value of the bribe regardless, then it was the taking of the third party's money that was the wrong, not any 'theft' or 'misappropriation' of any particular 'trust asset'. (And note, you cannot have it both ways.)

13.126   There are two further considerations to bear in mind which strongly counsel against imposing a constructive trust to strip a wrongdoer of his gains: the rules of tracing do not operate to strip a wrongdoer of gains that result from his wrong, and the rules of tracing are 'bent'. The first consideration is that if the concern of the disgorgement remedy is to ensure that the defendant does not gain by his wrong, then imposing a constructive trust on the gain, and of course, its traceable proceeds, is unlikely to achieve that result. As we know from *Foskett v McKeown* (11.155 et seq), tracing is a transactional inquiry, not a causal one. By that I mean that tracing tracks the transactions a person makes with the property rights at his disposal; it does not track the value of the gain initially received or any subsequent gain for which the initial gain was a 'but for' cause. So, presumably, if one wanted to ensure that X does not gain from his wrongdoing, not only would one wish to strip him of the immediate gain like the receipt of bribe money, but also any increase in his wealth for which the receipt of bribe money was a 'but for' cause; thus, if, because of the bribe money, X was able to make a profitable investment, we would want to strip him of that enrichment too, *irrespective of what funds he actually used to make the investment*, that is, irrespective of whether that enrichment was the traceable proceeds of any use of the bribe money. Assuming that we want to ensure that wrongdoers do not gain in any way from their wrong, the post-initial enrichment causal inquiry should be to determine whether there has been any subsequent enrichment which would not have occurred but for the initial, wrongful, gain. Similarly, and contrariwise, where there is no causal connection between the receipt of an illicit gain and a particular profit, there would seem to be no reason to strip X of this second profit—and diminish his estate for the rest of his creditors—just because the gain was the traceable proceeds of a transaction expending the bribe money. Claims against traceable proceeds vindicate equitable beneficial ownership interests; they are not in any way a substitute for gain-stripping as a matter of principle, and they are a very poor facsimile in practice, as the facts in *Foskett* itself make abundantly clear.

13.127   As to the second consideration, we know (11.130) that tracing rules are 'bent' in favour of the victims of wrongdoers. When tracing through bank accounts, which will commonly be the case if a bribe taker receives the bribe in the form of money, the victim of the wrong, as beneficiary of the constructive trust, will be able to 'cherry-pick' the expenditures which result in profitable (or least loss-making) 'investments' of the bribe money, to the disadvantage of the bribe taker's other general creditors. This 'cherry-picking' result is now justified on the basis that the beneficiary of a trust may trace into such withdrawals as he pleases (within the arithmetic limits of what he and the trustee contributed) on the principle that all reasonable inferences will be made against a wrongdoer whose own act gave rise to the factual difficulty of determining whose money went where. It is too late now to revisit this result as regards beneficiaries of express trust interests, but it cautions us against imposing proprietary liability against wrongdoers where our only legitimate aim is to strip the wrongdoer of his unauthorised gains. Where the wrongdoer is bankrupt by the time of the action, which will again commonly be the case, the 'cherry-picking rule' will allow the victim not only to obtain the windfall of the ill-gotten gain, but artificially to enhance the value of that windfall, as he pleases, at the expense of the wrongdoer's general creditors. In other words, the application of the bent tracing rules through bank accounts will occasion the bankrupt wrongdoer's general creditors' *positively contributing* to the victim's windfall. One way around this problem might be to suggest that where the wrongdoer-constructive trustee's actual personal interests are out of the picture because he is bankrupt, so that the real conflict is between innocents, the innocent victim of the wrong and the innocent general creditors, we should not apply the 'cherry-picking' rule, adopting instead a neutral rule for tracing through bank accounts. But that is most certainly not the present law, and until such a suggestion is adopted, imposing proprietary liability upon wrongdoers for their ill-gotten gains is liable to work substantial injustice against their general creditors, for no principled reason.

13.128 A final concern is that we must determine what we are trying to do here. If the evil we mean to address is taking a bribe to do something wrong, and let us remind ourselves that *FHR* was *not* a case of anyone being bribed, then this is something that both fiduciaries and non-fiduciaries are equally capable of. Again, it seems that we are pursuing people, bribees, for the breach of BFBDL, which applies to fiduciaries, but not only to them. The remedial response of stripping the bribe of his gain lies squarely within the law of disgorgement or restitution for wrongs. Unfortunately, the law of restitution for wrongs is, arguably, in as bad a state as any area of private law (Burrows 2011, Part 4; Stevens, (2007), 79–84). None of the judges or commentators agree on what the law is or what it should be. If some restitution lawyers want to have a go at saying that equity—in its 'auxiliary jurisdiction' (1.13) of assisting the common law to provide adequate remedies for torts or breaches of contract (Reid clearly breached his contractual obligations to the Attorney-General of Hong Kong, a security guard clearly breaches his contractual obligations to his employer by letting the thieves in)—should require the wrongdoers to hold their ill-gotten gains on trust, so be it; but such an argument would have nothing to do with the liability to account that trustees or other fiduciaries have, and so the proprietary liability of trustees to account should not serve as a model for the development of the law of restitution for wrongs in these cases. The two have nothing to do with each other.

Equitable compensation for breach of fiduciary obligation

13.129 As we have seen in respect of the no conflict rule, the standard response of equity is to strip the defendant of any profit earned by participating in a transaction in conflict of interest. In the case of the self-dealing and fair dealing rules, the court will reverse the transaction, if possible, and, if not, again will strip the false fiduciary of any profit. However, in certain circumstances the breach of fiduciary obligation will not give rise to any profit to the false fiduciary, or not only do that, but may actually give rise to a loss on the part of the fiduciary's principal. In such a case the fiduciary must compensate his principal for the loss, and this compensation for loss is styled *equitable compensation*, which we have already encountered (11.35). The leading modern case that establishes the jurisdiction of equity to award equitable compensation for breach of fiduciary obligation is *Nocton v Lord Ashburton* (1914). Nocton, a solicitor, advised Lord Ashburton to advance £60,000 on a mortgage as part of a scheme to develop land. Nocton derived personal advantages under the scheme of which he did not inform Ashburton. Later Nocton advised Lord Ashburton to release a property from the mortgage, which made the mortgage loan less secure, and which again unbeknownst to Lord Ashburton benefited Nocton. The scheme failed to be profitable, and the value of the property securing the mortgage fell far short of what Lord Ashburton had advanced. The HL unanimously decided that, although Nocton had not intended to defraud Lord Ashburton, he was in breach of his fiduciary obligations to him in advising him to act so as to benefit Nocton, and the court affirmed the lower court's direction to inquire into the amount of Lord Ashburton's losses.

13.130 The principles underlying equitable compensation for breach of fiduciary duty were considered, as we have seen, by Lord Browne-Wilkinson in *Target Holdings* (1996) (11.46 et seq), although in the context of the measure of liability to restore the trust when the account is falsified, so you should review what he said there now. These principles were considered by the CA in *Swindle v Harrison* (1997). Mrs Harrison, at the instigation of her son, mortgaged her house to provide capital to purchase the Aylesford Hotel, in order that together they could operate a family res-taurant business. She contracted to buy the hotel and paid a £44,000 deposit, which would have been forfeited if she did not pay the remainder of the sale price and complete the purchase. Unfortunately, by the date of completion, she and her son were unable to obtain sufficient money to complete the purchase. Her solicitor, the engagingly named Mr Swindle, arranged for his firm to provide a bridging loan so that she could complete. In breach of fiduciary duty, Mr Swindle failed to inform her of certain pertinent facts, in particular his firm's profit on the loan. It was clear that, but for the bridging loan, Mrs Harrison would not have been able to purchase the restaurant, and she would have lost her £44,000 deposit. The restaurant business turned out to be a disaster, resulting in the loss of the entire sum she had raised on the equity in her home. Because the solicitor failed to disclose material facts to her in breach of his fiduciary duty, she was clearly entitled to rescind the bridging loan agreement; indeed, by the time of trial, that loan agreement had been rescinded by agreement. It was argued that the solicitors' firm was liable for any losses that would not have resulted 'but for the loan', ie all the losses resulting from the restaurant business.

13.131   The CA unanimously found against Mrs Harrison. Unfortunately, all three judges gave ex-tensive judgments that used different terminology and provided different rationales for doing so. Essentially, however, all three agreed that the particular breach in question, the failure to inform Mrs Harrison of the profit Mr Swindle's firm was taking on the loan, did not lead to the losses caused by her entering the restaurant business.

13.132   Another example is *Gwembe Valley Development v Koshy* (2003): in conflict of interest, a dir-ector made a massive profit on currency transactions contracts he arranged for his company. While he was liable, of course, to disgorge those unauthorised profits, the court held that these contracts had not contributed to the ultimate failure of the development venture, so he was not liable to compensate the company for the resultant losses. In *Hilton v Barker, Booth & Eastwood* (2005) (13.42), a solicitors' firm was held liable for the losses suffered when, in breach of its contract of retainer with its client it failed to advise him of facts important to his decision whether to proceed with a transaction, and it was liable for the losses he suffered by proceeding. Because the contractual duty to advise a client of all material facts known to the solicitor is a duty 'rooted in the fiduciary relationship between solicitor and client', and indeed, is arguably a fiduciary obligation in its own right deriving from the solicitor's duty generally to act in the best interest of his client, this is a case where the award against the solicitors could be framed both as damages for breach of contract and as equitable compensation for breach of fiduciary obligation.

Secondary liability for breach of fiduciary obligation

13.133   As we have seen (11.15), where a fiduciary misappropriates his principal's property, say where a company director fraudulently draws a cheque from the company bank account in his own favour, equity regards this as equivalent to a breach of trust and the normal breach of trust remedies against third parties, ie for knowing receipt or knowing assistance, will apply. Making third parties liable in the case of a true breach of fiduciary obligation is, however, a more vexed question (see Mitchell (2002); Davies (2015a), 264–69). There are, of course, some breaches of fiduciary obligation that necessarily involve misapplications of the principal's property, ie breaches of the self-dealing and fair dealing rules, and there would seem to be no objections in principle to making third parties who dishonestly assist such breaches, or receive property via them, to be held liable. The same might be said for those cases in which a fiduciary is properly held to hold an unauthorised profit on constructive trust for his principal, ie those cases in which the unauthorised profit can fairly be said to be a misappropriation of the principal's property (13.121–13.127). In these cases the analogy with knowing receipt and knowing assistance is straightforward.

13.134   For example, in *CMS Dolphin Ltd v Simonet* (2001), Collins J treated a director's exploitation for himself of a maturing business opportunity 'as appropriating for himself [the property of his company]'. The new company he formed, which took the benefit of the opportunity (and which was deemed to have his knowledge), was liable either as a 'participant' in a breach of trust, or alternatively as a knowing recipient of trust property transferred in breach of trust (see also *Comax Secure Business Services v Wilson* (2001); *Dilmun v Sutton* (2004)). While the reasoning that a maturing business opportunity is a company's 'property' is questionable (13.49 et seq), the principle upon which the company was found liable seems a straightforward application by analogy of the rules governing secondary liability for breach of trust.

13.135   Nevertheless, the cases do not speak with one voice. In *Satnam Investments Ltd v Dunlop Heywood & Co Ltd* (1999) the claimant's competitor was assisted in its purchase of a site for development, a site in which the claimant was also interested, by the unauthorised release of confidential information by the claimant's agent, which the court treated as a breach of its fiduciary obligation. The CA refused to hold that the competitor held the site on constructive trust for the claimant. Distinguishing *Boardman* on the basis that there the defendants had placed themselves in a fiduciary position vis-à-vis the beneficiaries, the court said that it would be contrary to commercial good sense to hold a competitor, which of course had no prior fiduciary duty to the claimant, liable as a fiduciary for taking advantage of the claimant's agent's breach and stripping it of the asset it had acquired. This case seems to suggest that merely knowingly receiving a benefit that would not have come to one but for another's breach of fiduciary obligation is insufficient to render one liable to the wronged principal. Notice one can analyse this case on the basis that the acquisition of the site for development could be regarded as something that its agent should have acquired for its principal if for anyone; there seems little doubt that had the agent acquired the site itself, it would have been liable to hold it on trust for the principal. Thus, as a case equivalent to a 'misappropriation of trust property' case, it seems directly to conflict with *CMS Dolphin*.

13.136   The CA's decision in *Novoship UK v Nikitin* seems to confirm (at [77]; the trial judge explicitly endorsed the point) that a third party is not accountable for the fiduciary's own unauthorised gain, ie is not liable to pay over a sum equivalent to the unauthorised gain which the fiduciary himself acquired. *Novoship* also decides that a third party who *dishonestly* participates in a transaction in which the fiduciary acts in conflict of interest, is liable to account for his own gain to the fiduciary's principal, but the gain must be the causal result of his participation, on conventional principles of 'but/for' causation. This reasoning coheres with the result vis-à-vis the third parties in *Regal Hastings* (13.43 et seq): recall that besides the directors, the company's solicitor subscribed for shares, and one director subscribed for shares for third parties. Neither the solicitor nor the third party were stripped of their profits, although, on the facts, it could hardly be clearer that the solicitor knowingly participated in and benefited from the scheme, and the third party benefited from the scheme. Neither was the director who subscribed for others liable secondarily for those others' gains. This was so even though all of them knowingly participated in a scheme that would not have come off but for their participation, and which they were in a position to realise, if they had thought about it, was a scheme reflecting a conflict of interest. But it would be hard to characterise any of these third parties as dishonest.

13.137 In *Akita Holdings v AG of the Turks and Caicos Islands* (2017), a government minister of the Turks & Caicos Islands purchased land under a Crown Land Policy scheme, which allowed individuals to first rent and develop land, then buy it if the conditions were satisfied. He obtained a private valuation of the land which showed it to have a much higher value than the price he paid for it under the outdated valuation relied upon by the government. After development of the land, and before he exercised his right to buy the land, the minister transferred the right to the company Akita Holdings, a company jointly owned by him and his brother. Further development continued and the land increased further in value.

13.138 The UKPC held that Akita, 'having acquired [the minister's] right to buy the property at the discounted price, with full knowledge of his breach of fiduciary duty, it is in principle liable to account to the government in the same way as him', that is, for all the profits the company earned on the development of the land. The decision is arguably correct but the reasoning can be criticised. The court referred to the minister's 'breach of fiduciary duty' without specifying what that was. On the facts it is clear that he breached the fair-dealing rule by failing to inform the government of the private valuation. By pursuing the minister's profits, it is clear that any profits he acquired through the increase in the value of his shares in Akita Holdings could also be claimed by the government. So far so simple. The only real question, which was not explored, was whether his brother's profits from Akita's developments should also be claimable by the government. Assuming that his brother was 'dishonest' on *Novoship* principles, he would be. If that assumption was correct, we would have the correct result. But the court should not have short-circuited this inquiry by treating Akita as a 'knowing recipient' of property transferred in breach of fiduciary duty, such that all of Akita's profits could be claimed by the government. Consider this case. Let us assume that Akita's shares were owned by the minister and a genuine third party investor, acting in good faith. Why should that person be stripped of her profits, ie the value of her shares, just because those profits were earned by Akita's development of the land? The right of the principal is to strip *the fiduciary* of any profits he earns in a transaction which breaches his fiduciary relationship with the principal, not to strip everyone else who might profit from the impugned transaction just because they would not, on a but for causal basis, have earned those profits but for the transaction taking place. If that were the law then a principle in such circumstances would be able to set aside the transaction irrespective of its effect on third parties acting in good faith, and that is clearly not the law.

The finding of a fiduciary relationship in untypical cases

13.139 Trustees, agents, and company directors are the classic cases of fiduciary relationship, but the concept has been stretched to cover other cases, sometimes appropriately, sometimes not. A sensible extension of the concept brings the solicitor and client relationship (see eg *Longstaff v Birtles* (2002)), and similar cases of authoritative advice-giving, into the fold. While a solicitor does not usually have true legal powers to affect his client (he does not typically act as the client's agent, strictly speaking), the solicitor does advise his client how to deal with third parties in circumstances where the client essentially follows the solicitor's advice, and so in that sense the solicitor has strong practical powers to affect his client's legal position vis-à-vis those third parties. Clearly if a solicitor were to advise a client to settle an action against a company, not because that was what the client's legal position indicated, but because the solicitor was interested in the company, this would be a breach of loyalty and good faith, which is essentially equivalent to the trustee's or agent's breach of fiduciary obligations.

13.140   However, various inappropriate extensions of the concept have been made, typically in cases where the person named as a 'fiduciary' has committed a legal wrong; a legal wrong that is not just wrong, but can be characterised as one that shows a breach of BFBDL. We have already considered the case of *M (K) v M (H)* (1992) (13.22 et seq) (see also *Norberg v Wynrib* (1992)). Another example of a case where the fiduciary relationship was distorted to achieve a particular result is *Reading v A-G* (1951). A sergeant in the British Army stationed in Egypt assisted smugglers by riding in their lorries wearing his uniform so that they would not be stopped at check points. The British authorities seized £20,000 of the money he was paid for these services. In an action to recover the money Reading argued that while he had obtained it wrongfully, the Crown had no right to retain it; the HL held that as a non-commissioned officer he stood in a fiduciary relationship to the Crown and therefore he was liable to account to the Crown for any profits he obtained by the misuse of his position. Only on the very strained rationale that Reading, by wearing his uniform, had the practical power to affect the Crown's practical interests, by affecting the reputation of the Crown in Egypt, could Reading be regarded as a fiduciary.

13.141   Much the better explanation is simply that the terminology of fiduciary was fictitiously applied to Reading in order to provide a basis for stripping him of his ill-gotten gain, ie to treat it as an 'unauthorised profit' (13.76 et seq); the case would better have been dealt with openly as one in which the principles of restitution or gain-stripping for a wrong should be applied (see Jones (1968); 12.67; 13.128).

13.142   The case of bare trusts raises an interesting question regarding the scope and nature of fiduciary obligations. Recall that for fiduciary obligations to arise, there must be some scope for discretion or leeway in the fiduciary's performance of his duties. No such discretion or leeway arises in the case of the nomineeship (2.13) because, in such cases, the trustee is only to follow his beneficiary's instructions exactly. If the nominee breaches the trust in some way, he will certainly be liable for breach of trust but, as we know (13.6 et seq), not all breaches of trust are breaches of fiduciary obligation. For example, a nominee might mistakenly do something he was not directed to do such as paying trust money away to the wrong person; that would not constitute a breach of fiduciary obligation, because it would not be a consequence of the trustee favouring his own self-interests over those of his beneficiary. Now here's the tricky issue: since a nominee is not empowered to take decisions off his own bat that legally bind his beneficiary, *any* decision he takes off his own bat will be a wrong per se, a clear breach of trust, because in that case he will not be following his beneficiary's instructions. And as we have just seen, the mere commission of a wrong does not become a breach of fiduciary obligation because it shows that the wrongdoer favoured his own interest over that of the person he wronged. Thus, one can argue that, because the nominee never undertook to act as a decision-maker for his beneficiary, he cannot be a fiduciary to him, and so cannot commit a breach of fiduciary obligation. In other words, since there are no decisions that he could *legitimately* take off his own bat, while he can commit various wrongs (breaches of trust) there is nothing that he can do which could amount to a breach of fiduciary obligation. This reasoning seems to underlie the Canadian decision in *RH Deacon & Co Ltd v Varga* (1972). A stockbroker was instructed to buy shares in a company in which it itself held an interest. The court found no breach of fiduciary obligation, since the broker did not exercise any discretion in making the purchase. As Weinrib (1975) puts it: 'There was nothing that had to be controlled by the imposition of the fiduciary obligation.'

13.143   While this line of reason is appealing, and seems to flow from a cogent characterisation of the rationale behind the imposition of fiduciary obligations outlined earlier, it was not accepted by Cross J in *Re Brooke Bond & Co Ltd's Trust Deed* (1963). The case concerned a *custodian trustee* (10.63), a nominee who takes directions from a *managing trustee* rather from the beneficiaries. Clearly the managing trustee had fiduciary obligations to the beneficiaries, but did the custodian trustee? In this case the custodian trustee was an insurance company, and the managing trustee decided that the trust should take out a policy of insurance to protect the beneficiaries' interests in the trust fund. The managing trustee decided to take out the trust policy with the custodian trustee in its capacity as an insurance company. Now if the custodian trustee was a regular trustee with fiduciary obligations, taking out an insurance policy for the trust with itself would have been prohibited, because there would have been a clear conflict of interest, and a violation of the self-dealing rule. But why was such a transaction prohibited here, given that the managing trustee had made the decision, the custodian trustee having no discretion to make the policy with itself? Cross J held that the transaction could be set aside, although the reasons he gave for his decision do not go to the root of the matter in any detailed way. Rather, he seems to have just felt that a trustee of whatever kind, including a custodian trustee, is subject to the self-dealing rule so long as the trustee is a party to a contract entered into on behalf of the trust.

13.144   In *Paragon Finance plc v Thakerar & Co* (1999), however, a clearly wrongful act by a fiduciary, indeed a trustee, who dealt with the trust property held under a bare trust with mandate in a way that (if the allegations of fraud were correct) clearly manifested his acting in his own best interests in total disregard of those of his beneficiary, was not regarded as a breach of any fiduciary obligation under the trust. As it appears that the obligations the solicitors had with respect to the trust property were limited to carrying out the terms of the land purchase trust, which gave them no discretion as to how to deal with the trust money, this decision seems to affirm the view that there can be no breach of a fiduciary obligation except where a person acts to favour his own self-interest within the scope of a discretion undertaken to permit him to serve the interests of another. Since the solicitors had no discretions to exercise over the trust money, they therefore had no fiduciary obligations in respect of it, and therefore their fraudulent disposition of the money could not be a breach of any fiduciary obligation in respect of it—rather, it was just a fraud. Their being solicitor-trustees just put them in a good position to carry it out. They did, however, clearly breach the BFBDL.

FURTHER READING

Birks (ed) (1994b, vol II, Pt IV; 1997b)

Brownbill (1993, Pt VI)

Chambers (2005b, 2013b)

Conaglen (2007)

Crilley (1994)

Davies (2015a)

Dignam and Lowry (2010), ch 14

Edelman (2010)

Ho (1998)

Lowry (1997)

Lowry and Edmonds (1998)

Miller (2011, 2013, 2014)

Millett (1998a)

Penner (2012, 2014c, 2014d, 2019b)

Smith (2003b, 2013a, 2014a)

Swadling (1997)

Valsan (2016)

Watt (2013)

Weinrib (1975)

Must-read cases: *Re Duke of Norfolk's Settlement Trusts* (1981); *Keech v Sandford* (1776); *Re Gee* (1948); *Boardman v Phipps* (1966); *Regal (Hastings) Ltd v Gulliver* (1942); *Lister & Co v Stubbs* (1890); *Holder v Holder* (1968); *A-G for Hong Kong v Reid* (1993); *Sinclair Investments (UK) Ltd v Versailles Trade Finance Ltd* (2011); *FHR European Ventures LLP v Mankarious* (2013)

SELF-TEST QUESTIONS

1.   Discuss the scope and rationale for the conflict of interest rule as it governs a fiduciary's personal profits, and the remedies available to a principal or beneficiary where the fiduciary is liable under the rule.

2.   Andrew is a farmer, who farms his own land and also manages and farms the land of Frank. Andrew recently purchased a load of seed cheaply, and now realises it is more than he can use on his own farm. He plants a ton of the seed on Frank's land, and charges Frank the going price, making a profit of £600. An agent of Superseeds Ltd rings up Andrew at his manager's office on Frank's farm and asks whether Frank will grow a new genetically modified tomato Superseeds has developed. Frank has a policy against growing genetically modified crops, and Andrew offers to grow the tomato on his own farm. The crop does spectacularly well, earning Andrew a profit of £20,000. Finally, Andrew offers to purchase half of Frank's acreage. He provides Frank with the accounts of his management of Frank's farm; they are in such disarray that it is impossible to determine how profitable the operation is, but Frank sells anyway. Discuss Andrew's liability to Frank.

3.   In what circumstances, if any, should a fiduciary hold any unauthorised profit on constructive trust for his principal?

4.   Arthur is the director and chief operating officer of Smartco, a clothing manufacturer. In 2003, he purchased, on behalf of the company, £15,000 worth of fabric from a company in which both he and his wife have a major shareholding. Later in the same year, he moved the head office of Smartco to Guildford, in Surrey, where he lives, so as to reduce his need to commute. The move cost the company approximately £150,000. The company's solicitor, Derek, carried out the necessary conveyancing work, earning a fee of £20,000. In early 2004, Smartco acquired a controlling interest in Splash Ltd, a swimwear manufacturer, and Arthur used the Smartco shares in Splash to vote himself on to

Splash's board of directors, taking £10,000 director's fees. As a director of Splash, Arthur discovered it was undervalued, and purchased the remaining shares of Splash for himself. Following a reorganisation of Splash largely brought about through Arthur's efforts, its shares have increased in value by 50 per cent. Advise Smartco.

5.   'Fiduciary obligations are not 'free-standing' like the duty to take care in making trust investments, or the duty to keep the trust accounts. As the various rules governing fiduciaries demonstrate, they are 'auxiliary' rules in the sense that they ensure that the fiduciary exercises his various powers with the proper motive in mind.' Discuss.

14

Charitable trusts

SUMMARY

Introduction
Fiscal benefits
The conditions for charitable status
The charitable character of public purpose trusts
Trusts for the relief of poverty
Trusts for the advancement of education
Trusts for the advancement of religion
Trusts for other purposes beneficial to the community
The public benefit requirement
A charity must be for exclusively charitable purposes
Preservation from failure: the cy-près doctrine

Introduction

14.1   Charity has no essential connection with the law of trusts, as Matthews (1996) explains:

> [Charity] derived from the ecclesiastical jurisdiction, not from that of the Chancery.
> Charity did not need to be performed through the medium of the trust. It was not so
> in English law at the outset, and even today it need not be. It could, for example, be
> carried out through a company. And many legal systems have well developed laws of
> charity without recourse to, indeed without any knowledge of, trusts. It is a historical
> accident that the Court of Chancery hijacked the charitable gift and squeezed it (with
> some difficulty) into the pre-existing framework of the trust.

While there are some particular features of charitable trusts (as opposed to charitable
corporations) that concern their nature as trusts per se (eg aspects of the cy-près doctrine,
14.56 et seq), this topic largely comprises particular aspects of the law of charities. Be warned,
therefore, that what you learn here will, for the most part, have only marginal relevance to what
else you have learned in this book, which is why it is at the end. The topic is, however, invariably
covered in trusts courses, most likely because it is easy, providing at least one exam question on
which all can do well. It also makes a welcome change for those who dislike studying trusts, and
for those who dislike teaching it.

14.2   Charitable purposes are (1) purposes that benefit the public, which (2) on the authority of statute and common law are 'charitable'. Not all publicly beneficial purposes are considered by the law to be charitable. The question, 'What counts as a charitable purpose?' has been the source of a constant supply of case law, and has been the subject of recent legislation in the form of the Charities Acts 2006 and 2011. The 2011 Act, which came into force on 14 March 2012, repeals and replaces the Recreational Charities Act 1958, the Charities Act 1993, and most of the substantive provisions (without significant changes) of the 2006 Act save for Part 3, which concerns fund-raising.

14.3   Charitable trusts are not subject to the requirement of certainty of objects, or at least not in the same sense as private trusts are. A testamentary trust for 'charitable objects', without further speci-fication, is valid. The court (or the Charity Commissioners) will specify those objects to which the trust funds should be devoted. Moreover, as has been confirmed by the UKSC in *Shergill v Khaira* (2014), where a settlor creates a trust in general or vague terms, the trustees have the power and the obligation to execute a trust deed which gives practical contours to how the trust funds are to be spent, so long as it does not conflict with the broad purpose the settlor intended. Charitable trusts are also not subject to the beneficiary principle (9.2). Charitable trusts are valid purpose trusts that are enforced, not by beneficiaries, but by the Attorney-General or, more recently, by the Charity Commission (formerly the Charity Commissioners). The Charity Commission is the regulator of charities in England and Wales, which not only registers charities, but has broad powers to moni-tor the accounts of charitable trusts, investigating the running of charities to check abuses, and ad-vise charitable trustees. (For a comprehensive consideration of the role of the Charity Commission in maintaining and reviewing the register of charities, see Mitchell (2000).) An appeal from deci-sions of the Commission lies in the first instance to the First Tier Tribunal or the Upper Tribunal, depending on the issue. Charitable trusts can last forever, and on that score are not subject to the rule against perpetuities (3.49). (Charitable gifts that are determinable or made upon condition subsequent, are, however, subject to the rule as it applies to gifts of that kind.)

Fiscal benefits

14.4   Charities are generally exempt from income tax, capital gains tax, corporation tax, and stamp duty, although, with minor exceptions, they do have to pay VAT on the goods and services they purchase. They are also able to claim an 80 per cent rebate on business rates for their non-residential property and local councils may refund the remaining 20 per cent on a discre-tionary basis. Relief from inheritance tax, capital gains tax, and income tax is also available for donors who give to charities. Charities are not taxed on the profits they earn from trading so long as the profits are applied to charitable purposes and the trading carries out the purpose of the charity (14.55). Finally, charities may also reclaim income tax paid by donors on money given to charity; thus a charity will be able to claim £20 from Revenue and Customs if it receives a gift of £100 from a donor who pays income tax at the basic rate of 20 per cent.

Dissociating validity from exemption from taxation

14.5   In *Dingle v Turner* (1972) Lord Cross suggested in an *obiter dictum* that:

[T]he courts—as I see it—cannot avoid having regard to the fiscal privileges accorded to charities…[T]hey enjoy immunity from the rules against perpetuity and uncertainty and although individual potential beneficiaries cannot sue to enforce them the public interest arising under them is protected by the Attorney-General. If this was all there would be no reason for the courts not to look favourably on the claim of any 'purpose' trust to be considered a charity if it seemed calculated to confer some real benefit on those intended to benefit by it whoever they might be and if it would fail if not held to be a charity. But that is not all. Charities automatically enjoy fiscal privileges which with the increased burden of taxation have become more and more important and in deciding that such and such a trust is a charitable trust the court is endowing it with a substantial annual subsidy at the expense of the taxpayer…It is, of course, unfortunate that the recognition of any trust as a valid charitable trust should automatically attract fiscal privileges, for the question whether a trust to further some purpose is so little likely to benefit the public that it ought to be declared invalid and the question whether it is likely to confer such great benefits on the public that it should enjoy fiscal immunity are really two quite different questions.

14.6   Misgivings about the automatic provision of fiscal benefits to charities have a long history (see in particular the dissenting judgments of Lord Halsbury LC and Lord Bramwell in *Income Tax Special Purposes Comrs v Pemsel* (1891)). The concern, well expressed by Lord Cross, is that there seems to be no obvious reason why fiscal benefits should automatically be accorded to every non-private purpose, since such purposes will vary in the extent to which they confer genuinely public benefits. Consider, for example, student unions. These are charitable on the grounds that they contribute to the education of university students, the concept of 'education' obviously being construed broadly here. Does a student union really provide public benefits in the way that, say, a charity for research into the causes and prevention of cancer does? To take another example, is the practice of religious rites or the education provided by public schools as beneficial to the public as the support of cultural institutions such as the National Gallery?

14.7   The idea is sometimes mooted that the state ought to give money directly to those 'true' charities which confer a genuinely public benefit (eg Chesterman (1999)). But the difficulties with dissociating fiscal advantages from charitable status must also be acknowledged. If the law were changed so that only charities providing certain public benefits received fiscal advantages, this would require a new definition of, or graded scale for, 'public benefit', and this might be complex and hard to apply, and might seem to raise the question why purposes with insufficient public benefit should be treated as charitable at all, never mind the fiscal advantages. In other words, while there seems to be obvious force in Lord Cross's *obiter dictum*, it might beg the question: the real problem is not dissociating fiscal advantage from charitable status, but rather that charitable status has, over time, with the expansion of purposes deemed to be charitable (14.9 et seq), become only weakly connected to public benefit in at least some cases—if qualifying as a charity indeed entailed that the purpose provided a genuinely public benefit, then every charity would *deserve* its advantages drawn from the *public* purse because every charity would indeed genuinely benefit the *public*; it would, in these circumstances, be irrational or perverse for the public to tax charities, for by doing so it would only be taxing itself. Moreover, the proposal that automatic fiscal benefits should be replaced by direct government grants to particular charities has difficulties of its own. If the government of the day were able to subsidise whichever charities in whatever amounts it liked, then one is faced with the concern that the independence of charities to pursue public goals that might be politically unpopular would be discouraged, leading some charities at least to tailor their purposes for political reasons; furthermore, smaller charities that could not muster the political support to lobby for a state subsidy would be unfairly disadvantaged. In any case, it is clear that the question of justifying fiscal benefits is intertwined with the requirement that charities confer a *public* benefit, and so the fiscal background should be borne in mind when we consider that requirement in detail later (14.33 et seq). A last point can be made here about fiscal advantages: occasionally, students declare in their exam scripts that one of the main purposes of creating a charity is to obtain tax advantages, but this is misconceived: no settler of a charitable trust personally receives any ongoing tax advantages from doing so. It is the charity itself which obtains ongoing tax relief, tax relief which benefits the charity, not anyone else. By creating a charity one devotes property to a *public* purpose; one does not engineer a private benefit with special tax advantages. Trying to use the law of charity to achieve this sort of result is impermissible in principle though, as we will see (14.40), there are borderline cases.

The conditions for charitable status

14.8 In order for a purpose to be charitable:

- the *character* of the purpose must be charitable;
- the purpose must, on balance, be beneficial rather than detrimental;
- the purpose must benefit a section of the public, not a collection of private individuals or an artificially restricted class;
- the purpose must be *exclusively* charitable, and in particular, the purpose must not be political; and
- the purpose must not include making a financial profit, not in the sense that a charity like a university cannot make an operating profit in any one year, but in the sense that a charity may not distribute profits to investors in the way a private business can.

The charitable character of public purpose trusts

14.9 The Charities Act 2011 provides a list of those purposes which the law regards as charitable, though one can only make sense of and interpret this new statutory list of charitable purposes in light of the previous law, so we will look at that in some detail. The relevant sections of the act are as follows:

2   Meaning of 'charitable purpose'

(1) *For the purposes of the law of England and Wales, a charitable purpose is a purpose which—*

(a) *falls within section 3(1), and*

    (b) is for the public benefit (see section 4).

  (2) Any reference in any enactment or document (in whatever terms)—

    (a) to charitable purposes, or

    (b) to institutions having purposes that are charitable under the law relating to charities in England and Wales, is to be read in accordance with subsection (1).

  (3) Subsection (2) does not apply where the context otherwise requires.

  (4) This section is subject to section 11 (which makes special provision for Chapter 2 of this Part onwards).

3   *Descriptions of purposes*

  (1) A purpose falls within this subsection if it falls within any of the following descriptions of purposes—

    (a) the prevention or relief of poverty;

    (b) the advancement of education;

    (c) the advancement of religion;

    (d) the advancement of health or the saving of lives;

    (e) the advancement of citizenship or community development;

    (f) the advancement of the arts, culture, heritage or science;

    (g) the advancement of amateur sport;

    (h) the advancement of human rights, conflict resolution or reconciliation or the promotion of religious or racial harmony or equality and diversity;

    (i) the advancement of environmental protection or improvement;

    (j) the relief of those in need because of youth, age, ill-health, disability, financial hardship or other disadvantage;

    (k) the advancement of animal welfare;

    (l) the promotion of the efficiency of the armed forces of the Crown or of the efficiency of the police, fire and rescue services or ambulance services;

    (m) any other purposes—

      (i) that are not within paragraphs (a) to (l) but are recognised as charitable purposes by virtue of section 5 (recreational and similar trusts, etc.) or under the old law,

      (ii) that may reasonably be regarded as analogous to, or within the spirit of, any purposes falling within any of paragraphs (a) to (l) or sub-paragraph (i), or

      (iii) that may reasonably be regarded as analogous to, or within the spirit of, any purposes which have been recognised, under the law relating to charities in England and Wales, as falling within sub-paragraph (ii) or this sub-paragraph.

  (2) In subsection (1)—

    (a) in paragraph (c), 'religion' includes—(i)a religion which involves belief in more than one god, and(ii)a religion which does not involve belief in a god,

    (b) in paragraph (d), 'the advancement of health' includes the prevention or relief of sickness, disease or human suffering,

(c) paragraph (e) includes—
    (i) rural or urban regeneration, and

    (ii) the promotion of civic responsibility, volunteering, the voluntary sector or
         the effectiveness or efficiency of charities,

(d) in paragraph (g), 'sport' means sports or games which promote health by
    involving physical or mental skill or exertion,

(e) paragraph (j) includes relief given by the provision of accommodation or care
    to the persons mentioned in that paragraph, and

(f) in paragraph (l), 'fire and rescue services' means services provided by fire and
    rescue authorities under Part 2 of the Fire and Rescue Services Act 2004.

(3) Where any of the terms used in any of paragraphs (a) to (l) of subsection (1), or
    in subsection (2), has a particular meaning under the law relating to charities in
    England and Wales, the term is to be taken as having the same meaning where it
    appears in that provision.

(4) In subsection (1)(m)(i), 'the old law' means the law relating to charities in England
    and Wales as in force immediately before 1 April 2008.

14.10 We will refer to each these provisions as we go along, but look first at ss 2(1)(a) and 3(1).
Together they could be said to give the statutory meaning of charitable purpose, but it is important to see that this does *not* constitute a legal *definition* of charitable purpose in any real
sense. All it does is refer to a list of charitable purposes. A true definition would be some
characterisation of charitable purpose which could be applied by itself to a prospective purpose to determine if it were charitable. These provisions clearly do not do that. The list of
charitable purposes in s 3(1), elaborated in some cases in s 3(2), only makes sense against the
categorisation of charitable purposes which operated prior to the 2006 and 2011 Acts and, indeed s 3(1)(m)(i) preserves as charitable any purpose recognised under the pre-2008 law, so it
is to that prior learning that we now turn.

14.11 Prior to the 2006 and 2011 Acts the law recognised as charitable those purposes found in the
Preamble to the Charitable Uses Act 1601, or purposes that the case law held to be 'analogous'
to those in the Preamble and within its 'spirit and intendment'. The relevant section of the
Preamble is as follows:

> some [property given] for relief of aged, impotent and poor people, some for the
> maintenance of sick and maimed soldiers and mariners, schools of learning, free
> schools, and scholars in universities; some for repair of bridges, ports, havens, causeways,
> churches, sea banks and highways; some for education and preferment of orphans;
> some for or towards the relief, stock, or maintenance of houses of correction; some
> for marriages of poor maids; some for supporting, aid and help of young tradesmen,
> handicraftsmen and persons decayed; and others for relief or redemption of prisoners
> or captives, and for aid or ease of any poor inhabitants concerning payment of fifteens,
> setting out of soldiers and other taxes…

It seems that in 1601 this list consisted almost entirely of purposes that would directly work
a public benefit by lowering the local rates, since the persons and projects named would
otherwise have been financially supported by the parish; thus an individual who devoted his
funds to such purposes provided a very tangible public benefit indeed. There is a school of
thought that holds that even today tax relief afforded to charities can only be justified to the

extent that these charities provide services that would otherwise require the allocation of state funds. (Consider this point in relation to our discussion of fiscal advantages in 14.5 – 14.7.)

14.12   Basing himself on the guidance the Preamble provided, in *Income Tax Special Purposes Comrs v Pemsel* (1891), Lord Macnaghten produced his famous fourfold characterisation of what is charitable:

> *Charity in its legal sense comprises four principal divisions: trusts for the relief of pov- erty; trusts for the advancement of education; trusts for the advancement of religion; and trusts for other purposes beneficial to the community, not falling under any of the preceding heads.*

The first three divisions appear as the first three charitable purposes in the new statutory list, while the remaining purposes in the list are fruitfully regarded as the 'spelling out' of the last, catch-all category.

Growth by analogy

14.13   In *Scottish Burial Reform and Cremation Society Ltd v Glasgow Corpn* (1968) the HL decided that the Scottish Burial Reform Society, a non-profit-making company whose main object was the inexpensive, sanitary disposal of the dead, particularly by cremation, was a charity. Lord Reid stated:

> *[The] benefit [must be] of a kind within the spirit and intendment of the [Charitable Uses Act 1601]. The preamble specifies a number of objects which were then recognised as charitable. But in more recent times a wide variety of other objects have come to be recognised as also being charitable. The courts appear to have proceeded first by seeking some analogy between an object mentioned in the preamble and the object with regard to which they had to reach a decision. Then they appear to have gone further, and to have been satisfied if they could find an analogy between an object already held to be charitable and the new object claimed to be charitable.*

A perhaps strained use of this extension of charitable purposes by analogy occurred in *Vancouver Regional Freenet Association v Minister of National Revenue* (1996). The Canadian Federal Court of Appeal drew an analogy between the provision of free internet access, ie access to the 'information highway', to the Preamble's 'repair of bridges, ports, havens, causeways, churches, sea banks and highways', to decide that such provision was charitable.

14.14   This 'extension by analogy' approach to the identification of new charitable purposes has at times been regarded as out of date (see the judgment of Russell LJ in *Incorporated Council of Law Reporting for England and Wales v A-G* (1971)), but as is clear from s 3(1)(m)(ii) and (iii) of the 2011 Act, the use of analogy to extend the scope of charitable purposes has now been given a statutory footing.

14.15   The history of this expansion by analogy is not a particularly honourable one. Worries about testators disinheriting their families through gifts to the Church and other charities led to the Mortmain and Charitable Uses Act 1736 (now repealed), which made most gifts of land on trust to charities void. Apparently favouring disinherited family members over charities, judges slowly expanded the boundaries of what counted as charitable so as to bring about the failure of as many gifts as possible under the Act. In particular, the wide scope for what counts as religion can be explained in part by the fact that a wide definition ensured that gifts of land to all sects were equally struck down. In the famous case of *Thornton v Howe* (1862), a gift on trust to publish the writings of Joanna Southcott, 'an ignorant and foolish woman' who believed herself with child by the Holy Spirit and about to give birth to the new Messiah, was held to be charitable, therefore void under the Act.

14.16 Very occasionally, a purpose once regarded as charitable ceases to be so. In 1993 the Charity Commissioners deregistered gun and rifle associations (formerly found to be charitable in *Re Stephens* (1892)) as no longer charitable in view of changed social circumstances (*The City of London Rifle and Pistol Club; The Burnley Rifle Club* (1993)). When an organisation seeks registration as a charity, both the Charity Commission and the courts (*Southwood v A-G* (2000)) will consider the organisation's activities and proposed activities when trying to determine whether its purpose is charitable, although this is to be understood as evidence going to help the court determine the nature of the purpose itself. Where an organisation's purpose is charitable, any activities the organisation undertakes which fail to advance that purpose do not undermine the charitability of the purpose itself; rather, the carrying out of those activities with charitable funds will be a breach of charity law (*Independent Schools Council v Charity Commission for England and Wales* (2011)).

Trusts for the relief of poverty

14.17 Poverty does not mean destitution; trusts for poverty are for those who would otherwise have to 'go short' (*Re Coulthurst* (1951)), so trusts for 'ladies of limited means' (*Re Gardom* (1914)) and for 'decayed actors' (*Spiller v Maude* (1881)) were valid. The charity can be limited to particular classes so long as it does not name individuals, nor include those who might not be poor. So trusts for poor employees (*Dingle v Turner* (1972)), or an individual's poor relations (*Re Scarisbrick* (1951); *Re Segelman* (1996)) are good, but a trust benefiting the working classes was not because being a member of the working class did not necessarily entail poverty (*Re Sanders' Will Trusts* (1954)), nor was a trust for providing clothing to boys aged 10–15 years in a certain district, since eligibility was not restricted to the poor (*Re Gwyon* (1930)). In *Re Niyazi's Will Trusts* (1978) a trust for a working man's hostel in Famagusta, Cyprus, where there was a grave housing shortage, was upheld as charitable, although Megarry VC opined that the trust was 'desperately near the border-line'.

Trusts for the advancement of education

14.18 This head obviously includes conventional education and training: thus trusts for schools, colleges, universities, and other institutions of learning are valid. But this head extends to cover research, artistic and aesthetic education (*Royal Choral Society v IRC* (1943)), museums (*British Museum Trustees v White* (1826)), sport facilities provided for the young at school (*Re Mariette* (1915)), student unions (*London Hospital Medical College v IRC* (1976)), and professional bodies so long as they advance education (*Royal College of Surgeons of England v National Provincial Bank Ltd* (1952)). However, courts are careful to ensure that this head is not used to provide charitable status for political purposes masquerading as education or research (14.22).

14.19   Education of the young must be taken in a broader sense than mere classroom learning. In *IRC v McMullen* (1980) a trust for the provision of facilities to play association football or other sports in schools or universities was held valid. In *Baldry v Feintuck* (1972) the charitable status of student unions was affirmed as part of the educational enterprise, but the devotion of funds to political campaigns by student unions on issues not related to university education (see further 14.47) was not, and could be restrained by injunction (see also *Webb v O'Doherty* (1991)). However, the fact that a student union provides facilities to political clubs does not invalidate its charitable status.

14.20   The education head also covers the dissemination of useful knowledge. It was upon this basis that the CA decided that the production of the Law Reports was a charitable advancement of education in *Incorporated Council of Law Reporting v A-G*. It also covers the promotion of culture: in *Re Delius* (1957) a charity to promote the music of Delius was good.

14.21   Carrying out useful research is charitable under the education head as well, but the limits of charitable research are not entirely clear: in *Re Shaw* (1957) George Bernard Shaw's testamentary gift of funds to be devoted to research into a 40-letter alphabet for English and the translation of one of his works into the new alphabet was held to be not charitable; this was probably a narrow decision, based on the idea that the gift did not contemplate education or teaching. In contrast, in *Re Hopkins' Will Trusts* (1965) a gift to the Francis Bacon Society 'to be earmarked and applied towards finding the Bacon-Shakespeare manuscripts', ie to finding evidence that Francis Bacon wrote the works attributed to Shakespeare, was valid under the education head, on the basis that such a discovery would be of immense importance. In *McGovern v A-G* (1982) Slade J summarised the principles:

> A trust for research will ordinarily qualify as a charitable trust if, but only if, (a) the subject matter of the proposed research is a useful subject of study; and (b) it is contemplated that knowledge acquired [thereby] will be disseminated to others; and (c) the trust is for the benefit of the public, or a sufficiently important section of the public. (2) In the absence of a contrary context, however, the court will [readily construe] a trust for research as importing subsequent dissemination of the results thereof. (3) Furthermore, if a trust for research is to constitute a valid trust for the advancement of education, it is not necessary either (a) that a teacher/pupil relationship should be in contemplation or (b) that the persons to benefit from the knowledge to be acquired should be [students] in the conventional sense. (4)...[the court] must pay due regard to any admissible extrinsic evidence which is available to explain the wording of the will in question or the circumstances in which it was made.

14.22   The production of mere propaganda is not the advancement of education. *Re Hopkinson* (1949) is one of several cases in which trusts for educating adults in the principles of particular political parties were held invalid, in which the oft-cited words of Vaisey J appear: 'political propaganda . . . masquerading as education is not education within the statute of Elizabeth'. *Re Koeppler's Will Trusts* (1986) concerned a trust for carrying on the work of the 'Wilton Park' Institution, which ran conferences for representatives of member nations of major Western organisations to exchange views on political, economic, and social issues; although political figures participated, the conferences did not further any particular political viewpoint, and the trust was charitable under the education head.

Trusts for the advancement of religion

14.23   In general, the law of charities assumes that any religion is better than none but, as between religions, stands neutral (*Neville Estates Ltd v Madden* (1962) *per* Cross J). Case law prior to the 2006 Act held that religion required a spiritual belief or faith in some higher unseen power, and some worship or veneration of that higher power; the consequence was that promoting morality or particular ethical ways of life did not count as a religious purpose. Thus, in *Re South Place Ethical Society* (1980) Dillon J said: 'Religion is concerned with man's relations with God, and ethics are concerned with man's relations with man.' The trust in question, one for the study and dissemination of ethical principles and the cultivation of a rational religious sentiment, was not charitable under the religion head, but was as a trust for the advancement of education, as well as under the fourth head as contributing to mental or moral improvement. In *Shergill v Khaira* (2014) a dispute arose between two factions over the proper interpretation of a trust for religious purposes. Overturning the view of the CA who held that the court could not pronounce on issues regarding who was right or wrong on religious matters, as being non-justiciable, the UKSC held that although the court could not pronounce on the truth of religious doctrines, where rights over the proper applications of trust funds were concerned the court might in the right case have to decide such religious issues as could be objectively determined. The decision was interlocutory, concerning permission to amend the particulars of the claimants' claim, so the court did not have to apply this ruling to the facts. The central question was whether a particular individual was rightly the 'successor saint' to a predecessor, and it would have been interesting to see how the court might have objectively determined that. In *R v Registrar General, ex p Segerdal* (1970) the 'Church' of Scientology, based upon the American L Ron Hubbard's theory of 'dianetics', was held to be a philosophy of existence, not a religion, so not a charity. In the Australian case, *Church of the New Faith v Comr for Payroll Tax* (1983), Scientology was held charitable under the religion head: the court considered any 'belief in a supernatural Being, Thing, or Principle' to be sufficient so long as that belief was combined with canons of conduct giving effect to that belief. By contrast the Charity Commissioners (1999) considered an application by the Church of Scientology for registration as a charity, but denied it charitable status. While adherents believed in a higher power, their practices of training and auditing were more akin to therapy or study than to worship, so Scientology was held not to be a religion. Scientology also failed the public benefit test (14.33 et seq) because its activities were only for the private benefit of its practising adherents. You will see, however, that s 3(2)(a) widens the definition of religion to ensure that multi-deity faiths (such as Hinduism) or *non-deity faiths* (such as some types of Buddhism) now also clearly qualify. This raises the question whether the 'worship and veneration' requirement mentioned above continues to operate, since where a religion has no deity it is not clear there is anything to venerate or worship. In part relying upon these provisions, the UKSC has recently held in *Hodkin v Registrar General of Births, Deaths and Marriages* (2013) that the Church of Scientology is a religion for the purposes of the Places of Worship Registration Act 1855. Although the court's finding that Scientology fell within the definition of religion under s 3(2)(a) is strictly speaking *obiter* as regards the application of the Charities Act, it would be unlikely in the extreme for a subsequent UKSC or the Charity Commission to take a different view. Section 3(2)(a) shows that, in bringing in the new Act, the government did not question whether the recognition of the advancement of religion as charitable (so providing religion with the fiscal benefits flowing from that) was justified in a predominantly secular society. If charitable status had been withdrawn from religion that would not, of course, have meant that religious organisations would lose all association with charity. Many, perhaps most, religious organisations carry out non-religious charitable activities, such as the relief of poverty, the provision of education, the maintenance of historic buildings, and so on, and so religious organisations carrying out these activities would to that extent remain charitable; a proposal to deny charitable status to religion per se would deny that status to those activities such as the performance of religious rites, to proselytising, and so on. It is the according of charitable status to activities of that kind to which a reform of charities law would be directed, simply because it is not clear how these activities benefit the public (14.33 et seq), rather than just the adherents of the particular religion, whose beliefs are often very controversial (see also Penner (2016)). As has been said before, the problem with the death of God is not that people believe in nothing, but that people will believe in anything: crystals, dolphins, the summer solstice, heaven only knows what nonsense; where, one might ask, is the public benefit in such belief? Since the coming into force of the 2006 Act there has not, apparently, been a stampede to register new religious charities. Thank heaven for small mercies.

Trusts for other purposes beneficial to the community

14.24 For obvious reasons, this is the most difficult category for which to define what counts as charitable, and the 'growth by analogy' approach is most evident here. Perhaps the easiest case is a gift to a locality, such as a village or town (eg *Re Allen* (1905)), or even England (*Re Smith* (1932)), which will be treated as a gift for charitable purposes unless non-charitable purposes for the gift are clearly specified (eg *A-G Cayman Islands v Wahr-Hansen* (2001), where the objects included 'worthy individuals'). In *Williams' Trustees v IRC* (1947) there was a gift on trust to establish and maintain an institute, to be known as the 'London Welsh Association', the purposes of which included maintaining an institute for the benefit of Welsh people in London, and promoting their language and culture. The various activities of the institute included lectures, dances, games, and provision of facilities for clubs. These purposes and activities not being exclusively charitable, the trust failed. Lord Simonds quoted Viscount Cave LC in *A-G v National Provincial and Union Bank of England* (1924):

> it is not enough to say that the trust in question is for public purposes beneficial to the community; you must also show it to be a charitable trust;

Nor did the gift count as a gift to a locality. Lord Simonds said:

> If the purposes are not charitable per se, the localisation of them will not make them charitable.

Thus for a purpose under the fourth head to be charitable, it must be one of those found to be so in the 'old law' (s 3(1)(m)(i), (4)), or one of those listed in s 3(1) of the 2011 Act, or one that the courts are prepared to hold for the first time is analogous to one of those (s 3(1)(m)(ii) and (iii)). Simply because the gift is beneficial to a particular community is entirely insufficient.

14.25 The Preamble specifically mentions the 'relief of aged, impotent and poor people'. This passage is construed disjunctively, and this is reflected in s 3(1), so trusts for the provision of housing for the aged are charitable (*Joseph Rowntree Memorial Trust Housing Association Ltd v A-G* (1983)), as are trusts for blind children (*Re Lewis* (1955)), the seriously ill or wounded (*Re Hillier* (1944)), the permanently disabled (*Re Fraser* (1883)), and trusts for hospitals, even if they charge fees to patients, so long as they are not profit-distributing (*Re Resch's Will Trusts* (1969)); the same reasoning applied to make independent schools that charge fees charitable (*Independent Schools Council* (2011), 14.16, 14.33 et seq). Trusts for the relief of victims of disasters are charitable (*Re North Devon and West Somerset Relief Fund Trusts* (1953)), but only in so far as they provide relief from poverty, or in the case of sickness or disability, the class is a public one (14.42). The Charity Commission strongly advises those considering launching an appeal to consider whether the funds sought are to be used exclusively for charitable purposes or not and to inform prospective donors accordingly (Charity Commission (2002)).

14.26   Certain public services and facilities are charitable under the fourth head, such as the production of the Law Reports (*Incorporated Council of Law Reporting v A-G* (1971)) and the work of the National Trust (*Re Verrall* (1916)).

14.27   Although apparently far from the concerns evident in the Preamble, trusts for animal welfare such as the Society for the Prevention of Cruelty to Animals (*Tatham v Drummond* (1864)) and the preservation of wildlife through animal sanctuaries (*Re Wedgwood* (1915) (Wild Fowl Trusts)) were charitable even before the coming into force of the 2006 Act. However, in *Re Grove-Grady* (1929), the CA held that a gift for an animal sanctuary that specifically excluded humans so that the animals would not be molested, was not charitable, because such a gift produced no public benefit. Section 3(1)(k) now makes clear that the advancement of animal welfare is a charitable purpose, and *Re Grove-Grady* might be decided differently today applying s 3(1)(i), which provides that environmental protection or improvement is a valid charitable purpose.

14.28   Trusts for sport or recreation have had a difficult time in the past. In *Re Nottage* (1895) trusts for mere sport, here yacht racing, were held not to be charitable purposes. Similarly, in *IRC v City of Glasgow Police Athletic Association* (1953) the HL accepted that trusts that promote the efficiency of the police or the armed forces are charitable, but held that a trust for the purpose of promoting athletic sports and general pastimes for the Glasgow police was not, being more in the nature of a private trust for the advantage of the members. On the other hand, the provision of land for a recreation ground for public use by the community at large is charitable (*Re Hadden* (1932)). In 2003 the Charity Commissioners recognised the promotion of amateur sport as charitable, and this position was confirmed by s 3(1)(g), (2)(d).

14.29   In *IRC v Baddeley* (1955) a trust to be administered by Methodist leaders for the promotion of religious, social, and physical well-being of persons resident in West Ham and Leyton, by the provision of facilities for religious services and instruction and for the social and physical training and recreation of persons, who for the time being were or were likely to become members of the Methodist Church who had insufficient means to otherwise enjoy these advantages, was held not charitable by the HL. These recreational purposes were not charitable because there was insufficient public benefit. Viscount Simonds said that one must observe the distinction:

> between a form of relief accorded to the whole community yet by its very nature advantageous only to the few, and a form of relief accorded to a selected few out of a larger number equally willing and able to take advantage of it...I should in the present case conclude that a trust cannot qualify as a charity within the fourth class...if the beneficiaries are a class of persons not only confined to a particular area but selected within it by reference to a particular creed. The Master of the Rolls in his judgement cites a rhetorical question asked by [counsel]...: 'Who has ever heard of a

bridge to be crossed only by impecunious Methodists?' The reductio ad absurdum is sometimes a cogent form of argument, and this illustration serves to show the danger of conceding the quality of charity to a purpose which is not a public purpose.

The Recreational Charities Act 1958; Charities Act 2011, s 5

14.30   Lord Reid dissented in *Baddeley*, and the law was felt to be in some confusion. In response the Recreational Charities Act 1958 was passed, which is now superseded by s 5 of the 2011 Act, which states:

> **5   Recreational and similar trusts, etc.**
>
> (1)   It is charitable (and is to be treated as always having been charitable) to provide, or assist in the provision of, facilities for—
>
>   (a)   recreation, or
>
>   (b)   other leisure-time occupation, if the facilities are provided in the interests of social welfare.
>
> (2)   The requirement that the facilities are provided in the interests of social welfare cannot be satisfied if the basic conditions are not met.
>
> (3)   The basic conditions are—
>
>   (a)   that the facilities are provided with the object of improving the conditions of life for the persons for whom the facilities are primarily intended, and
>
>   (b)   that—
>
>   (i) those persons have need of the facilities because of their youth, age, infirmity or disability, poverty, or social and economic circumstances, or
>
>   (ii) the facilities are to be available to members of the public at large or to male, or to female, members of the public at large.
>
> (4)   Subsection (1) applies in particular to—
>
>   (a)   the provision of facilities at village halls, community centres and women's institutes, and
>
>   (b)   the provision and maintenance of grounds and buildings to be used for purposes of recreation or leisure-time occupation, and extends to the provision of facilities for those purposes by the organising of any activity.
>
> But this is subject to the requirement that the facilities are provided in the interests of social welfare.
>
> (5)   Nothing in this section is to be treated as derogating from the public benefit requirement.

The Act makes clear that such facilities are subject to the public benefit requirement (s 5(5)), and so it is not clear that it does much more than restate the prior law, except in so far as s 5(3)(b)(1) allows facilities restricted to a class limited on the basis of social and economic circumstances that do not, apparently, simply mean poverty; the other restrictions appear to define classes that have an independent status in the law of charities: gifts for the poor, aged, and impotent are good anyway, and recreational facilities for youth are generally treated as charitable as advancing education. Section 5 does not seem to overturn *Williams v IRC*, *Baddeley*, or the *Glasgow Police* cases.

14.31 In *IRC v McMullen* (1980) the HL decided that the gift for sports fell under the education head, and so did not consider the Recreational Charities Act, but in its 1979 decision in the case the CA did: the majority held that the gift was not 'provided in the interests of social welfare', because it did not merely provide facilities for those deprived; secondly, it was not intended to 'improve the conditions of life of those for whom the facilities were primarily intended', because it was intended as a gift for pupils generally, but would only benefit those who played, irrespective of their conditions in life. Bridge LJ dissented from this 'deprived class' view, saying, 'Hyde Park improves the conditions in life for residents in Mayfair and Belgravia as much as for those in Pimlico or the Portobello Road'. His dissent won the day in the HL in *Guild v IRC* (1992), where a gift for a public sports centre was held to be charitable.

'New' charitable purposes under the 2006 and 2011 Acts

14.32 Section 3(1)(e) and (h) provide that the advancement of 'citizenship or community development' and 'human rights, conflict resolution or reconciliation or the promotion of religious or racial harmony or equality or diversity' are charitable purposes. It is likely, perhaps, that these purposes might have been regarded as charitable prior to the Act in any case, as analogous extensions from purposes such as religion, education, and research, but their specification in the Act makes their status clear. Charities carrying out these purposes are, because of their character, likely to benefit most from the Commission's facilitative attitude toward political campaigning by charities (14.47).

The public benefit requirement

14.33 The law concerning the public benefit requirement has recently been thoroughly reviewed by the Upper Tribunal (Tax and Chancery Chamber), *Independent Schools Council v Charity Commission for England and Wales* (2011). As the decision makes clear, there are two aspects to the public benefit requirement: the first is that for a purpose to be beneficial to the public, it must actually be *beneficial*, not of no value or worse, detrimental; the second is that the purpose must be of benefit to the public as opposed to some private group or artificially restricted section of the public. A charity that operates abroad satisfies the public benefit test if its activities would be charitable if carried out in England (*Re Carapiet's Trust* (2002)).

A detrimental purpose cannot be charitable

14.34 Occasionally the courts make decisions about the ultimate benefits of certain purposes. In *National Anti-Vivisection Society v IRC* (1948), the purpose was found not be charitable as a political purpose (14.43), but in addition to holding that the HL decided to weigh the conflicting moral and material utilities of, on the one hand, the advancement of morals and education that would result from a suppression of vivisection and, on the other, the benefits to medical science and research vivisection afforded. It decided that on balance the suppression of vivisection was not beneficial to the public. It departed from the earlier case *of Re Foveaux* (1895), which held that the court stood neutral on the public benefit of abolishing vivisection. In *Re Hummeltenberg* (1923) a gift for the training of spiritual mediums was held to provide no public benefit, and in the course of his decision in *Re Pinion* (1965), Harman J gave the illustration of schools for prostitutes or pickpockets as purposes that would not be charitable on this score. In the *Independent Schools Council* case, the tribunal rejected the argument that fee-paying schools are detrimental because they impair social mobility and are socially divisive; in the court's view, the issues raised in such an argument required political, not judicial, resolution. In *McGovern v A-G* (14.44) the court considered the possible detriment that Amnesty International's activities might have in the conduct of foreign affairs by the government.

14.35 In the case of religion the court appears to allow charities that it regards as having no benefit whatsoever, as in the case of *Thornton v Howe* (14.15). With respect to detrimental religious purposes, the Church of Scientology was formerly held not to be charitable (14.23), and this may in part have reflected the pronouncements of judges in other cases not concerning Scientology's charitable status: in *Hubbard v Vosper* (1972), Lord Denning said that Scientology was 'dangerous material', and it was described by Goff J as 'pernicious nonsense' in *Church of Scientology v Kaufman* (1973).

The requirement that a section of the public must benefit

14.36 Section 4 of the 2011 Act provides:

> **4   The public benefit requirement**
>
> (1) In this Act 'the public benefit requirement' means the requirement in section 2(1)(b) that a purpose falling within section 3(1) must be for the public bene-fit if it is to be a charitable purpose.
>
> (2) In determining whether the public benefit requirement is satisfied in relation to any purpose falling within section 3(1), it is not to be presumed that a purpose of a particular description is for the public benefit.
>
> (3) In this Chapter any reference to the public benefit is a reference to the public benefit as that term is understood for the purposes of the law relating to charities in England and Wales.
>
> (4) Subsection (3) is subject to subsection (2).

Section 4 of the 2006 Act and ss 14, 15(2) and (3), and 17 of the 2011 Act require the Charity Commission to issue guidance to charities and prospective charities on the public benefit re-quirement: see Charity Commission (2013a, 2013b).

14.37 Section 4(2) provides that there is no presumption that any particular purpose is for the public benefit. In the *Independent Schools Council* case, the tribunal held that there was no legal 'presumption' of benefit in the pre-2006 Act law; rather, the determination of public benefit was always context sensitive, turning on the particular purpose under consideration. The tribunal quashed the Charity Commission's guidance on the public benefit in relation to independent schools which charged substantial fees out of the reach of many, in particular anyone poor. Whilst the tribunal found that any organisation which positively excluded the poor from benefiting from its purpose could not be charitable, none of the independent schools in question had this as part of their organising purposes. The schools did not charge substantial fees in order to exclude the poor; rather, they could not afford not to charge substantial fees if they were to carry out their educational purposes. It was the duty of the trustees to ensure that in carrying out their educational purposes the poor were not entirely excluded from benefit. If they did effectively exclude the poor beyond a token or *de minimis* level, it would not indicate that the purpose of the organisation was not charitable; rather, it would mean that the trustees were in breach of their duty properly to carry out their charitable purpose. Moreover, determining how best to carry out their charitable purpose was primarily a matter for the judgment of the trustees themselves. The Charity Commission could not fetter the exercise of this judgment by setting out a requirement that a school devote such and such proportion of its fee-income to bursaries in favour of students who could not afford the fees.

14.38 Trusts for the education of residents of specific localities, or for the children of members of various professions are valid. In *Oppenheim v Tobacco Securities Trust Co Ltd* (1951) however, a trust for the education of children of employees or former employees of the British-American Tobacco Company, the employees of which numbered over 110,000, was held to be not charitable by the HL, on the ground of insufficient public benefit, employing what has been called the 'personal nexus' test: if a class is defined by a personal nexus to someone, and in this case the children's connection with their parent's employer stands on the same footing as one's connection with a relation, then that class is not a section of the public. Lord MacDermott dissented, asking whether there should be a difference between a trust for the children of coalminers before all the pits were nationalised, which would be charitable, and one for the same children afterwards, which would fail since they would all be joined by the employment nexus to the National Coal Board. He rejected the test and said that the court must consider all the circumstances of the case, and would have held the gift charitable. In *Dingle v Turner* (1972) Lord MacDermott's criticism of the personal nexus test was accepted by the HL, although this was *obiter*, as the gift in that case was a gift to relieve poverty, in respect of which there are no similar tests on the extent of the class.

14.39 Indeed, in respect of trusts to relieve poverty, it appears that the public benefit test means no more than that the trusts cannot be for named individuals; a gift for one's poor relations is perfectly valid (*Re Scarisbrick* (1951)). *Dingle v Turner* (1972) concerned a trust to pay pensions to poor employees. Being restricted to the poor, the trust was valid, but the HL unanimously joined Lord Cross in rejecting the personal nexus test in favour of determining a trust's validity on the basis of all the circumstances of the case. Lord Cross did, however, consider that certain schemes such as the educational scheme in *Oppenheim* were, perhaps, akin to fringe benefits for employees that should not be subsidised by the taxpayer.

14.40 The 'fringe benefit' issue appeared to be central in two cases that concerned the preferential treatment of a private class in educational trusts. *Re Koettgen's Will Trusts* (1954) concerned a trust for the promotion of commercial education for members of the public who could not afford it, which, however, contained a provision stating that a preference should be given to the families of employees of a named company of up to 75 per cent of the total fund; it was held charitable, although it is clearly very close to the line, if not incompatible with *Oppenheim*. The CA's decision in *IRC v Educational Grants Association Ltd* (1967) may better reflect the law. Here, there was a fund devoted to the advancement of education in general terms, which was therefore charitable; the fund was maintained by payments from the Metal Box Company; in one year, however, when the claim was made for tax relief, between 76 per cent and 85 per cent of the income was paid for the education of children of persons connected with the company; the tax relief was denied, because it was held that it was not spent for charitable purposes only—the non-charitable payments were ultra vires.

14.41   In the case of trusts for the advancement of religion, the requirement that a section of the public benefits is elusive. In *Neville Estates Ltd v Madden* (1962) a gift to the Catford synagogue was good, because the court:

> is entitled to assume that some benefit accrues to the public from the attendance at places of worship of persons who live in this world and mix with their fellow citizens.

In *Gilmour v Coats* (1949) the HL held that a gift to a contemplative order of nuns was not charitable, reasoning that intercessory prayer on behalf of members of the public was not a sufficient public benefit; there must be some engagement with the public. In *Re Heatherington* (1990) a gift for the saying of masses for the repose of the donor's husband and relations was charitable on the basis that the masses were said in public.

14.42   Under the 'other purposes' fourth head of charitable purposes, purposes will fail if the benefit appears to be unnecessarily or artificially restricted, as in *Baddeley*, or restricted to what amounts to a class of private individuals, as in *Glasgow Police*. Such a gift is not bad on this count if the benefits are restricted to residents of a particular community. Nor does the trust's being restricted to victims of a disaster create an invalid class (*Re North Devon and West Somerset Relief Fund Trusts*), although being the victim of a disaster alone does not make one an object of charity—one is a proper object of charity only if, and to the extent that, one is thereby impoverished, or disabled, etc. So if a millionaire loses his rose garden in a flood, he is not the proper object of a disaster relief charity.

A charity must be for exclusively charitable purposes

14.43   It has always been the law that a purpose, to count as charitable, must be wholly charitable. Trusts have failed for being expressed to be for more than charitable purposes. A classic example is *Morice v Bishop of Durham* (1805), where a trust for 'charitable or benevolent' purposes failed, since not every benevolent purpose would count as a charity under the law. (The Charitable Trusts (Validation) Act 1958 overturns the actual decisions in such cases, providing that where, within the terms of a gift, the property *could* be used entirely for charitable purposes, it shall be treated as a gift confined to those charitable purposes.). However, charitable trusts may engage in subsidiary purposes or activities that are not themselves charitable, such as fund-raising, which contribute to the fulfilment of their main purposes. It is, however, the issue of charities engaging in political activity that has raised some of the thorniest issues. In general, political purposes are not charitable. The orthodox rationale for this was explained by Lord Simonds in the *National Anti-Vivisection Society* case:

> [Quoting Tyssen on Charitable Bequests:] 'However desirable the change may really be, the law could not stultify itself by holding that it was for the public benefit that the law itself should be changed. Each court in deciding on the validity of a gift must decide on the principle that the law is right as it stands.'... Lord Parker [in Bowman v Secular Society

(1917)] uses slightly different language, but means the same thing, when he says that the court has no means of judging whether a proposed change in the law will or will not be for the public benefit. It is not for the court to judge and the court has no means of judging.

Furthermore, Lord Simonds pointed out that the Attorney-General must supervise and enforce charities, and, in some cases, formulate a scheme for their execution, and he should not be put in the position of forwarding a purpose that he and his government might feel to be quite against the interests of the general welfare.

14.44   *McGovern v A-G* (1982) concerned a trust set up by Amnesty International for those of its purposes that it felt were charitable. The relevant purposes were to secure the release of prisoners of conscience, to procure the abolition of torture and other cruel, inhumane, or degrading treatment of prisoners, to undertake research into the maintenance and observation of human rights and to disseminate the same. Slade J held that where the political purpose was one of a change in the laws of a foreign country, there was no danger of the court 'stultifying' itself by having both to regard a law that it was bound to apply as both right and needing to be changed, since the law was a foreign one. But such a trust would still fail the public benefit test for the court would in such a case have even less means of judging whether the proposed change in the law was of benefit to the local inhabitants. Furthermore, the court would have to take into account the substantial risk that such activity by a UK charity would prejudice the foreign relations of the UK with that country. Precisely the same dangers would apply to changing the administrative practice of a foreign government if the purpose could be achieved by that end. Therefore trusts whose central purposes involved a change in the law, government policy, or administrative practice either in the UK or abroad were political and thus not charitable.

14.45   On the requirement that trust purposes must be wholly and exclusively charitable, Slade J said:

[Each] and every object or purpose designated must be of a charitable nature. Otherwise, there are no means of discriminating what part of the trust property is intended for charitable purposes and what part for non-charitable purposes and uncertainty in this respect invalidates the whole trust. Nevertheless,…a distinction of critical importance has to be drawn between (a) the designated purposes of the trust, (b) the designated means of carrying out these purposes and (c) the consequences of carrying them out. Trust purposes of an otherwise charitable nature do not lose it merely because, as an incidental consequence of the trustees' activities, there may enure to private individuals benefits of a non-charitable nature. Thus, for example, in Incorporated Council of Law Reporting the Court of Appeal rejected contentions that the Council of Law Reporting was a non-charitable body merely because publication of the law reports supplied members of the legal profession with the tools of their trade. Similarly, trust purposes of an otherwise charitable nature do not lose it merely because the trustees, by way of furtherance of their purpose, have incidental powers to carry on activities which are not themselves charitable…The distinction is… one between (a) those non-charitable activities authorised by the trust instrument and which are merely subsidiary or incidental to a charitable purpose, and (b) those non-charitable activities so authorised which in themselves form part of the trust purpose. In the latter but not the former case, the reference to non-charitable activities will deprive the trust of its charitable status.

14.46 Slade J found that both securing the release of prisoners of conscience and securing the abolition of torture and other degrading or inhuman punishments were not charitable purposes. As
to the former, the purpose:

> must be regarded as being the procurement of the reversal of the relevant decisions of
> governments and governmental authorities in those countries where such authorities
> have decided to detain prisoners of conscience, whether or not in accordance with local
> law. The procurement of the reversal of such decisions cannot, I think, be regarded as
> one possible method of giving effect to the purposes…it is the principal purpose itself.

Making reference to the Amnesty International statutes, Slade J construed the latter purpose as
including the abolition of capital and corporal punishment, and found as its main object:

> to procure the passing of the appropriate reforming legislation for the purpose of abol-
> ishing inhuman or degrading punishments by process of law, including capital and
> corporal punishment…

Had research into human rights and dissemination of the result thereof been the only purpose,
Slade J would have found the trust charitable, but given that the other purposes were not, it
fell with the rest. The general orientation of Slade J's approach continued in the CA decision
in *Southwood v A-G* (2000), where an organisation seeking charitable status whose purposes
included 'propos[ing] alternative policies to achieve disarmament' failed to do so, the purpose
being found to be political (see Garton (2000)).

14.47 The Charity Commission produces guidance from time to time on the allowable political activity by charities. The guidance has become less and less restrictive of political activities over
the years (compare Charity Commissioners (1995) and the Charity Commission (2008)). Most
recently, the Charity Commission has emphasised the positive aspects of political advocacy
by charities: owing to the high regard in which they are held, their strong links to local com-
munities, and the diversity of their activities, it is argued that they are well situated to comment on government policy and offer alternative ways of engaging in public debate and give
voice to otherwise under-represented groups or interests. The 2008 Guidelines suggest that,
in the eyes of the Charity Commission at least (although it is difficult to know how far the
courts would go), the ambit of acceptable political activity by charities is now very wide, up to
and including supporting the policies of a particular political party and devoting all of their
resources, for a time, to political campaigning if this best serves the purpose of the charity
(Charity Commission (2008)). In *Aid/Watch Incorporated v Commissioner of Taxation* (2010)
the High Court of Australia reviewed the 'no political purposes' rule and held charitable an
organisation, Aid/Watch, the principal purpose of which was to review the efficacy of various
aid programmes and to generate discussion of their findings, with the understanding that this
might influence government policy. The majority of the court said:

> the Commissioner submitted that the Full Court should have decided the appeal in
> his favour on the ground that the main or predominant or dominant objects of Aid/
> Watch itself were too remote from the relief of poverty or advancement of education
> to attract the first or second heads in Pemsel. It is unnecessary to rule upon these
> submissions by the Commissioner. This is because the generation by lawful means of
> public debate…concerning the efficiency of foreign aid directed to the relief of poverty,
> itself is a purpose beneficial to the community within the fourth head in Pemsel.

It also is unnecessary for this appeal to determine whether the fourth head encompasses the encouragement of public debate respecting activities of government which lie beyond the first three heads (or the balance of the fourth head) identified in Pemsel and, if so, the range of those activities. What, however, this appeal should decide is that in Australia there is no general doctrine which excludes from charitable purposes 'political objects' and has the scope indicated in England by McGovern v Attorney-General.

It may be that some purposes which otherwise appear to fall within one or more of the four heads in Pemsel nonetheless do not contribute to the public welfare… But that will be by reason of the particular ends and means involved, not disqualification of the purpose by application of a broadly expressed 'political objects' doctrine.

14.48 Disapproval of the 'political objects' doctrine was also expressed in *Re Greenpeace of New Zealand Inc* (2014), a decision of the New Zealand Supreme Court. (For misgivings about this trend, see Penner (2016).) The majority (Elias CJ, McGrath and Glazebrook JJ) allowed the appeal against the Court of Appeal's holding that a political purpose cannot be charitable, holding that:

[59] We do not think that the development of a standalone doctrine of exclusion of political purposes, a development comparatively recent and based on surprisingly little authority (as the discussion at paragraphs [32] to [47] indicates), has been necessary or beneficial.

14.49 The majority went on to say that:

[60] The label 'political' itself has been used in a number of different senses (party political, controversial, law-changing, opinion-moulding, among others) and is apt to mislead.

14.50 The majority did not accept that the 'political objects' doctrine, as commonly framed, is only confined to excluding promotion of changes in legislation from being charitable. But even so, they doubted that all advocacy for legislative change should be excluded from being recognised as charitable, citing the kind of promotion of law reform undertaken by law commissions (which aims to keep laws updated for modern usage) as one example of the kind of law reform that might well be seen as charitable if undertaken by a private body. Furthermore, citing several older English authorities, the majority also failed to see a meaningful distinction between promoting legislative change and promoting change in government policy. Interestingly, the majority also accepted that:

[63] . . . in the circumstances of modern participatory democracy and modern public participatory processes in much administrative and judicial decision-making, there is no satisfactory basis for a distinction between general promotion of views within society and advocacy of law change (including through such available participatory processes).

14.51 Turning to broader concerns, the majority observed that:

[69] A conclusion that a purpose is 'political' or 'advocacy' obscures proper focus on whether a purpose is charitable within the sense used by law. It is difficult to construct any adequate or principled theory to support blanket exclusion. A political purpose or advocacy exclusion would be an impediment to charitable status for organisations which, although campaigning for charitable ends, do not themselves directly undertake tangible good works of the type recognised as charitable.

14.52   The majority also said that a strict exclusion 'risks rigidity in an area of law which should be responsive to the way society works.' The majority cited the variety of endeavours in which public benefit has been recognised, from philanthropy in easing the burden on parishes of alleviating poverty in post-Reformation Elizabethan England, to law reporting in the twentieth century. The idea is that changes in society may throw up new philantrophic endeavours which may need to be properly treated as charitable.

14.53   In sum, the majority agreed with the view expressed by Kiefel J in *Aid/Watch Incorporated v Commissioner of Taxation* (2010) that charitable and political purposes are not mutually exclusive:

> [72] The better approach is not a doctrine of exclusion of 'political' purpose but acceptance that an object which entails advocacy for change in the law is 'simply one facet of whether a purpose advances the public benefit in a way that is within the spirit and intendment of the statute of Elizabeth I'.

14.54   As an olive branch of sorts, the majority was prepared to accept that the circumstances in which advocacy of particular views is shown to be charitable will not be common. However, they argued that that does not justify a rule that all non-ancillary advocacy is properly characterised as non-charitable. An assessment of whether advocacy or promotion of a cause or law reform is a charitable purpose will depend on:

> [76] . . . consideration of the end that is advocated, the means promoted to achieve that end and the manner in which the cause is promoted in order to assess whether the purpose can be said to be of public benefit within the spirit and intendment of the 1601 Statute . . .

A charity must be non-profit-distributing

14.55   Charitable trusts may engage in activities to raise funds, including charging fees for their services (*Re Resch's Will Trusts* (1969); *Independent Schools Council* (2011)). They must absolutely not distribute profits. This goes for charitable companies as well as charitable trusts, obviously. As for earning profits, in *Oxfam v Birmingham City District Council* (1976), the HL held that a charity shop was not entitled as a charity to relief from rates, because it was used for the purpose of fund-raising and was not directed to the charitable purposes themselves. The general rule, therefore, is that the profit-earning activities of charities are liable to the same rates and taxes, such as VAT, as are any other businesses, although various exceptions exist. For example, the Rating (Charity Shops) Act 1976 overturned the *Oxfam* ruling in respect of those shops that are used solely or mainly for the sale of donated goods, the proceeds of which are used solely for charitable purposes. Detailed guidance on trading by charities and the tax implications can be found in Charity Commission (2007).

Preservation from failure: the cy-près doctrine

14.56   Where a charitable purpose would fail because the means chosen by a testator for its implementation are either impractical or impossible to carry out, the cy-près doctrine, and more recently, Part 6 of the Charities Act 2011, can be applied so that it will not fail. 'Cy-près' is law French, originally meaning something like 'as near as possible'. The cy-près power of the courts allows the court to direct that the trust property be applied to a purpose as close as possible to the one intended by the settlor. Cy-près can save charitable trusts from failure at the outset, or from subsequent failure when carrying out the purpose becomes impossible or impractical. Given, as we have seen, that when a private trust fails an automatic resulting trust arises (Chapter 5), it is not obvious why, when a charitable trust fails, the court ought to be empowered to devote the trust funds to a new charitable purpose, and it is, in fact, not an easy matter to justify the court's jurisdiction to do so (see Garton (2007)).

Preservation from failure at the outset

14.57   The cy-près doctrine can save a charitable trust from failure at the outset because the charitable purpose is impractical or impossible to carry out. NB: The doctrine only applies to a purpose *that already counts as a charitable purpose*, ie to relieve poverty, or advance education, or some other charitable purpose. Students regularly make the mistake in exams of thinking that the court can use the cy-près doctrine to turn a non-charitable purpose into a charitable one—the court cannot; if the proposed purpose is not charitable, the court has no power to make it so. In order for the court to redirect money intended for a charitable purpose that fails by applying the cy-près doctrine, the court must find that the donor manifested a 'general' or 'paramount' charitable intention, ie an intention to give the money to charitable purposes of which the particular gift was but a specification; if the intention was to give only to the specific charity or charitable purpose, and the charity is defunct or the purpose impossible to carry out, then the gift fails.

14.58   What is a general charitable intention? In *Re Lysaght* (1966) Buckley J said:

> A general charitable intention...may be said to be a paramount intention on the part of a donor to effect some charitable purpose which the court can find a method of putting into operation, notwithstanding that it is impracticable to give effect to some direction by the donor which is not an essential part of his true intention—not, that is to say, part of his paramount intention. In contrast, a particular charitable intention exists where the donor means his charitable disposition to take effect if, but only if, it can be carried into effect in a particular specified way, for example, in connection with a particular school to be established at a particular place, Re Wilson (1913), or by establishing a home in a particular house: Re Packe (1918).

14.59   The courts have employed cy-près effectively to strike out conditions on trusts for scholarships. In *Re Lysaght* (1966) an endowment of medical studentships at the Royal College of Surgeons was to be restricted to recipients not of the Jewish or Roman Catholic faith; the College would not accept the gift because the condition was 'so invidious and so alien to the spirit of the college's work as to make the gift inoperable in that form'. In *Re Woodhams* (1981) music scholarships were restricted to boys from two particular groups of orphans' homes. In both cases the condition was regarded as an inessential element of the testator's bequest, specifying particular means of carrying out his general charitable intention to fund the said scholarships, and the conditions were deleted.

14.60   Many cases in which charitable gifts are saved from failure at the outset concern testamentary gifts to charitable institutions or bodies that operated when the testator made his will but have since been amalgamated with others or have gone defunct. Three cases must be distinguished. The first concerns gifts to particular named charities that no longer exist in their own right, but the purposes of which are continued by other charities. In *Re Faraker* (1912) there was a testamentary gift to 'Mrs Bayley's Charity, Rotherhithe', which had, with other local charities, been consolidated into a trust for the poor in Rotherhithe. The CA held that the gift should go to the consolidated charity because it continued the named charity. This is not an example of cy-près, because the gift is regarded as being successfully made to the intended charity. This is so even in the circumstances where, as in *Faraker*, the continuing charity has substantially different overall purposes; the original charity was for poor widows, and the consolidated charity was for the poor generally, so that there was no guarantee that any of the gift actually went to poor widows.

14.61   Secondly, where the particular charitable institution named to be the recipient of the gift no longer exists, the gift will not fail if on a true construction of the testator's intentions he intended to create a charitable purpose trust and merely indicated this institution to serve as the trustee. This, too, is not an example of cy-près: since a trust will not fail for want of a trustee, the court will find another trustee to carry out the charitable purpose. This construction is much more likely in the case of a gift to an unincorporated charitable body than an incorporated one, for the following reasons given by Buckley J in *Re Vernon's Will Trusts* (1972):

> *Every bequest to an unincorporated charity by name without more must take effect as a gift for a charitable purpose. No individual or aggregate of individuals could claim to take such a bequest beneficially. If the gift is to be permitted to take effect at all, it must be as a bequest for a purpose, viz., that charitable purpose which the named charity exists to serve. A bequest which is in terms made for a charitable purpose will not fail for lack of a trustee…A bequest to a named unincorporated charity, however, may on its true interpretation show that the testator's intention to make the gift at all was dependent upon the named charitable organisation being available at the time when the gift takes effect to serve as the instrument for applying the subject matter of the gift to the charitable purpose for which it is by inference given. If so and the named charity ceases to exist in the lifetime of the testator, the gift fails: In re Ovey (1885). A bequest to a corporate body, on the other hand, takes effect simply as a gift to that body beneficially, unless there are circumstances which show that the recipient is to take the gift as a trustee. There is no need in such a case to infer a trust for any particular purpose…the natural construction is that the bequest is made to the corporate body as part of its general funds, that is to say, beneficially and without the imposition of any trust. That the testator's motive in making the bequest may have undoubtedly been to assist the work of the incorporated body would be insufficient to create a trust.*

14.62   This reasoning is inventive but unpersuasive. Surely most testators do not know whether the institutions to which they give are unincorporated or not and, secondly, most probably do not register a distinction between a gift to a charitable body as an accretion to its funds or a gift for the charitable purposes it carries out; how, then, can such a distinction be used to discern the testator's intentions? Nevertheless, the distinction is accepted as good law; it was applied in *Re Finger's Will Trusts* (1972), so that a gift to a now defunct unincorporated association was valid as a purpose trust, whereas a gift to a defunct incorporated body failed, although the latter was saved by applying the money cy-près. *Re Vernon* and *Re Finger* were both cited with apparent approval by the CA in *Re Koeppler's Will Trusts* (1986). Such a purpose trust is a trust for that specific purpose only, a particular charitable institution serving as trustee must not treat the gift as a general accretion to its funds, but must apply it only to the specific purpose (*Re Spence* (1979)). In contrast, testamentary gifts to an incorporated charity that took effect following a court order that it be wound up, but before its actual dissolution were, on the same principles, held by Neuberger J not to be gifts on trust for a charitable purpose, but gifts in accretion to the corporation's funds; the gifts went into the general assets of the charitable corporation for distribution to its creditors (*Re ARMS (Multiple Sclerosis Research) Ltd* (1997)).

14.63   True cases of cy-près only occur where the intended charitable gift actually fails, as in the gift to the incorporated body in *Re Finger's Will Trusts* above. In *Re Rymer* (1895) the testator gave money to a particular seminary, which at the time of the testator's death had ceased to exist, although its current students were transferred to another seminary. The gift could only be saved by application of the cy-près doctrine, but since the court found that the gift was to the particular seminary only, there was no general charitable intention, so cy-près could not be applied.

14.64   *Re Harwood* (1936) established something of a general rule that a gift to a particular charity that once existed but is now defunct, is interpreted, unless there are indications to the contrary, as a gift intended for that body alone, disclosing no general charitable intention, whereas in the case of a gift to a named charity that never existed it is much easier to find a general charitable intention. In *Re Spence*, Megarry VC extended the principle to the case where the testator has selected a particular charitable purpose, here the purpose of benefiting the residents of a particular old peoples' home, which at the testatrix's death ceased to exist. He explained the rule's rationale as follows:

> I do not think that the reasoning of the In re Harwood line of cases is directed to any feature of institutions as distinct from purposes. Instead, I think the essence of the distinction is in the difference between particularity and generality. If a particular institution or purpose is specified, then it is that institution or purpose, and no other, that is to be the object of the benefaction. It is difficult to envisage a testator as being suffused with a general glow of broad charity when he is labouring, and labouring successfully, to identify some particular specified institution or purpose as the object of his bounty. The specific displaces the general. It is otherwise where the testator has been unable to specify any particular charitable institution or practicable purpose, and so, although his intention of charity can be seen, he has failed to provide any way of giving effect to it. There, the absence of the specific leaves the general undisturbed. It follows that in my view in the case before me, where the testatrix has clearly specified a particular charitable purpose which before her death became impossible to carry out, [there is] that level of great difficulty in demonstrating the existence of a general charitable intention which was indicated by In re Harwood.

14.65   Section 63 of the 2011 Act usefully provides that where collections are on public appeal for a charitable purpose, such as purchasing a work of art for the National Gallery so that it remains within the UK, which fails at the outset (eg not enough money is raised for the purpose), the money will be applicable cy-près as if given for charitable purposes generally.

Preservation from subsequent failure

14.66   When a charitable trust has been effectively carried out for a time, but then its purposes become impossible or impractical to carry out, the court may modify the purposes, on the basis that they are giving effect to the settlor's intention to give property 'out and out' to charity. Up to the turn of the century, the cy-près power to modify the terms of a trust was narrowly construed, and only if the original terms were actually impossible or impractical to carry out would the court intervene. So, as Martin (2001, at 446) remarks, cumbersome, uneconomical, and inconvenient trusts for 'the distribution of loaves to the poor or of stockings for poor maidservants' continued well into the last century. Section 62(1)(e)(i) of the 2011 Act expands the scope for the doctrine, in particular providing that a cy-près modification may occur where the original purposes have been adequately provided by other means, which encompasses statutory services in a welfare state. The predecessor s 13 of the Charities Act 1993, although often used by the Charities Commissioners, has not been frequently litigated. In *Re JW Laing Trust* (1984) it was held that s 13 applied only to permit alterations in the purposes of a trust, not variations of settlors' directions that were merely administrative, although in this case such a direction, that the capital and income be fully distributed within a short time period, was deleted under the court's inherent jurisdiction (10.66). *Varsani v Jesani* (1999) is an interesting case. The court employed its power under s 13 to divide the assets of a religious sect between two rival factions following a fundamental disagreement over the true tenets of the faith.

FURTHER READING

Charity Commission (2008, 2013a, 2013b)

Chesterman (1999)

Economist (1995)

Garton (2005, 2007)

Gravells (1977)

Mitchell (1999a, 1999b, 2000)

Moffat (1999), ch 18

Must-read cases: *Shergill v Khaira* (2014); *Independent Schools Council v Charity Commission for England and Wales* (2011); *McGovern v A-G* (1981); *Hodkin v Registrar General of Births, Deaths and Marriages* (2013); *Re Lysaght* (1965); *Incorporated Council of Law Reporting for England and Wales v A-G* (1972); *IRC v McMullen* (1981); *IRC v Baddeley* (1955); *Oppenheim v Tobacco Securities Trust* (1951); *Dingle v Turner* (1972); *Re Faraker* (1912); *Re Vernon's Will Trusts* (1960); *Re Finger's Will Trusts* (1971); *Re Spence* (1978)

SELF-TEST QUESTIONS

1. Are the following purposes charitable?
    - To set up a sporting institute to train Great Britain's most promising young athletes.
    - To provide birth control to students in schools in London.
    - To provide tennis rackets to the unemployed of Manchester.
    - To provide a national health service in a poor developing country where the predominant religion prohibits blood transfusions.

- To further the activities of a religious sect that counsels its adherents to withdraw from the world and live in remote communes.
- To establish a sixth form college for dyslexic pupils which charges high fees, 5 per cent of the annual fee income being devoted to bursaries for pupils from poorer families.
- To abolish the use of animal testing to assess the efficacy of newly developed drugs.
- To provide scholarships to assist students to learn ballroom dancing while at university, with the condition that the trustees may, in applying up to 75 per cent of the income of the trust, give preference to children of employees of Y Ltd.
- To provide funds to the Sisters of 2001, an association of Roman Catholic nuns whose sole purpose is to persuade the Vatican to allow the ordination of women priests.
- To purchase tracts of land in the Amazon basin of Brazil so as to preserve the natural habitat, where possible in areas that are currently subject to logging authorised by the government.
- To convert British Muslims to Christianity.

2. What is the public benefit requirement? Has the requirement been changed by the Charities Acts 2006 and 2011?

3. How does the law operate to save charitable trusts from initial failure? Describe and critically assess the law governing the court's finding of a 'general charitable intention'.

4. 'The Charities Acts 2006 and 2011 represent a missed opportunity to reform charities law.' Discuss.

5. 'The prohibition on charities advancing political purposes or engaging in political activities has always been difficult to apply, and is made even more difficult in view of the recognition of certain purposes as charitable under the Charities Act 2011.' Discuss.

Select bibliography

Abbreviations

CLJ *Cambridge Law Journal*

CPL *Conveyancer and Property Lawyer*

JoE *Journal of Equity*

LMCLQ *Lloyd's Maritime and Commercial Law Quarterly*

LQR *Law Quarterly Review*

MLR *Modern Law Review*

OJLS *Oxford Journal of Legal Studies*

TLI *Trust Law International*

American Law Institute (1937). *Restatement of Restitution*. St Paul, MN, American Law Institute.

American Law Institute (1959). *Restatement of Trusts*. St Paul, MN, American Law Institute.

Baker, J. H. (2002). *An Introduction to English Legal History*, Butterworths LexisNexis.

Bant, E. (1998). '"Ignorance" as a ground of restitution: Can it survive?' LMCLQ: 18.

Bell, A. P. (1989). *Modern law of personal property in England and Ireland*. London, Butterworths.

Bennett, M. (2017). 'Competing views on illusory trusts: The *Clayton v Clayton* litigation in its wider context.' JoE 11: 48–79.

Birks, P. (1985). *An Introduction to the Law of Restitution*. Oxford, Clarendon Press.

Birks, P. (1991). 'The English recognition of unjust enrichment.' LMCLQ: 473.

Birks, P. (1992). 'Mixing and tracing.' CLP 45(2): 69.

Birks, P. (1993). 'Persistent problems in misdirected money: A quintet.' LMCLQ: 218.

Birks, P. (1994a). '*In rem or in personam? Webb v Webb.*' TLI 8: 99.

Birks, P. (1994b). *The Frontiers of Liability*. Oxford, Oxford University Press.

Birks, P. (1996b). 'Equity in the modern law: An exercise in taxonomy.' *University of Western Australia Law Review* 26: 1.

Birks, P. (1997a). 'On taking seriously the difference between tracing and claiming.' TLI 11: 2.

Birks, P. (1997b). *Privacy and Loyalty*. Oxford, Clarendon Press.

Birks, P. (2002). Receipt. *Breach of Trust*. P. Birks and A. Pretto. Oxford, Hart: 213.

Birks, P. (2005). *Unjust Enrichment*. Oxford, Oxford University Press.

Birks, P. and A. Pretto (2002). *Breach of Trust*. Oxford, Hart.

Bridge, M. G. (2002). *Personal Property Law*. Oxford, Oxford University Press.

Brownbill, D. (1992). 'Anatomy of a trust deed Parts I–III.' *Journal of International Planning* 1: 35, 100, 165.

Brownbill, D. (1993). 'Anatomy of a trust deed Parts IV–VI.' *Journal of International Trust and Corporate Planning* 2: 49, 103, 164.

Brownbill, D. (1994). 'Anatomy of a trust deed Parts VII–VIII.' *Journal of International Trust and Corporate Planning* 3: 50, 166.

Brownbill, D. (1995). 'Anatomy of a trust deed Parts IX.' *Journal of International Trust and Corporate Planning* 4: 51.

Bryan, M. (2012). Boardman v Phipps: Doing Equity Inequitably. *Landmark Cases in Equity*. C. M. P. Mitchell. Oxford, Hart: 581.

Burn, E. H. and J. Cartwright (2011). *Cheshire and Burn's Modern Law of Real Property*. Oxford, Oxford University Press.

Burrows, A (2002) 'We do this at common law but that in equity' 22 OJLS 1.

Burrows, A. (2011). *The Law of Restitution*. Oxford, Oxford University Press.

Burrows, A. (2017). 'Illegality after Patel v Mirza.' CLP 70: 55–71.

Chambers, R. (1997). *Resulting Trusts*. Oxford, Clarendon Press.

Chambers, R. (2001). 'Comment on Lohia v Lohia.' TLI 15: 26.

Chambers, R. (2001–2). 'Constructive trusts in Canada.' TLI 15: 214; 'Constructive trusts in Canada.' TLI 16: 2.

Chambers, R. (2005a). The importance of specific performance. *Equity in Commercial Law*. S. Degeling and J. Edelman. Sydney, Law Book Co: 463.

Chambers, R. (2005b). 'The consequences of breach of fiduciary duty.' *King's College Law Journal* 16: 186.

Chambers, R. (2006). Resulting trusts. *Mapping the Law*. A. Burrows and L. R. o. Earlsferry. Oxford, Oxford University Press: 247.

Chambers, R. (2007). 'Knowing receipt: Frozen in Australia.' JoE 2: 40.

Chambers, R. (2009). Two Kinds of Enrichment. *Philosophical Foundations of the Law of Unjust Enrichment*. R. Chambers, C. Mitchell and J. Penner. Oxford, Oxford University Press: 240.

Chambers, R. (2010a). Is There a Presumption of Resulting Trust? *Constructive and Resulting Trusts*. C. Mitchell. Oxford, Hart: 267.

Chambers, R. (2013a). Trust and theft. *Exploring Private Law*. E. Bant and Harding. Cambridge, Cambridge University Press: 223.

Chambers, R. (2013b). 'Constructive trusts and breach of fiduciary duty.' CPL 77: 73.

Chambers, R. (2013c). *An Introduction to Property Law in Australia*. Sydney, Thomson Law Book.

Chambers, R. and J. E. Penner (2008). Ignorance. *Unjust Enrichment in Commercial Law*. S. Degeling and J. Edelman. Sydney, Thomson LLP.

Charity Commissioners (1995) 'Political activities and campaigning by charities.' (1995) CC9.

Charity Commissioners (1999) 'Decision of the Charity Commissioners: Application by the Church of Scientology for registration as a charity.' (1999).

Charity Commissioners (2002) 'Disaster appeals: Attorney-General's guidelines.' (2002) CC40.

Charity Commissioners (2007) 'Trustees, Trading and Tax: How Charities May Lawfully Trade.' (2007) CC35.

Charity Commission (2008) 'Speaking Out—Guidance on Campaigning and Political Activity by Charities.' (2008) CC9.

Charity Commission (2009) 'Public Benefit Assessment Reports.' (2009) on file with the author.

Charity Commissioners (2013a) 'Public benefit: the public benefit requirement.' (2013).

Charity Commissioners (2013b) 'Analysis of the Law Underpinning Charities and Public Benefit.' (2013).

Chesterman, M. (1999). 'Foundations of charity law in the new welfare state.' MLR 62: 333.

Committee, L. R. (1982). 23rd Report: The Powers and Duties of Trustees, Cmnd 8733.

Conaglen, M. (2003). 'Equitable compensation for breach of fiduciary dealing rules.' LQR 119: 246.

Conaglen, M. (2007). *Fiduciary Loyalty: Protecting the Due Performance of Non-Fiduciary Duties*. Oxford, Hart.

Conaglen, M. (2016). 'Equitable Compensation for Breach of Trust: Off *Target*.' *Melbourne University Law Review* 40: 126–167.

Crawford, M. (2014). 'Theft, trust and property rights: Is equity's cure worse than the disease.' JoE 8: 338–366.

Crilley, D. (1994). 'A case of proprietary overkill.' *Restitution Law Review*: 57.

Cullity, M. (1975). 'Judicial control of trustees' discretions.' *University of Toronto Law Journal* 25: 99.

Cullity, M. (1985). 'Liability of beneficiaries: A rejoinder.' *Estates and Trusts Quarterly* 7: 35.

Cullity, M. (1986). 'Liability of beneficiaries: A further rejoinder to Mr Flannigan.' *Estates and Trusts Quarterly* 8: 130.

D'Angelo, N. (2014). 'The trust as a surrogate company: The challenge of insolvency.' JoE 8: 299–337.

Davies, P. S. (2015a). *Accessory Liability*. Oxford, Hart.

Davies, P. S. (2015b). 'Remedies for breach of trust.' MLR 78: 672–694.

Dignam, A. and J. Lowry (2010). *Company Law*. Oxford, Oxford University Press.

Economist (1995). 'Not as deserving as they seem.' *The Economist* 15 July: 22.

Edelman, J. (2010). Four fiduciary puzzles. *Exploring Private Law*. E. Bant and M. Harding. Cambridge, Cambridge University Press: 298–318.

Edelman, J. (2010). 'When do Fiduciary Duties Arise?' LQR 126: 302.

Edelman, J. (2017). An English Misturning with Equitable Compensation. *Equitable Compensation and Disgorgement of Profit*. S. Degeling and J. N. Varuhas. Oxford, Hart Publishing: 91–109.

Elliot, D. (1960). 'The power of trustees to enforce covenants in favour of volunteers.' LQR 76: 100.

Elliott, S. and C. Mitchell (2004). 'Remedies for dishonest assistance.' MLR 67: 16.

Emery, C. (1982). 'The most hallowed principle: Certainty of beneficiaries of trusts and powers of appointment.' LQR 98: 551.

Endicott, T. (1997). 'Vagueness and legal theory.' Legal Theory 3: 37.

Evans, S. (1999). 'Rethinking tracing and the law of restitution.' LQR 115: 469.

Flannigan, R. (1984). 'Beneficiary liability in business trusts.' *Estates and Trusts Quarterly* 6: 278.

Flannigan, R. (1986). 'The control test of principal status applied to business trusts.' *Estates and Trusts Quarterly* 8: 37.

Ford, H. and I. Hardingham (1987). Trading trusts: Rights and liabilities of beneficiaries. *Equity and Commercial Relationships*. P. Finn. Sydney, The Law Book Co: 48–88.

Gardner, S. (1998). 'A detail in the construction of gifts to unincorporated associations.' CPL: 8.

Gardner, S. (2010). Reliance-based Constructive Trusts. *Constructive and Resulting Trusts*. C. Mitchell. Oxford, Hart: 63.

Gardner, S. (2013). Persistent Rights Appraised. *Modern Studies in Property Law*. N. Hopkins. Oxford, Hart Publishing. 7: 321–357.

Garton, J. (2000). 'Comment on *Southwood v A-G*.' TLI 14: 233.

Garton, J. (2003). 'The role of the trust mechanism in the rule in *Re Rose*.' CPL: 364.

Garton, J. (2005). 'The legal definition of charity and the regulation of civil society.' *King's College Law Journal* 16: 29.

Garton, J. (2007). 'Justifying the cy-près doctrine.' TLI 21: 134.

Getzler, J. (2014). Ascribing and Limiting Fiduciary Obligations: Understanding the Operation of Consent. *Philosophical Foundations of Fiduciary Law*. A. S. Gold and P. B. Miller. Oxford, Oxford University Press: 39–62.

Gleeson, S. (1995). The involuntary launderer: The banker's liability for deposits of the proceeds of crime. *Laundering and Tracing*. P. Birks. Oxford, Clarendon Press: 115.

Glister, J. (2004a). 'Trusts as quasi-securities? The Law Commission's proposals for the registration of security interests.' LMCLQ: 460.

Glister, J. (2010a). The Presumption of Advancement. *Constructive and Resulting Trusts*. C. Mitchell. Oxford, Hart: 289.

Glister, J. (2010b). 'Section 199 of the Equality Act 2010: How Not to Abolish the Presumption of Advancement.' MLR 73: 807.

Glister, J. (2014a). 'Breach of trust and consequential loss.' JoE 8: 235–258.

Glister, J. (2014b). 'Breach of trust and conversion in a falling market' LMCLQ 4: 511–536.

Goff, R. and G. Jones (1966). *The Law of Restitution*. London, Sweet & Maxwell.

Goff, R. and G. Jones (2016). *The Law of Unjust Enrichment*. London, Sweet & Maxwell.

Goodhart, W. (1996). Trust law for the twenty-first century. *Trends in Contemporary Trust Law*. A. Oakley. Oxford, Oxford University Press: 257.

Goudkamp, J. (2017). 'The end of an era? Illegality in private law in the Supreme Court.' LQR 133: 14–20.

Grantham, R. and C. Rickett (1996). 'Restitution, property and ignorance: A reply to Mr Swadling.' LMCLQ: 463.

Gravells, N. (1977). 'Public purpose trusts.' MLR 40: 397.

Green, B. (1980). 'The dissolution of unincorporated non-profit associations.' MLR 43: 626.

Green, B. (1984). 'Grey, Oughtred, and Vandervell: A contextual reappraisal.' MLR 47: 385.

Gretton, G. (2000). 'Trusts without Equity.' *International and Comparative Law Quarterly* 49: 599.

Grubb, A. (1982). 'Powers, trusts and classes of objects.' CPL: 432.

Hackney, J. (1987). *Understanding Equity and Trusts*. London, Fontana.

Harpum, C. (1986). 'The stranger as constructive trustee.' LQR 102: 114, 267.

Harpum, C. (1990). 'Overreaching, trustee's powers, and the reform of the 1925 legislation.' CLJ 49: 277.

Haskett, T. (1996). 'The medieval English Court of Chancery.' *Law and History Review* 14: 245.

Hayton, D. (1990). 'Developing the law of trusts for the twenty-first century.' LQR 106: 87.

Hayton, D. (1994). 'Uncertainty of subject-matter of trusts.' LQR 110: 335.

Hayton, D. (1996). The irreducible core content of trusteeship. *Trends in Contemporary Trust Law*. A. Oakley. Oxford, Oxford University Press: 47.

Hayton, D. (1999). 'English fiduciary standards and trust law.' *Vanderbilt Journal of Transnational Law* 32: 555.

Hayton, D. (2001a). 'Developing the obligation characteristic of the trust.' LQR 117: 96.

Hayton, D. (2001b). *Hayton and Marshall: Commentary and Cases on the Law of Trusts and Equitable Remedies*. London, Sweet & Maxwell.

Hayton, D. (2007). 'Lessons from knowing receipt, liability and unjust enrichment in Australia.' TLI 21: 55.

Hayton, D., P. Matthews and C. Mitchell (2006). *Underhill and Hayton: Law of Trusts and Trustees*. London, Butterworths.

Hayton, D. and C. Mitchell (2005). *Hayton and Marshall: Commentary and Cases on the Law of Trusts and Equitable Remedies*. London, Sweet & Maxwell.

Heydon, J., M. Leeming and P. Turner (2015). *Meagher, Gummow & Lehane's Equity: Doctrines & Remedies*. Australia, LexisNexis Butterworths.

Hicks, A. (2001). 'The Trustee Act 2000 and the modern meaning of "investment".' TLI 15: 203.

Ho, L. (1998). 'Attributing losses to a breach of fiduciary duty.' TLI 12: 66.

Ho, L. (2010). Trustee's duties to provide information. *Exploring Private Law*. E. Bant and M. Harding. Cambridge, Cambridge University Press: 343–359.

Ho, L. (2010). Trustees' duties to provide information. *Exploring Private Law*. E. Bant and M. Harding. Cambridge, Cambridge University Press: 343–359.

Ho, L. (2016). 'An Account of Accounts.' *Singapore Academy of Law Journal* 28: 849–883.

Ho, L. (2017). Causation in the Restoration of a Misapplied Trust Fund: Fundamental Norm or Red Herring? *Equitable Compensation and Disgorgement of Profit*. S. Degeling and J. N. Varuhas. Oxford, Hart Publishing: 159–174.

Ho, L. (2018). 'Breaking Bad': Settlors' Reserved Powers. *Trusts and Modern Wealth Management*. R. C. Nolan, K. F. K. Low and H. W. Tang. Cambridge, Cambridge University Press: 34–56.

Hodge, D. (1980). 'Secret trusts: The fraud theory revisited.' CPL 44: 341.

Hohfeld, W. N. (1913). 'The Relations Between Equity and Law.' *Michigan Law Review* 11: 537–571.

Hopkins, J. (1971). 'Certain uncertainties of trusts and powers.' CLJ 29: 68.

Hornby, J. (1962). 'Covenants in favour of volunteers.' LQR 78: 228.

Institute, A. L. (1959). *Restatement of the law, second, trusts 2d: as adopted and promulgated by the American Law Institute at Washington, D.C., May 23, 1957*, American Law Institute Publishers.

Jones, G. (1968). 'Unjust enrichment and the fiduciary's duty of loyalty.' LQR 84: 472.

Jones, N. (1997). 'Uses, Trusts, and a Path to Privity.' CLJ 56: 175.

Kodilinye, G. (1982). 'A fresh look at the rule in Strong v Bird.' CPL: 14.

Khurshid, S. and P. Matthews (1979). 'Tracing Confusion.' LQR 95: 78.

Langbein, J. (1994). 'The new American Trust Investment Act.' TLI 8: 123.

Langbein, J. (2005). 'Questioning the trust law duty of loyalty: Sole interest or best interest?' Yale LJ 114: 929.

Langbein, J. and R. Posner (1980). 'Social investing and the law of trusts.' *Michigan Law Review* 79: 72.

Lau, J. (2018). 'Legal and Beneficial Entitlement to Joint Bank Accounts with Volunteers.' *Banking and Finance Law Review* 33(3): 345.

Lau, M. W. (2011). *The Economic Structure of Trusts*. Oxford, Oxford University Press.

Law Commission (1999). Trustees' Powers and Duties, Law Com No 262.

Law Commission (2002). Trustee Exemption Clauses, Consultation Paper 171.

Law Commission (2003). Registration of Security Interests: Company Charges and Property Other Than Land, Consultation Paper 164.

Law, M. and R. Ong (2017). '"He who comes to Equity need not do so with clean hands?" illegality and resulting trusts after *Patel v Mirza*, what should the approach be?' *Trusts & Trustees* 23: 880–891.

Lewin on Trusts—see Mowbray et al.

Lim, E. (2017). '*Ex Turpi Causa*: Reformation not Revolution.' *Modern Law Review* 80: 927–941.

Lowry, J. (1997). 'Directorial self-dealing; constructing a regime of accountability.' *Northern Ireland Legal Quarterly* 48: 211.

Lowry, J. and R. Edmonds (1998). 'The corporate opportunity doctrine: The shifting boundaries of the duty and its remedies.' MLR 61: 515.

Macdonald, R. (1993–4). 'Reconceiving the Symbols of Property: Universalities, Interests and Other Heresies.' *McGill Law Journal* 39: 761.

Macnair, M. (1988). 'Equity and volunteers.' *Legal Studies* 8: 172.

Macnair, M. (2007). 'Equity and conscience.' OJLS 27: 659.

Maitland, F. W. (1929). *Equity, Also the Forms of Action at Common Law: Two Courses of Lectures*. Cambridge, Cambridge University Press.

Martin, J. (1997). *Hanbury and Martin's Modern Equity*. London, Sweet & Maxwell.

Martin, J. (2001). *Hanbury and Martin's Modern Equity*. London, Sweet & Maxwell.

Matthews, P. (1979). 'The true basis of the half-secret trust?' CPL: 360.

Matthews, P. (1989). 'The efficacy of trustee exemption clauses in English law.' CPL: 42.

Matthews, P. (1994). 'Resulting trusts and subsequent contributions.' *Trust Law International* 8: 43.

Matthews, P. (1995a). 'A problem in the construction of gifts to unincorporated associations.' CPL: 302.

Matthews, P. (1995b). The legal and moral limits of common law tracing. *Laundering and Tracing*. P. Birks, Clarendon Press: 23.

Matthews, P. (1995c). 'Protectors: Two cases, twenty questions.' TLI 9: 108.

Matthews, P. (1996). 'The new trust: Obligations without rights? *Trends in Contemporary Trust Law*. A. Oakley. Oxford, Oxford University Press: 1.

Matthews, P. (2000). 'Trustee exoneration clauses and comparative law.' TLI 14: 103.

Matthews, P. (2002). From obligation to property, and back again. *Extending the Boundaries of Trusts and Similar Ring-Fenced Funds*. D. Hayton. London, Kluwer: 203.

Matthews, P. (2005). 'All about bare trusts: Parts 1 and 2.' *Private Client Business* 6: 266, 336.

Matthews, P. (2006). 'The comparative importance of the rule in Saunders v Vautier.' LQR 122: 274.

Matthews, P. (2010). The Words Which Are Not There: A Partial History of the Constructive Trust. *Constructive and Resulting Trusts*. C. Mitchell. Oxford, Hart: 3.

McFarlane, B. and R. Stevens (2010). 'The nature of equitable property.' JoE 4: 1.

McKay, L. (1974). 'Re Baden and the third class of uncertainty.' CPL 38: 269.

McKnight, A. (2004). 'Review of Swadling (ed) *The* Quistclose *Trust*.' TLI 18: 231.

Mee, J. (2010). 'Automatic' Resulting Trusts: Retention, Restitution, or Reposing Trust? *Constructive and Resulting Trusts*. C. Mitchell. Oxford, Hart: 207.

Mee, J. (2014) 'Presumed resulting trusts, intention and declaration' CLJ 73: 86–112

Mee, J. (2017). 'The Past, Present, and Future of Resulting Trusts.' CLP 70(1): 189–225.

Miller, P. (2011). 'The *Quistclose* Trust—a reply.' *Trusts & Trustees* 17: 7.

Miller, P. B. (2011). 'A Theory of Fiduciary Liabiilty.' *McGill Law Journal* 56: 235–288.

Miller, P. B. (2013). 'Justifying Fiduciary Duties.' *McGill Law Journal* 58: 969–994.

Miller, P. B. (2014). The Fiduciary Relationship. *Philosophical Foundations of Fiduciary Law.* A. S. Gold and P. B. Miller. Oxford, Oxford University Press: 63–90.

Millett, P. (1985). 'The *Quistclose* trust: Who can enforce it?' LQR 101: 269.

Millett, P. J. (1998a). 'Equity's place in the law of commerce: Restitution and constructive trusts.' *Law Quarterly Review* 114: 214–227.

Millett, P. (1998b). 'Review Article: Resulting Trusts' [reviewing Robert Chambers, Resulting Trusts (Oxford: Clarendon, 1997)].' *Restitution Law Review*: 283.

Millett, P. (2000). 'Pension schemes and the law of trusts: The tail wagging the dog?' TLI 14: 66.

Millett, P. (2005). Proprietary Restitution. *Equity in Commercial Law.* S. Degeling and J. Edelman. Sydney, Law Book Co.

Mitchell, C. (1994). *The Law of Subrogation.* Oxford, Oxford University Press.

Mitchell, C. (1999a). 'Redefining charity in English law.' TLI 13: 21.

Mitchell, C. (1999b). 'Charity taxation under review.' TLI 13: 107.

Mitchell, C. (2000). Reviewing the register. *Foundations of Charity.* C. Mitchell and S. Moody. Oxford, Hart: 175.

Mitchell, C. (2002). Assistance. *Breach of Trust.* P. Birks and A. Pretto. Oxford, Hart: 139.

Mitchell, C. (2010b). *Hayton and Mitchell Commentary and Cases on the Law of Trusts and Equitable Remedies.* London, Sweet & Maxwell.

Mitchell, C. (2013). 'Equitable Compensation for Breach of Fiduciary Duty.' CLP 66: 307–339.

Mitchell, C. (2014). 'Stewardship of Property and Liability to Account.' CPL 78: 215-228.

Mitchell, C. and S. Watterson (2010). Remedies for Knowing Receipt. *Constructive and Resulting Trusts.* C. Mitchell. Oxford, Hart: 115.

Moffat, G. (1999). *Trusts Law: Text and Materials.* London, Butterworths.

Mowbray, J., L. Tucker, N. Le Poidevin, E. Simpson and J. Brightwell (2008). *Lewin on Trusts.* London, Sweet & Maxwell.

Murphy, W. (1991). 'The oldest social science? The epistemic properties of the common law tradition.' MLR 54: 182.

Nicholls, L. (1995). 'Trustees and their broader community: where duty, morality, and ethics converge.' TLI 9: 71.

Nicholls, L. (1998). Knowing receipt: The need for a new landmark. *Restitution: Past, Present and Future.* J. O'sullivan and W. R. Cornish. Oxford, Hart.

Nobles, R. (1992a). 'Charities and ethical investment.' CPL: 115.

Nobles, R. (1992b). 'The exercise of trustees' discretion under a pension scheme.' *Journal of Business Law*: 261.

Nolan, R. (2002). '*Vandervell v IRC*: A case of overreaching.' CLJ 61: 169.

Nolan, R. (2004). 'Property in a fund.' LQR 120: 108.

Nolan, R. C. (2016). '"The execution of a trust shall be under the control of the court"; A Maxim in Modern Times.' *Canadian Journal of Comparative and Contemporary Law* 2: 469–496.

Nolan, R. C. (2018). Trustees and Third-Party Powers. *Trusts and Modern Wealth Management.* R. C. Nolan, K. F. K. Low and H. W. Tang. Cambridge, Cambridge University Press: 57–75.

Oakley, A. (2003). *Parker and Mellows Modern Law of Trusts.* London, Sweet & Maxwell.

Ontario Law Reform Commission (1984). *Report on the Law of Trusts.* Toronto, Ministry of the Attorney-General.

Penner, J. (2017). 'Sort of' Backwards Tracing. *Equity, Trusts and Commerce.* P. S. Davies and J. Penner. Oxford, Hart Publishing: 123–149.

Penner, J. E. (1996a). 'Voluntary obligations and the scope of the law of contract.' *Legal Theory* 2: 325.

Penner, J. E. (2000). 'Review of Baxendale-Walker, *Purpose Trusts* (London: Butterworths).' TLI 14: 118.

Penner, J. E. (2002). Exemptions. *Breach of Trust.* P. Birks and A. Pretto. Oxford, Hart: 241.

Penner, J. E. (2004). Lord Millett's analysis. *The Quistclose Trust.* W. Swadling. Oxford, Hart: 41.

Penner, J. E. (2005). 'Contribution between wrongdoers: *Alexander v Perpetual Trustees.*' TLI 19: 105.

Penner, J. E. (2006a). Duty and liability in respect of funds. *Commercial Law: Perspectives and Practice*. J. Lowry and L. Mistelis. London, Butterworths.

Penner, J. E. (2006b). The common law controversy over the nature of the trust. *Los Patrimonios Fiduciarios y el Trust*. S. Nasarre and M. Garrido. Madrid, Colegio Notarial de Cataluña.

Penner, J. E. (2009b). Value, Property, and Unjust Enrichment: Trusts of Traceable Proceeds. *Philosophical Foundations of the Law of Unjust Enrichment*. R. Chambers, C. Mitchell and J. E. Penner. Oxford, Oxford University Press: 304.

Penner, J. E. (2010a). Resulting Trusts and Unjust Enrichment: Three Controversies. *Constructive and Resulting Trusts*. C. Mitchell. Oxford, Hart: 237.

Penner, J. E. (2010b). 'An Untheory of the Law of Trusts, or Some Notes Towards Understanding the Structure of Trusts Law Doctrine.' CLP 63: 653.

Penner, J. E. (2012). 'The difficult doctrinal basis for the fiduciary's proprietary liability to account for bribes.' *Trusts and Trustees* 18: 1000.

Penner, J. E. (2014a). 'The (True) Nature of a Beneficiary's Equitable Proprietary Interest Under a Trust.' *Canadian Journal of Law and Jurisprudence* 27: 473–500.

Penner, J. E. (2014b). 'Purposes and rights in the common law of trusts.' *Revue Juridique Themis de l'Universite de Montreal* 48: 579–597.

Penner, J. E. (2014c). Is Loyalty a Virtue, and Even If It Is, Does It Really Help Explain Fiduciary Liability? *Philosophical Foundations of Fiduciary Law*. A. S. Gold and P. B. Miller. Oxford, Oxford University Press: 159–175.

Penner, J. E. (2014d). 'Distinguishing Fiduciary, Trust, and Accounting Relationships.' JoE 8: 202–234.

Penner, J. E. (2016). 'Autonomy, Religion and Politics: Reflections on Matthew Harding's Charity Law and the Liberal State.' *Australian Journal of Legal Philosophy* 41: 126–138.

Penner, J. E. (2017). Falsifying the Trust Account and Compensatory Equitable Compensation. *Equitable Compensation and Disgorgement of Profit*. S. Degeling and J. N. Varuhas. Oxford, Hart: 143–157.

Penner, J. E. (2018a). The Beneficiary's Performance Interest in a Trust: *AIB v Redler* and the March of the Compensatory Principle. *Trusts and Modern Wealth Management*. R. C. Nolan, K. F. K. Low and H. W. Tang. Cambridge, Cambridge University Press: 277–306.

Penner, J. E. (2018b). 'We All Make Mistakes: A 'Duty of Virtue' Theory of Restitutionary Liability for Mistaken Payments.' *Modern Law Review* 81: 222–246.

Penner, J. E. (2019a). Equity, Justice, and Conscience: Suitors Behaving Badly? *Philosophical Foundations of the Law of Equity*. D. Klimchuk, I. Samet and H. E. Smith. Oxford, Oxford University Press.

Penner, J. E. (2019b). Fiduciary Law and Moral Norms. *Oxford Handbook of Fiduciary Law*. E. J. Criddle, P. B. Miller and R. H. Sitkoff. Oxford, Oxford University Press.

Penner, J. E. (2019c). Hohfeld's Equity. *The Legacy of Wesley Hohfeld: Edited Major Works, Select Personal Papers, and Original Commentaries*. S. Balganesh, T. Sichelman and H. E. Smith. Cambridge, Cambridge University Press.

Perrins, B. (1985). 'Secret trusts: The key to the dehors.' CPL: 248.

Piska, N. (2008). 'Intention, Fairness and the Presumption of Resulting Trust after *Stack v Dowden*.' MLR 71: 120.

Polden, P. (1994). 'Panic or Prudence—T Thellusson Act 1800 and Trusts Accumulation.' *Northern Ireland L Quarterly* 45: 13–29.

Pollard, D. (2003). 'Case note: *Schm Rosewood Trust*.' TLI 17: 90.

Rickett, C. (1980). 'Unincorporated asso and their dissolution.' CLJ 39: 88.

Rickett, C. (1999). 'The classification *New Zealand Universities Law Revi*

Rickett, C. (2001). 'Completely con inter vivos trust: Property rules?'

Sheridan, L. (1951). 'English an trusts.' LQR 67: 314.

Simpson, A. (1986). *A History o* Oxford, Clarendon Press.

Sitkoff, R. H. (2014). An Eco Fiduciary Law. *Philosophic*

Fiduciary Law. A. S. Gold and P. B. Miller. Oxford, Oxford University Press: 197–208.

Smith, L. (1994). 'Tracing, "swollen assets" and the lowest intermediate balance: Bishopsgate Investment Management Ltd v Homan.' TLI 8: 102.

Smith, L. (1995). 'Tracing in *Taylor v Plumer*: Equity in the Court of King's Bench.' LMCLQ: 240.

Smith, L. (1997). *The Law of Tracing.* Oxford, Clarendon Press.

Smith, L. (2000). 'Unjust enrichment, property, and the structure of trusts.' LQR 116: 412.

Smith, L. (2003a). 'Access to information: *Schmidt v Rosewood Trust Ltd.*' *Estates, Trusts & Pensions Journal* 23: 1.

Smith, L. (2003b). The motive, not the deed. *Rationalising Property, Equity, and Trusts.* J. `etzler. London, Butterworths: 53.

L. (2004). Understanding the power. *The* ⁻lose *Trust.* W. Swadling. Oxford, Hart: 67.

(2004). 'Unravelling Proprietary n.' *Canadian Business Law Journal*

'. 'Trust and Patrimony.' *Revue* ⁻it 38: 379.

ᵖhilosophical Foundations ᴿemedies. *Philosophical w of Unjust Enrichment.* ʰell and J. E. Penner. `y Press: 281.

⁻laims to traceable ⁻w 125: 338–348.

⁻d Dispositions `uebec Law.'

he
for
egal

idt v

ciations

of trusts.'
ew 18: 305.
tituting an
CPL: 515.
Irish secret

the Land Law.

nomic Theory of
al Foundations of

and the

the

83

Fiduciary Law. A. S. Gold and P. B. Miller. Oxford, Oxford University Press: 141–158.

Smith, L. D. (2014b). 'Fiduciary Relationships: Ensuring the Loyal Exercise of Judgement on Behalf of Another.' *Law Quarterly Review* 130: 608–634.

Smith, S. A. (2016). The Deed, Not the Motive: Fiduciary Law Without Loyalty. *Contract, Status, and Fiduciary Law.* P. B. Miller and A. S. Gold. Oxford, Oxford University Press: 213–237.

Smith, S (forthcoming) *Private Law Remedies: Foundation, Scope, and Structure*

Stebbings, C. (2002). *The Private Trustee in Victorian England.* Cambridge, Cambridge University Press.

Stevens, R. (2007). *Torts and Rights.* Oxford, Oxford University Press.

Stevens, R. (2017). Floating Trusts. *Equity, Trusts and Commerce.* P. S. Davies and J. Penner. Oxford, Hart Publishing: 113–122.

Stevens, R. (2018). 'The Unjust Enrichment Disaster.' *Law Quarterly Review* 134: 574–601.

Sullivan, G. (1979). 'Going it alone: *Queensland Mines v Hudson.*' MLR 42: 711.

Swadling, W. (1987). 'The conveyancer's revenge.' CPL: 451.

Swadling, W. (1994). Some lessons from the law of torts. *The Frontiers of Liability.* P. Birks. Oxford, Oxford University Press: 41.

Swadling, W. (1996a). 'A new role for resulting trusts?' *Legal Studies* 16: 110.

Swadling, W. (1996b). 'A claim in restitution?' LMCLQ: 63.

Swadling, W. (1997). Property and unjust enrichment. *Property Problems: From Genes to Pension Funds.* J. Harris. London, Kluwer: 130.

Swadling, W. (1998). 'Property and conscience.' TLI 12: 228.

Swadling, W. (2000). Property: General principles. *English private law.* P. Birks. Oxford, Oxford University Press: 203–384.

Swadling, W. (2004). *The* Quistclose *Trust.* Oxford, Hart.

ıdling, W. (2005a). 'Rescission, property, and the common law.' LQR 121: 123.

ᵥadling, W. (2005b). The vendor–purchaser constructive trust. *Equity in Commercial Law.*

S. Degeling and J. Edelman. Sydney, Law Book Co: 431.

Swadling, W. (2007). 'The common intention constructive trust in the House of Lords: An opportunity missed.' LQR 123: 511.

Swadling, W. (2008). 'Explaining resulting trusts.' LQR 124: 72.

Swadling, W. (2010). The Nature of the Trust in *Rochefoucauld v Boustead*. *Constructive and Resulting Trusts*. C. Mitchell. Oxford, Hart: 95.

Swadling, W. (2011). 'The Fiction of the Constructive Trust.' CLP 64: 399.

Swadling, W. (2016). 'Substance and Procedure in Equity.' JoE 10: 1–25.

Swadling, W. (2017). The Nature of 'Knowing Receipt'. *Equity, Trusts, and Commerce*. P. S. Davies and J. Penner. Oxford, Hart Publishing: 303–330.

Tarrant, J. (2009). 'Thieves as trustees: In defence of the theft principle.' JoE 3: 170.

Treitel, G. (2003). *The Law of Contract*. London, Sweet & Maxwell.

Trust Law Committee (1999). *Report and Consultation Papers: Report on Rights of Creditors against Trustees and Trust Funds; Consultation Papers on Capital and Income of Trusts, Trustee Exemption Clauses*.

Turner, P. (2012). 'Understanding The Constructive Trust Between Vendor and Purchaser.' LQR 128: 582.

Turner, P. (2018). The Entitlement of Objects as Defining Features of Discretionary Trusts. *Trusts and Modern Wealth Management*. R. C. Nolan, K. F. K. Low and H. W. Tang. Cambridge, Cambridge University Press: 242–276.

Valsan, R. (2016). 'Fiduciary Duties, Conflict of Interest, and Proper Exercise of Judgment.' *McGill Law Journal* 62: 1–40.

Virgo, G. (2006). *The Principles of the Law of Restitution*. Oxford, Oxford University Press.

Virgo, G. (2016a). '*Patel v Mirza*: one step forward and two steps back.' *Trusts & Trustees* 22: 1090–1097.

Virgo, G. (2016b) 'Restitution and Unjust Enrichment in the Supreme Court: Reflections on *Bank of Cyprus UK Ltd v Menelaou*.' Legal Studies Research Paper Series, 1–24.

Virgo, G. (2018). *The Principles of Equity & Trusts*. Oxford, Oxford University Press.

Waggoner, L. (2014). 'From here to eternity: The folly of perpetual trusts.' *Michigan Law Public Theory and Legal Theory Research Paper Series* Paper 259.

Waters, D. (1996). The protector: New wine in old bottles? *Trends in Contemporary Trust Law*. A. Oakley. Oxford, Clarendon Press: 63.

Watkin, T. (1981). 'Cloaking a contravention.' CPL: 335.

Watts, P. (2013). '*Tyrrell v Bank of London*—an inside look at an inside job.' LQR 129: 527.

Watts, P. (2016). 'Agents' Disbursal of Funds in Breach of Instructions.' LMCLQ 2016: 118–134.

Watts, P. (2016). '"Unjust Enrichment"—the Potion that Induces Well-meaning Sloppiness of Thought.' CLP 69(1): 289–325.

Weinrib, E. J. (1975). 'The Fiduciary Obligation.' *University of Toronto Law Journal* 25: 1–22.

Willoughby, P. (1999). *Misplaced Trust*. Saffron Walden, Gostick Hall.

Worthington, S. (1996). *Proprietary Interests in Commercial Transactions*. Oxford, Clarendon Press.

Youdan, T. (1984). 'Formalities for trusts of land, and the doctrine in *R v Boustead*.' CLJ 43: 306.

Index